W9-AHX-771

Networking with Microsoft TCP/IP

Certified Administrator's Resource Edition

Drew Heywood

Rob Scrimger

New Riders Publishing, Indianapolis, Indiana

Networking with Microsoft TCP/IP, Certified Administrator's Resource Edition

By Drew Heywood and Rob Scrimger

Published by:
New Riders Publishing
201 West 103rd Street
Indianapolis, IN 46290 USA

Printed in the United States of America 2 3 4 5 6 7 8 9 0

Library of Congress Cataloging-in-Publication Data

CIP data available upon request

ISBN: 1-56205-791-X

Warning and Disclaimer

This book is designed to provide information about TCP/IP. Every effort has been made to make this book as complete and as accurate as possible, but no warranty of fitness is implied.

The information is provided on an "as is" basis. The authors and New Riders Publishing shall have neither liability nor responsibility to any person or entity with respect to any loss or damages arising from the information contained in this book or from the use of the discs or programs that may accompany it.

Associate Publisher *David Dwyer*
Publishing Manager *Laurie Petrycki*
Marketing Manager *Kourtnaye Sturgeon*
Managing Editor *Sarah Kearns*
Director of Development *Kezia Endsley*

Product Development Specialist and Acquisitions Editor
Sean Angus

Development Editor
Ami Frank

Project Editor
Suzanne Snyder

Copy Editors
Jennifer Clark
Keith Cline, Karen Walsh

Technical Editor
Glenn Berg

Coordinator of Editorial Resources
Suzanne Snyder

Software Product Developer
Steve Flatt

Software Acquisitions and Development
Dustin Sullivan

Assistant Marketing Manager
Gretchen Schlesinger

Acquisitions Coordinator
Amy Lewis

Manufacturing Coordinator
Brook Farling

Cover Designer
Dan Armstrong

Cover Production
Nathan Clement

Book Designer
Glenn Larsen

Director of Production
Larry Klein

Production Team Supervisor
Laurie Casey

Graphics Image Specialists
Kevin Cliburn, Wil Cruz, Tammy Graham, Oliver Jackson

Production Analysts
Dan Harris
Erich J. Richter

Production Team
Lori Cliburn, Kim Cofer, Mary Hunt, Kristy Nash, Elizabeth San Miguel, Scott Tullis

Indexer
Tim Wright

About the Authors

Drew Heywood, author of the the first and second editions of this book, first became involved with computers when he was ensnared by the come-hither look of an Apple II in 1978, and they've been eating up large parts of his paychecks ever since. He first started conversing with the ether in 1985 when a LAN crossed his path, and has spent so much time with networks that he's not good for much of anything else. After several years of running networks he fell into book development at New Riders Publishing, where he launched many of the best-selling network books in the industry. While at New Riders, a dormant writing bug—squashed by a couple of flops in the early 1980s—reasserted itself, and Drew once again started pounding the keys late into the night as he authored and co-authored a variety of popular network titles. In 1994, he left New Riders to try writing full-time. Now with three successful books, Drew is well on the way to enjoying the occupational benefits of the writing profession: failing eyesight, pallid skin, and deadline stress—and, thankfully, the kind comments of a number of readers, for which he is extremely grateful.

On the rare occasions when he is not in his office staring at a monitor, Drew enjoys activities with his wife, Blythe. A seasoned computer professional herself, Blythe keeps Drew honest and keeps the business running smoothly. Together they enjoy music and dance concerts and travel to historic areas.

Rob Scrimger, MCSE, MCT, is the author responsible for the certified edition of this book. Born in Cold Lake, Alberta, Canada, he was an Air Force brat until his family moved to Ottawa, Ontario. After his start with an Apple II in high school (Lisgar Collegiate), he began to write programs in Basic. From there he moved on to create inventory systems and work with a Wang OIS system, and a group of Wang PC's (with 12 MB hard disks). His career then moved to various parts of the Information Technology field (though that term didn't exist yet) at such companies as Bell Canada International, Ricoh, and Canada Post.

Now after nearly twenty years, Rob has done everything with computers except design the boards and sell them (something not likely to ever occur). In the last eight years, his primary endeavor has been training, starting with many different applications and moving in the last few years to working exclusively with Network Operating Systems and related topics (such as TCP/IP). Rob is currently a Microsoft Certified Systems Engineer and a Microsoft Certified Trainer. His goal is to pass every exam in the MCSE track (currently he's passed 18 out of a possible 23) within the next year.

Having a head for bizarre and twisted facts, Rob has enjoyed these years of training and will continue to enjoy them as long as he can still see the light come on when someone "gets it."

Rob's personal time is spent with his wife Juudy (two u's because she's unique) and daughter Tawni. They spend a lot of time with his parents notably stealing away on the family boat.

Dedications

From Drew Heywood: For Woody from his proud father.

From Rob Scrimger: I wrote this book for three people: my wife Juudy to make her proud, myself to prove I could do it, and my daughter Tawni, who wants a Nintendo.

Acknowledgments

From Drew Heywood:

My sincere thanks go out to:

Blythe for her patience, support, and business expertise that support me every day. My mother for always helping out in a crisis. New Riders Publishing for giving me yet another opportunity. To everyone at New Riders, many thanks. Julie Fairweather for solving problems. Jack Belbot for getting me what I needed when I needed it. Karanjit Siyan for being a good friend, an exemplar of professionalism, and an outstanding technical resource. Chris Stone for his technical editing. Microsoft for ensuring that Windows NT keeps moving ahead.

From Rob Scrimger:

First, I want to acknowledge the contributions of the Technical (Glenn) and Development (Ami) Editors who made this book look good (they converted from binary for you). I will also acknowledge Sean and Jason for making this possible. I want to acknowledge Drew Heywood for writing Networking with Microsoft TCP/IP upon which this is (loosely at times) based. I want to acknowledge all the people that I have been able to introduce to TCP/IP over the years; your questions helped form this book.

Contents at a Glance

PART I: TCP/IP Theory 13

1 *Introduction to TCP/IP* 15
2 *Introduction to Microsoft Networking* 31
3 *The Application Layer* 55
4 *The Transport Layer* 67
5 *The Internet Layer* 77
6 *Subnetting* 93
7 *Routing* 113

PART II: Microsoft TCP/IP Services 125

8 *Microsoft TCP/IP Services* 127
9 *Internet Information Server* 153
10 *TCP/IP Printing Services* 183
11 *Dynamic Host Configuration Protocol (DHCP)* 197

PART III: NetBIOS Over TCP/IP 233

12 *NetBIOS Name Resolution* 235
13 *The Windows Internet Name Service* 257
14 *The Browser Service and TCP/IP* 299

PART IV: TCP/IP Services 317

15 *Microsoft DNS Server* 319
16 *TCP/IP Utilities* 405
17 *Management Utilities: SNMP and the Performance Monitor* 479
18 *Remote Access Service and TCP/IP* 509

PART V: Microsoft TCP/IP Implementation 559

19 *Troubleshooting TCP/IP* 561
20 *Designing a TCP/IP Internetwork* 589

PART VI: Appendices 607

A *Overview of the Certification Process* 609
B *All About TestPrep* 619

Table of Contents

Objectives Matrix 1

A .... Planning
B .... Installation and Configuration
C .... Connectivity
D .... Monitoring and Optimization
E .... Troubleshooting

Introduction 5

The Planning Process 6
Estimating Your Needs 6
Internet or Intranet? 7
Who Should Read This Book? 8
Special Elements in this Book 9
Practice Sections 9
Notes, Tips, Cautions, Sidebars 9
New Riders Publishing 10

Part I: TCP/IP Theory 13

1 Introduction to TCP/IP 15

A Brief History of TCP/IP 17
Request for Comments—Defining the Internet 19
Why Use TCP/IP? 22
Overview of TCP/IP Addresses 24
Summary 26
Test Yourself 27
Test Yourself Answers 28

2 Introduction to Microsoft Networking 31

The OSI Reference Model 32
What Is Microsoft Networking? 32
Layers on Layers 34
Application/File System Drivers 36
Transport Driver Interface 36
The Transport Protocols 37
Network Driver Interface Specification 38
Adapter Card Drivers 38

The TCP/IP Model 42
Components at the Application Layer 43
The Transport Layer Protocols 45
The Internet Layer 46
Network Access Layer 50
Summary 51
Test Yourself 51
Test Yourself Answers 52

3 The Application Layer 55

Getting into WinSock 56
How the Process Works 56
NetBIOS Over TCP/IP 61
NBT 61
NBTSTAT 62
Name Resolution Overview 63
Summary 64
Test Yourself 64
Test Yourself Answers 65

4 The Transport Layer 67

Headers 68
TCP Headers 68
UDP Header 69
Pseudo Headers 70
Transmission Control Protocol (TCP) 71
Session Establishment 71
Byte Stream Communications 72
Sliding Windows 72
User Datagram Protocol 74
Summary 75
Test Yourself 75
Test Yourself Answers 75

5 The Internet Layer 77

What Is a Subnet Mask? 78
Introduction to Routing 78
Finding Another Machine's Address 80
Creating an IP Datagram 84
Fragmentation and Reassembly of Datagrams 86
Error Detection and Reporting 87
Summary 89
Test Yourself 89
Test Yourself Answers 90

6 Subnetting 93

Remembering Binary 94
How Do You Subnet? 96
Determining Your Addressing Needs 97
Defining Your Subnet Mask 97
Finding Out How Many Networks, How Many Hosts 98
Subnetwork IDs 99
Host IDs 102
Supernetting 104
Summary 106
Test Yourself 106
Test Yourself Answers 109

7 Routing 113

What Is Routing? 114
What Is a Router? 114
NT as a Router 115
Static Routing 115
Dynamic Routing 118
Summary 121
Test Yourself 121
Test Yourself Answers 122

Part II: Microsoft TCP/IP Services 125

8 Microsoft TCP/IP Services 127

Using Microsoft TCP/IP andWindows NT 4 128
New Features in Windows NT 4 128
Services Available in NT 129
TCP/IP Support for RFCs 131
Installing Microsoft TCP/IP 134
The Network Settings Dialog Box 134
Testing the TCP/IP Configuration 141
Microsoft TCP/IP Properties Overview 145
Summary 150
Test Yourself 150
Test Yourself Answers 150

9 Internet Information Server 153

Installing IIS 154
Preparing for Installation 154
The Installation Process 155

Using the Product Documentation 157
Testing the Installation 158
Managing IIS 158
Selecting IIS Views 160
Setting Up the IUSR_*computername* Account 160
Configuring the HTTP Server (WWW Service) 161
Configuring the FTP Service 174
Configuring the Gopher Service 175
Practice 176
Exercise 0—Installing IIS 176
Exercise 1—Changing the IUSR_*computername* Password 177
Exercise 2—Adding an Alias to the FTP Server 179
Summary 179
Test Yourself 180
Test Yourself Answers 180

10 TCP/IP Printing Services 183

Printing with Windows NT 184
The Print Process 184
Installing a Printer 188
Installing TCP/IP Printing Services 189
Connecting to an LPD Server 189
Sharing Your Printer Using LPD 191
Practice 193
Exercise 1—Installing the TCP/IP Printing Service 193
Exercise 2—Creating a Demonstration Printer 194
Exercise 3—Turning On the TCP/IP Print Server 194
Exercise 4—Printing to the TCP/IP Printer 194
Exercise 5—Hooking Up to the LPD Service 195
Summary 196
Test Yourself 196
Test Yourself Answers 196

11 Dynamic Host Configuration Protocol (DHCP) 197

DHCP Concepts and Operation 198
Installing DHCP Servers 202
Setting Up DHCP Scopes 202
Enabling DHCP Clients 205
Viewing and Managing Active Leases 206
Modifying Properties for an Active Lease 208
Deleting Active Leases 209

Establishing Reservations 209
Activating, Deactivating, and Deleting Scopes 212
Managing Leases 212
Managing Multiple DHCP Servers 213
Managing the DHCP Database 213
Compacting the DHCP Database 214
Starting and Stopping the DHCP Server 214
Repairing a Corrupted DHCP Database 215
Creating a New DHCP Database 216
DHCP Configuration Options 217
Managing Default, Global, and Scope DHCP Options 218
Managing Client-Specific Options for Reservations 219
DHCP Options for Microsoft TCP/IP 220
Configuring DHCP in the Registry 221
Viewing and Editing DHCP-Related Values in the Registry 223
DHCP-Related Registry Values 224
DHCP Relay Agent 226
Practice 227
Exercise 1—Installing the DHCP Server 228
Exercise 2—Configuring a DHCP Scope 228
Exercise 3—Adding Scope and Global Options in the DHCP Server .. 228
Exercise 4—Configuring a Second DHCP Scope 229
Exercise 5—Adding Client Reservations 230
Exercise 6—Checking the Information 230
Summary 230
Test Yourself 231
Test Yourself Answers 231

Part III: NetBIOS Over TCP/IP 233

12 NetBIOS Name Resolution 235

Methods of Name Resolution 237
NetBIOS Name Cache 237
Broadcast 238
The LMHOSTS File 239
NetBIOS Name Server 242
The HOSTS File 244
DNS 245
Order of Resolution 246
B-Node 247
P-Node 248
M-Node 248

H-Node 248
Viewing and Setting the Node Type 249
Practice 251
Exercise 1—Sample LMHOSTS 251
Exercise 2—Creating a Simple LMHOSTS File 251
Summary 254
Test Yourself 254
Test Yourself Answers 255

13 The Windows Internet Name Service 257

The WINS Process 258
Name Registration 258
NetBIOS Name Renewal 261
NetBIOS Name Release 262
Name Resolution 263
Installing WINS Server 265
Installing the WINS Clients 268
Configuring a Statically Addressed WINS Client 268
Configuring WINS Proxies 268
Configuring DHCP Clients as WINS Clients 269
Managing WINS Servers 272
Adding WINS Servers to WINS Server Manager 273
Monitoring WINS 273
Viewing the Database 274
Setting WINS Manager Preferences 276
Configuring WINS Server Properties 277
Viewing WINS Server Details 279
Configuring Static Mappings 281
Special Names 282
Backing Up the Database 284
Restoring the WINS Database 285
Scavenging and Compacting the Database 286
Replicating the WINS Database 287
Adding Replication Partners 289
Manually Triggering Replication 290
WINS Registry Entries 291
DbFileNm 291
DoStaticDataInit 292
InitTimePause 292
LogDetailedEvents 292
LogFilePath 292
LoggingOn 293
McastIntvl 293

McastTtl ... 293
NoOfWrkThds ... 293
PriorityClassHigh ... 293
RefreshInterval ... 294
TombstoneInterval ... 294
TombstoneTimeout ... 294
UseSelfFndPntrs ... 294
VerifyInterval ... 295
Practice ... 295
Exercise 1—Installing the WINS Server ... 295
Exercise 2—Learning About WINS Server Configuration ... 296
Exercise 3—Adding Static Mappings to the Database ... 296
Summary ... 297
Test Yourself ... 297
Test Yourself Answers ... 298

14 The Browser Service and TCP/IP 299

The Browsing Process ... 300
The Microsoft Browser Service—Basics ... 300
Configuring Browsers ... 304
Browser Elections ... 305
Supporting Domain Activity ... 307
A Quick Review of NT Directory Services ... 307
User Logon ... 308
Browsing Multiple Subnets ... 308
Using LMHOSTS ... 309
Using WINS to Enable NBT ... 313
Summary ... 314
Test Yourself ... 314
Test Yourself Answers ... 315

Part IV: TCP/IP Services 317

15 Microsoft DNS Server 319

Overview of Domain Name System ... 320
Hierarchies ... 320
The Domain Name Space ... 321
Domain Administration ... 324
Resolving DNS Queries ... 325
Organization of the Internet Domain Name Space ... 327
Obtaining Domain Information with WHOIS ... 342
Mapping Addresses to Names ... 344

DNS Under Windows NT 4 345
Deciding Whether to Implement DNS 346
Name Resolution with HOSTS Files 347
Getting Ready for DNS 348
Managing Microsoft DNS Server 348
DNS Configuration Options 350
Creating BIND Database Files 351
The BOOT File 351
Domain Database Files 353
Reverse-Matching Database Files 360
The Localhost Database File 362
The Cache File 362
Setting Up a Secondary Name Server 365
Managing the DNS Server 366
Installing the Microsoft DNS Server 367
Initializing the DNS Server 367
Server Roles 369
Adding the Reverse-Lookup Zones 369
Adding a Primary Zone 370
Adding Resource Records 371
Modifying Zone Properties 376
Resolving Names with WINS 381
Managing Multiple DNS Servers 382
Creating a Secondary DNS Server 383
Adding Subdomain Zones 384
Updating the Database Files 386
Setting DNS Manager Preferences 386
DNS Server Statistics 387
Porting Data from BIND Servers 388
Enabling DNS Clients 389
Windows NT Name Resolution 390
Nslookup 391
Making Non-Interactive Queries 391
Making Interactive Queries 393
Practice 396
Exercise 1—Installing the DNS Server 396
Exercise 2—Configuring DNS Domains 397
Exercise 3—Adding Hosts 398
Exercise 4—Adding Other Records 399
Exercise 5—Testing the DNS Server 400
Summary 401
Test Yourself 401
Test Yourself Answers 402

16 TCP/IP Utilities 405

File Transfer Utilities 406
FTP 406
TFTP 411
RCP 412
Interactive Utilities 414
Internet Explorer 414
Telnet 424
RSH 426
REXEC 426
Printing Utilities 427
LPR 427
LPQ 428
Troubleshooting 429
Ping 429
IPCONFIG 433
Finger 434
NSLOOKUP 434
HOSTNAME 439
NETSTAT 440
NBTSTAT 442
ROUTE 444
TRACERT 446
ARP 448
Network Monitor 449
Installing Network Monitor 451
Setting Up Network Monitor Security 451
Describing Your Network Cards 453
Capturing Network Frames 453
Saving Captured Data 454
Creating an Address Database 454
Selecting the Network to be Monitored 456
Managing the Capture Buffer 456
Avoiding Dropped Frames 457
Using Capture Filters 458
Using Logical Operators 462
Using Capture Triggers 462
Saving Capture Data 463
Examining Captured Data 463
Practice 471
Exercise 1—Using the FTP Command to Move Files 471
Exercise 2—Entering and Removing Entries from the ARP Cache 473
Exercise 3(A)—Using the Network Monitor and Agent 473

Summary ... 476
Test Yourself ... 476
Test Yourself Answers ... 477

17 Management Utilities: SNMP and the Performance Monitor 479

SNMP Roles ... 480
MIBs (Management Information Base) ... 480
Communities ... 482
Installing and Configuring SNMP ... 483
The Agent Tab ... 484
The Traps Tab ... 485
The Security Tab ... 485
Testing SNMP ... 486
Performance Monitor ... 487
Using Performance Monitor ... 487
Counters for Transmission Control Protocol ... 493
Counters for User Datagram Protocol ... 494
Chart Settings for Performance Monitor ... 494
The Log Setting ... 496
Using a Log File ... 497
Practice ... 499
Exercise 1—Installing the Protocol ... 499
Exercise 2—Using SNMPUTIL to Test SNMP ... 500
Exercise 3—Monitoring Real-Time Performance ... 501
Exercise 4—Logging TCP/IP Activity ... 503
Summary ... 504
Test Yourself ... 504
Test Yourself Answers ... 505

18 Remote Access Service and TCP/IP 509

Understanding RAS ... 510
Installing the Hardware ... 513
Adding Serial Ports ... 513
Installing Modems ... 514
Setting Telephony Properties ... 518
Configuring RAS to Dial Out ... 519
Dial-Up Networking ... 521
Adding Phonebook Entries ... 521
Editing Entries ... 524
Dialing with a Phonebook Entry ... 530
User Preferences ... 532
Logon Preferences ... 535

Dial-Up Networking Monitor 535
Monitor Settings 536
Using RAS as an Internet Router 539
Configuring a RAS Server 541
RAS Setup 541
Remote Access Admin 544
Using the Point-to-Point Tunneling Protocol 546
Configuring PPTP 548
Enabling PPTP Filtering 549
Monitoring Server PPTP Support 549
Enabling Client PPTP Support 550
Practice 551
Exercise 0—Adding a Null Modem 551
Exercise 1—Installing Remote Access Service 552
Exercise 2—Creating Phonebook Entries 552
Exercise 3—Editing Phonebook Entries 553
Exercise 4—Configuring RAS as a Server 553
Exercise 5—Assigning Permissions 554
Summary 554
Test Yourself 555
Test Yourself Answers 556

Part V: Microsoft TCP/IP Implementation 559

19 Troubleshooting TCP/IP 561

The Basics 562
Where Is the Problem? 562
What Changed? 563
Tools and Utilities 568
Ping 568
IPCONFIG 568
NETSTAT 568
NBTSTAT 569
ROUTE 569
TRACERT 569
ARP 569
Network Monitor 569
Performance Monitor 569
Event Viewer 570
NT Diagnostics 571
Checking Connectivity 573

Troubleshooting TCP/IP Services 574
The Internet Information Server 574
TCP/IP Printing 574
DHCP 575
WINS 575
The Browser Service 576
DNS 576
Summary 577
Test Yourself 577
Scenario 1—Troubleshooting an FTP Server 577
Scenario 2—A Subnetting Problem 578
Scenario 3—Finding Configuration Errors 578
Scenario 4—Troubleshooting Clients 580
Scenario 5—Client Configuration Problems 580
Test Yourself Answers 583

20 Designing a TCP/IP Intranetwork 589

Looking at IP 593
Linking the Sites 594
Services 598
Adding DHCP Servers 598
Adding WINS Servers 599
Adding DNS Servers 600
Adding the Internet Information Server 600
The RAS Server 601
Using a Proxy Server 602
Summary 602
Test Yourself 602
Scenario 1—Designing a High-Security Network 603
Scenario 2—Planning to Use the Internet as Your WAN 604
Scenario 3—Creating a Private Network 604
Test Yourself Answers 604

Part VI: Appendices 607

A Overview of the Certification Process 609

How to Become a Microsoft Certified Product Specialist (MCPS) 610
How to Become a Microsoft Certified Systems Engineer (MCSE) 611
How to Become a Microsoft Certified Solution Developer (MCSD) 616
Becoming a Microsoft Certified Trainer (MCT) 617

B All About TestPrep 619

Question Presentation 620
Scoring 620
Non-Random Mode 620
Instructor Mode 621
Flash Cards 621

Index 623

Objectives List for Internetworking with Microsoft™ TCP/IP on Microsoft Windows NT™ 4.0

Objectives Matrix

A Planning

Planning	Chapter/Page Reference
A.1 Given a scenario, identify valid network configurations.	*Introduction, page 6*

B Installation and Configuration

Planning	Chapter/Page Reference
B.1 Given a scenario, select the appropriate services to install when using Microsoft TCP/IP on a Microsoft Windows NT Server computer.	*Chapter 8, page 129* *Chapter 20, page 598*
B.2 On a Windows NT Server computer, configure Microsoft TCP/IP to support multiple network adapters.	*Chapter 7, page 115*
B.3 Configure scopes by using DHCP Manager.	*Chapter 11, pages 202, 217*
B.4 Install and configure a WINS server. ◆ Import LMHOSTS files to WINS. ◆ Run WINS on a multihomed computer. ◆ Configure WINS replication. ◆ Configure static mappings in the WINS database.	*Chapter 13, pages 265, 266, 268, 272, 281, 282, 287*
B.5 Configure subnet masks.	*Chapter 2, page 46* *Chapter 6, page 97*
B.6 Configure a Windows NT Server computer to function as an IP router. ◆ Install and configure the DHCP relay Agent.	*Chapter 7, pages 115, 120* *Chapter 8, pages 148, 149*

continues

continued

Planning	Chapter/Page Reference
B.7 Install and configure the Microsoft DNS Server service on a Windows NT Server computer. ◆ Integrate DNS with other name servers. ◆ Connect a DNS server to a DNS root server. ◆ Configure DNS server roles.	*Chapter 15, pages 350, 357, 362, 366, 369, 370, 379, 383, 388*
B.8 Configure HOSTS and LMHOSTS files.	*Chapter 12, pages 239, 244* *Chapter 14, pages 309, 310*
B.9 Configure a Windows NT Server computer to suppport TCP/IP printing.	*Chapter 10, page 189*
B.10 Configure SNMP	*Chapter 17, page 483*

C Connectivity

Planning	Chapter/Page Reference
C.1 Given a scenario, identify which utility to use to connect to a TCP/IP-based Unix host.	*Chapter 16, pages 406, 414, 427*
C.2 Configure a RAS server and dial-up networking for use on a TCP/IP network.	*Chapter 18, pages 519, 521, 526, 539, 541, 546*
C.3 Configure and support browsing in a multiple-domain routed network.	*Chapter 14, pages 310, 314*

D Monitoring and Optimization

Planning	Chapter/Page Reference
D.1 Given a scenario, identify which tool to use to monitor TCP/IP traffic.	*Chapter 16, pages 440, 442, 449* *Chapter 17, page 487*

E Troubleshooting

Planning		Chapter/Page Reference
E.1	Diagnose and resolve IP addressing problems.	*Chapter 1, page 24*
E.2	Use Microsoft TCP/IP utilities to diagnose IP configuration problems. ◆ Identify which Microsoft TCP/IP utility to use to diagnose IP configuration problems.	*Chapter 16, page 429* *Chapter 19, page 568*
E.3	Diagnose and resolve name resolution problems.	*Chapter 3, page 63* *Chapter 12, pages 237, 246* *Chapter 16, page 434* *Chapter 19, pages 575, 576*

Introduction

In today's world, because IS managers seek to base their systems on standards and because everyone wants to connect to the Internet, TCP/IP has become unavoidable for anyone working with LANs. That doesn't make TCP/IP any less imposing, however.

TCP/IP is an extremely rich set of network protocols—probably the richest. After all, no other protocols have the Internet with its millions of users—many bent on making the Internet do more, which often means adding to TCP/IP. As a result, the family of TCP/IP can and has become a professional preoccupation for many people in the networking community. The vastness of TCP/IP forces any author addressing the subject to select a subset of the field that will meet the needs of the book's readers.

An additional purpose of this book is to provide all the necessary information for computer professionals who need to prepare for the *Internetworking with Microsoft TCP/IP on Microsoft Windows NT 4* certification exam #70-59.

The Planning Process

Objective A.1

As you read through this text, you should consider that all the details covered here are required to implement the overall strategy that your organization intends to use. Before you need to concern yourself with the details of implementation, you should have some idea of what you will implement. You need to consider several keys points. Some of these are listed here:

- How many users does the network need to host?
- What line speed will be available to connect the offices together?
- Where are the offices located in relation to each other?
- What services are going to be required from the network?
- Are there going to be roaming users (moving from desk to desk in your office), or traveling users (going to sites where they are away from the network)?

The main thing that you need to keep in mind is that every network that you will work with either in the planning stages, the implementation, or the support phase is different. Always take the time to consider what it is that the corporate entity requires, and figure out how best to suit those needs. Whether this is the office suite that they want to run that you are deciding on, or the way that they will run it (from the network or a stand-alone station), remember that there is always more than one way to accomplish the task. A good network engineer looks at all the ways, and finds a best solution. Always leave your preferences at the door—the solution that you are creating in this type of role is more important than selling another network of brand x. There will be times when NT doesn't fit the bill, because it has grown into such a robust network operating system.

Estimating Your Needs

Another thing that you need to keep in mind is that the network is not more important than the organization (sorry to say). The network is there to service the needs of the organization that creates it, not the other way around. There are cases where you will need to look at fiber, and there are cases where the standard (cheap) Ethernet card will work fine.

You must always look at the number of users, but also at the amount of traffic passing the network. Additionally, you need to guess at the future of the computer industry to see what is coming. If you are building a network for a three-station LAN, and the client is already sold on Ethernet, there is no point in trying to sell the client on fiber; the client doesn't need it. By the same token, there is little point in telling a company that it can go 10BaseT when the company has 7,000 users on 4 segments—they need to break down the network further, and should look at a higher-speed network system.

When you estimate the needs, remember that you need to consider the amount of background noise on the network. Many different types of broadcasts take place in NT networking because of the broadcast nature of the NetBIOS networking base that NT is built on.

Another critical area that you must estimate is the dial-in traffic that you expect, and the amount of traffic that you expect to hit the corporation's web presence. The World Wide Web has become a very busy place, with many different people all trying to compete to have you find their area, their company, their presence on the WWW. Inescapably, you need to give ample consideration to this. Some factors make this a nightmare as well.

Always check with the individual or the firm that will develop the WWW site. The web site developer may have many different requests. Building a simple home page on the web these days is no longer enough. Many different sites are out there, and if you want people to visit your site you must provide something different.

Many organizations are using video and audio and fancy graphics to grab the attention of people passing by. Two pieces of advice on web design: keep it simple, and if that is not an option, give the client an option of a test-only page.

The other area in which you need to estimate bandwidth is in the link between the different sites. There are main different types, and traffic needs to flow from site to site. If your network cannot keep up with it, you (or your client) can't provide your clients with the needed when needed.

If you will be looking at links between sites, you should look at estimating the amount of traffic carried not only for the information that you need to pass but also for the other services such as account replication. This is far outside the scope of this book, and is not covered in this text.

Internet or Intranet?

Another decision you face is whether to set up an intranet or an Internet connection. Although having an Internet connection 100 percent of the time is, with the right security, highly desirable for some organizations (such as research firms), it is not required for most.

In a lot of cases, you do not need to have a connection to the Internet, or at least not a permanent connection for every system. The next section discusses the use of a proxy service. This is an option that enables you to use the Internet, yet still use any address that you want to use.

Whether your organization uses the Internet or an intranet is something that you need to decide on. Remember also to address the ever-present and important security issues. If you have permanent access to the Internet, you must remember that the Internet has permanent access to you.

Always keep straight which server is publishing to the Internet and which to the intranet. If you mix the two up, you will assuredly run into problems.

Who Should Read This Book?

This book is ideal for network administrators and engineers alike. Anyone responsible for installing and managing Windows NT Server on a network with Windows 95 or NT Workstation clients will find in this book what they cannot in the Microsoft documentation. If you are a consultant who has to make recommendations to an organization or the person who actually implements the system, this book is an invaluable resource, organized in a user-friendly manner.

This book is also for computer professionals who need to pass the *Internetworking with Microsoft TCP/IP on Microsoft Windows NT 4* certification exam as they move toward Microsoft Certified Systems Engineer (MCSE) certification.

Note MCSE is the Microsoft Certified Professional category for those computer professionals who work with Microsoft networks.

This book is a comprehensive volume for the knowledge base required for the TCP/IP exam, which is an elective exam.

If you are interested in becoming certified, this book offers the following assistance:

- This book comprehensively covers the information needed to pass the TCP/IP exam as part of its discussion of any topic related to the exam.
- An icon appears before every topic that includes information needed for the exam.
- Hands-on, step-by-step instructions on performing tasks help you gain practical knowledge about the skills required for the exam.
- Questions and answers at the end of each chapter provide an opportunity to test your understanding of the material in the chapter.
- A matrix of test topics and where they are covered within this book is located after the book's Table of Contents. An icon, such as this one in the margin, pinpoints the corresponding information on the page indicated in the matrix. Together, the matrix and icons make it easy for you to find exactly what you need as you make certain that you have covered all the knowledge bases you need.

Objective X.X

Don't expect to read this book as if it were a novel. You can flip from chapter to chapter, section to section, as your needs demand. Between the test topic matrix and the index, New Riders is confident that you will easily find exactly what you looking for.

Special Elements in this Book

Networking with Microsoft TCP/IP, Certified Administrator's Resource Edition includes several special elements and textual features aimed at enhancing the presentation of the material herein. It is the goal that this enhanced presentation will add meaning in terms of the "type" of information presented and enable you, the reader, to learn from this information in the most efficient manner possible.

Practice Sections

At the end of some chapters, a section entitled "Practice" is included. This section is set up as a lab of several exercises that build on each other. The exercises ask you to carry out specific actions that encompass what was discussed in the chapter. These give you an opportunity to get hands-on practice for material covered on the exam, or day-to-day tasks that you will face as an administrator.

Notes, Tips, Cautions, Sidebars

Networking with Microsoft TCP/IP, Certified Administrator's Resource Edition features several special "asides" set apart from the normal text. These asides add extra meaning by illustrating graphically the kind of information being presented. This book offers four distinct asides:

- Notes
- Tips
- Cautions
- Sidebars

Note

A Note includes "extra"—and useful—information that complements the discussion at hand rather than being a direct part of it. A Note might describe special situations that can arise when you install or configure TCP/IP, and tells you what steps to take when such situations do arise. Notes also might tell you how to avoid problems with your software or hardware.

Tip

A Tip provides you with quick instructions for getting the most from your TCP/IP network system as you follow the steps outlined in general discussion. A Tip might show you how to conserve memory in some setups, how to speed up a procedure, or how to perform one of many time-saving and system-enhancing techniques.

Caution A Caution tells you when a procedure might be dangerous—that is, when you run the risk of losing data, locking your system, or even damaging your hardware. Warnings generally tell you how to avoid such losses, or describe the steps you can take to remedy them.

Sidebars Offer Additional Information

A Sidebar, conceptually, is much like a Note—the exception being its length. A Sidebar is by nature much longer than a Note, but offers the same extra, complementary information. Sidebars often include information that is a refresher for material that you may or may not already know. You will know from the title whether or not you need to read the Sidebar. If it's a topic you already understand, save your time and skip it. If it's a topic you aren't familiar with, take a minute and get the basics.

New Riders Publishing

The staff of New Riders is committed to bringing you the very best in computer reference material. Each New Riders book is the result of months of work by authors and staff who research and refine the information contained within its covers.

As part of this commitment to you, New Riders invites your input. Please let us know if you enjoy this book, if you have trouble with the information and examples presented, or if you have a suggestion for the next edition.

Please note, though: New Riders staff cannot serve as a technical resource for Windows NT Workstation 4, or for questions about software- or hardware-related problems. Please refer to the documentation that accompanies NT 4 or to the applications' Help systems.

If you have a question or comment about any New Riders book, there are several ways to contact us. We respond to as many readers as we can. Your name, address, or phone number will never become part of a mailing list and will never be used for any purpose other than to help us continue to bring you the best books possible. You can write us at the following address:

New Riders Publishing
Attn: Associate Publisher
201 W. 103rd Street
Indianapolis, IN 46290

If you prefer, you can fax New Riders Publishing at 317-817-7448.

NRP is an imprint of Macmillan Computer Publishing. To obtain a catalog or information, or to purchase any Macmillan Computer Publishing book, call 800-428-5331.

Thank you for selecting *Networking with Microsoft TCP/IP, Certified Administrator's Resource Edition*!

Part I

TCP/IP Theory

1 *Introduction to TCP/IP* 15

2 *Introduction to Microsoft Networking* 31

3 *The Application Layer* 55

4 *The Transport Layer* 67

5 *The Internet Layer* 77

6 *Subnetting* 93

7 *Routing* 113

CHAPTER 1

Introduction to TCP/IP

As computers first began to emerge from the lab into the business world, a surprising number of different vendors were providing systems. Unfortunately, the vendors had all developed these systems independently. This meant that everyone (and indeed anyone) who wanted to create a computer could and did—following their own rules.

Often, many different people used the larger systems at the same time. This meant that not only did the system developers have to design hardware that could run applications, they also had to devise a method to enable many different users to access the system simultaneously. This normally meant designing communications protocols to allow terminals to access the resources of a central computer. One of the best examples of this is the System Network Architecture (SNA) that IBM developed—this architecture made it possible for a central computer to track the sessions of multiple virtual devices internally. All that was needed was to establish a method of communicating with the remote devices, such as IBM 3270 terminals.

Dozens of network architectures populated the computers of the '70s and '80s. Equipment from the hardware companies such as IBM, Digital, Sperry, Burroughs, and Honeywell ended up as electronic islands, unable to communicate with one another because each company had designed a proprietary communications protocol (network architecture). Because the computer vendors made most of their money by selling systems (integrated hardware and software), they tended to view a proprietary network architecture as a way to bind their customers to specific brands of computer and network equipment.

As personal computers became more and more common, businesses and individuals began connecting them to local area networks (LANs) as a way to share information and resources with each other. Again because of a lack of standards, the LANs also tended to use proprietary protocols. Novell promoted its IPX/SPX protocol suite, Apple had AppleTalk, and IBM and Microsoft (working together at that point) focused on NetBEUI. Enabling computers on one type of network to communicate with computers on a competing network presented a large challenge. Providing for communications with a mainframe or mini-computer reduced the emerging power of the PC to the same level as a dumb terminal.

Sharing data between different systems became an expensive proposition, and required that a gateway between the networks be created—often from scratch. Frequently, even moving data from one system to another required the services of network integrators, which was also very expensive.

By the end of the '80s, many different organizations had made significant investments in their computer operations, and the computer had become a part of everyday life. The expense and inconvenience of moving data between different networks had become a large part of the cost of doing business, and companies were beginning to look around for a solution to the problem.

Left to their own resources, computer manufacturers would likely still be disputing the design of a common network architecture. Fortunately for the business community, a standard did exist that enabled the different computer systems to talk to each other and therefore enabled the different networks to share information with each other: TCP/IP.

This standard was found on the Internet, a loosely associated group of educational institutions and research organizations that had, in conjunction with the United States Department of Defense (DOD), developed a group of standards (protocols) that enabled them to exchange information with each other, regardless of the hardware involved. For more than 20 years, the Internet had provided a medium for internetworking thousands of computers spread throughout the world. TCP/IP was and still is the language of the Internet. It has also become the standard for corporate networks with vendors such as Microsoft, Novell, and Banyan all moving to it as the default protocol.

This chapter provides a broad overview of several aspects of TCP/IP. Because it is important to understand the reasons behind the development of TCP/IP, the first topic of discussion is the evolution of TCP/IP, starting with its early roots in the United States Department of Defense. This discussion introduces you to many of the networking problems that have stimulated the design and evolution of TCP/IP.

Next, this chapter examines the TCP/IP standardization process. Unlike vendor proprietary protocols, which tend to evolve in manufacturers' laboratories, TCP/IP standardization is open and public. As you become involved with TCP/IP, you should know about the standardization process so that you can monitor changes that might affect you.

A Brief History of TCP/IP

Perhaps no organization has more complex networking requirements than the U.S. Department of Defense. Simply enabling communication among the wide variety of computers found in the various services is not enough. DOD computers often need to communicate with contractors and organizations that do defense-related research (that includes most universities). Defense-related network components must be capable of withstanding considerable damage so that the nation's defenses remain operable during a disaster. TCP/IP enables such communication, regardless of vendor or hardware differences, to occur.

The fact that the DOD initiated research into networking protocols (investigating the technology now known as *packet switching*) is not surprising. In fact, research on the protocols that eventually became the TCP/IP protocol suite began in 1969. Among the goals for this research were the following:

- **Common protocols.** The DOD required a common set of protocols (communications rules) that could be specified for all networks. Common protocols would greatly simplify the procurement process because the systems could communicate with each other.
- **Interoperability.** If equipment from various vendors could interoperate, the system development efficiency could be improved and competition among vendors would be promoted.
- **Robust communication.** A particularly dependable network standard was required to meet the nation's defense needs. These protocols needed to provide reliable, high-performance networking with the relatively primitive wide area network technologies then available.
- **Ease of reconfiguration.** Because the DOD depended on the network, reconfiguring the network and adding and removing computers without disrupting communication needed to be possible.

In 1968, the DOD Advanced Research Project Agency (then called DARPA, but since renamed ARPA) initiated research into networks using the technology now called *packet switching*—the capability to address a packet and move it to the destination through different networks. The first experimental network connected four sites: the University of California at Los Angeles (UCLA), the University of California at Santa Barbara (UCSB), the University of Utah, and SRI International. Early tests were encouraging, and additional sites were connected to the network. The ARPAnet, as it came to be called, incorporated 20 hosts by 1972.

Note You will encounter the terms Internet and internet, and should be aware of an important distinction between them. An *internet* (short for internetwork) is any network comprised of multiple, interconnected networks, normally within one company (also referred to as an intranet). The *Internet* is the global internetwork that traces its lineage back to the ARPAnet.

In 1986, groundwork was laid for the commercialization of the ARPAnet. The ARPAnet backbone was dismantled, replaced by a network funded by the National Science Foundation. NSFnet now functions as the Internet backbone. The Advanced Network Services (ANS) manages the NSFnet.

Debate on the Internet protocols has always taken place in a public forum. Consequently, no particular company "owns" these protocols. Responsibility for setting Internet standards rests with an Internet Activity Board.

The initial set of TCP/IP protocols was developed in the early '80s. These protocols became the standard protocols for the ARPAnet in 1983. The protocols gained popularity in the user community when TCP/IP was incorporated into version 4.2 of the BSD (Berkeley Standard Distribution) Unix. This version of Unix is used widely in educational and research institutions. It became the foundation of several commercial Unix implementations, including Sun's SunOS and Digital's Ultrix. Because BSD Unix established a relationship between TCP/IP and the Unix operating system, the vast majority of Unix implementations now incorporate TCP/IP.

Evolution of the TCP/IP protocol suite continues in response to the evolution of the Internet. In recent years, access to the Internet has extended well beyond the original community and is available to virtually anyone who has a computer. This dramatic growth has stressed the Internet and has pushed the design limitations of several protocols. On the Internet, nothing is permanent except change.

The IP protocol currently in use is version 4. It uses a 32-bit address. Only a limited number of addresses are available, and this is becoming a major problem. The next version of IP will be IPng (IP v6). This version will use 128-bit addressing and is already in testing. You can expect to see IPng in the next 2–3 years.

Request for Comments—Defining the Internet

Many different people were involved in the development of the TCP/IP protocol suite. This presented a need to facilitate the sharing of ideas. A process did evolve that enabled everyone to comment on the proposed definitions of the different standards. Basically, someone would draft a standard and the document would be published for review. This became the Request for Comments (RFC) process. Anyone could, and can, contribute to the RFC process. As you review documentation about the TCP/IP protocol in Windows NT, you will see references to the many RFCs that the product supports.

On its way to becoming a standard, a protocol passes through different stages. The protocol starts as a Proposed Standard. It may be promoted to a Draft Standard, and finally to a full-fledged Standard. At each stage, the protocol faces review, debate, implementation, and testing. Proposed Standards, for example, go through at least six months of review before they may be promoted to a Draft Standard. In general, promoting a standard requires two independent implementations of the protocol.

Obviously this process would break down if no one actually monitored it and made decisions when required. The body that takes care of this for the TCP/IP protocol (and therefore also for the Internet) is the Internet Activities Board (IAB). Established in 1983, it is best described as "an independent committee of researchers and professionals with a technical interest in the health and evolution of the Internet system." The IAB coordinates design, engineering, and management of the Internet. The IAB has two task forces: the Internet Engineering Task Force (IETF) and the Internet Research Task Force (IRTF).

Two organizations work with the IAB: the Federal Networking Council and the Internet Society. The Federal Networking Council represents all agencies of the United States federal government involved with the Internet. The Internet Society is a public organization that takes its membership from the entire Internet community. Both organizations provide input on Internet policy and standards.

The IETF is responsible for specifying the Internet protocols and architecture. By its own description, the IETF is not a traditional standards organization, although many specifications produced become standards. The IETF is made up of volunteers who meet three times a year to fulfill the IETF mandate. The IETF has no membership. Anyone may register for and attend meetings.

As figure 1.1 shows, the work of the IETF is organized into various areas that change over time.

Figure 1.1

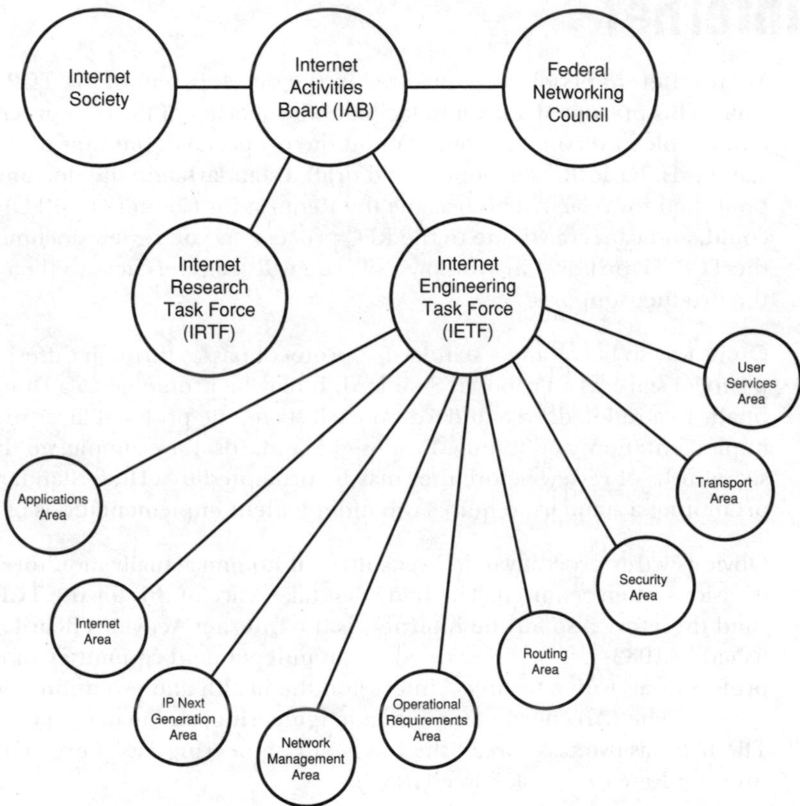

Organizations involved with the Internet.

The directors for the technical areas comprise the Internet Engineering Steering Group, which is responsible for recommending protocol standards. The current IETF areas are as follows:

- Applications
- Internet
- IP Next Generation
- Network Management
- Operational Requirements
- Routing

- Security
- Transport
- User Services

The IRTF is the research organization of the IAB. Membership of the IETF and the IRTF overlap considerably to promote technology transfer.

A memo titled "Internet Official Protocol Standards" describes the standards for protocols to be used on the Internet. It also includes a thorough discussion of the standards process, which has been simplified considerably in this discussion. The memo is updated quarterly and is RFC 2000 as of this writing.

It is important to note that not all RFCs are standards. Many RFCs, for example, have been posted to provide industry input to the process of updating the IP standard. Although not all RFCs are standards, all Internet standards are defined in RFCs and are assigned a standard number.

All documents are assigned RFC numbers for tracking purposes. After a document has been assigned an RFC number and is published, it can never be revised by using the same RFC number. Any published revisions are assigned a new RFC number. If a new RFC replaces an older RFC, the obsolete RFC is identified on the title page. Also, the old RFC is labeled as obsolete and classified as historical. The concern, therefore, is not having the *latest* version of a particular RFC, because only one version of a given RFC ever exists. The concern is having the current RFC for a given standard. (In the second edition of this book, for example, the Internet Official Protocol Standards RFC was number 1920; it is now 2000.)

Internet protocols can have several designations, depending on their state in the standards process. The designation describes the status of the protocol that the RFC describes. The main designations are as follows:

- **Proposed Standard.** Protocols under consideration for standardization in the future.
- **Draft Standard.** Protocols in the final stages of study prior to approval as a standard.
- **Standard.** An official standard protocol for the Internet.
- **Experimental.** Protocols undergoing experimentation but not on the standards track.
- **Historical.** Protocols that have been superseded or are otherwise no longer under consideration for standardization.
- **Informational.** Protocols that interest the Internet community but have not been through the IAB standards review process.

As well as a designation, the requirement level for the protocol is defined in each RFC. This requirement level describes the intended use of the RFC. The main requirement levels are as follows:

- **Required.** Must be implemented by all systems connected to the Internet.
- **Recommended.** Should be implemented.
- **Elective.** May be implemented if desired.
- **Limited.** May be useful in some systems. Experimental, specialized, and historic protocols might receive this classification.
- **Not Recommended.** Historical, specialized, or experimental protocols not recommended for use on the Internet.

In recent years, new technologies have appeared rapidly on the Internet. A case in point is the World Wide Web, which depends on the HyperText Transfer Protocol (HTTP). The web and HTTP were in wide use long before RFC 1945 established an Internet standard for HTTP version 1.0. Increasingly, evolution of the Internet is being led by network heavy hitters such as Microsoft and Netscape. The slow standards process fails to satisfy vendors who want to establish themselves as leaders on the Net.

If you want to obtain information about a particular protocol, you should obtain the RFCs that contain its definition. Obviously the best way to get an RFC is to find it on the Internet. You can easily obtain all the RFCs as well as FYIs and FAQs by visiting the Internic site. Internic is essentially the IAB site on the Internet, and is found at:

```
www.internic.net
```

Note An FYI is a *For Your Information* document that attempts to condense the information from one or more RFCs into something a larger group of people can digest. FYIs are a subset of RFCs and can be found at the Internic site. FAQs are the *Frequently Asked Questions.* These are found on many sites. These documents normally describe (in general terms) the purpose of a site, protocol, newsgroup, and so on. FAQs are written to answer the most often asked questions.

Why Use TCP/IP?

From the discussion thus far, you might be getting the impression that the TCP/IP protocol suite is based on compromise—meaning that many interests are included in the final standard. You might even wonder whether the whole thing can really work given the number of fingers in the pie. The great thing about TCP/IP, however, is that everyone is supporting and pushing it as the protocol of the future.

Through luck or planning or a combination of the two, the TCP/IP protocol suite has turned out to be a robust networking technology that is flexible enough for all the network vendors to use it. It is also open enough so that many different groups can develop applications that work with it. The other main advantage for the network vendors is that TCP/IP has been developed based on the work of the DOD, meaning that the specifications for it are in the public domain.

The only other serious work that has been done comes from the International Standards Organization in the form of the Open Systems Interconnection (OSI). As work on the OSI protocols progressed, it was widely assumed that they would replace TCP/IP as the open protocol solution. The United States government announced that future computer purchases would conform to a government subset of the OSI protocols (called GOSIP). The DOD indicated that GOSIP would replace TCP/IP on military networks.

As often happens with international bodies, however, negotiations on the OSI protocol suite have bogged down. In part because the designers are attempting to make the protocols be everything for everyone, the OSI protocols have been slow to emerge. In fact, development appears to have stalled, and interest in OSI has waned as the fortunes of TCP/IP have prospered. Many industry analysts have argued that OSI is not needed because a functional, open protocol suite is already available in TCP/IP. The DOD has backed off from its declaration that future procurements would require GOSIP. Although OSI might yet be resurrected, the immediate future of TCP/IP appears to be secure. Given the growth of the Internet into a worldwide entity, it is difficult to see how TCP/IP could be dislodged.

One consequence of this compromise is that TCP/IP has evolved into an extremely rich suite of protocols and applications. The name by which the protocol suite is most commonly known is misleading because TCP (Transmission Control Protocol) and IP (Internet Protocol) are only two of dozens of protocols—rules for communicating on a network—that constitute the protocol suite. To emphasize the distinction that TCP/IP is much more than just TCP and IP, some refer to the suite as the Internet protocol suite or the DOD protocol suite.

Here are but a few examples of protocols and services associated with TCP/IP:

- **Telnet.** A remote terminal emulation protocol that enables clients to log on to remote hosts on the network.
- **FTP.** A file transfer application that enables users to transfer files between hosts.
- **SNMP (Simple Network Management Protocol).** Used to remotely manage network devices.
- **DNS (Domain Name Service).** Puts a friendly face on the network by assigning meaningful names to computers.
- **HTTP (HyperText Transfer Protocol).** This protocol, the core of the World Wide Web, facilitates retrieval and transfer of hypertext (mixed media) documents.

In the chapters that follow, you will learn about many different protocols. The word protocol will become confusing because it is used to refer to many different parts of the stack. You will see essentially three types of protocols: services (these protocols enable you to provide services such as WWW Publishing Service), clients (applications that enable you to use services such as Internet Explorer, for example), and the actual transport protocols (these protocols—TCP, UDP, and IP, for example—actually move the data on the network).

Overview of TCP/IP Addresses

Objective E.1

To make TCP/IP work, each and every device on a TCP/IP network requires a unique address. An IP address identifies the device to all the other devices on the network. IP addresses are made up of two parts. The first identifies your network ID. With the Internet spanning the entire globe, every network or part of a network must have a unique ID. This ID is used to route the information being sent to the correct network. The other part of your IP address is the host ID, a unique number that identifies each computer and device on your network that talks using TCP/IP.

An IP address is very similar to your street address. If your address is 110 Main Street, the address identifies which street you are on—Main Street. It also identifies your house on that street—number 110. The only difference between a street address and a TCP/IP address is that the street addresses are reversed. If this were a TCP/IP address, it would look like this: Main Street, 110.

How much of the address describes the network ID depends on the type of address you have. Three main classes of addresses exist: Class A, B, and C. A TCP/IP address is, simply put, a 32-bit binary number. Looking at an address as 32 zeros or ones is difficult for humans, so the address is viewed as a dotted decimal address in the following format: 198.53.147.153. In this case, you are on network 198.53.147, and you are host number 153. Each of the four numbers represents 8 bits of the address and is referred to as an octet. To understand TCP/IP and some of the concepts that make it work, it is important to be familiar with the binary form of the address.

Understanding binary is relatively easy. Look at the number 238, for example. In conventional math, this is two hundred and thirty-eight. Automatically, you see the 2 as two groups of one hundred, the 3 is three groups of ten, and there are eight groups of one. Each of the digits is multiplied by a positional value to make the total. That value is always ten times the value to the right because there are ten different numbers: 0 1 2 3 4 5 6 7 8 9.

Normally, you need only to work with binary numbers that are 8 digits long. Table 1.1 shows the values for those first 8 positions:

TABLE 1.1
Bit Position Values

128	64	32	16	8	4	2	1

In binary, there are only two numbers, 1 and 0. Where the decimal system is a base ten system, the binary system is a base two system. Like the decimal system, the positional values increase. Here, however, they increase by two times the previous value (exponentially). Using table 1.1, you should be able to figure out that the binary code 110110 does not represent one hundred and ten thousand, one hundred and ten. Instead, it represents one group of thirty-two, one group of sixteen, no groups of eight, one group of four, one group of two, and no groups of one. That is, 110110 represents the number 54 if you express it in decimal.

If you were to take the 198 from the example address 198.53.147.153, you could express this number as 128+64+4+2 (or 11000110). Remember that each of the 4 numbers represents 8 bits of the address, making up the total of 32 bits.

The most obvious difference between the three main types of addresses is the number of octets used to identify the network ID. Class A uses the first octet only; this leaves 24 bits (or three octets) to identify the host. Class B uses the first two octets to identify the network, leaving 16 bits (two octets) for the host. Class C uses three octets for the network ID, leaving 8 bits (one octet) for the host.

A couple of rules determine what you can and cannot use for addresses. Neither the network ID nor the host ID can be represented by all 0's or by all 1's, because each of these conditions has a special meaning. As well, the network with the first octet 127 is used solely for loop back tests (a test where the classes of networks also differ in how their addresses start in binary). Class A addresses start with 0. Class B addresses start with 10. Class C addresses start with 110. You can tell which class of address a host has by the first octet of its TCP/IP address. Knowing that the first octet represents the first 8 bits of the address, and by knowing the starting bits for the classes of addresses, you can see the first octet ranges for the respective classes in table 1.2:

TABLE 1.2
TCP/IP Address Classes—First Octet

Class	Start (Binary)	Finish (Binary)	Start (Decimal)	Finish (Decimal)
A	00000001	01111111	1	127
B	10000000	10111111	128	191
C	11000000	11011111	192	223

Because the Class A addresses use only the first octet to identify the network ID, there are a limited number of them (126, to be exact; 127 is reserved). Each of these 126 networks, however, can have many hosts on it: 2^{24} (the remaining 24 bits) hosts minus two (the host IDs that are all 0's and all 1's) equals 16,777,214 hosts on a single network (albeit impossible).

Class B addresses use the first two octets. The first 2 bits, however, are set to binary 10. This leaves 14 bits that can be used to identify the network: 2^{14} possible combinations (6 bits in the first octet and 8 from the second)—16,384 network IDs (because the first two digits are 10, you don't have to worry about an all 0's or all 1's host ID.) Each of those network IDs has 16 bits left to identify the host or 65,534 hosts ($2^{16} - 2$).

Class C networks use three octets (or 24 bits) to identify the network. The first three bits, however, are always 110. This means that there are five bits in the first octet and eight in the other two that can be used to uniquely identify the network ID or 2^{21} possible networks (2,097,152)—each of which has 8 bits for hosts or 254 (2^8–2).

Table 1.3 summarizes all the possible TCP/IP addresses.

Table 1.3
Address Class Summary

Address Class	First Octet Start	Finish	Number of Networks	Hosts Each
A	1	126	126	16,777,214
B	128	191	16,384	65,534
C	192	223	2,097,152	254

You will encounter much more about addressing in other chapters in this book.

Summary

The next few chapters introduce the various components that make TCP/IP workable, and explain how TCP/IP works in Microsoft Windows NT (the fastest-growing network operating system today). The next chapter covers NT networking architecture, explaining where TCP/IP fits in and how NT deals with it. The focus then changes to a discussion of all the layers of TCP/IP. This discussion should help you understand just what happens when data is transferred.

Test Yourself

1. What problem did TCP/IP address?
2. What was Microsoft's original protocol?
3. What was the main organization that drove the development of TCP/IP?
4. What was the original name for the Internet?
5. What were the main design goals for TCP/IP?
6. What do the following acronyms stand for, and what is a brief definition of each one?

   RFC

   FYI

   TCP

   IETF
7. What are the three levels of RFC designations a protocol might have?
8. Where can you find copies of RFCs?
9. What are some of application protocols and services that are available in TCP/IP?
10. How does the computer see a TCP/IP address? How do users see it?
11. What are the two pieces of a TCP/IP address?
12. Convert the following to decimal:

    10110100

    00101110

    11011010

    01010010

    11100000

    00101111

    11010111

    10101101

    01000101

    11111111

13. Convert the following to binary:

    253

    127

    64

    78

    156

    187

    45

    63

    65

    198

14. For the following network addresses, indicate the class of address to which they belong:

    198.53.235.0

    2.0.0.0

    190.25.0.0

    192.25.15.0

    128.56.0.0

15. What are the first 3 bits in a Class C address?

16. Complete the following chart:

Address Class	First Octet Start	Finish	Number Of Networks	Hosts Each
A	1	126		16,777,214
B		191	16,384	
C	192			254

Test Yourself Answers

1. TCP/IP was developed to addresses issues of interoperability between computers manufactured by different vendors.
2. Microsoft originally used NetBEUI.
3. The Department of Defense in the United States.

4. Originally the Internet was called DARPA (DOD Advanced Research Project Agency) and was then changed to ARPA, and eventually to ARPAnet.
5. The main goals for TCP/IP included common protocols, interoperability, dependable (robust) networking, and easy configuration.
6. **RFC** Request For Comments: The working documents of the Internet

   FYI For Your Information: Summaries of RFCs related to important protocols

   TCP Transmission Control Protocol: One of the main protocols in the TCP/IP protocol suite

   IETF Internet Engineering Task Force: The body that handles the implementation of new standards
7. RFCs for protocols that are being implemented start as a Proposed Standard, then become a Draft Standard, and finally, if approved, achieve Standard status.
8. The best place to find an RFC is the Internic web site at:

   `www.internic.net.`
9. Some examples include Telnet, FTP, SNMP, DNS, and HTTP.

   The computer views an address as a string of 32 bits, we look at addresses as a series of 4 octets in dotted decimal notation.

11. A TCP/IP address is made up of a Network ID and a Host ID.
12. **10110100** 180

    00101110 46

    11011010 218

    01010010 82

    11100000 224

    00101111 47

    11010111 215

    10101101 173

    01000101 69

    11111111 255
13. **253** 11111101

    127 01111111

    64 01000000

    78 01001110

    156 10011100

187	10111011
45	00101101
63	00111111
65	01000001
198	11000110

14.

198.53.235.0	C
2.0.0.0	A
190.25.0.0	B
192.25.15.0	C
128.56.0.0	B

15. The first three bits are 110.
16.

Address Class	First Octet Start	Finish	Number Of Networks	Hosts Each
A	1	126	126	16,777,214
B	128	191	16,384	65,534
C	192	223	2,097,152	254

CHAPTER 2

Introduction to Microsoft Networking

If you were to study the internal combustion engine, you would have to know how that relates to the entire automobile and just where all the pieces fit together. This sense of proportion helps to make the learning easier by putting all the pieces together. Just like the automobile engine, before you can really understand the TCP/IP protocol stack, you have to understand the way that Microsoft networking fits together.

This chapter looks at all the parts of Microsoft networking. This is not specific to the Windows NT product, but generally describes the way that any Microsoft network operating system works.

The OSI Reference Model

Chapter 1, "Introduction to TCP/IP," mentioned the Open Systems Interconnection (OSI) reference model. Every networking model is built on layers. The OSI reference model was designed as a guide for vendors to use as they built their own networking architectures. (It is not an actual architecture.) Windows NT networking fits the OSI model. This discussion uses it as a comparison to the TCP/IP model, which is different, yet manages to achieve the same purpose (and which NT also fits). The layers in the OSI model have the following functions:

- **Application.** Generates the requests and processes the requests that it receives.
- **Presentation.** Creates the SMB (Server Message Block) (in NT's case) that tells the other system what is requested, or contains the response to the request. This layer also deals with type conversions when the communicating hosts are different.
- **Session.** Provides a method for creating and maintaining a logical connection between two hosts. It also tracks the resources currently in use.
- **Transport.** Puts the information into a "language" that the other system understands.
- **Network.** Deals with directing which system or systems receive the information on the other end. In other words, it tracks which MAC (Media Access Control—the unique number that each network card has) address to send to.
- **Data Link Control.** Deals with the framing of the information sent on the wire.
- **Physical.** Puts the information on to the physical network and receives packets (or frames) from the network.

A discussion of Microsoft networking architecture should help you understand that when data is being moved between two systems, the information from each of the layers becomes the data of the layer that resides below it. In this manner, an SMB (Server Message Block), which is created by the Application and Presentation layers, becomes the data for the Session layer (or in NT, the TDI boundary).

What Is Microsoft Networking?

Microsoft provides a great deal of flexibility in networking by providing the layered approach to the networking components. Primarily, Microsoft uses NetBIOS (Network Basic Input/Output System) as its internal networking protocol. NetBIOS provides the following several services essential to networking:

- **Name management.** In NetBIOS networking, computer names are used to identify the different systems on a network. This function allows for NetBIOS names to be registered at a computer and enables the computer to know to which requests to respond. NetBIOS names are 16 bytes in length with the 16th byte being used to identify the service that registered the name (for example, workstation, server, and so on).
- **Connection-oriented data transfer.** This function enables the transfer of data from one system to another by using a session, and also enables a series of checks and balances to ensure that the data being transferred is correct.
- **Connectionless data transfer.** This part of NetBIOS enables computers to make announcements and send queries to all computers on the network without having to create sessions. It is used to locate other computers on the network, or to let other computers know about this one. This provides a transport for such purposes as logon validation, server announcements, name queries, and so on.
- **Session management.** This service tracks and maintains sessions with other computers on the network, enabling the system to keep track of other computers with which you work so that those computers can communicate with each other more quickly. Rather than having to identify yourself every time you communicate with another system, you can just use the session.

NetBIOS uses a structure called an SMB (Server Message Block) to communicate between the system requesting the service and the system that will provide the service. On the system that generates the request, an SMB is created by the redirector (the component that gets access to the other computer) that, in Microsoft Windows NT networking, is the workstation service. The SMB describes what the other system is to do (put this data on the drive, send some data to the SMB, start a session, and so forth) and includes that actual data where required.

The redirector and the server services are the Application layer discussed earlier in relation to the OSI model. These actually create the requests and respond to them. These services also handle the Presentation layer; they create the SMBs (how requests are formatted for the other computer).

As figure 2.1 shows, the SMB is a method of communications between a redirector and a server. No other parts of the network architecture use the SMB. Instead, all the lower layers carry the data.

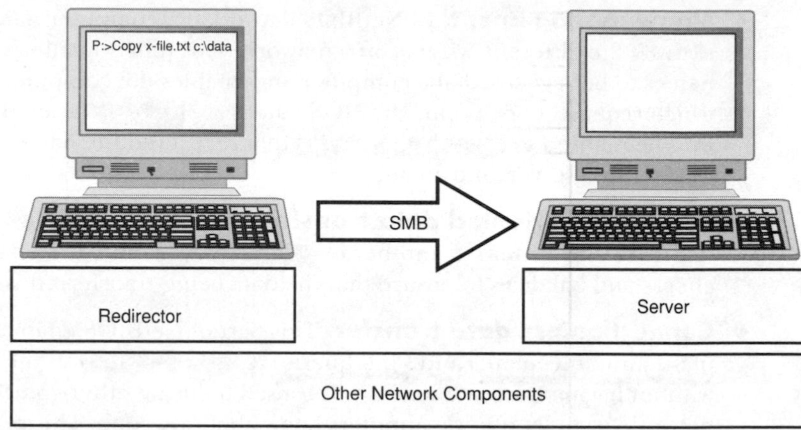

Figure 2.1
Depiction of communications between a Redirector and Server.

Layers on Layers

One of the great strengths of Microsoft networking is the layered approach. By taking this approach, Microsoft has created an environment where it is possible to add in many different components to the network architecture without having to re-create the whole operating system. Another advantage is that only any one layer has to understand the layer that it directly communicates with—this means that a programmer writing an application does not need to be concerned about the network topology, not even if a network is available. Programmers need only concern themselves with what the application is meant to do.

This isolation from the details is an important move forward; it enables quicker development of applications and makes it possible for developers to concentrate on one area. This isolation also extends to other areas of the network architecture. You can create your own transport protocol, for example, which you can add into the NT stack. The transport protocol you create only needs to be able to communicate with the layer above (which is the TDI layer) and the layer below (NDIS) (see fig. 2.2).

Essentially, the Microsoft network has five main layers. The following list describes these layers in detail:

- **Application/File System Drivers.** These are the high-end components that are going to formulate your requests, and service requests from other systems. The components at this layer are implemented in one of two ways: either as an API (Application Programming Interface), which is a series of routines that other programs can call on; or as a file system driver, which provides basic input/output services. This layer is equivalent to the Application and Presentation layers in the OSI model.

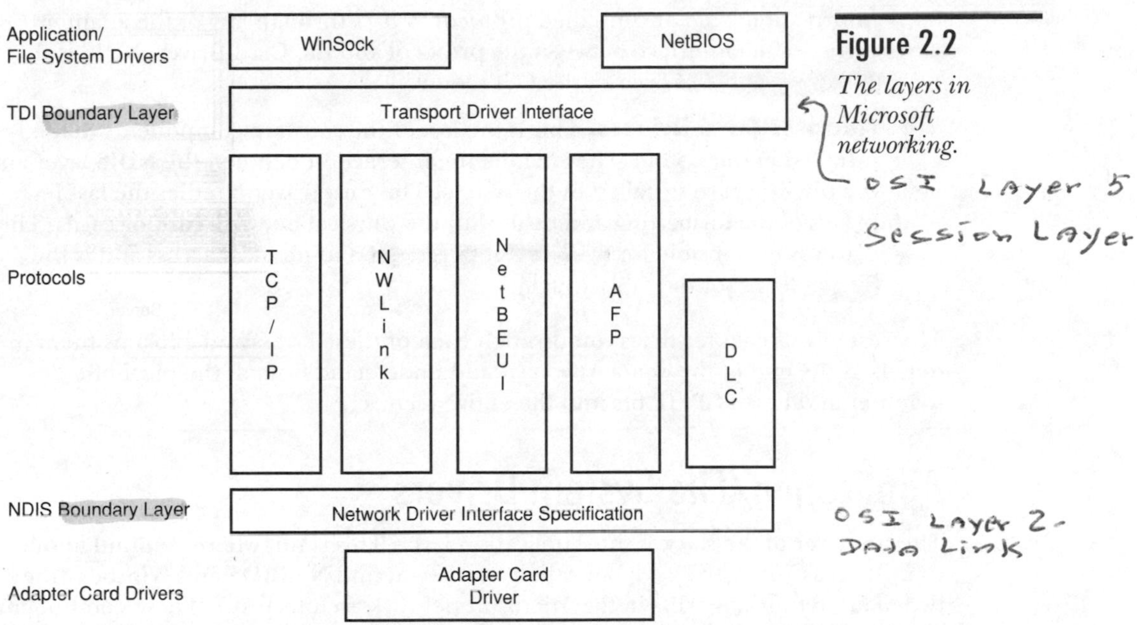

Figure 2.2

The layers in Microsoft networking.

- **TDI (Transport Driver Interface).** This layer acts, as the name suggests, as an interface, and is referred to as a boundary layer (meaning that it is a standard set of calls, not an actual file). The upper layer components call on the TDI layer to pass requests to and from the various protocols installed on the system. The TDI layer is based mainly on NetBIOS, and is installed as the NetBIOS Interface—though it does handle more than just NetBIOS traffic. The TDI layer also takes care of the session services and, therefore, maps to the Session layer of the OSI model.
- **Protocols.** In Microsoft networking, you have great flexibility as to which protocol your computer runs: You can choose one protocol, or run all the available protocols. This is true for all the platforms from the lowly DOS client (which can run TCP/IP, NWLink, NetBEUI, and DLC) through to Windows NT 4. The protocols are responsible for transporting and formatting the data so that the other system can understand them. Protocols are the language of networks and handle the Transport and Network layers in the OSI model. You can also add protocols—in some cases, they have been added so that the Microsoft environment could communicate with other environments. One case in point is the Banyan Vines IP stack for Windows NT.
- **NDIS (Network Driver Interface Specification).** This is the other boundary layer; it interfaces between the protocols installed in the computer and the network card drivers that are installed. NDIS provides the logical connections between the protocols and the adapter card drivers that enable

information from any installed protocol to pass through any of the adapter cards. As the interface between the protocol and the Card Driver, NDIS is the Data Link Control layer of the OSI model.

- **Adapter Card Drivers.** This is the last of the software components that is installed in the system. They handle the interaction between the NDIS layer and the physical card installed in the system. The card driver handles the last few pieces of the formatting and deals with the physical network card or cards. The driver is responsible for Media Access Control and physical access and is the Physical layer of the OSI model.

The rest of this chapter takes you through each of these layers and explains them in detail. At the end of the chapter, you should understand how all the pieces fit together and how TCP/IP fits into the entire picture.

Application/File System Drivers

The top layer of the stack is the Application layer. This is not where you find applications such as Word or Excel, but rather where you find NetBIOS and Winsock (the two main networking APIs in the Microsoft network architecture). These components provide services to the actual applications that can call on the network by using these network APIs. As stated, the APIs provide a standard method for programmers to call on the services of the underlying network without having to know anything about it.

Sitting at this layer, you might also add an NCP (Netware Core Protocol) component to enable you to talk with or provide services to the Novell world, or maybe add an NFS component to enable you to work with the Network File System that is popular on the Unix platforms. This capability to add in other network components comes from the modular design.

The main components installed at this layer include the workstation service and the server service. These are the NetBIOS services that enable you to use the resources available at another computer or that make it possible for other computers to use your resources. When you install TCP/IP (or IPX/SPX), you also get Winsock, which acts as both the server and workstation for non-NetBIOS services. This chapter discusses these as they relate to TCP/IP later.

Transport Driver Interface

On the next layer, all the applications and installed file systems talk to the TDI. The TDI layer is responsible for taking the information from the layer above and moving it down to the appropriate protocol so that the information from the upper layer can be encapsulated into a packet to be sent on the wire. The information from the various redirectors and servers that is being passed down is nothing more than the data that the TDI is asking the protocols to deliver. The TDI layer does this, and keeps track of the different computers with which it communicates.

The TDI also works with other services such as the NWNBLink and NBT, enabling it to provide NetBIOS services over IPX/SPX and TCP/IP respectively. The TDI layer must also deal with Winsock to enable these communications.

The Transport Protocols

The next part in the architecture is the actual protocols. It is important to note that the TCP/IP protocol is only one of the protocols that Microsoft networking can use. Windows NT comes with several protocols, including TCP/IP (of course), NWLink, NetBEUI, AFP, and DLC. The properties of these protocols are explained in the following list:

- **TCP/IP (Transmission Control Protocol/Internet Protocol).** The de facto industry standard protocol for wide area networking. The TCP/IP protocol is an entire suite of protocols that enables end-to-end connections as well as multicasting (sending the same information to many computers) connections. TCP/IP is available on most operating systems and networks, enabling it to communicate between different types of computers over different network topologies and configurations by routing your data through each of them.
- **NWLink (Netware Link).** The Microsoft implementation of the standard IPX/SPX (Internetwork Packet Exchange/Sequenced Packet Exchange) protocol used by Novell servers. This protocol is also routeable (it can move between different networks,) but is geared mainly to the simple movement of data from point A to point B.
- **NetBEUI (NetBIOS Extended User Interface).** This is the original protocol used in Microsoft networking, and has been updated constantly. Although it is the fastest protocol included in the NT suite of protocols, it is intended for a single segment (all the computers connected to a single network) network and best supports between 20 and 200 computers. NetBEUI is not routeable and is therefore not suitable to wide area networking.
- **AFP (Apple File Protocol).** Apple computers use this protocol. It is included to enable NT Server to support Apple networking. Though the AFP is a routeable protocol, it is not as flexible as TCP/IP or NWLink.
- **DLC (Data Link Control).** This protocol is not intended to be used for computers to communicate with each other and therefore does not have all the services the other protocols do. It is included in Windows NT to enable communications with HP JetDirect printers, and between an NT systems and an IBM mainframe using 3270 emulation software.

Network Driver Interface Specification

The NDIS layer is the next layer. Simply put, this is a standard interface between a protocol and a network adapter card. In NT 4, the NDIS layer is NDIS 4.0. In essence, NDIS creates a logical connection (binding) between the protocol and the network adapter card. Each of the bindings is assigned a number. The TDI layer uses that number to determine which path the data should take. The process takes each of the network protocols and binds them to each of the adapters, assigning each of these a number starting at 0. The number for a binding is referred to as the LANA (Local Area Network Adapter) Number (see fig. 2.3).

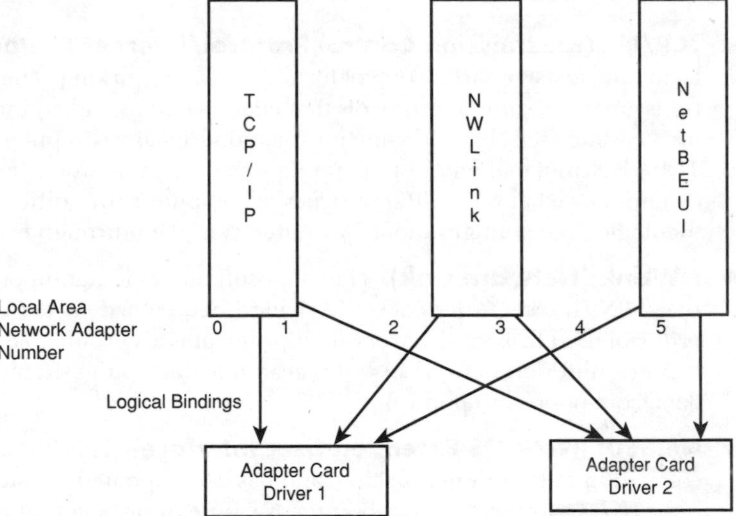

Figure 2.3
An illustration of the binding process and LANA Numbers.

This method of binding protocols to network adapter cards means that only one instance of any protocol ever exists; just as only one instance of each adapter driver exists. This reduces the overhead you might experience when working with multiple network protocols and adapters.

Adapter Card Drivers

Finally, the card driver frames the data that started at the top of the architecture for the particular network topology, and the by the network adapter physically merges the data on to the wire.

To put all this together, consider the process of sending a piece of data from one system to another. First you drag a file from your system and drop it on a network drive.

In figure 2.4, Explorer (or whatever you used) now calls the network APIs to access the network. These APIs call on the Workstation server (assuming you are talking to a NetBIOS server) to create an SMB. This contains information about what the server should do when it gets the SMB and up to 64 K worth of data. (If the file is large, you may need many SMBs to transport the file to the remote system.)

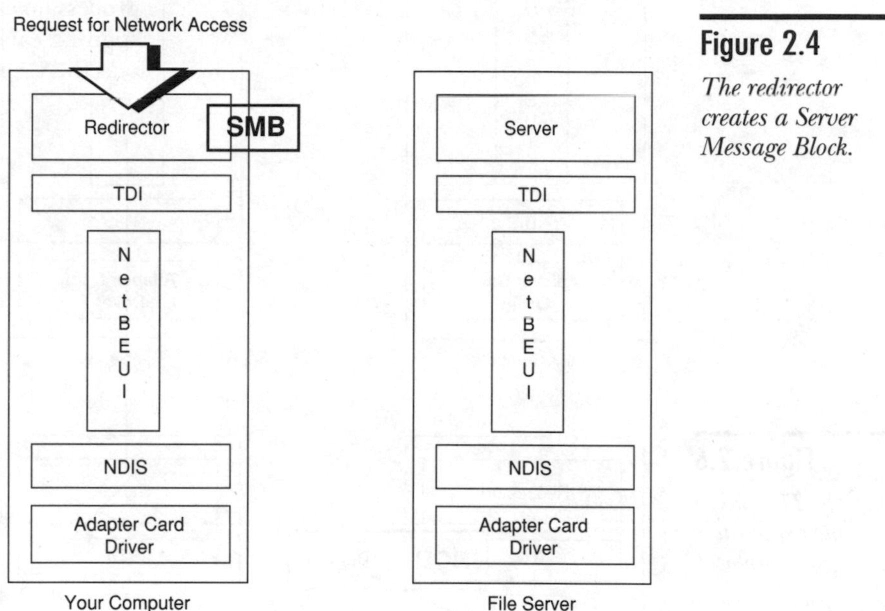

Figure 2.4
The redirector creates a Server Message Block.

The redirector now passes the SMB to the TDI as data, and the TDI generates an NCB (Network Control Block) based on where the data is to be sent (see fig. 2.5). The TDI checks its session table and locates the correct path to send the data to the remote system—identified by the LANA Number. With this information, the TDI now passes the data and NCB to the protocol.

The protocol takes the request (generated as an NCB) and translates the request (where and how to send the data) to its own set of instructions (see fig. 2.6).

The NDIS layer now takes the instructions from the protocol and passes them to the appropriate network card (based again on the LANA Number). The driver for the card takes the information and data from the protocol and treats it all as data. NDIS delivers the actual information to be placed on the wire to the Adapter Card Driver (see fig. 2.7).

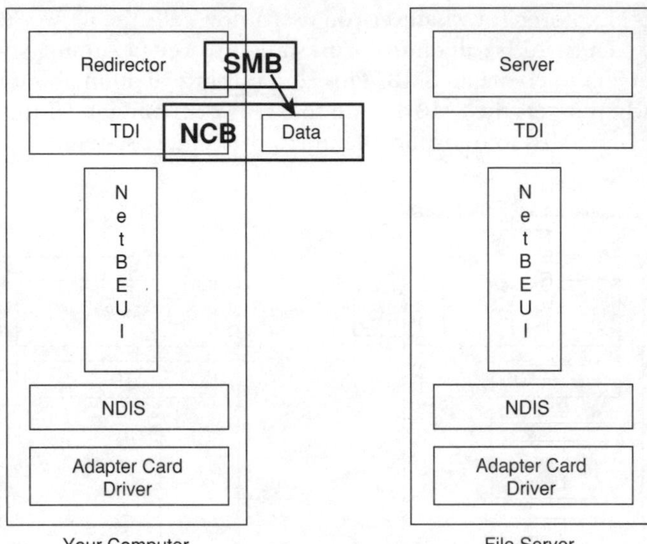

Figure 2.5
The TDI layer creates an NCB with the SMB as data.

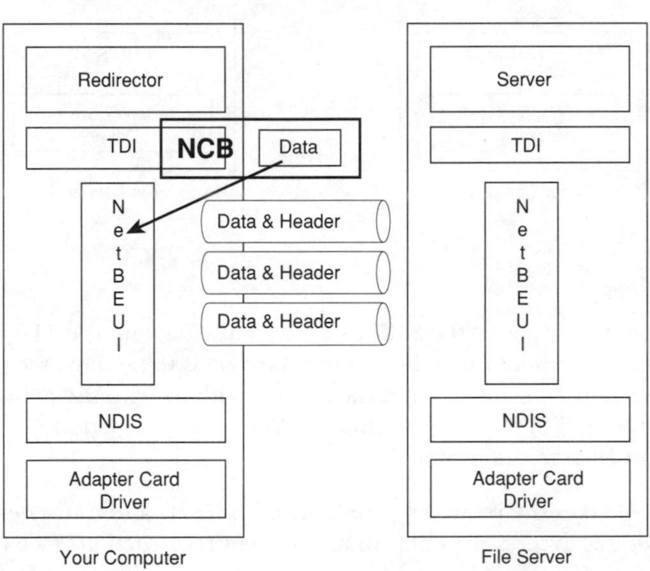

Figure 2.6
The TDI passes the request to a protocol.

The Adapter Card Driver formats it for the topology it uses (for example, Token Ring, Ethernet, FDDI). It now sends the data to the other system where the reverse process takes place (see fig. 2.8).

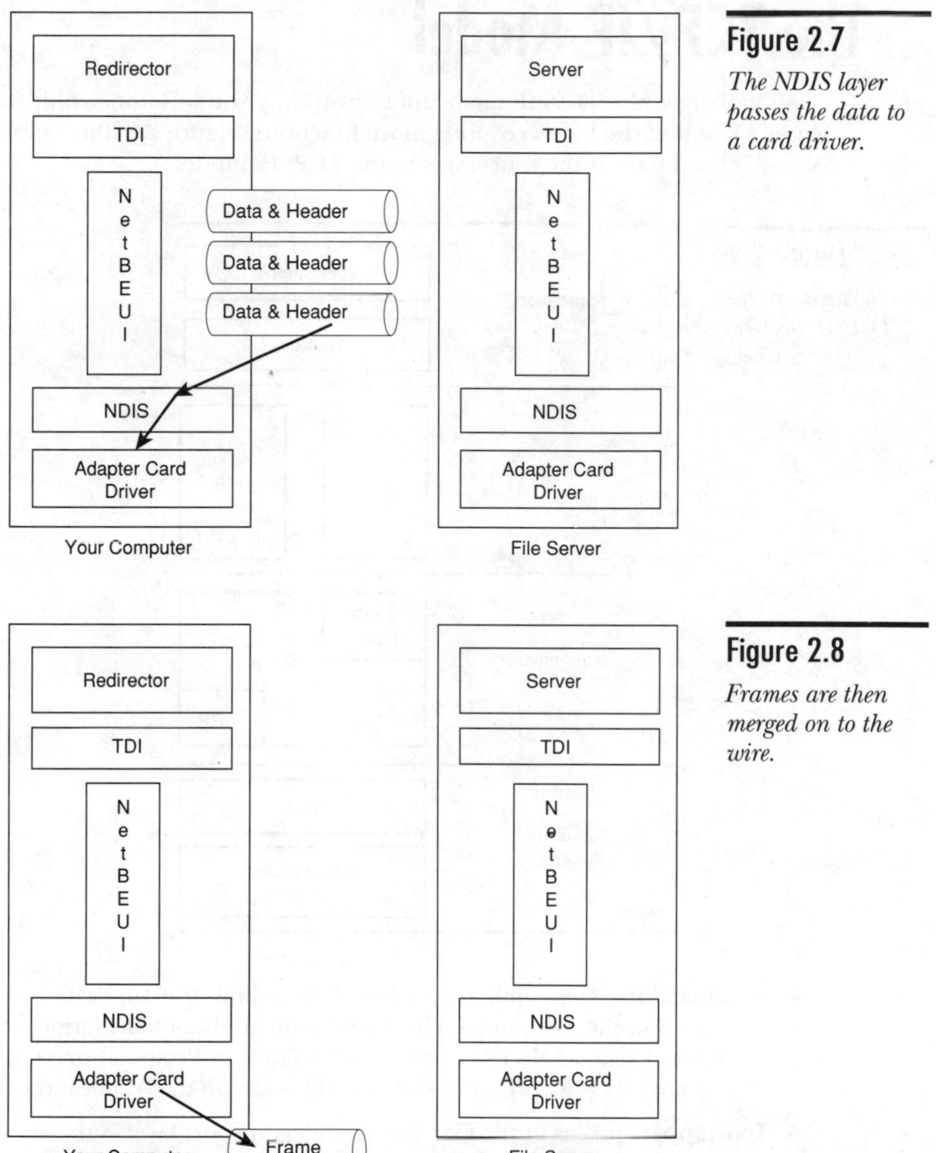

Figure 2.7

The NDIS layer passes the data to a card driver.

Figure 2.8

Frames are then merged on to the wire.

The TCP/IP Model

When looking at the TCP/IP model for networking, you will notice only four layers. This is a result of the layers covering more functions. Figure 2.9 illustrates and the following list discusses the four layers of the TCP/IP model.

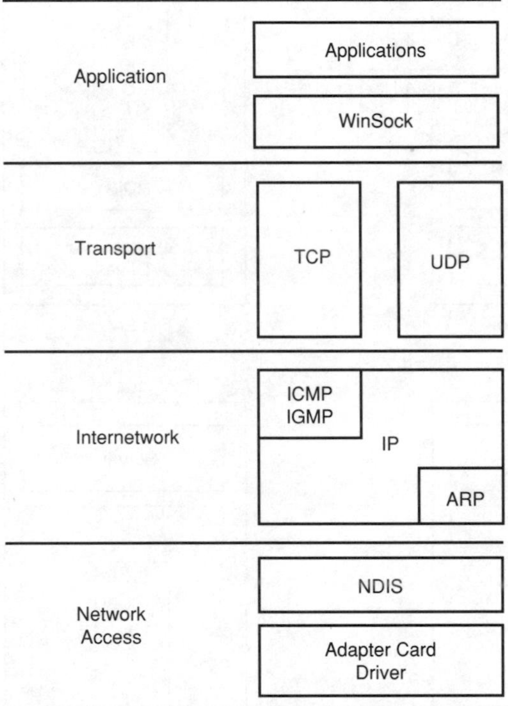

Figure 2.9
The layers in the TCP/IP protocol stack.

- **Application.** This combines the functions of both the Application and Presentation layers in the OSI model. The Application layer contains various services (protocols) such as NNTP (Network News Transfer Protocol) or SMTP (Simple Mail Transfer Protocol). The WinSock API is also in the Application layer.
- **Transport.** Just as in the OSI model, the Transport layer is the actual language of the network. All requests use one of two different transport protocols—either TCP (Transmission Control Protocol) or UDP (User Datagram Protocol).
- **Internet.** This replaces the network layer in the OSI model, and deals not only with finding other hosts (computers) on the same network, but with routing information (in the form of packets) to other networks.
- **Network Access.** Replaces the Data Link Control and Physical layers by treating them as one. This layer still handles framing the data and merging it to the wire, but the IP layer takes care of deciding which systems to send to.

TCP/IP does not use computer names in its communications. Rather, it uses the IP address of the host as the destination for the packet it will send. This means that some method of turning \\sparky (a NetBIOS computer name) or `www.microsoft.com` (a host name) into an IP address must exist. Otherwise you would have to memorize many different IP addresses.

Now that you have seen what the layers are, it's time to take a closer look at each of them.

Components at the Application Layer

Many different protocols (for this discussion of TCP/IP applications, the word protocol is used to describe most of the pieces that are TCP/IP) can be located at this layer. All the TCP/IP protocols (applications) and the NetBIOS services, however, rely on the services of two main APIs: WinSock and NBT (normally referred to as NetBIOS. It is NBT or NetBIOS over TCP/IP, however, that provides the capability of SMB networking to happen over TCP/IP).

WinSock

WinSock provides socket-oriented services to the TCP/IP utilities that can exist at the Application layer and also provides services to NetBIOS. The socket provides a simple reference point that enables each system to send to a specific port number on the other (see fig. 2.10). The numbers are not normally the same on both ends; services usually use well defined and well known port numbers. These well defined port numbers are controlled and assigned by the Internet Assigned Numbers Authority.

Figure 2.10

Host communications using WinSock.

When you start a service on your system (such as the Internet Information Server's HTTP Publishing Service), the service registers its assigned port number in the system and anything that comes in for that port is sent to that service (see fig. 2.11). Again, this allows the WinSock interface and all the underlying layers to ignore what the information is and to just move it from point to point. Included in the information is the address, transport layer protocol (UDP or TCP), and socket number that sent the information; this information enables the application to respond directly to that client running on the remote system.

Figure 2.11

A service opens its port (or socket).

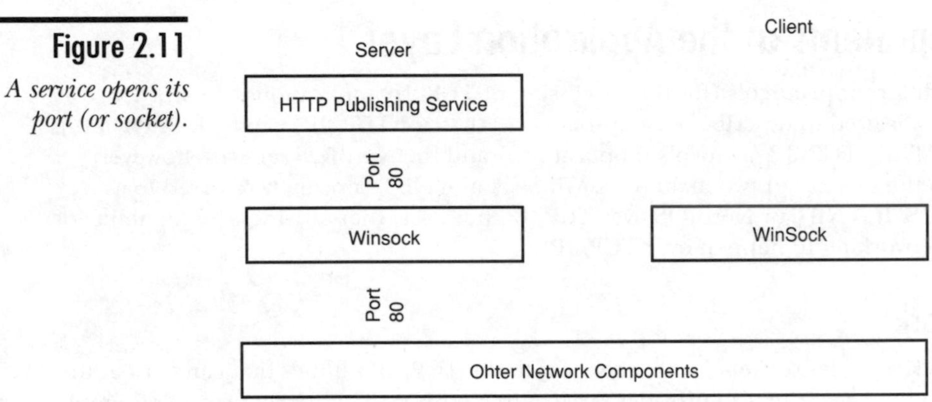

The first 1,024 ports are reserved and are used only for services. Any port number up to 65,536, however, is valid. To look at the whole process, the service starts on the server and registers its port number (thereby monitoring that port as shown in figure 1.12).

Figure 2.12

The client also registers a port.

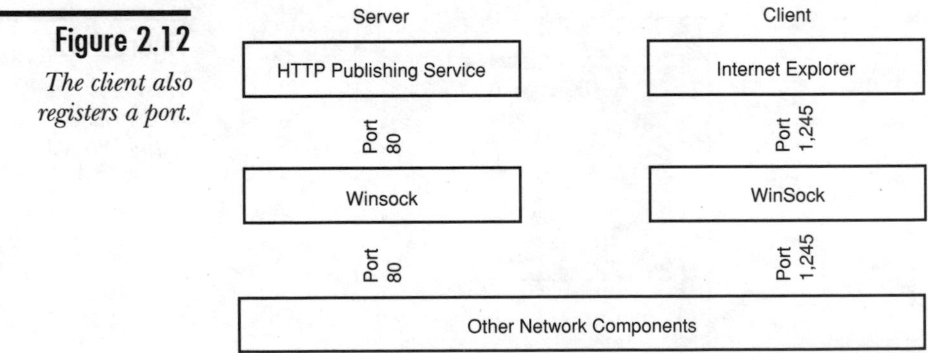

On the other host, the client side application starts. It also registers a port number that it will use (any available port above 1023). The client application can now start to send information to the server by sending to the IP address, transport protocol, and socket number. The server then responds to the IP address, protocol, and socket from which it received the information.

In this way, there is no reliance on computer names or other upper-level information and absolutely no restriction on which port any particular service can use.

NetBIOS

As stated earlier, Windows NT uses NetBIOS when you work with its redirector and server services (the base Application layer components of Microsoft networking). This means that it requires the underlying protocol to handle requests in the forms of NetBIOS commands. You have just seen that the TCP/IP stack does not use names, nor does it register each service with a name/number combination. On the surface, this indicates that in fact NT cannot use TCP/IP for a protocol; however, it does. To do this, another layer has to be brought in that maps (or translates) the NetBIOS command into a series of TCP/IP port numbers. This enables the NetBIOS to have a port for transmitting and receiving data, establishing and releasing sessions, and handling NetBIOS names—all over TCP/IP. Not surprisingly, the component that handles this function is called NBT or NetBIOS over TCP/IP. It is responsible for the mapping of, and communications between the NetBIOS interface and the various WinSock ports (see fig. 2.13).

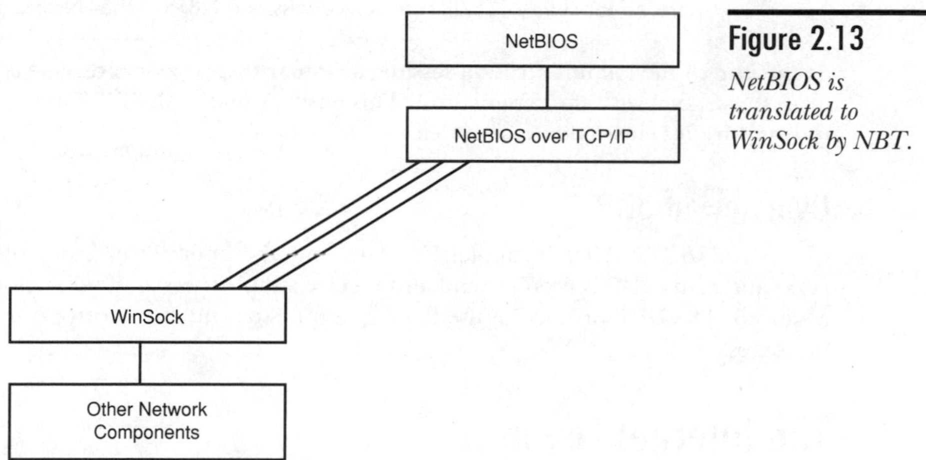

Figure 2.13
NetBIOS is translated to WinSock by NBT.

This means that all communications over TCP/IP must go through the WinSock interface.

The Transport Layer Protocols

WinSock has to rely on the Transport layer to deal with data moving to and from it. This is handled by the two Transport layer protocols. Computers can have different types of conversations with each other. Just like humans, computers can send a package by regular post and hope that it gets there (like mailing a letter), or they can send it by registered mail and have a guarantee of delivery. UDP (User Datagram Protocol) is like sending it regular mail—no guarantee. TCP (Transmission Control Protocol), on the other hand, creates a session, and can therefore guarantee delivery.

Overview of TCP

TCP is used, as stated several times earlier, to provide a connection-oriented delivery service for the higher-level protocols. To do this, TCP must first establish a session with the remote communicating host. It does this by means of a three-way handshake.

First the host initiating the communications sends a packet to the other host that contains information about itself and a SYN (or synchronize flag) telling the other host that a session is requested. The other host receives this packet and responds with information about itself—the SYN flag and an ACK (acknowledgment) of the information that it received. Finally the first host ACKs the information it received from the other, and a session now exists between the two systems.

Note You can view the sessions that your system currently has by using the NETSTAT command for strictly TCP/IP communications and NBTSTAT for NetBIOS sessions.

At the end of the communication session, a similar three-way handshake is used to drop the session with the remote host. This ensures that both of the hosts are through transmitting. It closes the session cleanly.

Overview of UDP

Compared to TCP, UDP is simple: The data from the upper-layer protocol is encapsulated and sent. UDP is used to send and receive simple messages; no session is required. The UDP protocol is used, for example, to send and receive broadcast messages.

The Internet Layer

The Internet layer has four main protocols. These protocols work together to provide a best-effort delivery service (guarantees are the responsibility of TCP or higher-level applications). IP (Internet Protocol) needs only to know which IP address to send the data to and the protocol on the other system (TCP or UDP) that should receive it.

The Internet Protocol (IP Layer)

Objective B.5

All devices that use TCP/IP have an Internet layer that includes the routers that provide the backbone for communications across the network. The IP is responsible for taking the packet and determining whether the packet is for the local network. If not, the IP must find a route for the packet to the destination network and eventually the destination host. To understand how the IP determines whether a host is on the local network, you must look at the subnet mask and what its function is.

As you saw in Chapter 1, the IP address that each host has is a combination of the network ID and the host ID. The address itself is 32 bits long. A varying number of bits are used to identify the network and the host. The discussion here keeps the subnetting simple and works with the standard subnet masks. In a later chapter, you will look at using custom subnetting and supernetting.

To understand a subnet mask, you must again venture into binary, and use logical operators with binary. A good and well known (yet readily overlooked) example is the attributes that you can place on a file. All the attributes for a file on a standard FAT partition are stored in one byte in the directory entry. Remembering that one byte is eight bits, you can see that there are eight different on/off states that we can store. The attributes are Read Only, Archive, System, Hidden, Directory, and Volume Label. Table 2.1 shows a list of bytes versus bits.

TABLE 2.1
Breakdown of File Status Bytes into Bits

R	A	S	H	D	V
0	1	0	1	0	0

That means a decimal value of 20. If you want to know the state of a single attribute, however, you might have a problem unless you understand the logical AND. A logical AND enables you to compare two binary numbers and come up with a third that describes the state of the other numbers. What makes it important is that you can use it to pull out a single bit from the byte. An AND returns (bitwise) the values in table 2.2.

TABLE 2.2
Results of Bitwise ANDing

Bit 1	Bit 2	Result
1	1	1
1	0	0
0	1	0
0	0	0

If you want to see whether a file is hidden, you can mask (get rid of) the unimportant information by assigning a zero to the bit positions that you are not interested in and then extracting the required information. Table 2.3 shows an example of masking a bit.

Table 2.3
Example of Masking a Bit

	R	A	S	H	D	V
Attributes	0	1	0	1	0	0
Mask	0	0	0	1	0	0
Result	0	0	0	1	0	0

This makes sense if you look at it, and it is a common technique used in programming. As you can see, binary is going to become more important as you get further into the book. Anyway, that is the same process that your system uses to see whether an address is local or remote. If you take a Class C address such as 198.53.147.0 (the 0 means that you are referring to the entire network), for example, and look at two systems (hosts) on that network (say 198.53.147.45 and 198.53.147.98), you can compare them by using the standard Class C subnet mask of 255.255.255.0. Take a look at the binary. Table 2.4 shows the AND process where the IP addresses are on the same subnet.

Table 2.4
ANDing IP Addresses and Subnet Masks—Local Host

198.53.147.45	11000110	00110101	10010011	00101101
255.255.255.0	11111111	11111111	11111111	00000000
Result	**11000110**	**00110101**	**10010011**	**00000000**
198.53.147.98	11000110	00110101	10010011	01100010
255.255.255.0	11111111	11111111	11111111	00000000
Result	**11000110**	**00110101**	**10010011**	**00000000**

As you can see, the results match exactly. This tells the system that the network ID in both cases is the same. Therefore the systems are on the same network. Table 2.5 demonstrates the AND process with a remote host such as 131.107.2.200.

TABLE 2.5
ANDing IP Addresses and Subnet Masks—Remote Host

198.53.147.45	11000110	00110101	10010011	00101101
255.255.255.0	11111111	11111111	11111111	00000000
Result	**11000110**	**00110101**	**10010011**	**00000000**
131.107.2.200	10000011	01101101	00000010	11001000
255.255.255.0	11111111	11111111	11111111	00000000
Result	**10000011**	**01101101**	**00000010**	**00000000**

Here the network IDs don't match, and the system can determine that the other host is on another network. In the case of a host on a different network, the IP layer would then try to find out on which gateway (router), as discussed in later chapters, to send the packet.

Address Resolution Protocol

Address Resolution Protocol (ARP) is now used to send the information to another host on your network. The host you send to is always on your network—either the computer you want to talk to, or to the local interface for your router (in the case of remote system). The problem is that your card can only talk to other cards on your local network.

Therefore ARP, using either its cache of resolved addresses or by broadcast, finds the MAC address to send the packet to. In the case of a local machine, this is the actual machine. In the case of a remote system, it is the router. Remember that the router also has the IP layer and therefore ARP. The router finds the MAC address or the host (or another router) on the other network. You never receive the information about the other hosts MAC address; it would be pointless.

After ARP has the address, IP sends the packet to that address. Sometimes, however, when talking to hosts on other networks, your packet will have problems. When this happens, you receive notification.

Internet Control Messaging Protocol

ICMP is a diagnostics and messaging protocol used in the TCP/IP stack to enable communications to continue. ICMP handles such routine functions as PING. It also handles important issues such as reporting unreachable networks.

When you are considering a network that spans the globe, you have to expect that problems connecting with specific hosts will sometimes arise. A few protocols now in place help to prevent this. Dynamic Routing is one that provides alternative routes if a link goes down. Another is the time out value that is given to each packet on the Internet. The time out represents (in theory) the maximum number of hops that a packet can make. By default in Windows NT, the time out or Time To Live (TTL) is 32 seconds. Each router is supposed to decrement the TTL by one for every second that the packet is in the router.

Today on the Internet, you will find that many routers decrement your TTL by far more than one. If the TTL expires or there is no route to the network you are trying to reach, you receive an ICMP message (request timed out or destination host unreachable).

ICMP also works to manage the flow of data on the Internet by directing traffic. If your router becomes overloaded, for example, and is unable to keep up, it might send a source quench message to your system. This tells your system to stop sending for a while. Routers also send an ICMP message if they detect that a better route to your destination is available. This would be an ICMP redirect message, telling your system to use another router.

Internet Group Management Protocol

This is the last of the protocols that reside in the lower layers of the TCP/IP stack. IGMP handles sending and receiving when groups of computers are involved. Sending to groups of computers is used to provide the systems that receive the information with a live feed. (Several radio stations do this on the Internet.) This is multicasting, which was mentioned earlier. In multicasting, you send the information from your system to a special IP address (a Class D address). You should remember that there were Class A, B, and C address. Class D, however, is only mentioned here; it is not valid as a host IP address.

When a system multicasts, it chooses an IP address (this has to be unique on the network) and sends all the information to that address. If you want to receive the information, you must tell your system to listen for that address. The problem is that your router does not know that it should listen for that address, and the packets don't get into your network. IGMP tells your router that you wish to listen to that address, enabling you to receive multicasts.

Network Access Layer

Just as in the OSI model, the Network Access layer is responsible for framing the packets of information for the underlying topology and merging the data on the wire. The Network Access layer also grabs the frames off the network. If they are for that MAC address or for broadcast/multicast, the Network Access layer passes them up to the appropriate protocol.

Summary

This chapter has provided an overview of Microsoft networking. You have also been introduced to the TCP/IP stack. You have learned that Windows NT (and Microsoft networking) in general fits either the OSI model or the TCP/IP model. NetBIOS has been shown as the main protocol for internal portions of NT networking. You have also learned that a translation layer is used to allow this to run on top of Winsock. The next chapters discuss more of the details for the main layers in the TCP/IP stack.

Test Yourself

1. What are the four main services provided by NetBIOS?
2. What is the unit of communications between a redirector and server in NetBIOS?
3. What are the five main layers in the Windows NT networking architecture?
4. Which of the layers are boundary layers?
5. What is the main advantage of using a layered approach?
6. What are the two main APIs found at the application/file system driver layer?
7. How many redirectors can you add to Microsoft NT?
8. What protocols come with Windows NT?
9. Which protocol is not intended for host-to-host communications?
10. Which of the protocols are not routeable?
11. Which protocol enables you to work with a Novell network?
12. What is a LANA Number?
13. What is the main advantage of NDIS?
14. At the TDI layer, what is created to direct the SMB to the correct protocol?
15. How many layers are there in the OSI reference model? In TCP/IP?
16. What is a socket?
17. Which socket numbers are reserved for services to use?
18. What will use sockets?
19. When you use sockets, how is the data being transferred addressed so that it reaches the correct destination?
20. What is the main difference between TCP and UDP?
21. What are the protocols at the IP layer?
22. What is the first function that IP must perform? How does it do it?

23. For the following IP address and subnet masks, determine the network ID:

145.42.36.45	**255.255.0.0**
198.53.14.6	**255.255.255.0**
205.47.18.5	**255.255.255.0**
75.25.255.42	**255.0.0.0**
128.45.6.245	**255.255.0.0**

24. What does ARP do?
25. What address will ARP look for if the host your are communicating with is a local host? For a remote host?
26. What is the purpose of ICMP?
27. When is IGMP used?

Test Yourself Answers

1. The services provided by NetBIOS are: name management, connection-oriented data transfer, connectionless data transfer, and session management.
2. Redirectors and servers talk to each other using SMBs (Server Message Blocks).
3. The five main layers in Windows NT networking architecture are: application/file system driver, transport driver interface (TDI), protocols, network driver interface specification (NDIS), and adapter card drivers.
4. The TDI and NDIS layers are the boundary layers.
5. The layered approach allows more flexibility as to what can be added to each layer. Developers need only be concerned with communicating with the layer above and the layer below.
6. The two main APIs in Microsoft networking are the NetBIOS API and the WinSock API.
7. As many as you want. System performance might suffer, however, if too many are installed.
8. Windows NT has five protocols: TCP/IP, NWLink (an IPX/SPX-compatible protocol), NetBEUI, AFP, and DLC.
9. The DLC (Data Link Control) protocol is intended for communications between a system and an HP Jetdirect card, or using a 3270 emulation with an IBM mainframe.
10. Both NetBEUI and DLC are not routable.
11. NT uses NWLink to work with Novell Netware networks.

12. A LANA Number is a Local Area Network Adapter number and it describes a logical link between the protocols and the network cards.
13. NDIS allows multiple protocols to bind (or work with) multiple network cards without having to load multiple instances of either driver.
14. The TDI layer creates a NCB or Network Control Block to move the SMB (as data) to the correct protocol.
15. The OSI model uses seven layers to describe a networking model. The TCP/IP protocol uses only four. The main reason for the difference is increased responsibility at the Application layer and an isolation, and the Network Access layer because TCP/IP is topology-independent.
16. A socket is a number that represents the location of a service. Sockets provide endpoints for communications between two hosts.
17. The first 1,024 sockets are reserved. These are under the control of the Internet Assigned Numbers Authority.
18. All communications over TCP/IP use a socket, including NetBIOS traffic.
19. The addressing includes the IP address, transport protocol (TCP or UDP), and the port (socket) number to which the data should be delivered.
20. TCP is a connection-oriented transport protocol, meaning that it can guarantee delivery of the packet to the other system. UDP is connectionless and delivers data on a "best-effort" basis.
21. At the IP layer, four main protocols are: IP (Internet Protocol), ICMP (Internet Control Messaging Protocol), IGMP (Internet Group Messaging Protocol), and ARP (Address Resolution Protocol).
22. IP must first determine whether the address is a local or remote address. IP performs this function by ANDing the local IP address with subnet mask to determine the local network ID. Then IP will AND the subnet mask with the remote host to determine a pseudo-network address (it might be incorrect). The two network addresses assume the other host is local. Otherwise, it is remote.
23.

145.42.36.45	**255.255.0.0**	145.42.0.0
198.53.14.6	**255.255.255.0**	198.53.14.0
205.47.18.5	**255.255.255.0**	205.47.18.5
75.25.255.42	**255.0.0.0**	75.0.0.0
128.45.6.245	**255.255.0.0**	128.45.0.0

24. ARP or Address Resolution Protocol is used to find the hardware (MAC) address of a host you are communicating with.
25. In the case of a local host, ARP attempts to find the host MAC address. In the case of a remote host, ARP finds the address of the default gateway.
26. The Internet Control Messaging Protocol is used to report error conditions of a packets in transit. It can also be used, to control the flow of data on the network.
27. Internet Group Messaging Protocol is used to communicate with systems that are multicasting. Multicasting enables one system to send to a special address. Many systems can then receive the same information from that one transmission.

CHAPTER 3

The Application Layer

As stated already, the Application layer is the interface top layer of the networking architecture. The Application layer serves as the gate between the programs that you run on your computer and the underlying network transport layers. At the Application layer, you can find both the components required for you to share resources (services) with the network and to gain access to network resources.

You have also already read about the two main APIs that reside at the Application layer: WinSock and NetBIOS. WinSock is used to support the purely TCP/IP applications (such as Internet Information Server or IIS, FTP, and PING). NetBIOS is used to support the Windows networking architecture (Network Neighborhood, NET USE). This chapter discusses how these APIs work with the Application layer and what makes them work.

Getting into WinSock

WinSock acts as a connection point for the services running on your computer (such as IIS) and for the applications (or clients such as Internet Explorer) that reach across the network to work with these services. Because all communications across TCP/IP must use the WinSock interface, it is important for you to understand how WinSock works.

WinSock uses ports (numbered between 1 and 65,536) as the connection point for the service or client registering with the WinSock interface. A port is a logical connection point, and can be used by a client to identify to which service the client wants to talk. The FTP service that you can run on Windows NT uses port 21 as a control port and port 20 as the data port, for example, so a client will look for FTP on port 21 when it first attempts to connect to the service. It is important to note that these are the standard numbers assigned by the Internet Assigned Numbers Authority. You can, however, change these port numbers for added security.

When a service opens (or registers) a port number with WinSock, it performs what is referred to as a passive open. This means that it opens the connection; however, it does not actively do anything with the port unless traffic comes in on that port. Basically, the service is letting the WinSock interface know that any information that comes in on that port number should be forwarded to the service.

The service sits there waiting for activity on that port. An example of such a wait is the World Wide Web Publishing Service (HTTP). It opens port 80 and then waits for activity on that port before doing anything.

The client does not open a port passively; it opens the port in an active state because the client typically is trying to connect with a service on another computer. An active open tells WinSock that the port is about to be used. As stated in Chapter 2, "Introduction to Microsoft Networking," the port number for a client is any available port number above 1,024.

How the Process Works

To follow this all the way through, take a look at a connection between the Internet Explorer and an IIS server running a web site (see fig. 3.1).

The following steps take you through the example:

1. The WWW Publishing service starts (for example, at `www.microsoft.com`), performing a passive open on port 80 (see fig. 3.2). WinSock now knows to send any information it gets for port 80 to this service.
2. You might start up the Internet Explorer. This performs an active open on some port number (1,734, as an example only), telling WinSock that a connection attempt is coming through that port.

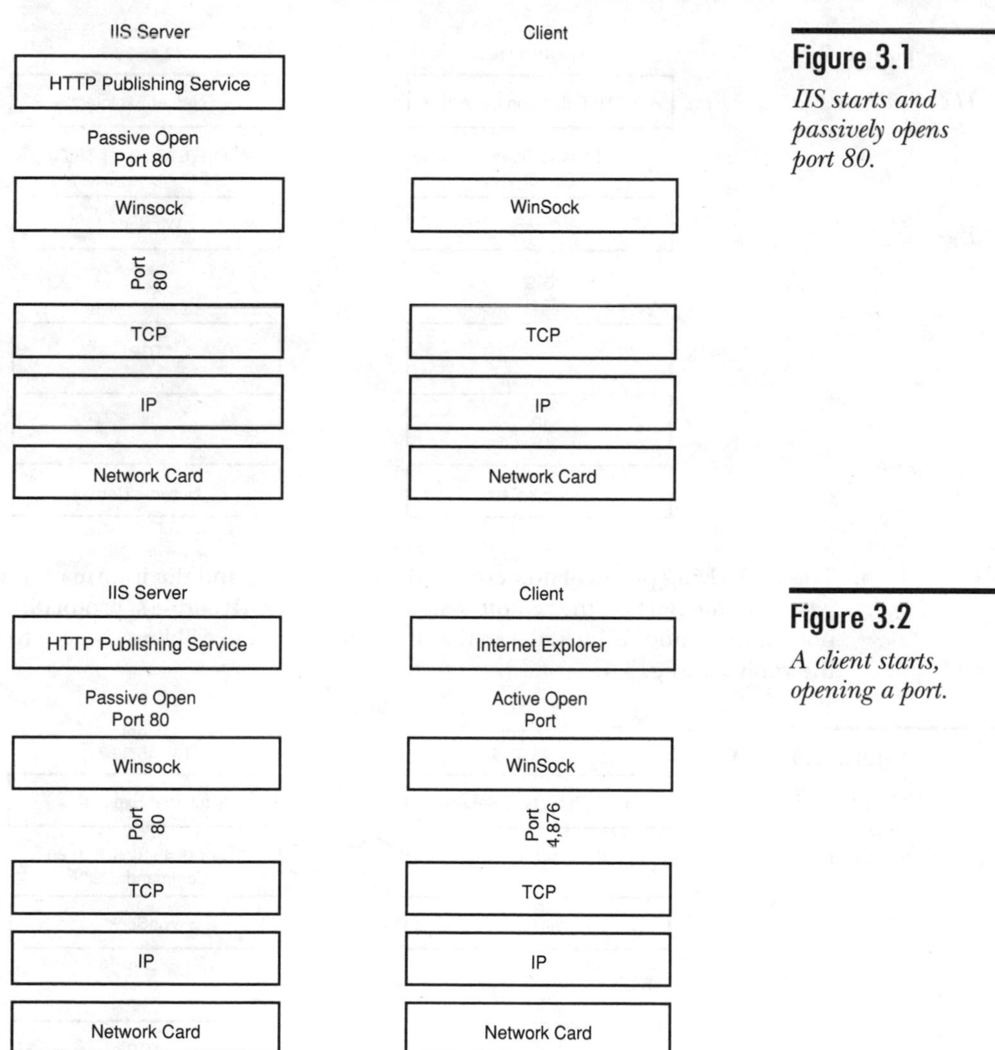

Figure 3.1
IIS starts and passively opens port 80.

Figure 3.2
A client starts, opening a port.

3. The client opens the site, in this case the Get command is formulated to get the default web page and pass it to WinSock (see fig. 3.3). The information being passed is the IP address (actually `www.microsoft.com` will need to be resolved first, more on this later), transport protocol (TCP in this case), and the socket number for the service to which you want to connect along with the command (which is data to WinSock.)

Figure 3.3

The client issues a Get command.

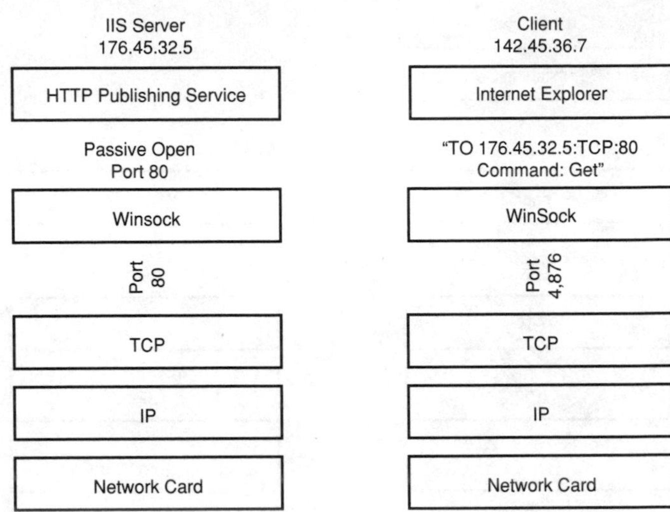

4. The underlying protocol now creates the connection, and the information is passed to the port on the remote system. As well, the IP address, protocol, and port of the sender is included so that the remote system will know where to send the reply (see fig. 3.4).

Figure 3.4

Using a TCP session, the request is sent.

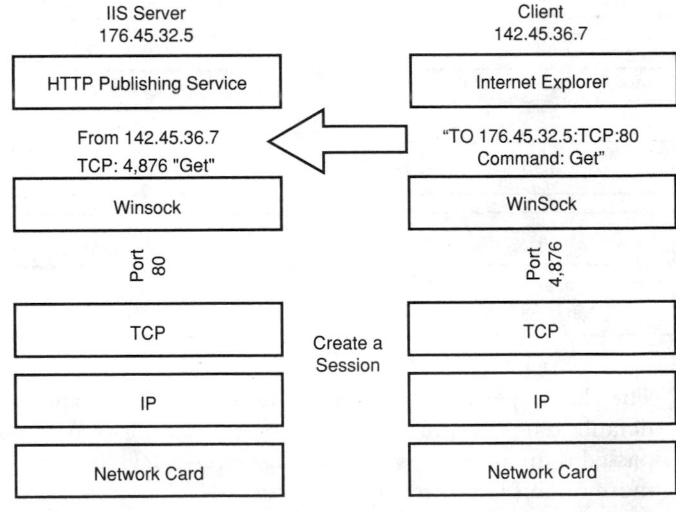

5. The publishing service receives the request and responds with (in this case) the page of information the client requested (see fig. 3.5).

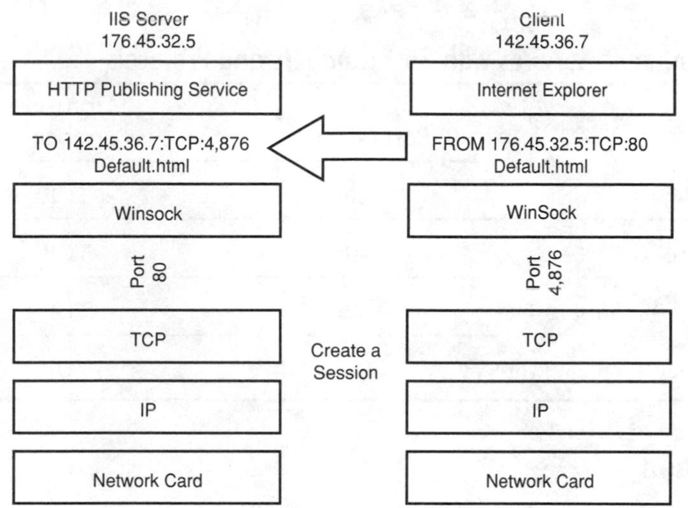

Figure 3.5

The server returns the page to the remote socket.

As you can see from the walk-through of the communications process, the services identify themselves by the IP address, the transport layer protocol, and the port number to which you want to connect. Table 3.1 lists some of the better known port numbers.

TABLE 3.1
Common Services with Port Numbers and Protocols

Service	Port Number	Transport Protocol
Echo Service (PING)	7	TCP or UDP
FTP Data Channel	20	TCP
FTP Control Channel	21	TCP
Telnet	23	TCP
Simple Mail Transfer Protocol	25	TCP
Domain Name Service	53	TCP
Trivial File Transfer Protocol	69	UDP
Gopher	70	TCP

continues

TABLE 3.1, CONTINUED
Common Services with Port Numbers and Protocols

Service	Port Number	Transport Protocol
World Wide Web	80	TCP
Post Office Protocol (3)	110	TCP
Network News Transfer Protocol	119	TCP
Simple Network Management Protocol	161	UDP

NETSTAT Command

To view the connection that you have made with other systems or to view connections to your system, you can use the NETSTAT command. A sample output might look like the following:

```
Active Connections

  Proto  Local Address          Foreign Address        State
  TCP    tawni:1025             LOCALHOST:1026         ESTABLISHED
  TCP    tawni:1026             LOCALHOST:1025         ESTABLISHED
  TCP    tawni:1066             OTT.NOTES:nbsession    TIME_WAIT
  TCP    tawni:1067             OTT.NOTES:nbsession    TIME_WAIT
  TCP    tawni:1069             OTT.NOTES:nbsession    TIME_WAIT
  TCP    tawni:1070             OTT.NOTES:nbsession    ESTABLISHED
```

The switches you can use with the NETSTAT command are shown in the following output from NETSTAT /?:

```
NETSTAT [-a] [-e] [-n] [-s] [-p proto] [-r] [interval]

  -a            Displays all connections and listening ports. (Server-side
                connections are normally not shown.)
  -e            Displays Ethernet statistics. This may be combined with the -s
                option.
  -n            Displays addresses and port numbers in numerical form.
  -s            Displays per-protocol statistics. By default, statistics are
                shown for TCP, UDP and IP; the -p option may be used to specify
                a subset of the default.
```

```
  -p proto      Shows connections for the protocol specified by proto; proto
                may be tcp or udp. If used with the -s option to display
                per-protocol statistics, proto may be tcp, udp, or ip.
  -r            Displays the contents of the routing table.
interval       Redisplays selected statistics, pausing interval seconds
                between each display. Press CTRL+C to stop redisplaying
                statistics. If omitted, NETSTAT will print the current
                configuration information once.
```

Although WinSock serves as a connection between the TCP/IP clients on a personal computer and TCP/IP applications from the network, consideration must be given to running NetBIOS networking over the TCP/IP stack. As you will see, this can be handled by providing NetBIOS service ports.

NetBIOS Over TCP/IP

As you saw in the last chapter, NetBIOS is the basis for Microsoft networking. This means that you must be able to handle the basic NetBIOS functions: name management, session management, and connectionless and connection-oriented data transfer. TCP/IP does not perform all these functions directly. You can, however, use the functions that do exist in TCP/IP to handle all of these. The data transfer mode is handled easily by the differences between TCP and UDP. As long as NetBIOS knows which to use, no problem will arise.

Session management is also something TCP can handle; this is one of the functions that the TCP protocol handles for you. Name management, however, is something that TCP/IP does not handle well (and which is covered in detail in later chapters). Because TCP/IP works with IP addresses, that could be a stumbling block. Because NetBIOS does work over TCP/IP, there is a solution. You have even heard of it: NetBIOS over TCP/IP, or NBT.

NBT

NBT handles the direction of NetBIOS traffic to either TCP or UDP, depending on whether the traffic is connection-oriented. Connection-oriented traffic requires a session. NBT requests TCP to create the session and then tracks the session to ensure it remains active.

There still remains the problem of name management, which is handled by NBT providing a name service that runs on a separate port that all the NetBIOS systems know about. This enables NetBIOS to register names and the name service. Because name management (that is, registering, resolution, and releasing) is all handled normally by broadcasts, this service uses UDP ports (137 and 138 to be exact).

Table 3.2 lists important NetBIOS port numbers and the services that use them.

Table 3.2
NetBIOS Port Numbers and Protocols

Service	Nickname	Port	Protocol
NetBIOS Name Service	nbname	137	UDP
NetBIOS Datagram Service	nbdatagram	138	UDP
NetBIOS Session Service	nbsession	139	TCP

To make all this work, the application you are using talks to the regular NetBIOS API. This passes the request to the NBT layer, which calls on the port numbers previously mentioned to actually perform the services.

NBTSTAT

Just like other connections, you can view NetBIOS connections that you make over WinSock. NBTSTAT -S gives you a report similar to the code listing.

```
NetBIOS Connection Table

Local Name              State     In/Out  Remote Host             Input   Output
--------------------------------------------------------------------------------
TAWNI           <03>  Listening
SCRIM           <03>  Listening
TAWNI           <00>  Connected    Out    198.53.147.2              0B     174B
```

The other switches for NBTSTAT as seen from NBTSTAT /? include the following:

```
NBTSTAT [-a RemoteName] [-A IP address] [-c] [-n]
        [-r] [-R] [-s] [-S] [interval] ]

  -a   (adapter status) Lists the remote machine's name table given its name
  -A   (Adapter status) Lists the remote machine's name table given its
                        IP address.
  -c   (cache)          Lists the remote name cache including the IP addresses
  -n   (names)          Lists local NetBIOS names.
  -r   (resolved)       Lists names resolved by broadcast and via WINS
  -R   (Reload)         Purges and reloads the remote cache name table
  -s   (sessions)       Lists sessions table converting destination IP
                        addresses to host names via the hosts file.
```

```
-S   (Sessions)        Lists sessions table with the destination IP addresses

RemoteName             Remote host machine name.
IP address             Dotted decimal representation of the IP address.
interval               Redisplays selected statistics, pausing interval seconds
                       between each display. Press Ctrl+C to stop redisplaying
                       statistics.
```

Name Resolution Overview

Objective E.3

For all this to work, there has to be some method of resolving the NetBIOS name or the host name to a TCP/IP address. You already know that the WinSock interface uses only IP addresses to communicate; that is equally true for NetBIOS communications, and it is also true for TCP/IP utilities.

The type of name you are resolving is normally determined (rather, the order is determined) by the command that you use. If you use a NetBIOS command, the resolution is in the NetBIOS order discussed in detail later. If you use a host name, it is host name resolution that you use. Whichever method that you use, several different means provide the resolution.

Note The type of resolution that you use depends on the command you issue. If the command is a TCP/IP utility (FTP, Internet Explorer), you use host name resolution. Using NT Explorer or the command-line utility NET USE causes you to use NetBIOS name resolution. Both of the methods back up each other.

The methods available can all be configured and include the following:

- **NetBIOS Name Cache.** This is a list of the NetBIOS names that have already been resolved to TCP/IP addresses. These names can be configured (as you will see) to either be static (permanent) or dynamic.
- **NetBIOS Name Server (NBNS).** These are systems that exist on the network. They have a service running that takes a name query for a NetBIOS name and resolve it to an IP address. You will later look at WINS (Windows Internet Naming Service), which is an example of an NBNS.
- **Broadcast.** NetBIOS has always been based on broadcast, as this is the type of topology around which it was designed. A broadcast can be used to resolve addresses that cannot be found otherwise, or to register or release a name. It is important to note that most routers do not pass NetBIOS broadcasts—they would cause too much traffic at the router and prevent it from sending real data.

- **LMHOSTS.** This is the LAN Manager hosts file that was used in LAN Manager to enable systems to resolve TCP/IP addresses. There are several special tags that will be looked at in this text file in a later chapter.
- **HOSTNAME.** Basically, this decides whether you are trying to talk to yourself. You can check your host name by entering HOSTNAME at a prompt.
- **HOSTS file.** The BSD (Berkeley Software Distribution) 4.2 standard text file that enables you to resolve host names. Very similar to an LMHOSTS file. It does not, however, have any special tags.
- **DNS (Domain Name Service).** A DNS service runs on a computer and resolves host names to IP addresses, or IP addresses to host names (reverse lookup). You can use the NSLOOKUP command to test your DNS service and see whether it is functioning correctly.

Please note that the order of these is important. It is very different from the order done by HOST name resolution. The issues relating to this are covered on the exam.

All these methods are discussed in several chapters later in the book. Understanding which method is used and when is important. This is a key issue in troubleshooting. Understanding this will also help you pass the exam.

Summary

This chapter examined the two main networking APIs: WinSock and NetBIOS. You also started to look at the different parts that appear in the Application layer. This chapter also introduced name resolution. At the Application layer—the very top layer of the network—you find the services and clients. This chapter also introduced the concept of sessions. You will continue to look at them from the Transport layer.

Test Yourself

1. What are the two types of open for a WinSock port, and what type of protocol uses each method?
2. Will the client and the service both use the same port number?
3. Name five common port numbers and the service each one represents.
4. What command can you use to view the TCP/IP connections that you have with other computers?
5. What allows the use of NetBIOS networking over TCP/IP?

6. What are the three main port numbers and their use when working with NetBIOS over TCP/IP?
7. What command can you use to view NetBIOS of TCP/IP connections?
8. What has to happen before NetBIOS can create a session over TCP/IP? Why?
9. What are the methods of NetBIOS name resolution?

Test Yourself Answers

1. A WinSock port can be opened in active or passive mode. When a service opens a port, it opens it passively, waiting for data to come in. The client opens the port in active mode to start sending data immediately.
2. The client and service normally use different port numbers. The services typically use one of the well-defined port numbers. A client, on the other hand, uses any port number after the first 1,024 (which are reserved).
3. Any five of the following:

Service	Port Number	Transport Protocol
Echo Service (PING)	7	TCP or UDP
FTP Data Channel	20	TCP
FTP Control Channel	21	TCP
Telnet	23	TCP
Simple Mail Transfer Protocol	25	TCP
Domain Name Service	53	TCP
Trivial File Transfer Protocol	69	UDP
Gopher	70	TCP
World Wide Web	80	TCP
Post Office Protocol (3)	110	TCP
Network News Transfer Protocol	119	TCP
Simple Network Management Protocol	161	UDP

4. The NETSTAT command enables you to view both the connections to your system and those that you have with others.
5. This is facilitated by the NetBIOS over TCP/IP component, referred to as NBT.

6. The ports and uses are:

Service	Nickname	Port	Protocol
NetBIOS Name Service	nbname	137	UDP
NetBIOS Datagram Service	nbdatagram	138	UDP
NetBIOS Session Service	nbsession	139	TCP

7. You can use the NBTSTAT command to view the current sessions and other information relating to NBT.
8. The IP address of the target host must be known. This is required because TCP/IP uses IP addresses for communications, and NetBIOS uses computer names.
9. You can use six methods to resolve a NetBIOS name: NetBIOS name cache, NetBIOS name server, broadcast, the LMHOSTS file, the HOSTS file, and a DNS server.

CHAPTER 4

The Transport Layer

The Transport layer is responsible for taking the data from Winsock and putting it into packages that can be sent on the network. The Transport layer is also responsible for creating the data segments it is sending to WinSock on the remote computer, as well as addressing the packets to a TPC/IP address.

When a call comes through the WinSock interface, it is passed to UDP or TCP, depending on the type of service required. The Transport layer knows what port the data came from, and because it is sent to the appropriate protocol, all the WinSock interface needs to do is tell the transport protocol to which IP address to send. This chapter discusses that process in detail. You will learn about headers and pseudo headers. This chapter also explains the TCP protocol and how it works in detail.

Headers

The data from Winsock becomes the data segment (normally UDP does not have a data segment) and then both a header and pseudo header are created. A *header* is a special data structure added to the data Winsock sent down. This header provides information about the destination and host computers, the protocols being used. The header also contains information that enables TCP to guarantee delivery. The purpose of the header is very different depending on whether it is TCP or UDP. It is, however, information for the corresponding protocol on the receiving hosts. The *pseudo header* is used to tell IP where the information is to be sent.

TCP Headers

TCP is a connection-oriented protocol, with a mechanism that guarantees delivery of information from one place to another. The header, therefore, must contain things such as the segment ID (so that you know whether you received them all), a CRC (cyclic redundancy check—a form of checksum verifies the information is intact). The TCP header looks like the image shown in figure 4.1.

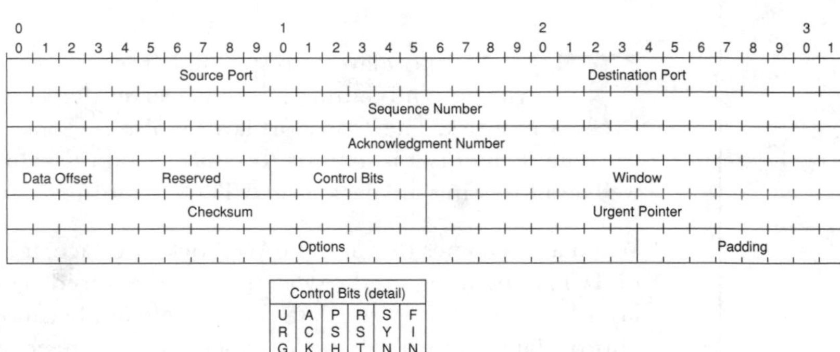

Figure 4.1
The format of a TCP header.

The information in the header is broken down into fields. The fields contain information required to enable the hosts to communicate. Included in the key information are the ports that each host is using, Sequence and Acknowledgment numbers, and the control bits. The following list identifies the entire contents of the header:

- **Source Port (16 bits).** Specifies the WinSock port sending the information.
- **Destination Port (16 bits).** Specifies the WinSock port to use on the receiving host.
- **Sequence Number (32 bits).** Specifies the sequence position of the first data byte in the segment. This enables the hosts to guarantee delivery by providing unique numbers for each segment that can be acknowledged by that number.

- **Acknowledgment Number (32 bits).** Specifies the next Sequence number expected by the sender of the segment. TCP indicates that this field is active by setting the ACK bit, which is always set after a connection is established.
- **Data Offset (4 bits).** Specifies the number of 32-bit words in the TCP header. Options are padded with 0-value octets to complete a 32-bit word when necessary. This tells the system what the header is and what is data.
- **Reserved (6 bits).** Must be zero. Reserved for future use.
- **Control Bits (6 bits).** The six control bits are as follows:

  URG. When set (1), the Urgent Pointer field is significant. When cleared (0), the field is ignored.

  ACK. When set, the Acknowledgment Number field is significant.

  PSH. Initiates a push function.

  RST. Forces a reset of the connection.

  SYN. Synchronizes sequencing counters for the connection. This bit is set when a segment requests the opening of a connection.

  FIN. No more data. Closes the connection.

- **Window (16 bits).** Specifies the number of bytes, starting with the byte specified in the Acknowledgment Number field, which the sender of the segment can currently accept.
- **Checksum (16 bits).** An error control checksum that covers the header and data fields. It does not cover any padding required to have the segment consist of an even number of octets.
- **Urgent Pointer (16 bits).** Identifies the Sequence number of the octet following urgent data. The urgent pointer is a positive offset from the Sequence number of the segment.
- **Options (variable).** Options are available for a variety of functions, including end of options list, no-operation, maximum segment size, and maximum segment size option data.
- **Padding (variable).** 0-value octets are appended to the header to ensure that the header ends on a 32-bit word boundary.

UDP Header

UDP also uses a header in communications. Because it is connectionless, however, the header format is much simpler (see fig. 4.2).

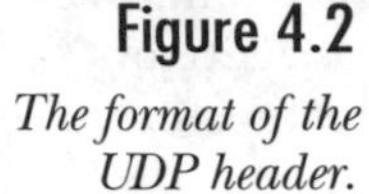

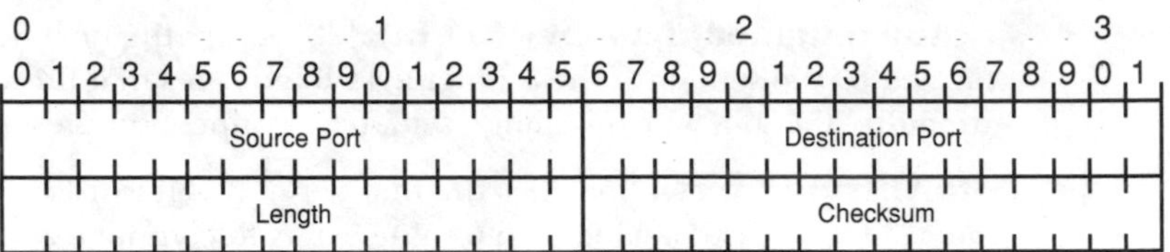

Figure 4.2
The format of the UDP header.

Compared to the TCP header, the UDP header is considerably simpler, as is the protocol itself. There is no need to have the extra information for error correction because this protocol does not guarantee delivery. The following list describes all the required fields:

- **Source Port (16 bits).** This field is optional and specifies the source WinSock port when enabling the receiver of the datagram to send a response if necessary. Otherwise, the source port value is 0.
- **Destination Port (16 bits).** The destination WinSock port at the remote host.
- **Length (16 bits).** The length in bytes of the datagram, including the header and data. The minimum value is 8 to allow for a header. Consequently, a UDP datagram is limited to a maximum length of 65,535 bytes, making 65,527 bytes available for data.
- **Checksum (16 bits).** A checksum value.

The headers are bundled with the data to create either a TCP segment or a UDP header. This is passed to the IP layer. To prevent the IP layer from having to open the packet, a pseudo header is also passed to the IP layer.

Pseudo Headers

In addition to the headers just discussed, pseudo headers are also generated. Just like the NCB discussed earlier, these pseudo headers are used to tell the underlying layers (IP in this case) what to do with the packet.

The pseudo header includes source and destination addresses, the protocol, and the segment length. This information is forwarded with the TCP or UDP segments to IP to provide the information required to move the information across the network and to the correct protocol on the other host (see fig. 4.3).

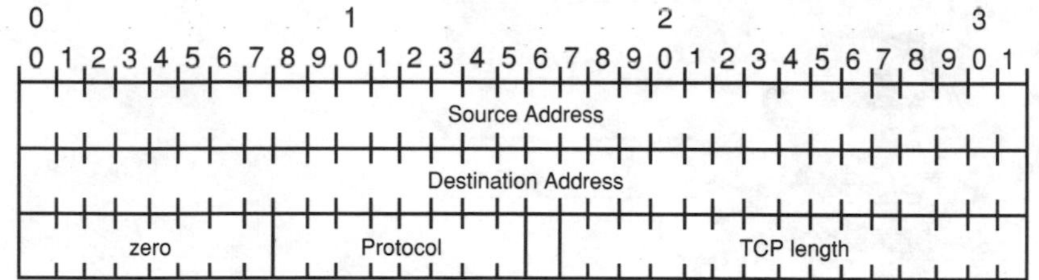

Figure 4.3

Breakdown of the pseudo header.

Transmission Control Protocol (TCP)

TCP provides reliable communication between processes that run on interconnected hosts. This Transport layer functions independently of the network structure. TCP is not concerned with routing data through the internetwork; the network infrastructure is the responsibility of the IP layer. As you have seen, TCP on one host communicates directly with TCP on another host, regardless of whether the hosts are on the same network or remote from each other.

In fact, TCP is oblivious to the network. A wide variety of network technologies can be accommodated, including circuit switching and packet switching on local and wide area networks. TCP identifies hosts by using IP addresses and does not concern itself with physical addresses.

The main functions of TCP are discussed in the following sections, including:

- Session establishment
- Byte stream communications
- Sliding windows

Session Establishment

Applications using the TCP protocol must be able to open, close, and check the status of sessions to allow them to communicate. To perform this function, TCP uses a three-way handshake as discussed earlier (see fig. 4.4). The handshake is important not only to create the session, but also in allowing the hosts to exchange data about their capabilities.

The handshake starts when one host is asked by Winsock to open a connection (or session). A TCP segment is generated to start the session, and the SYN control bit is turned on. This tells the other host that a session is requested. The host also includes in the TCP header the starting Sequence number for this connection and the current window size.

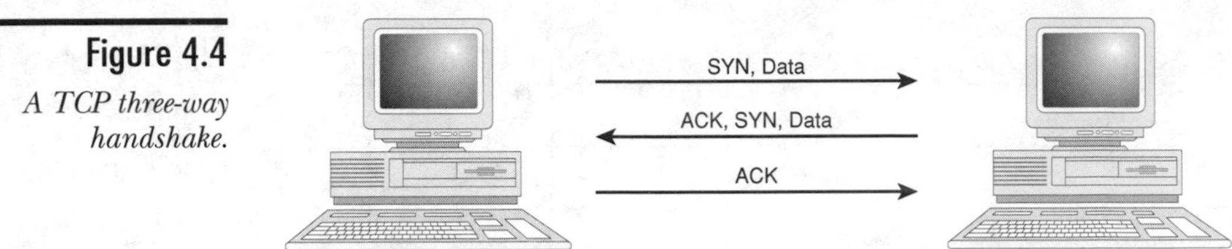

Figure 4.4
A TCP three-way handshake.

The TCP segment is now sent to the other host, who acknowledges the segment, including its window size. The segment sent to acknowledge the first host also includes the SYN control bit. Finally, the process ends when the first host acknowledges the receipt of the other's segment.

After the hosts have completed their communications, the connection is closed in a similar manner, the difference being that the FIN control bit is set rather than the SYN bit.

Byte Stream Communications

When a connection (session) is established, the upper-layer protocol uses this connection to send data to the other host. The upper-layer protocols do not concern themselves with formatting data to fit the underlying topology, but send the data as a continuous stream.

This process, called *byte stream communications*, means that TCP must have some method for dealing with a large volume of data that has no boundaries. Every byte in a stream is assigned a Sequence number, enabling every byte sent to be acknowledged. If TCP sent each byte as a single package, this would be unmanageable. TCP therefore bundles the data stream it sends into segments; a segment contains chunks of data.

The TCP header specifies the segment Sequence number for the first byte in the data field, and each segment also incorporates an Acknowledgment number. Because you do not know which byte will be the first in a given segment, you must give each byte a Sequence number. When TCP sends a segment, it retains a copy of the segment in a queue (transmit window), where it remains until an acknowledgment is received. Segments not acknowledged are retransmitted.

When TCP acknowledges receipt of a segment, it relieves the sending TCP of responsibility for all data in that segment. The receiving TCP then becomes responsible for delivering the data in the segment to the appropriate upper-layer process.

Sliding Windows

This is all necessary because of the way the Internet (or your intranet) works. The segments that you send could each take a different route. This might happen because routers can become busy or links could fail. Data must be buffered on the sending host until the remote host has acknowledged it.

The Sliding Window is the buffer that enables byte stream communications, and enables TCP to guarantee the delivery of segments of data. During the session establishment, the two hosts exchange the current size of the receive window. This information is also included in the TCP header of each and every segment sent. A host that is communicating sets the size of its send window to match the other host's receive window (see fig. 4.5).

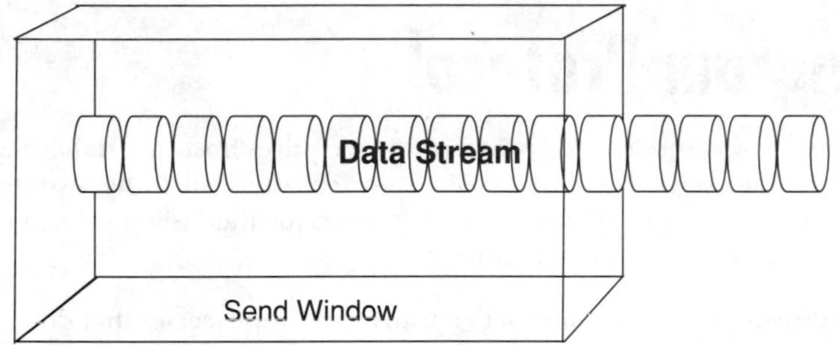

Figure 4.5

Data in a Send Window.

If you look at the data being transmitted, you would see a series of bytes. If you overlay a window at the start of the data, you can see that a portion of the data falls into the window. This is the only data with which the TCP layer can work. The window cannot slide (move to cover more data) until all the data currently in the window is sent and acknowledged.

As the data in the window is transmitted to the remote host, the retransmit timer is set for each segment sent. The receiving host acknowledges the segments when its receive window fills to a predetermined amount (in NT this is two consecutive segments). When the acknowledgment is received by the sender, its transmit window slides past the acknowledged data and the next segments are transmitted.

In the process of moving the data from point A to point B, many things might happened to the segments being transmitted. They could be lost due to congestion at the routers, or could be received out of sequence.

If a packet is lost, the retransmit timer expires on the sending host, the segment is retransmitted, and the retransmit timer is set to two times the original value. This continues until the segment is acknowledged or the maximum number of retries has been made (about 16 seconds). If the data cannot be transmitted, TCP reports the condition and you get an error message.

In a case where the segments are received out of order, the receiving host sets the delayed acknowledgment timer for the segment it did receive, and waits for other segments to arrive. If the delayed acknowledgment timer (hard-coded to 200 ms) expires, TCP on the receiving host sends an acknowledgment for the segment it did receive.

TCP Window Size

You can adjust the size of the sliding window. Great care should be taken in adjusting the window size. If the window size is set too small, only a few packets can be sent at a time. This means that the system transmits the packets and then must wait for acknowledgments. If the size is set too large, network traffic delays the transmission. You can adjust the TCP window size under `HKEY_LOCAL_MACHINE\System\CurrentControlSet\Services\TCPIP\Paramters`. The default is 8760, which is tuned for Ethernet. This setting affects only TCP, because UDP does not use a sliding window.

User Datagram Protocol

TCP is a connection- or session-oriented protocol that requires hosts to establish a session, which is maintained for the duration of a transfer, after which the session is closed. The overhead required to maintain connections is justified when reliability is required but often proves to be misspent effort.

User Datagram Protocol provides an alternative transport for processes that do not require reliable delivery. UDP is a datagram protocol that does not guarantee data delivery or duplicate protection. As a datagram protocol, UDP need not be concerned with receiving streams of data and developing segments suitable for IP. Consequently, UDP is an uncomplicated protocol that functions with far less overhead than TCP.

In the following several situations, UDP might be preferred over TCP as a host-to-host protocol:

- **Messages that require no acknowledgment.** Network overhead can be reduced by using UDP. Simple Network Management Protocol (SNMP) alerts fall into this category. On a large network, considerable SNMP alerts are generated because every SNMP device transmits status updates. Seldom, however, is loss of an SNMP message critical. Running SNMP over UDP, therefore, reduces network overhead.
- **Messages between hosts are sporadic.** SNMP again serves as a good example. SNMP messages are sent at irregular intervals. The overhead required to open and close a TCP connection for each message would delay messages and bog down performance.
- **Reliability is implemented at the process level.** Network File System (NFS) is an example of a process that performs its own reliability function and runs over UDP to enhance network performance.

Summary

In this chapter, you have looked at the Transport layer. This layer handles TCP sessions and both connection-oriented (or session-oriented) transmissions and connectionless (with no session) transfers. You have seen that all the work at this layer is done by either TCP or UDP. The next chapter examines the Internet layer, which services both these protocols.

Test Yourself

1. What is the purpose of the Transport layer?
2. What two pieces are added to the data at the Transport layer?
3. What is the purpose of the TCP header?
4. What is the purpose of the pseudo header?
5. What are the three main functions of TCP?
6. How is a TCP session established? What control bit is involved?
7. What control bit is used to end a TCP session?
8. What does byte stream communications provide?
9. What is used to ensure that the sent data is received?
10. What is a TCP sliding windows? When is the size of the window set?
11. Where would UDP be used?

Test Yourself Answers

1. The Application layer is used to communicate with the Transport layer on the remote host. It receives instructions from the Application layer, which it packages with instructions for the remote system's Transport layer. The packages created at this layer are passed as data to the IP layer.
2. The Transport layer adds both a header and a pseudo header.
3. The header adds control and error checking information to the information being sent.
4. The pseudo header is used much like the NCB is at the TDI layer. It tells the underlying protocol what to do with the information being passed to it.
5. The three main functions of TCP are session establishment and termination, byte stream communications, and Sliding Windows.

6. TCP creates a session with the remote host by way of a three-way handshake. The host that initiates the communications starts by sending a packet that contains information about itself, and in which the SYN flag is raised. The other host receives the packet, and acknowledges it. In the acknowledgment, the SYN flag (control bit) is raised, and data about that host is included. Finally, the initiating host sends an acknowledgment back to the target host, and a session now exists between the two hosts.
7. Ending a TCP session is identical to creating one with one important difference: the FIN control is raised rather than the SYN control bit.
8. Byte stream communications provide a seamless transfer mechanism that treats all the data from the upper layers as one long stream of information. This means that there are message boundaries or protocols that the upper-layer applications need to understand. This means that data transfer across the network is the same to the application as sending data to the local hard disk.
9. TCP sends a Sequence number with every packet of information that it sets. This number represents the position of the first byte of data in the packet within the entire stream being sent. Each of the packets sent requires an acknowledgment of that number. As well, every packet includes a checksum value that ensures that data sent is the same as that received.
10. On each system that uses TCP, there is a receive and transmit window. The transmit window is set to the size of the other host's receive window during the TCP three-way handshake. The transmit window is now placed over the data stream to be sent, and the information in the window is sent. The window remains over that information until the receiver acknowledges receipt of the information, at which time, the window slides past that information and sends the next.
11. Typically, UDP is used in cases where the sender does not require a confirmation of the transmission. This might include server announcements, SNMP packets, and name query broadcasts. UDP can also be used if the upper layers are ensuring the delivery, such as NFS does.

CHAPTER 5

The Internet Layer

Both TCP and UDP pass information to the IP layer. This layer is responsible for actually moving the data from one machine on the network (or internetwork) to another. The IP layer handles a number of different tasks required for communications to exist. The IP layer, however, does not guarantee delivery—as you have seen, this is done by TCP.

Some of the functions handled at this layer include the following:

- Routing of datagrams
- Resolution of IP addresses to MAC addresses
- Fragmentation and re-assembly of datagrams
- Error detection and reporting

This chapter discusses each of these topics. This is the important part of the TCP/IP stack. Because this is where routing takes place, this chapter first covers the basics of routing. Then it examines resolution of addresses. You will learn to never send information to a TCP/IP address, but always to a MAC address.

What Is a Subnet Mask?

You learned in Chapter 2, "Introduction to Microsoft Networking," how the subnet mask can be used to determine whether a host is a local or remote host. To review, the IP address is ANDed with the subnet mask to extract the network ID for the local network on which the host resides. The IP address that IP receives in the pseudo header is now ANDed with the subnet mask to determine a network ID.

It is important to note that the network ID generated might be incorrect. If the host attempting to send is a Class C host using 255.255.255.0 as the subnet mask, ANDing generates an incorrect address if the remote host is a Class B. This does not matter, however, because the network IDs will not match (remember the first octet differs, depending on the class of network).

As you can see, therefore, the subnet mask enables you to extract the network ID. This information is used to see whether the datagram is for the local network. If it is not, the system needs to look at the remote IP address and use the routing table to figure out where to send it.

Introduction to Routing

After the network IDs are known, they can be compared. The only case where they should match is if the two hosts are on the same network. If the host that you are trying to reach is on the same network, the IP layer finds that host and transmits the data to it. If not, you need to look for a route to the host. This will be done in the routing table. All devices that have IP have a routing table. The following is an example of a routing table from an NT system:

```
Active Routes:

  Network Address          Netmask  Gateway Address       Interface  Metric
          0.0.0.0          0.0.0.0    206.51.250.69   206.51.250.69       1
        127.0.0.0        255.0.0.0        127.0.0.1       127.0.0.1       1
     206.51.250.0    255.255.255.0    206.51.250.69   206.51.250.69       1
    206.51.250.69  255.255.255.255        127.0.0.1       127.0.0.1       1
   206.51.250.255  255.255.255.255    206.51.250.69   206.51.250.69       1
        224.0.0.0        224.0.0.0    206.51.250.69   206.51.250.69       1
  255.255.255.255  255.255.255.255    206.51.250.69   206.51.250.69       1
```

If you want to look at your routing table, you can use the ROUTE command. The syntax for the ROUTE command is as follows:

```
Manipulates network routing tables.

ROUTE [-f] [command [destination] [MASK netmask] [gateway] [METRIC metric]]

  -f           Clears the routing tables of all gateway entries. If this is
               used in conjunction with one of the commands, the tables are
               cleared prior to running the command.

  -p           When used with the ADD command, makes a route persistent across
               boots of the system. By default, routes are not preserved
               when the system is restarted. When used with the PRINT command,
               displays the list of registered persistent routes. Ignored for
               all other commands, which always affect the appropriate
               persistent routes.

  command      Specifies one of four commands
                 PRINT     Prints a route
                 ADD       Adds a route
                 DELETE    Deletes a route
                 CHANGE    Modifies an existing route

  destination  Specifies the host.

  MASK         If the MASK keyword is present, the next parameter is
               interpreted as the netmask parameter.

  netmask      If provided, specifies a sub-net mask value to be associated
               with this route entry. If not specified, it defaults to
               255.255.255.255.

  gateway      Specifies gateway.

  METRIC       specifies the metric/cost for the destination

All symbolic names used for destination are looked up in the network database
file NETWORKS. The symbolic names for gateway are looked up in the host name
database file HOSTS.
If the command is print or delete, wildcards may be used for the destination
and gateway, or the gateway argument may be omitted.
```

In the case of a host, the routing table generally does not contain actual routing information, except for the default gateway (router) address. Any packet not on the local network is normally sent to the default gateway. IP on the gateway then looks in its routing table for a route to the remote network. Occasions will arise where you have entries in the local host's routing table. In those cases, this table is consulted to find the first hop in the route.

A routing table contains the following five pieces of information:

- **Network Address.** The actual network ID to which the entry describes a route. This is the real network ID, not the one generated earlier when checking, if the host is local or remote.
- **Netmask.** The subnet mask that can be used to generate the network ID. The system runs through the table and ANDs the IP address you are trying to reach with each of the netmasks. Then it can compare the result to the Network Address to see whether they match. If they match, a route has been found.
- **Gateway Address.** Where to send the packet if it is a remote network ID to which the computer is sending.
- **Interface.** Which network interface to send the packet from. Normally you only have one network card, and this is the same for all entries. (The exception here is the loopback and multicasting addresses.)
- **Metric.** How far away this network is. This is the number of routers (gateways) that the packet must travel through to get to the remote.

There will often be an entry for network 0.0.0.0 with a netmask of 0.0.0.0. This is the entry for the default gateway and is checked last. If you work it out in binary, you will see that all addresses match this one.

Figure 5.1 summarizes the process that IP uses to determine where it should send the packet.

Finding Another Machine's Address

Whether the packet that you are sending is going to a host on your network or to a host on a remote network, the packet is always sent to a MAC address (the hardware address of the network card). The only difference in sending to the local or the remote network is that the address you send for a remote network is the router. Remember that a router is a simple device that connects two (or more) networks; it has a network interface on each network (with an IP address on each subnet) and the IP layer to enable it to route packets between different networks based on the routing table. In the case of a packet going to a remote system, the system finds the MAC address of the default gateway's IP address on the local subnet (see fig. 5.1).

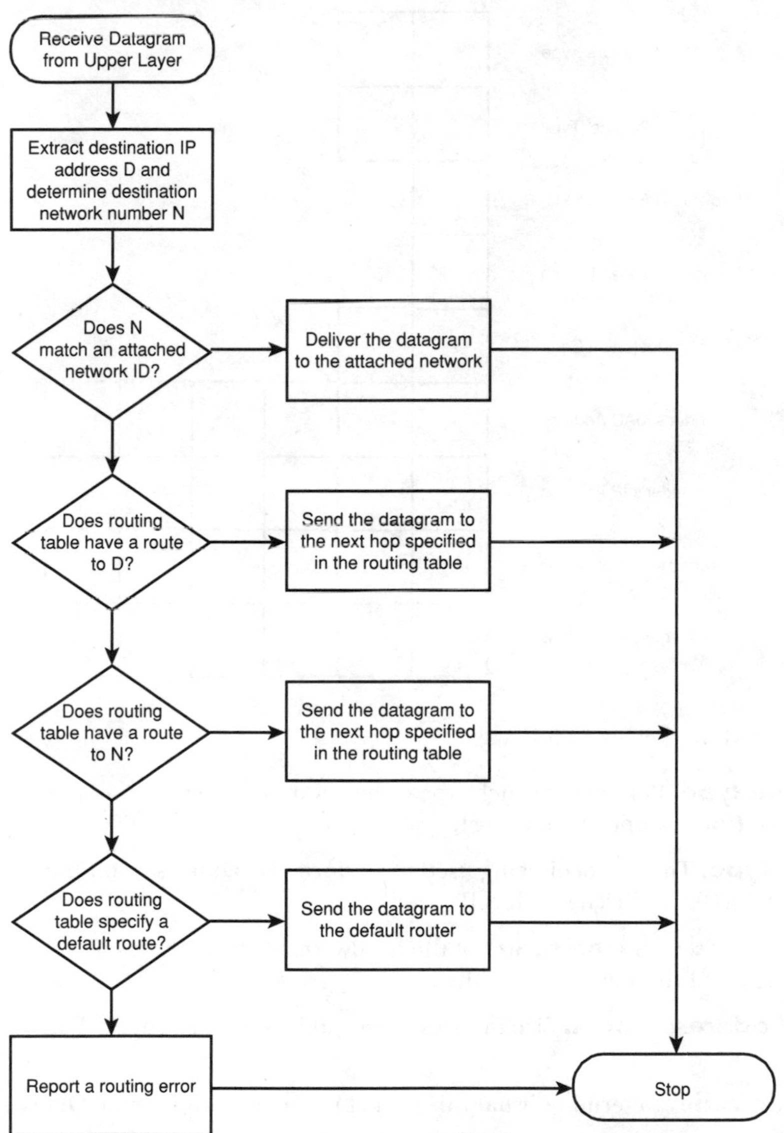

Figure 5.1

How IP chooses a route.

The protocol that handles the resolution of hardware addresses, as previously mentioned, is the ARP (Address Resolution Protocol). ARP first checks the ARP cache to see whether it has recently resolved the address. If it has, it can pass that to IP so that the packet can be sent. Otherwise, ARP creates a broadcast packet that is sent on the network (see fig. 5.2). The packet contains the IP address your system wants to resolve. It also contains the IP address and MAC address of your machine.

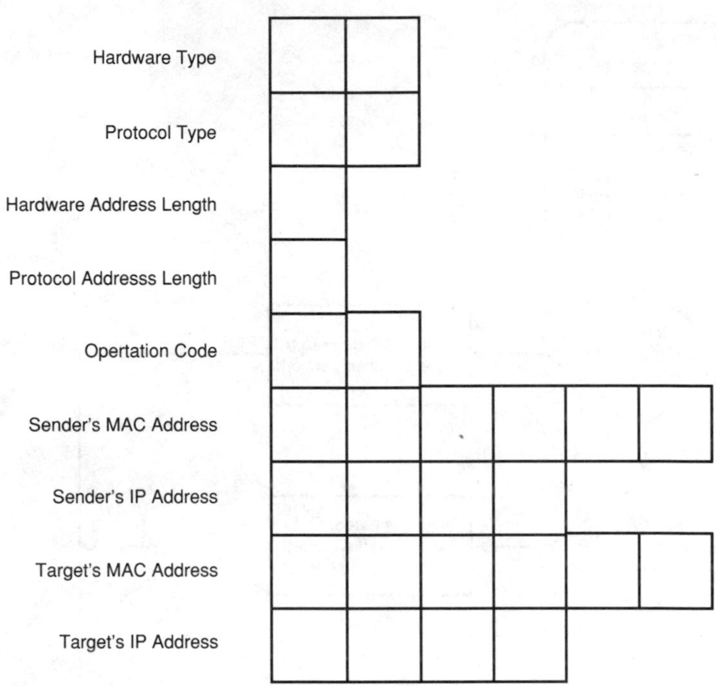

Figure 5.2
Breakdown of the ARP packet.

The parts of the ARP packet are as follows:

- **Hardware type.** References which type of hardware is being used to access the network (for example, token ring).
- **Protocol type.** The protocol being used to perform the address resolution. Normally set to 0800 (hex), which is IP.
- **Hardware address length.** Size of the hardware address in bytes. For Token Ring and Ethernet, this is 06 (hex).
- **Protocol address length.** Size in bytes of the address being sought. This is 04 (hex) for IP.
- **Operation code.** Determines what this packet is. Operations include Query and Reply.
- **Sender's addresses.** Both the MAC and IP addresses. This is added to the target machine's ARP cache, and is used to reply.
- **Target's addresses.** The information being sought. The IP address is known, and the MAC address is returned.

When the ARP packet is broadcast on the network, all the systems receive the packet and pass it up to their own IP layer. ARP sees whether the IP address being sought is its own IP address. If it is, it takes the IP address and MAC address of the other host and adds it to its own table. Then it creates an ARP reply to tell the other system its MAC address. Both systems now know each other's IP and MAC addresses.

You should, however, remember a couple of things about the ARP cache: Entries in the ARP cache expire after a short period of time; if the address is not used again, the entry lasts for two minutes; if it is used, it is kept for ten minutes. An entry could also be removed if the cache is getting full—in this case, ARP removes the oldest entries first. You can also add a static entry in the ARP cache. It remains, however, only until the system is restarted.

This might seem a little severe. Entries in the ARP cache, however, are the hardware addresses of the network cards in other hosts. This could very possibly change for a given host, and would (if your entries were permanent) require all the hosts to be updated. To work with your ARP cache, you can use the ARP command. Following is the help text for the ARP command:

```
C:\users\default>arp /?

Displays and modifies the IP-to-Physical address translation tables used by
address resolution protocol (ARP).

ARP -s inet_addr eth_addr [if_addr]
ARP -d inet_addr [if_addr]
ARP -a [inet_addr] [-N if_addr]

  -a            Displays current ARP entries by interrogating the current
                protocol data. If inet_addr is specified, the IP and Physical
                addresses for only the specified computer are displayed. If
                more than one network interface uses ARP, entries for each ARP
                table are displayed.
  -g            Same as -a.
  inet_addr     Specifies an internet address.
  -N if_addr    Displays the ARP entries for the network interface specified
                by if_addr.
  -d            Deletes the host specified by inet_addr.
  -s            Adds the host and associates the Internet address inet_addr
                with the Physical address eth_addr. The Physical address is
                given as 6 hexadecimal bytes separated by hyphens. The entry
                is permanent.
  eth_addr      Specifies a physical address.
  if_addr       If present, this specifies the Internet address of the
                interface whose address translation table should be modified.
                If not present, the first applicable interface will be used.
```

Creating an IP Datagram

The data that came down from TCP or UDP is now ready to be sent to the destination address (MAC). IP now creates the IP datagram. Just like TCP and UDP did, the IP layer adds a header to the data that came from the upper-layer protocol (see fig. 5.3). The header contains all the information required for the packet to be delivered to the destination host.

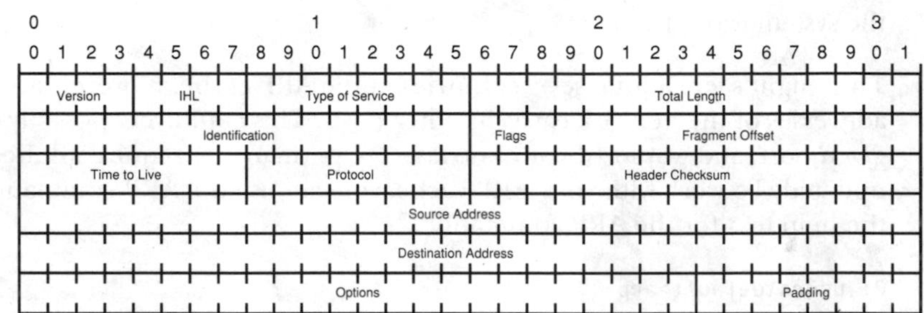

Figure 5.3
Parts of the IP header.

The parts of the IP header are as follows:

- **Version (4 bits).** Indicates the format of the Internet header. The current version as described in RFC 791 is version 4.
- **Internet Header Length (IHL; 4 bits).** Informs the other system of the number of 32-bit words in the header. The minimum size for a correct header is five words.
- **Type of Service (8 bits).** Data in this field indicate the quality of service desired.

  Bits 0, 1, and 2 Precedence. Deals with what type of traffic this packet is. The valid values are as follows:

  111—Network Control

  110—Internetwork Control

  101—CRITIC/ECP

  100—Flash Override

  011—Flash

  010—Immediate

  001—Priority

  000—Routine

The effects of values in the precedence fields depend on the network technology employed, and values must be configured accordingly.

Bit 3 - Delay. Indicates whether the packet is normal (0—Normal Delay) or urgent (1—Low Delay).

Bit 4 - Throughput. Requests throughput for the packet to be normal (0) or high (1).

Bit 5 - Reliability. Set to normal (0) or high (1)

Bits 6, and 7 Reserved.

Not all options in this field are compatible. When special service is desired, a choice must be made among options of low delay, high reliability, and high throughput. Better performance in one area often degrades performance in another. Few cases call for setting all three flags.

- **Total length (16 bits).** The length of the datagram in bytes, including the IP header and data. This field enables datagrams to consist of up to 65,535 bytes. The standard recommends that all hosts be prepared to receive datagrams of at least 576 bytes in length.
- **Identification (16 bits).** An identification field used to aid reassembly of the fragments of a datagram.
- **Flags (3 bits).** This field contains the following three control flags:

  Bit 0 Reserved. Must be 0.

  Bit 1 (DF - Do not Fragment). 0=May fragment; 1=Do not fragment.

  Bit 2 (MF - More Fragments). 0=Last fragment; 1=More fragments. (If a datagram is fragmented, the MF bit is 1 in all fragments except the last.)

- **Fragment Offset (13 bits).** For fragmented datagrams, indicates the position in the datagram of this fragment.
- **Time to Live (8 bits).** Indicates the maximum time the datagram can remain on the network. If this field has a value of 0, the datagram is discarded. The field is modified during IP header processing and generally is measured in seconds. Each IP module that handles the datagram, however, must decrement Time to Live by at least 1. This mechanism ensures that undeliverable datagrams are eventually removed.
- **Protocol (8 bits).** The upper-layer protocol associated with the data portion of the datagram.
- **Header Checksum (16 bits).** A checksum for the header only. This value must be recalculated each time the header is modified.

- **Source Address (32 bits).** The IP address of the host that originated the datagram.
- **Destination Address (32 bits).** The IP address of the host that is the final destination of the datagram.
- **Options (0 to 11 32-bit words).** May contain 0 or more options.

Fragmentation and Reassembly of Datagrams

IP is responsible for delivering datagrams through the internetwork. An IP datagram can be as large as 64 K. Many networks, however, cannot support data units of that size. An Ethernet frame, for example, can support only 1500 bytes of upper-layer data. Other network types are further restricted in the message sizes that can be accommodated. The MTU (*maximum transfer unit)* describes the number of bytes in the maximum frame size that a network can deliver without fragmentation.

In an internetwork, different network segments can have different MTU specifications. Consider the internetwork in figure 5.4. The token ring has an MTU of 3000; the Ethernet network has an MTU of 1500; and the intermediate WAN has an MTU of 520 (allowing for a 20 byte IP header and 500 bytes of data). If host 1 sends a 3000 byte datagram to host 2, router A must fragment the original datagram for transfer through the WAN. Router B must re-assemble the fragments to recover the original datagram and then refragment it for delivery to host 2.

The IP protocol specification states that all hosts must be prepared to accept and reassemble datagrams of at least 576 bytes. All routers must be able to manage datagrams up to the maximum message size of the networks to which they are attached, and must always be able to handle datagrams of up to 576 bytes.

IP has the task of fragmenting large datagrams into datagrams that are compatible with the physical layer being used. The header for each fragment includes information that enables IP at the receiving host to identify the position of the fragment and to re-assemble the original datagram.

When an oversize datagram must be fragmented, the header for each fragment includes an offset parameter that specifies where the first byte in the fragment is located in the overall datagram. In the preceding case, an original datagram—containing 1300 bytes in its data field—must be fragmented to accommodate a network with an MTU of 520. Allowing for the header, each fragment can contain 500 bytes of data. Three fragments are generated with offsets of 0, 500, and 1000 respectively.

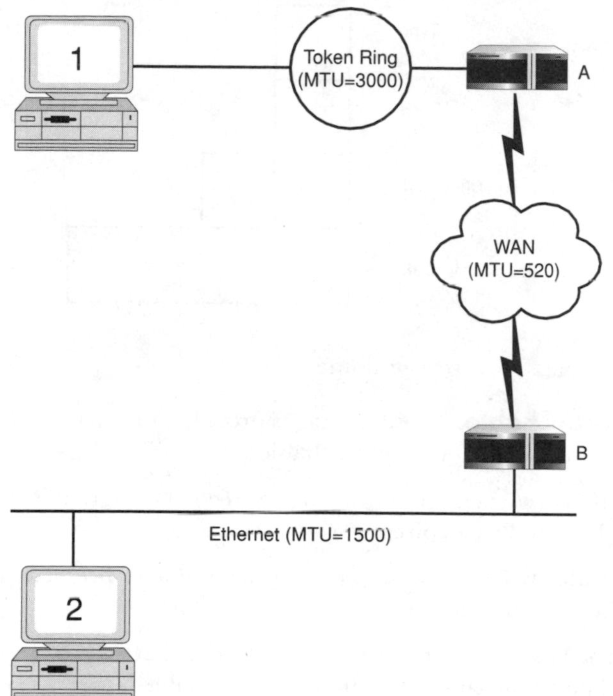

Figure 5.4
Sample internetwork with various maximum transfer units.

Note Note that each of the fragments is a standard IP datagram. The headers of the fragments are nearly identical to the header of the original datagram, except that the MF bit in the flags field is used to indicate whether the datagram is an intermediate fragment or the last fragment in a datagram.

No error detection and recovery mechanisms are implemented in the IP protocol. If a fragment of an overall datagram is damaged or lost, IP cannot request retransmission of the fragment. Instead, IP is forced to report an error to the upper-layer protocol, which must then retransmit the entire datagram. This can be highly inefficient, requiring a large datagram to be retransmitted because a small fragment was lost.

Error Detection and Reporting

Although there is no error correction for the data (remember IP does not guarantee delivery), there is a method to report errors that happen in transit. This is handled by the ICMP (Internet Control Messaging Protocol). ICMP handles sending messages for controlling data streaming and for error reporting purposes.

An ICMP packet is very simple (see fig. 5.5).

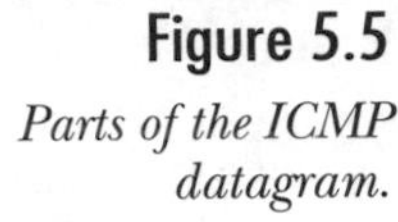

Figure 5.5
Parts of the ICMP datagram.

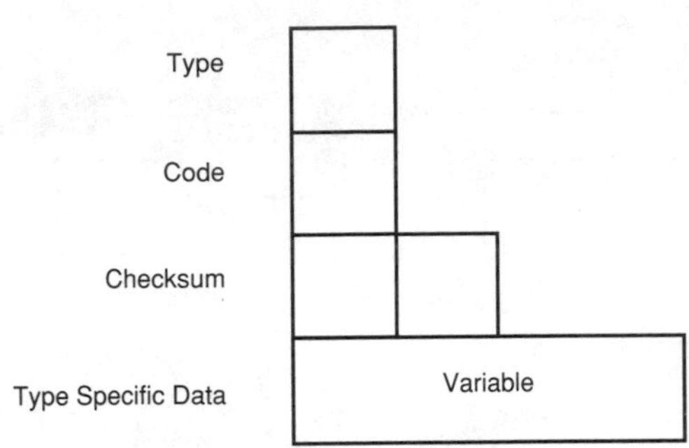

Some of the main ICMP messages are as follows:

- **Destination Unreachable.** These messages provide information when a host, net, port, or protocol is (are) unreachable.
- **Time Exceeded.** These messages notify the source if a datagram is undeliverable because its Time to Live expired.
- **Parameter Problem.** These messages report a parameter problem and the octet in which the error was detected.
- **Source Quench.** These messages may be sent by destination routers or hosts forced to discard datagrams due to limitations in available buffer space, or if for any reason a datagram cannot be processed.
- **Redirect.** These messages are sent to a host when a router receives a datagram that could be routed more directly through another gateway. The message advises the host that was the source of the datagram of a more appropriate router to receive the datagram.
- **Echo Request and Echo Reply Messages.** These messages exchange data between hosts.
- **Timestamp Request and Timestamp Reply.** These messages exchange timestamp data between hosts.
- **Information Request and Information Reply.** These messages can be used to enable a host to discover the network to which it is attached.

ICMP provides basic connectivity utilities used by upper-layer protocols—utilities such as PING use these to perform their functions.

Summary

This chapter has looked at the IP layer and introduced the concept of routing. You have also seen that no matter where the IP datagram is sent, it always goes to a MAC address, not an IP address. This layer has three main protocols: IP, ARP, and ICMP. As you have seen, these protocols all work together to provide the capability to actually send data. The next two chapters look at subnetting and routing in great detail, and explain the basis for using TCP/IP in wide-area networking.

Test Yourself

1. On what type of system is the IP layer present?
2. What are some of the main functions of the IP layer?
3. What is the function of a subnet mask?
4. What is the standard subnet mask for a Class C address?
5. On what types of systems do you find a routing table?
6. What command can you use to look at the routing table?
7. What command would you issue to add a route to network 142.53.0.0 (subnet mask 255.255.0.0) so that data goes to a local router at 125.32.45.7?
8. In the routing table, what does the interface refer to?
9. What is the entry 0.0.0.0 in the routing table for?
10. What happens after IP determines that the system is a local system?
11. How long is an entry in the ARP cache retained?
12. Why would it be unwise for ARP to retain an entry permanently?
13. Other than responding to the request, what else does ARP do on the target host?
14. The header of the IP datagram has many fields. What is the purpose of the following ones?

    Fragment Offset

    Time to Live

    Protocol

15. When is fragmentation required?
16. Which IP layer protocol is used to handle the reporting of errors?
17. What are examples of some of the errors that might be handled?

Test Yourself Answers

1. All devices that have an IP address have the IP layer, including both computers and routers.
2. The IP layer is responsible for routing datagrams, resolving IP address to MAC addresses, fragmentating and re-assembing packets too large for the underlying topology, and error detection and reporting.
3. The subnet mask allows IP to strip the host ID from the IP address, leaving the network ID.
4. The Class C subnet mask is 255.255.255.0.
5. All systems that use IP have a routing table. The routing table for most computers, however, points all data for networks other than the local network to the default gateway (router).
6. The ROUTE command enables the viewing and modifying of the routing table.
7. The command would be

   ROUTE ADD 142.53.0.0 MASK 255.255.0.0 125.32.45.7
8. The interface refers to the network card in the local machine that sends out the information.
9. This is the entry for the default gateway.
10. The IP layer will now use ARP to find the MAC address.
11. Entries in the ARP cache have a maximum lifetime of ten minutes. If the entry is not used again within two minutes, however, it is removed.
12. ARP resolves the IP address to the MAC address; the MAC address is part of the network card. If the network card ever needed to be changed, the entry would have to be removed by hand and then re-entered.
13. ARP adds the IP address and MAC address of the sending host. It does this assuming that more communications will follow.

14. Fragment Offset is used to re-assemble datagrams that have been fragmented in transit.

    Time to Live is the maximum number of "seconds" that a packet can remain active on the network. When the TTL reaches zero, the packet is discarded.

    Protocol Used is used to tell the IP layer on the target hosts which protocol to send the information up to.

15. Fragmentation occurs if the datagram travels over networks of different topologies. The topologies all have different maximum transfer unit sizes. In the case of a packet that moves from a network with a large MTU to a small one, the datagram must be fragmented.
16. Error reporting is a function of the Internet Control Messaging Protocol.
17. The ICMP protocol handles many errors and other messages including Destination Unreachable, Time Exceeded, Parameter Problem, Source Quench, Redirect, Echo Request, Echo Reply, Timestamp Request, Timestamp Reply, Information Request, and Information Reply.

CHAPTER 6

Subnetting

In a perfect world, everyone who wants to have a network ID can have one. In the real world, however, only a limited number of network IDs are available. This has begun to cause a problem—the increased popularity of the Internet in the last few years is quickly depleting the supply of network IDs.

Note It should be clearly understood that this section applies only if you are planning on connecting to the World Wide Internet (the backbone that enables you to visit WWW sites and exchange e-mail). If you work only with computers in your own organization, you can use any address you feel like using—this is called a *Private Network Address*. This is the case as well when you use a firewall or proxy server.

In previous chapters, you looked at various classes of networks—A, B, and C. Each of these enables you to have a different number of hosts. Larger organizations usually have more than one segment on a network, but they still only get one Internet address (normally). This means that any host you want to enable on the Internet must be on the segment that has the router. Obviously you cannot put 16,384 hosts on one segment, never mind 16,777,214.

The solution is very simple, just like cutting a cake so that a large group can each have a piece: you can cut your IP address into slices. This is the process of subnetting. *Subnetting* enables you to take a single IP address from your ISP (or the Internic) and make a group of networks out of it. You can then route between these networks internally and through your main router externally.

Subnetting is an important concept to understand if you are organizing a large network. To the outside world, the network ID looks like a single network—your network could be 160.16.0.0, for example. This is a valid class B address, and means that you could have up to 65,534 hosts on that network. This, of course, is impossible.

Because understanding what happens in subnetting requires understanding the TCP/IP address as a 32-bit binary address, this chapter starts with a recap of binary. After covering that essential, the chapter examines the process of subnetting, and then finishes off with a look at supernetting.

Remembering Binary

Chapter 5, "The Internet Layer," covered how the IP layer uses the subnet mask to determine whether a host is on the local network or a remote network. To do this, the bits in the subnet mask are turned on for the portion that represents the network ID. In a class B address, for example, the standard subnet mask is 255.255.0.0, which means all the bits are "on" (1s) for the first two octets. The ANDing process pulls the first 16 bits from the IP address, which is the network ID. Table 6.1 shows an example of this.

Table 6.1
Extracting a Network ID Using a Standard Subnet Mask

IP Address 160.16.45.3	10100000	00010000	00101101	00000011
Subnet Mask 255.255.255.0	11111111	11111111	00000000	00000000
Network ID 160.16.0.0	10100000	00010000	00000000	00000000

Note This chapter usually lists the IP address in the first column, and then breaks that into the binary for each of the octets of the address. This setup enables you to see the binary versions of the IP addresses and subnet masks. You will probably find (as most people do) that it is easier to understand if you look at it in binary.

When a network is subnetted, all that happens is that you set two or more extra bits to "on" in the subnet mask. In this way, the IP layer sees more of the hosts with which you are communicating as being on a remote network—including some of the addresses within your organization. Table 6.2 shows a network ID extract using a custom subnet mask.

Table 6.2
Extracting a Network ID Using a Custom Subnet Mask

IP Address 160.16.45.3	10100000	00010000	00101101	00000011
Subnet Mask 255.255.240.0	11111111	11111111	11110000	00000000
Network ID 160.16.32.0	10100000	00010000	00100000	00000000

Notice that the network ID extract in table 6.1 differs from that in table 6.2—even though the IP address is the same. This is because extra bits are used to identify the network. In this case, four extra bits are used. Assume, for example, that you are trying to contact a host with an address of 160.16.154.23, as shown in table 6.3.

TABLE 6.3
Extracting the Target Network ID Using Standard and Custom Masks

IP Address 160.16.154.23	10100000	00010000	10011010	00010111
Subnet Mask 255.255.0.0	11111111	11111111	00000000	00000000
Network ID 160.16.0.0	10100000	00010000	00000000	00000000
Subnet Mask 255.255.240.0	11111111	11111111	11110000	00000000
Network ID 160.16.144.0	10100000	00010000	10010000	00000000

As table 6.3 shows, if you use the standard subnet mask, the network IDs match—your system will know that the host is a local host. If you use the custom subnet mask, however, the network IDs differ—this means that the target host is remote.

Remember that the IP address is a 32-bit binary address with the first part as the network ID, and the remainder as the host ID on that network. Obviously if you use more bits for the network ID (to subnet it), it has fewer for the hosts; you reduce the number of hosts per network (see fig. 6.1).

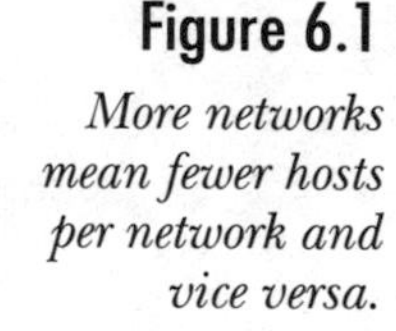

Figure 6.1
More networks mean fewer hosts per network and vice versa.

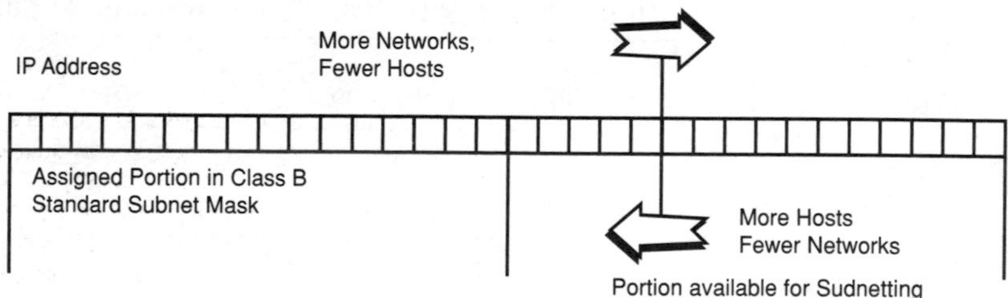

How Do You Subnet?

Subnetting is usually done only once, and falls into the planning stages of the network. Changing the subnetting scheme after a network is in place generally requires visiting each station on the network and reconfiguring it.

Determining Your Addressing Needs

You must determine two critical factors when choosing how to subnet your network. First you need to know how many different subnets are needed, and then you need to know the maximum number of hosts required on any one subnet. Remembering that your network will probably grow at some time in the future, you should always design your network so that the growth you expect (and more) can be accommodated.

Some points that you want to consider in planning the subnetting of your network include where your users are physically located, and how much network traffic different types of users are going to generate. General guidelines include the following:

- Locate users that share data with each other on the same subnet
- Put a domain controller on each subnet that users log on to
- Place users with heavy network usage on less populated subnets
- Reserve a network ID for each Wide Area Link
- Allow for the most subnets possible—use the desired maximum number of hosts per segment as the limiting factor
- Where possible, put users on the same subnet as the servers they will use
- If required, put multiple network cards in servers that server multiple subnets

All these help to reduce the load on your routers. You should also plan redundancy into your router scheme, making alternate routes available in case one fails.

Defining Your Subnet Mask

Objective B.5

For an IP address to be a remote address, the network portion of the address must be different (in binary) from your own. In the case of subnetting, that means the bits in the portion you are using to subnet have to change. The easiest way to figure out how many bits you need is to write the number in binary. Twelve subnets, for example, would be 1100. It takes 4 bits to write the number 12 in binary. To allow for at least 12 unique binary combinations, therefore, you need to use 4 bits for your subnet mask.

You can add the bits to the standard subnet mask to generate a custom subnet mask. When the bits are added to the subnet mask, all the required bits are set to 1. In the class B example used earlier in this chapter, it would look like table 6.4.

TABLE 6.4
Creating a Custom Subnet Mask by Adding Subnetting Bits

Standard Mask	11111111	11111111	00000000	00000000
Additional Bits			11110000	
Custom Subnet Mask	11111111	11111111	11110000	00000000

You might want to move the bits you want to use to the beginning of the octet (as in table 6.4, for example). Because the network ID is always the first part of the IP address, the subnetting bits (which are an extension of the network ID) are the always the first bits after the standard mask.

Finding Out How Many Networks, How Many Hosts

As you might have guessed, there are actually more than the 12 subnets required. In fact, four bits generate 16 unique combinations (or 2^4). This means that a total of 14 subnets are available, because just like host IDs and network IDs, the subnet IDs cannot be all 0s or all 1s.

Calculating what the subnet mask requires is very simple now. In fact, you have already done it. Table 6.4 shows the custom subnet mask—you can just convert it to decimal 255.255.240.0. You can also figure out how many hosts each subnet will have. Remember that the subnet mask is used to remove the host ID so that only the network ID remains. All the bits that you are masking out (0s), therefore, are used for the host ID.

In this case, the third octet has 4 and the last octet has 8, meaning 12 bits are used for the host ID. The number 2 put to the power of 12 gives you the number of hosts that are supported per subnet. Remember, though, to subtract 2 from the product because the address with all 0s is this subnet's ID, and the address with all 1s is the broadcast for this subnet. So 2^{12} is 4,096 minus 2 is 4,094 hosts available on each subnet.

Because you always include the bits that you want to subnet with immediately after the standard subnet mask, only certain numbers work for the subnet mask. Obviously 255 and 0 are available—they make up the standard subnet mask. As you saw in the preceding example, you took the 4 bits and put them on the left side of the octet; the rest was padded with 0s. This is the same procedure you follow for all custom subnetting. Table 6.5 shows all the valid numbers for subnet masks.

TABLE 6.5
Valid Subnet Numbers

Bits Used	Octet in Binary	Decimal Value
1	Not valid	Not valid
2	11000000	192
3	11100000	224
4	11110000	240
5	11111000	248
6	11111100	252
7	11111110	254
8	11111111	255

Notice that subnetting on one bit is not valid. This makes sense if you remember that the subnet ID cannot be all 1s or all 0s. Because the only possible subnet IDs with one bit would be a 1 or a 0, you cannot use this.

Subnetwork IDs

Now that the hard work is done, you can figure out the subnetwork IDs. By figuring these, you can calculate the valid host IDs for each subnet. Using the same example as earlier, 16 possible combinations exist in the subnetted octet. Looking at them as an entire octet, they can be converted to decimal. This gives you the subnet IDs. Table 6.6 shows the calculation of subnet IDs using binary.

TABLE 6.6
Calculating the Subnet IDs Using Binary

Octet in Binary	Decimal Equivalent	Full Network ID
0000 0000	0	Not Valid
0001 0000	16	160.16.16.0
0010 0000	32	160.16.32.0

continues

TABLE 6.6
Calculating the Subnet IDs Using Binary

Octet in Binary	Decimal Equivalent	Full Network ID
0011 0000	48	160.16.48.0
0100 0000	64	160.16.64.0
0101 0000	80	160.16.80.0
0110 0000	96	160.16.96.0
0111 0000	112	160.16.112.0
1000 0000	128	160.16.128.0
1001 0000	144	160.16.144.0
1010 0000	160	160.16.160.0
1011 0000	176	160.16.176.0
1100 0000	192	160.16.192.0
1101 0000	208	160.16.208.0
1110 0000	224	160.16.224.0
1111 0000	240	Not Valid

Again two values are not valid because they consist of all 0s and all 1s. Looking at table 6.6, you might notice that the subnet ID always increases by 16. If you look at the first half of the octet (the part being subnetted), this is being increased by 1 each time, and the 4 other bits are ignored. Therefore you are counting by 16s.

This in fact works for all the possible subnetting scenarios. You always end up counting by the position value of the last bit in the subnet mask. To look at another example, consider what happens if you subnet on 3 bits (see table 6.7).

TABLE 6.7
Subnet IDs for a Three-Bit Subnet Mask

Octet in Binary	Decimal Equivalent	Full Network ID
000 00000	0	Not Valid

Octet in Binary	Decimal Equivalent	Full Network ID
001 00000	32	160.16.32.0
010 00000	64	160.16.64.0
011 00000	96	160.16.96.0
100 00000	128	160.16.128.0
101 00000	160	160.16.160.0
110 00000	192	160.16.192.0
111 00000	224	Not Valid

In this case, the last bit in the subnet mask has a position value of 32. To calculate the subnet IDs, therefore, all you need to do is look at the position value for the last bit in the subnet mask. This is the first valid subnet ID, and the value by which to increment.

Table 6.8 summarizes all the information that you have looked at so far.

TABLE 6.8
Table for Calculating Subnet Mask, IDs, and Number of Subnets

Position Value	64	32	16	8	4	2	1
Subnet Bits	2	3	4	5	6	7	8
Subnets Available	2^2-2 =2	2^3-2 =6	2^4-2 =14	2^5-2 =30	2^6-2 =62	2^7-2 =126	2^8-2 =254
Subnet Mask	128+64 =192	192+32 =224	224+16 =240	240+8 =248	248+4 =252	252+2 =254	254+1 =255
Host Bbits	6	5	4	3	2	1	0

Using table 6.8, look at a network with the given class B address of 152.42.0.0. In this case, you need at least 28 subnets with a maximum of 300 hosts per subnet (segment). In this case, there *is* more than one right answer.

Knowing that you need 28 subnets, the obvious answer is to use 5 bits for subnetting—as you can see, that gives you up to 30 subnets. You might, therefore, use the 255.255.248.0 as the subnet mask. This leaves 3 bits for hosts in the third octet plus the 8 in the last for a total of 11 bits. That works out to 2,046 hosts per segment (211–2.)

This is perfectly valid—you have the correct number of subnets, and meet (exceed) your maximum number of hosts per network. Because you don't want to end up with segments (subnets) that have 2,046 hosts each (too much traffic), however, you might look at this the other way around. If you need to have 300 unique host IDs, you can write that number in binary (just like you did for the subnet bits in the beginning) and see how many bits you need. The number 300 in binary is 100101100, which is nine bits. Because the last octet has eight bits, you really one need one from the third to make nine.

You can, therefore, use 7 bits for the subnet mask, giving you 27–2 subnets (126). That leaves you a lot of room for growth while still maintaining the maximum number of hosts per subnet to maintain acceptable performance. Both answers are correct, but remember to allow for growth.

Host IDs

The last step in subnetting is to figure out the actual host IDs (IP addresses) for each of the subnets that you are creating. This is now very simple. The IDs available for each network are all the possible bit combinations between the subnet ID and the broadcast address for the subnet. If the subnet ID is 160.16.32.0 and the subnet mask is 255.255.240.0, for example, the range is 160.16.32.1 to 160.16.47.254.

Maybe that's not completely obvious. The first step is to figure out the next subnet ID. In the preceding case, the subnet mask is 255.255.240.0, which tells you that the subnet mask has 4 bits. The last bit in the subnet mask, therefore, is in the 16 position, hence you increment by 16. You can see now that the next valid subnet ID is 160.16.48.0.

Remembering that the IP address is really just a 32-bit number, you can increment by 1. This gives you the first host's ID, as shown in table 6.9.

Table 6.9
Finding the First Host ID by Addition

Subnet ID 160.16.32.0	10100000	00010000	00100000	00000000
Plus 1	00000000	00000000	00000000	00000001
First Host ID 160.16.32.1	10100000	00010000	00100000	00000001

Finding the end of the valid host IDs is also simple. Take the next subnet ID (in the case of the last subnet, use the subnet mask—which is the subnet with all 1s) and subtract 1, as shown in table 6.10. This gives you a case where all the hosts bits are on in the previous subnet. Because this is the broadcast address, you should back up one more to get the last host ID.

TABLE 6.10
Finding the Last Host ID by Subtraction

Next Subnet ID 160.16.47.255	10100000	00010000	00110000	00000000
Minus 1	00000000	00000000	00000000	00000001
Broadcast for Previous Subnet 160.16.47.255	10100000	00010000	00101111	11111111
Minus 1	00000000	00000000	00000000	00000001
Last Host ID 160.16.47.254	10100000	00010000	00101111	11111110

Finding the host IDs becomes very obvious if you look at it this way, notably in the case of a subnetted class A or B address. You can apply the same math, however, when subnetting a class C address. In this case, it is not so obvious because the numbers are not familiar.

Take 198.53.202.0, for example, as a network address. You want two subnets. You end up with 198.53.202.64 and 198.53.202.128 as the two subnet IDs (subnet mask 255.255.255.192). Following the logic set out previously, the valid hosts are as follows in table 6.11:

TABLE 6.11
Host IDs for a Subnetted Class C Address

Subnet ID	Starting Host ID	Last Host ID
198.53.202.64	198.53.202.65	198.53.202.126
198.53.202.128	198.53.202.129	198.53.202.190

Supernetting

As the world runs out of TCP/IP addresses, larger companies face a problem: class A or even many class B addresses are no longer available. If a company has 620 hosts on its network, it must have multiple class C addresses because it cannot obtain a class B. This means having multiple routers to connect to the Internet, and multiple addresses that the Internet has to handle for a single company.

Supernetting came about as a way to relieve this problem. In the preceding example, the company requires at least three class C addresses. This, however, does not leave much room for growth. Additionally, if the distribution of the systems does not match the distribution of addresses (say 300 hosts at each of two locations, and 20 at the head office), the WAN links might become problematic.

When you look at subnetting, you can see that because of the way binary works you can break large networks into a group of smaller ones. It makes sense then that you should be able to join together smaller networks into one large one. If you treat class C addresses as a subnetted class B address, using 8 bits for the subnet mask, the problem just about resolves itself.

If you consider the company previously mentioned as a single subnet on a class B network, you would look at the 620 hosts as a maximum number of hosts per segment. This means that you need 10 bits for host IDs (620 in binary is 1001101100 - 10 bits). You could subnet a class B on 6 bits, therefore, leaving 2 bits in the third octet and 8 in the last for the host ID.

Although this sounds great, a class C address is not really a class B address. Therefore you can't really do this. You can, however, fake it. The third octet has 2 bits being used for the host ID in this example, meaning there are four possible combinations. If you take four class C addresses where the only difference is the last 2 bits of the third octet, you can actually combine them together.

This actually gives you four class C addresses. It is not important which addresses are used, only that they are sequential and all possible combinations of the last 2 bits of the third octet are included. Table 6.12 shows four addresses that work in this case.

Table 6.12
Binary View of a Supernet

198.53.212.0	11000110	00110101	11010100	00000000
198.53.213.0	11000110	00110101	11010101	00000000
198.53.214.0	11000110	00110101	11010110	00000000
198.53.215.0	11000110	00110101	11010111	00000000

As you can see, all that changes is the last 2 bits in the third octet (you might also notice that, in supernetting, all 0s and all 1s are actually valid). In this case, you can treat these four addresses as a subnetted class B address: 198.53.212.0. Using the standard class B subnet of 255.255.0.0, you must add the 6-bit subnet mask of 252, which gives you 255.255.252.0.

This has to be handled in conjunction with your Internet Service Provider (ISP). ISPs have large banks of addresses (mainly class C) and frequently have to do this for large organizations. Now consider a slightly larger case.

Your new company has 85,765 hosts on its network, and you require full Internet access from each host. To support 85,765 hosts, you normally require a class A address (wasting over 16 million addresses). You could combine two class B addresses. It is hard to get a class B address, however, and getting two in sequence is nearly impossible.

Again you start by expressing the number 85,765 in binary 1 01001111 00000101. The number is larger, but the process is still the same. In this case, you treat a group of class C addresses as a subnetted class A. Because this subnet requires 17 bits for the host ID, and because 24 bits are available for hosts in a class A network, you can see that the subnet mask needs to use 7 bits. The standard class A subnet mask is 255.0.0.0; adding the 7-bit subnet mask to that, it becomes 255.254.0.0. You can now find a group of class C addresses where the first 15 bits are always the same. To figure out the addresses, it is easiest to think of them in binary (see table 6.13).

TABLE 6.13
Finding Class C Addresses for a Class A Supernet

Subnet Mask	11111111	11111110	00000000	00000000
Starting Class C	110XXXXX	XXXXXXX0	00000000	00000000
Ending Class C	110XXXXX	XXXXXXX1	11111111	00000000

You can add in any valid combination of bits for the Xs. This results in the range of networks you require. For example, 205.126.0.0 works with the subnet mask of 255.254.0.0. This range includes 512 (you are using 9 bits, or 29 class C networks) networks. The actual network IDs range from 205.126.0.0 to 205.127.255.0. Notice again that all 0s and all 1s are valid (and required) in supernetting.

Summary

Simply put, subnetting is the hardest concept that you will have to deal with. The unfortunate part is that you may need to deal with subnetting fairly often in your organization. This chapter has looked at the why and then the how of subnetting. It also has given you the information you need to deal with it. The single largest stumbling block is normally trying too hard. It is really very simple, as long as you don't let the binary scare you. Building on the subnetting that you have seen here, the next chapter looks at IP routing, which is basically why you need to subnet.

Test Yourself

1. Why is subnetting required?
2. What does subnetting do from a binary perspective?
3. What is the least number of bits that you can subnet on?
4. How many different subnet masks are required for an organization with 17,938 hosts?
5. For each of the following number of networks, determine the number of bits needed in the subnet mask and how many networks there will be in total.

   48

   156

   12

   64

   6

   78

   312

   56

   127

   7

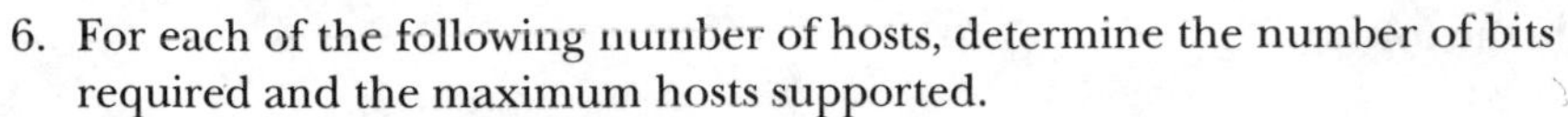

6. For each of the following number of hosts, determine the number of bits required and the maximum hosts supported.

   50

   250

   125

   300

   800

   2,000

   60

   95

   4,000

   1,500

7. Complete Subnet Mask and Hosts per Subnet columns in the following chart.

Network ID	Subnets Required	Subnet Mask	Hosts per Subnet
152.42.0.0	10	___	___
120.0.0.0	250	___	___
187.16.0.0	100	___	___
210.125.36.0	2	___	___
160.106.0.0	33	___	___

8. What numbers are valid in a subnet mask.

9. For each of the following, give the first three valid subnet IDs.

   152.42.0.0 mask 255.255.240.0

   120.0.0.0 mask 255.255.0.0

   187.16.0.0 mask 255.255.254.0

   210.125.36.0 mask 255.255.255.192 (only two)

   160.106.0.0 mask 255.255.248.0

Complete the following table:

Position Value	64	32	16	8	4	2	1
Subnet bits	—	—	—	—	—	—	—
Subnets Available	—	—	—	—	—	—	—
Subnet Mask	—	—	—	—	—	—	—
Host bits	—	—	—	—	—	—	—

11. For each of the following subnet IDs, give the range of valid host IDs.

    152.42.64.0 mask 255.255.240.0

    160.106.64.0 mask 255.255.192.0

    198.78.16.64 mask 255.255.255.224

    15.56.0.0 mask 255.255.0.0

    131.107.64.0 mask 255.255.252.0

12. For each of the following host IDs, determine the range of hosts for the subnet.

    175.42.36.52 mask 255.255.248.0

    189.64.125.12 mask 255.255.192.0

    164.53.47.8 mask 255.255.240.0

    45.36.25.4 mask 255.255.0.0

    160.106.78.52 mask 255.255 224.0

13. What is the purpose of supernetting?
14. Who do you have to work with to perform supernetting? Why?
15. For each of the following number of hosts, determine the number of class C addresses required for supernetting and the subnet mask.

    12,245

    160,782

    852

    6,254

    85,765

Test Yourself Answers

1. Subnetting is required to enable organizations that have a large number of hosts to take the assigned network ID and break down into small pieces. This is generally done for performance reasons or to accommodate different physical locations.
2. Subnetting is basically the process of using more bits to identify the network than the standard mask uses. The extra networks generated this way become a division that can be managed internally.
3. Subnetting requires that the subnet ID not be all 0s or all 1s. This means you cannot use 1 bit to subnet. The least number of bits you can subnet on, therefore, is 2.
4. One. When you plan the network, all the hosts on the network should use the same subnet mask—regardless of the number of hosts.
5. The answers are as follows:

48	6 bits	62
156	8 bits	255
12	4 bits	14
64	7 bits	126
6	3 bits	6
78	7 bits	126
312	9 bits	510
56	6 bits	62
127	8 bits	255
7	4 bits	14

6. The answers are as follows:

50	6 bits	62
250	8 bits	254
125	7 bits	126
300	9 bits	510
800	10 bits	1,022
2,000	11 bits	2,046

60	6 bits	62
95	7 bits	126
4,000	12 bits	4,094
1,500	11 bits	2,046

7. When completed, the table should look like this:

Network ID	Subnets Required	Subnet Mask	Hosts per Subnet
152.42.0.0	10	255.255.240.0	4,094
120.0.0.0	250	255.255.0.0	65,534
187.16.0.0	100	255.255.254.0	510
210.125.36.0	2	255.255.255.192	62
160.106.0.0	33	255.255.248.0	2,046

8. The numbers valid in a subnet mask are 0, 192, 224, 240, 248, 252, 254, 255.

9. The valid subnet IDs are as follows:

   For 152.42.0.0 mask 255.255.240.0

   152.42.16.0, 152.42.32.0, 152.42.48.0

   For 120.0.0.0 mask 255.255.0.0

   120.1.0.0. 120.2.0.0, 120.3.0.0

   For 187.16.0.0 mask 255.255.254.0

   187.16.2.0, 187.16.4.0, 187.16.6.0

   For 210.125.36.0 mask 255.255.255.192 (only two)

   210.125.36.64, 210.125.36.128

   For 160.106.0.0 mask 255.255.248.0

   160.106.8.0, 160.106.16.0, 160.106.24.0

10. When completed, the table should look like this:

Position Value	64	32	16	8	4	2	1
Subnet bits	2	3	4	5	6	7	8
Subnets Available	2^2-2 2	2^3-2 6	2^4-2 14	2^5-2 30	2^6-2 62	2^7-2 126	2^8-2 254

Subnet Mask	128+64 =192	192+32 =224	224+16 =240	240+8 =248	248+4 =252	252+2 =254	254+1 =255
Host bits	6	5	4	3	2	1	0

11. The ranges are as follows:

    For 152.42.64.0 mask 255.255.240.0

    152.42.64.1 to 152.42.79.254

    For 160.106.64.0 mask 255.255.192.0

    160.106.64.1 to 160.106.65.254

    For 198.78.16.64 mask 255.255.255.224

    198.78.16.65 to 198.78.16.94

    For 15.56.0.0 mask 255.255.0.0

    15.56.0.1 to 15.56.255.254

    For 131.107.64.0 mask 255.255.252.0

    131.107.64.1 to 131.107.67.254

12. The ranges are as follows:

    For 175.42.36.52 mask 255.255.248.0

    175.42.32.1 to 175.42.39.254

    For 189.64.125.12 mask 255.255.192.0

    189.64.64.1 to 189.64.127.254

    For 164.53.47.8 mask 255.255.240.0

    164.53.32.1 to 164.53.47.254

    For 45.36.25.4 mask 255.255.0.0

    45.36.0.1 to 45.36.255.254

    For 160.106.78.52 mask 255.255 224.0

    160.106.64.1 to 160.106.95.254

13. Supernetting enables you to combine groups of class networks in a single network ID. This is required to get around the lack of available addresses.

14. You must work with your ISP to obtain a supernetted address. Your ISP needs to allocate you a series of consecutive class C address.

15. The number of class C addresses and the subnet masks are as follows:

Hosts	Number of Addresses	Subnet Mask
12,245	64	255.255.192.0
160,782	1,024	255.252.0.0
852	4	255.255.252.0
6,254	32	255.255.224.0
85,765	512	255.254.0.0

CHAPTER 7

Routing

Now that you have an understanding of subnetting, and have looked at all the parts of the TCP/IP protocol stack, you need to look at the process of routing. This is the piece that makes TCP/IP as popular as it is. This chapter briefly defines routing, and then spends some time discussing NT as a router format. This chapter discusses both static and dynamic routing.

What Is Routing?

In its simplest form, routing is the process of moving a packet of information from one network to another based on known information. The process of routing takes place on all IP-enabled equipment. This includes routers, but can also include any NT (or other) hosts that use TCP/IP as a protocol.

What Is a Router?

To understand what the process of routing does, you must have a very clear idea of what a router is. In basic terms, a *router* is a physical link between two networks. This link sits there passively until it receives a packet from a host on either network. It then sends the packets to a host on the opposite network. Routers should not be confused with bridges which, in effect, "pay attention" to all traffic. Routers are passive in that they do not actively seek packets that have to be moved to the other network; instead the packet is sent directly to the router. Bridges listen to all the traffic on the networks it is connected to, finding out which systems (MAC addresses) are on each side. It can then move data bound for a particular MAC address to the network on which that address resides.

Both a router and a bridge have a physical network interface on both networks with which it connects. This physical link is a Network Interface Card (NIC), just like the one that you would find inside your system. Routers also have the IP layer built into them. It is the IP layer that enables the router to route the packets from one network to another.

Routing is a function of the IP layer of the TCP/IP protocol stack. As mentioned previously, the IP layer uses the routing table to figure out where the packet should be sent next. As you should recall, the IP datagram contained the source and destination addresses for the packet being sent. You should also recall the process of ANDing that you used to figure out the network ID. These are both functions of the IP layer.

The routing table is the key that allows a router to route the packets. The routing table is basically a list of all the networks that the router knows about. The ROUTE command is used to modify or view the routing information in an NT system (see Chapter 5, "The Internet Layer").

NT as a Router

You can implement two types of routing with NT: static and dynamic. As a static router, NT knows only about the networks that you tell it about or that it is physically connected to. To route to other networks, you must build up the entire routing table and maintain it. In cases where you participate in a large intranet or communicate with the Internet, building a manual routing table is an impossible task. To facilitate this, dynamic routing was developed. Routing protocols are used to enable routers to share information about the networks they are aware of. The following sections cover static and dynamic routing in detail.

Note This discussion focuses on NT as a router. There are many other types of systems that are capable of routing, however, including Unix workstations and even dedicated Cisco routers.

Static Routing

Windows NT can act as a router; this makes sense, because NT can support multiple network cards and has an IP layer. It is important to remember that Windows NT is not sold as a router; routing support is just a capability it has because of the implementation of IP.

Objective B.2

If you want to use NT as a router, you must provide the system with a physical connection to the networks that it will route between. To complete the process, use the following steps:

Objective B.6

1. Install two (or more) network cards. In fact, trying to put two or more network cards into a single computer is probably the hardest part.
2. Assign an IP address to each of the two cards that is valid for the network to which they are connected.
3. After the cards are in and functioning, enable IP routing. This is done in the TCP/IP Configuration dialog box by checking the Enable IP Forwarding check box on the Routing tab.

Your Windows NT system is now a static router. The routing table now includes the information required to move the data between the two networks to which you are connected.

To illustrate this, look at a network with two subnets that you are connecting using an NT system as the router (see fig. 7.1). The routing table for the NT system automatically has a reference to both networks, and can route between them.

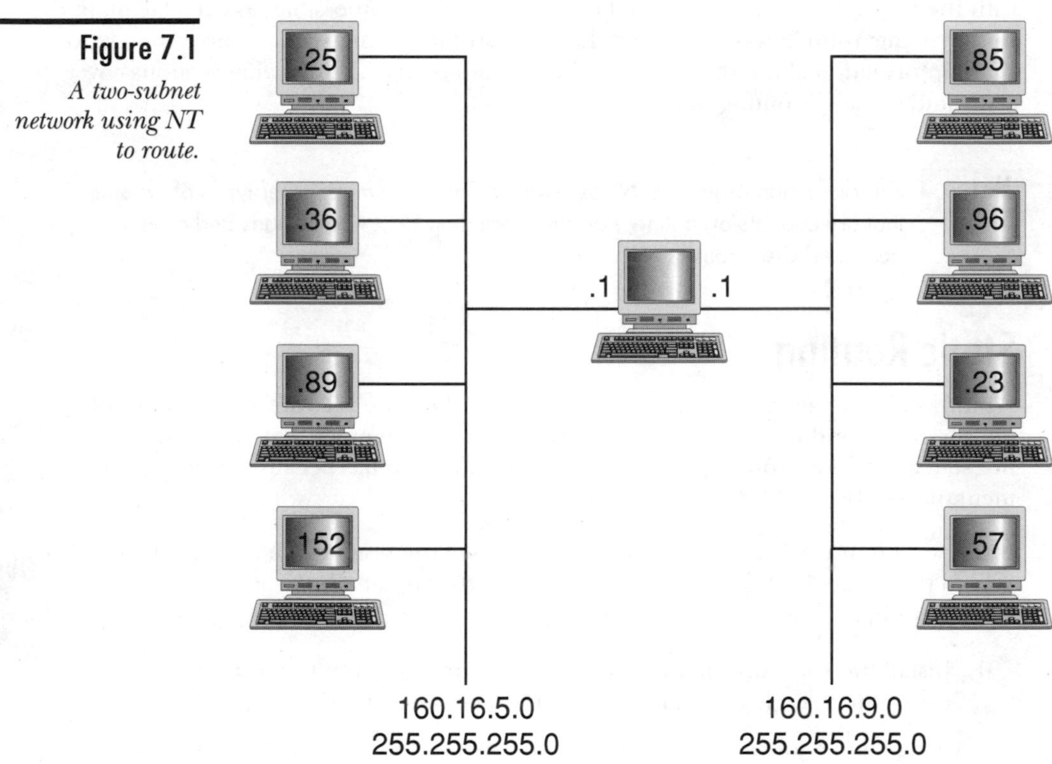

Figure 7.1 *A two-subnet network using NT to route.*

In figure 7.1, the NT router knows about networks 160.16.5.0 and 160.16.9.0. It will, therefore, automatically have a static route from one to the other. The entries would look like what you see in table 7.1.

TABLE 7.1
Routing Table for a Two-Subnet Router

Network ID	Subnet Mask	Gateway
160.16.5.0	255.255.255.0	160.16.5.1
160.16.9.0	255.255.255.0	160.16.9.1

In this case, all the hosts on the 5.0 subnet use 5.1 as the default gateway; the hosts on the 9.0 subnet use 9.1. When a host, say 5.89, attempts to send a packet to 9.23, the packet goes to the router, the router looks at the destination IP address and finds that a route exists (packets for 160.16.9.0 are sent to 160.16.9.1).

If all networks were this simple, this chapter would be complete. By adding even one more network, however, you make the scenario problematic.

In figure 7.2 the first router still knows about networks 160.16.5.0 and 160.16.9.0. The second router, which has been added, knows about 160.16.9.0 and 208.23.25.0. Neither router knows about the entire network—this means that the host 160.16.5.89 cannot communicate with 208.23.25.64. You can solve this problem in one of two different ways.

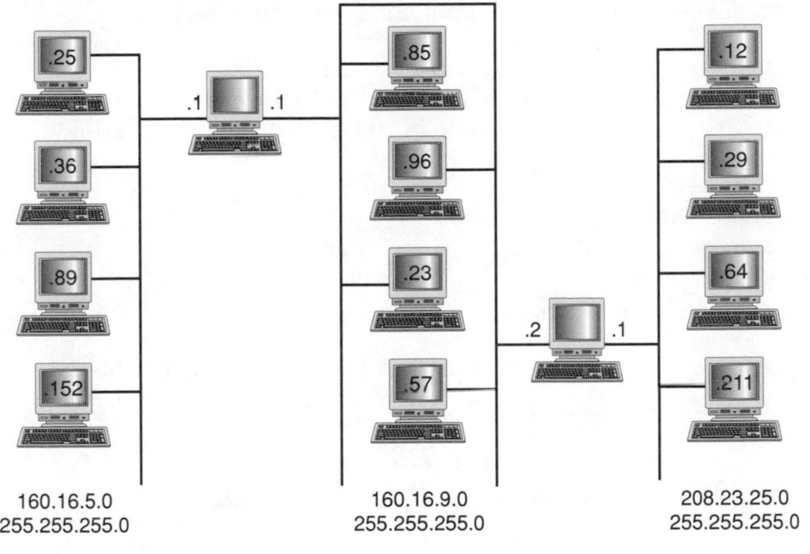

Figure 7.2

A routing with three networks.

If you remember the routing table you looked at in Chapters 5 and 6, there was an entry for network ID 0.0.0.0 with a subnet mask of 0.0.0.0—obviously this is going to catch every possible IP address. This entry is the default gateway, which is essentially used as a place to send packets for unknown networks. Routers also have a default gateway so that they can forward packets to more powerful routers. (The router put in your office by your ISP probably does this.)

If you look at the problem in figure 7.2, you see that if the first router doesn't know about the address you are trying to contact, the second router should. The opposite is also true, meaning that in this case, the two routers combined know about every network that exists. If you were to tell the first router that anything it doesn't know about should be sent to the second, and vice versa, the whole network should be able to communicate. The entries in the routing table on the first router would now look like what you see in table 7.2.

Table 7.2
Routing Table for a Three-Subnet Network Using Default Gateway

Network ID	Subnet Mask	Gateway
160.16.5.0	255.255.255.0	160.16.5.1
160.16.9.0	255.255.255.0	160.16.9.1
0.0.0.0	0.0.0.0	160.16.9.2

This solves the problem. After each router becomes the other's default gateway, communications can be established. If there are more than three subnets, figuring out the default gateways could be tricky. As well, any one router going down would be a break in the chain, and communications would no longer be possible.

Your other solution is to add a static route to each router to tell it how to get to the other networks with which it needs to communicate. To do this, you use the route command. On the first router, you add a route to 208.23.25.0 and on the second router to 160.16.5.0.

```
COMMAND AT THE FIRST ROUTER
ROUTE -P ADD 208.23.25.0 MASK 255.255.255.0 160.16.9.2
COMMAND AT THE SECOND ROUTER
ROUTE -P ADD 160.16.5.0 MASK 255.255.255.0 160.16.9.1
```

The routing table in the first router would now look like what you see in table 7.3.

Table 7.3
Routing Table for a Three-Subnet Network Using Static Entries

Network ID	Subnet Mask	Gateway
160.16.5.0	255.255.255.0	160.16.5.1
160.16.9.0	255.255.255.0	160.16.9.1
208.23.25.0	255.255.255.0	160.16.9.2

Dynamic Routing

As you can see, if there was no other method of maintaining routing information, system administrators would spend most of their time entering and updating routes to all the networks (and subnets) on a company's internal network and on the Internet. This is where the dynamic router comes into play. A dynamic router is a router that has some method of sharing its routing information with the other routers on the network. There are a couple of different methods for doing this such as OSPF (Open Shortest Path First) and RIP (Routing Internet Protocol), Windows NT supports only RIP routing, and this is covered in the following section.

RIP Routing

NT has supported dynamic routing since the release of service pack 2 for NT 3.51. The support for dynamic routing came in the form of the Routing Information Protocol (RIP).

RIP is a distance vector routing protocol. In other words, RIP is concerned not only with finding a method for moving the information from point A to point B, but also with the costs (not cash, but primarily the number of hops) involved in connecting with the remote host. This information is used to calculate the best route to the destination host. The cost information is kept as the routing metric.

Note You can see the entries in the routing table for your computer by using the command ROUTE PRINT.

The actual working of RIP is very simple. Every so often (30 seconds in the case of NT), the router broadcasts its routing table to the network. This might seem to be a problem: If a router in Singapore broadcasts its routes, might that not overload another router in New York City? The truth of the matter is that in reality it would. Therefore the maximum metric that a router can keep a route for is 15 (the router only keeps the address of the remote network and the next router to which it forwards the datagrams to reach that network).

Note Even keeping track of the next 16 hops could be a problem with some of the routers on the Internet. This is handled by increasing the amount of memory in the router. In some cases, the router even has a hard disk to back up the information so that the table does not need to be created from scratch again.

As a router broadcasts its routing table to the local networks to which it is connected, the other routers take that information and enter it into their own routing tables (adding 1 to the metric to represent the hop to the router that made the broadcast). What is added is the network for which there is a route, and addresses of the router that broadcasted the information. The router that receives the information now broadcasts everything it knows to the networks to which it is connected, and so on. In this way it is possible to propagate the routing information to many different routers on an intranet or indeed on the Internet.

Through this process, all the routers on the network will eventually know about all the networks that are 16 or less hops away. This process of information sharing is known as convergence.

Although this all sounds like a wonderful idea, the RIP protocol has some drawbacks. The main problems that you might encounter include the following:

- **Table size.** The basis of RIP is that every router knows what its neighbor knows, and what that neighbor knows, and so on until you reach a metric of 16 (meaning a depth of 16 networks). This means that the routing table on any one router can grow to include entries for a good number of different networks. This is currently addressed by adding RAM to the routers to increase the size of list that they are able to keep.
- **Broadcast traffic.** Like so many other protocols, RIP relies on broadcast traffic. Because there is a limit on the amount of traffic that a network can carry, the added broadcast traffic from RIP routing can cause network load problems.
- **Dead routers.** The entries in the routing table are based not only on the next router, but also on the one after that and the next one. Even though a route entry has a time-out value of three minutes, there can be a significant amount of time before the route clears entries from routers that are 5 or 6 or 16 networks away.

Installing RIP

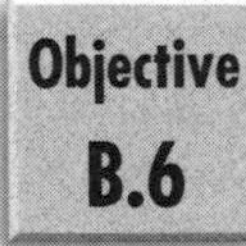

Before you install RIP, you should ensure that you have two network cards in and functioning, and that you have enabled IP forwarding. To install RIP, follow these steps:

1. Open the Network dialog box.
2. Select the Services tab, and then choose Add.
3. Select RIP for TCP/IP networks, and then click OK.
4. Close the Network dialog box.
5. Restart your system.

As a final note, you can install RIP on your NT systems that do not act as routers. This enables you to view the routes being broadcast by other RIP enabled routers only. This type of system does not broadcast because it does not have any networks to advertise, and is known as a Silent RIP Router. Its only purpose is to enable you to view the networks that your routers have found.

Summary

This chapter has covered the basics of routing and has looked at both dynamic and static routing. NT can act as either type of router, and you have seen both in this chapter. This chapter also discussed RIP routing and what that protocol adds to NT. This chapter completes an overview of the TCP protocol started in Chapter 1. The rest of this text looks at the services available in NT and what they can be used for.

Test Yourself

1. What is a router?
2. What is the difference between a router and a bridge?
3. Describe the two types of routing?
4. What conditions must be met to allow NT to act as a router?
5. Can Windows NT act as a dynamic router?
6. How often does RIP broadcast? What does it broadcast?
7. How many hops can a routing table have for using RIP?
8. Can you install RIP on a computer with only one network card?

The next few questions all relate to figure 7.3.

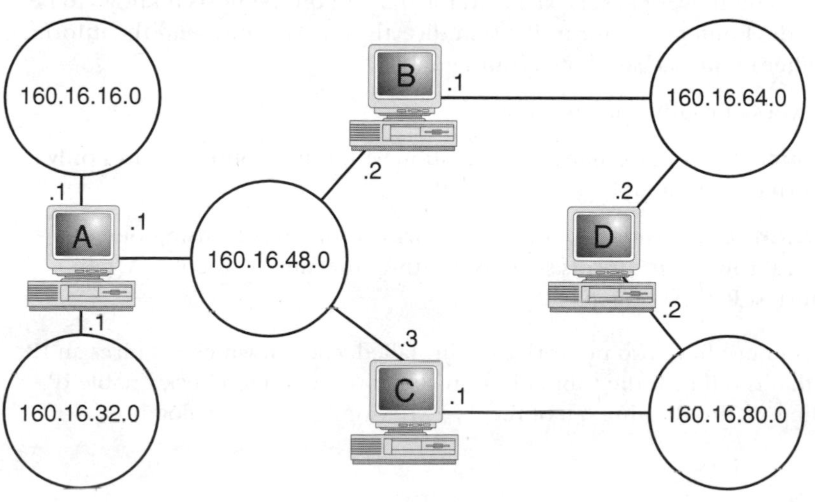

Figure 7.3

A sample network.

9. Given that the network shown uses static routing, what commands should be given at each router if the subnet mask is 255.255.240.0?
10. What are all the routes in router A?
11. What default gateway should be assigned for hosts on 160.16.80.0 who talk primarily to hosts on 160.16.64.0?
12. Can the default gateway setting be used on this network to handle all routing? If so, what could the default gateways be set to?
13. Ignoring networks 160.16.16.0 and 160.16.32.0 and router A, the network is set up with routing based on default gateways where B defaults to D which defaults to C which defaults back to B. For each of the three networks (160.16.48.0, 160.16.64.0, and 160.16.80.0), what would be reachable if the link between router D and 160.16.80.0 were to go down?
14. What metric would be reported in the routing table of router A for the network 160.16.80.0?
15. If RIP was installed on this network, how many routers would exist for network 160.16.64.0 to reach 160.16.16.0?

Test Yourself Answers

1. A router is a physical device that connects to two or more networks and moves packets between them.
2. A bridge is an active device that scans traffic on both networks to which it is connected, and moves packets back and forth based on the hosts it knows to be on each side. Routers wait for traffic sent directly to them, and send the information to other networks based on a routing table.
3. The two types of routing are as follows:
    - **Static.** Does not exchange information with other routers; it uses only its internal routing table
    - **Dynamic.** Learns about other networks automatically, using one of several routing protocols such as Routing Internet Protocol or Open Shortest Path First.
4. The system must have two network cards installed, each of which requires an IP address that is valid for the subnet it is on. Then you need to check Enable IP Forwarding on the Routing tab of the TCP/IP Configuration dialog box.

5. Windows NT 4 ships with RIP routing. To install RIP routing, go to the Services tab of the Network dialog box and choose Add. RIP for Internet Protocol is listed.
6. The RIP protocol broadcasts the routing table of a RIP-enabled router every 30 seconds.
7. The furthest network can be 16 networks away or 15 hops. The biggest metric, therefore, is 15.
8. A system that uses RIP with only one card does not broadcast any routes. Therefore it is called a Silent RIP Router.
9. The commands are as follows:

   Router A

   ROUTE -P ADD 160.16.64.0 MASK 255.255.240.0 160.16.48.2

   ROUTE -P ADD 160.16.80.0 MASK 255.255.240.0 160.16.48.3

   Router B

   ROUTE -P ADD 160.16.16.0 MASK 255.255.240.0 160.16.48.1

   ROUTE -P ADD 160.16.32.0 MASK 255.255.240.0 160.16.48.1

   ROUTE -P ADD 160.16.80.0 MASK 255.255.240.0 160.16.64.2

   ROUTE -P ADD 160.16.80.0 MASK 255.255.240.0 160.16.48.3

   Router C

   ROUTE -P ADD 160.16.16.0 MASK 255.255.240.0 160.16.48.1

   ROUTE -P ADD 160.16.32.0 MASK 255.255.240.0 160.16.48.1

   ROUTE -P ADD 160.16.64.0 MASK 255.255.240.0 160.16.80.2

   ROUTE -P ADD 160.16.64.0 MASK 255.255.240.0 160.16.48.2

   Router D

   ROUTE -P ADD 160.16.16.0 MASK 255.255.240.0 160.16.64.1

   ROUTE -P ADD 160.16.16.0 MASK 255.255.240.0 160.16.80.1

   ROUTE -P ADD 160.16.32.0 MASK 255.255.240.0 160.16.64.1

   ROUTE -P ADD 160.16.32.0 MASK 255.255.240.0 160.16.80.1

   ROUTE -P ADD 160.16.48.0 MASK 255.255.240.0 160.16.64.1

   ROUTE -P ADD 160.16.48.0 MASK 255.255.240.0 160.16.80.1

10. The routes are as follows:

160.16.16.0	160.16.16.1
160.16.32.0	160.16.32.0
160.16.48.0	160.16.48.1
160.16.64.0	160.16.48.2
160.16.80.0	160.16.48.3

11. The gateway should be 160.16.80.2.

12. It is possible to use a default gateway to route on this network. You can set the gateways one of two ways: They could go A to B to D to C to A, or A to C to D to B to A.

13. The following will be true:

    160.16.48.0 could see 160.16.64.0 through router B, and 160.16.80.0 through router C.

    160.16.64.0 could see 160.16.48.0 through router B, but couldn't see 160.16.80.0.

    160.16.80.0 could see 160.16.48.0 through router C, and could send only to 160.16.64.0 through router C and B. There would be no response, however, because the response must come through router D.

14. The metric would be 2, one hop for router A and one for router C.

15. Two routes would be available. Packets could be sent to router B with a metric of 2, or to router D with a metric of 3.

Part II

Microsoft TCP/IP Services

8 *Microsoft TCP/IP Services* 127

9 *Internet Information Server* 153

10 *TCP/IP Printing Services* 183

11 *Dynamic Host Configuration Protocol (DHCP)* .. 197

CHAPTER 8

Microsoft TCP/IP Services

The preceding chapters provided a basic introduction to the technologies and protocols in the TCP/IP protocol suite. This chapter puts TCP/IP to work with Microsoft networking products.

This chapter focuses on Windows NT Server, because NT Server serves as the backbone technology for any extensive Microsoft TCP/IP network. Although Windows 3.1, Windows for Workgroups 3.11, Windows 95, and Windows NT Workstation can function in a TCP/IP network, you need at least one Windows NT computer if you want to provide services such as automatic IP address assignment or a Windows naming service.

First this chapter explains how Microsoft TCP/IP and Windows NT work together, what the new features are, and the services available with Windows NT. After discussing the actual installation process, the chapter then moves on to cover reconfiguration of TCP/IP, including adding and removing TCP/IP protocols and network adapters.

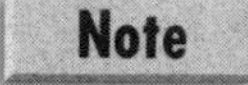

The rest of the chapters assume that you are reasonably comfortable with Windows, particularly with Windows NT. You are shown all the steps for accomplishing any given procedure, but not all the operations of Windows management.

Using Microsoft TCP/IP and Windows NT 4

This book concentrates on Microsoft TCP/IP and has as its main focus Windows NT 4 Server. If you are serious about supporting TCP/IP in a Windows NT environment, you should consider upgrading to version 4. Although version 3.5x provides excellent protocol support, many of Microsoft's current and future TCP/IP tools require version 4.

For that reason, this section focuses on how Microsoft TCP/IP works with NT 4. This section reviews the new features, and then discusses the many different services available in Windows NT.

New Features in Windows NT 4

One of the most prominent tools that requires TCP/IP to run is the Internet Information Server (IIS), which is included with and requires Windows NT Server 4. IIS is becoming a very popular Internet server, supporting World Wide Web, FTP, and Gopher server functionality. A steady flow of new products is emerging from Microsoft, most of which are dependent on NT 4, and on the IIS as their management tool. This includes products such as Proxy Server, Transaction Server, and NetShow.

It is entirely possible to construct Internet servers using NT version 3.5x. Many third-party web servers are available, and NT Server 3.5x includes Microsoft's own FTP server. If you are pursuing a Microsoft-centric TCP/IP strategy, however, you really have very little choice but to follow Microsoft's lead and upgrade to Windows NT 4.

Another service that uses TCP/IP is the DNS (Domain Name Server) services, which are now included with Windows NT 4. The Windows NT Resource Kit for Windows NT 3.5x included a DNS server that was compatible with BIND (Berkeley Internet Name Domain). It was configured using static files and had no graphic interface. The new NT 4 DNS server can be configured using static, BIND-compatible files, but it also provides a Windows interface that supports on-the-fly management and the capability to integrate with WINS to provide dynamic DNS. Under NT Server 4, you can manage DNS by using the familiar Windows interface, and you can avoid the need to restart the DNS server to make changes in the DNS name space.

Yet another prominent new feature supported by Windows NT 4 is the Multiprotocol Router, which supports RIP on Windows NT routers. If your network is at all complex, you will find that RIP can greatly simplify routing management as demonstrated in the preceding chapter.

Services Available in NT

Objective B.1

Many different services are available in Microsoft TPC/IP for Windows NT. The next few pages introduce these to you. All the services here are discussed in later chapters.

Internet Information Server

The Internet Information Server (IIS) is just that, a service that enables your computer to provide standard Internet service. The primary services that it handles for you include World Wide Web (WWW) publishing, File Transfer Protocol (FTP), and Gopher publishing. IIS also comes with an Internet Service Manager (ISM). The Internet Service Manager is used to handle all Internet services installed on an NT system. Chapter 9, "Internet Information Server," discusses the ISM in more detail.

IIS provides several advantages over other methods of publishing. IIS provides built-in IP address filtering (using ISAPI—Internet Server Application Programming Interface—filters), the capability to restrict access to NT domain users only (with encrypted passwords), the capability to add server extensions as a DLL (instead of a separate process that has to be launched every time someone hits the page), and many other features.

The ISM is designed so that all the other TCP/IP services that you add can be managed from a single tool. Other services out already include Proxy server, NetShow, and Transaction Server.

Line Printer Daemon

TCP/IP has long been the protocol for the Unix world. As such, many different protocols and services were developed in that environment. This obviously includes some method of network printing. Services that run on a Unix system are called a *daemon.* To enable NT to integrate with a Unix environment, it was necessary for Microsoft to include the capability to print between the two platforms. Included with NT, therefore, is the TCP/IP Printing Service. This enables connection to and use of the services of a Unix system's printer (using Print Manager) by creating an LPR (Line Printer Request) port that uses the daemon on the Unix system for printing.

As well, you can start the TCP/IP Print Server. That enables the reverse to happen and set the NT system up as a daemon that the Unix stations can use.

Dynamic Host Configuration Protocol (DHCP)

After having looked at IP addressing, it becomes clear that maintaining IP addresses in a changing network can pose a significant challenge. Doing so is one problem DHCP can help correct.

Very few hosts require fixed IP addresses. Routers and DNS servers are examples of hosts to which you should assign fixed IP addresses because those addresses frequently are entered into the configurations of hosts as the Default Gateway or the DNS server address. Most host computers, however, do not require a fixed IP address and can be assigned any valid host ID.

Microsoft's DHCP server removes the need to assign fixed IP addresses to the majority of hosts. Microsoft's DHCP enables administrators to specify groups of IP addresses called scopes that are leased to clients depending on which subnet they are on. When a host is configured to obtain its IP address from a DHCP server, it is automatically assigned an address from a DHCP scope appropriate for its current subnet.

DHCP also enables administrators to specify numerous parameters that tune the operation of IP, TCP, and other protocols that are given to the host when it receives its address. Because DHCP is centrally managed, administrators can manage many characteristics of the hosts for which they are responsible without having to physically visit the workstations.

DHCP Boot Relay Agent

DHCP, as previously described, requires that the client requiring an address be able to perform a broadcast. In this case, it is not a NetBIOS broadcast, but something referred to as a BOOTP (Boot Protocol) broadcast. Most routers can forward BOOTP broadcasts. In cases where they cannot, however, the Relay Agent handles the process by acting as a go-between, accepting the BOOTP broadcast and forwarding the request to a DHCP server somewhere on the network.

Windows Internet Name Service (WINS)

As you may recall, Chapter 2, "Introduction to Microsoft Networking," discussed the use of computer names by Microsoft networking. Obviously there must be some method by which NetBIOS names can be resolved to IP addresses. When you work with NetBIOS names (rather than host names, which are normally resolved by DNS), the standard naming service is WINS, which is a NetBIOS name service.

Without WINS, a computer seeking to enter the network attempts to register itself by broadcasting messages on the local network. If no other computer challenges the name, the computer establishes itself on the local network and announces itself. This mechanism works well on a single segment network, but fails on an internetwork because broadcast messages do not cross routers.

Note NetBIOS uses broadcast for many different reasons. This broadcast traffic can be significant, and can cause congestion at the routers. Routers can pass these broadcasts, but they are normally configured not to so that the routers do not become congested with broadcast traffic.

WINS provides a way to integrate NetBIOS naming conventions with TCP/IP. NetBIOS over TCP/IP provides a way to disseminate NetBIOS names throughout an internetwork (the NetBIOS name service—UDP port 137). Only one WINS server is required for most networks. This is possible due to the capability of a WINS server to exchange information with other WINS servers (WINS replication), which you will see in Chapter 11, "Dynamic Host Configuration Protocol (DHCP)."

WINS is the Microsoft implementation of a NetBIOS name server. Under NT 4, however, WINS can work in conjunction with DNS. This enables your company to put itself on the Internet and use WINS and DNS to manage its local domain name space.

DNS Server

As mentioned earlier, DNS being packaged with NT is new to Windows NT 4. The DNS server included with NT is very flexible and easy to use. As you probably already guessed, this service enables you to find other computers on the network when you are not using NetBIOS networking.

DNS is discussed in great detail in Chapter 15, "Microsoft DNS Server," where you will look at installing and configuring the DNS server, and at using Microsoft DNS to service both internal and external clients.

TCP/IP Support for RFCs

Microsoft has been including TCP/IP support in network products since LAN Manager. TCP/IP was Microsoft's choice as a routable protocol for use when the non-routable NetBEUI was not functional. TCP/IP is available for DOS, Windows 3.x, Windows for Workgroups 3.1x, Windows 95, and Windows NT clients. There is also a client that works with OS/2.

Table 8.1 summarizes the main RFCs that comprise Microsoft's implementation of TCP/IP supports.

TABLE 8.1
RFCs Supported by Microsoft NT TCP/IP

RFC	Title
768	User Datagram Protocol (UDP)
783	Trivial File Transfer Protocol revision 2 (TFTP) 791 Internet Protocol (IP)
792	Internet Control Message Protocol (ICMP)
793	Transmission Control Protocol (TCP)
816	Fault Isolation and Recovery
826	Ethernet Address Resolution Protocol (ARP)
854	Telnet Protocol (TELNET)
862	Echo Protocol (ECHO)
863	Discard Protocol (DISCARD)
864	Character Generator Protocol (CHARGEN)
865	Quote of the Day Protocol (QUOTE)
867	Daytime Protocol (DAYTIME)
894	Transmission of IP Datagrams over Ethernet
919	Broadcasting Internet Datagrams
922	Broadcasting Internet Datagrams in the Presence of Subnets
959	File Transfer Protocol (FTP)
1001, 1002	NetBIOS Service on a TCP/UDP Transport: Concepts, Methods, and Specifications
1034, 1035	Domain Name System
1042	Transmission of IP Datagrams over IEEE 802 Networks (SNAP)
1055	Transmission of IP Datagrams over Serial Lines: SLIP

RFC	Title
1112	Host Extensions for IP Multicasting
1122	Requirements for Internet Host Communication Layers
1123	Requirements for Internet Host Application and Support
1134	Point-to-Point Protocol (PPP)
1144	Compressing TCP/IP Headers for Low-Speed Serial Links
1157	Simple Network Management Protocol (SNMP)
1179	Line Printer Daemon Protocol
1188	Transmission of IP Datagrams over FDDI
1191	Path MDU Discovery
1201	Transmitting IP Traffic over ARCNET Networks
1231	IEEE 802.5 Token Ring MIB
1332	PPP Internet Protocol Control Protocol (IPCP)
1334	PPP Authentication Protocols
1518	An Architecture for IP Address Allocation with CIDR
1519	Classless Inter-Domain Routing CIDR: An Address Assignment and Aggregation Strategy
1533	DHCP Options and BOOTP Vendor Extensions
1534	Interoperability between DHCP and BOOTP
1541	Dynamic Host Configuration Protocol (DHCP)
1542	Clarifications and Extensions for the Bootstrap Protocol (BOOTP)
1547	Requirements for an Internet Standard Point-to-Point Protocol (PPP)
1548	Point-to-Point Protocol (PPP)

continues

Table 8.1, Continued
RFCs Supported by Microsoft NT TCP/IP

RFC	Title
1549	PPP in High-Level Data Link Control (HDLC) Framing
1552	PPP Internetwork Packet Exchange Control Protocol (IPXCP)
1553	Compressing IPX Headers over WAN Media
1570	PPP Link Control Protocol (LCP) Extensions
Draft	NetBIOS Frame Control Protocol (NBFCP)
Draft	PPP over ISDN
Draft	PPP over X.25
Draft	Compression Control Protocol

Installing Microsoft TCP/IP

If you have installed Windows NT, you already appreciate the general simplicity of the Windows NT installation process. That simplicity carries over to the procedures for installing TCP/IP. All procedures are performed from the graphic interface, using the Network utility in the Control Panel.

The Network Settings Dialog Box

TCP/IP installation and configuration is performed by using the Network utility, which is one of the tools in the Control Panel. Because this utility is so important in configuring TCP/IP on Windows NT, this section examines it in detail.

Figure 8.1 shows the Network dialog box, which displays the Identification tab when it is first started. Take the time to examine each of the tabs, following the order in which you use the tabs to configure networking.

The Identification Tab

The Identification tab contains two vital bits of information that must be established before the computer can successfully log on to a Windows NT domain (see fig. 8.1).

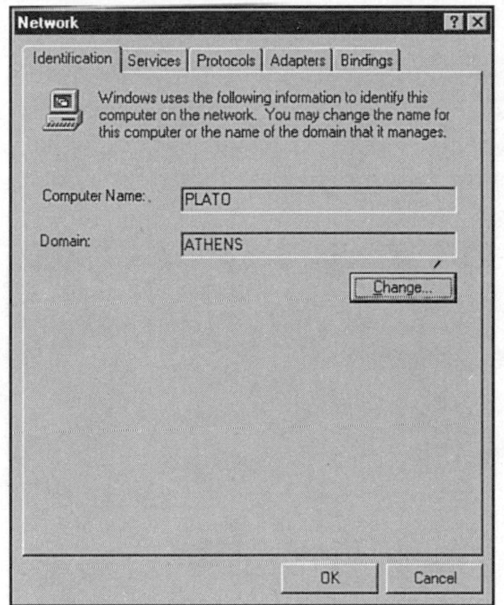

Figure 8.1

The Network dialog box Identification tab.

The Computer Name field sets the NetBIOS name of the computer. The NetBIOS name is the native (NetBIOS) name of the computer on the Windows NT network and is the name used to advertise the computer, enable the computer to receive messages, and enable the computer to log on to a network domain.

The Domain field indicates to which domain this computer attempts to connect when it logs on to the network.

The Change button opens the Identification Changes dialog box. In this box, you can change the computer name and domain, but be aware of the following considerations:

- A Windows NT computer cannot be managed by a domain unless a computer account has been created in the domain for that specific computer. If you change the computer name, the computer can no longer be managed by the domain until a new computer account has been created.
- Changing the name of a computer disrupts any sharing links that have been established with the computer. If you change a computer name, users can no longer use the established connections to shared directories or printers on that system.

The name you enter as the NetBIOS computer name serves as the initial TCP/IP host name. This name is restricted to 15 characters and should not contain spaces or other special characters.

The Services Tab

Network services extend the capability of Windows NT in a variety of ways. In later chapters, you use the Services tab to add and manage a variety of services, including DHCP, WINS, and IIS (see fig. 8.2). Services are managed much like protocols, and the procedures are covered in the appropriate chapters.

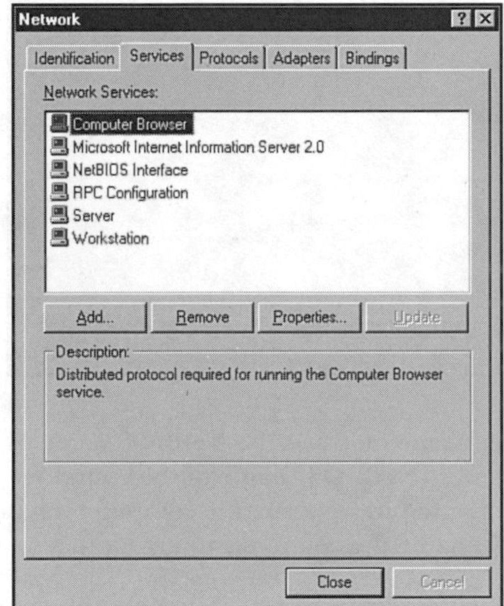

Figure 8.2
The Services tab.

The Protocols Tab

Recall from Chapter 2 that the Windows NT architecture permits multiple protocols to be installed on the same computer. The Protocols tab is used to install, remove, and configure network protocols, and is operated very much like the Adapters tab. Figure 8.3 shows the Protocols tab after TCP/IP has been installed.

Installing TCP/IP Protocols

To install TCP/IP protocol support, follow these steps:

1. Click Add in the Protocols tab to open the Select Network Protocol dialog box.
2. Select TCP/IP Protocol in the Network Protocol list and choose OK.
3. The next prompt asks, `Do you wish to use DHCP?` If this computer will obtain its IP address from DHCP, choose Yes. If this computer will be configured with a static IP address, choose No.
4. When prompted, supply the path where Setup can locate the driver files.

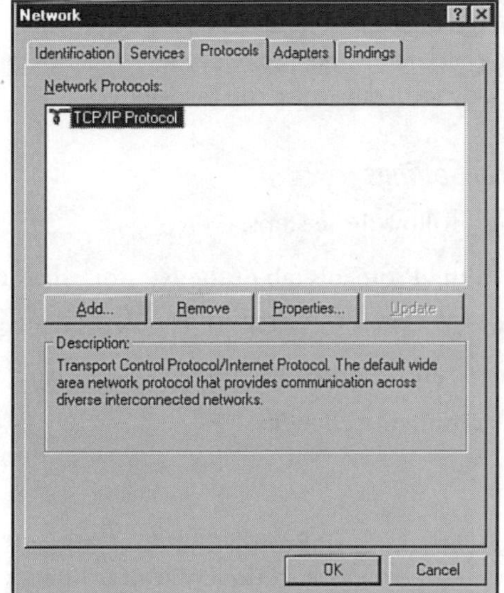

Figure 8.3

The Protocols tab.

5. Choose Close to exit the Network dialog box. After recalculating the bindings (LANA numbers), setup shows you a Microsoft TCP/IP Properties dialog box that will, at first, be blank.
6. If more than one adapter has been installed, select the adapter to be configured in the Adapter list.
7. If this computer will obtain its address configuration from DHCP, click the Obtain an IP address from a DHCP server radio button.
8. If this computer will be configured with static addresses, click the Specify an IP address radio button and complete the following fields:

   IP Address (Required)

   Subnet Mask (Required. Setup suggests the default subnet mask appropriate for the IP address you enter.)

   Default Gateway
9. Choose OK and restart the computer to activate the settings.

Note that because duplicate IP addresses can cause havoc on the network, Microsoft TCP/IP clients automatically detect duplicate addresses (however, only on the local subnet). If you attempt to add a client to the network using an IP address already present on the local network, you receive an error message and TCP/IP is disabled on the client you are adding. The client currently using the IP address also receives an error message, although it continues to function.

Note Microsoft TCP/IP detects a duplicate IP address on the local subnet only. This is because it uses ARP to check for the duplicate. Because ARP does not (by its design) need to cross routers, only local duplicates can be detected.

Reconfiguring TCP/IP Protocol Settings

To reconfigure TCP/IP settings, follow these steps:

1. Select TCP/IP Protocol in the Protocols tab of the Network dialog box.
2. Choose Properties to open the Microsoft TCP/IP Protocols dialog box.
3. Make any required changes, and choose OK.
4. Restart the computer to activate the changes.

Removing TCP/IP Protocols

To remove TCP/IP protocols, select TCP/IP Protocol in the Protocols tab of the Network dialog box and choose Remove. Restart the computer to activate the changes. Before removing a protocol, ensure that doing so will not disrupt any vital network communication.

The Adapters Tab

The Adapters tab is used to add, remove, and configure any network interface devices on the computer. Although only one adapter appears in figure 8.4, a computer can be equipped with multiple adapters if required. A computer that operates as an IP router, for example, must be configured with at least two adapters.

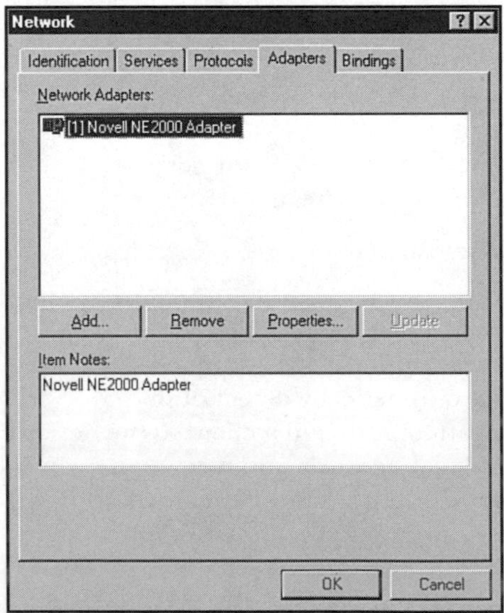

Figure 8.4

The Adapters tab.

Install and configure the network card hardware before you start NT. The vast majority of network cards now being made are configured using a software utility. Because NT prevents programs from directly manipulating hardware, the configuration utilities must usually be executed under DOS. Therefore, you cannot change the settings after NT is started.

Adding a Network Adapter

To add an adapter, follow these steps:

1. Click Add in the Adapters tab to open the Select Network Adapter dialog box.
2. Select an adapter in the Network Adapter list and choose OK.

Note Note that if your adapter is not listed and you have a driver disk provided by the vendor for the adapter, choose Have Disk and follow the prompts to install the drivers.

3. If an adapter is already installed that uses the same driver you are installing, a Setup Message box prompts you that `A network card of this type is already installed in the system. Do you want to continue?` Choose OK to confirm addition of the second adapter.
4. Next, specify the hardware settings for the adapter you are installing in the Network Card Setup dialog box, what is displayed.

Caution Be certain that you enter the correct settings in step 4. NT does not always detect these settings for you and cannot confirm that the settings you enter are correct. Nor can NT confirm that the settings you enter do not conflict with other devices in the computer.

5. If your computer is equipped with more than one expansion bus (ISA and PCI, for example), an Adapter Bus Location dialog box prompts you to specify the bus in which the adapter is installed. First select a bus type. Then, if the computer has more than one bus of that type, select a bus number.
6. When prompted, supply the path where Setup can locate the driver files. For an Intel x86 computer, the files are located in the \I386 directory on the installation medium (for example, D:\I386).
7. When prompted, restart the computer to activate the adapter drivers.

If you are installing PCI network adapters, the installation details probably differ from the generic procedure just described. For one thing, PCI adapters are typically configured automatically, and there is no need to specify hardware settings. Also, in many cases, the driver setup routines have unique features. The setup software for Intel EtherExpress Pro/100B adapters, for example, detects and displays all installed adapters, enabling you to select which hardware adapter you want to configure. Consult the product documentation for your hardware for the details.

Changing Properties for a Network Adapter

To change the settings for an installed adapter, follow these steps:

1. Select the adapter in the Network Adapters list.
2. Choose Properties to open a Network Card Setup dialog box in which you can alter the hardware settings for the adapter.
3. When prompted, restart the computer to complete the change.

Removing a Network Adapter

To remove an adapter, select the adapter and choose Remove. Restart the computer to complete the change. Before removing an adapter, be certain that you are not disrupting any vital network communication.

The Bindings Tab

A relationship that establishes communication between two network drivers is a *binding*. When TCP/IP is configured to communicate with a specific network adapter, a binding is established between TCP/IP and that adapter.

Bindings are reviewed and managed in the Bindings tab of the Network Settings dialog box. The bindings displayed are determined by the Show Bindings for field, which can have the following values: all services, all protocols, and all adapters.

The order in which protocols appear is important because it determines the order in which NT consults the available protocols to search for information on the network. Of particular significance is the sequence in which browsers are consulted.

Suppose that your network consists of a mix of configurations. Some computers are configured with NetBEUI, some with TCP/IP, and some with both—in which case separate browser environments will be maintained in the NetBEUI and TCP/IP environments. If you are working on a computer configured with both NetBEUI and TCP/IP, the bindings order determines whether your attempts to browse the network consult NetBEUI or TCP/IP browser first. If the protocol you use most frequently is raised to the top of the bindings list, your average connection time decreases. If you use both TCP/IP and NetBEUI, but access TCP/IP services infrequently, move NetBEUI to the top of the list. Improperly adjusted bindings orders can degrade performance. In extreme cases, if the bindings order is configured incorrectly, your browsing attempts may time out before an appropriate browser is located.

If TCP/IP is the primary protocol on your network, you probably want tasks such as name resolution to be performed via TCP/IP in preference to NetBEUI or NWLink. To raise the binding priority for TCP/IP, open the bindings under the Workstation service and select a protocol. Then click Move Up or Move Down to adjust the position of the protocol in the bindings order.

You can use the Bindings tab to disable bindings not currently required. If, for example, you have installed multiple network adapter cards but are not using one of them at present, you can reduce memory requirements by disabling the unused adapter. Just select the adapter entry and choose Disable. Use the Enable button to enable a disabled adapter.

Note If the adapter is no longer used, you should remove it. Disabling is normally used only to shut down a subnet for a period of time.

Testing the TCP/IP Configuration

Installing the TCP/IP connectivity utilities adds several useful troubleshooting tools to the computer. Two of the utilities, ping and ipconfig, are useful for checking out the network connections of TCP/IP hosts. They are illustrated in the context of the simple network shown in figure 8.5, consisting of two hosts with IP addresses 128.1.0.1 and 128.1.0.2.

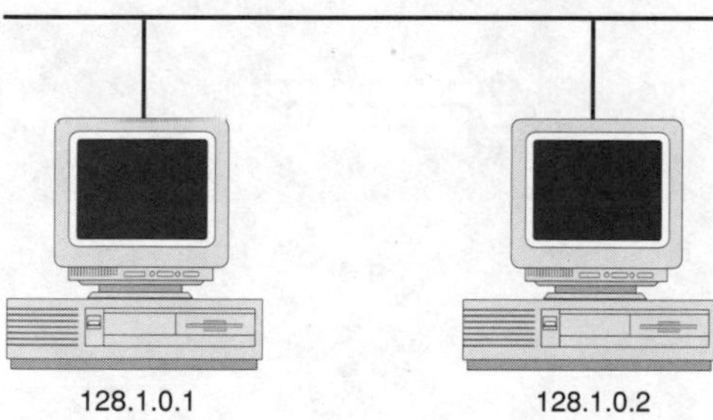

Figure 8.5
An example network.

Using Ping

Ping (Packet Internet Groper) is used to verify connections between hosts by sending ICMP echo packets to the specified IP address. Ping waits up to one second for each packet it sends and reports the numbers of packets sent and received. By default, ping sends four echo packets that consist of 32 bytes of data each.

Figure 8.6 shows the results of successfully and unsuccessfully pinging a host. When a host does not respond, ping displays the message `Request timed out`.

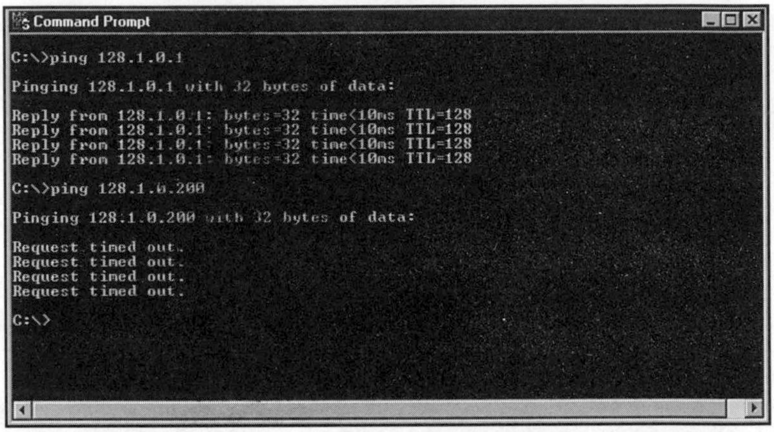

Figure 8.6

The results of a successful ping.

```
Command Prompt

C:\>ping 128.1.0.1

Pinging 128.1.0.1 with 32 bytes of data:

Reply from 128.1.0.1: bytes=32 time<10ms TTL=128
Reply from 128.1.0.1: bytes=32 time<10ms TTL=128
Reply from 128.1.0.1: bytes=32 time<10ms TTL=128
Reply from 128.1.0.1: bytes=32 time<10ms TTL=128

C:\>ping 128.1.0.200

Pinging 128.1.0.200 with 32 bytes of data:

Request timed out.
Request timed out.
Request timed out.
Request timed out.

C:\>
```

You might recall from Chapter 1, "Introduction to TCP/IP," that network ID 127 was reserved for diagnostic functions. You will encounter a special address, called the loopback address, which refers to any valid address that has a network ID of 127. The network adapter reflects back any packet sent to the loopback address without letting it enter the network. Pinging the loopback address tests the configuration of the local TCP/IP interface. Figure 8.7 demonstrates what it looks like.

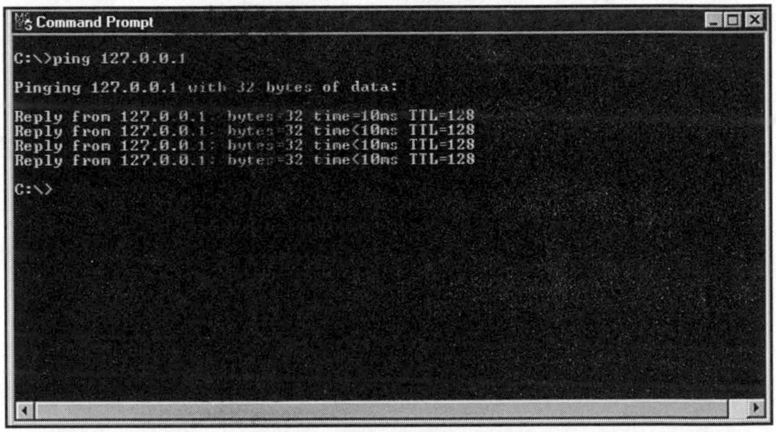

Figure 8.7

Pinging the loopback adapter.

```
Command Prompt

C:\>ping 127.0.0.1

Pinging 127.0.0.1 with 32 bytes of data:

Reply from 127.0.0.1: bytes=32 time=10ms TTL=128
Reply from 127.0.0.1: bytes=32 time<10ms TTL=128
Reply from 127.0.0.1: bytes=32 time<10ms TTL=128
Reply from 127.0.0.1: bytes=32 time<10ms TTL=128

C:\>
```

When you add a TCP/IP computer to the network, it is a good idea to use ping to test it. To use ping to test a TCP/IP computer added to the network, follow these steps:

1. Ping the loopback address 127.0.0.1. (This ensures that the protocol is in and functioning correctly.)
2. Ping the host's own IP address. (This tests the binding between the protocol and the adapter card.)

3. Ping other hosts on the network, particularly servers to which the host will connect. (This verifies that you are connected to the local network, and that your subnet mask is not too restrictive—using too many bits.)
4. Try to ping hosts on another network. (This checks to see that you can get to the router, and that your subnet mask is not too open—using too few bits.)

Note Ping can accept IP addresses or DNS host names. If you can ping a host by its IP address but not by its host name, a name resolution problem exists (see fig. 8.8).

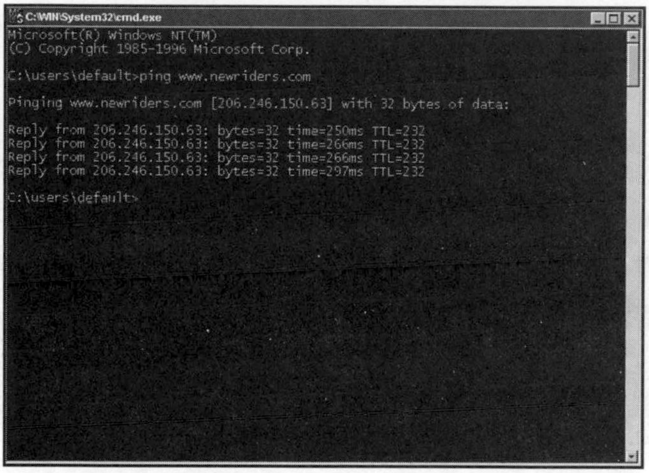

```
C:\WIN\System32\cmd.exe
Microsoft(R) Windows NT(TM)
(C) Copyright 1985-1996 Microsoft Corp.

C:\users\default>ping www.newriders.com

Pinging www.newriders.com [206.246.150.63] with 32 bytes of data:

Reply from 206.246.150.63: bytes=32 time=250ms TTL=232
Reply from 206.246.150.63: bytes=32 time=266ms TTL=232
Reply from 206.246.150.63: bytes=32 time=266ms TTL=232
Reply from 206.246.150.63: bytes=32 time=297ms TTL=232

C:\users\default>
```

Figure 8.8
Ping using a host name.

The following is a listing from ping without parameters, showing the command line arguments that you can use with ping.

```
Usage: ping [-t] [-a] [-n count] [-l size] [-f] [-i TTL] [-v TOS]
            [-r count] [-s count] [[-j host-list] ¦ [-k host-list]]
            [-w timeout] destination-list

Options:
    -t             Ping the specifed host until interrupted.
    -a             Resolve addresses to hostnames.
    -n count       Number of echo requests to send.
    -l size        Send buffer size.
    -f             Set Don't Fragment flag in packet.
    -i TTL         Time To Live.
    -v TOS         Type Of Service.
    -r count       Record route for count hops.
    -s count       Timestamp for count hops.
```

```
-j host-list   Loose source route along host-list.
-k host-list   Strict source route along host-list.
-w timeout     Timeout in milliseconds to wait for each reply.
```

Using Ipconfig

The ipconfig utility displays TCP/IP configuration settings for a host. Figure 8.9 shows the output from the command `ipconfig /all`, which displays complete details about a host's TCP/IP configuration. This utility is particularly useful when the host dynamically obtains address information from DHCP.

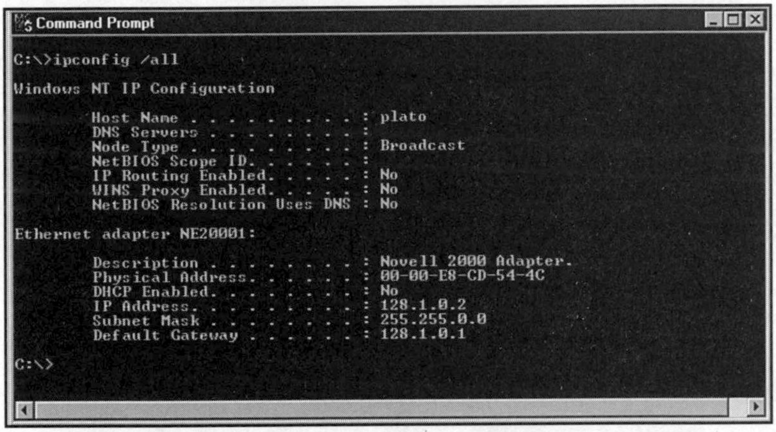

Figure 8.9

Output of ipconfig /all.

```
Command Prompt

C:\>ipconfig /all

Windows NT IP Configuration

        Host Name . . . . . . . . . : plato
        DNS Servers . . . . . . . . :
        Node Type . . . . . . . . . : Broadcast
        NetBIOS Scope ID. . . . . . :
        IP Routing Enabled. . . . . : No
        WINS Proxy Enabled. . . . . : No
        NetBIOS Resolution Uses DNS : No

Ethernet adapter NE20001:

        Description . . . . . . . . : Novell 2000 Adapter.
        Physical Address. . . . . . : 00-00-E8-CD-54-4C
        DHCP Enabled. . . . . . . . : No
        IP Address. . . . . . . . . : 128.1.0.2
        Subnet Mask . . . . . . . . : 255.255.0.0
        Default Gateway . . . . . . : 128.1.0.1

C:\>
```

The following code list shows the switches available for ipconfig:

```
Windows NT IP Configuration

usage: ipconfig [/? ¦ /all ¦ /release [adapter] ¦ /renew [adapter]]

       /?       Display this help message.
       /all     Display full configuration information.
       /release Release the IP address for the specified adapter.
       /renew   Renew the IP address for the specified adapter.

The default is to display only the IP address, subnet mask and default gateway
for each adapter bound to TCP/IP.

For Release and Renew, if no adapter name is specified, then the IP address
leases for all adapters bound to TCP/IP will be released or renewed.
```

In place of ipconfig, Windows 95 substitutes a GUI utility named WINIPCFG. (The command version in NT 4 enables you to use it in scripts and command files.) To run WINIPCFG, open the Start menu, choose the Run command, and enter WINIPCFG in the Open field of the Run dialog box.

Microsoft TCP/IP Properties Overview

You have already examined some of the TCP/IP protocol properties, such as IP addresses and subnet masks. You will examine others in later chapters. It is a good idea at this time, however, to briefly flip through the options.

To access the Microsoft TCP/IP Properties, go to the Network dialog box, select the Protocols tab, select TCP/IP Protocol in the Network Protocols list, and choose Properties.

IP Address Properties

The first tab you see is IP Address, shown here in figure 8.10. Figure 8.10 shows the entries on this tab. The following list describes the entries:

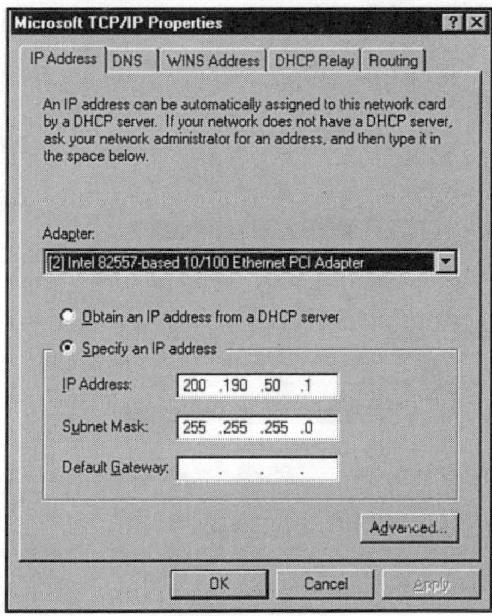

Figure 8.10

The IP Address tab.

- **Adapter.** On multihomed hosts, this field enables you to select the interface currently being configured.
- **Obtain an IP address from DHCP server.** This button enables this host as a DHCP client.

- **Specify an IP address.** This button enables manual addressing and activates the three address fields.
- **IP Address.** If manual addressing is active, you must specify the host IP address in this field.
- **Subnet Mask.** If manual addressing is active, you must specify the network subnet mask in this field. All hosts attached to the same IP network segment must be configured with the same subnet mask.
- **Default Gateway.** This field is optional and specifies a default router address. This field is required if you want to talk to hosts on other networks.

DNS Properties

As was introduced in Chapter 3, "The Application Layer," DNS is basically the process of resolving a host name to an actual IP address so that the system can figure out whether the address is local or remote and resolve it to a MAC address. This is one of the methods available for resolving the names. Primarily this resolves names for utilities that use the WinSock API—in other words, names other than NetBIOS names (see fig. 8.11).

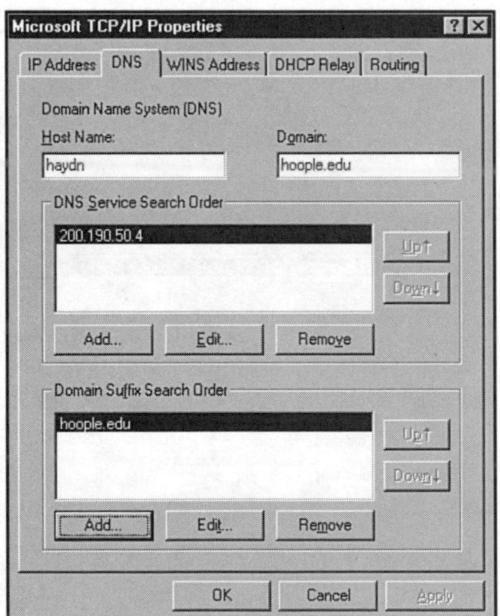

Figure 8.11

The DNS Properties page.

The following list briefly describes the fields and their purposes:

- **Host Name.** This is the name that other hosts see you as. By default, this is the same as the NetBIOS computer name and in most cases should be left as such.
- **Domain.** This is not an NT domain; rather this is the domain that your company has registered on the Internet (for example, Learnix.ca or Microsoft.com). This, together with your host name, makes up your Fully Qualified Domain Name (FQDN)—the name your computer has on the Internet.
- **DNS Service Search Order.** This is a list of computers that run a Domain Name Service. This resolves the FQDNs into TCP/IP addresses. Windows NT can act as a DNS server. (This is covered in a later chapter.)
- **Domain Suffix Search Order.** To speed up searches for computers from your own domain, you can enter the domain suffix (the Domain you entered already). The DNS first looks for the host in the domain files for the suffix you specify.

WINS Address Properties

The WINS Address tab is really a general purpose tab for configuring NetBIOS name resolution options (see fig. 8.12). Just as you need to have a way to resolve the FQDNs such as `www.newriders.com`, you also need some way for your computer to find the other NetBIOS host on your network. WINS (Windows Internet Naming Service) enables you to do this. WINS even handles the dynamic addressing that you receive from DHCP. (NetBIOS name resolution is done differently than host name resolution. These are covered in Chapter 12, "NetBIOS Name Resolution," and Chapter 15 respectively.)

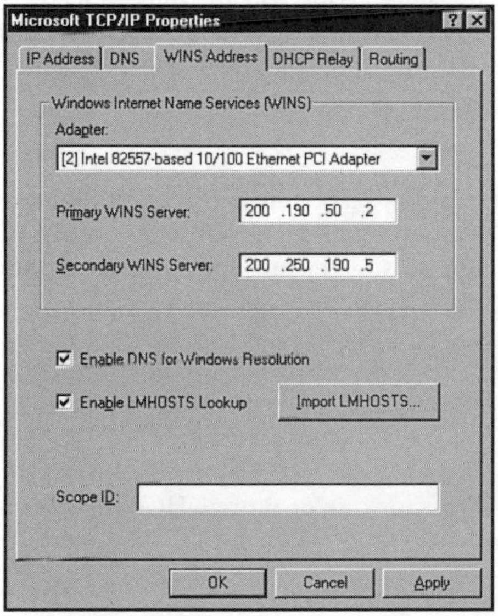

Figure 8.12

The WINS Address tab.

Here is a brief list and an explanation of the contents of the WINS Address tab:

- **Adapter.** Each of the adapters in the computer can use a different WINS server. This is not usual.
- **Primary WINS Server.** WINS servers are identified by their IP addresses. To enable a host as a WINS client, enter the IP address of a WINS server in this field.
- **Secondary WINS Server.** Any network that uses WINS should be configured with at least two WINS servers (to provide backup in case one fails). You can specify the IP address of a fallback WINS server in this field.
- **Enable DNS for Windows Resolution.** If you check this box, DNS becomes the host's preferred means of resolving host names. This is useful only in cases where the majority of hosts on the network are using Unix or some other non-Microsoft operating system.
- **Enable LMHOSTS Lookup.** If you check this box, the host consults LMHOSTS files if other resources cannot resolve a name. Chapter 12 examines the LMHOSTS file in greater detail.
- **Import LMHOSTS.** If you have already created an LMHOSTS file that is correct for this network, you can use this button to open a browse box where the file can be selected for import. The file is placed (by default) in C:\winnt\system32\drivers\etc.
- **Scope ID.** This field is usually left blank except in high-security environments. Scope IDs establish groups of computers that can communicate with each other, and only hosts that have the same scope ID can communicate using NetBIOS. By default, the Scope ID field is left blank, and all hosts with a blank scope ID can communicate. Note that this does not affect Winsock communications.

DHCP Relay Agent

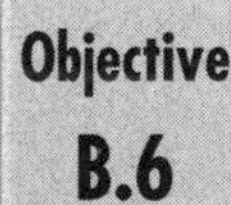

The DHCP Relay Agent enables an NT server sitting on one subnet to act as a go-between for DHCP clients on that subnet and a DHCP server on another subnet. This makes automatic IP configuration possible even if the client cannot normally broadcast to the DHCP server (see fig. 8.13).

The options for the Relay Agent include the following:

- **Maximum hops.** The greatest number of networks that can be crossed trying to get to the DHCP server.
- **DHCP Servers.** The address for one or more DHCP servers that can provide an address on this network.

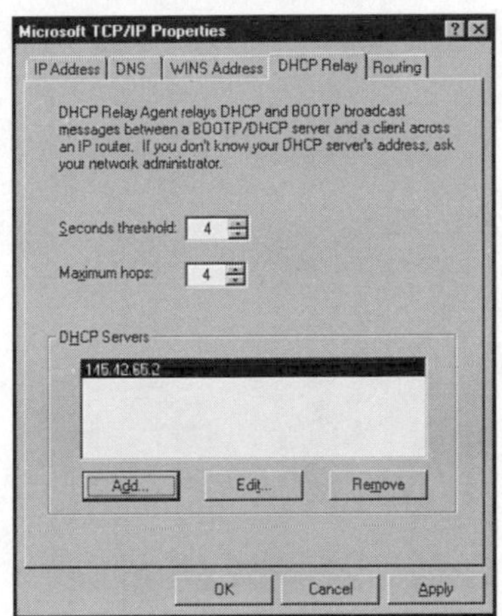

Figure 8.13

The DHCP Relay tab.

Routing

The Routing tab contains only one option: the Enable IP Forwarding check box (see fig. 8.14). Checking this box enables a multihomed NT computer to function as an IP router (as discussed in the preceding chapter, "Routing").

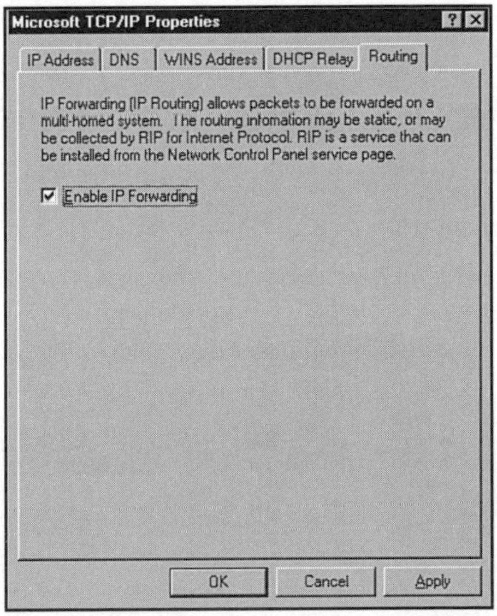

Objective B.6

Figure 8.14

The Routing tab of the TCP/IP Properties window.

Summary

This chapter has concentrated on two areas: the services available in NT, and installing TCP/IP in Windows NT. The information on the services provides an introduction to the rest of the text where all these services are covered. The installation section marks the transition from theoretical information to practical information.

Test Yourself

1. Name three new features of Windows NT 4.
2. What other TCP/IP-related services are included with NT?
3. Which of the services included in Windows NT are used primarily for network management? How?
4. What parameters are required for TCP/IP function on an intranet?
5. Where do you change the computer name? The host name? What is the difference?
6. How many adapters will an NT-based host support?
7. What two utilities can you use to test TCP/IP after it is installed?
8. What is the host 127.0.0.1?
9. What series of steps do you perform using `ping`? What does each test?
10. What command would you use to display the IP address for your DNS server?
11. Where do you enter the IP address of a WINS server?
12. If your network has three subnets connected by routers that are not BOOTP-enabled, what can you add to enable DHCP to function?

Test Yourself Answers

1. New features included for TCP/IP in Windows NT 4 include the following:

   Internet Information Server

   Routing Internet Protocol

   Domain Name System

   DHCP Boot Relay Agent

2. Line Printer Daemon, Dynamic Host Configuration Protocol, and Windows Internet Naming Service
3. The services used for network management are as follows:

   DHCP is used to assign addresses and host configuration dynamically

   DHCP Boot Relay enables DHCP on networks that don't route BOOTP requests.

   RIP is used to build and maintain routing tables in multihomed systems.

   WINS is used to dynamically register names. It also enables name resolution without the need for broadcast traffic.

   DNS provides host name resolution on the network, and when integrated with WINS provides a dynamic host naming system.
4. You need an IP address, a subnet mask, and a default gateway suitable for your subnet.
5. The computer name is changed on the Identification tab of the Network Settings dialog box. The host name is changed on the DNS tab in the TCP/IP Configuration dialog box. The host name is used for TCP/IP networking and can be combined with you Internet domain name to give your Fully Qualified Domain Name. The host name or FQDN can then be resolved to a TCP/IP address. The computer name is strictly for NetBIOS networking, and is used by a client to connect to your system.
6. NT enables you to add as many adapters as you wish. The only limit is the number of adapters you can add to your hardware.
7. The utilities generally used to test TCP/IP are ping and ipconfig.
8. The host ID 127.0.0.1 is the internal loopback adapter that can be used to test the protocol.
9. When you are using ping to test TCP/IP, follow these steps:

Ping 127.0.0.1	This tests that the protocol has been installed correctly, and is initialized.
Ping *your_IP_address*	This ensures that the TCP/IP is correctly bound to the network adapter.
Ping *local_hosts*	This checks that you are connected to the local network. It also verifies that your subnet mask is not too restrictive.
Ping *remote_hosts*	This checks that you can talk to the router, and that your subnet mask is not too open.
Ping *host_name*	Verifies that you have some form of host name resolution.

10. The command ipconfig /all displays all configuration information. This includes the IP address of your DNS server.
11. This is entered in the TCP/IP Configuration dialog box on the WINS Addressing tab.
12. The DHCP Relay Agent could be configured on two of the three subnets to forward DHCP broadcast to the DHCP server by directed transmission.

CHAPTER 9

Internet Information Server

With the recent industry attention to the Internet, much importance has been placed on the capability to publish documents to the web. Microsoft has positioned NT to become one of the leaders in publishing with the inclusion of the Internet Information Server (IIS) version 2.0 in the Windows NT 4 retail product. Currently, version 3.0 ships with Service Pack 2 for Windows NT 4.

As stated in the last chapter, IIS is the building block on which Microsoft will leverage many different Internet tools. Already many products are available that build up on the foundations of IIS. This is possible mainly because of ISAPI (Internet Server Application Programming Interface), which enables you to plug extensions easily into IIS and share resources with the IIS process.

This chapter examines the Internet Information Server 2.0 because this is the version that currently ships with NT. It is a robust and very powerful server that will only continue to gain acceptance in the marketplace because of its extensibility and flexibility. As it ships with Windows NT, IIS 2.0 includes the following:

- World Wide Web server
- File Transfer Process (FTP) server
- Gopher server

This text covers only the basics of these protocols (the subject is broad enough for its own book). Indeed, Microsoft has a separate course on this topic, and separate exam.

You can use these services whether you are working with the Internet or just wanting to set up an internal site on your own intranet. Intranet sites tend to be more informal and to contain information for internal use only. A site on the Internet is quite literally the face you wear for the entire world. Obviously, you must take care to ensure that items intended for an internal site do not end up on the external site.

This discussion looks at using IIS for internal purposes. If you want to publish to the Internet, however, you should consider the following steps:

1. Establish a secure Internet connection, preferably with a solid firewall.
2. Obtain a domain name and become registered on a DNS name server.

You will probably work with an Internet Service Provider (ISP organizations such as Sprint, MCI, and iStar) to accomplish both tasks. Most ISPs maintain your Internet domain name space for you, freeing you of the responsibility of running a DNS name server. (For more information, see Chapter 15, "Microsoft DNS Server.")

Installing IIS

Installation can be broken down into the following three steps:

- Preparing for installation
- Installation
- Testing IIS

Preparing for Installation

Very little preparation is required. To get ready, perform the following steps:

- Configure TCP/IP in the computers that will be participating. If you use a firewall (and you should), IIS should be outside the firewall. (A firewall is essentially a router. The systems inside the firewall use a set of address completely separate from the outside addresses that are used. Firewalls can also block different ports incoming or outgoing or different sites.)
- Identify a Windows NT Server computer that will host IIS. If you expect IIS to be heavily used, this server should be dedicated to the task of providing IIS services. (Because of the architecture, an SMP—Symmetric Multiprocessing PC—can increase performance.)

- Remove any existing third-party WWW, FTP, or Gopher servers that you may be running on the computer that will be the IIS, otherwise IIS installation may fail because another service is already installed on the port.
- Format the volumes on the server with NTFS or convert existing FAT volumes to NTFS. (Although this is optional, it ensures the highest possible level of security.)
- Enable auditing if you feel you need to closely monitor the server for security breaches. (Again this is optional. If the server will be heavily used, this can slow down performance.)
- Set up a name resolution method. (You have already read about both DNS and WINS—both of which are discussed forthwith.

The Installation Process

The installation process is very simple. If you performed a standard install of Windows NT, it is already there. If not, NT has a shortcut on the desktop to install IIS. In fact, you can install IIS in the following three ways:

- Select the Install Microsoft Internet Information Server box when you are installing Windows NT Server 4.
- Select the Install Internet Information Server icon on the Windows NT Server 4 desktop.
- Install the Internet Information Server as a service by using the Network utility in the Control Panel.

During the installation, you receive prompts for information. For most of the information, you just accept the given default. The following list identifies some of the things asked.

- **License Agreement.** You must read and accept the license agreement.
- **Products to Install.** You are presented with a screen asking you which components to install (see fig. 9.1). Select those you will be using.
- **Directory to Install.** Figure 9.1 shows a default directory. You can change the directory at this point, if you wish (if the directory suggested is on the same drive as NT, you should change it for increased security).
- **Home Directories.** Where the home directories will be for the services that you are installing (see fig. 9.2). (Again this should not be the same drive that NT is on.)
- **ODBC Drivers.** Next, you are asked to select the ODBC drivers to be installed. At this time, the only option is to install drivers for Microsoft SQL Server. You can, however, add any ODBC drivers. ODBC (Open Database Connectivity)

enables you to create pages that can query a database and present results on your web page.

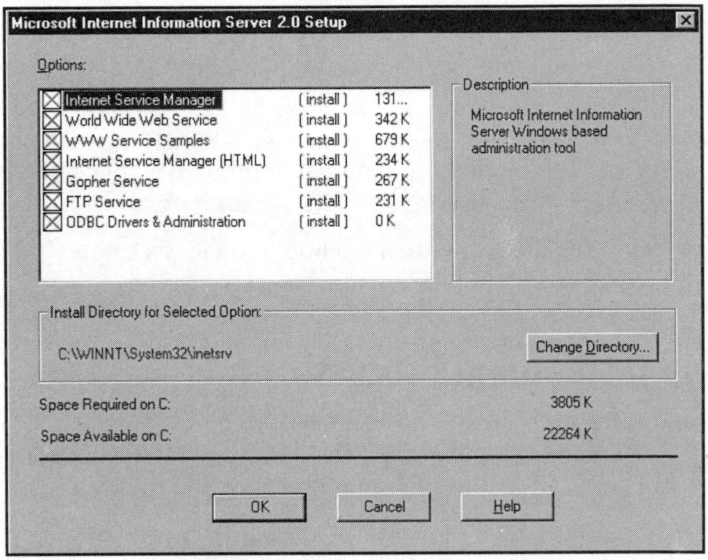

Figure 9.1

The installation options for IIS 2.0.

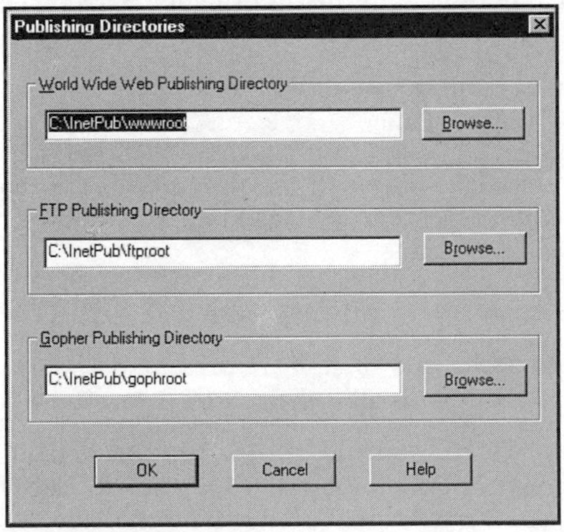

Figure 9.2

Choosing the Home Directories for your services.

The installation process makes some changes to the NT system on which you are installing IIS. These changes include a new common program group added to the Start menu. This program group contains the following four options:

- Internet Information Server Setup

- Internet Service Manager
- Key Manager
- Product Documentation

You will also find that a new user account has been created: the IUSR_*computername* account. This is the account that anonymous users of your site use to log on. (By default, every time you connect to a site—WWW, FTP, and so on—you are identified to the system. Normally you are identified as anonymous.) The account has the right to "log on locally" because IIS on the local machine performs the logon. By default, this account has no password—you should change this immediately through the User Manager for Domains. You must also change it in the Internet Service Manager (which you will see shortly).

Using the Product Documentation

All the online documentation is contained in Hypertext Markup Language (HTML) files that can be read with a WWW browser. The Microsoft Internet Explorer is included with Windows NT Server 4 and appears as an icon on the desktop. To use the Internet Explorer to view the documentation, select the Product Documentation option in the Microsoft Internet Server program group. (If you have configured a different browser, it will be started rather than Internet Explorer.) Figure 9.3 shows the main documentation table of contents in the Microsoft Internet Information Server Installation and Administration Guide. Moving around is just a matter of clicking on the highlighted text—just like a normal web site.

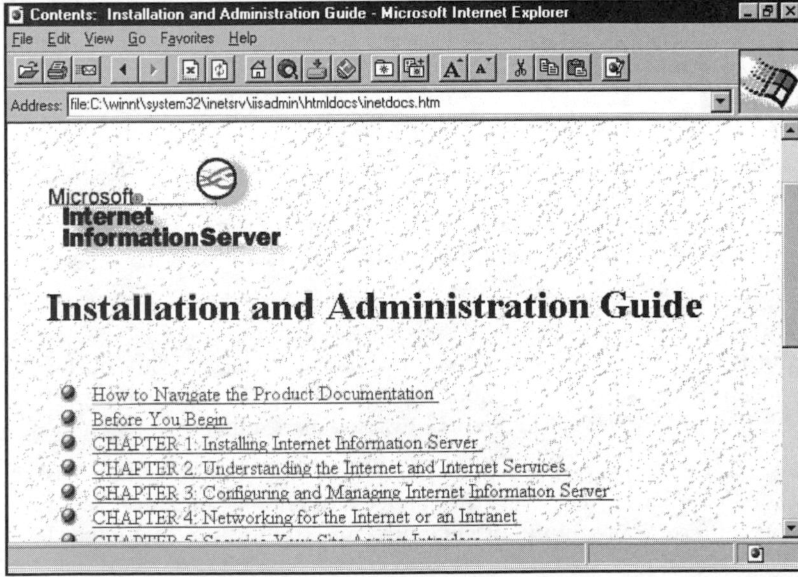

Figure 9.3
Online documentation for IIS 2.0.

Testing the Installation

To test the server, start Internet Explorer on a network computer on the same subnet, choose File, Open, and then enter the computer name for the computer running IIS. Figure 9.4 shows the sample page that appears. In this example, working on the local Microsoft network, the computer name is its NetBIOS name. (This works because the methods of host name resolution and NetBIOS name resolution back each other up.)

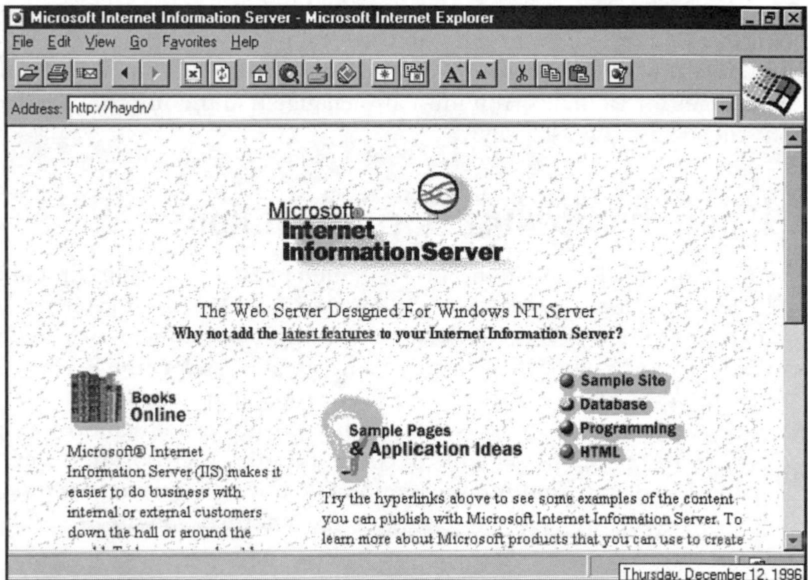

Figure 9.4

The sample page that comes with IIS.

Managing IIS

All IIS services are managed from the Internet Service Manager (see fig. 9.5). The window lists the services installed on a computer and indicates the state of the service. As you can see, you can manage more than one IIS server from the same Internet Server Manager. In this case, two Internet Information Servers are shown.

The services you are looking at can be in any of the three following states:

- **Running.** A Running service is started and operating normally. You can start a service by selecting the service and choosing the Start Service command in the Properties menu or by clicking the Start button on the toolbar.
- **Paused.** A Paused service continues to operate, but does not permit new users to connect. To pause a service, select the service and choose the Pause Service command in the Properties menu, or click the Pause button on the toolbar.

- **Stopped.** A Stopped service is no longer operating. You stop services by using the Stop Service command in the Properties menu or by clicking on the Stop button on the toolbar.

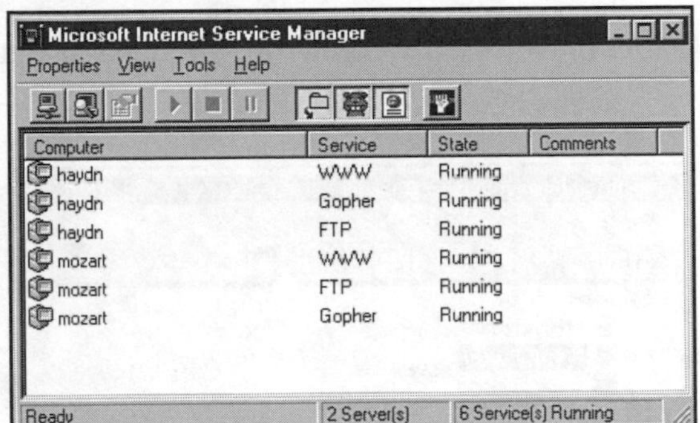

Figure 9.5

The Internet Service Manager.

Note You can also start and stop IIS services by using the Services utility in the Control Panel.

Figure 9.5 also shows a toolbar. The options (left to right) are as follows:

- **Connect to a Server.** Connects the Internet Service Manager to a specific IIS. Once connected, you can observe the services running on that server (assuming you have permissions).
- **Find Internet Servers.** Searches the network to identify all running servers. This search can take considerable time. Identified servers display in the Internet Service Manager.
- **Properties.** Opens the Properties dialog box for a service. (You can also double-click the service from the list.)
- **Start Service.** Starts the selected service.
- **Stop Service.** Stops the selected service.
- **Pause/Continue Service.** Pauses the selected service.
- **View FTP Servers.** When this button is depressed, FTP servers are listed.
- **View Gopher Servers.** When this button is on, Gopher servers are listed.
- **View WWW Servers.** When this button is activated, WWW servers are listed.

Selecting IIS Views

Besides the Report View shown previously, you can also select from two other formats for display. To select the Servers View (shown in figure 9.6), choose Servers View in the View menu. You can open the servers as shown to view the status for each service. A traffic signal specifies whether the service is running (green), paused (yellow), or stopped (red).

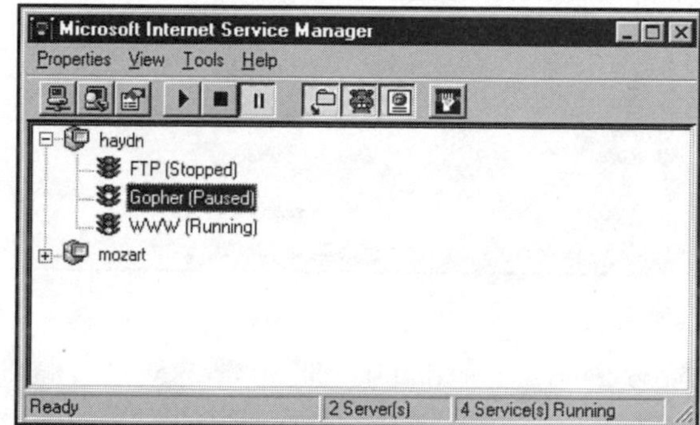

Figure 9.6
The Server View in the Internet Service Manager.

The Services View lists all servers under the services they offer. Open this view by choosing Services View in the View menu (see fig. 9.7).

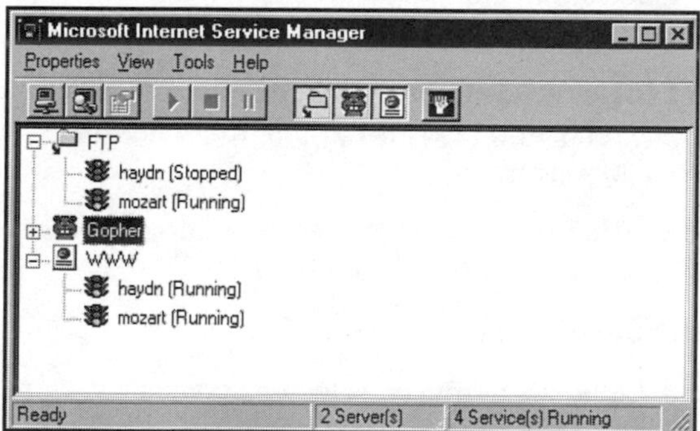

Figure 9.7
The Services View of the ISM.

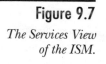

Setting Up the IUSR_*computername* Account

All users who access your WWW server inherit the permissions given to the IUSR_*computername* account. These permissions are typically limited to Read permissions in the WWW, FTP, and Gopher directory trees. (This account will, however, also have permissions granted to the group Everyone. You should take care when using this group to set permissions.) It is recommended that you change the password for this account. You can change it in the User Manager for Domains and in the properties for the various services. You should also note that you can use a different account for each service.

Configuring the HTTP Server (WWW Service)

Setting up a WWW server is not especially difficult. A WWW server provides HTTP services that enable your users to connect to your web pages. Most of the work involves creating the HTML pages that will be displayed on the server. Windows NT 4 includes an excellent tool for this called FrontPage.

This section describes how to configure the WWW Publishing Service that comes with NT. The configuration is done in the Internet Service Manager.

Managing WWW Server Properties

To configure a WWW server, select the server and choose Service Properties in the Properties menu, or click the Properties button on the toolbar. The Properties dialog box for a WWW server appears (see fig. 9.8). Four tabs are used to configure the WWW server.

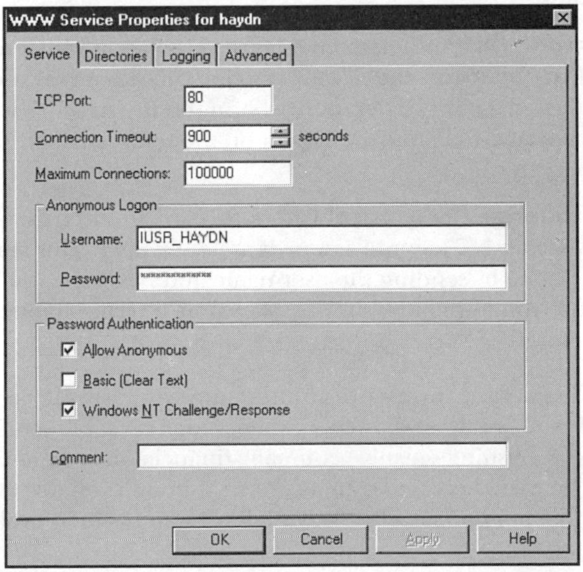

Figure 9.8

The Service tab of the WWW Service Properties.

You must make several different choices when configuring the WWW server. The Service tab, the Directories tab, the Logging tab, and the Advanced tab all present you with different options. The following sections highlight each tab.

The Service Tab

The Service tab includes basic service settings. The fields in this tab are as follows:

- **Connection Timeout.** The value in this field determines how long the server permits a connection to remain idle (no traffic) before the connection is broken at the server. This time out ensures that improperly closed connections are eventually released.
- **Maximum Connections.** This value determines the number of users who can connect at a given time. Decrease this number if users begin to experience performance problems.
- **Anonymous Logon Username.** The normal mode for using a WWW server is to permit users to log on anonymously—that is, without entering a user name and password. Users who connect anonymously gain the access permitted to the specified user name . The default user name is IUSR_*computername*. The password you specify is for use only within Windows NT. To permit anonymous logons, you must check the Allow Anonymous check box.
- **Allow Anonymous.** When this box is checked, users can connect to the server without entering a user name or password. If you do not permit anonymous logons, users must log on using an account configured under User Manager for Domains.
- **Basic (Clear Text).** Check this box to enable users to log on with a user name and a password. Clear text logon enables users to log on with any WWW browser, but provides no security from users who snoop the network with protocol analyzers because the password is sent on the network in clear text (that is, it is not encrypted).
- **Windows NT Challenge/Response.** Check this box to force users to log on with a secure Windows NT logon. Passwords are encrypted. This feature is supported automatically (by sending the user name and password you logged on to your computer with to the web site) by Microsoft Internet Explorer version 2.0 and later.

The majority of web servers permit any user to connect anonymously. IIS can also function in that mode. There are times, however, when a high level of security is desired. Suppose you are publishing sensitive company financial data on your internal web server so that it can be easily accessed by managers. Although you want the information available with a minimum of hassle, you don't want it freely available to anyone with a web browser.

Windows NT Challenge/Response provides a means for offering secure access to your web server. Logon is controlled by standard Windows NT access controls, including user accounts and passwords.

At present, users are required to use the Microsoft Internet Explorer version 2.0 or later to connect to a web server using the challenge/response protocol. Be certain to disable basic (clear text) authentication if you wish to force users to log on using the challenge/response protocol.

The Directories Tab

WWW browsers are essentially a way of viewing HTML document files stored in content directories on the WWW server. Although you can place all your HTML files in a single content directory, it is often advantageous to configure multiple content directories (see fig. 9.9).

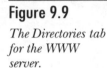

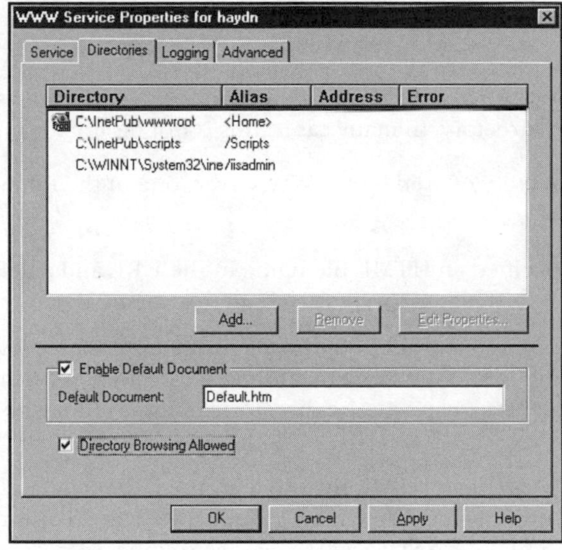

Figure 9.9

The Directories tab for the WWW server.

Note

If your files are stored in multiple directories or on multiple servers, you need to configure virtual directories to make these available to users. Virtual directories are discussed later in this chapter.

It is also possible to configure virtual servers that enable a single WWW server to have multiple domain web sites (FQDN-type domains). A single WWW server, for example, could support virtual WWW sites for several companies. Virtual servers must work with DNS, placing the topic beyond the scope of this chapter. Later in this chapter, you learn how to configure a virtual server on IIS.

As noted, you will see how to configure directories and servers shortly. The remaining options on the Directories Tab are as follows:

- **Enable Default Document.** Default documents automatically display only if this box is checked.
- **Default Document.** If you want to change the file name for your default document files, edit this field.

Note Users can request a specific file by specifying the file name in an URL. In many cases, however, the user just specifies a directory to be accessed. You can create a default document that displays when a user accesses a WWW directory without specifying a file name. These first two options are used to set that file sent by default.

- **Directory Browsing Allowed.** If this is enabled, users can see a list of all the files in the home directory. In many cases, this is not desirable.

When a user accesses a directory offered by a WWW server, one of the following three things can happen:

- If the user has not specified an HTML file name in the URL and a default document file resides in the directory, the default document is sent to the user.
- If the user has not specified an HTML file name in the URL and a default document is not found, the WWW server can send a directory browsing document that enables the user to browse the directories supported by the WWW server (see fig. 9.10).
- If the user has not specified an HTML file name in the URL, a default document is not found, and directory browsing is not enabled, an error is returned to the user informing the user `You do not have permission to open this item.` You receive an "Access Forbidden" message.

The Logging Tab

The Logging tab enables you to manage logging for the WWW server (see fig. 9.11). Particularly if your server is connected to the Internet, you will want to enable logging to assist you to maintain tight security. The options in this tab are as follows:

- **Enable Logging.** This box is checked by default.
- **Automatically open new log.** When this box is checked, new log files open when the specified conditions are met. The option you choose depend on the rate at which your log files grow.

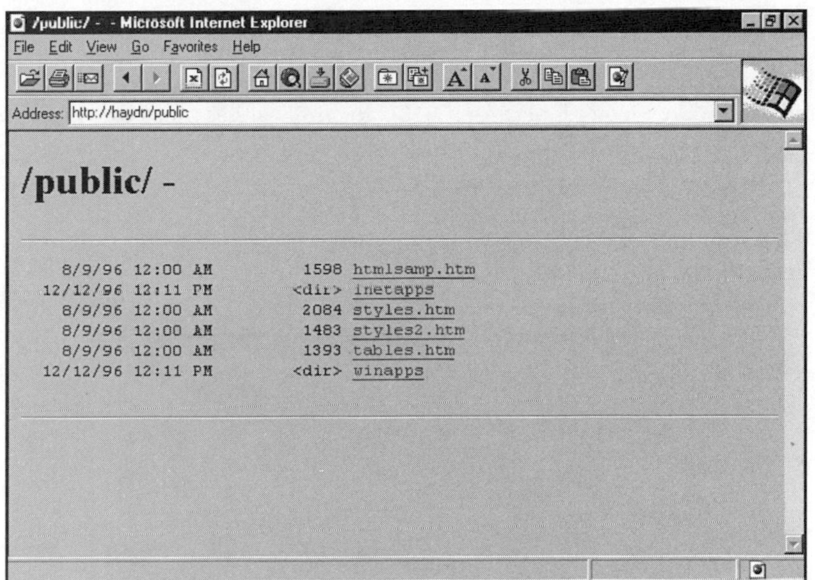

Figure 9.10

An HTML browsing document.

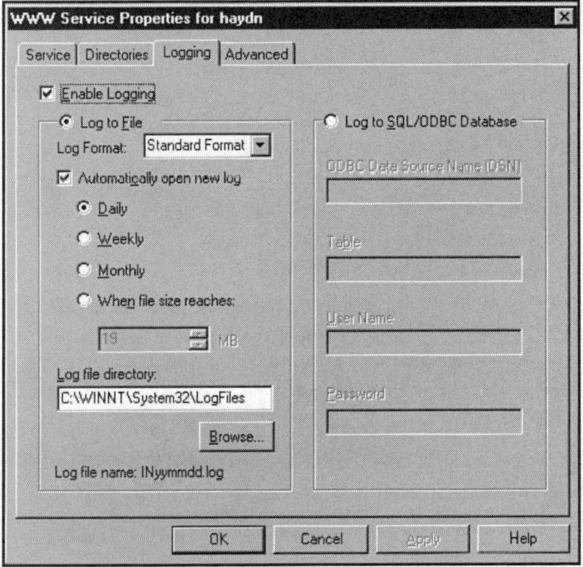

Figure 9.11

The Logging tab for the WWW service.

- **Log file directory.** In this field, specify the directory in which log files will be stored. The log file is named by date. The file name format depends on how often a new file is opened.

- **Log to SQL/ODBC Database.** If ODBC support is installed, you can direct logs to an SQL database. If this option is enabled, complete the remaining fields as required. Note that in cases where you must get every ounce of performance, you should use the text logging because ODBC logging carries more overhead.

The Advanced Tab

The Advanced tab, shown in figure 9.12, enables you to set some access and network traffic limits. The settings are as follows:

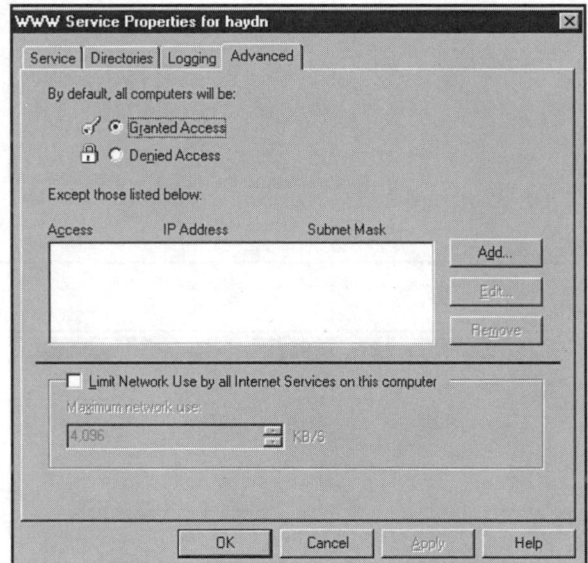

Figure 9.12
The Advanced tab for the WWW service.

- **Granted Access.** If this button is selected, computers with all IP addresses are permitted access. Exceptions can be specified in the Access list.
- **Denied Access.** If this button is selected, computers with all IP addresses are denied access. Exceptions can be specified in the Access list.
- **Access.** Computers listed in this box are the exceptions to the Granted Access or Denied Access (set in the preceding items). You can add addresses to this list by choosing Add.
- **Limit Network Use by all Internet Services on this computer.** An Internet server can get very busy and can affect the performance of an entire network. If you want to limit the network traffic generated by this server, check this box and adjust the value of the Maximum Network Use field.

Caution The only limitations supported by the Advanced tab are based on the IP address of the sender. Unfortunately, a technique called *IP address spoofing* enables knowledgeable users to fake an IP address that can slip around address-based security. Do not ever trust a security system that depends on IP addresses. Be certain to get a good firewall if you are connecting critical systems to the Internet. If you require a high level of security, the best approach is to require challenge/response logons when connecting to the server.

Home Directories

Each IIS service has a home directory, which is the root directory for that service. This home directory is the directory retrieved by the basic URL for the service. You can change the home directory for a service by doing the following:

1. Open the Property dialog box for the service (double-click the service in the Internet Service Manager).
2. Select the Directories tab.
3. In the Directory list, select the directory that lists the alias <Home>.
4. Choose Edit Properties to open the Directory Properties dialog box (see fig. 9.13).

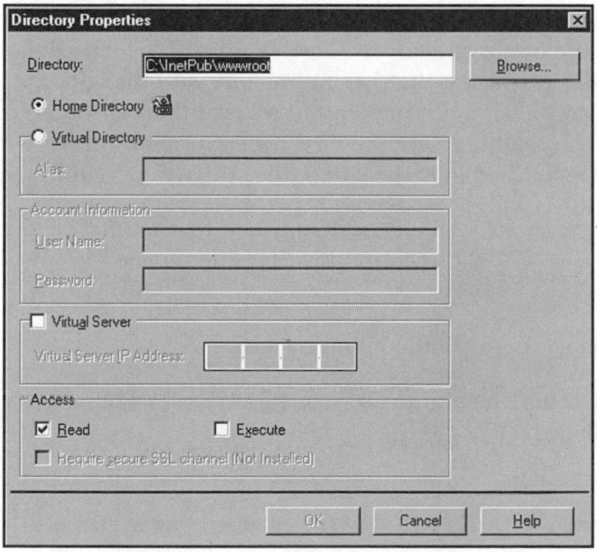

Figure 9.13
Editing directory properties.

5. In the Directory box, specify the home directory for this service. Click the Browse button to browse for the directory if desired.
6. In the Access box, specify whether users should have Read and/or Execute access to the directory.
7. Choose OK to save the changes.

Changing the directory in this procedure does not create the new directory or delete the old directory structure. You must create or delete the directories and their contents separately.

Setting Up Virtual Directories

To this point, it has been assumed that the web server will be publishing from a single directory, the home directory. That is pretty restrictive, however, and IIS makes it possible to publish from multiple directories, which can be located on local drives or on drives accessed through the network. These directories that supplement the home directory are called virtual directories.

You don't want to just throw multiple directories at the users—otherwise the URLs could get quite confusing. If you want users to use your site, you can't really expect users to enter an URL such as `http://www.hoople.edu/d:\basketweaving`. Too much typing and too much confusion takes place between forward and backslashes.

Consequently, virtual directories are made to appear as subdirectories of the home directory. Even though the home directory is C:\wwwroot and the virtual directory is D:\basketweaving, the user can access the virtual directory with the URL `http://www.hoople.edu/baskets`, which is a bit simpler and relieves the user of the responsibility for remembering the volume where the directory is located. Notice also that basketweaving has been simplified to baskets to reduce the typing requirement.

When a virtual directory is created, an alias is established that simplifies access to the virtual directory. You create virtual directories by using the service's Property dialog box.

To create a virtual directory, perform the following steps:

1. Open the Property dialog box for the service (double-click the service in the Internet Service Manager).
2. Select the Directories tab.
3. Choose Add to open the Directory Properties dialog box (see fig. 9.14).

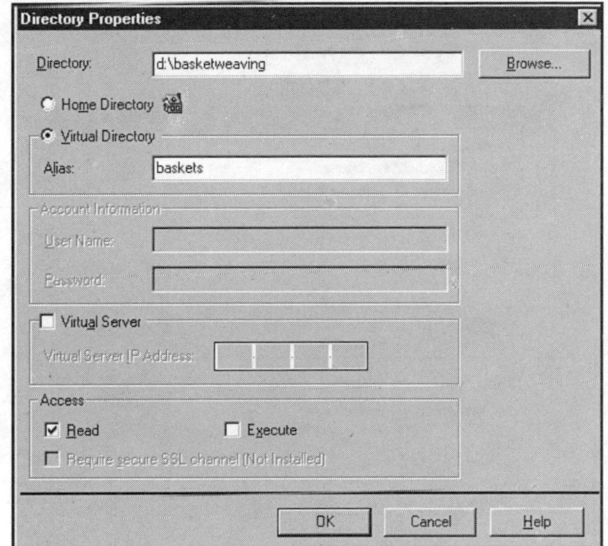

Figure 9.14
The Directory Properties dialog box.

4. In the Directory box, specify the directory for which you want to establish an alias. Click the Browse button to browse for the directory, if desired. If the directory is on the network, you can enter the UNC (Universal Naming Convention) name—you should also enter a user name and password with access to the network share.
5. Select the Virtual Directory button.
6. In the Alias field, enter the name that will be associated with the virtual directory.
7. In the Access box, specify whether users should have Read and/or Execute access to the directory.
8. Choose OK to save the virtual directory definition.

Figure 9.15 shows the directory properties for the WWW service, including definitions for two virtual directories.

Planning Virtual Servers

There are times when you want one server to do the work of two or more. Suppose that your company markets two distinct product lines, for example, and you want each to be advertised on its own web server. Must you set up two Internet Information Servers? That seems like overkill and, in fact, it is.

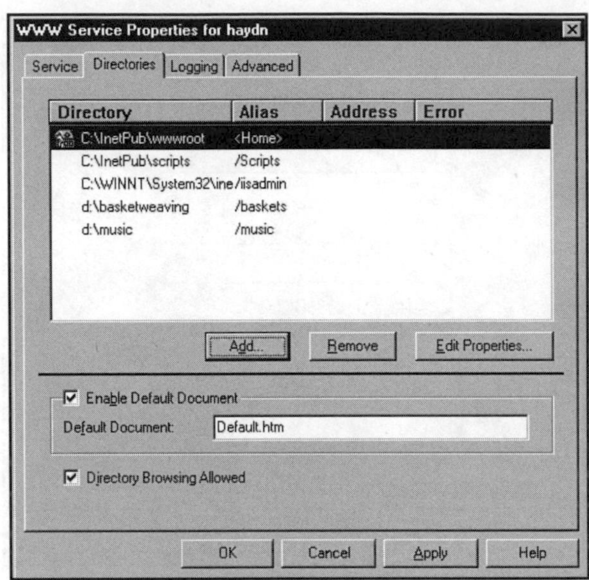

Figure 9.15
Virtual directories for a WWW service.

IIS has the capability of supporting virtual servers. Although the virtual servers appear to be separate and distinct, they are actually running on the same IIS. Each virtual server has its own IP address and DNS name, giving it a separate identity, but your administrative labor is significantly reduced.

To prepare to set up a virtual server, do the following:

1. Obtain a separate IP address for each virtual server.
2. Register each virtual server with DNS.
3. Create a content directory for each virtual server.

Look at the following scenario for setting up virtual servers.

Setting Up Virtual Servers

Suppose the University of Hoople already operates a web server, `www.hoople.edu`. The School of Music and the School of Basketweaving also want a web server, but the university doesn't want to budget for three web servers. That's not a problem, because the current web server can operate virtual servers created for the Schools of Music and Basketweaving.

Each virtual server must have its own DNS entry, IP address, and home directory. If a single IP address is configured on a computer running IIS, all directories are associated with the same IP address. When multiple IP addresses are configured, however, it is possible to associate each IP address with its own home directory. That is the central trick that makes it possible to set up virtual servers. When users connect with IIS, the home directory they view depends on the IP address they use to make the connection.

The settings for the virtual servers are as follows:

DNS Entry	IP Address	Home Directory
www.hoople.edu	200.190.50.1	C:\wwwroot
music.hoople.edu	200.190.50.100	C:\music
baskets.hoople.edu	200.190.50.101	D:\baskets

It is important to realize that the name of the home directory is arbitrary and has nothing to do with the way the virtual server is accessed. The DNS name determines the name of the virtual server, not the file system directory name.

Configuring the IP Addresses

The first step is to assign both IP addresses to the network interface on IIS. This is done in the Network dialog box as follows:

1. Open the TCP/IP Properties dialog box and click Advanced to open the Advanced IP Addressing dialog box (see fig. 9.16).

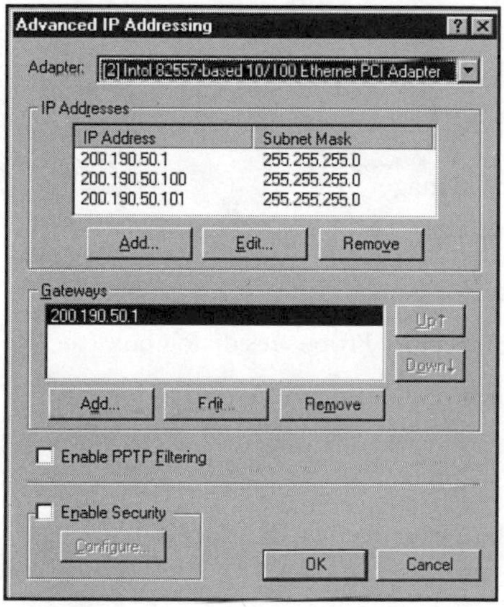

Figure 9.16
Adding an IP address for a network adapter.

2. Use the Add button to add multiple IP addresses to the interface.
3. Restart the computer to activate the new addresses.

Adding the DNS Names

You must enter the virtual server names into DNS or WINS to enable users to resolve the names. Figure 9.17 shows the DNS server for hoople.edu, in which the entries for music and baskets have been entered.

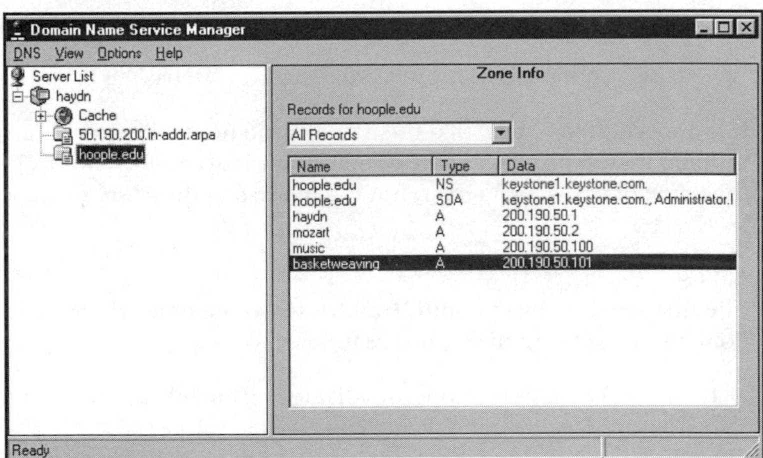

Figure 9.17
DNS entries for hoople.edu.

Creating the Virtual Server Home Directories

To set up the virtual server, do the following:

1. Open the Internet Service Manager.
2. Double-click the WWW service to display its properties.
3. Select the Directories tab.
4. Choose Add to open the Directory Properties dialog box (see fig. 9.18).
5. Click Browse, and then browse the server to locate the home directory for the virtual server.
6. Check Virtual Server.
7. Enter the IP address in the Virtual Server IP Address field.
8. Choose OK.
9. Repeat steps 4 through 8 for each virtual server that is to be established. Figure 9.19 shows the results.

10. By default, the wwwroot directory is not associated with an IP address. Unless an IP address is assigned to that directory, it becomes the default home directory for all TCP/IP addresses assigned to the server. Therefore, if virtual servers are configured, you should add an IP address to the properties of the wwwroot directory. Open the Directory Properties dialog box by double-clicking the wwwroot entry. Then check Virtual Server and enter the IP address.

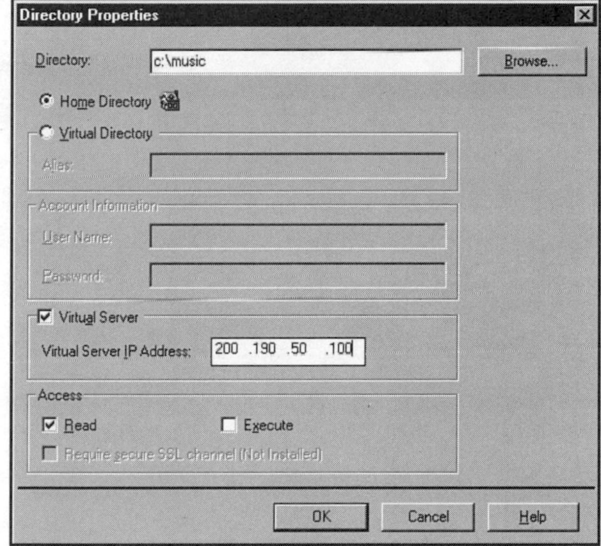

Figure 9.18

Directory properties for the virtual server.

WWW Service Properties for haydn

Service | Directories | Logging | Advanced

Directory	Alias	Address	Error
C:\InetPub\wwwroot	<Home>	200.190.50.1	
c:\music	<Home>	200.190.50.100	
d:\baskets	<Home>	200.190.50.101	
C:\InetPub\scripts	/Scripts		
C:\WINNT\System32\ine	/iisadmin		

Add... Remove Edit Properties...

Enable Default Document

Default Document: Default.htm

Directory Browsing Allowed

OK Cancel Apply Help

Figure 9.19

A server configured.

Configuring the FTP Service

After going over the options for the WWW service, you will be happy to know that the configurations that you have already looked at apply verbatim to the FTP service. There are only two exceptions: the Messages tab (see fig. 9.20) in the FTP service properties, and a few changes to the Directories tab.

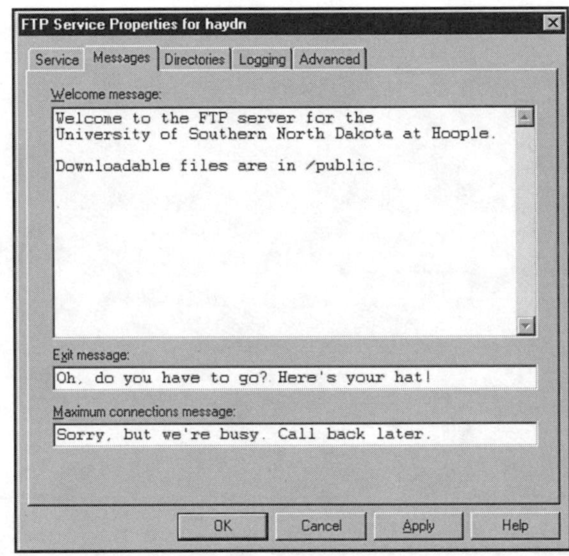

Figure 9.20
FTP service Messages tab.

The options are fairly simple; they include the following:

- **Welcome message.** This is the message that FTP users receive when they first connect to your system.
- **Exit message.** A message to send when the user logs off.
- **Maximum connections message.** The message to send if you are already at your maximum connections.

Figure 9.21 shows the changes to the Directories tab.

Notice that there are no virtual servers. (You can tell because there are no addresses listed.) The other difference is the choice of directory listing, Unix (the default), or MS-DOS.

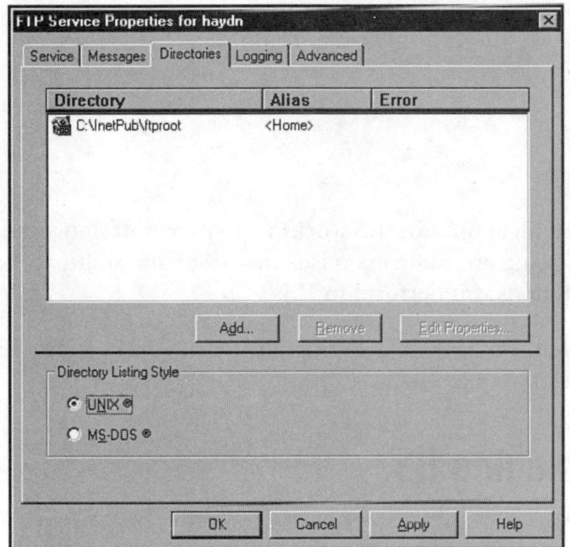

Figure 9.21
The FTP Directories tab.

Configuring the Gopher Service

Configuring the Gopher service is almost identical to the procedures for configuring an FTP service. Again like FTP, there are no virtual gophers. The service properties are, however, slightly different (see fig. 9.22).

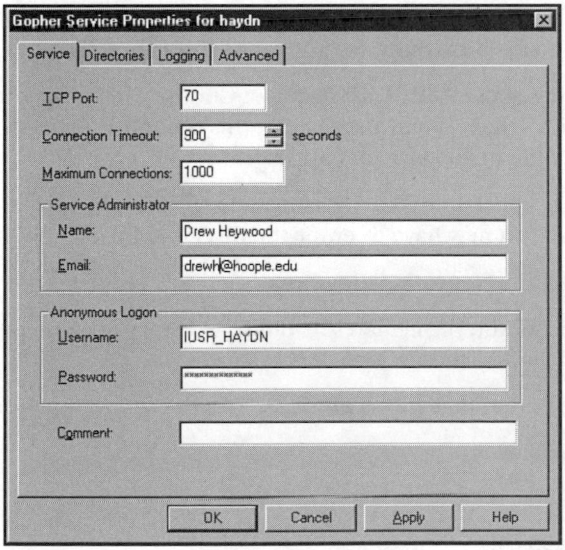

Figure 9.22
The Gopher service configuration.

As you can see, the only difference is the inclusion of the name and e-mail address of the administrator.

Practice

Now that you have learned all about how IIS works with Microsoft networking, it is time to practice. The following are some exercises that test your ability to execute some of the common functions you perform in IIS.

These exercises assume that you have installed IIS. If you have not, follow Exercise 0. If you have installed IIS, skip to Exercise 1.

Exercise 0—Installing IIS

This exercise has two sections. The first exercise applies only if you are not currently on a network. In this exercise, you add a "loopback" adapter normally used for testing. The second exercise actually installs IIS.

Adding Network Support

If you have not installed IIS because you don't have a network adapter, you can install the MS Loopback adapter, which will act as a fake network adapter for you. To install the MS Loopback adapter and TCP/IP, perform the following steps (this assumes you are running NT):

1. Open the Network dialog box (Start, Settings, Control Panel, Network).
2. On the Adapters tab, choose Add. A list displays. Choose MS Loopback Adapter from the list and click OK. You may be asked at this point for the source files directory. Enter it in the dialog box that appears.
3. On the Protocols tab, check that TCP/IP is present. If it is not, choose Add and select TCP/IP. Again you may have to enter the directory for the source files.
4. Click on Close to exit the Network dialog box.
5. The system now reviews and recalculates its binding. It may ask whether you want to use DHCP. If it does ask, choose No.
6. The TCP/IP configuration dialog box appears. Add the following information:

IP Address	148.53.64.8
Subnet Mask	255.255.192.0
Gateway	148.53.64.1

7. Click OK and the system will begin to add components. It stops at one point to warn you that `One or more network adapters have an empty primary WINS`. Click OK to continue.

8. Restart your system.

Adding IIS

At this point, you should have network services. Now you need to add IIS.

1. Right-click the Network Neighborhood and select Properties.
2. On the Services tab, click Add.
3. From the list that comes up, choose Internet Information Server and click OK. Again you need to enter the path for the source files.
4. The installation will ask you which services to install. Click OK to accept the defaults.
5. When you are prompted for the home directories, click OK to accept the defaults. (Normally you would move these to a different drive.)
6. If prompted, restart your computer.

Exercise 1—Changing the IUSR_*computername* Password

At this point, this discussion reviews how to change the password on the IUSR_*computername* account.

Accessing the Web Site

First, make certain that you can get to your web site. To do this, follow these steps:

1. Open the Internet Explorer.
2. From the menu choose File, Open.
3. Enter your computer name.

The default web site shown in figure 9.4 should appear.

Changing the Actual Password

You will now change the IUSR_*computername* password. This is done to increase security.

1. Open the User Manager for Domains.
2. Double-click the IUSR_*computername* account in the list.

3. Highlight the password and enter **TCP/IP**.
4. Click in the Confirm password text field and then enter that same password again.

   Stop and look. What groups does this user belong to, what options are set? Answer: The user is a member of Domain Guest, and User Cannot Change Password and Password Never Expires should be selected.
5. Click OK to change the user settings. Then close the User Manager for Domains.

Testing the New Password

Now you will test to see whether you can access the web site.

1. Open the Internet Explorer.
2. From the menu choose File, Open.
3. Enter your computer name.

What happened?

If things worked correctly, you should have received an access is denied error. (If not, try stopping and restarting the service as described in the following section.)

Fixing the Problem

If you did not receive an access is denied error, you will need to stop and restart the service as described in the following steps:

1. From the Start menu, choose Programs, Internet Information Server.
2. Choose the Internet Service Manager.
3. Double-click the WWW service that is running.
4. You should see the account information. Double-click the password to highlight it, and then enter **TCP/IP** as the password.
5. Click OK to close the Configuration dialog box.
6. Now stop and restart the service to do this. Ensure the WWW service is highlighted, and then choose Properties, Stop Service. After the service says Stopped, choose Properties, Start Service.
7. Attempt to connect to the site again.

If all the steps were followed, you should now be able to connect to the site.

Exercise 2—Adding an Alias to the FTP Server

In this exercise, you add an alias to the FTP server.

1. Create a directory called C:\FTP_TEST.
2. Copy some files into it. (Try copying the BMP files from the WINNT directory.)
3. Open the Internet Service Manager and double-click the FTP service.
4. Double-click the password and enter the password used in the last exercise.
5. Click the Directories tab.
6. Choose Add and enter **C:\FTP_TEST** as the directory.
7. In the Alias field, enter **Test**. Click OK to close this dialog box.
8. Click OK again to close the FTP Properties dialog box.
9. Stop and restart the service.

Testing the Directory

You can test your directory by following these steps:

1. Use Internet Explorer to open FTP://computername.

What do you see?

This should say Current directory is / and that's all.

2. Now open FTP://computer/test.

Do you see files listed? Are they the files you copied?

If everything is working, the answer to both should be yes. If you copied BMP—or any graphics files—try clicking the file name. The image should appear on-screen.

Summary

IIS has quickly become the best choice for web publishing. The integration of other services into IIS is a great incentive. This chapter is just a broad overview. Here you have seen how to perform a basic install, and how to configure the services. In most cases, this is enough.

Test Yourself

1. What are the three services that come with IIS? What does each do?
2. What is required on an NT server before installing IIS?
3. What is required to publish to the Internet rather than just your intranet?
4. Assuming that IIS is not already installed on your system, how can you add it?
5. What package do you use to control and configure IIS services?
6. Which installation option is *not* selected by default during IIS installation? (Note: Don't go by the figure in the book.)
7. Where should you not place the home directories for the different services?
8. What are ODBC drivers, and what two functions do they perform?
9. What changes will be made to the NT system on which IIS is installed?
10. Using the product documentation, determine what SSL is.
11. What is an alias?

Test Yourself Answers

1. The following services are included:

   HTTP Publishing Service—Used to create web pages that can be viewed by web browsers.

   FTP Publishing Service—Used to allow users to connect to a system to move files back and forth.

   Gopher Service—Another form of FTP, only with longer, friendly names.

2. The only absolute requirement is a TCP/IP address. Optionally you may wish to create an NTFS partition to install the files on and set up auditing. If you will use references to other systems in your home page, name resolution is required.
3. If you will be publishing to the Internet, you require a connection to the Internet. You also need to have a domain name that will be visible to the Internet.
4. Although IIS is usually installed during the installation of Windows NT 4, there are two ways to add it afterward if it was not. First, the installation places an Install Internet Information Server icon on the desktop. You can double-click the icon. Alternatively, you can go to the Network Settings dialog box, and on the Service tab choose Add. IIS is listed in the services available to be added.

5. IIS comes with the Internet Service Manager. This can be used to control and configure all the services that come with IIS. It also acts as the building block for other services added later.
6. The Internet Service Manager (HTML) is not selected by default.
7. The home directories should never be placed on the same drive as the NT installation. This can slow performance and increases the risk of someone getting at your system files.
8. The ODBC (Open Database Connectivity) drivers enable you to log access to your site directly to a database. This also enables you to create web pages that can query a database and post the results set.
9. The computer installation will add another group to the Start menu. As well, a new user account called IUSR_*computername* is created and granted the Log on Locally right.
10. SSL (Secured Sockets Layer) is a method of crcating secure web sites that can be used to pass encrypted information between the client and the server.
11. An alias is a directory entry in a service that enables clients to move to directories on different areas of the server (or on different servers) by adding a /alias_name to the name of the web site.

CHAPTER 10

TCP/IP Printing Services

One of the goals in designing Windows NT was to create an operating system that could interact with the many different environments that already existed. This meant having the capability to work with not only the file systems and servers on operating systems, but also to share printers with them.

For a long time now, TCP/IP has been associated with the Unix world and with the world of mainframe computers. To share printing services with these worlds, NT has to have the capability to work with a Line Printer Daemon (LPD). Further, to use printers shared in the Unix world and to share to the Unix world, NT itself must act as an LPD. This is only required to enable non-Microsoft systems to use the print services of NT. When Microsoft networking clients attempt to print, they use the Server service (NetBIOS networking). One of the most common problems that you will run across is a user who can't print. There are many reasons for this, too many in fact to cover in this text.

This chapter covers the basics of printing from NT. After the basics are covered, TCP/IP Printing Services is discussed. These services fall into two parts: using a remote LPD server, and setting NT up as an LPD server. Remember that LPD is a Line Printer Daemon normally used with Unix platforms.

Printing with Windows NT

The following section provides an overview of the printing process in Windows NT. Although many users will already be familiar with how to print from NT and how to create printers, this section also talks about the actual process used to print from Windows NT.

The Print Process

When you print from Windows NT, you normally go to the menu in the application (such as Word) that you are working with and choose File, Print. For many users, this is the extent of their knowledge on the printing process that NT performs. Many different components, however, are at work in the background and are needed to move the bytes of data from your system to the page.

The following list serves as an overview of the printing process:

1. You start the printing process by choosing File, Print from the application that you are working in.

2. If the system uses a network printer, the next step is to verify the version of the driver stored locally. With NT, the system can retrieve the driver from the print server, ensuring that the current and correct driver is always used when printing. The local system checks the version of the driver with the version on the print server. If that one is newer, the local system retrieves a copy.

3. Now the generic portion of the print driver (there are three parts to a print driver, which are covered shortly) is used, and in conjunction with the GDI (Graphics Device Interface) creates an Enhanced Metafile (EMF). An EMF file is a simple file similar in concept to an HTML (Hypertext Markup Language—a web page) document. When the printer needs to make something bold, a generic bold code is used. When the printer is turned off another generic code is used. The EMF format is common to Windows NT and Windows 95. This enables Windows 95 systems to send the jobs to the print server in this format—saving the local system the resources needed to complete the rendering process.

4. As the GDI and printer driver build the EMF file, it moves to a spool file on the local system. (This is a file on the local hard disk. There must be space available.) The local spooler contacts the spooler on the print server and creates an RPC (remote procedure call) to that system. The local spooler sends the print job to the print server over this connection. Obviously this does not occur if the user is printing to a local printer.

5. On the print server, the spooler service receives the print job and stores it to disk. It also lets the router know the file is there.
6. The router checks the type of data the file contains and calls on the print processor to complete the job of rendering the print job to the data format expected by the printer.
7. Now the print processor works with the master copy of the print driver to complete the rendering process. This involves removing all the code that the system put into the file in step 3, and replaces it with the actual codes required by the physical printer to perform the given function.
8. Another processor generates a separator page and adds it to the beginning of the file. The file is now ready to be copied to the printer.
9. Now the job is held in the spool and a port monitor is used to move the file from the spool file to the printer. The port monitors link the logical printers and the physical printer.
10. Finally the print job comes out of the physical printing device (if it is "online").

As you can see, the printing process in Windows NT consists of many different parts. If any of the parts fail, the whole printing process also fails. The NT printing system has four main parts: the printer driver, the print spooler, the print processor, and the port monitors. The next few sections look at each of these.

Print Drivers

The print drivers in NT are broken down into three sections: graphics driver, printer interface, and characterization data files. All three of these need to function together to enable NT to print.

Graphics Driver

The graphics driver is the part of the print driver that works with the GDI to create the EMF file. It knows about the type of printer to which you are printing. There are three main types of printers: raster, PostScript, and plotters. Each of these types of printers has a different graphics driver that knows how that type of printer prints. The three graphics drivers are as follows:

- **RASDD.DLL.** This is used for raster printers. A raster printer is the most common form of printer. These printers create their image with a series of dots. This is most evident with the older dot matrix form of printers. The same method is used, however, by most laser printers. RASDD.DLL can call on other files where it is required to complete the process. An example is HPPCL.DLL, which is used with most of the HP LaserJet printers.

- **PSCRIPT.DLL.** Your system uses this graphics driver when you are working with a PostScript printer. These printers use a programming language to describe the page and how it will look using vectors. Vectors use a starting point, direction, and distance to build your page out of a series of lines. A common example of a PostScript printer is the Apple Laserwriter.
- **PLOTTER.DLL.** As you might guess from the name, this is used in a case where you are using a plotter. Plotters, of course, create a page just like you do. They use a pen and move the pen across the paper (or the paper across the pen), lifting the pen and lowering it to start and stop marking.

Printer Interface

The printer interface is just that, your interface to the settings of the printer with which you are working. Because there are the three main types of printers, there are also three main types of printer interface files.

- **RASDDUI.DLL.** Used for raster printers.
- **PSCRPTUI.DLL.** This is used for PostScript printers.
- **PLOTUI.DLL.** Used with plotters.

The printer interface reads information from the characterization file so that you know what options are available on the printer, and then it enables you to set the options.

Characterization Data File

Nearly every printer that NT supports has its own characterization data file. (In some cases, several printers share a common characterization file.) These files are the key piece to putting the whole thing together. They provide the information for the printer interface so that it knows what the capabilities are. They also contain the codes used to transform the EMF file to a printer-ready state.

Print Spooler

The print spooler is responsible for storing the print job on the hard disk and moving it through the various stages on the way to the printing device. It runs as a service on NT and can be seen in the Services icon in the Control Panel.

Note If your printer seems to be "jammed," you can usually fix it by stopping and restarting the spooler service.

Print Processor

When you print from a Windows application, your file ends up as an EMF. If you print from a DOS application, it will be raw text or formatted printer data. If you print from a Macintosh, the file ends up as a PSCRIPT1 file. The printer needs to see the data as formatted printer data if it is to actually print the file.

The print processor handles the conversion between the different types of files. The processor (WINPRINT.DLL) handles the data types (where mentioned), and can convert them to the data type the printer requires. If this is a print server, the processing is handled on the server, not the client. In this way, the burden is moved off the client computer, leaving more processing power of the applications on that computer.

Port Monitor

This is the link between the logical printer that the users connect to and the physical printer where the paper comes out. Many different port monitors support the different types of connections that can be used for printers. The following list covers some of the available port monitors:

- **LOCALMON.DLL.** This handles any printer connected locally to the computer (LPT1:, COM1:, and so on) and any printers to which you have created a connection (for example, using NET USE LPT3: \\server\printer).
- **LPRMON.DLL.** This is the reason for the discussion. This enables you to connect to and use the services of a LPD server.
- **HPMON.DLL.** Used to communicate with HP JetDirect printers.
- **SFMMON.DLL.** Windows NT provides support for Macintosh computers and the capability to share files and printers with them. This monitor enables NT to use a Macintosh printer on the network.
- **DECPSMON.DLL.** This monitor works with DEC network interface printers.
- **LEXMON.DLL.** The monitor of Lexmark Vision series network printers.
- **PJLMON.DLL.** This monitor is used for any printers that follow the Printer Job Language communications standards.

This separation of the logical and physical printers has enabled Microsoft to add extra functionality to the printing process. First there is the capability to link several different logical printers to a single physical printer (many network operating systems do this). This means that you can have different settings on the different logical printers and then use the same printing device. You can, for example, create a logical raster printer and a logical PostScript printer that both print to the same multimode physical printer.

The other somewhat unique function is the capability to connect several physical printers to the same logical printer. This creates a printer pool. Many different printing devices all accept jobs from one logical printer. This works well in areas where there is high demand and often a long queue. Creating a printer pool increases the number of pages-per-minute that you can process without having to purchase very expensive high-end printers.

Installing a Printer

The process of installing a printer is very straightforward. A wizard walks you through the entire process. The steps vary slightly depending on the type of printer that you are installing, and on the type of port that it will attach to, but the general steps are as follows:

1. Open the My Computer icon, and then double-click on the Printers icon.
2. Double-click on the Add Printer icon.
3. Choose either My Computer if the printer is connected directly, or Network Print Server if it is not.
4. If the printer is connected directly, you are asked to tell the system which port the printer is connected to. (If you choose Enable Print Pooling, you may choose more than one port.) You can, if required, click on Add Port or Configure Port.
5. Next you need to choose the Manufacturer from the list on the left side, and the model from the list on the right. (If the printer is not listed, but you have a driver disk, click on Have Disk.) Then choose Next.
6. Name the printer whatever you want to (up to 31 characters), and choose whether this is the default printer. Choose Next to continue.
7. If you want to share the printer, you can choose Shared. If you do, enter the share name and the platforms of the users that will connect to the printer. (This tells NT to add the drivers for these other platforms so that the clients can retrieve the driver from your server. Choose Next.
8. Now you can try the printer by printing a test page. When done, click on Finish.

This should provide you with the basics of printing. You could learn many other things about printing from NT. Because this book is about TCP/IP, however, this chapter concentrates on TCP/IP Printing Services.

Installing TCP/IP Printing Services

The installation and configuration of the services for TCP/IP printing support is simple. You must first have TPC/IP up and functioning correctly; additionally, if you use host names, you must have some method of resolving them. (Chapter 15, "Microsoft DNS Server," covers host name resolution.)

Objective B.9

Assuming that you have met these criteria, the following steps describe how to install the services:

1. Open the Network dialog box (right-click on Network Neighborhood and choose Properties).
2. On the Services tab, choose Add.
3. Select Microsoft TCP/IP Printing, and choose OK (see fig. 10.1).

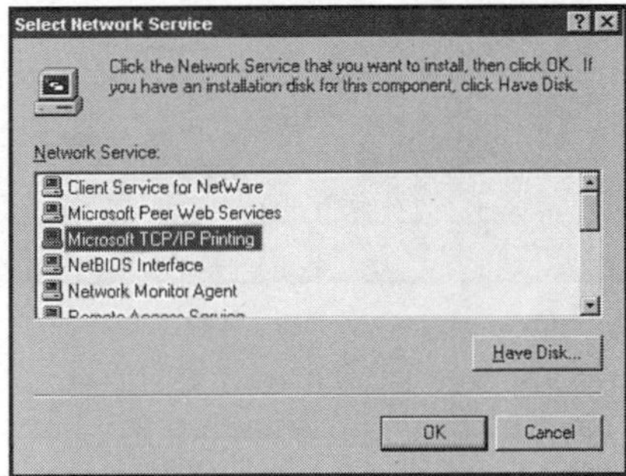

Figure 10.1
The Select Network Service dialog box.

4. Enter the directory for your source files.
5. Select Close from the Network dialog box. Then choose Yes to restart your computer.

That is all there is to adding the services. After they are in, you can configure your system to either make use of an existing LPD server or to become one.

Connecting to an LPD Server

The process of moving print files from the queue to the physical printing device in NT is handled by a monitor. Many different monitors are available that enable you to print to many different types of printers.

When you want to connect to an LPD server, you must create a printer (unless you just want to redirect an existing printer). You have already seen how to install a printer under Windows NT, so now it is time to concentrate on the LPR (Line Printer Request) Port monitor.

You enter the settings for the LPR port on the Ports tab of the Printer Properties dialog box (see fig. 10.2).

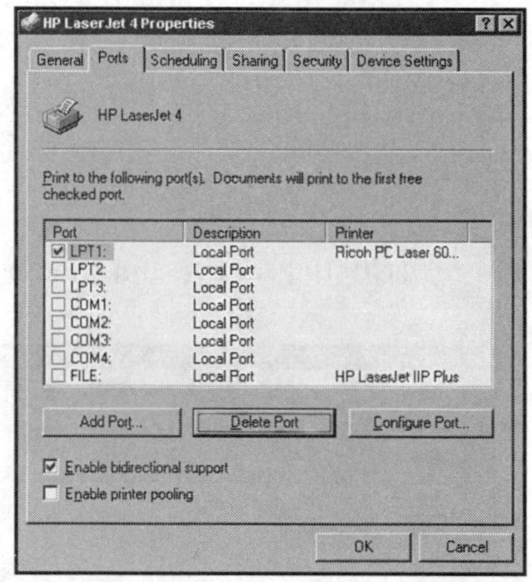

Figure 10.2

The Ports tab on a Printers Properties dialog box.

Choose Add Ports. This brings up a screen similar to that shown in figure 10.3. You may not have the same choices as illustrated (possibly you will have more). If you have installed TCP/IP printing, however, you will see the LPR Port option.

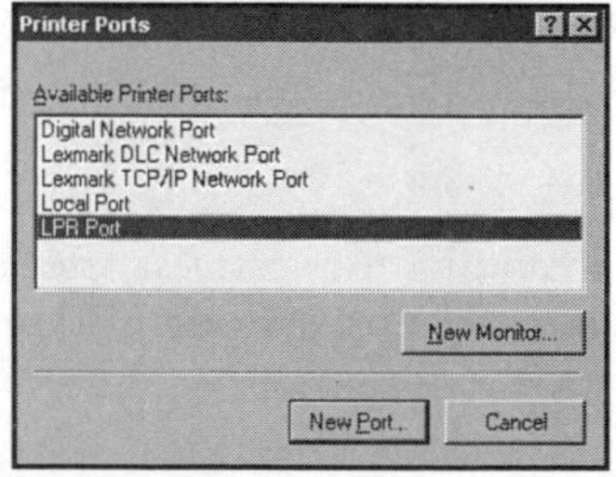

Figure 10.3

The Printer Ports dialog box.

Select LPR Port, and then click on the New Port button. You now have a dialog box that looks like that shown in figure 10.4. In the first box, put the host name or IP address of the server that will control the printer. In the second box, enter the name of the printer.

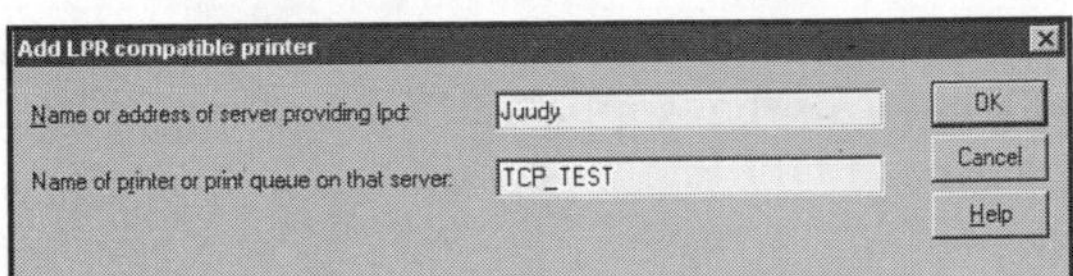

Figure 10.4
Adding the LPR-compatible printer.

If you enter a host name that cannot be resolved, the following error message appears:

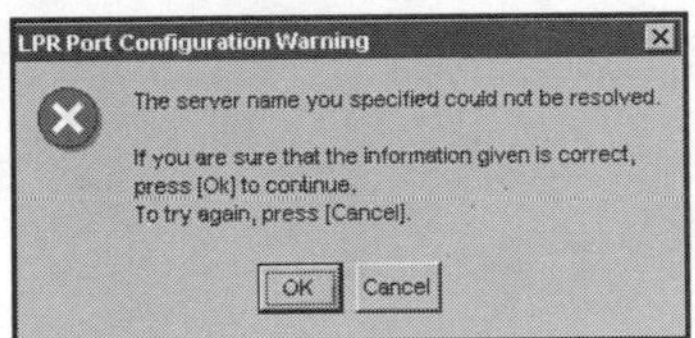

Figure 10.5
An error message indicating the name cannot be resolved.

If everything worked correctly, you now have another port in the list of available ports. This is the connection to the LPD server (see fig. 10.6).

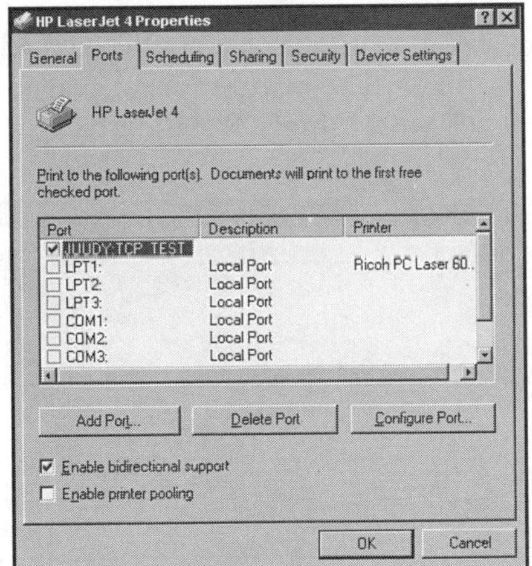

Figure 10.6
A new port will be listed in the Printer Properties dialog box.

Sharing Your Printer Using LPD

So far you have learned where to add a port to talk to an LPD server. As previously stated, Windows NT can also act as an LPD server itself (both NT Workstation and NT Server). The LPD server, like most other servers, is implemented as a service. There are basically two steps involved in sharing your printer using LPD services.

First, you need to share your printer normally (see fig. 10.7). You should keep the name simple because not all platforms that support LPR also support long share names. Here the printer is shared as HPLJ4.

Figure 10.7

Sharing a printer in the Printer Properties dialog box.

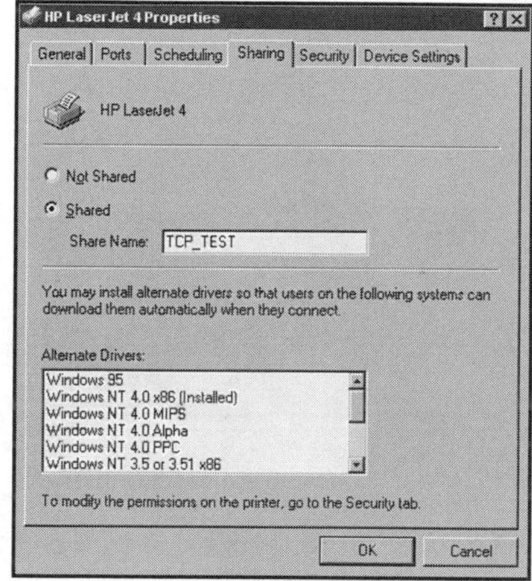

After you have shared the printer, you need only start the LPD service in the Services icon of the Control Panel (see fig. 10.8). The printer is now available to other users, even from the other platforms that support the LPR standards.

Figure 10.8

Starting the TCP/IP print service.

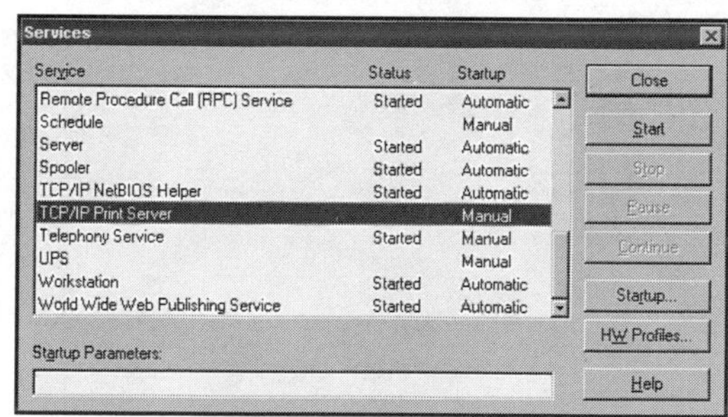

If you want to have the service start automatically every time you start your system, select the Startup button and change the Startup Type to Automatic (see fig. 10.9).

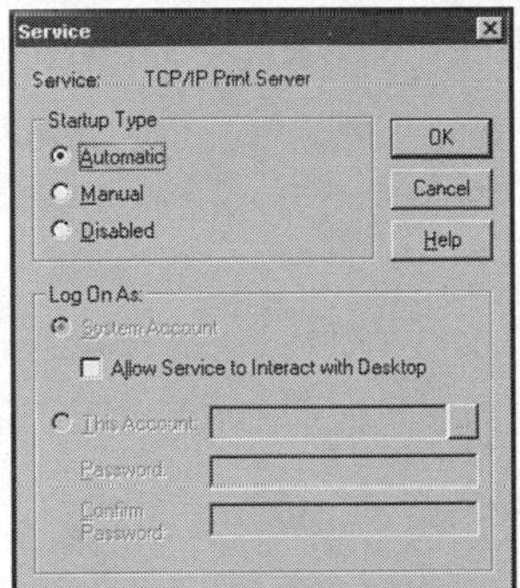

Figure 10.9
Configuring the TCP/IP Print Server to start automatically.

Practice

Now it is time to put what you have learned in this chapter to good use. Following are some exercises that utilize the information in this chapter in real world ways.

Exercise 1—Installing the TCP/IP Printing Service

In this lab, you create an LPD printer and send a job to it. You also connect (virtually) to an LPD printer using an LPR port. This assumes you have TCP/IP installed and functioning. If not, see Exercise 0 in the "Practice" section of Chapter 9.

1. Open the Network dialog box (right-click on Network Neighborhood).
2. On the Services tab, choose Add, then highlight Microsoft TCP/IP Printing and choose OK.
3. Enter the directory for your Windows NT source files.
4. Choose close from the Network dialog box. When prompted, restart your system.
5. When restarted, open the Control Panel and double-click the Services icon.
6. Scroll down and verify that TCP/IP Print Server is listed.

Exercise 2—Creating a Demonstration Printer

In this exercise, you create a printer that you can use for demonstration purposes, so as not to destroy the setting for your real printer.

Note If you have a printer on LPT3:, turn it off during this lab, otherwise you may end up printing to the printer by accident rather than the one you will install.

1. From the Start menu, choose Settings, Printers.
2. Double-click on the Add Printer icon.
3. By default, My Computer should be selected. If not, select it and click Next.
4. For the port, choose LPT3: and click Next.
5. From the list, choose any printer that you like and click Next.
6. In the Printer Name field enter TCP_TEST. Do not set this up as the Windows default printer; instead choose Next.
7. Select Shared, and click Next. Choose No for the Test Page and click Finish.
8. Enter the location of your source files.

Exercise 3—Turning On the TCP/IP Print Server

Now that you have a printer, it is time to turn on the TCP/IP Print Server.

1. In the Control Panel, click the Services icon.
2. Choose the TCP/IP Print Server and click Start.

Exercise 4—Printing to the TCP/IP Printer

Now you can print to the TCP/IP printer.

1. From the Start menu, choose Settings and Printers (this dialog box may still be open).
2. Right-click the TCP_TEST printer and choose Pause Printing from the pop-up menu.
3. Close the Printers dialog box.
4. Start a command prompt (Start, Programs, Command Prompt).

5. Enter the following: **LPR -Scomputername -PTCP_TEST c:\autoexec.bat**

Note The -S and the -P are case sensitive. If you do not have an autoexec.bat, you can use a text file. Substitute your computer name for computername.

6. To verify the printing worked, type the following command: **LPQ -Scomputername -PTCP_TEST**

   The output should look like this:

```
Windows NT LPD Server
                                 Printer TCP_TEST(Paused)
Owner           Status       Jobname           Job-Id     Size     Pages  Priority
-------------------------------------------------------------------------------------
Scrim (152.     Waiting      \autoexec.bat     2          48       0      1
```

Exercise 5—Hooking Up to the LPD Service

Finally, you hook up to an LPD service from the printer created in Exercise 2.

1. Open the Printers dialog box. Right-click the TCP_TEST printer, and choose Properties.
2. On the Ports tab, choose Add.
3. Click LPR Port in the list, and then click the New Port button.
4. If you are asked, enter the source file location.
5. Enter your computer name in the Name or Address field. Then enter **TCP_TEST** as the printer name.
6. Click OK to add the port and Close to return to the Printer Properties dialog box.

You should notice that the printer's properties are different, the new port is listed, and that it is checked. You can now delete the printer and remove Microsoft TCP/IP Printing.

Summary

This chapter covered three main areas: printing from Windows NT, using an LPD server on the network, and becoming an LPD server. As you have seen, TCP/IP printing is very simple (as long as the underlying transport is in place). Using a remote LPD server is a matter of adding a port; becoming a server is just a matter of starting the service.

Test Yourself

1. What does the TCP/IP printing services do?
2. What does LPD stand for?
3. How will an LPR port appear in the Printer Ports dialog box?
4. At the command prompt, type **LPR** /?. Read the information that appears. Now type **LPQ** /? and read about it. What is each used for?

Test Yourself Answers

1. TCP/IP printing services enable you to print to and accept jobs from all types of TCP/IP hosts such as a Unix workstation.
2. LPD stands for Line Printer Daemon. Daemon is the name given to a service running on a Unix system.
3. The standard is host_name:printer_name.
4. LPR or Line Printer Request is used to send a job to a Line Printer Daemon. LPQ or Line Printer Query is used to view the jobs on the printer.

CHAPTER 11

Dynamic Host Configuration Protocol (DHCP)

The DHCP can make TCP/IP network administration much more efficient by dynamically assigning IP addresses to hosts, practically eliminating the need to configure host addresses manually. A DHCP client host can even move to a different subnet and obtain a new IP address without any need for manual reconfiguration.

DHCP also provides a mechanism for local management of the majority of TCP/IP clients on the internetwork. Parameters such as default gateway can be configured centrally without visiting each host and making changes manually.

This chapter provides an overview of DHCP, defines it, and explains how it works. Then the chapter proceeds to examine DHCP, beginning with installation. It also examines configuration and management issues.

DHCP Concepts and Operation

The DHCP process requires both DHCP servers, which assign IP addresses, and DHCP clients, which request IP addresses. Figure 11.1 illustrates a simple network that consists of a single DHCP server and a few clients. As shown, a single DHCP server can supply addresses for more than one network. To support DHCP on an internetwork, routers must be configured with BOOTP forwarding. DHCP clients and hosts communicate using BOOTP (which is a broadcast-based protocol). BOOTP is an older, less versatile protocol also used to assign IP addresses automatically.

Note BOOTP (or Bootstrap protocol) is the forerunner of DHCP. They differ primarily in the way the addresses are assigned. All the addresses in BOOTP are assigned in a boottab (Boot table). Essentially this is the same as reserving an address for every client on the network.

The other main change is the fact that it is a lease, so it does run out. In BOOTP, because the addresses are statically assigned, there is no time out period.

The DHCP server maintains pools of IP addresses, called *scopes.* When a DHCP client first starts up, it requests and is granted (in most cases) a lease to use an address from an appropriate scope for a specific period of time. If the DHCP server is on a different subnet, the BOOTP protocol tags each of the requests for an IP address with the network's broadcast address. This information enables the DHCP server to assign an address to the client that is appropriate for their subnet.

The concept of leasing is important because DHCP clients are not ordinarily granted permanent use of an address. Instead, they receive a lease of limited duration. Periodically they must renew the lease. This approach guarantees that hosts receive new configuration parameters on a routine basis.

As you can see in figure 11.1, a single DHCP server can support clients on several networks in an intranet. Clients configured for DHCP that are moved to different subnets are assigned IP addresses by the DHCP server, appropriate to the new subnet.

Figure 11.2 shows the dialog that takes place when a DHCP client obtains a lease from a DHCP server. If a client does not receive an offer from a DHCP server to lease it an address, it repeats the request four times at 2-, 4-, 8-, and 16- second intervals, varying the intervals by a random amount between 0 and 1,000 milliseconds. If it still fails to receive a DHCPOFFER message, the client stops trying and waits for five minutes before renewing its attempt (you will of course receive a message). If a DHCP server is unavailable, the client is unable to bind to TCP/IP and cannot enter the network.

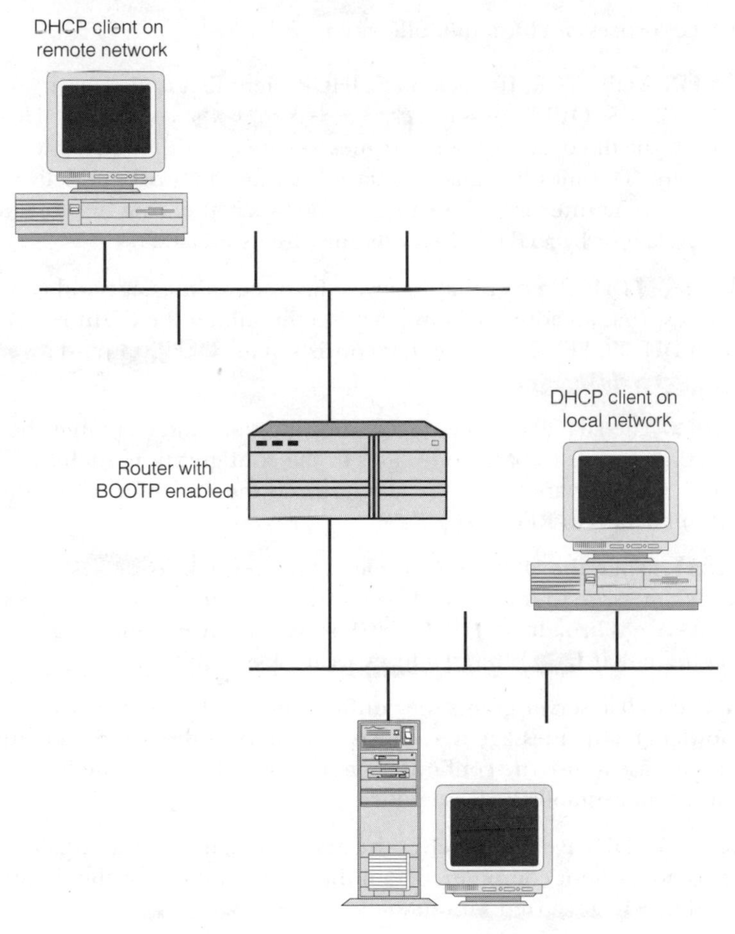

Figure 11.1

An example of a network running DHCP.

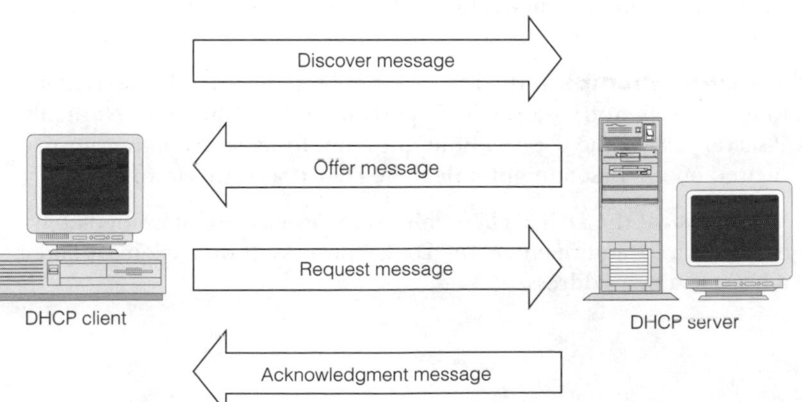

Figure 11.2

The process used to obtain a DHCP lease.

The steps in the DHCP process include the following:

1. **DHCPDISCOVER.** As the TCP/IP stack on a DHCP client first initializes, it broadcasts a DHCPDISCOVER message to the local network. To enable DHCP servers to reply to the discover message, the message includes the MAC address of the DHCP client. This message may be relayed to other networks to deliver it to DHCP servers on the Internet. This can be done by a router that supports RFC 1542 (BOOTP Relay) or by a DHCP Relay Agent (discussed later).
2. **DHCPOFFER.** Each DHCP server that receives the discover message and can service the request (has an address appropriate to the subnet the client is on) responds with a DHCPOFFER message that consists of an IP address and associated configuration information.
3. **Selecting state.** The DHCP client enters a selecting state and examines the offer messages that it receives based on values in the configuration, such as the lease duration. If all offers are equal, the client selects the first offer received. (You can find full details in RFC1541.)
4. **DHCPREQUEST.** When the DHCP client selects an offer, it broadcasts a DHCPREQUEST message to the network requesting the offered configuration. Because the message is broadcast, other DHCP servers receive the message as well, notifying them that their offered addresses are not required.
5. **DHCPACK.** The DHCP server grants the configuration with a DHCPACK (DHCP acknowledgment) message that consists of the IP address and configuration along with a lease to use the configuration for a specific time. The local network administrator establishes lease policies.
6. **Initialization.** The DHCP client receives the acknowledgment and initializes the IP configuration. Client computers retain the configuration for the duration of the lease and may be restarted without negotiating a new lease.
7. **First renewal attempt.** When the lease has been active for 50 percent of the permitted lease duration, the client attempts to renew its lease with the DHCP server.
8. **Second renewal attempt.** If the lease cannot be renewed at 50 percent of the time to live, the client tries again at 75 percent and 87.5 percent. Normally the DHCP server renews the lease without question. In most cases, therefore, the lease is renewed on the first attempt unless the DHCP server is down.
9. **Failure to renew.** If the DHCP client fails to renew its lease, it immediately unbinds the IP address and re-enters the DHCP process. It then requests and is assigned a lease to a new address.

Notice that the client initiates all DHCP activity. A client can pull configuration changes in from a DHCP server, but a DHCP server cannot push changes out to a client. For this reason, all leases should have a limited duration. Only when all leases have expired can you be certain that changes made to the DHCP configuration have been distributed to all clients.

Unless errors are encountered, the process of requesting, assigning, and renewing is completely transparent to the client and requires little ongoing maintenance on the part of the network administrator.

When a DHCP client restarts and logs on to the network, it attempts to re-establish its existing lease by broadcasting a DHCPREQUEST rather than a DHCPDISCOVER packet. The request packet contains a request for the DHCP address most recently assigned.

The DHCP server should respond with a DHCPACK after attempting to grant the request. If the request cannot be granted, the server sends a DHCPNACK (DHCP Negative Acknowledgment) message, and the client must enter an initializing state and request a new address lease.

Although the majority of clients are assigned an IP address selected from a pool, DHCP can be configured to assign specific addresses to specific hosts. This enables administrators to use DHCP to set host protocol options while retaining fixed address assignments. It is also required to enable some printers to obtain an address by using BOOTP protocol.

Microsoft DHCP does not include the capability to send software with the lease, which is defined in the DHCP standards. Because this is optional, Microsoft has not included it. This means that DHCP cannot service some types of printers (and other hardware) because it cannot supply the required software.

Several types of hosts must be assigned fixed, manual addresses so that other hosts can enter the addresses into their configurations, including, among others, the following examples:

- Routers (gateways)
- WINS servers
- DNS servers

Installing DHCP Servers

You can install DHCP Server services on computers running Windows NT Server. To install DHCP services, follow these steps:

1. Install TCP/IP on the computer that will act as a DHCP server. You must configure DHCP servers with static IP addresses. Every other computer can, if desired, obtain its IP address from the DHCP server.
2. Go to the Network dialog box (right-click Network Neighborhood).
3. On the Services tab, choose Add.
4. In the Network Service list, select Microsoft DHCP Server and then click OK.
5. Supply the path to the installation files when prompted.
6. Close the Network dialog box.
7. If required, edit the TCP/IP properties. Make certain that the interface adapters are configured with static IP addresses.
8. Restart your system.

Note If you are upgrading to Windows NT Server 4 from Windows NT Server 3.51, you must convert the DHCP database. The first time the DHCP service starts, it detects the old database and attempts to convert it by using JETCONV.EXE. The user is informed that conversion must take place, and the user must confirm the procedure. (Information on the DHCP database is given in the following section.)

Setting Up DHCP Scopes

Objective B.3

Before DHCP clients can obtain IP addresses from a DHCP server, at least one scope must be created. A *scope* is a range of IP addresses along with a set of configuration options that apply to clients that receive IP addresses assigned from the scope. All scopes have the following properties:

- A series of IP addresses
- A subnet mask
- A lease duration

DHCP is administered using the DHCP Manager utility. An icon for DHCP Manager is created in the Administrative Tools group on the Start menu when DHCP Server services are installed. Figure 11.3 shows the DHCP Manager window.

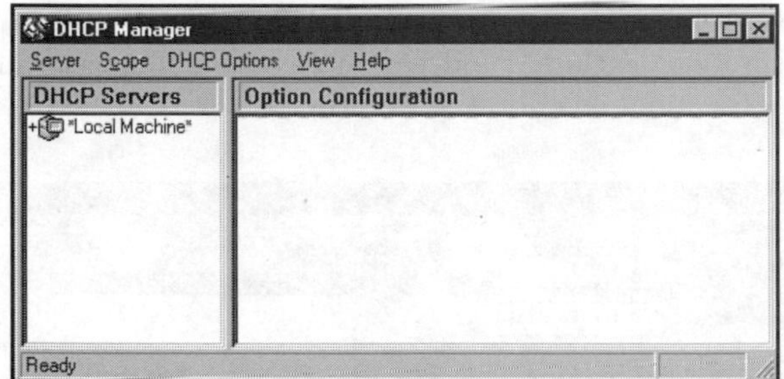

Figure 11.3

The Windows NT DHCP Manager window.

In this figure no scopes have been defined. Before defining a scope, you should determine the following:

- The starting IP address of the range to be assigned to the scope
- The ending IP address to be assigned
- The subnet mask to be in effect
- Any addresses in the range that are not to be made available to clients obtaining addresses from the scope
- The duration of the lease (default value is three days)
- The name of the DHCP Scope

To create a scope, perform the following steps:

1. Start DHCP Manager, which is installed in the Administrative Tools group of the Start menu. Figure 11.3 shows DHCP Manager before defining any scopes. If a DHCP Server service is running on this computer, it is identified as Local Machine. If this is the first time the DHCP Manager is run, it automatically skips to step 4.

2. Select one of the DHCP servers you have added to the list of DHCP servers. The example creates a scope on Local Machine. A scope is always created on a specific DHCP server.

3. In the DHCP Manager dialog box, choose Create in the Scope menu. The Create Scope dialog box opens (see fig. 11.4). Data fields in the figure have been filled to reflect typical scope properties.

4. Enter the appropriate addresses in the Start Address, End Address, and Subnet Mask fields.

5. If required, you can exclude an address or range of addresses. Under Exclusion Range, enter the appropriate addresses in the Start Address and End Address fields. (An end address is not required when you exclude a single address.) Then

choose Add to move the addresses to the Excluded Addresses list. If you make a mistake, you can remove an excluded address range by selecting the range in the Excluded Addresses list and then choosing Remove.

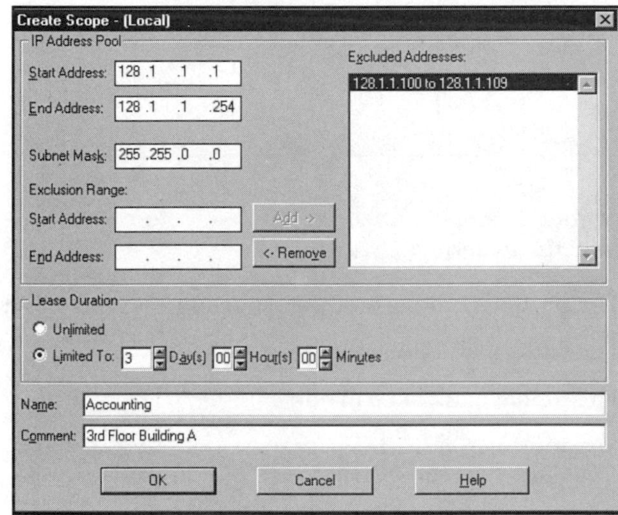

Figure 11.4

The DHCP Scope Configuration dialog box.

6. Choose Unlimited if leases for this scope are to be unlimited in duration (this is not recommended because the client will never need to update configuration parameters). Choose Limited To and enter a period in days, hours, and minutes to set a lease duration for the scope. The duration of the lease depends on the volatility of your environment—if things change often, use a short lease; otherwise use a longer lease to decrease traffic and server load.
7. If you wish, enter a name and comment for the scope in the Name and Comment fields. This information helps identify the scope in the DHCP Manager, making administration easier.
8. Click OK to return to the DHCP Manager main dialog box. For a new scope, you receive the message shown in figure 11.5. To activate the scope, choose Yes.

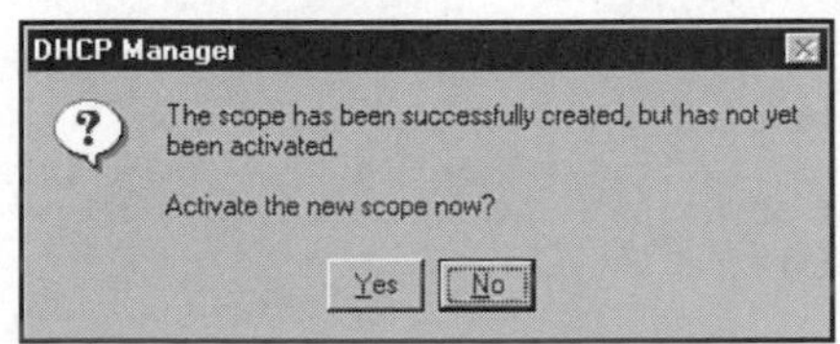

Figure 11.5

Choose Yes to activate the new scope.

9. As figure 11.6 shows, the scope you define appears under the DHCP server for which the scope was defined. Because it was activated, the light bulb icon illuminates.

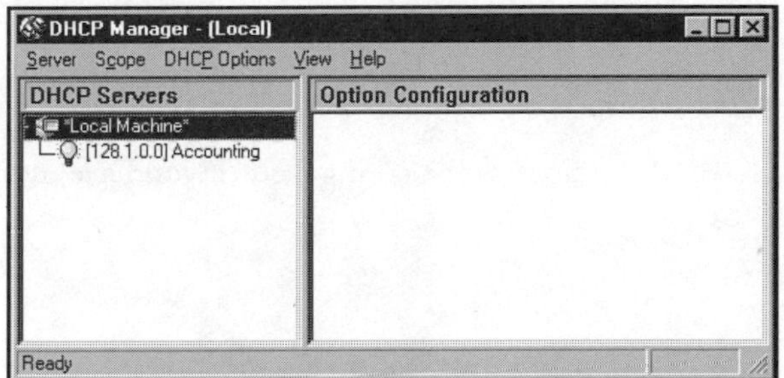

Figure 11.6
DHCP Manager with the new scope configured.

Note If you need to modify a scope, select the scope in the DHCP Manager and choose Properties in the Scope menu. A Scope Properties dialog box opens. In this you can change scope properties. Click OK after you make the necessary changes. If you are changing the available addresses, you must add or remove them in 32 address blocks.

Caution Be certain that the scope address range does not include the IP addresses of any hosts for which addresses have been manually assigned. This includes all servers. Fixed IP addresses must be outside the scope address range or must be excluded from the scope.

Enabling DHCP Clients

After you have created a DHCP scope, DHCP clients can begin to lease addresses. All the following Microsoft clients can use DHCP:

- Windows NT
- Windows 95
- Windows 3.11 with the 32-bit TCP/IP client (from the NT Server CD-ROM)
- MS-DOS Client version 3.0 (also from the NT Server CD-ROM)
- MS DOS Client for LAN Manager 2.2c (also from the NT Server CD-ROM (supports RPL, Remote Program Load)

Enabling a client usually requires that you select the Obtain Address Automatically from DHCP server option in the TCP/IP configuration for the client. In the case of Windows NT, the exact steps are as follows:

1. Open the Network dialog box by right-clicking Network Neighborhood.
2. Select TCP/IP Protocol in the Protocols tab and choose Properties. The Microsoft TCP/IP Properties dialog box opens.
3. In the Adapter list, select the adapter to be configured (if you have more than one).
4. Select Obtain an IP Address from a DHCP server.
5. Choose Apply.
6. Close the Network dialog box and restart the computer.

The option to Obtain an IP Address from a DHCP server is not available if DHCP Server services or WINS Server services are installed on the computer. You must configure DHCP or WINS servers using fixed IP addresses.

Note Note that if you have configured any of the parameters in the TCP/IP Setting dialog box yourself (other than IP Address and Subnet Mask), these settings persist and override the settings from the DHCP server.

If you are using DHCP, you can find out what address you are using by typing **IPCONFIG** at a prompt (**WINIPCFG** for Windows 95 users). You can also use IPCONFIG/ALL to view all the information, including when your lease will be renewed, where your DHCP server is, and so on. (Windows 95 users use the Advanced button.)

Viewing and Managing Active Leases

Assuming that you have completed all the configurations, you can now start to manage the DHCP server. One of the first things you might want to do is to view the leases that a DHCP server has issued.

To view active leases, perform the following steps:

1. Select a scope in the DHCP Servers box.
2. Choose Active Leases from the Scope menu.

Figure 11.7 shows a scope with two active leases.

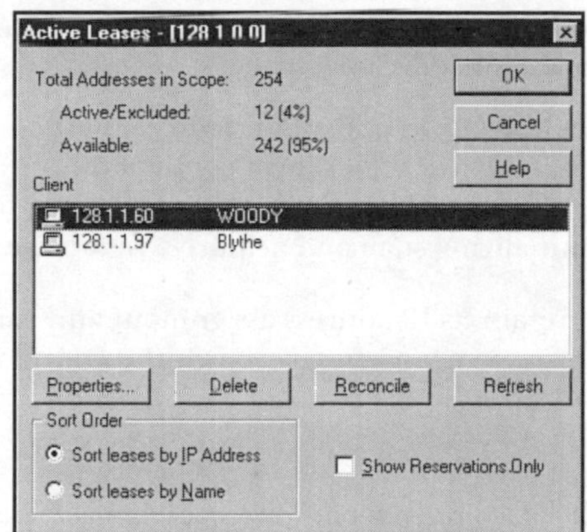

Figure 11.7

Active leases in a scope.

The following information is available in the Active Leases dialog box:

- **Total Addresses in Scope.** The total number of addresses in the scope.
- **Active/Excluded.** The number of addresses currently unavailable for leasing. This number is the total number of active leases, excluded addresses, and reserved addresses.

Note No direct way exists for determining the number of active leases. To determine the number of active leases, record the total number of active/excluded addresses. Then check the Show Reservations Only box to determine the number of reserved addresses. Subtract the number of reservations from the total of active/excluded addresses to determine the number of nonreserved leases. Then subtract the number of excluded addresses, which you must determine from the scope properties.

- **Available.** This is the number of addresses the DHCP server has available for clients.
- **Client.** The NetBIOS name and the leased address of the computers that have obtained DHCP lease.
- **Sort Order.** Determines how the leases shown will be sorted either by IP address or by name.
- **Show Reservations Only.** Whether normal DHCP leases should be displayed along with DHCP reservations.

When a DHCP client restarts, the events that take place depend on whether the client holds a lease to an IP address.

- If the DHCP client does not hold an address lease, it enters an initializing state in which it attempts to obtain an address lease.
- If the DHCP client holds a lease to an address, it sends a message to DHCP declaring its configuration. A DHCP server must confirm this information if the client is to continue using the lease. If the DHCP server sends a negative reply, the client must enter an initializing state and acquire a new lease.

Usually, a client is permitted to retain its IP address assignment and can use the same address indefinitely. Changes in scope properties can force the DHCP client to accept a new IP address lease when it restarts.

Note When a client starts TCP/IP, it transmits an ARP request frame to determine whether the IP address is active on the network. If it is discovered that another host is using the IP address, TCP/IP is not started and the client reports an error message. You must resolve the conflict before attempting to restart the client. In the case of DHCP, use **IPCONFIG /RENEW** to force the station to a initialization state.

Modifying Properties for an Active Lease

If you wish to view or modify the properties for a lease, select the lease in the Active Leases dialog box and choose Properties. The Client Properties dialog box opens (see fig. 11.8).

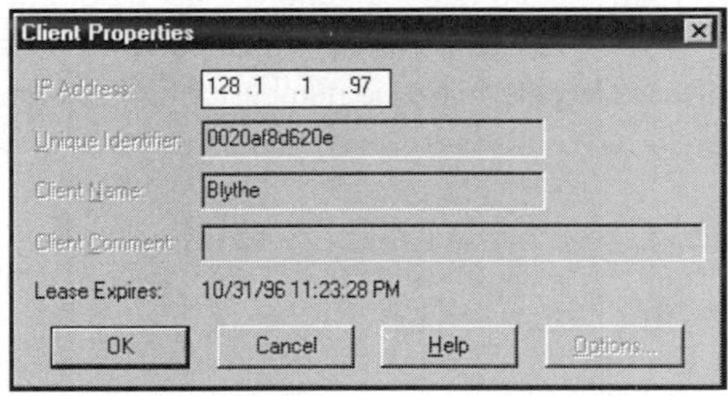

Figure 11.8
Modifying a client configuration.

For leases assigned from a scope address pool, you cannot modify any fields in the Client Properties dialog box. If the lease has been assigned to a reserved address, however, you can modify the following three fields:

- Unique Identifier
- Client Name
- Client Comment

You cannot modify the IP Address field. If you need to change the IP address reserved for the client, you must delete the current reservation and create a new one. You must also force the client to release and renew its old address, which you do by executing the command **IPCONFIG/RENEW** at a command prompt on the client computer. Windows 95 users can run the WINIPCFG command at a Run prompt and choose the Renew button to accomplish the same result.

Deleting Active Leases

Deleting an active lease is not quite what it appears. Selecting a lease in the Active Leases dialog box and choosing Delete removes the lease from the display but leaves the client free to use the lease for the duration of the current session.

The client is not forced off the network but continues to use the IP address until the client is restarted. The next time it restarts, the client enters a renewing state. DHCP denies the client's request to renew the lease on its old address. This forces the DHCP client into a rebinding state, in which the client requests a new address lease from DHCP.

Note Do not delete an active lease when a client is logged on using that lease. The client can continue to use the IP address until it logs off the network. The IP address, on the other hand, is returned to the pool of available addresses and can be leased by other DHCP clients. As a result, two active clients might find themselves sharing the same IP address.

To force a client to release its current lease and free up its IP address, enter the command **IPCONFIG /RELEASE** at the command prompt of the client. Windows 95 users should run the WINIPCFG program at a Run prompt and choose Release. Doing so forfeits the client's IP address and effectively disconnects it from the network. Restarting the client and logging back in to the network to obtain a new IP address is necessary.

Establishing Reservations

In some cases, it is important that a client always obtains the same IP address, but it remains advantageous to manage the other IP configuration properties through DHCP. To support clients that require fixed addresses, you can specify reservations in DHCP Manager. Essentially a reservation consists of an IP address and associated properties, keyed to the physical (MAC) address of a specific computer. Only that computer can obtain a lease for the IP address.

You can configure all computers to obtain their addresses from DHCP, except for computers running DHCP server services or WINS server services. Here are some examples of situations that might require reserved IP addresses:

- ◆ A constant address is required, such as the address of a default gateway or a DNS server.
- ◆ A domain controller obtains its address from an LMHOSTS file.
- ◆ A host does not obtain its address from DHCP, and address conflicts must be prevented.

To define a reservation, the physical address of the client must be determined. After TCP/IP protocols are installed on a computer, either of the following procedures can be used to identify the physical address:

- ◆ Enable the computer as a DHCP client and have it obtain a lease to an address in any active scope. Then view the properties for the client as described in the section "Viewing and Managing Active Leases," earlier in this chapter. One of those properties is the host's physical address. You can copy this address to the Clipboard by selecting it and pressing CTRL+C (shortcut for Edit, Copy). This makes pasting the address into the reservation properties easy.
- ◆ At the client host, open an MS-DOS prompt and enter the command **IPCONFIG/ALL**. One of the items in the resulting list reports the physical address of the computer. The Windows 95 WINIPCFG utility displays similar data. Run WINIPCFG from the Run command in the Start menu.

To create a reservation, perform the following steps:

1. Start DHCP Manager.
2. In the DHCP Servers dialog box, select the scope in which to define the reservation.
3. Choose Add Reservations in the Scope menu to open the Add Reserved Clients dialog box (see fig. 11.9).

Figure 11.9

Adding a DHCP-reserved address.

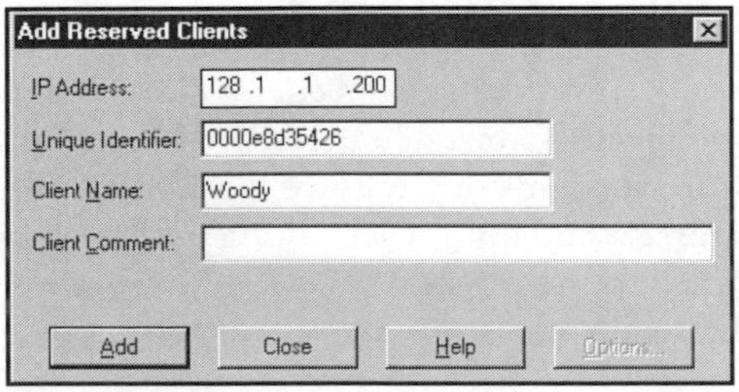

Add Reserved Clients

IP Address: 128 .1 .1 .200

Unique Identifier: 0000e8d35426

Client Name: Woody

Client Comment:

Add | Close | Help | Options...

4. In the IP Address field, enter the IP address to be reserved. This address must fall within the range of available and non-excluded addresses of the scope selected in step 2.
5. In the Unique Identifier field, enter the physical address of the client for which the address is being reserved. This address is often reported with punctuation such as 00-00-6e-44-9f-4f. Do not, however, include any punctuation in the Unique Identifier field. If you copied the address of the computer to the Clipboard, you can paste it by selecting the Unique Identifier field and pressing CTRL+V (shortcut for Paste).
6. Enter the client's name in the Client Name field.
7. If you want, enter a description in the Client Comment field.
8. Choose Add to store the reservation.

Reservations are listed in the Active Leases dialog box. As figure 11.10 shows, reserved leases are identified with the label "Reservation" and state the reserved IP address.

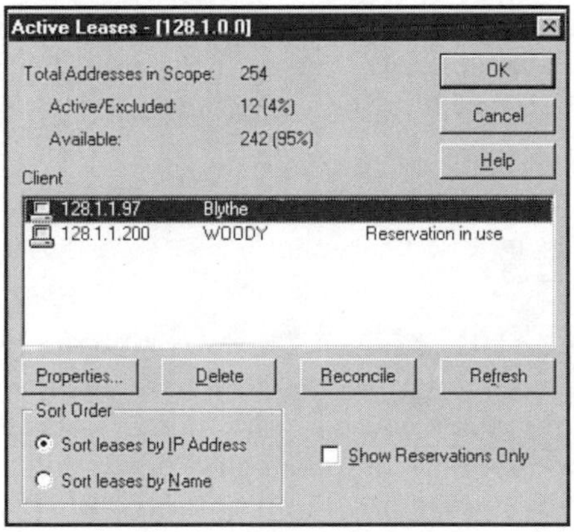

Figure 11.10

A DHCP scope showing a reservation.

Note

Assigning a reservation to a client currently connected using an address leased from a scope does not force the client to release its current lease and obtain the reserved IP address. Instead, the client's current lease is deleted (expired), forcing the client to obtain a new address lease the next time it connects with the network. At that time, the client obtains the IP address reserved for it.

As with deleting active leases, therefore, you should add a reservation only after the client has released its current lease. Otherwise duplicate IP addresses can be assigned to the original client and to a new client that leases the address.

Activating, Deactivating, and Deleting Scopes

Scopes may be active or inactive. An active scope services DHCP requests and is indicated in DHCP Manager by an illuminated (yellow) light bulb icon to the left of the scope name. An inactive scope does not service DHCP requests and is indicated by a darkened (gray) light bulb icon to the left of the scope name.

If you wish to deactivate an active scope, select the scope in DHCP Manager and choose Deactivate in the Scope menu. To reactivate it, select the scope in DHCP Manager and choose Activate in the Scope menu.

If you need to delete a scope, you must first deactivate the scope. Then choose Delete in the Scope menu.

After a scope is deactivated or deleted, currently logged-on clients can continue to utilize the address leases assigned to them. When a client restarts or must renew an expired lease, it must obtain a lease from a different scope.

After deactivating or deleting a scope, you can force a DHCP client to obtain a lease from another scope by entering the command **IPCONFIG/RENEW** at a command prompt on the client. It might be necessary to restart the client. The Windows 95 WINIPCFG program provides a Renew button that accomplishes the same task.

Managing Leases

One of the key issues in running a DHCP server is to determine the length of the lease. Although it is an option, it is strongly recommended that you not use the Unlimited option. This means that the client never has to renew its address, and therefore will never update the configuration parameters. If you will be using an Unlimited lease period, think about including the IPCONFIG/RENEW command in the network logon scripts.

In a case where the network configuration changes frequently, choose fairly short lease times so that addresses that become available can be reassigned quickly and so that the TCP/IP parameters are updated often.

After a client lease expires, it remains in the DHCP database for approximately one day. The DHCP client can attempt to renew its old lease within that period. The delay accommodates DHCP clients and servers in different time zones or those that don't have synchronized clocks.

The Active Leases dialog box reports the sum of active and excluded addresses for the scope selected.

Managing Multiple DHCP Servers

A network can support any desired number of DHCP servers. Multiple DHCP servers enable DHCP address assignment to continue if one of the DHCP servers fails. Unfortunately, having redundant DHCP servers for the same scope is impossible. DHCP does not provide a mechanism that enables DHCP servers to exchange information regarding which addresses have been leased and which are open. If any IP addresses appear in the scope definitions for two DHCP servers, therefore, duplicate IP addresses might be assigned.

One way around this, suggested by Microsoft, is to split the pool of DHCP addresses into two. This way, you can place most of the addresses (75 percent of the range) on the DHCP server closest to the subnet, and the rest on another server.

All DHCP servers can be managed centrally by a manager who has Administrator permissions for the servers. To add a DHCP server to the DHCP Manager, perform the following steps:

1. Start DHCP Manager.
2. In the Server menu, choose Add.
3. In the Add DHCP Server to Server List dialog box, enter the IP address of the DHCP server that you want to add.
4. Click OK.

Managing the DHCP Database

The key DHCP database files are stored by default in C:\winnt\system32\dhcp. (If your system files are stored in a directory other than C:\WINNT, substitute the appropriate directory path). The files you will find are as follows:

- **DHCP.MDB.** The DHCP database file.
- **DHCP.TMP.** A file used by DHCP to store temporary working data.
- **JET.LOG and JET*.LOG.** These files record transactions performed on the database. You can use this data to recover the DHCP database in the event of damage.
- **SYSTEM.MDB.** Holds information about the structure of the DHCP database.

Caution Do not attempt to open these files. Because these are database files, opening the file while the DHCP server is running can easily lead to file corruption.

Windows NT Server periodically backs up the DHCP database and Registry entries. The default backup interval is 15 minutes, configurable using a Registry key.

Compacting the DHCP Database

Windows NT 4 automatically compacts the DHCP database from time to time, making it seldom necessary to compact the database manually. If you are running DHCP on Windows NT Server 3.51 or earlier, however, you must compact the database manually. Microsoft recommends compacting DHCP.MDB when it reaches 10 MB in size. To compact the database, follow this procedure:

1. Open a command prompt.
2. Enter the command **NET STOP DHCPSERVER** to stop the DHCP Server service on the computer. Users cannot obtain or renew DHCP leases while the DHCP Server service is stopped. (You can also stop the service using the Services icon in the Control Panel.)
3. Change to the DHCP directory. If the directory is in the default location, enter the command **CD \WINNT\SYSTEM32\DHCP**.
4. Enter the command **JETPACK DHCP.MDB TEMP.MDB** to compact the database. DHCP.MDB is the file to be compacted, and TEMP.MDB is a name for a temporary file that JETPACK uses during the compacting process.
5. After receiving the message JETPACK completed successfully, restart DHCP with the command **NET START DHCPSERVER** (or the Services icon).
6. To close the command prompt, enter the command **EXIT**.

You can use JETPACK to compact only the DHCP.MDB file. Do not compact the SYSTEM.MDB file, period, per Microsoft, because this is encrypted, and could become corrupted easily.

Starting and Stopping the DHCP Server

You might need to periodically stop and restart the DHCP server. You might also need to determine whether DHCP Server services are started. If users experience difficulty obtaining addresses from DHCP, the first troubleshooting step is to make certain that the DHCP Server service is started.

As explained in the previous section, you can start and stop the DHCP Server service from the command prompt. You can also use the Server Manager from the Administrative Tools group on the Start menu. Using the Server Manager, you can start and stop services not only on your system but also on other computers in your network.

Using the Server Manager involves the following steps:

1. From the Start menu, choose Programs, Administrative Tools, and run the Server Manager.
2. Select the Server you want to start or stop the service on and choose Computer, Services from the menu.
3. Scroll through the list of services to locate the entry Microsoft DHCP Server. The status of the server is described by entries in two columns:
   - The Status column states whether the service is started. If no entry is found, the service is not started.
   - The Startup column indicates whether the service starts automatically when the system restarts. Automatic and Manual indicate whether manual intervention is required to start the service. You cannot start a disabled service from the Services dialog box.
4. To change the startup mode for a service, choose Startup and change the Startup Type in the Services dialog box.
5. To stop a started service, select the service and choose Stop. To start a stopped service, select the service and choose Start.
6. Choose Close to close the list of Services, and choose Computer, Exit to close the Server Manager.

Repairing a Corrupted DHCP Database

The DHCP database files are backed up at periodic intervals. The default location for the backup copies of the database files is the directory C:\winnt\system32\dhcp\backup\jet.

If the DHCP Server service is started but users still cannot obtain leases from DHCP, the DHCP database might have become corrupted, which would make DHCP unavailable. Restoring the DHCP database from the backup copy might be possible. To force DHCP to restore its database from the backup, stop and restart the DHCP Server service, using the techniques described in the preceding two sections. If the DHCP Server service identifies a corrupted database during startup, it automatically attempts to restore from the backup database.

The section entitled "Configuring DHCP in the Registry," later in this chapter, discusses the RestoreFlag key in the Registry. You can set this key to force DHCP to restore its database when the computer is restarted.

If neither procedure restores the database satisfactorily, stop the DHCP Server service. Then copy all files in C:\winnt\system32\dhcp\backup to C:\winnt\system32\dhcp. Finally, restart the DHCP Server service.

After you restore the database, you need to bring the database up to date on active leases not recorded in the backup copy of the database. This procedure is called "reconciling the DHCP database." To reconcile the DHCP database, follow these steps:

1. Start DHCP Manager.
2. Select a scope in the DHCP Scopes dialog box.
3. Choose Active Leases in the Scope menu.
4. Click the Reconcile button in the Active Leases dialog box.

Note The DHCP database is not fault-tolerant, even though it is periodically backed up. A system crash during the backup process can corrupt both the database and the backup database.

Creating a New DHCP Database

If the database is corrupted and a valid backup is unavailable, you can force DHCP to create a new database by performing the following steps:

1. Stop the DHCP Server service.
2. Copy the file C:\winnt\system32\dhcp\dhcp.mdb to another directory.
3. Delete all files in the directory C:\winnt\system32\dhcp (the default primary directory).
4. Delete all files in the directory C:\winnt\system32\dhcp\backup\jet (the default backup directory).
5. Copy the file System.mdb from the installation CD-ROM or disks to the directory C:\winnt\system32\dhcp.
6. Restart the DHCP Server service. The following four steps reconcile the new DHCP database with active leases.
7. Start DHCP Manager.
8. Select a scope in the DHCP Scopes dialog box.
9. Choose Active Leases in the Scope menu.
10. Choose the Reconcile button in the Active Leases dialog box. When they renew their leases, clients are matched with active leases to complete rebuilding the database.

Note You can force a client to renew its DHCP lease by entering the command **IPCONFIG /RENEW** at a command prompt on the client computer. With Windows 95, choose the Renew button in the WINIPCFG utility, which you can start by entering the command **WINIPCFG** in a Run dialog box.

DHCP Configuration Options

ective
3.3

Your organization might choose to implement DHCP even though IP addresses are not assigned dynamically. DHCP options enable network administrators to configure many settings that affect the TCP/IP protocols (see fig. 11.11). These DHCP options can be applied to any computer that obtains its address from DHCP, whether the address is dynamically allocated or reserved.

- Global options apply to all scopes on a given DHCP server unless overwritten by scope or client options.
- Scope options apply to all clients within the scope unless overridden by client options. Scope properties might be used to set options for a department or for hosts on a specific network.
- Client options supersede scope and global options for a specific client. You can configure client-specific options for clients having DHCP reservations.

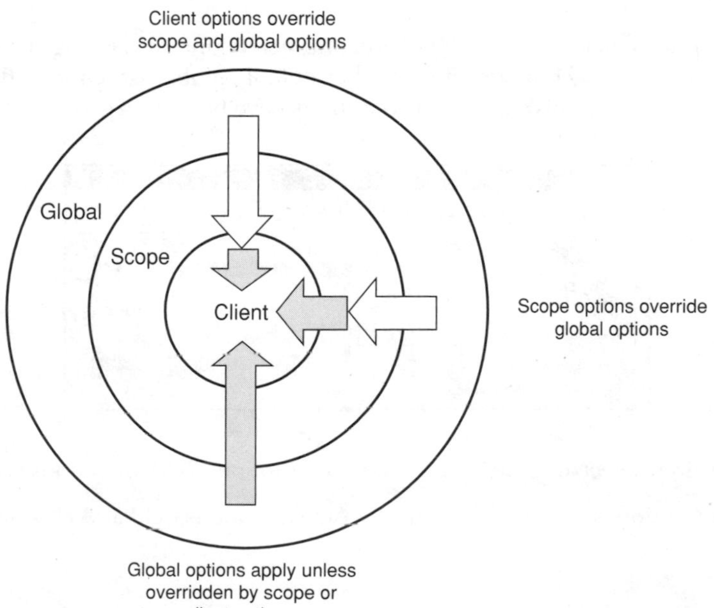

Figure 11.11

Priority of DHCP options.

Specifying default options is another possibility. Specifying a default option establishes default values for any parameters associated with the option, but does not put the option into effect. Options go into effect only when specified as global, scope, or client options.

A Microsoft DHCP packet can support a DHCP data payload of 312 bytes, which is generally sufficient. If too many DHCP options are configured, some can exceed the 312-byte capacity, making it necessary to trim options of lower priority.

Managing Default, Global, and Scope DHCP Options

Options are added, configured, and removed within DHCP Manager. Default, global, and scope options are managed from the DHCP Manager dialog box. To change options, follow these steps:

1. Start DHCP Manager.
2. Select an existing scope.
3. To set default parameter values for an option, choose the Default command in the DHCP Options menu.

   To set options for all scopes on the DHCP server, choose the Global command in the DHCP Options menu.

   To set options for the selected scope, choose the Scope command in the DHCP Options menu.
4. The DHCP Options dialog box is used to add and delete options (see fig. 11.12). The legend for the dialog box specifies whether default, global, or scope options are being configured. In this example, two options have been added.

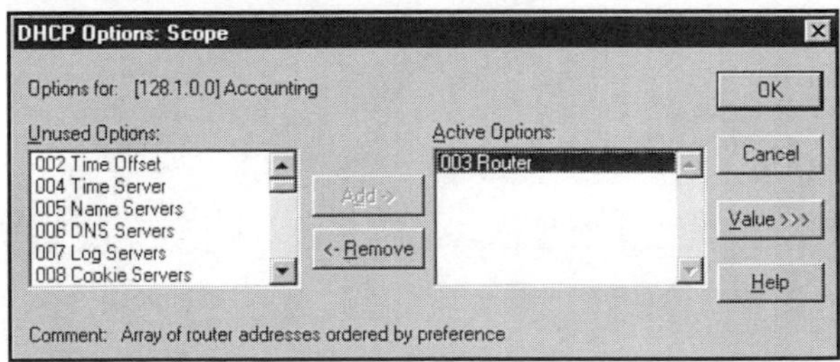

Figure 11.12
The DHCP Options dialog box.

5. To add an option, select an option in the Unused Options field and choose Add.
6. To remove an option, select an option in the Active Options field and choose Remove.

7. Many options accept or require configuration values. To change the values of an option, select the option in the Active Options field and choose Value. The DHCP Options dialog box expands to display the currently assigned value or values (see fig. 11.13).

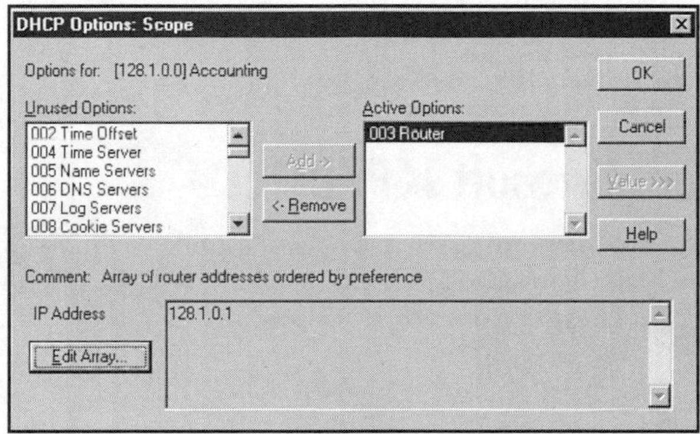

Figure 11.13
After you choose the values button, you can enter values.

8. If required, you can choose Edit Array. An appropriate editor opens. Figure 11.14 shows the IP Address Array Editor dialog box. In this box, you can add or remove values from the array of addresses. (The order of the options determines their priority, and values should be added in order of priority.)

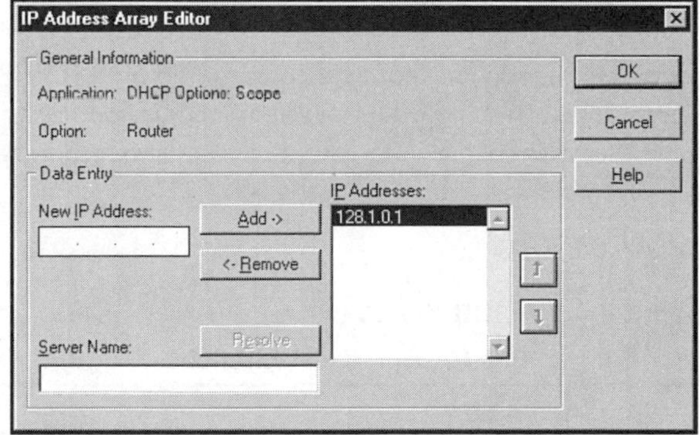

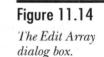

Figure 11.14
The Edit Array dialog box.

Managing Client-Specific Options for Reservations

You can assign client-specific options to reservations only. You can only assign options to leases by assigning default, global, and scope options.

To assign options to a reservation, follow these steps:

1. Select the scope supporting the reservation in the DHCP Manager dialog box.
2. Choose the Active Leases command in the Scope menu.

3. Select the reservation in the Active Leases dialog box and choose the Properties button to open the Client Properties dialog box.
4. For reservations, the Options button in the Client Properties dialog box is active. Choose Options to open the DHCP Options: Reservation dialog box, which is similar to the dialog box shown in figure 11.12. Use this box to add and configure options for the reservation.
5. Choose OK to exit the DHCP Options dialog box.

DHCP Options for Microsoft TCP/IP

Table 11.1 summarizes the most common DHCP options applied to Microsoft TCP/IP clients. Several RFC1533 DHCP options are configured in the Create Scope or Scope Properties dialog box. These options are as follows:

- 1. Subnet mask
- 51. DHCP Lease time
- 58. DHCP Renewal (T1) time
- 59. DHCP Rebinding (T2) time

Options 51, 58, and 59 are all functions of the lease duration specified in the Create Scope or Scope Properties dialog box.

Note RFC1533 specifies many other options not applicable to Microsoft TCP/IP clients. If non-Microsoft clients will be obtaining addresses from the Microsoft DHCP Server, you can include non-Microsoft options in the properties of the appropriate scopes and reservations.

Table 11.1
DHCP Options for Microsoft Clients

Code	Name	Description
1	Subnet Mask	Specifies the client subnet mask. This option is configured in the Create Scope or Scope Properties dialog box and cannot be directly configured as a scope option.
3	Router	Specifies a list of IP addresses for routers on the client's network.

Code	Name	Description
6	DNS servers	Specifies a list of IP addresses for available DNS servers.
15	Domain name	Specifies the domain name to be used when resolving DNS host names.
44	WINS/NBNS	Specifies a list of IP addresses for NetBIOS name servers (NBNS).
46	WINS/NBT	Specifies the NetBIOS over TCP/IP node type. Values: 1=b-node, 2=p-node, 4-m-node, 8=h-node.
47	NetBIOS ID	Specifies a string to be used as the NetBIOS over CP/IP scope ID.

Configuring DHCP in the Registry

The Registry is a database in which configuration data is stored for Windows NT computers. Several Registry parameters are related to DHCP and can, like other Registry parameters, be modified using the Registry Editor.

Caution The Registry includes configuration data for virtually every part of the Windows NT system. Obviously, a great deal of damage can be done if errors are introduced into the Registry. Therefore, when browsing the Registry with the Registry Editor, you should choose Read Only Mode in the Options menu to prevent accidental changes. If your Registry becomes corrupted, and you do not have a backup, you will have to re-install the operating system.

The Registry is organized into four subtrees. Each of the subtrees has a window within Registry Editor (see to fig. 11.15). The following list delineates the subtrees:

- **HKEY_LOCAL_MACHINE.** Current configuration parameters for the computer. This is the main Registry subtree.
- **HKEY_CURRENT_USER.** The profile for the current user. The information here is also stored in HKEY_USERS.
- **HKEY_USERS.** Stores user profiles for the currently logged-on user, and the default user.

- **HKEY_CLASSES_ROOT.** Performs object linking and embedding (OLE) and file class associations. This is also under HKEY_LOCAL_MACHINE\SOFTWARE\CLASSES.

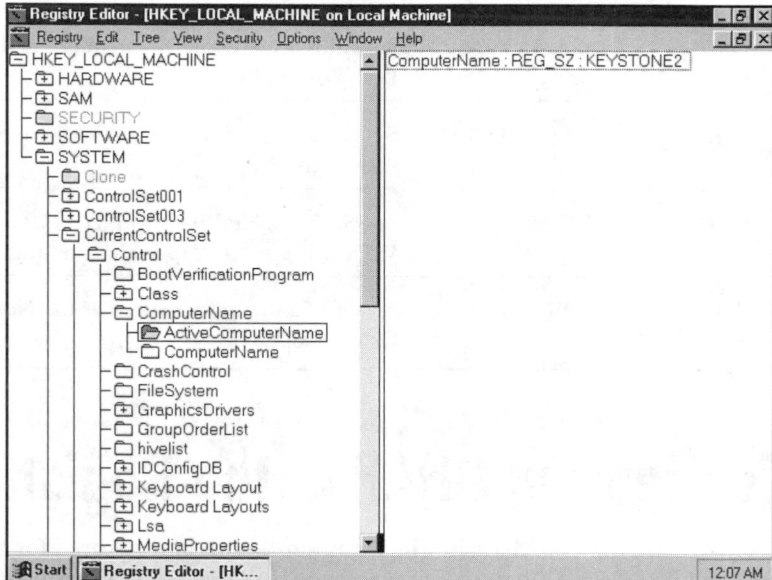

Figure 11.15

The Windows NT Registry.

Data associated with DHCP are stored in the HKEY_LOCAL_MACHINE subtree. The window for this subtree has been expanded in figure 11.15 to show the database structure. Note the similarity between the structure of the Registry and of the NT hierarchical file system. The equivalents of the directory in the Registry database are called keys. Data stored in Registry keys are called values.

Keys can contain other keys. In figure 11.15, for example, SYSTEM is a key that contains several subkeys such as ControlSet001 and CurrentControlSet.

In figure 11.15, the CurrentControlSet branch has been opened for several levels, revealing the ComputerName key. This key contains one value, describing the NetBIOS name assigned to this computer. Keys can contain an indefinite number of values. All values have the following three components:

- A name, in this example, ComputerName
- A data type, such as REG_SZ
- A value, here, KEYSTONE2

Registry data has one of the following five data types:

- **REG_BINARY.** Raw binary data, the form used to store most hardware data.
- **REG_DWORD.** Numeric data up to 4 bytes in length, in decimal, hexadecimal, or binary form.
- **REG_EXPAND_SZ.** Expandable data strings that contain system variables. An example of this variable type is %SystemRoot\system32.
- **REG_MULTI_SZ.** Data consisting of multiple strings in lists. Often used to store lists of human-readable values.
- **REG_SZ.** Character data, usually human-readable text.

The data types that apply to DHCP Registry entries are discussed along with the associated values. See the section titled "DHCP-Related Registry Values" later in this chapter.

Viewing and Editing DHCP-Related Values in the Registry

DHCP-related Registry values are stored in the HKEY_LOCAL_MACHINE subtree in the following subkey:

SYSTEM\CurrentControlSet\Services\DHCPServer\Parameters

To observe or modify the DHCP Registry values, follow these steps:

1. To start the Registry Editor, choose the Run command in the Program Manager File menu. In the Command Line field for the Run command, enter the command **regedt32** and click OK.
2. If no subtrees are shown, choose the Open Local command in the Registry menu.
3. Expand the window for the HKEY_LOCAL_MACHINE subtree.

   Click the following keys to expand the appropriate branch of the tree:

   - SYSTEM
   - CurrentControlSet
   - Services
   - DHCPServer
   - Parameters

   Completed, the window resembles that shown in figure 11.16.

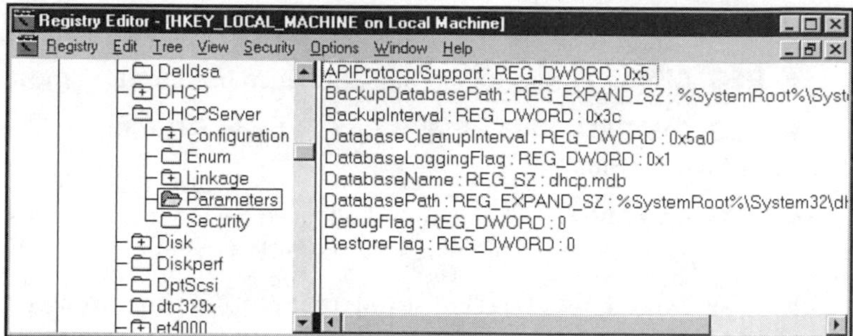

Figure 11.16

DHCP values in the Registry.

4. To change a value, double-click the value entry to open the appropriate editor. The editor that appears supports entry only of data that conform to the data type associated with this value. The example shown in figure 11.17 shows the DWORD editor, which accepts only a binary, decimal, or hexadecimal value. A String Editor is used to enter string-type values.

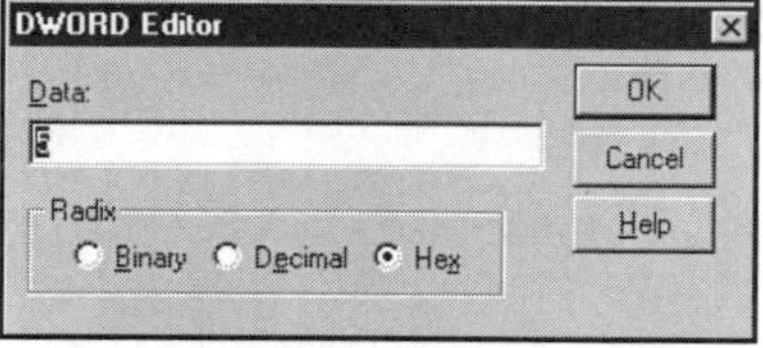

Figure 11.17

One of the Registry Editing dialog boxes (DWORD in this case).

Edit the value and, if necessary, click the button associated with the data format. Then choose OK to save the value to the Registry.

5. To save changes, choose Close in the Registry menu.

DHCP-Related Registry Values

This section lists each of the Registry values and describes their specifications in detail. You can view and edit them by using the procedure described in the preceding section.

APIProtocolSupport

Data Type:	REG_DWORD
Range:	0x1, 0x2, 0x4, 0x5, 0x7
Default:	0x7

The APIProtocolSupport value specifies the protocols supported by the DHCP server. Edit this parameter to allow different computers to access the DHCP server. Available values are as follows:

0x1	RPC over TCP/IP
0x2	RPC over named pipes
0x4	RPC over local procedure call (LPC)
0x5	RPC over TCP/IP and RPC over LPC
0x7	RPC over TCP/IP, named pipes, and LPC

BackupDatabasePath

Data Type:	REG_EXPAND_SZ
Range:	path name
Default:	%SystemRoot%\system32\dhcp\backup

Using BackupDatabasePath, you can specify the directory in which DHCP backup files are stored. The default value places the backup files on the same hard drive as the primary files, making both vulnerable to a single hardware failure. If the system has more than one hard drive, locating the backup directory on an alternative hard drive is preferable. This directory must be on a local hard drive because DHCP Manager cannot access a network drive.

BackupInterval

Data Type:	REG_DWORD
Range:	no limit
Default:	15 minutes

This option sets the interval in minutes between DHCP database backups.

DatabaseCleanupInterval

Data Type:	REG_DWORD
Range:	no limit
Default:	0x15180

DHCP periodically cleans up the database, removing expired records. This parameter specifies the interval in minutes between DHCP cleanup operations. The default value sets an interval of one day (0x15180 is 86,400 seconds, equivalent to 24 hours).

DatabaseLoggingFlag

Data Type:	REG_DWORD
Range:	0 or 1
Default:	1

If the value of this parameter is 1, database changes are recorded in the JET.LOG file. If the value is 0, changes are not recorded. The JET.LOG file is used to recover changes that have not been made to the database file. It might be desirable to turn off logging to improve system performance.

DatabaseName

Data Type:	REG_SZ
Range:	file name
Default:	dhcp.mdb

This value is just the name of the DHCP database file.

DatabasePath

Data Type:	REG_EXPAND_SZ
Range:	path name
Default:	%SystemRoot%\System32\dhcp

This tells the DHCP server in which directory database files are created and opened.

RestoreFlag

Data Type:	REG_DWORD
Range:	0 or 1
Default:	0

If this value is 0, the database is not restored from the backup database when the DHCP Server service is started. Set this value to 1 to force DHCP to retrieve the backup database. This parameter is automatically set to 0 after a successful database restoration.

DHCP Relay Agent

When you are working with multiple subnets, you must have some way of moving the DHCP request from subnet to subnet. In this chapter, you have seen that this is often left to the router. NT Server, however, also has a method.

In the configuration for the TCP/IP protocol is the DHCP Relay Agent tab discussed earlier. As shown in figure 11.18, the configuration is fairly straightforward. Before this configuration can take effect, however, you must install the service.

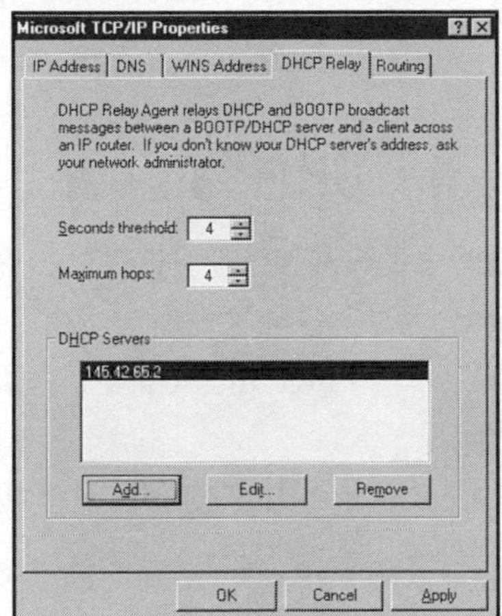

Figure 11.18

The DHCP Relay Agent configuration.

The installation is simple, just follow these steps:

1. Open the Network dialog box, and choose the Services tab.
2. Click Add and select the DHCP Relay Agent from the list.
3. Click OK and enter the directory for your source files.
4. Close the Network dialog box and restart your system.

The configuration options seen in figure 11.18 include the following:

- **Seconds.** Maximum time that it can take for the DHCP Relay Agent to contact the DHCP server
- **Hops.** Maximum number of hops that the Relay Agent can make to get to the DHCP server.
- **DHCP Servers.** The addresses of the DHCP servers on your network.

Using the DHCP Relay Agent enables you to disable the BOOTP relay in the routers. This can be beneficial because it restricts broadcast traffic to the local subnet. It should also be noted here that Relay Agent works with both BOOTP and DHCP requests.

Practice

In this lab, you install and configure a DHCP server. Because various readers will be using different networks, this lab does not require you to install a client. If you have multiple stations, please feel free to try this on a client.

If you do not have networking installed, see Exercise 0 from the lab for Chapter 9, "Internet Information Server."

Exercise 1—Installing the DHCP Server

1. Open the Network Settings dialog box. From the Services tab choose Add.
2. Select Microsoft DHCP Server and click OK.
3. Enter the path for your Windows NT source files. Close the Network Settings dialog box and restart your computer.
4. From the Start menu, choose Programs, Administrative Tools. Verify that the DHCP Manager is installed.

Exercise 2—Configuring a DHCP Scope

1. Start the DHCP Manger. Double-click the Local Machine to determine whether you are connected to it.
2. Choose Scope, Create from the menu. The Create Scope dialog box appears.
3. Enter the following information for the IP Address Pool:

Start Address	**148.53.66.1**
End Address	**148.53.127.254**
Subnet Mask	**255.255.192.0**

4. To add an exclusion, enter **148.53.90.0** into the Start Address and **148.53.90.255** in to the End Address. Click the Add button.
5. Leave the duration at default, and enter **"Test Subnet 1"** as the name. When everything is in, click OK.
6. A prompt appears for you to activate the scope. Choose Yes.

Exercise 3—Adding Scope and Global Options in the DHCP Server

1. Click the scope that was created in the preceding exercise.

Note If you get an error, click OK to continue. This is an undocumented feature (meaning, a bug). Close the DHCP Manager and reopen it to stop this.

2. From the menu, choose DHCP Options, Scope.
3. From the list of Unused Options, choose "003 Router" and click Add.
4. Click the Values button to see the rest of the dialog box. Currently no router is listed.
5. Choose Edit Array. In the dialog box that appears, enter **148.53.64.1** in the IP Address field. Click Add to add the address to the list.
6. Click OK to close the IP Address Array Editor, and then click OK to close the DHCP Options: Scope dialog box.

   The router option should appear in the Options Configuration panel.
7. Choose DHCP Options, Global from the menu, and add the following options:

   006 DNS Servers

   015 Domain Name

   044 WINS/NBNS Servers (You will get a message when you add this one.)

   046 WINS/NBT Node Type
8. After the options are in, add the configuration for them. Use the following values:

DNS Server	148.53.64.8
Domain Name	mcp.com
WINS/NBNS Servers	198.53.64.8
WINS/NBT Node Type	0x8
9. Click OK.

All the options should display in the Options Configuration panel.

Exercise 4—Configuring a Second DHCP Scope

1. Add another DHCP scope using the following values:

IP Address	Pool
Start Address	148.53.140.0
End Address	148.53.191.255
Subnet Mask	255.255.192.0

2. Set the lease duration for 14 days, and name the scope **"Test Subnet 2"**.

   There should be a number listed for each scope in the DHCP manager. The number given is the subnet ID for the scope. This scenario used a Class B address, which is split into two subnets, 148.53.64.0 and 148.53.128.0.

3. Set the default gateway for this scope to 148.53.128.1.
4. This scope will not be used immediately; therefore you will deactivate it. Do this by choosing Scope, Deactivate.

Exercise 5—Adding Client Reservations

1. Highlight the first subnet (148.53.64.0).
2. Choose Scope, Add Reservations from the menu.
3. In the Add Reserved Clients dialog box, change the IP address to 148.53.66.7.
4. Enter the unique identifier, **0000DE7342FA**, and enter the client name as **Rob**.
5. Click Add.
6. Enter the IP address **148.53.66.9**, with the unique identifier **00D4C9C57D34**. The client name is Judy. Click Add.
7. Choose Done.

Exercise 6—Checking the Information

From the menu, choose Scope, Active Leases.

Do you see the two reservations you entered in the preceding exercise?

If everything is all right, they should be listed.

How many total Addresses are there, and how many are Active/Excluded?

The total should be 15,870 with 258 being active or excluded.

Summary

This chapter has covered DHCP in general, its implementation, and its use. When you look at DHCP, remember the options that you can carry with the packet to the client. This capability to dynamically configure the hosts on the local subnet as well as remote make using TCP/IP relatively simple.

Test Yourself

1. What are the five possible broadcasts in the DHCP process?
2. Before a client can receive a DHCP address, what must be configured on the DHCP server?
3. To pass DHCP broadcasts, what must a router support?
4. What is the recommended method of providing backup to the DHCP server?
5. What is the effect of a lease duration of Unlimited?
6. In what environment is it advisable to have a short lease duration?
7. What portions of the DHCP process are initiated by the server?
8. How must an NT server be configured before you install a DHCP server?
9. What information is required to define a scope?
10. Which clients can use a DHCP server?
11. How do you configure a client to use DHCP?
12. What is the difference between a global and a scope option?
13. Why would you use a client reservation?
14. What is required for a client reservation?
15. What happens to the client if you delete its lease?
16. What must you do before compacting the database? What is the command to compact the database?
17. How can a client see the information about the DHCP lease?

Test Yourself Answers

1. The five broadcasts are DHCPDISCOVER, DHCPOFFER, DHCPREQUEST, DHCPACK, and DHCPNACK.
2. The server must have scope that is valid for the client's subnet.
3. Routers need to support BOOTP relay (as defined in RFC1542).
4. On the main server for a subnet, you configure the server with 75 percent of the addresses and on another server you configure 25 percent of the addresses.
5. The client will never need to renew its lease, and therefore will never update the configuration parameters.

6. In situations where the network frequently changes, if your environment is extremely dynamic, you should use a short lease duration.
7. None. The client initiates all steps in the DHCP process.
8. The server needs to have at least one network adapter configured with a static IP address.
9. You need to have a series of IP addresses, a subnet mask, and to know the duration you wish to use.
10. DHCP clients include Windows NT, Windows 95, Windows for Workgroups with the TCP/IP protocol from the NT server CD-ROM, MS Client 3.0 for MS-DOS (and Windows 3.1), and MS-LAN Manager Client 2.2c for DOS.
11. In most cases, you choose Obtain IP Address Automatically. For Windows for Workgroups (and NT 3.51) select Enable Automatic DHCP Configuration. For the DOS clients, run setup, and for the TCP/IP protocol choose DHCP configuration.
12. Global options affect all the scopes on the server; scope options affect only the single scope. The DNS server address is an example of the global options, and router is an example of a scope option.
13. In a case where the system is required to have a static IP address but you want to be able to dynamically update the other parameters, you can use a client reservation.
14. You need the unique MAC address for the client.
15. Nothing happens until the client attempts to renew. At that point, the server sends a DHCPNACK, and the client begins the DHCP process all over.
16. Before you can compact the DHCP database, you need to stop the DHCP service. You compact the database by using JETPACK DHCP.MDB TEMP.MDB, which you run in the \%winroot%\system32\dhcp directory.
17. By using the IPCONFIG /ALL, the client can see all the information relating to DHCP.

PART III

NetBIOS Over TCP/IP

12 NetBIOS Name Resolution 235

13 The Windows Internet Name Service 257

14 The Browser Service and TCP/IP 299

CHAPTER 12

NetBIOS Name Resolution

As you have seen, there are really two different ways that computers will be communicating over Microsoft TCP/IP. This book has already discussed WinSock and NetBIOS, and hopefully you are understanding the differences. One of the main differences is that NetBIOS networking requires the use of NetBIOS computer names. This chapter is going to provide you with the details on name resolution.

Name resolution is quite simply the process of taking a NetBIOS name and providing the underlying transport (TCP or UDP) with the TCP/IP addresses for that name. The tricky part is that you must use the underlying transport to find out what the name is.

When you work with Microsoft networking, each computer and each user has a name, and so will the users. The names that can be used are 15 characters in length with an additional character that defines the type of name, making the total 16 characters. Just as you use port numbers when working with the WinSock interface, you use this sixteenth character to provide an end point for the communication. Table 12.1 summarizes some of the common name types showing what the sixteenth character would be for these services—the values are in hex.

TABLE 12.1
NetBIOS Name Types

Common NetBIOS Names	Service That Registers the Name
<computer name>[00h]	Workstation (your NetBIOS Redirector)
<computer name>[03h]	Messenger (listens for messages sent to the computer)
<computer name>[20h]	Server (Shares your resources to the network)
<user name>[03h]	Messenger (listens for messages sent to your logon ID)
<domain name>[1Dh]	Master Browser (see Chapter 14, "The Browser Service and TCP/IP")
<domain name>[1Bh]	Domain Master Browser (see Chapter 14)

As your system starts up, or even as you log on, the computer you are working at must register the name(s) that you are using on the network. This is done in one of two ways: by broadcasting a Name Registration or sending a Name Registration to a NetBIOS Name Server. These are, of course, handled by WinSock (all TCP/IP communications use WinSock) over the NetBIOS Name Service port—UDP port 137. This port is normally disabled on routers, relieving the routers of the need to pass broadcast traffic (also known as noise).

The NetBIOS Name Service port handles the following four main functions:

- **Name Registration.** This occurs whenever a system starts up, or even when a new user logs on. This is verifying that the names that need to be unique are in fact unique (computer and user names) on the network.
- **Name Query.** When you want to connect to another computer across the network, your system has to be capable of finding that computer. In the case of TCP/IP, this requires that you have the IP address. The Name Query is sent on the network (like the ARP packet that will follow), requesting a response from the computer that has this name registered. The current limit for registered NetBIOS names on a single computer is 250.
- **Positive Name Query Response.** As implied, this is the response to the Name Query that was just described. Note that the Name Query packet that was sent as a broadcast packet is received and accepted by every host on the local network. Each passes the packet up to IP, which passes it to UDP, which passes it to the NetBIOS Name Service port. This means that every computer needs to spend CPU time checking to see whether the queried name is one of theirs.

- **Name Release.** As you shut down your system, a Name Release broadcast is sent on the wire. This informs hosts with which you are communicating that you are shutting down. Notably though, this releases your user name that is also registered. By doing this, there will not be problem with duplicate names should you log on at a different workstation.

Note To view the NetBIOS names registered on your computer, use **"NBTSTAT -n"**. (The "n" is case-sensitive.)

Methods of Name Resolution

Objective E.3

Six different methods of NetBIOS name resolution are available to Windows NT. The following list shows each of these methods:

- NetBIOS Name Cache
- The LMHOSTS file
- Broadcast
- NetBIOS Name Server
- The HOSTS file
- A DNS Server

NetBIOS Name Cache

The NetBIOS name cache is an area of memory that contains a list of NetBIOS computer names and the associated IP address. The address in the Name Cache can get there one of two ways: you have resolved that address or the address was preloaded. The Name Cache provides a quick reference to IP addresses that will be used frequently.

The NetBIOS Name Cache, however, cannot keep every address on your network. In fact the NetBIOS cache (again like ARP) keeps entries for a short period of time only—10 minutes by default. The exception is preloaded entries (discussed in the following section, "The LMHOSTS File"), which remain in cache.

You cannot directly modify the NetBIOS name cache. You can, however, add preloaded entries in the LMHOSTS file. If you do this (or if you wish to clear the Name Cache), use **"NBTSTAT -R"**—again, the "R" is case-sensitive. This purges and reloads the Name Cache. If you wish to view the resolved names, you can use **"NBTSTAT -r"**. (Now you see why it is case-sensitive.)

You should be aware of a couple of Registry entries that affect the way the Name Cache works. The entries are found under

```
HKEY_LOCAL_MACHINE\SYSTEM\CurrentControlSet\Services\NetBT\Parameters
```

The entries are as follows:

- **Size: Small/Medium/Large.** Determines the number of names kept in the Name Cache. The settings are Small (1 maintains only 16 names), Medium (2 maintains 64 names), or Large (3 holds 128 names). The default is 1. This is sufficient for most client stations.
- **CacheTimeout.** The time in milliseconds that an entry remains in cache. The default is 927c0 (hex) or 600,000 (which is 10 minutes).

Broadcast

If the name cannot be found in the NetBIOS Name Cache, the system attempts to find the name by using a broadcast on the local network. Broadcast is a necessary evil. Although it takes up bandwidth, in many cases it is the simplest way to move the information.

NetBIOS Name Queries use UDP to send a packet to each and every computer on the local network. Every computer must then take the packet and pass it all the way up the protocol stack to NetBIOS so that the name can be checked against the local name table. Some of the problems with this system are the overload of traffic on the network, and CPU cycles wasted on checking names that don't exist.

UDP handles the broadcasts for NetBIOS names, specifically on ports 137 and 138. The problem is that these ports are normally blocked at the router, so Name Queries never pass the router, and this form of resolution doesn't work on an internetwork.

You are going to see methods that enable you to resolve names without broadcast traffic. It should be noted that broadcasts are a throwback to the early days of networks where the computers were slower, and the bandwidth of the networks was more than enough to cover the occasional broadcast.

You can use a couple of Registry entries to customize the Broadcast function. These entries are under

```
HKEY_LOCAL_MACHINE\SYSTEM\CurrentControlSet\Services\NetBT\Parameters
```

The entries are as follows:

- **BcastNameQueryCount.** This setting specifies the number of times the system retries the broadcast for the name. The default is 3.

- **BcastQueryTimeout.** The amount of time to wait before retrying the Name Query broadcast. The default is 7.5 seconds.

The LMHOSTS File

Objective B.8

Obviously, Microsoft has been building network operating systems for a long time now. Before NT, Microsoft had put out a product called LAN Manager. LAN Manager was based on NetBEUI. As you may recall, NetBEUI has one major problem: it cannot be routed from network to network. The reason that Microsoft had gone with NetBEUI in the first place was that NetBEUI as a protocol was compatible with the NetBIOS networking model that Microsoft was using.

In an effort to make LAN Manager more acceptable as a Network Operating System, Microsoft included TCP/IP as an alternative protocol for medium to large organizations that wanted to use their product (which was based on Microsoft OS/2 version 1.3). There was a problem: how do you resolve NetBIOS names using TCP/IP on a routed network? On the local network, this was not a problem because the system could use the NetBIOS Name Service port and broadcast a request for the local name.

Note NT checks only the LMHOSTS file if a broadcast on the local network fails to resolve the address.

The solution was relatively easy: create a list of the systems that the computer would have to talk to (given, peer-to-peer networking had not become vogue—there you are allowed only a limited number anyway). In this file, you could put both the IP address and the NetBIOS name. It was an obvious solution that could work. Some situations arose, however, when the client would not be talking to a single machine, but rather looking at any machine with a particular service (the Netlogon service, for example).

The list is of course the file LMHOSTS (no extension), which is located in the \%winroot%\system32\drivers\etc directory. A sample LMHOSTS file was also added during installation. This file is called LMHOSTS.SAM. You should edit the LMHOSTS file by using the EDIT command rather than NOTEPAD. (When creating a file, NOTEPAD saves it in Unicode. That renders the LMHOSTS file nonfunctional.)

Note If you can imagine, all the hosts on the Internet used to be listed in a single file at Stanford Research Institute's Network Information Center. Whenever you tried to connect to another host, your system had to consult this file on their server to find the IP address. The file was called hosts.txt.

The solution to the problem of contacting a service rather than a particular computer was solved by the inclusion of tags. Several tags were introduced that enabled systems to send a request to all the computers that had a particular service running. (The #DOM tag, for example, tells your system that a particular system should be running the Netlogon service.)

The result was a system that could communicate across routers even though it internally used NetBIOS. A very workable compromise (sort of). As time went on, the amount of time spent updating the LMHOSTS file increased. Because this file needs to be located on each and every host, the task was even more difficult.

Tags were a good solution once, and again proved they could resolve the issue. New tags were added that enabled the computers to read a central LMHOSTS file. They still needed one locally so that the system would know where and how to find the central one. This did, however, reduce the required number of lines from 70 or 80 or more to 5 or 6.

Windows NT supports and uses several tags. Table 12.2 provides a list of tags and an explanation as to what they do.

Table 12.2
Tags Available for Use by Windows NT

Tag	Use
#PRE	This is what the section on the NetBIOS Name Cache was leading to. A #PRE tag tells the computer to preload the entry to the cache during initialization or after the NBTSTAT -R command has been issued. Entries with the #PRE have a life of -1 (static), meaning it is always in cache.
#DOM:domain_name	This tag indicates to the system that the computer is a domain controller and the domain that it controls. This enables NT to handle domain functions, domain logon, and browsing services among other things.
#NOFNR	Prevents the use of NetBIOS-directed name queries in the LAN Manager for Unix environments.
#INCLUDE	Tells the computer the location of a central LMHOSTS file. The file is specified using a UNC-type name such as \\MIS\Information\LMHOSTS. It is important that MIS as a computer name must be able to be resolved to an IP address and should be included in the local LMHOSTS file and must be preloaded. Otherwise NT ignores it.

Tag	Use
#BEGIN_ALTERNATE	This is used in conjunction with the #INCLUDE. This entry marks the beginning of a list of alternative locations for the centralized LMHOSTS file that can be used if the first entry is not available. Only one central LMHOSTS is used.
#END_ALTERNATE	You probably already guessed that this would end the list of alternative locations for a central LMHOSTS file. Between the two entries, add as many alternatives as you like. NT tries each in sequence (remember the names must resolve to IP addresses.).
#MH	Multihomed computers may actually appear in the LMHOSTS file more than once, this tag tells the system that this is one of those cases where it should not ignore the others entries in the list.

Note The LMHOSTS file is scanned from top to bottom. Therefore, your most frequently used servers should be listed first. Any entries to preload a server address should be at the bottom because they are already in the NetBIOS Name Cache.

The following listing shows an example of what an LMHOSTS file might contain:

```
152.42.35.2      victoria1     #DOM:MYCORP
152.42.9.255     london2       #DOM:MYCORP
152.42.160.45    ottawa8
152.42.97.56     houston4
#INCLUDE \\victoria1\INFO\LMHOSTS
#BEGIN_ALTERNATE
#INCLUDE \\ottawa8\INFO\LMHOSTS
#INCLUDE \\houston4\INFO\LMHOSTS
#END_ALTERNATE
152.42.193.5     capetown4     #PRE #DOM:MYCORP
152.42.194.255   capetown8     #PRE #DOM:MYCORP
```

Note Just a reminder, use "NBTSTAT -R" to flush the NetBIOS Name Cache and reload from the LMHOSTS file. This enables you to test an LMHOSTS file as you create it.

Of course nothing in this world is perfect, so keep the following things in mind when using the LMHOSTS file:

- If the IP address is wrong, your system will resolve the address, but you cannot connect. Normally this shows up as a `Network Name not Found` error.
- Although NT is good, if the name is spelled wrong in the LMHOSTS file, NT cannot do anything to resolve it. (Note: the names are not case-sensitive.)
- If the LMHOSTS file contains multiple entries, the address for the first one is returned. If it is wrong, it acts the same as in first point.

Only one Registry entry deals with LMHOSTS. It can, however, be easily changed in the Network Settings dialog box. The entry is Enable LMHOSTS. If it is not selected, the system ignores the LMHOSTS file. This is selected by default in NT and Windows 95, but unselected in Windows for Workgroups.

To change the Enable LMHOSTS setting, perform the following steps:

1. Open the Network dialog box.
2. Select the Protocol tab and open the Properties for TCP/IP.
3. To turn on Enable LMHOSTS, ensure there is a check in the Enable LMHOSTS Lookup check box on the WINS Addressing tab. Clear the check box if you want to turn off Enable LMHOSTS.
4. Close the TCP/IP Settings dialog box and the Network dialog box.
5. Restart your computer.

NetBIOS Name Server

The LMHOSTS file does have some limitations. Even using a central LMHOSTS file, there is a great deal of updating. If you don't use a central LMHOSTS file, and you attempt to update a host's address, you must visit each and every station on your entire network. There is also the issue of broadcast traffic. The LMHOSTS file does not reduce that traffic unless every entry is preloaded (meaning the system never has to perform a NetBIOS Name Query broadcast).

As the size of networks around the world began to increase, another method of name resolution had to be found. The method needed to reduce broadcast traffic and update itself without intervention. TCP/IP already had a DNS service—a simple system that computers could query to find the IP address for a given host name. The problem with DNS was that there was only the basic host name—you could not find the services sometimes being sought.

The DNS system required a large (but at least centralized) file to be kept with a listing of all the IP address to host name mappings. Looking at the three functions of NetBIOS naming—registration, resolution, and release—the DNS service only fit one of the criteria.

A new type of name service had to be built, therefore, that would enable systems to register their own IP addresses and that could respond to queries from these systems about the IP addresses of others. The system that emerged was the NetBIOS Name Server (NBNS). Windows NT implements this in the form of the WINS (Windows Internet Naming Service), which is discussed in the next chapter.

Just like TCP/IP, hosts had always had a DNS server entry. The NetBIOS world could now use an NBNS (or WINS, which is the NBNS that comes with NT) server entry. The process was aided by the capability of the routers that were available to pass directed transmission over UDP ports 137 and 138. A set of three basic commands was established, and NetBIOS networking could now really talk to the world.

Figure 12.1 shows the TPC/IP Settings dialog box in which you enter the WINS server address and a secondary WINS server address. This is all that is required to use a WINS server as your NBNS.

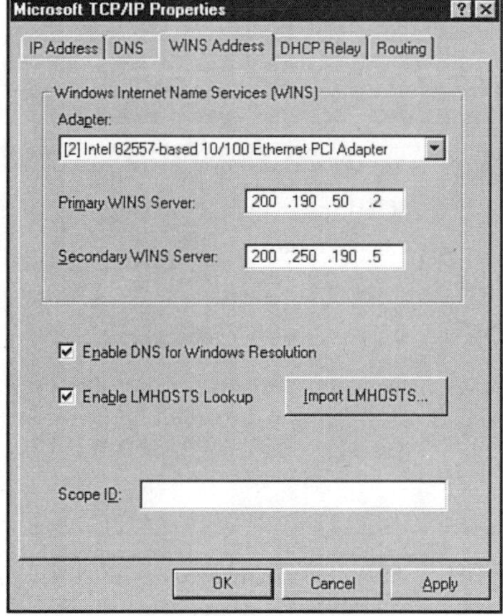

Figure 12.1
The TCP/IP Settings dialog box.

The commands defined include the following:

- **Name Registration.** The transmission registers a computer name with the NBNS. In this way, the NBNS was made to be a dynamic system that required little or no maintenance on the part of the network administrators.
- **Name Query.** Normally all the systems in an organization use the same NBNS, making it very easy to resolve a name and to send the NetBIOS Name Query to the NBNS. The server responds with the IP address if the system has registered with it. (The next chapter discusses replication in more detail. That chapter also discusses making a group of NBNS's act as a single unit.)

- **Name Release.** Some names—such as user names—can move from one computer to another, and therefore from one IP address to another. By including the capability to release a registered name, conflicts in the database are avoided.

You accrue some major advantages when using an NBNS, such as WINS, if you use TCP/IP as your networking protocol with Windows products. These advantages include the following:

- Reduction in broadcast traffic
- Less administrative overhead for maintenance
- Facilitates domain activity over a WAN
- Provides browsing services across multiple subnets

Note This book fully investigates these advantages in the next two chapters.

You can customize a couple of Registry entries for the NBNS. These entries are under

```
HKEY_LOCAL_MACHINE\SYSTEM\CurrentControlSet\Services\NetBT\Parameters
```

- **NameServerPort.** This is the UDP port used for NetBIOS Name Queries going to the NBNS. The default is 137 (89 hex.)
- **NameSrvQueryCount.** Indicates the number of times your system should try each NBNS. The default is 3.
- **NameSrvQueryTimeout.** How long your computer should wait for a response from the NBNS. Default is 15 seconds (5dc hex milliseconds).

The HOSTS File

Objective B.8

Because you are looking at NetBIOS name resolution, you might think that including the HOSTS file here is out of place. The HOSTS file is normally associated with host name resolution. In fact, the HOSTS file is primarily for host name resolution. NT uses the HOSTS file, however, if all other methods of name resolution have failed.

Host names are the TCP/IP names given to the computer. Normally the host name is the same as the NetBIOS name (without the sixteenth character), but they don't have to be. The host name also includes the Internet domain name—these parts together make up the Fully Qualified Domain Name (FQDN). The host name can be any length. THISISAWEBSERVER.MYCROP.COM, for example, is a valid FQDN; it is not, however, a valid NetBIOS name (more on this in Chapter 15, "Microsoft DNS Server").

The HOSTS file, which is located in the \%winroot%\system32\drivers\etc directory, is very similar in makeup to the LMHOSTS file discussed earlier. The difference is that the HOSTS file is simpler in the following two ways:

- There are no tags in the HOSTS file.
- More than one name can be associated with a host by entering the names all on the same line, separated by spaces.

Here is what a sample HOSTS file might look like:

```
160.16.5.3      www www.scrimtech.com     # corporate web server
38.25.63.10     www.NTworld.com           # NT associate page
127.0.0.1       localhost
```

As discussed earlier, it is simple. The first entry resolves WWW as well as WWW.SCRIMTECH.COM to the IP address 160.16.5.3. You might have noticed the # signs. These indicate comments in the HOSTS file that are always placed at the end of the line.

The entry for localhost at 127.0.0.1 is a default entry that NT adds. This enables you to ping your own computer by name to ensure the HOSTS file is working.

DNS

Just like with the HOSTS file, you might think that using DNS to resolve NetBIOS names is a little out of place. NT can, however, use a DNS server to resolve a host name. In environments that will be working with the Internet almost exclusively, having a DNS server makes sense. You can even use it rather than WINS. If you want to do this, just check the Enable DNS for Windows Resolution check box shown in figure 12.1.

Note In NT 4, the WINS server and DNS server can be easily integrated to give you the best of both worlds. It is rumored that in the next release, the products will become a single Name Server product.

Configuring NT to use a DNS server is very simple. All that you need to do is enter a DNS server address in the DNS tab of the TCP/IP Settings dialog box (see fig. 12.2).

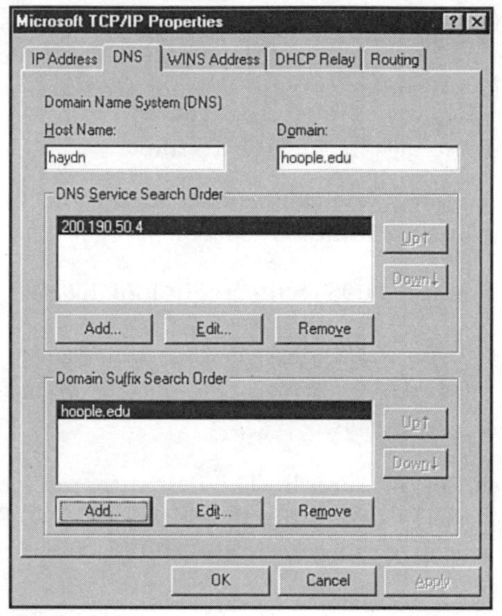

Figure 12.2
The DNS tab from the TCP/IP Configuration dialog box.

Order of Resolution

Objective E.3

As you have just seen, Windows NT has six different ways to resolve a NetBIOS name to an IP address. Each way works, though as discussed, some have limitations that make them impractical for a large-scale WAN. Thankfully this does not matter because the methods of resolution back each other up and enable whichever method can resolve to do so.

A problem can arise, though, if you are not careful. Does it make sense, for example, if you first read the HOSTS file and then broadcast the NetBIOS Name Query to the local subnet? Perhaps checking with the DNS server should be next. The point is that the order in which you use the methods of resolution is more important than the resolution. You are fairly well assured that the name will be resolved (if you spelled it right). Going through the resolution methods in the wrong order, however, can slow down the process.

Remember that this is the order of resolution for NetBIOS names only. Resolving host names uses a different method. You look at that in Chapter 15. For now though, bear in mind that this is NetBIOS name resolution. This is what occurs when you use the NetBIOS interface rather than the WinSock interface. All the normal Microsoft products—NT Explorer, User Manager, NET.EXE—use this method of resolution.

The actual order of resolution is set by the NetBIOS Node Type. You can set this by either editing the Registry or via the DHCP server (if you are using DHCP to allocate IP addresses and services). Note that the default is B-Node (Broadcast) unless a WINS server address is entered; in this case, it defaults to H-Node (Hybrid). The type of Nodes that can be set are as follows:

- B-Node (Broadcast Node).
- P-Node (Peer-to-Peer Node). Uses an NBNS.
- M-Node (Mixed Node). Tries B-Node first and then P-Node.
- H-Node (Hybrid Node). Tries P-Node first and than B-Node.

Note Microsoft's version of B-Node is an enhanced form of the B-Node standard. Because Microsoft already had an LMHOSTS file that had been used successfully with LAN Manager, Microsoft included searching this file in the B-Node form of resolution.

B-Node

The simplest way to resolve a name on the network is to ask all those on the network if this is their name. Obviously this has to be done as a broadcast to the network with every host on the network responding to the broadcast.

Broadcasted NetBIOS Name Queries can take up a significant amount of bandwidth from the network, and also take CPU time from every host on the network. This causes the overall network performance to not only seem slower, but to actually be slower. NT attempts three times to resolve the name using broadcasting, waiting 7.5 seconds between each attempt.

The actual steps that a B-Node system goes through to resolve a name are as follows:

1. NetBIOS Name Cache
2. Broadcasting a NetBIOS Name Query
3. Checking the LMHOSTS file (Microsoft Enhanced B-Node only)
4. Checking a HOSTS file
5. Checking with a DNS server

P-Node

As you saw, you can resolve a NetBIOS name in better ways. The best way is to ask a central system that has a list of every host's IP address and NetBIOS name. This is what P-Node does for you.

With P-Node, a NetBIOS Name Query is still sent on the network. Instead of having to send the query as a broadcast, however, it is sent directly to an NBNS. In this way, the resolution is made quicker, and less CPU time is taken up on the other hosts on the network. Like the B-Node, P-Node makes three attempts to contact an NBNS, waiting for 15 seconds each time.

The order of resolution for P-Node is as follows:

1. NetBIOS Name Cache
2. Asking a NetBIOS Name Server
3. HOSTS file
4. DNS

M-Node

An M-Node system tries every method of resolution. This and the H-Node are combinations of the B-Node and P-Node systems just discussed. The only difference is the order in which Windows NT resolves the names.

For M-Node, the order of resolution is as follows:

1. NetBIOS Name Cache
2. Broadcasting a NetBIOS Name Query
3. Checking the LMHOSTS file
4. Asking a NetBIOS Name server
5. Checking the HOSTS file
6. Consulting the DNS

H-Node

The H-Node is a combination of the P-Node and B-Node resolution methods you have already seen. Unlike M-Node, H-Node reduces the amount of broadcast traffic on your network by consulting the NBNS first before attempting a broadcast.

If you put a WINS address into the TCP/IP configuration, NT automatically uses the H-Node. The steps in H-Node resolution are as follows:

1. NetBIOS Name Cache
2. Asking a NetBIOS Name server
3. Broadcasting a NetBIOS Name Query
4. Checking the LMHOSTS file
5. Checking the HOSTS file
6. Consulting the DNS

Viewing and Setting the Node Type

Because the node type is important to the performance of the system you are using, you should be able to see the node type currently in use. You should also be able to change it if a better method is available.

To check the current node type, you can use the command **IPCONFIG/ALL**, which you have seen several times already. Figure 12.3 shows the output from this command. Note that the node type is Broadcast (also note that no WINS server is listed).

```
Command Prompt
C:\>ipconfig /all

Windows NT IP Configuration

        Host Name . . . . . . . . . : plato
        DNS Servers . . . . . . . . :
        Node Type . . . . . . . . . : Broadcast
        NetBIOS Scope ID. . . . . . :
        IP Routing Enabled. . . . . : No
        WINS Proxy Enabled. . . . . : No
        NetBIOS Resolution Uses DNS : No

Ethernet adapter NE20001:

        Description . . . . . . . . : Novell 2000 Adapter.
        Physical Address. . . . . . : 00-00-E8-CD-54-4C
        DHCP Enabled. . . . . . . . : No
        IP Address. . . . . . . . . : 128.1.0.2
        Subnet Mask . . . . . . . . : 255.255.0.0
        Default Gateway . . . . . . : 128.1.0.1

C:\>
```

Figure 12.3

The output from the IPCONFIG / ALL Command.

You can set your node type manually. By default, you are a B-Node system. If you want to become an H-Node, just add the address of a WINS server into the TCP/IP configuration screen (refer back to fig. 12.1). If you want to be a different node type, you must edit the Registry. The entry is under

```
HKEY_LOCAL_MACHINE\SYSTEM\CurrentControlSet\Services\NetBT\Parameters
```

The entry is NodeType, which can be set to the following values:

- 1 (hex) - B-Node
- 2 (hex) - P-Node
- 4 (hex) - M-Mode
- 8 (hex) - H-Node

You can also set the node type automatically by using the DHCP server. The DHCP Options that you should set are 044 - WINS/NBNS Server and 046 WINS/NBT Node Type (see figs. 12.4 and 12.5). These options enable an administrator to set the node type for all machines that use DHCP.

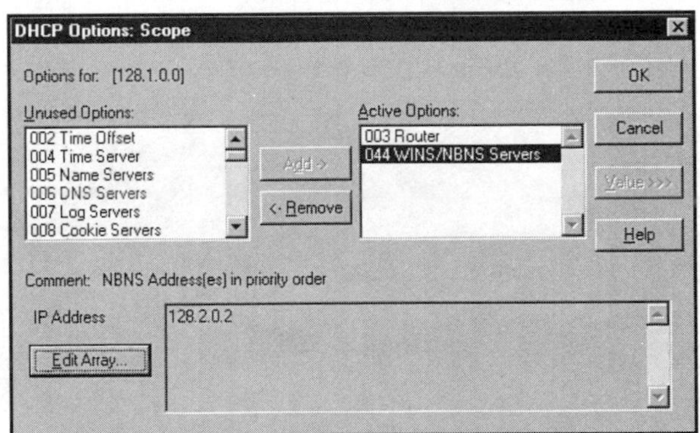

Figure 12.4

Setting the WINS/NBNS Address at the DHCP server.

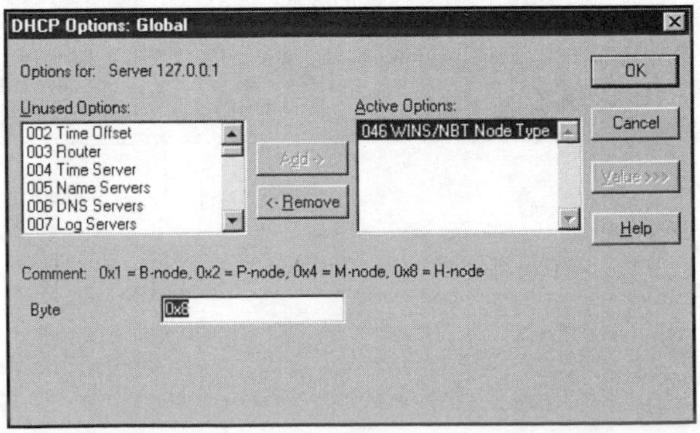

Figure 12.5

Setting the WINS/NBT Node Type at the DHCP server.

Practice

This lab concentrates on the LMHOSTS file and the HOSTS file. Other sections cover both WINS and DNS.

Exercise 1—Sample LMHOSTS

In this exercise, you look at the sample LMHOSTS that comes with Windows NT.

1. Start a command prompt.
2. Change to the \%winroot%\system32\drivers\etc directory.
3. Edit the LMHOSTS.SAM file("EDIT LMHOSTS.SAM").
4. Review the file.

Exercise 2—Creating a Simple LMHOSTS File

In this exercise, you create a simple LMHOSTS file.

Note If you are currently using an LMHOSTS file, please back it up before proceeding.

1. Review the sample network shown in figure 12.6.

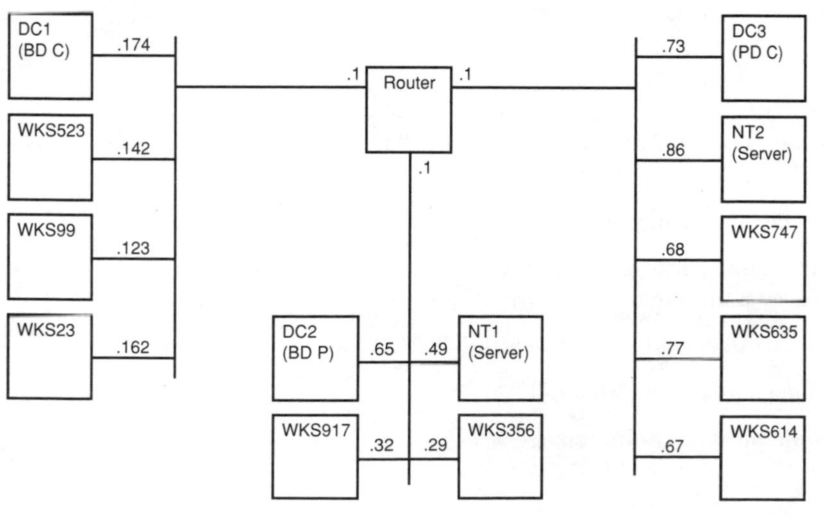

Figure 12.6

A sample network for LMHOSTS exercise.

2. If you were to use a central LMHOSTS file, where do you think it should go?

   The best location in this case is the NT server that is routing between the networks.

3. If you assume that only NT servers or domain controllers provide network services, which systems will these be?

   The following systems provide network services:

   Primary Domain Controller at 148.53.96.86.

   Back Domain Controllers at 148.53.32.174 and 148.53.64.65.

   NT Servers at 148.53.64.49, 148.53.96.73.

   The router at .1 for all subnets.

4. What entries in the LMHOSTS file require tags?

   Only the three domain controllers require tags. You may have suggested that the computer with the central LMHOSTS file should be added as a #PRE. Because it is local to all subnets, however, regular broadcast resolves the name.

5. Create the LMHOSTS file.

   Your file should look like this:

   ```
   148.53.32.174    DC1      #DOM:Training
   148.53.64.65     DC2      #DOM:Training
   148.53.96.86     DC3      #DOM:Training
   148.53.64.49     NT1
   148.53.96.73     NT2
   ```

6. Add the #PRE to all the entries. Save the file as \%winroot%\system32\drivers\etc\lmhosts. (Place the period on the end so that there will be no extension.)

7. Run another command prompt.

8. Check the names in your NetBIOS Name Cache by executing NBTSTAT -c (Note that -r shows names that are resolved, -c shows all names in cache).

9. Now purge and reload the Cache with NBTSTAT -R.

10. Check the names again, what did you get?

    You should have the following:

```
Node IpAddress: [0.0.0.0] Scope Id: []

           NetBIOS Remote Cache Name Table

    Name          Type              Host Address      Life [sec]
    -----------------------------------------------------------
    DC3        <03>  UNIQUE          148.53.96.86          -1
    DC3        <00>  UNIQUE          148.53.96.86          -1
    DC3        <20>  UNIQUE          148.53.96.86          -1
    DC2        <03>  UNIQUE          148.53.64.65          -1
    DC2        <00>  UNIQUE          148.53.64.65          -1
    DC2        <20>  UNIQUE          148.53.64.65          -1
    DC1        <03>  UNIQUE          148.53.32.174         -1
    DC1        <00>  UNIQUE          148.53.32.174         -1
    DC1        <20>  UNIQUE          148.53.32.174         -1
    NT2        <03>  UNIQUE          148.53.96.73          -1
    NT2        <00>  UNIQUE          148.53.96.73          -1
    NT2        <20>  UNIQUE          148.53.96.73          -1
    NT1        <03>  UNIQUE          148.53.64.49          -1
    NT1        <00>  UNIQUE          148.53.64.49          -1
    NT1        <20>  UNIQUE          148.53.64.49          -1
```

11. What entries are required if all Windows clients have peer networking enabled (that is, file and print sharing)?

    The file would look like the following:

```
148.53.32.174     DC1       #DOM:Training
148.53.64.65      DC2       #DOM:Training
148.53.96.86      DC3       #DOM:Training
148.53.64.49      NT1
148.53.96.73      NT2
148.53.32.142     WKS523
148.53.32.123     WKS99
148.53.32.162     WKS23
148.53.64.32      WKS917
148.53.64.29      WKS356
148.53.96.68      WKS747
148.53.96.77      WKS635
148.53.96.67      WKS614
```

12. If you were to install a WINS server and enable all clients to use it for name resolution, what do you need in the LMHOSTS file?

    Nothing, WINS can handle all resolution.

Summary

When you are looking at Microsoft networking, it is critical to resolve NetBIOS names. You should keep in mind, however, that this is only one form of name resolution. Chapter 15 deals with host name resolution. NetBIOS name resolution takes place for any application that uses the NetBIOS API. Host name resolution takes place for any application that uses WinSock directly. You have also looked at how the host name resolution backs up the NetBIOS resolution. You will see that the reverse is also true. This function is critical to implementing wide area networks with NT. The next chapter looks at WINS, which is Microsoft's NBNS. The chapter after that looks at supporting browsing and domain activity over a wide area network.

Test Yourself

1. What is the sixteenth character in the NetBIOS name used for?
2. Which WinSock port is used for name services?
3. What are the four NetBIOS Name functions?
4. Why is there no Negative Name Query Response?
5. How can you see what names are registered to your computer?
6. How many names can a computer register on the network?
7. What are the six methods of NetBIOS name resolution over TCP/IP?
8. What is the command used to see which names your system has resolved on the network?
9. What layer does a NetBIOS Name Query broadcast have to get to?
10. How many times will your computer try broadcasting?
11. Where is the LMHOSTS file located?
12. When is an LMHOSTS file required?
13. What do the #BEGIN_ALTERNATE and #END_ALTERNATE tags do in the LMHOSTS file?

14. If there is a central LMHOSTS file on a server called NCRSRV43 in a share called INFO, what line do you include in the LMHOSTS file to enable your system to use it?
15. What does the #PRE tag do?
16. If there are two entries for the same computer in the LMHOSTS file, both with different addresses, which is used?
17. Give an example of a NetBIOS Name Server?
18. What are some of the benefits of WINS?
19. How is the HOSTS file different from the LMHOSTS file?
20. What are the four node types?
21. If your host is set for H-Node, what order of NetBIOS name resolution will you use?

Test Yourself Answers

1. The sixteenth character is used to identify the server that registered the name on the network.
2. The NetBIOS Name Service runs on UDP port 137.
3. The NetBIOS Name functions are Name Registration, Name Query, Positive Name Query Response, Name Release.
4. Name Queries are sent to all hosts on the local network, not a specific host. If every host who did not have that name responded, the amount of traffic would swamp the network.
5. Using "NBTSTAT -n". This command shows you all the names that NetBIOS has registered on the local computer.
6. The current limit is 250 names that can be registered by one computer.
7. The methods that Microsoft TCP/IP can use include NetBIOS Name Cache, NetBIOS Name Server, Broadcast, the LMHOSTS file, the HOSTS file, and using a DNS server.
8. The command is "NBTSTAT -r". This lists all resolved names in the cache.
9. NetBIOS Name Queries have to be passed all the way up the network stack to the NetBIOS layer.
10. Three times at 7.5 second intervals. These values can be changed in the Registry.
11. The LMHOSTS file is in the \%winroot%\system32\drivers\etc directory.

12. LMHOSTS is required if you will require services from remote hosts, and no WINS server is available.

13. These tags surround a list of alternative sites where your system can find a copy of the central LMHOSTS file. There would be one or more #INCLUDE lines between them.

14. The line would be:

    #INCLUDE \\NCRSRV43\INFO\LMHOSTS

15. This tells NetBIOS over TCP/IP to load the entry into your Name Cache when it initializes, or if the cache is reloaded using "NBTSTAT -R".

16. The file is read from top to bottom; therefore the first is used. The exception to this is a case where the address is preloaded.

17. WINS is the native NT NetBIOS Name Server.

18. WINS reduces the amount of broadcast traffic. It also registers names dynamically, meaning no manual updating of an LMHOSTS file. WINS also facilitates browsing over a wide area network and provides a basis for domain activity (NT Domains) in a routed environment.

19. The HOSTS file has no tags. As well, the HOSTS file is used primarily for host name resolution.

20. The node types available in Microsoft Networking include Broadcast B-Node (Enhanced), Peer-to-Peer P-Node, Mixed M-Node, and Hybrid H-Node.

21. The steps in H-Node resolution are as follows:

    NetBIOS Name Cache

    NetBIOS Name Server

    Broadcasting on the local subnet

    The LMHOSTS file

    The HOSTS file

    Using a DNS server

CHAPTER 13

The Windows Internet Name Service

As discussed in the last chapter, there is a requirement for the computers on a network to be able to resolve the name of other computers to IP addresses. Two main methods have been discussed thus far: Broadcast and NetBIOS Name Servers.

When you looked at Broadcast, you saw that there was a lot of overhead that is involved in using Broadcast, even on the local network, because the NetBIOS Name Service sits at the Application layer of the NT networking architecture. This means that every system has to not only receive the broadcast, but must act on it, passing it all the way up the stack.

Another of the major problems that you saw in the last chapter was the inability of the broadcast traffic to pass IP routers. This is not a problem. NetBIOS was designed with a small single segment network in mind. This means that bandwidth is not a problem, so NetBIOS uses a lot of broadcasts. The amount of broadcast traffic that a single system might generate is relatively insignificant. If you have 300 or 400 hosts that are all broadcasting, however, the amount of information that must be handled is enormous.

It was decided, therefore, that routers should generally not carry this broadcast traffic. The reasons are twofold: First, the router would have to handle many more packets of information, and the chances that a router would become congested are high; second, routers were used in many cases to pass packets across leased lines. These lines frequently had limited bandwidth, and in some cases you were charged for packets sent. These two factors made it impractical for routers to carry NetBIOS broadcasts.

Obviously, Microsoft still wanted to sell network operating systems, so it came up with two different solutions. Both of the solutions were actual tried and true methods that were borrowed from the Internet. You saw the first method, LMHOSTS file(borrowed from the HOSTS file); the second is the NetBIOS Name Server—WINS. This chapter discusses WINS at some length and looks at configuring WINS from both the server end and the client end. This chapter also examines the process and the functions it performs.

This chapter also shows you how to use WINS as a small network in a single organization, as well as how to work with WINS in a worldwide network.

The WINS Process

The process used by WINS is very simple. If you remember, a NetBIOS server needs to perform three main functions with respect to name resolution. The functions are as follows:

- Name registration and renewal
- Name release
- Name resolution

Name Registration

When a WINS client initializes, NetBIOS over TCP/IP (NetBT) sends a name registration query (called a NAMEREGISTRATIONREQUEST) message directly to the primary WINS server for that client. The name registration query includes the source (WINS client) IP address, the destination (WINS server) IP address, and the NetBIOS name to be registered.

As you saw earlier, NetBIOS names are 16 characters in length. The first 15 characters are user-defined, such as the computer name. The last character is a hexadecimal number, 00 through FF, that identifies the NetBIOS service registering the NetBIOS name. The WINS database, for example, may contain the names FRODO[00h] and

FRODO[03h], which are the computer names of a WINS client registered by the client's Workstation Service and Messenger Service, respectively. Table 13.1 shows other NetBIOS names and the services that register them.

TABLE 13.1
NetBIOS Names Registered in a WINS Server Database

Common NetBIOS Names	Service that Registers the NetBIOS Name
<computer name>[00h]	Workstation
<computer name>[03h]	Messenger
<computer name>[06h]	Remote Access Service (RAS) Server
<computer name>[1Fh]	Network Dynamic Data Exchange (NetDDE)
<computer name>[20h]	(LAN Manager) Server
<computer name>[21h]	RAS Client
<computer name>[BEh]	Network Monitoring Agent
<computer name>[BFh]	Network Monitoring Utility
<user name>[03h]	Messenger
<domain name>[1Dh]	Master Browser
<domain name>[1Bh]	Domain Master Browser
<domain name>[00h]	Workstation
<domain name>[1Ch]	Domain Controller
<domain name>[1Eh]	Browser Election

If the WINS server is available and the NetBIOS name is not already registered in the database, the server replies to the client with a positive name registration response message (also called a NAMEREGISTRATIONRESPONSE). This response includes the IP address of the WINS client and WINS server to route the message to the WINS client, the NetBIOS name that has been registered, and the renewal interval, which is a Time to Live (TTL) duration for the NetBIOS name registration. After the renewal interval expires, the NetBIOS name is removed from the database unless the WINS client renews the registration and is given a new renewal interval. There is, of course, no reason for the WINS server not to renew the name. The only time a client is removed is if the client is shut down for a long period of time or there are problems connecting with the server.

If the WINS server is available and the database already contains a duplicate of the NetBIOS name that was requested to be registered by the WINS client, the WINS server sends a challenge to the currently registered owner of the NetBIOS name in question. The challenge is sent as a name query request (NAMEQUERYREQUEST), three times at 500-millisecond intervals. The purpose of the challenge is to see whether the original owner of the NetBIOS name is still using that NetBIOS name. If a computer tries to register its computer name in a WINS server that already has that computer name registered, for example, the WINS server sends a message to the original owner of the computer name to see whether that computer name is still in use on the network.

A multihomed computer in TCP/IP terminology has more than one network interface installed that is bound to TCP/IP. If the registered owner of a NetBIOS name is a multihomed computer, the WINS server sends up to three challenges to each network interface on the multihomed computer to ensure that the challenge message reaches the multihomed host. WINS stops sending challenges as soon as it receives a reply from any of the addresses.

If the current owner of a registered NetBIOS name responds to the name query challenge from the WINS server, the WINS server sends a negative name query response (NAMEQUERYRESPONSE) to the new WINS client attempting to register the duplicate NetBIOS name. The offending WINS client is not allowed to register that name, and an error message is displayed or recorded at the offending WINS client.

If the WINS server does not respond to the first name registration request, the WINS client sends two more requests and then sends up to three requests to the secondary WINS server if one has been configured for the WINS client. If neither WINS server responds, the WINS client initiates a B-Node broadcast to register its NetBIOS names on the local network.

Note LAN Manager 2.2c for MS-DOS and Microsoft Network Client 3.0 WINS clients does not register NetBIOS names with a WINS server, although they can use the WINS server database for NetBIOS name resolution.

NetBIOS Name Renewal

To continue using a registered NetBIOS name, a WINS client must periodically renew its WINS name registrations in the WINS server database. If the client does not renew its registrations during the renewal interval, the name registration expires, and that NetBIOS name to IP address mapping is marked as released (no longer registered) in the WINS server database. The renewal interval is set on the WINS server in the WINS Server Configuration dialog box of the WINS Manager tool found in the Administration Tools group on the Start menu. By default, the renewal interval is 144 hours (four days).

The renewal interval normally should not be changed from the default duration of 144 hours. If the interval is shortened, network traffic increases and performance will likely decrease. The interval can be lengthened, but then the database might be less likely to remain accurate. You should always ensure that the renewal interval is the same for primary and backup WINS servers so that the backup WINS server is not utilized until necessary.

When a WINS client first registers its names on a WINS server, the client is not given a renewal interval to use. Instead it attempts to renew or refresh the registrations every one-eighth (1/8) of the initial refresh timeout, a value set in the Windows NT Registry. By default, the initial refresh timeout is 16 minutes, and thus the initial registration refresh is attempted 2 minutes after the initial registration.

The WINS client sends a name refresh request directly to the primary WINS server. The name refresh request contains the source (WINS client) and destination (WINS server) IP addresses and the NetBIOS name to be refreshed. If the WINS client gets no response, it tries again every one-eighth of the initial refresh timeout until one-half, or 50 percent, of the initial refresh timeout has expired. After 50 percent of the initial refresh timeout has expired, the WINS client begins again with a new renewal interval, acting as if 0 percent of the renewal interval has expired. This time, however, it starts sending name refresh requests to the secondary WINS server—if configured—every one-eighth of the renewal interval until 50 percent of the renewal interval has expired again. Then the WINS client goes back to trying to register with the primary WINS server.

Note

The WINS client continuously attempts to renew its name registration every one-eighth of the initial refresh timeout until it gets a response from the primary or secondary WINS server. Regardless of this fact, the WINS servers still mark the registration as released when the first renewal interval has expired if it does not receive the renewal request from the WINS client.

When a WINS server receives a name refresh request, it sends a name refresh response directly to the WINS client. The name refresh response contains the WINS client IP address as the destination; the WINS server IP address as the source; the NetBIOS name registered; and the new renewal interval, which by default is 144 hours.

After a WINS client has received its first renewal from the WINS server, from then on it attempts to renew its registration only after 50 percent of the renewal interval has expired, or until the WINS client is restarted.

Note A WINS client registration is not assigned a renewal interval or TTL until after it has renewed its initial registration. Until that point, it attempts to renew its registrations every one-eighth of the initial refresh timeout, or every two minutes, by default.

NetBIOS Name Release

When a WINS client initiates a normal shutdown of the host, meaning that the operating system is shut down before rebooting, the WINS client sends one name release request directly to the WINS server for each of its registered NetBIOS names. The NetBIOS name release request contains the WINS client and WINS server IP addresses, as well as the NetBIOS name to be released in the WINS database.

When the WINS server receives a name release request, it consults the local WINS database to ensure that the name exists and is registered to the WINS client that sent the name release request. If the name requested to be released is found in the database and is mapped to the IP address of the client sending the name release request, the WINS server marks that database entry as released and sends a positive name release response to the WINS client that sent the name release request. The positive name release response is directed to the WINS client IP address. It contains the released NetBIOS name and a renewal interval or TTL of zero.

If the NetBIOS name requested to be released was not registered in the WINS database or was registered with a different IP address, the WINS server replies with a negative name release response to the WINS client that sent the name release request.

The WINS client treats a negative name release response the same as a positive name release response. After the WINS client receives either type of name release response from the WINS server, it no longer responds to name request registration challenges sent from the WINS server when another host wants to register the same NetBIOS name.

If the WINS client does not receive a name release response from the primary WINS server, it sends up to three B-Node broadcasts of the name release request to the local network. All B-Node-enabled clients, including WINS clients, receiving the name release request then ensure that the NetBIOS name is removed from their local NetBIOS Name Caches.

Name Resolution

When a host running NetBIOS over TCP/IP (NetBT) attempts to execute a command containing a NetBIOS name, that NetBIOS name must be resolved to an IP address. If the command "NET USE P: \\SERVER01\PUBLIC" is executed, for example, NetBT must make a connection to the computer SERVER01 in order to map the drive P: to the PUBLIC share on SERVER01. To make this connection, NetBT must know the IP address of the computer SERVER01. In other words, NetBT must resolve the NetBIOS name to an IP address.

The process of NetBIOS name resolution involves checking the NetBIOS name mapping tables in various places until an entry is found that maps the NetBIOS name to an IP address. As you have seen, the NetBIOS name to IP address mappings can be found in some or all of the following places, depending on which components are implemented on the internetwork:

- The local NetBIOS Name Cache, found in memory on the local or source host.
- A WINS server database.
- An LMHOSTS. file, which is a text file on the local host containing the NetBIOS name to IP address mappings.
- A HOSTS. file, which is a text file on the local host containing host name to IP address mappings—the host name is often the same as the NetBIOS computer name.
- A Domain Name Service (DNS) database, which will also contain host name to IP address mappings.
- The host that owns the particular NetBIOS name can respond to a B-Node broadcast name query if that host is on the same subnet as the source host.

Depending on the configuration of the NetBT implementation, any number of the preceding methods of resolving NetBIOS names can be used in an order determined by the NetBIOS node type.

Note Remember that the default for a host configured to use WINS for NetBIOS name resolution is the H-Node (hybrid) NetBIOS name resolution order.

To verify which NetBIOS name resolution node type is being used by a host, enter **IPCONFIG /ALL** from a command prompt. For example:

```
Windows NT IP Configuration
        Host Name . . . . . . . . . : frodo.middle_earth.com
        DNS Servers . . . . . . . . : 200.20.16.122
        Node Type . . . . . . . . . : Hybrid
        NetBIOS Scope ID. . . . . . :
        IP Routing Enabled. . . . . : No
        WINS Proxy Enabled. . . . . : No
        NetBIOS Resolution Uses DNS : Yes
```

In the preceding sample output, the NetBIOS node type is hybrid, or H-Node, meaning that it uses a NetBIOS name server (WINS) and B-Node broadcasts to resolve NetBIOS names.

After the NetBIOS name has been resolved to an IP address, NetBT adds the NetBIOS name and IP address mapping to the local NetBIOS Name Cache and does not need to query by using any of the other methods. The NetBIOS names are periodically cleared from the NetBIOS Name Cache. The default time an entry resides in cache is 10 minutes, but you can configure this in the Registry (see the section "WINS Registry Entries," later in this chapter).

The NetBIOS Name Cache contains several names registered by the local host, including the computer name, user name, domain name, and any other names that have been recently resolved and added to the NetBIOS Name Cache. To view the current contents of the NetBIOS Name Cache, enter the command **NBTSTAT -n** from a command prompt. Sample output is shown here:

```
Node IpAddress: [200.20.1.30] Scope Id: []
            NetBIOS Local Name Table
   Name               Type         Status
-----------
FRODO          <00>  UNIQUE       Registered
FRODO          <20>  UNIQUE       Registered
HOBBITS        <00>  GROUP        Registered
HOBBITS        <1C>  GROUP        Registered
HOBBITS        <1B>  UNIQUE       Registered
BILBO          <03>  UNIQUE       Registered
ADMINISTRATOR  <03>  UNIQUE       Registered
```

As a review, look at the resolution order for an H-Node system. The NetBIOS name query is performed in the following order:

1. The local name cache is consulted for a NetBIOS name to IP address mapping.
2. If no mapping is found, a name query request is sent directly to the configured primary WINS server. The name query request contains the NetBIOS name to be resolved as well as the source (WINS client) and destination (WINS server) IP addresses.

   If the primary WINS server does not respond to the name query request, the WINS client resends the request two more times to the primary WINS server. If the primary WINS server still does not respond, the WINS client then sends up to three name query requests to the secondary WINS server, if one is configured on the WINS client.

   If either WINS server resolves the name, a name query response is sent to the WINS client along with the requested NetBIOS name and IP address mapping.

   If a WINS server receives the name query request but the name does not exist in the WINS database, the WINS server sends a `Requested Name Does Not Exist` response to the WINS client that initiated the request.
3. If no WINS server responds to the name query request or the WINS client receives the response `Requested Name Does Not Exist`, the WINS client then sends three B-Node broadcasts of the name request query to the local network.
4. If no name query response is received, the WINS client checks the local LMHOSTS. file, the HOSTS. file, and then the DNS server, if the client is configured to use any of these methods.

After the WINS client has received a mapping for the NetBIOS name, it adds the mapping to its local NetBIOS Name Cache. It can then use the Internet Protocol (IP) to route datagrams to the destination NetBIOS host.

If the requested NetBIOS name cannot be resolved to an address, NetBIOS cannot use TCP/IP to communicate with that host. If TCP/IP is the only protocol capable of reaching that host—for example, if the NetBEUI protocol is not being used—the requested NetBIOS command fails, and the host may report an error message such as `The network path was not found.`

Installing WINS Server

Of all the services that come with Windows NT Server, the WINS Server service is probably the easiest to install and configure. You need to look at only the following few things before you can install the WINS Server:

Objective B.4

- NT Server installed
- TCP/IP running on the server with a static IP address

Note WINS can be installed on a multihomed system (a system with multiple network adapters). This enables you to use WINS on an NT router, which can increase the resolution as requests are not required to cross routers. This functionality was added in NT 3.51 Service Pack 4 and refined in Service Pack 5. (See the section "Static Routing" in Chapter 7, "Routing," for information on installing multiple network cards.

Objective B.4

After you have met those two simple criteria, you can install the WINS Server on NT. The installation follows the same basic steps as you have used to install all the services that you have looked at thus far. Specifically, the steps are as follows:

1. Open the Network dialog box.
2. On the Services tab, choose Add.
3. From the list that appears, select the Windows Internet Naming Service (at the bottom).
4. Click OK and enter the directory for your source files.
5. Click Close to shut down the Network dialog box.
6. Finally (as always), choose Yes to restart the system.

Now that the server is installed on the Windows NT box, your clients can start to use it (provided they are configured to use WINS). That is all there is to it. There is no configuration required in a simple network scenario. The only exception to this rule might be importing the LMHOSTS file; this would enable your system to generate static entries for the systems already listed in the file. (This is discussed in more detail in later sections.)

If you will be installing WINS in a larger intranet, you should undertake some planning before you proceed. The first question when planning for WINS is: How many WINS servers does the network require? Microsoft guidelines state that a dedicated WINS server can support up to 10,000 computers.

Because WINS resolution increases network traffic, however, you should consider distributing WINS servers throughout the network. Consider placing a WINS server on each network segment, for example, to reduce the WINS traffic that must be routed, particularly through slow WAN links.

At a minimum, you should have two WINS servers, configured to mutually replicate their databases. This provides a measure of fault tolerance in case a WINS server fails. Be certain that your clients are configured with the IP addresses of each of the WINS servers on the network. The easiest way to do that is to configure the clients using DHCP.

When a WINS client is turned off, it releases its WINS registration. When the client restarts, it registers its name with the WINS server, receiving a new version ID. This re-registration results in entries in the WINS database that must be replicated with other WINS servers. Remember that a given NetBIOS computer can be associated with multiple NetBIOS names associated with the services running on the client. Each NetBIOS name registered with WINS increases the WINS replication (the process of copying changes to the database between servers—only the changes are replicated) traffic.

Roving WINS clients generate traffic in a different way. When a client moves to a different network and is restarted (for example, a laptop user), it attempts to register its name with WINS. A registration already exists for that client on the old network. WINS must challenge the existing name registration before it can be released for use by the client on the new network. This challenge is another source of increased traffic generated by WINS.

Note In a multiple WINS server environment, these sorts of challenges can also happen if the name release that the client station performed as it shut down on the previous network has not replicated with the WINS server on the network that it is currently joining.

All this is to say that you must be sensitive to WINS traffic demands when planning and monitoring your network. On small networks, WINS traffic will probably be insignificant. As networks grow to many hosts, however, WINS traffic can become significant. Proper placement of WINS servers can reduce routed WINS traffic. Additionally, scheduling WINS replication for periods of low network demand can reduce WINS bandwidth requirements.

WINS servers separated by WAN links should be replicated frequently whenever possible. Consider a WAN consisting of sites in New York and San Francisco. Typically, clients are configured so that their primary services are provided by local servers, and WINS servers would be located at each site. Each site should have at least two WINS servers, which should be synchronized frequently, perhaps at 15-minute intervals. With proper planning, it should be sufficient to synchronize the WINS servers between New York and San Francisco at longer intervals, such as 6 to 12 hours. Remember, however, that with long replication intervals, the time required to converge the entire network on a change is extended as well. It might be necessary to force replication to take place when significant changes occur.

Installing the WINS Clients

Objective B.4

Now that the server is configured and the WINS server is up and running, you need to configure the clients on the network to be able to use the WINS server. This can be handled in one of two ways: You can either visit each client on the network and add the WINS server address into the TCP/IP configuration, or you can set the Address Type and Node Type in the DHCP server so that the clients obtain the information automatically.

Configuring a Statically Addressed WINS Client

Objective B.4

Clients configured using static IP addresses are enabled as WINS clients by supplying one or more WINS server addresses for the client's TCP/IP configuration. Figure 13.1 shows the TCP/IP configuration of a computer that includes an address for a primary WINS server. If you are configuring a multihomed computer, be certain to add at least one WINS server address for each network adapter.

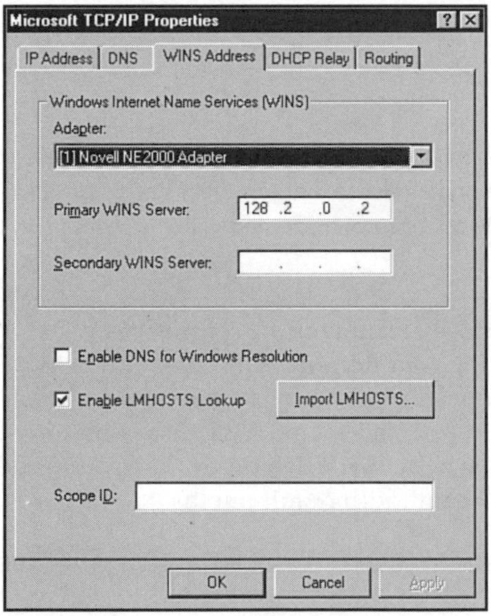

Figure 13.1

Configuring a TCP/IP host as a WINS client.

Configuring WINS Proxies

WINS proxies enable non-WINS clients to resolve names on the internetwork. When a WINS proxy receives a B-Node broadcast attempting to resolve a name on a remote network, the WINS proxy directs a name query to a WINS server and returns the response to the non-WINS client. This is similar to the DHCP Relay Agent you saw in previous chapters.

Windows NT, Windows 95, and Windows for Workgroups computers can be configured as WINS proxies, enabling them to receive broadcast B-Node name requests from non-WINS clients and to resolve them using directed H-Node queries to WINS servers. WINS proxies enable B-Node computers to obtain name resolutions from WINS.

For Windows for Workgroups and Windows NT 3.5x computers, the WINS proxy feature is enabled in the Advanced Microsoft TCP/IP Configuration dialog box by checking the box labeled Enable WINS Proxy Agent.

For Windows NT and Windows 95 computers, you must edit the Registry. Change the value of the EnableProxy value entry to 1 (type REG_DWORD). This value entry is found under the following Registry key:

```
HKEY_LOCAL_MACHINE\SYSTEM\CurrentControlSet\Services\Netbt\Parameters
```

Configuring DHCP Clients as WINS Clients

Obviously, if you will be using the DHCP server, it makes sense to use WINS. With DHCP there is a possibility that the computer's IP address will change. This means that some method of dynamic name resolution has to be available. It is fairly normal to see both WINS and DHCP on the same server.

If you are using DHCP, configuring the clients is simple. The clients must be assigned the following two DHCP options:

- **44 WINS/NBNS Servers.** This option specifies the WINS servers that the computers will attempt to use. Because hosts in different scopes will probably access different servers, this option should probably be assigned at the scope level.
- **46 WINS/NBT Node Type.** This option specifies the address resolution mode the WINS client will employ. In the vast majority of cases, all hosts should be configured in H-Node mode, and it may be appropriate to assign this as a global option that applies to all scopes on a DHCP server.

To add option 44 to a scope, follow these steps:

1. Start DHCP Manager.
2. Select a scope in the DHCP Servers box.
3. Choose Scope (or Global) in the DHCP Options menu.

4. In the DHCP Options: Scope dialog box, select 044 WINS/NBNS Servers in the Unused Options box and then choose Add (see fig. 13.2). Before the option is added to the Active Options box, you receive a warning, `Warning: In order for WINS to function properly, you must now set option 46(WINS/NBT Node Type), and set it to either 0x02(P-Node), 0x04(M-Node) or 0x08(H-Node). Click OK to continue.`

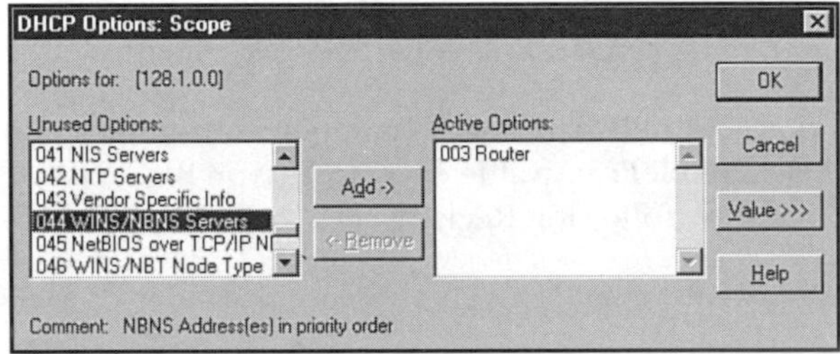

Figure 13.2
The DHCP Options: Scope dialog box.

5. Choose Value to expand the dialog box and display the current values of the option (see fig. 13.3). At first, of course, the IP address list will be empty. Your next task is to add the addresses of WINS servers.

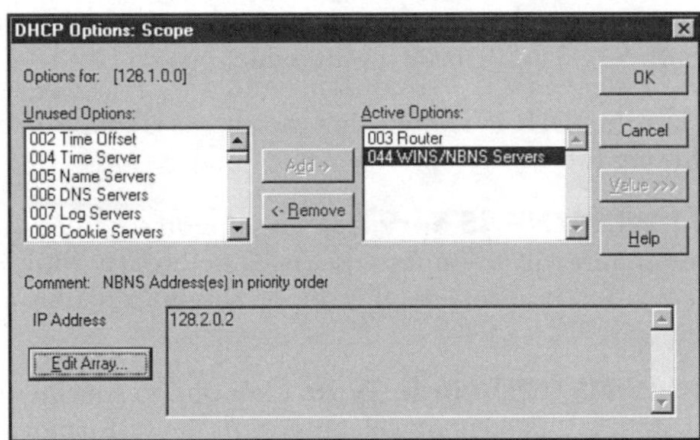

Figure 13.3
The WINS/NBNS option in the DHCP Options dialog box.

6. Option 44 accepts one or more addresses of WINS servers. To change the values, choose the Edit Array button to open the IP Address Array Editor (see fig. 13.4).

7. To add the address of a WINS server to the array, enter the address in the New IP Address field and choose Add to copy the address to the IP Addresses field. In figure 13.4, address 128.1.0.1 is being added to the array.

   You can also start by entering a WINS server name in the Server Name field. Then choose Resolve to generate the IP address associated with the name you have entered. After the IP address is added to the New IP Address field, choose Add to copy the address to the IP Addresses list.

   To remove an address, select the address in the IP Addresses field and choose Remove.

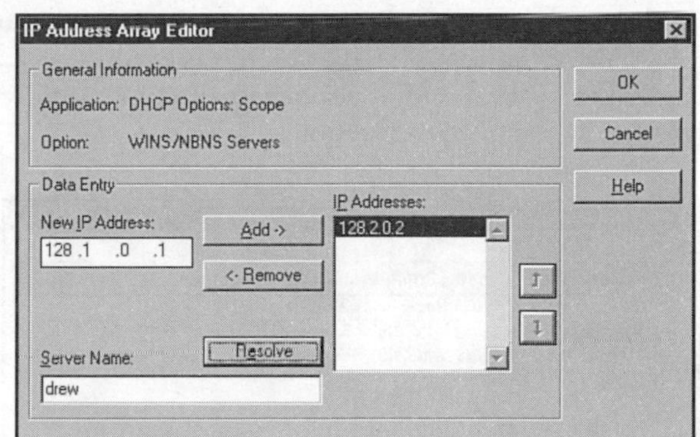

Figure 13.4

The IP Address Array Editor dialog box.

8. After addresses have been configured, click OK and return to the DHCP Manager main window.

Global options apply to all scopes unless overridden by a scope option. Because all WINS clients will be configured to use H-Node name resolution, option 46 is added as a global option as follows:

1. Start DHCP Manager.
2. Select a scope in the DHCP Servers box.
3. Choose Global in the DHCP Options menu.
4. In the DHCP Options: Global dialog box, select 046 WINS/NBT Node Type in the Unused Options box and choose Add.
5. Choose Value to expand the dialog box and display the current values of the option (see fig. 13.5). Option 46 requires one of four values that specifies an NBT node type. In general, option 0x8, H-node is the preferred choice. Enter the desired value and click OK.

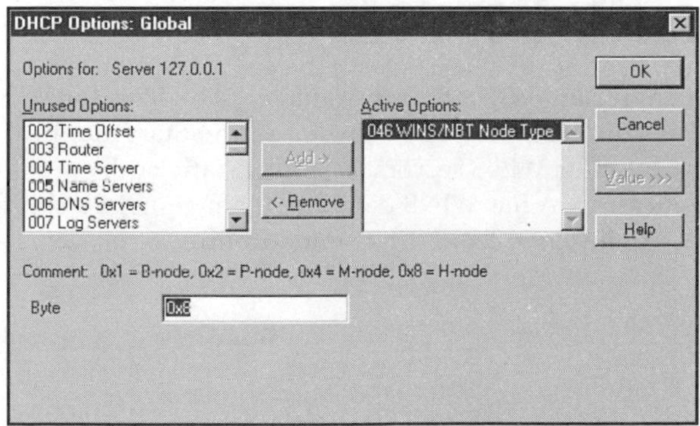

Figure 13.5

Editing the WINS/NBT Node Type option.

After the required options have been entered, they appear in the DHCP Manager main window (see fig. 13.6). Notice that option 046, which was entered as a global option, is identified by a global icon. This option applies to all scopes defined on this DHCP server unless overridden by a scope-level option.

Figure 13.6

DHCP Manager after the WINS options are added.

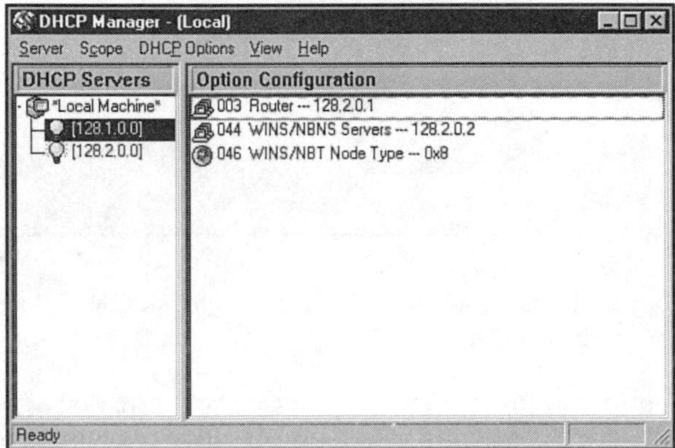

After the WINS options have been added to the appropriate DHCP scopes, it is necessary to force the DHCP clients to release their leases so that they can acquire new leases with the WINS options. You can delete the leases in the Active Leases dialog box, but clients cannot acquire new leases until their current leases expire.

Note

To force Windows NT and Windows 3.1x DHCP clients to update their current configurations, enter the command **IPCONFIG /RENEW** at a command prompt on the client computer. For Windows 95, use the command **WINIPCFG** at a command prompt and choose the Renew button.

Managing WINS Servers

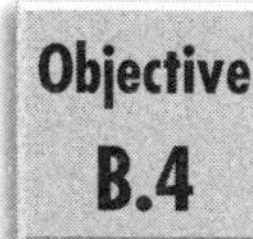

WINS functions are managed using WINS Server Manager. The icon for WINS Server Manager is installed in the Administrative Tools group on the Start menu. WINS Server Manager is used to monitor WINS servers, establish static address mappings, and manage database replication. A few WINS database management tasks, such as compacting the database, are initiated from the command line.

Adding WINS Servers to WINS Server Manager

Figure 13.7 shows the main window for WINS Server Manager. WINS Manager has been configured to manage two WINS servers. You can use a single WINS Service Manager to monitor all WINS servers on your intranet.

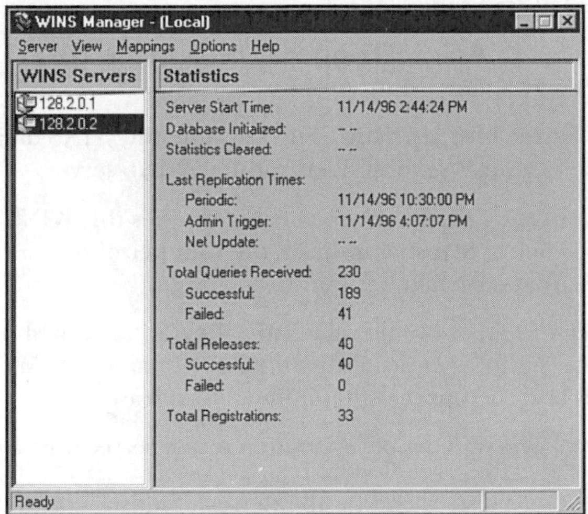

Figure 13.7
The WINS Server Manager.

If WINS Server Manager is run on a computer running the WINS Server service, the computer is listed in the WINS Servers list. To add a WINS server to the list of managed servers, perform the following steps:

1. Choose the Add WINS Server command in the Servers menu to open an Add WINS Server dialog box.
2. Enter the IP address of the new WINS server in the WINS Server entry box and choose OK. The server is added to those in the WINS Servers box.

   To remove a WINS server from the list, select the server and choose the Delete WINS Server command in the Server menu.

Monitoring WINS

The main window of WINS Server Manager displays several statistics about the WINS server selected in the WINS Servers box. The statistics are as follows:

- **Server Start Time.** The date and time when the WINS server was started. This is the time the computer was started. Stopping and starting the WINS Server service does not reset this value.

- **Database Initialized.** Static mappings can be imported from LMHOSTS files. This value indicates when static mappings were last imported.
- **Statistics Cleared.** The date and time when the server's statistics were cleared with the Clear Statistics command in the View menu.
- **Last Replication Time: Periodic.** The last time the WINS database was updated by a scheduled replication.
- **Last Replication Time: Admin Trigger.** The last time a WINS database replication was forced by an administrator.
- **Last Replication Time: Net Update.** The last time the WINS database was updated in response to a push request from another WINS server.
- **Total Queries Received.** The number of name queries this WINS server has received from WINS clients. Statistics indicate the number of queries that have succeeded and those that have failed.
- **Total Releases.** The number of messages indicating an orderly shutdown of a NetBIOS application. Statistics indicate the number of names the WINS server released successfully and the number that it failed to release.
- **Total Registrations.** The number of registration messages received from clients.

When you want to refresh the statistics, choose the Refresh Statistics command in the View menu or press F5. To clear the statistics, choose the Clear Statistics command in the View menu.

Viewing the Database

Once configured, WINS generally requires little maintenance. Some tasks should be performed periodically, however, to improve the efficiency of WINS and to reduce the size of WINS database files. Additionally, when clients experience name resolution problems, you might need to view the contents of the WINS database to diagnose problems.

To view the database for a WINS server, select the server in the WINS Manager main window. Choose the Show Database command in the Mappings menu to open the Show Database dialog box (see fig. 13.8).

If you want to display all database records for all managed WINS servers, select Show All Mappings. To restrict the display to database records owned by a specific WINS server, select Show Only Mappings from Selected Owner and select a WINS server in the Select Owner box. The owner of a WINS mapping record is the WINS server that first recorded the mapping.

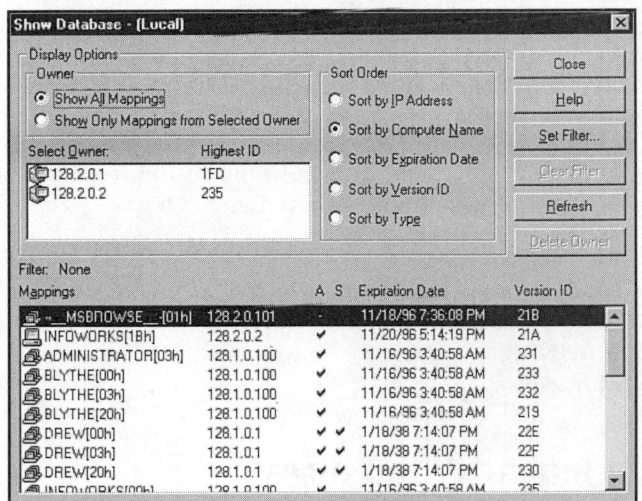

Figure 13.8

A WINS server database.

Each record in the Mappings box includes the following data fields:

- **Icon.** A single terminal icon indicates a unique name. A multiterminal icon indicates a group, Internet group, or multihomed name. (See the section "Special Names," later in this chapter.)
- **Computer Name.** Some computer names, such as _MSBROWSE_, are special names. User names also are shown in this listing. All are tagged with the hex number stored in byte 16 to identify the NetBIOS name type. (See the discussion in the section titled "Special Names.")
- **IP address.** The IP address associated with the name. Notice that several names can be associated with a single IP address.
- **A.** Indicates whether the system is active or not. If there is a check mark, the name is active.
- **S.** Indicates whether the name is established statically. If the name is a static mapping, there will be a check mark in this column.
- **Timestamp.** The day and time when the record expires.
- **Version ID.** A stamp indicating the sequence in which the entries were established. When a pull replication partner requests new data, it requests entries with a revision number higher than the last record revision received from the push partner.

Note The database display does not update dynamically. Choose Refresh to update the display.

The Sort Order box offers several options for sorting database records. You can also restrict displayed records by establishing a filter. Choose Set Filter and enter a computer name or IP address in the Set Filter dialog box to restrict the display to a specific computer.

If a WINS server is no longer available, you can remove the entries from it by selecting the server in the Select Owner box and then choosing Delete Owner.

As discussed in the section "Special Names," NetBIOS names fall into several categories, identified by byte 16 of a Microsoft-compliant NetBIOS name. Each name in the Mappings box of the Show Database dialog box is tagged with the value assigned to byte 16 of its name. (The WINS Show Database window uses the letter *h* to identify hex values. The value 01h is equivalent to 0x1.)

Setting WINS Manager Preferences

You can use the Preferences command in the Options menu to set a variety of optional features for WINS Manager. Figure 13.9 shows the Preferences dialog box. (In the figure, the Partners button has been clicked on to open the push and pull partner configuration options.)

Figure 13.9

The WINS Manager Preferences dialog box.

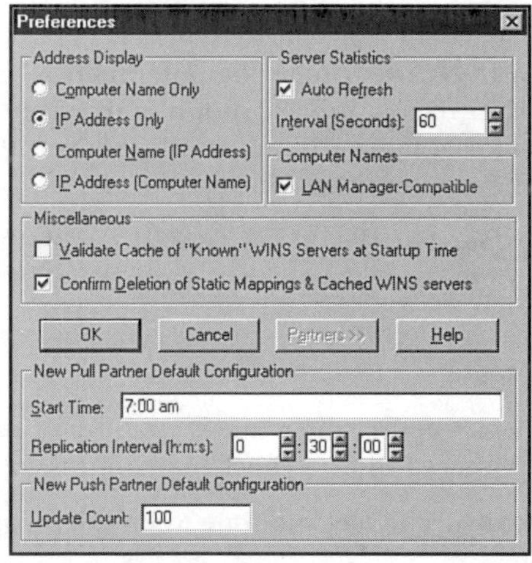

Options in this dialog box are as follows.

- **Address Display.** Contains four options that determine how WINS servers are listed in the WINS Servers list. The options are Computer Name Only, IP Address Only, Computer Name (IP Address), and IP Address (Computer Name).

- **Server Statistics: Auto Refresh.** Check this box to specify that statistics in the WINS Manager be automatically updated. Enter an update interval in the Interval (Seconds) field.
- **Computer Names: LAN Manager-Compatible.** Generally, this box should be checked to force computer names to conform to LAN Manager rules, which limit names to 15 characters. (Some NetBIOS environments use 16 character names.) LAN Manager uses the sixteenth byte to indicate the service on the computer (server, workstation, messenger, and so on). All Windows network products follow LAN Manager naming conventions.
- **Validate Cache of "Known" WINS Servers at Startup Time.** Check this option if the system should query all known servers when starting up to determine whether the servers are available.
- **Confirm Deletion of Static Mappings & Cached WINS servers.** Check this option if a warning message should be displayed when static mappings or cached names are deleted.
- **New Pull Partner Default Configuration: Start Time.** This value specifies a default start time that will be applied to newly created pull partners. Specify a default replication interval in the Replication Interval field. This value should be equal to or less than the lowest replication interval set for any active WINS replication partners.
- **New Push Partner Default Configuration: Update Count.** This value specifies the default for the number of registrations and changes that will cause a push partner to send a replication trigger. The minimum value is 5.

Configuring WINS Server Properties

You can adjust a number of properties for each WINS server. These properties are configured by selecting a WINS server in the WINS Server Manager and choosing the Configuration command in the Servers menu. Figure 13.10 shows the WINS Server Configuration dialog box. (In figure 13.10, the Advanced button was clicked to open the Advanced WINS Server Configuration box.) The options in this dialog box are as follows:

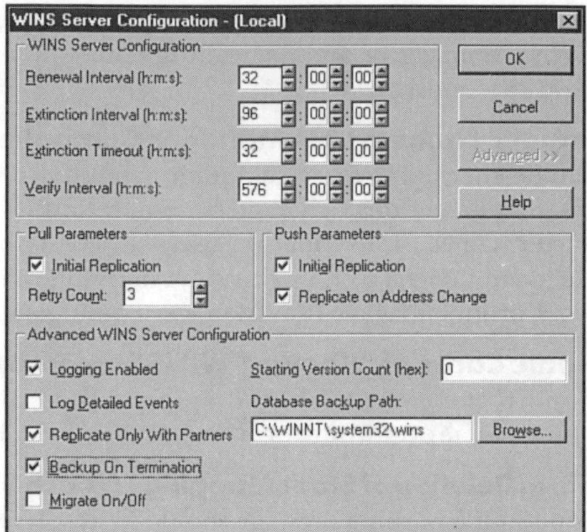

Figure 13.10

The WINS Server Configuration dialog box.

- **Renewal Interval.** This option determines how frequently a client must re-register its name. A name not re-registered within the renewal interval is marked as released. Forcing clients to re-register frequently increases network traffic. A value of 32 hours enables a client to retain a registration from day to day, while ensuring that the registration is released in a reasonable period of time if it is not used. The maximum value for this field is 144 hours (4 days).
- **Extinction Interval.** This option determines how long a released name can remain in the database before it is marked extinct and is eligible to be purged. Try setting this value to three or four times the renewal interval.
- **Extinction Timeout.** Specifies the interval between the time a record is marked extinct and the time when the record is actually purged from the database. The minimum value is one day.
- **Verify Interval.** Specifies how frequently the WINS server must verify the correctness of names it does not own. The maximum value is 24 days.

Note Setting renewal and extinction intervals is a balancing act between the needs of your users, keeping the WINS database up-to-date, and generation of network traffic. If you force renewal and extinction to occur at frequent intervals, network traffic increases and users can lose their name reservations if they are away from the office for a few days. On the other hand, if these intervals are too long, the database becomes cluttered with obsolete entries.

- **Pull Parameters: Initial Replication.** Check this box to have the server pull new data from its pull partners when it is initialized or when replication parameters change. Then specify a value in the Retry Count field to specify the number of times the server should attempt replication. If the server is unsuccessful, replication is retried according to the server's replication configuration.

- **Push Parameters: Initial Replication.** Check this box if the server should inform its push partners when it is initialized. If push partners should be notified when an address changes in a mapping record, check the Replicate on Address Change box.
- **Logging Enabled.** Check this box if database changes should be logged on to the Jet.log file.
- **Log Detailed Events.** Checking this box enables verbose logging. Due to the demand on system resources, this option should be used only when tuning WINS performance.
- **Replicate Only With Partners.** If this option is checked, an administrator cannot force a WINS server to push or pull from a WINS server not listed as a replication partner.
- **Backup On Termination.** If this option is checked, the database is backed up upon shutdown of WINS Manager, unless the system is being stopped.
- **Migrate On/Off.** Check this option if you are upgrading to Windows NT from a non-NT system. When checked, this option enables static records to be treated as dynamic so that they can be overwritten.
- **Starting Version Count (hex).** This value must be adjusted only if the WINS database is corrupted and must be restarted. In that case, set the value higher than the version number for this WINS server as it appears on all the server's replication partners, to force replication of records for this server. Version counts are visible in the View Database dialog box.
- **Database Backup Path.** Specifies the directory in which the database backup files are to be stored. If a path is specified, a backup is performed automatically at 24 hour intervals. This backup can be used to restore the main database if it becomes corrupted. Do not specify a network directory.

Note If you wish to have backups, you must enter a path in the Database Backup Path.

Viewing WINS Server Details

You can display detailed information for each WINS server by selecting the server and choosing the Detailed Information command in the Servers menu. Figure 13.11 shows a sample Detailed Information dialog box. The fields in this box are as follows:

- **Computer Name.** The NetBIOS name of the computer supporting the WINS server.

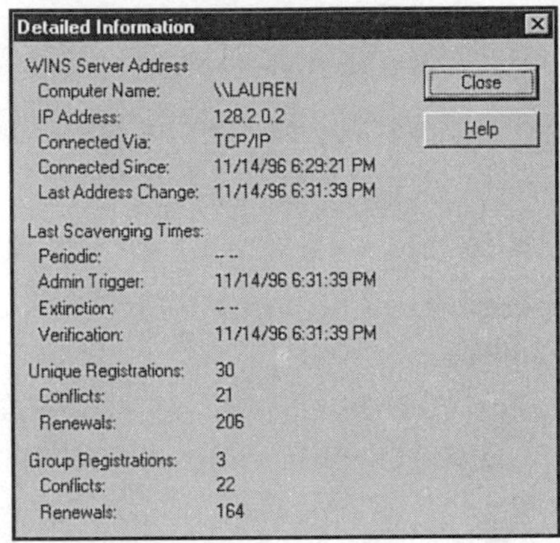

Figure 13.11
Detailed information about a WINS server.

- **IP Address.** The IP address of the WINS server.
- **Connected Via.** The connection protocol.
- **Connected Since.** The time when the WINS Server service was last activated. Unlike the Server Start Time statistic in the main window, Connected Since is reset when the WINS Server service is stopped and started.
- **Last Address Change.** The time when the last database change was replicated.
- **Last Scavenging Times.** The last time the database was scavenged to remove old data. Times are reported for the following scavenging events:
  - Periodic—Timed scavenging.
  - Admin Trigger—Manually initiated scavenging.
  - Extinction—Released records were scavenged because they had aged past the extinction time.
  - Verification—Last scavenging, based on the Verify interval in the WINS server configuration.
- **Unique Registrations.** The number of name registrations for groups that the WINS server has accepted. The Conflicts statistic indicates the number of conflicts encountered when registering names already registered. The Renewals statistic indicates the number of renewals that have been received for unique names.
- **Group Registrations.** The number of requests for groups that the WINS server has accepted. The Conflicts statistic indicates the number of conflicts encountered when registering group names. The Renewals statistic indicates the number of group name renewals received.

Configuring Static Mappings

Objective B.4

Sometimes dynamic name to address mappings are not desirable. At such times, creating static mappings in the WINS database proves useful. A *static mapping* is a permanent mapping of a computer name to an IP address. Static mappings cannot be challenged and are removed only when they are explicitly deleted.

To add static mappings in WINS Manager, use the following procedure:

1. Choose Static Mappings in the Mappings menu to open the Static Mappings dialog box, which lists all active static mappings (see fig. 13.12). The mappings for LAUREN are tagged with an individual icon because LAUREN was entered as a unique address mapping. The mappings for DREW are tagged by a group icon because DREW was entered as a multihomed mapping. Figure 13.13 shows how the static mapping for DREW was entered.

Figure 13.12
Static mappings.

2. To add a static mapping, choose Add Mappings to open the Add Static Mappings dialog box (see fig. 13.13).

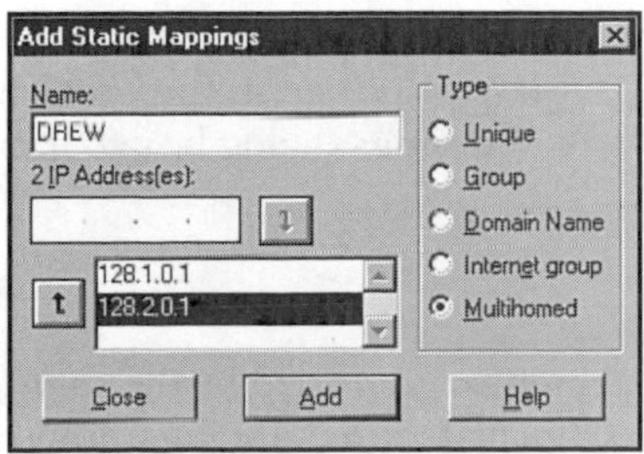

Figure 13.13
The Add Static Mappings dialog box.

3. Type the computer name in the Name field. WINS Manager supplies the \\ characters to complete the UNC name.
4. Enter the address in the IP Address field.
5. Click one of the buttons in the Type box. (Group, Internet group, and multihomed names are discussed further in the next section, "Special Names.") The following choices are available:
   - **Unique.** The name will be unique in the WINS database and will have a single IP address.
   - **Group.** Groups are targets of broadcast messages and are not associated with IP addresses. If the WINS server receives a query for the group, it returns FFFFFFFF, the IP broadcast address. The client then broadcasts on the local network.
   - **Domain Name.** A group associated with the IP addresses of up to 24 Windows NT domain controllers and the address of the primary domain controller, for a total of 25. This is used to facilitate domain activity.
   - **Internet group.** Similar to a Domain group, but it is a user-defined group that can include various resources such as routers or printers.
   - **Multihomed.** A name that can be associated with up to 25 addresses, corresponding to the IP addresses of a multihomed computer.
6. Choose Add.

To edit a static mapping, perform the following steps:

1. Choose Static Mappings in the Mappings menu.
2. Select the mapping to be modified in the Static Mappings dialog box and choose Edit Mapping.
3. In the Edit Static Mapping dialog box, make any required changes.
4. Click OK to save the changes.

Objective B.4

You can import static mappings for unique and special group names from files that conform to the format of LMHOSTS files, described in the preceding chapter. Choose Import Mappings in the Static Mappings dialog box to import mappings.

Special Names

WINS recognizes a variety of special names, identified by the value of the sixteenth byte of Microsoft-compatible names. Special names are encountered when setting up static mappings and when examining entries in the WINS database. The special names recognized by WINS are discussed in the following sections.

Normal Group Names

A normal group name is tagged with the value 0x1E in the sixteenth byte. Browsers broadcast to this name and respond to it when electing a master browser. In response to queries to this name, WINS always returns the broadcast address FFFFFFFF.

Multihomed Names

A *multihomed name* is a single computer name that stores multiple IP addresses, which are associated with multiple network adapters on the computer. Each multihomed name can be associated with up to 25 IP addresses. This information is established when TCP/IP configuration is used to specify IP addresses for the computer.

When the WINS Server service is running on a multihomed computer, the WINS service is always associated with the first network adapter in the computer configuration. All WINS messages on the computer, therefore, originate from the same adapter.

Multihomed computers with connections to two or more networks should not be configured as WINS servers. If a client attempts a connection with a multihomed WINS server, the server might supply an IP address on the wrong network, causing the connection attempt to fail.

Domain Group Names

A Domain group is used to register Windows NT Server computers in Domain groups, principally Windows NT Server domains. If the Domain group is not configured statically, member computers are registered dynamically as they enter and leave the group. Internet group names are identified by the value 0x1C in the sixteenth byte of the NetBIOS name. A Domain group can contain up to 25 members, preference being given to the nearest Windows NT Server computers. On a large internetwork, the Domain group registers the 24 nearest Windows NT Server computers and the primary domain controller. Windows NT Server v3.1 computers are not registered to this group dynamically and must be added manually in WINS Manager. Manually adding computers to the group makes the group static; it no longer accepts dynamic updates.

Other Special Names

Several other special names are identified by byte 16, including the following:

- **0x0.** Identifies the redirector name associated with the workstation service of a computer. This is the name usually referred to as the NetBIOS computer name.
- **0x1.** Identifies _MSBROWSE_, the name to which master browsers broadcast to announce their domains to other master browsers on the local subnet. WINS responds to queries to _MSBROWSE_ with the broadcast address FFFFFFFF.

- **0x3.** Identifies the Messenger service name used to send messages.
- **0x6.** Identifies the RAS Server service.
- **0x1B.** Identifies the domain master browser, which WINS assumes is the primary domain controller. If it is not, the domain master browser should be statically configured in WINS.
- **0x1F.** Identifies the NetDDE service.
- **0x20.** Identifies the Server service that provides access to file and printer shares.
- **0x21.** Identifies a RAS client.
- **0xBE.** Identifies a Network Monitor agent.
- **0xBF.** Identifies the Network Monitor utility.

Backing Up the Database

WINS performs a complete backup of its database every 24 hours. The file name and path are specified by Registry parameters, as discussed in the section "WINS Registry Entries." On occasion, you might want to execute an unscheduled backup. The procedure, which must be performed on the computer running the WINS Server service, is as follows:

1. Choose the Backup Database command in the Mappings menu to open the Select Backup Directory dialog box (see fig. 13.14).

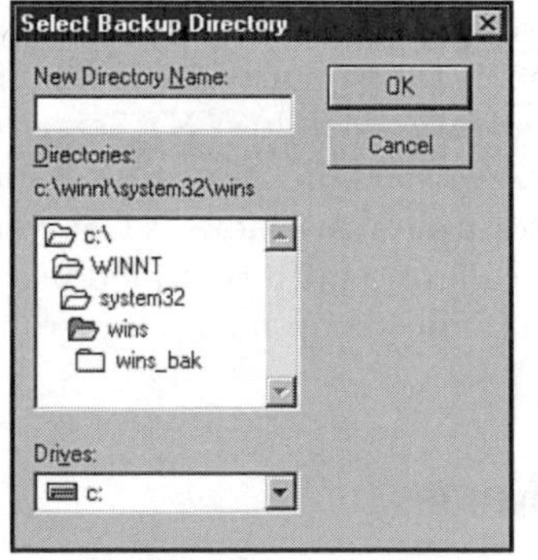

Figure 13.14
Selecting a WINS database backup directory.

2. If desired, select a disk drive in the Drives field. The best location is another hard disk so that the database files remain available if the primary hard disk fails.
3. Specify the directory in which backup files should be stored. WINS Manager proposes a default directory.
4. If desired, specify a new directory name to be created in the directory chosen in Step 3. By default, a subdirectory named wins_bak is created to store the backup files.
5. To back up only records that have changed since the last backup, check the Perform Incremental Backup check box. This option is meaningful only if a full backup has been previously performed.
6. Click OK to make the backup.

Restoring the WINS Database

If users cannot connect to a server running the WINS Server service, the WINS database may have become corrupted. In that case, you might need to restore the database from a backup copy. You can do this manually or by using menu commands. The procedure must be performed on the computer running the WINS service.

To use menu commands to restore the WINS database, perform the following steps:

1. Stop the WINS Service by using one of these methods:
    - Stop the Windows Internet Server Service by using the Services icon in the Control Panel or the Server Manager.
    - Open a command prompt and enter the command **NET STOP WINS**.
2. Start the WINS Manager, ignore any warning message that `The Windows Internet Naming Service is not running on the target machine,` or that the target machine is not accessible.
3. Choose the Restore Local Database command in the Mappings menu.
4. In the Select Directory To Restore From dialog box, specify the directory from which to restore.
5. Click OK to restore the database.
6. Start the WINS service by using one of the following methods:
    - Start the Windows Internet Server Service by using the Services icon in the Control Panel or the Server Manager.
    - Open a command prompt and enter the command **NET START WINS**.

To restore the database manually, follow this procedure:

1. Stop the WINS Server service.
2. Delete all files in the directory c:\winnt\system32\wins.
3. Copy the file System.mdb from the installation disks to the c:\winnt\system32\wins directory.
4. Make a backup copy of the file Wins.mdb to the c:\winnt\system32\wins directory.
5. Restart the WINS Server service.

The key WINS database files are stored by default in the directory C:\winnt\system32\wins. (If your system files are stored in a directory other than C:\winnt, substitute the appropriate directory path). The files are as follows:

- **Wins.mdb.** The WINS database file.
- **Winstmp.mdb.** Used by WINS to store temporary working data.
- **J50.log.** Records transactions performed on the database. (This was called Jet.log under Windows NT Server 3.5x.)

Caution Never remove or modify the WINS files.These files are not normal databases, and if you try to modify them the entire WINS database will become corrupted or be lost.

Scavenging and Compacting the Database

Over time, the WINS database becomes cluttered with released and old entries from other WINS servers. Scavenging the WINS database clears these old records (names that have not been renewed and have passed all three timeouts described previously). After scavenging, compacting the database to reduce the size of the data file is a good idea because it reduces the overall size of the database and therefore increases the speed at which queries can be processed.

Scavenging is performed periodically, as determined by parameters in the Registry. You can, however, choose to initiate scavenging manually before compacting the database. (Under Windows NT Server 3.51 or earlier, scavenging must be performed manually.)

To scavenge the database, choose the Initiate Scavenging command in the Mappings menu.

The WINS database is stored in the file named Wins.mdb, which is stored by default in the directory \winnt\system32\wins. To compact the WINS database, do the following:

1. Open a command prompt.
2. Enter the command **NET STOP WINS** to stop the WINS Server service on the computer. Users cannot resolve names on this server while the WINS Server service is stopped.
3. Change to the WINS directory. If the directory is in the default location, enter the command **CD \WINNT\SYSTEM32\WINS**.
4. Enter the command **JETPACK WINS.MDB TEMP.MDB** to compact the database. Wins.mdb is the file to be compacted, and Temp.mdb is a name for a temporary file that JETPACK uses during the compacting process.
5. After receiving the message `JETPACK completed successfully`, restart WINS by using the command **NET START WINS**.
6. To close the command prompt, enter the command **EXIT**.

Caution JETPACK should be used to compact the Wins.mdb file only. Do not compact the System.mdb file.

Replicating the WINS Database

Objective B.4

Having two or more WINS servers on any network is desirable. You can use a second server to maintain a replica of the WINS database that can be used if the primary server fails. On large intranets, multiple WINS servers result in less routed traffic and spread the name resolution workload across several computers.

You can configure pairs of WINS servers as replication partners. WINS servers can perform two types of replication actions: push and pull. A member of a replication pair functions as either a push partner or a pull partner.

All database replication takes place by transferring data from a push partner to a pull partner. A push partner, however, cannot unilaterally push data. Data transfers can be initiated in two ways.

A pull partner can initiate replication by requesting replication from a push partner. All records in a WINS database are stamped with a version number. When a pull partner sends a pull request, it specifies the highest version number associated with data received from the push partner. The push partner then sends any new data in its database that has a higher version number than was specified in the pull request.

A push partner can initiate replication by notifying a pull partner that the push partner has data to send. The pull partner indicates its readiness to receive the data by sending a pull replication request that enables the push partner to push the data.

In summary:

- Replication cannot take place until a pull partner indicates it is ready to receive data. A pull request indicates a readiness to receive data as well as the data the pull partner is prepared to receive. Therefore, the pull partners really control the replication process.
- All data is transferred from a push partner to a pull partner. Data is sent only in response to pull requests.

Pulls are scheduled events that occur at regular intervals. Pushes are triggered when the number of changes to be replicated exceeds a specified threshold. An administrator, however, can manually trigger both pushes and pulls.

Figure 13.15 illustrates a network that incorporates five WINS servers. In general, replication partners are configured for two-way record transfer. Each member of the partnership is configured as a push partner and a pull partner, enabling both servers to pull updated data from each other.

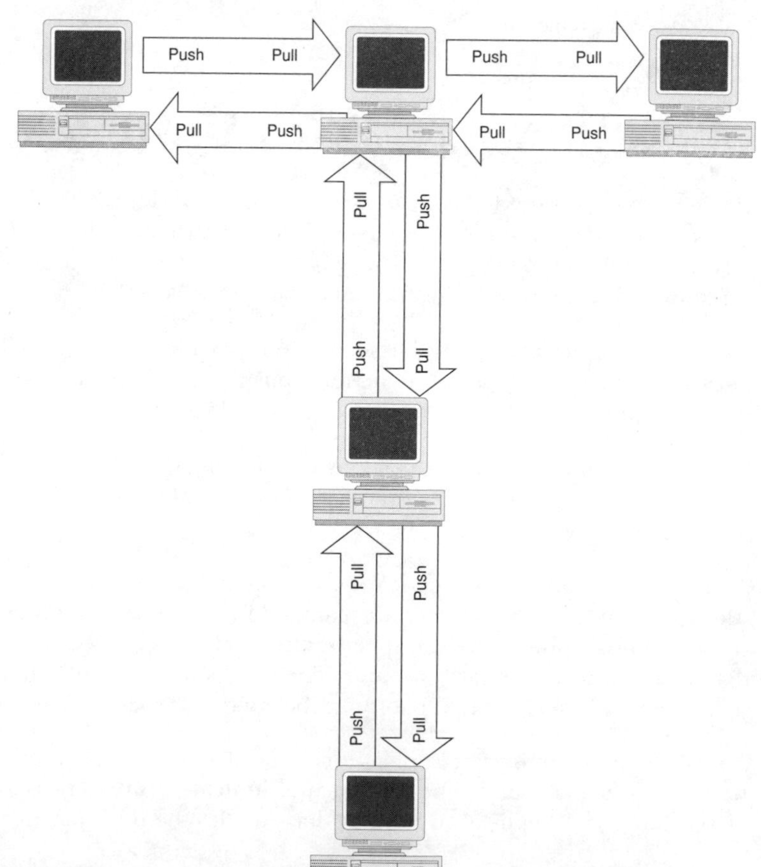

Figure 13.15

A network with several WINS servers.

Adding Replication Partners

To configure replication on a WINS server, perform the following steps:

1. Select a WINS server in the WINS Manager main window.
2. Choose the Replication Partners command in the Server menu to open the Replication Partners dialog box (see fig. 13.16).

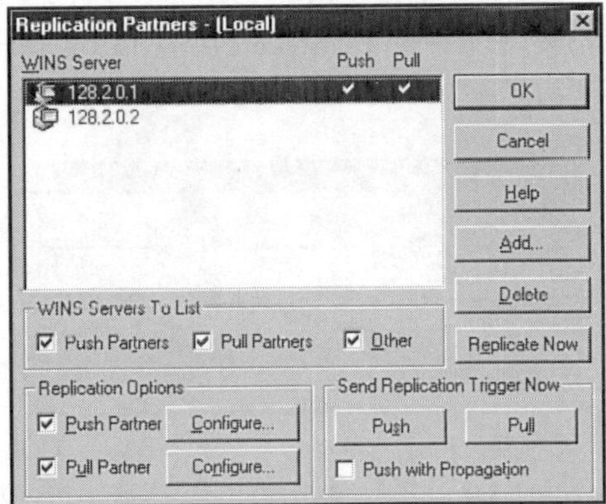

Figure 13.16
The Replication Partners dialog box.

3. The Replication Partners dialog box lists all WINS servers that have been added to the configuration of this WINS Manager.
4. To add a replication partner, choose Add and enter the name or the address of a WINS server in the Add WINS Server dialog box.
5. To specify a replication partner, choose a WINS server in the WINS Server box of the Replication Partners dialog box.

6a. To configure the selected server as a push partner, follow this procedure:

   i. Check the Push Partner check box under Replication Options.

   ii. Choose Configure to open the Push Partner Properties dialog box (see fig. 13.17).

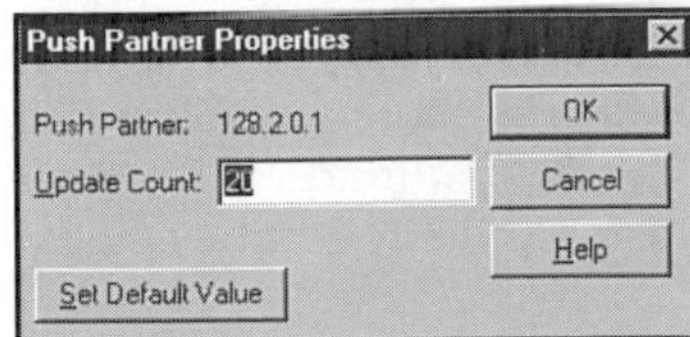

Figure 13.17
Push Partner configuration.

iii. Enter a value in the Update Count field that indicates the number of updates that should trigger a push. The minimum value is 5. Choose Set Default Value to enter the value you selected as a default in the Preferences dialog box.

iv. Choose OK to return to the Replication Partners dialog box.

6b. To configure the selected server as a pull partner, follow this procedure:

i. Check the Pull Partner check box under Replication Options.

ii. Choose Configure to open the Pull Partner Properties dialog box (see fig. 13.18).

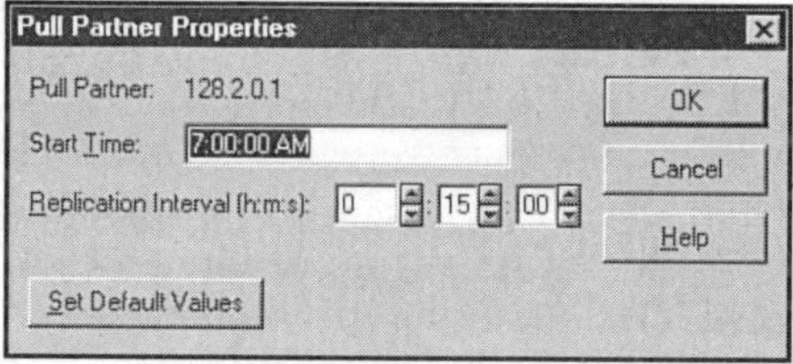

Figure 13.18
Pull Partner configuration.

iii. Enter a value in the Start Time field that specifies when in the day replication should begin. The time format must conform to the setting in the International option in the Control Panel. Also, specify a time in the Replication Interval field to determine the frequency of replication. Choose Set Default Values to enter the value you selected as a default in the Preferences dialog box.

iv. Click OK to return to the Replication Partners dialog box.

7. Configure other replication partners as required. You can configure a WINS server simultaneously as a push and a pull partner, which is required if two-way replication is to take place.

8. Click OK after replication partners are configured for this WINS server.

Manually Triggering Replication

After adding a WINS server, updating static mappings, or bringing a WINS server back online after shutting it down for a period of time, forcing the server to replicate its data with its replication partners may be required. WINS Manager enables administrators to manually trigger both push and pull replications.

To trigger a replication, follow these steps:

1. Choose a WINS server in the WINS Manager main window.
2. Choose the Replication Partners command in the Server menu.

3. Choose a replication partner in the WINS Server list of the Replication Partners dialog box.
4. Check the Push with Propagation check box if you want to trigger a push replication to be propagated to all WINS servers on the internetwork. If you do not check this box, only the immediate push partner receives the replicated data.

5a. To send a replication trigger, in the Send Replication Trigger Now box, choose Push or Pull.

A push trigger notifies the pull partner that the push partner has data to transmit. It does not force the pull partner to accept a push. Data is not transferred until the pull partner sends a pull request to the push partner that originated the trigger.

A pull trigger requests updated data from a push partner.

5b. To start immediate replication, select a replication partner and choose the Replicate Now button.

WINS Registry Entries

Unless otherwise specified, the Registry parameters related to WINS are stored in the HKEY_LOCAL_MACHINE subtree in the key \SYSTEM\CurrentControlSet\Services\Wins\Parameters. Not all parameters are inserted in the Registry during WINS installation. If you require the features associated with a parameter, use the Registry Editor to add the value to the Registry.

The Parameters key includes the subkey Datafiles, which specifies the files for WINS to use when it initializes the WINS database. The Registry values in the WINS Parameters key are described in the following sections.

DbFileNm

Data Type:	REG_SZ or REG_EXPAND_SZ
Range:	pathname
Default:	%SystemRoot%\system32\wins\wins.mdb

DbFileNm specifies the complete path name for the WINS database file.

DoStaticDataInit

Data Type: REG_DWORD
Range: 0 or 1
Default: 0

If this parameter is 1, the WINS database is initialized from files specified in the Datafiles subkey. Initialization takes place whenever WINS is started or when changes are made to parameters in the Parameters or Datafiles subkeys. If this parameter is 0, WINS does not initialize its database.

InitTimePause

Data Type: REG_DWORD
Range: 0 or 1
Default: 0

If this parameter is 1, the WINS Server service starts in a paused state until it has been replicated from one of its replication partners or until replication has failed at least once. If this parameter is 1, the \WINS\Partners\Pull\InitTimeReplication parameter should be set to 1 or removed from the Registry.

LogDetailedEvents

Data Type: REG_DWORD
Range: 0 or 1
Default: 0

This value ordinarily is set using the Log Detailed Events check box in the WINS Server Configuration dialog box. If 1, verbose logging is enabled. If 0, standard logging is enabled.

LogFilePath

Data Type: REG_SZ or REG_EXPAND_SZ
Range: pathname
Default: %SystemRoot%\system32\wins

The LogFilePath parameter specifies the directory in which to store WINS log files.

LoggingOn

Data Type:	REG_DWORD
Range:	0 or 1
Default:	0

If the value of this parameter is 1, logging takes place using the logging file specified by the LogFilePath parameter. This value ordinarily is set by checking the Logging Enabled check box in the WINS Server Configuration dialog box.

McastIntvl

Data Type:	REG_DWORD
Range:	2400 minimum
Default:	2400

This parameter specifies the interval in seconds at which the WINS server sends a multicast message to announce its presence to other WINS servers. The minimum value of 2400 sets an interval of 40 minutes.

McastTtl

Data Type:	REG_DWORD
Range:	1–32
Default:	6

Specifies the number of times a multicast announcement can cross a router.

NoOfWrkThds

Data Type:	REG_DWORD
Range:	1–40
Defaults:	Number of processors on the computer

Specifies the number of worker threads available to WINS. Can be changed without restarting the WINS server computer.

PriorityClassHigh

Data Type:	REG_DWORD
Range:	0 or 1
Defaults:	0

If this parameter is 1, WINS runs at a high priority, ensuring that it is not preempted by other processes on the computer. Use this parameter to emphasize WINS performance on a computer that functions primarily as a WINS name server. A value of 0 sets the WINS priority as normal.

RefreshInterval

Data Type:	REG_DWORD
Range:	Time in seconds, max 96h, 59m, 59s (hex)
Default:	96 hours

This parameter is a hex value that specifies the interval in seconds at which WINS names must be renewed on the server. The value ordinarily is set by specifying the Renewal Interval in the WINS Server Configuration dialog box.

TombstoneInterval

Data Type:	REG_DWORD
Range:	Time in seconds, max 96h, 59m, 59s
Default:	variable

This parameter is a hex value that specifies the interval after which non-renewed names are marked as extinct. The value ordinarily is set by specifying the Extinction Interval in the WINS Server Configuration dialog box.

TombstoneTimeout

Data Type:	REG_DWORD
Range:	Time in seconds, max 96h, 59m, 59s
Default:	variable

This parameter is a hex value that specifies the interval after which extinct names are removed from the WINS database. The value ordinarily is set by specifying the Extinction Timeout in the WINS Server Configuration dialog box.

UseSelfFndPntrs

Data Type:	REG_DWORD
Range:	0 or 1
Defaults:	0

If this parameter is 1 and the network routers support multicasting, a WINS server can automatically identify other WINS servers and identify push and pull replication partners. If routers do not support multicasting, WINS servers can automatically identify only those WINS servers on the same network or subnet. WINS server automatic identification adjusts automatically as WINS servers are started or gracefully shut down.

WINS server automatic identification is overridden if WINS Manager is used to establish replication.

VerifyInterval

Data Type:	REG_DWORD
Range:	Hex value for time in seconds
Default:	variable

This parameter is a hex value that specifies the interval after which the WINS server must verify entries in its database that it does not own. The value ordinarily is set by specifying the Verify Interval in the WINS Server Configuration dialog box.

Practice

This lab was designed to walk you through some of the steps in installing and configuring the WINS server. If your network configuration allows, please try working with both the proxy agents and WINS replication.

Note If you do not have networking installed, see exercise 0 from the lab for Chapter 9, "Internet Information Server."

Exercise 1—Installing the WINS Server

In this exercise, you install the WINS server on your computer.

1. Open the Network dialog box. On the Services tab, choose Add.
2. Select the Windows Internet Naming Service (at the bottom of the list). Now click OK.
3. A prompt asks for your NT source files.
4. Choose Close to exit the Network dialog box.
5. Restart your system.

Exercise 2—Learning About WINS Server Configuration

In this exercise, you begin to look at the WINS server and see where the configuration is done.

1. From the Start menu, choose Programs, Administrative Tools, WINS Manager. Click the server that is listed.
2. Check the Detail view of the server. Choose Server, Detailed View from the menu. When finished, choose Close to return to WINS manager.
3. Choose Server, Configuration from the menu. Click the Advanced button to display the rest of the dialog box.
4. Click the Browse button beside the Database Backup Path. In the directory window, choose the path c:\winnt\system32\wins. Enter **BACKUP** as the New Directory Name.
5. Click OK to save the information. Notice the full path in the Database Backup Directory field.
6. Click OK to close the Configuration dialog box.

Exercise 3—Adding Static Mappings to the Database

In this exercise, you add some static mappings to the database. (This will give you something to see when you look at the database.)

1. From the menu, choose Mappings, Static Mappings. The Static Mapping dialog box appears.
2. Click the Add Mappings button.
3. In the Name field, enter **Rob**, for the IP Address enter **148.53.66.7**. Click the Add button.
4. Add another mapping. Enter **Judy** for the name and **148.53.66.9** for the address. Click Add.
5. Click Close. This should bring the Static Mappings dialog box back up.

   How many mappings are listed? Why? There should be six mappings in total, three each. For each of the systems, WINS created a mapping for the Workstation Service, Messenger Service, and the Server Service.
6. Click Close to shut down the Static Mappings dialog box.

7. Choose Mappings, Show Database.

   You should see the six mappings listed in the database window.

8. Click Close and exit the WINS manager.

Summary

Working with Microsoft networking requires the use of NetBIOS names, which has been discussed many times in previous chapters. NetBIOS uses a lot of broadcasts to deal with name registration and release and resolution—in a TCP/IP environment, there is a problem because these broadcasts do not get forwarded by routers. This chapter has looked at WINS, a service that makes possible the use of NetBIOS names on a wide area network. You have looked at what WINS is, and you have seen how to install and configure WINS. The WINS service makes wide area networking with Microsoft TCP/IP possible.

Test Yourself

1. In a network with 26 subnets, how many WINS servers are required?
2. How many times will your client try to contact the WINS server?
3. At what point will a WINS client attempt to renew its name?
4. If you put a WINS address in the TCP/IP configuration of a client, do you need to change the node type?
5. Can a WINS server have a dynamic address?
6. What must be configured on the WINS server before the clients can begin using it?
7. When is it necessary to configure a static mapping in the WINS database?
8. Can a non-WINS client use the WINS server to resolve an address?
9. What do you have to do before WINS automatically backs up its database?
10. How do you configure a Windows for Workgroups system to act as a proxy?
11. There are three values, Renewal Interval, Extinction Interval, and Extinction Timeout. What are these values for?
12. What happens if the name that you are trying to register is already in the database?
13. What event triggers a pull replication? A push replication?

Test Yourself Answers

1. Generally only one is required. A second server, however, provides redundancy.
2. Three times at 15-second intervals.
3. Normally renewal takes place at 50 percent of the TTL.
4. No. Windows defaults to H-Node if there is a valid WINS server address.
5. No. The WINS server requires a static IP address.
6. Nothing. The configuration is done on the client end. The only configuration required is a WINS server address. This can be supplied manually or through DHCP.
7. *If* the client is a non-WINS client, a static mapping is required.
8. Yes. If the client is on the same subnet as a WINS proxy, the proxy takes the broadcast and checks the name with the WINS server.
9. You have to configure the server with a backup directory. Under Servers, Configuration, choose the Advanced tab and enter a directory.
10. In the TCP/IP Advanced Setting dialog box, check the Enable Proxy check box.
11. The purpose of the values is

    Renewal Interval. This is the TTL for the client's name. The client begins to attempt renewal at half this time.

    Extinction Interval. This is how long the WINS server keeps the address of a system that has not renewed its name before marking the system extinct.

    Extinction Timeout. The period of time from when an entry is marked extinct to when it is actually removed from the database.

12. The WINS server sends three challenges to the system that currently has the name registered. If the system does not respond, your system is registered with that IP address. If the system does respond, you cannot register that name.
13. Pull replication is triggered by a time period; push is triggered by the number of changes.

CHAPTER 14

The Browser Service and TCP/IP

You already know that Microsoft uses NetBIOS for its internal networking, and that NetBIOS uses broadcast traffic for many of the functions that it performs. This causes problems, of course, when it comes to running Microsoft networking over the TCP/IP protocol stack because NetBIOS broadcasts do not get forwarded by routers.

This chapter examines these problems and how they are overcome. There are two primary ways this can be done: LMHOSTS and WINS. This chapter shows how these two methods of name resolution make the Browser services possible and how they work to support Domain activity over TCP/IP even though both are broadcast based.

The Browsing Process

When you double-click the Network Neighborhood icon, you receive a list of computers available on your network. This list includes a system that has the capability to provide services to the network. As you should be aware, this capability to share resources is a function of having a server service. The next section looks at the process of starting a server service and how this server ends up in the list you see in the Network Neighborhood. The end of the section discusses some problems that arise, and how to get around them.

The Microsoft Browser Service—Basics

Figure 14.1 shows a server starting up. This computer (named NTS99) announces itself to the network as it initializes the server service, and will be announced on the network as NTS99(0x20)—remember that 0x20 indicates the server service. The server announces its presence to the network every minute for the first five minutes that it is up and running. After the initial period, the server continues to announce itself every 12 minutes. These announcements are made over the NetBIOS Datagram service port, which is port 138.

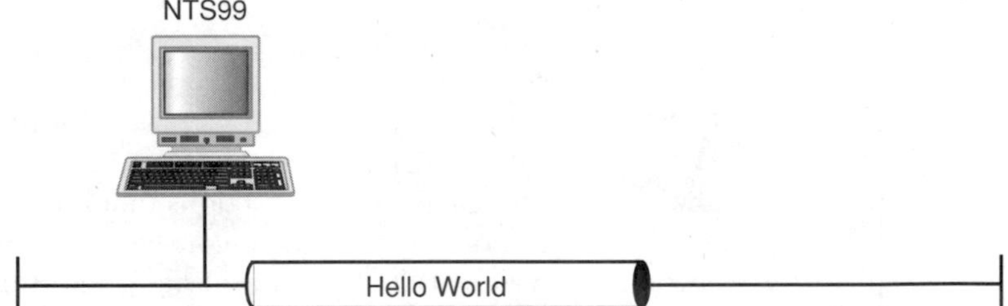

Figure 14.1

A server starts up and announces its presence to the network.

Obviously, if a server announces itself to the network, there should be some system listening to the announcements being made. In Microsoft networking, this system is the Master Browser. In figure 14.2, you can see that the Master Browser is also on the network. The Master Browser adds any servers that announce themselves to a list of servers that it keeps.

The Master Browser now has a copy of all the servers on the network. As figure 14.2 shows, the Master Browser is also included in the list (computer name NTS5). If you add another computer (NTS3) to this network, this computer also announces itself because it also has a server service (see fig. 14.3). For reasons soon to be evident, this system gets marked as a special system in the Master Browser list. Because of this, the system retrieves a copy of the list that the Master Browser has been building. This makes the system a Backup Browser.

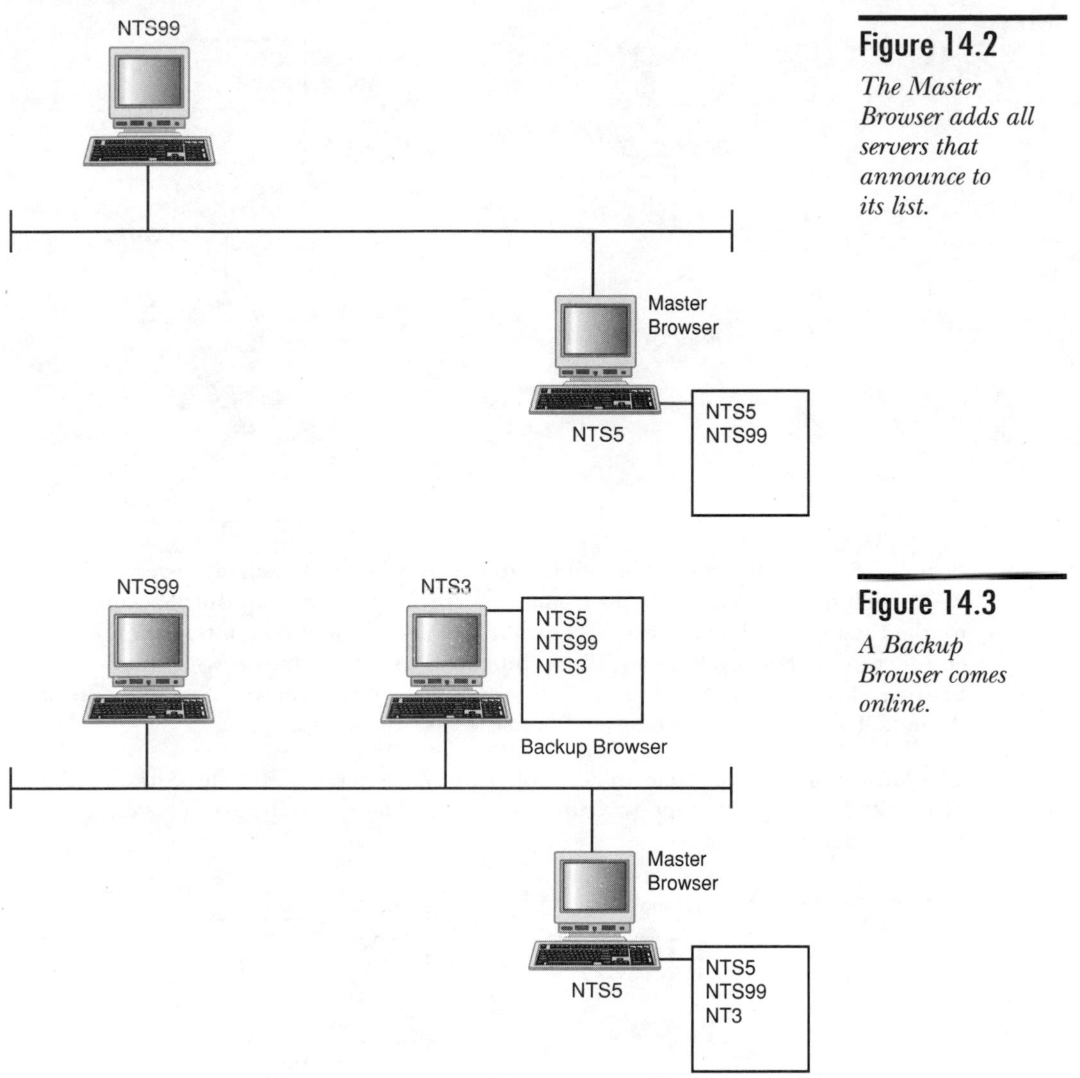

Figure 14.2
The Master Browser adds all servers that announce to its list.

Figure 14.3
A Backup Browser comes online.

The Backup Browser retrieves a new copy of the list (browse list) from the Master Browser every 15 minutes. In this way, the list of servers is always updated. You cannot change this time period.

At this point, all the basics of the browser service are in place. All that is needed is a workstation. In figure 14.4, a station called WKS454 is added. The user at this workstation wants to get a file from a share that is on NTS99.

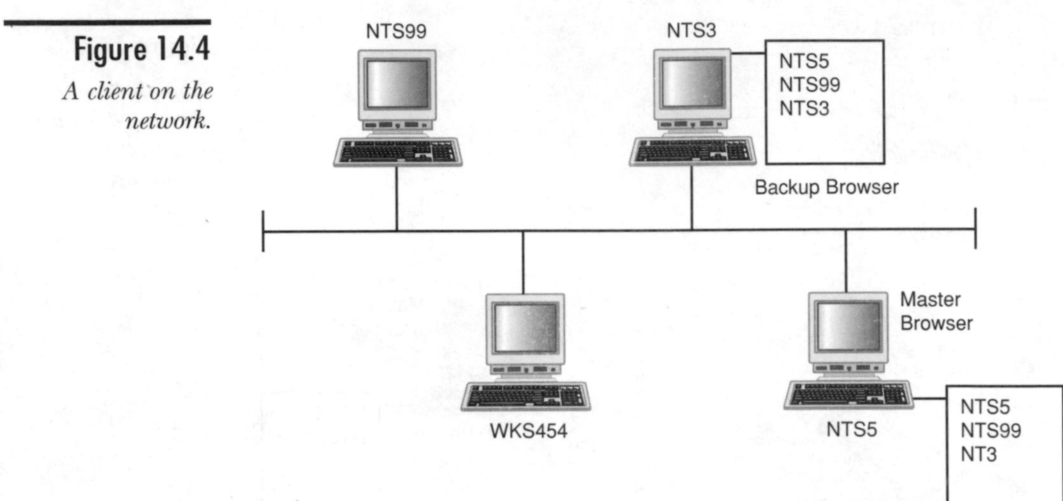

Figure 14.4
A client on the network.

If the workstation has not yet attempted to connect to another station over the network, it needs to retrieve a list of Backup Browsers (a list of all the specially marked systems in the browse list). From then on, the client computers always connect to the Backup Browser. If they all talked to the Master Browser simultaneously, this would overload the resources on that system. There is a problem here, though: The client does not know who the Master Browser is.

The Master Browser registers an additional NetBIOS name on the network called MBROWSE. The client, therefore, needs only to request this list from this name (see fig. 14.5).

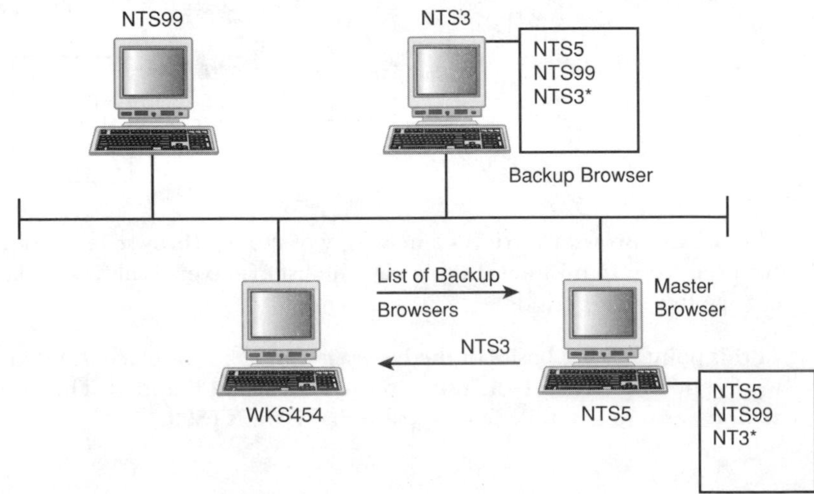

Figure 14.5
The client retrieves the list of Backup Browsers from the Master Browser.

Now that the client has a list of Backup Browsers, it does not have to talk to the Master Browser again. The only cases where it will are if the client restarts, or if none of the Backup Browsers respond. The client now retrieves a list of servers from one of the Backup Browser on the list the Master Browser gave it (see fig. 14.6).

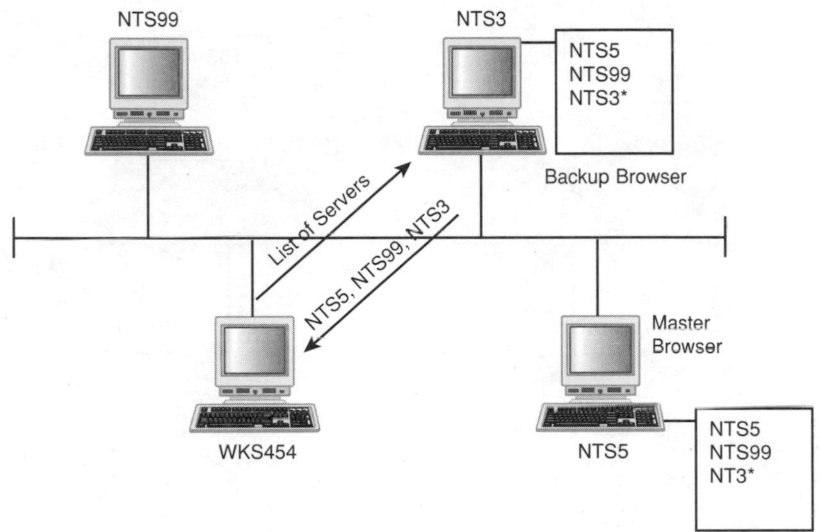

Figure 14.6

The client retrieves the browser list from the Backup Browser.

The client now has a list of all the servers present on the local subnet. Remember that the announcements cannot cross routers; therefore, only local systems are included. Next the client system displays the list for the user. As the user chooses the system to connect with, the user's system contacts that computer directly (see fig. 14.7). The user name and password of the current user is included in the contact so that only appropriate resources can be shown.

The user can now access the resource—usually. Sometimes when you click a system name in the Network Neighborhood, you receive an error explaining that the name cannot be found on the network. This happens if the system is down. If it's down, however, why is it in the list?

> **Note**
>
> One of the main problems—or in a better light, shortcomings—of this method of sharing names is that updating the information is not instantaneous. The Master Browser keeps an entry in its list until that entry has missed three announcement periods. That can be as long as 36 minutes (three periods of 12 minutes each). Further, because the Backup Browser retrieves a new copy of the list every 15 minutes only, the lag time can extend from 36 minutes to 51 minutes.

continues

This means that a system that dies an unnatural death (that is, crashes) can remain in the list for up to 51 minutes. Note that if it closes down gracefully (the user shuts the system down from the Start menu rather than the Power button), the name is removed from all lists. Remember the NetBIOS Name Release?

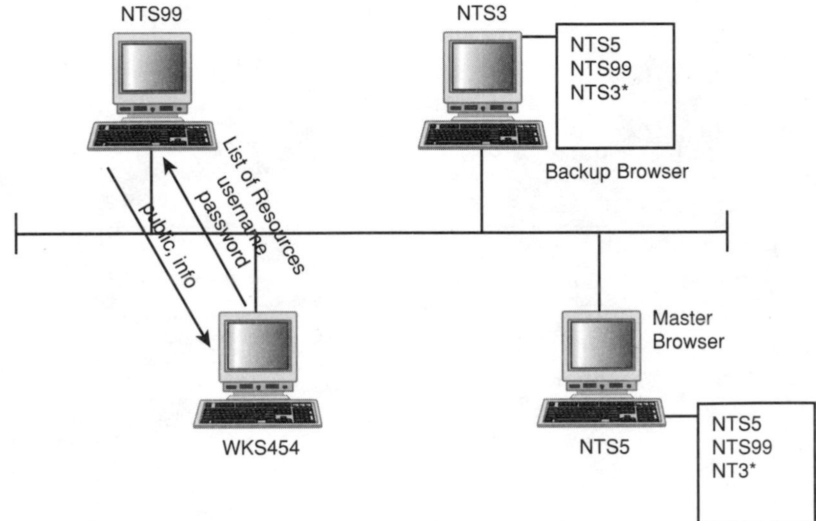

Figure 14.7
The client talks directly to the server.

Configuring Browsers

Two types of browsers have been involved on the network so far. This discussion first looks at some of the types of browsers that you will find on a network, and then examines how to configure them in a domain and in a workgroup model.

Types of Browsers

The following list describes the different types of browsers:

- **Domain Master Browser.** This is the Master Browser responsible for an entire domain. The PDC for a domain automatically becomes the Domain Master Browser (DMB).
- **Master Browser.** As you have seen, the Master Browser is the system that builds the browser list and distributes it to the Backup Browser when requested. On the subnet where the PDC is located, the DMB handles these functions. On other domains, this is usually a BDC. This can, however, be nearly any system if there is no BDC, including Windows for Workgroups, Windows 95, Windows NT Workstation, or Windows NT Server installed as a server.

- **Backup Browser.** In the domain model, this is just about always the BDC. Like the Master Browser, however, this can be very nearly any version of Windows. The Backup Browser retrieves a copy of the browse list from the Master Browser every 15 minutes, and provides the list to clients on request.
- **Potential Browser.** This is a system that can act as a browser, but is not currently a browser. Most systems fit into this category.
- **Non Browser.** You can configure a system to not participate in browsing (as described in the following section). If you do this, the system is a Non Browser.

Configuring the Browser Type

The configuration of the browser service on a particular computer depends on the operating system. For Windows NT and Windows 95, the configuration is done in the Registry. (Chapter 11, "Dynamic Host Configuration Protocol (DHCP)," covered editing Registry entries.) The key is:

```
HKEY_LOCAL_MACHINE\System\CurrentControlSet\Services\Browser\Parameters
```

The following settings in this key enable you to configure the browser service:

- **IsDomainMaster.** This tells the system to attempt to become the Master Browser. On the subnet that contains the PDC, this setting ensures only that the system becomes a Backup Browser. (The PDC always wins.) The setting can be either TRUE or FALSE. The default is FALSE.
- **MaintainServerList.** This setting tells your browser service whether to keep the browse list. This entry has three settings: Yes, No, and Auto. For the vast majority of systems, you should leave this at the default of Auto. If you choose Yes, the system usually becomes a Backup Browser. If you have a system more powerful on a particular subnet, you can consider setting this to Yes. Setting this to No ensures that this system does not participate in browsing. Use this setting for workstations that absolutely need every ounce of performance.

Browser Elections

The process of choosing the Master Browser is handled in a very democratic fashion. The computers on a subnet hold an election. The election process is a broadcast that determines the new Master Browser. Unlike a regular election, systems don't vote for each other; they all vote for themselves. The first one to cast the ballot wins. Two main criteria determine how long a system waits before casting its ballot:

- **Current browser role.** The Backup Browser wins over a Potential Browser.
- **Operating system and version.** NT 4 wins over 3.51. Both, however, win over Windows 95. Windows 95 wins over Windows for Workgroups.

Note The original networking components of Windows for Workgroups contained code that became invalid when NT 3.5 was released. A path on the NT Server CD that corrects this should be applied to any stations running Windows for Workgroups.

This of course means that a tie can sometimes result. There are, however, methods for tie-breaking. A tie is decided by the following:

- **Time up.** The system that has been up longer wins.
- **Computer name.** If the systems have been up an equal amount of time, the system with the first name (in alphabetic order) wins.

You should now be familiar with what the browser service does and with the election process. The next item to look at is the timing for an election. Three reasons determine that an election should be held. These reasons are as follows:

- **Master Browser shuts down.** If the Master Browser shuts down in a normal fashion, the last thing it does is call an election to determine its replacement.
- **Backup Browser fails to update its copy of the browser list.** If a Backup Browser attempts to contact the Master Browser to update the browser list and cannot, it calls an election.
- **A client fails to contact the Master Browser.** If a client attempts to get a list of Backup Browsers and fails, the client calls an election.

Calling an election is a simple process of sending a broadcast to the network. All the systems receive the broadcast, and the system with the highest criteria is the first to broadcast a reply, hence becoming the Master Browser.

Browsing Workgroups and Domains

One last concept must be covered before you look at how TCP/IP gets involved in the browsing process. You need to understand that the browsers and clients that talk to each other all have to be in the same domain or the same workgroup. If more than one domain or workgroup is on the same network, each has its own Master Browser and Backup Browsers.

There is always only one Master Browser. In the case of the domain model, the PDC will be the master browser on its network segment. On the other networks it is usually a BDC. (Why Microsoft has used BDCs becomes evident as you look at domain activity.)

In a domain model, the Backup Browsers are BDCs. You can have up to three BDCs acting as Backup Browsers on each subnet (but not more). Although this might seem silly, the PDC and BDCs have to be able to talk to each other anyway to allow for domain activity. Therefore, because these systems can talk to each other, they can exchange the browser list. The other consideration for using the BDCs as the Backup Browser is simple: They tend to be more powerful machines; therefore, they can better handle the extra load of being a Backup Browser.

The workgroup model is different. No systems always act in a main role. This is where the election process becomes very important and very common. In this scenario, though, you do not know what sort of systems will be acting as the Backup Browsers. There is, therefore, no guarantee they will have enough resources to handle the requests. To relieve the problem before it becomes a problem, Microsoft designed the system to choose one Backup Browser for every 32 active systems. Thus, if you have 78 systems on the network, there is one Master Browser and three Backup Browsers. In this way, no one system is overloaded with requests for information.

Supporting Domain Activity

Before examining the problems with the browser service and multiple subnets, this discussion considers the other big issue that needs to addressed when routers are used with Windows NT domains. Windows NT is usually configured as a domain controller or a server in a domain model. Working in the domain model has many advantages over the workgroup model. Most of these advantages deal with the centralized security that NT Directory Services provides. In a network that spans multiple subnets, however, a need still exists to communicate between domain controllers, even over routers (which don't pass the NetBIOS broadcasts that domain activity relies on).

A Quick Review of NT Directory Services

In the domain model, NT works with a Primary Domain Controller (PDC) and usually one or more Backup Domain Controllers (BDC). The whole advantage of using this model is that there is a single user database, meaning that all the user accounts are handled at a central level.

Thus, for any one user, there is only one account. The user is validated not by a single server, but by the domain's giving the user access to any system to which the user has privileges in the entire domain.

For this to happen, the domain controllers must share a single user accounts database. The accounts database is always on the PDC. Therefore, all changes made to the accounts database must be made on the PDC (an administrator adding an account, for example, or a user—somewhere—changing his password).

The BDCs have a copy of the accounts database. They keep a copy so they can validate user logons as well. Therefore, a process has to be in place that keeps the copy of the accounts database on each BDC in synchronization with the actual accounts database on the PDC. This process is the NETLOGON service that runs on all the domain controllers. The NETLOGON service provides three basic functions:

- **Logon validation.** The actual user logon. The logon process creates an access token for the user who establishes the user's security.
- **Pass through authentication.** In a multidomain model, this takes the use logon request and passes it to the trusted domain that contains the user's account.

Note Trust relationships are not covered in this text. Several good books that deal with this subject are available, however, such as *Inside Windows NT Server 4, Certified Administrator's Resource Edition* (also from New Riders).

- **Synchronization.** This is the process of synchronizing all the BDCs with the PDC.

All these processes depend on the capability of the systems to locate each other. This requires NetBIOS name resolution, which uses NetBIOS broadcasts for name resolution.

User Logon

The process that happens when a user attempts a logon also uses NetBIOS broadcast. In designing the network system, Microsoft decided that users should not have to be validated by a particular server. Instead, any domain controller should be able to handle the request. This makes sense. If a server goes down or is busy, the users can still log on to the domain.

You must remember, however, that because this is a broadcast, it cannot pass a router either. This creates a problem if the user is located on a subnet with one domain controller that goes down. The user could not be validated on the network, and therefore could not function.

Browsing Multiple Subnets

You can resolve both the problem of the browser service and the problem of domain activity in one of two ways. You can use the LMHOSTS file discussed in Chapter 13, "The Windows Internet Name Service," or you can use a NetBIOS Name Server such as WINS. The rest of this chapter covers how you can use these methods of NetBIOS name resolution to resolve the problems just described.

Using LMHOSTS

Objective B.8

Domain activity is easily handled using the LMHOSTS file. If you remember, a series of tags to handle various different requirements can be included in the LMHOSTS file. One of the tags, #DOM:*domain_name*, enables you to handle the problem of domain activity over a routed network.

The sample network, shown in figure 14.8, has three subnets. On each subnet is a domain controller that can handle the domain validation.

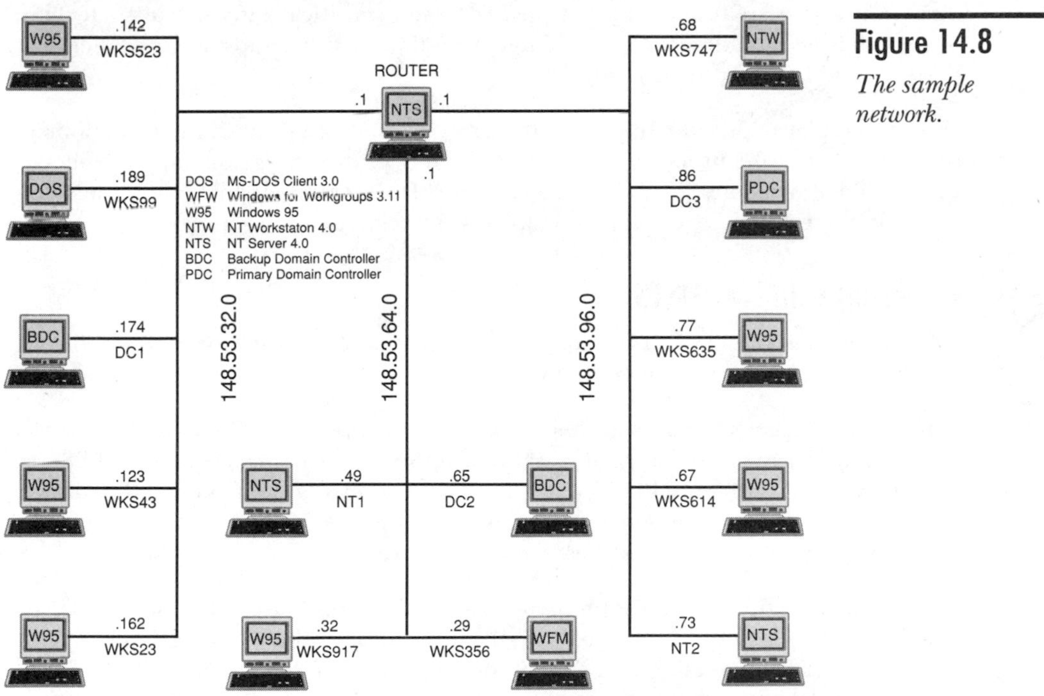

Figure 14.8
The sample network.

In this case, the three domain controllers cannot communicate with each other because they do not know each other's location. There is no way the broadcast can pass the router. Thus the domain cannot synchronize.

You should be aware here of a couple of effects. The users that reside on subnet 148.53.32.0 and on subnet 148.53.64.0 cannot make any changes to the accounts database because they cannot contact the PDC. This means the users cannot change their passwords.

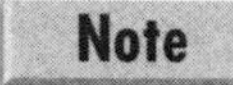

If users complain that they cannot change their passwords, you should verify whether they can see the PDC.

For the domain controllers to synchronize with each other, they need to be added to an LMHOSTS file which is placed on each of them. The file should give the address of the controllers, and using the #DOM tag identify the system as a domain controller. The file would look like this:

```
148.53.32.174      DC1    #DOM:training
148.53.64.65       DC2    #DOM:training
148.53.96.86       DC3    #DOM:training
```

Without this file, there is no way that any domain activity can happen. Notice that all three controllers are listed, and that the PDC is not specifically marked as such. This, of course, is because the PDC may change from time to time, and the controllers all have to be able to talk to each other.

You should place this same file on each user's station. In this way, if the local domain controller failed, the users could still log on to one of the other domain controllers. This would also enable the users to contact the PDC no matter which system was acting in the role, and thereby enable the users to change their passwords.

Objective B.8

Objective C.3

Browsing with LMHOSTS

As stated earlier, the browser broadcast travels only on the local subnet. Even the LMHOSTS file does not change that fact.

Solving this problem requires expanding the browsing services. First, there is always only one Master Browser for a domain. Look at the network shown in figure 14.8. Because you know that the PDC is the Master Browser, you might assume that the browser list would contain only the systems on subnet 148.53.96.0. This is not the case. Therefore, something else has to come into play.

What happens is the PDC takes on the role of the Domain Master Browser. This enables another system to act as a Master Browser. In fact, there will be a Master Browser on each subnet for each domain or workgroup on that subnet. The PDC acting as the Domain Master Browser coordinates the browser lists from each Master Browser, and creates what is known as the domain browser list. Then it can send back the list to each Master Browser on each subnet. The Master Browsers then give the list to the Backup Browsers.

In this way, a host on any subnet can see all the resources available on the entire network. The problem of how the Master Browser and the Domain Master Browser all find each other still exists. As discussed earlier, however, a BDC usually becomes the Backup Browser. If the BDC is on a different subnet, it can become the Master Browser for that subnet.

Because you have already seen the LMHOSTS file and know that it enables domain activity over the routed network, it makes sense now to use the BDCs as the Master Browsers for the other subnets because they already have a way to find the Domain Master Browser—the PDC. Thus, in addition to enabling domain activity, the #DOM tag tells the systems where the other Master Browsers are. Every 15 minutes, the Master Browser for each subnet can exchange lists with the Domain Master Browser.

A small problem still exists, though. Look again at figure 14.8. Consider, for example, that the user at WKS23 wants to connect to a file share on the system NT2. The following steps would take place:

1. When the system NT2 starts up, it announces itself.
2. The Master Browser for that subnet (here the Domain Master Browser) hears the broadcast and adds NT2 to its list.
3. Now the Domain Master Browser exchanges the list with the Master Browser on the remote subnet.
4. The Backup Browser(s) on that subnet calls the Master Browser and retrieves the browser list.
5. The client WKS23 starts and contacts the Master Browser for a list of Backup Browsers.
6. From the list of Backup Browsers, the client chooses and contacts one, asking for the browser list.
7. The client displays the browser list for the user who clicks on the NT2 system in that list.
8. Client WKS23 now attempts to contact the server. Because the client's LMHOSTS file has no mapping, there is no WINS server. Because the NT2 system is on a different subnet, the client cannot resolve the name.
9. Now the client station gives the user an error.

Obviously, the browser list is only part of the problem. The client still cannot work with the server because there is no way for the client to resolve the name that it received to an IP address. If the client needs to talk to the remote hosts, the LMHOSTS file needs to be modified. The new file would look like the following listing:

```
148.53.32.174       DC1     #DOM:training
148.53.64.65        DC2     #DOM:training
148.53.96.86        DC3     #DOM:training
148.53.96.73        NT2
```

This, however, solves only this particular problem. If the client station WKS635 wants now to talk to the server NT1, it goes through the steps just outlined. It cannot, however, resolve the name. The process is further aggravated if File and Print Sharing is enabled for all the Windows workstations on the network.

Note Unless there is a very good reason not to do so, File and Print Sharing should generally be turned off. If you think about it, every system that has a server service installed broadcasts its presence every 12 minutes. This means that if you have 400 stations on a segment, 400 broadcasts occur every 12 minutes.

There is also the problem of the size of the browser list. If every station in your intranet has the File and Print Sharing enabled, they are servers and are listed in the browser list. In a case where you have 10 or 15 systems, this is not a problem. If you have 10,000 or 15,000 systems in your network, however, each one is in that list.

The amount of CPU time used to coordinate the list, and the time spent transmitting the list every 15 minutes between the Domain Master Browser and the Master Browser on each subnet and then to the Backup Browser (probably three on each subnet) reduces the performance of your network noticeably. There is also the problem of the user's attempting to find a system in a list of 15,000.

As a rule of thumb, therefore, *do not* enable File and Print Sharing unless you absolutely have to.

If you wish to allow all the systems on all the networks to see every server, you need to change the LMHOSTS file. You must include every system that can share files using a NetBIOS server service (all Microsoft-based systems). In the case of the example network, that means the following LMHOSTS file:

```
198.53.32.142      WKS523
198.53.32.174      DC1         #DOM:training
198.53.32.123      WKS43
198.53.32.162      WKS23
198.53.64.49       NT1
198.53.64.32       WKS917
198.53.64.65       DC2         #DOM:training
198.53.64.29       WKS356
198.53.96.68       WKS747
198.53.96.86       DC3         #DOM:training
198.53.96.77       WKS635
198.53.96.67       WKS614
198.53.96.73       NT2
```

You must locate this file on each and every system in the network, or you can use a central LMHOST file, as discussed earlier. In either case, though, if you add another host that can share files, you must add it to the file. If you move a system from one network to another, you also need to update the file.

Obviously, this is not the solution to sharing NetBIOS resources across a routed network.

Using WINS to Enable NBT

As you have seen, many different potential problems can arise when using NetBIOS networking over TCP/IP-routed networks. These problems have led (in the days of LAN Manager) to many hours of laborious work for the system administrators of those networks. Thankfully, Windows NT comes with a service called WINS. This section examines how WINS solves these problems and enables both the building of large intranets using TCP/IP and the handling NetBIOS networking on top of it.

WINS, as you should recall, is a NetBIOS Name Server. This means that it handles the resolution of a NetBIOS computer name to a TCP/IP address. Even if that was all it did, that would solve a great portion of the problem. It does, however, do more than that.

WINS helps you get around the domain activity problem and also enables you to facilitate the browsing services better. As you should recall, when a station starts up, it registers its names with the WINS server. Because the WINS server can register all the NetBIOS name types, it can register services running on a computer as separate entries in the WINS database.

The WINS database contains a special group called the Domain Name Group. This group is used to register domain controllers that close to the WINS server. The group has space for 25 IP addresses, including the PDC and up to 24 BDCs. These are recognized with NetBIOS names that end with 0x1C. When a client needs to authenticate a user, the client can now ask the WINS server. The WINS server then provides the list of IP addresses for logon. The PDC is specially marked to differentiate it so that the change requests (such as a password change) can be sent to it directly.

Note As this implies, if you will have more than 25 domain controllers, you should have more than one WINS server.

This also enables the BDCs to find the PDC in the same way, thus permitting the NETLOGON service to handle the synchronization of the domain. As a side note, the NETLOGON service registers the computer name with the 0x1C attached.

Browsing with WINS

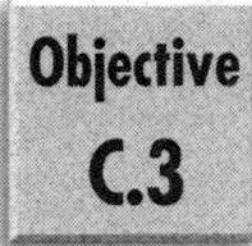

The WINS server also facilitates the browsing process. Obviously the capability to resolve the computer names in the browser list is an important part of it. As well, the registration of the domain controllers as members in the Domain Group enables the Master Browsers to talk easily with the Domain Master Browser.

In addition to the parts of browsing already presented, the Domain Master Browser makes a Domain Announcement every 15 minutes. This is usually done by a local broadcast. Because the Domain Master Browser is registered with the WINS server (as the PDC of the Domain), however, the Domain Master Browser can look up the domains and their PDCs in the WINS server.

Because the Domain Announcement contains the domain name and the address of the Domain Master Browser, this use of WINS removes the requirement for this broadcasting.

Summary

Over the years, Microsoft has been building better and better network operating systems while keeping NetBIOS as the foundation. This has meant that the core of the operating systems has stayed the same. This chapter laid out several of the problems that can arise when using NetBIOS and TCP/IP together. This chapter also showed you the solutions to these problems. You have looked at both the browser service and support domain activity. Although the browser service could be ignored, facilitating domain activity is crucial to enable NT to provide centralized management of the domain environment.

Test Yourself

1. From which system do you receive a list of servers?
2. In a workgroup model, how many Backup Browsers are there?
3. What are the three functions of NETLOGON?
4. Which system must be in the LMHOSTS file if no WINS server is used?
5. What tag in the LMHOSTS file enables domain activity over TCP/IP?
6. A user clicks on a system in the Network Neighborhood, and the system responds that the network name cannot be found. What can cause this?

7. How often does the server service announce itself?
8. When are systems removed from the browser list?
9. What type of group do domain controllers register in with the WINS server?
10. Which systems require an LMHOSTS file to enable the user accounts database to remain synchronized?
11. How do other domains become visible in the Network Neighborhood?
12. How many domain controllers can register in a Domain Group?
13. What types of computers make browser announcements?

Test Yourself Answers

1. The list of servers comes from the Backup Browser.
2. There will be one Backup Browser for every 32 systems in the workgroup.
3. The functions that NETLOGON handles include user validation, pass through authentication, and user account database synchronization.
4. The LMHOSTS file needs to provide address resolution for any system that registers a server service.
5. The #DOM:domainname tag facilitates domain activity over a TCP/IP network.
6. The system either could not resolve the NetBIOS name to an IP address, or the system crashed.
7. The server service announces every minute for the first five. After that, it announces every 12 minutes.
8. If a system shuts down correctly, it broadcasts a Name Release. This removes it from the browser list. The other case where a system is removed is if it misses three announcements.
9. The domain controllers register in the Domain Group.
10. Every domain controller requires an LMHOSTS file.
11. This is handled by the Domain Announcements that the Domain Master Browsers make every 15 minutes.
12. There will be the PDC and up to 24 BDCs in the Domain Group.
13. All systems that have a server service installed make announcements. This includes Windows for Workgroups, Windows 95, and Windows NT.

PART IV

TCP/IP Services

15 *Microsoft DNS Server* 319

16 *TCP/IP Utilities* 405

17 *Management Utilities: SNMP and the Performance Monitor* 479

18 *Remote Access Service and TCP/IP* 509

CHAPTER 15

Microsoft DNS Server

As an evolution of the HOSTS file, the TCP/IP world developed the DNS server. DNS (or Domain Name System) servers enable computers running WinSock applications (FTP or Internet Explorer, for example—applications that use the Winsock interface) to resolve host names easily by sending a query to a central server.

Windows NT 4 includes a DNS server. To fully understand the Windows NT DNS server, you should start with an overview of DNS as a whole.

Overview of Domain Name System

The Domain Name System (DNS—currently standardized in RFC 1034/1035) was introduced as a standard in 1983. DNS indexes host names in a hierarchical database that can be managed in a distributed fashion. Before examining DNS in any detail, looking at the characteristics of hierarchies in general, and of the DNS hierarchy in particular, should prove useful.

Hierarchies

You are already familiar with a common form of hierarchical organization: The hierarchical directory structure is used by virtually all operating systems, including Unix, DOS, and Windows. Figure 15.1 illustrates a Windows NT directory hierarchy, more commonly called a directory tree. Even though real trees and family trees—perhaps the oldest hierarchical databases—frequently place their roots at the bottom, database trees are always upended (see fig. 15.1). The upside-down trees commonly used to depict computer data structures are called *inverted trees.*

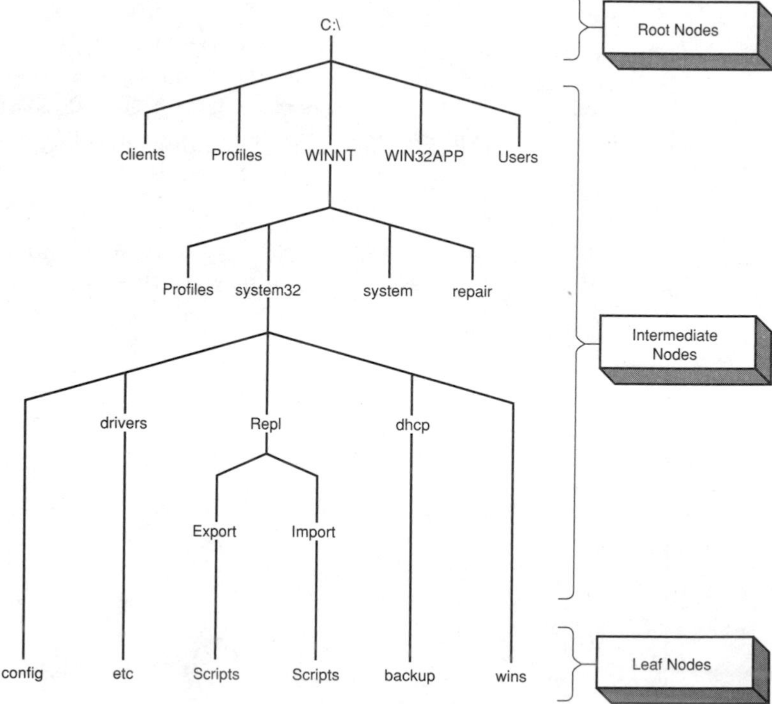

Figure 15.1
Example of a file system tree.

Data in a tree are represented by the intersections, or end points, of the lines that describe the tree structure. These points are called *nodes*, of which there are the following three kinds:

- **Root.** Every tree has exactly one root node. On a file system, this is called the root directory, represented by a \ (DOS and Windows) or a / (Unix).
- **Intermediate nodes.** An indefinite number of nodes can be made subordinate to the root node. Intermediate nodes may themselves have subordinate nodes. On file systems, intermediate nodes are called subdirectories and are assigned logical identifiers, such as WINNT.
- **Leaf nodes.** A leaf node is the end of a branch in the tree.

Nodes frequently are referred to as parent and child nodes. Leaf nodes are always children. Intermediate nodes are parents of their child (subordinate) nodes and children of their parent nodes. The root node is a parent to all first-level intermediate nodes. Nodes that are children of the same parent are known as siblings.

Any given node on the tree can be fully described by listing the nodes between itself and the root. Figure 15.1 shows an example identifying the node (in this case a subdirectory) \WINNT\system32\Repl\Export. Names that list all nodes between a node and the root are called *fully qualified names.*

Note Note that fully qualified names for file systems begin with the root and proceed down the tree to the node in question.

A fully qualified name can uniquely identify any node in the tree. The names \WINNT\clients and \WINNT\system describe separate nodes (subdirectories) in the directory tree.

Figure 15.2 illustrates an important rule of hierarchies: siblings may not have identical node names. Thus, the \WINNT directory cannot have two subdirectories named "system." Having two nodes named "clients" is perfectly all right, however, if their fully qualified names differ. Naming directories \clients and \WINNT\clients on the same file system, for example, is permissible.

The Domain Name Space

The DNS hierarchical database is called the domain name space. Each host in the domain name space has a unique, fully qualified name. Figure 15.3 shows a simple DNS hierarchy that an organization might use. The root node of a DNS tree is called either "root" or the "root domain." The root domain often is designated with empty quotation marks (" ").

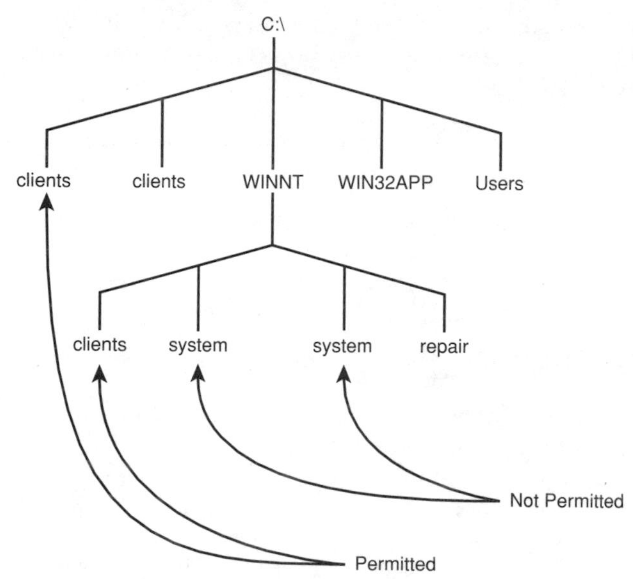

Figure 15.2
Each node in a hierarchy must have a unique fully qualified name.

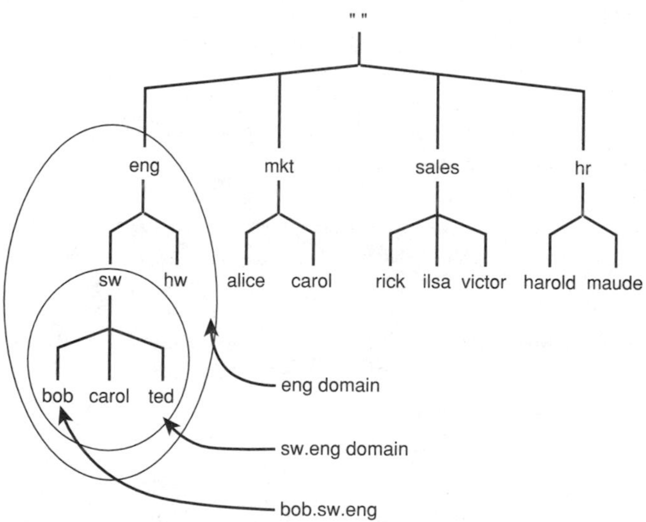

Figure 15.3
DNS tree for an organization.

Each node in the tree has a name, which can contain up to 63 characters. The fully qualified name for a DNS node is called the fully qualified domain name (FQDN). Unlike fully qualified path names in file systems, which start from the root, the FQDN convention in DNS starts with the node being described and proceeds to the root. Figure 15.3 illustrates bob.sw.eng as an example of an FQDN. The convention with DNS names is to separate node names with a period (referred to as "dot"). The root node may be represented by a trailing dot (as in bob.sw.eng.), but the trailing dot ordinarily is omitted.

DNS trees can be viewed in terms of domains, which are simply subtrees of the entire database. Figure 15.3 illustrates how subdomains can be defined within domains. The eng domain has two subdomains: sw.eng and hw.eng. The name of a subdomain is simply the FQDN of the topmost node in the domain. Subdomains always consist of complete subtrees of the tree, a node, and all of its child nodes. A subdomain cannot be designated to include both eng and mkt, which are located at the same level of the tree.

Subdomains are DNS management structures. Delegating management of any subdomain to distribute management responsibility for the complete name space is possible.

Figure 15.4 shows that DNS trees obey the same naming rules as directory trees: siblings must have unique node names. Nodes that are children of different parents may have the same node names.

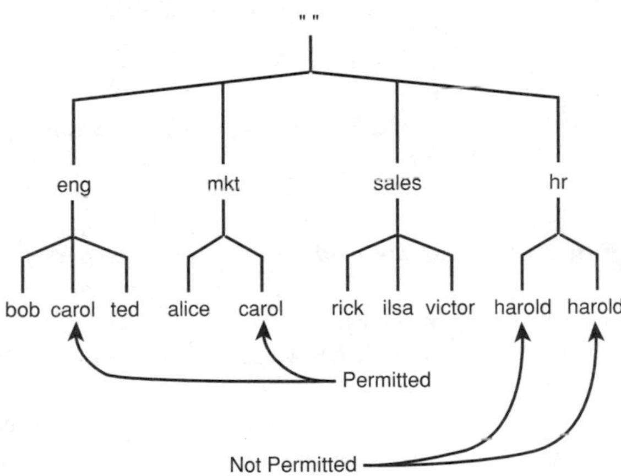

Figure 15.4

Naming rules for DNS nodes.

Note Domain names can be assigned *aliases*, which are pointers from one domain name to another. The domain to which the alias points is called the canonical domain name.

Domain and subdomain are relative terms and are used somewhat interchangeably. Technically speaking, every domain except root is literally a subdomain. When discussion focuses on a particular node, however, that node generally is referred to as a domain. Use of the terms domain and subdomain is primarily a function of perspective. DNS domains typically are referred to in the following terms of levels:

- **First-level domain.** A child of root. The more commonly used name for a first-level domain is top-level domain.
- **Second-level domain.** A child of a first-level domain.
- **Third-level domain.** A child of a second-level domain, and so forth.

Notice that eng.widgets may have two functions: it may serve as a name of a host in the DNS hierarchy, and also point to a particular IP address. eng.widgets is also a structure in the DNS database, however, that is used to organize its children in the database hierarchy. (This works much like a file system. A directory can contain files, but it can also contain other directories.)

Note Note that the term *domains*, as used with regard to DNS, has no relationship to Windows NT Server domains. Windows NT Server domains provide a way to organize Windows NT computers into manageable groups that share a common security database. DNS domains are related only to the Internet naming service. A Windows NT computer can participate in a Windows NT domain under one name and in a DNS domain with another name.

Domain Administration

DNS was designed to handle the Internet, which is too vast to be centrally administered as a single name space. Therefore, being able to delegate administration of subdomains was essential.

Name servers are programs that store data about the domain name space and provide that information in response to DNS queries. The complete name space can be organized into zones, which are subsets of the DNS tree. A given name server has authority for one or more zones. Figure 15.5 shows a sample tree as it might be organized into three zones. Notice that zones do not require regular boundaries. In the example, eng is maintained in a separate zone on its own name server. Notice that zones, unlike domains, need not be a simple slice of the DNS tree, but can incorporate different levels of different branches.

Figure 15.5

Zones and delegation of authority.

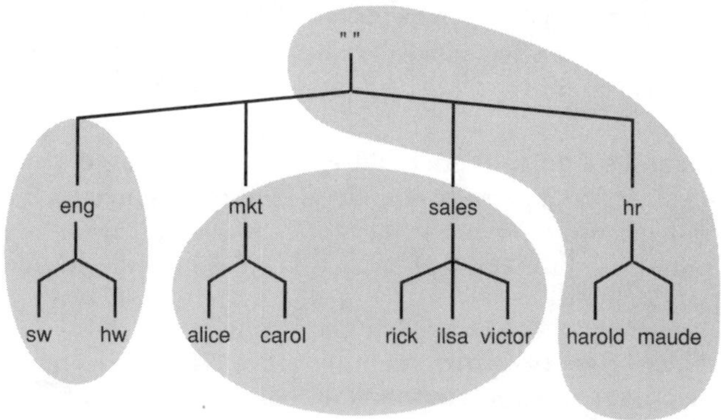

Administration for zones can be delegated to name servers as required. If administration for a domain is delegated to a name server, that name server becomes responsible for the domain's subdomains as well, unless administration for those subdomains is delegated away.

Each zone must be serviced by a primary master name server, which obtains the data for the zone from files on its host. Secondary master domain servers obtain zone data by performing zone transfers from the primary master name server for the zone. Secondary masters periodically update their databases from the primary to keep the various name servers for the zone synchronized.

DNS is very flexible in the way name servers and zones can be related. Recall that name servers may be authoritative for more than one zone. Beyond that, a name server can be a primary on some zone(s) and a secondary for other zone(s).

The provision for multiple name servers provides a level of redundancy that enables the network DNS to continue to function with secondaries, even in the event of a failure of the primary master name server.

Resolving DNS Queries

When an application requires DNS data, it uses a resolver to query a DNS server. A resolver is the client side of the DNS client-server relationship. The resolver generates a DNS query and sends it to a name server, processes the response from the name server, and forwards the information to the program that requested the data.

Resolver queries are fulfilled by DNS servers (see fig. 15.6). The resolver in a host is configured with the IP address of at least one DNS server. When the resolver requires an IP address, it contacts a known DNS server, which is responsible for processing the request.

Resolution is a matter of querying other DNS servers starting with one that is authoritative for the root domain. The root name server provides the address of a first-level domain in the queried name. If required, the first-level domain supplies the address of a second-level domain server, and so on, until it reaches a domain server that can satisfy the query.

Note

The most popular implementation of DNS is Berkeley Internet Name Domain (BIND), which was originally written for 4.3 BSD Unix and is now at version 4.8.3. BIND has been ported to most versions of Unix, and a Windows NT version is included with the Windows NT Resource Kit. BIND supports tree depths of 127 levels, sufficient to enable BIND to be used on the root name servers for the Internet.

BIND uses so-called stub resolvers. A *stub resolver* has no DNS search capability. It simply knows how to send a query to a DNS server. The name server performs the actual resolution of the query.

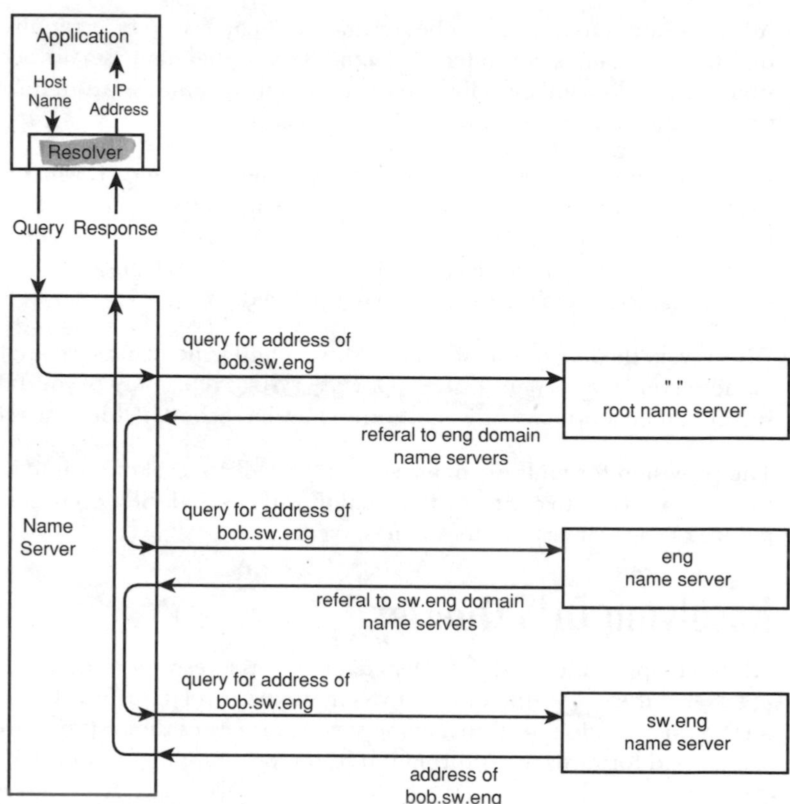

Figure 15.6
Resolution of a DNS query.

To diminish the effort required to resolve DNS queries, DNS servers cache the results of recent queries. Data in the cache can enable the server to satisfy a DNS query locally or to shorten the search by starting at a DNS server that is authoritative for a lower-level domain. In the event that cached information cannot be used to initiate a search, the process begins with the root domain. Entries in a DNS cache table are assigned a Time to Live (TTL), which the domain administrator configures. Entries that exceed the TTL are discarded, and the next time a resolver places a request for that domain, the name server must retrieve the data from the network.

Resolvers are actually components of applications and processes running on a host. When compiling programs, developers include library routines for the name service to be supported. Thus, programs such as FTP and Telnet are compiled with the capability to construct DNS queries and to process the response. The DNS server, however, is responsible for searching the database.

Clearly, the capability of supporting secondary DNS servers in domains is crucial to providing a reliable name service. If no DNS server is available for the root domain, for example, all name resolution eventually fails because entries in the cache tables in lower-level DNS servers expire and require renewal.

Organization of the Internet Domain Name Space

All the discussed DNS capabilities come into play on the Internet, certainly the largest name space on any network.

The critical nature of root name servers, along with the volume of DNS queries on the Internet, dictate the need for a large, broadly distributed base of root name servers. At this time, the Internet is supported by nine root name servers, including systems on NSFnet, MILNET, SPAN (NASA's network), and in Europe.

The root name servers are authoritative for the top-level domains in the Internet DNS database. On the Internet, no actual organization has a first-level domain name. Top-level domains (TLDs) organize the name space in terms of categories.

The only domains the Internet authorities administer are top-level domains. Administration of secondary and lower-level domains is delegated. Domain name registration is under the authority of the Internet Assigned Numbers Authority (IANA) and is administered by the Internet Registry (IR). The central IR is internic.net.

The Internet name space evolves too quickly to be centrally administered; it has been shown how the DNS name space can be organized into subdomains and zones to enable administration to be flexible, efficient, and local. After establishing a new domain, a management authority for the domain is designated. In many cases, second- and lower-level domains are administered by the entities that requested establishment of them. Organizations such as universities, companies, and government agencies maintain name servers that support the DNS database for their portions of the DNS tree.

RFC 1591, "Domain Name System Structure and Delegation," describes the domain name structure for the Internet, as well as guidelines for administration of delegated domains. TLDs fall into the following three categories:

- Generic world wide domains
- Generic domains for only the United States
- Country domains

Figure 15.7 shows the overall organization of the Internet DNS name space.

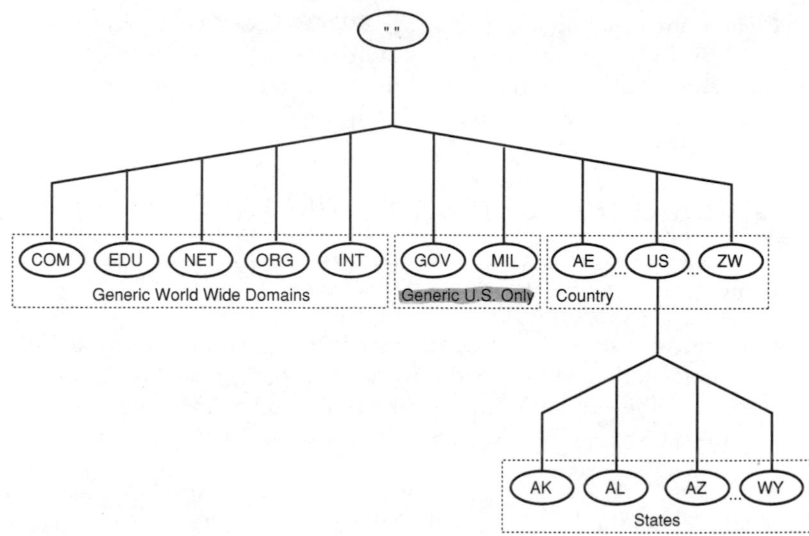

Figure 15.7
Organization of the DNS name space.

Generic World Wide Domains

If you have spent any time on the Internet, you have encountered these top-level domains, which organize the majority of Internet DNS names into the following five categories:

- **Com.** Identifies commercial entities. Because this domain comprehends virtually every company that has a presence on the Internet, the com name space is getting quite large, and consideration is being given to organizing it in subdomains (microsoft.com, for example).
- **Edu.** Originally embracing all educational institutions, this domain also is becoming quite extensive. Registration in this domain now is limited to four-year colleges and universities. Other schools and two-year colleges are registered under their respective country domains (berkeley.edu, for example).
- **Net.** Includes network providers and Internet administrative computers (internic.net, for example).
- **Org.** Anything that does not fit in the other generic categories (un.org, for example—for the United Nations.)
- **Int.** Organizations established by international treaties (nato.int, for example).

Registering second-level domains in these categories is the responsibility of the InterNIC (contact hostmaster@internic.net). InterNIC also is responsible for registering all new top-level domains.

Generic, United States-Only Domains

The following two top-level domains are reserved for the United States government:

- **Gov.** At one time applied to any government office or agency, it has since been decided that new registrations will include only agencies of the U.S. federal government. State and local government entities are now registered under country domains (nsf.gov, for example).
- **Mil.** The U.S. military (dca.mil, for example).

Registration of second-level domains in gov is the responsibility of the InterNIC (contact hostmaster@internic.net).

Second-level domains under mil are registered by the DDN registry at nic.ddn.mil.

Country Domains

Country TLDs are derived from ISO 3166. IANA recognizes the ISO as an international organization with mechanisms in place to identify bona fide countries.

The regional registry for Europe is the RIPE NCC (contact ncc@ripe.net). The registry for the Asia-Pacific region is APNIC (contact hostmaster@apnic.net). The InterNIC administers North America and other undelegated regions.

Table 15.1 lists most of the Internet top-level domains. These change frequently, however. The information was obtained from the WHOIS server at rs.internic.net. Later in this chapter, the section "Obtaining Domain Information with WHOIS" explains how to conduct WHOIS searches. (The search command was whois root-dom.) Pg 342

stands for domain

TABLE 15.1
Internet Top-Level Domains

Domain	Country
AD	Andorra
AE	United Arab Emirates
AG	Antigua and Barbuda
AI	Anguilla
AL	Albania (Republic of)
AM	Armenia (top-level domain)

continues

Table 15.1, Continued
Internet Top-Level Domains

Domain	Country
AN	Netherlands Antilles
AO	Angola (Republic of)
AQ	Antarctica
AR	Argentina (Argentine Republic)
ARPA	Advanced Research Projects Agency Domain
AT	Austria (Republic of)
AU	Australia
AW	Aruba
AZ	Azerbaijan
BA	Bosnia-Herzegovina
BB	Barbados
BE	Belgium (Kingdom of)
BF	Burkina Faso
BG	Bulgaria (top-level domain)
BH	Bahrain (State of)
BI	Burundi (Republic of)
BJ	Benin (Republic of)
BM	Bermuda
BN	Brunei
BO	Bolivia (Republic of)
BR	Brazil (Federative Republic of)
BS	Bahamas (Commonwealth of the)

Domain	Country
BW	Botswana (Republic of)
BY	Belarus
BZ	Belize
CA	Canada
CF	Central African Republic
CH	Switzerland (Swiss Confederation)
CI	Cote d'Ivoire (Republic of)
CK	Cook Islands
CL	Chile (Republic of)
CM	Cameroon
CN	China (People's Republic of)
CO	Colombia (Republic of)
COM	Commercial
CR	Costa Rica (Republic of)
CU	Cuba (Republic of)
CV	Cape Verde
CY	Cyprus (Republic of)
CZ	Czech Republic
DE	Germany (Federal Republic of)
DJ	Djibouti
DK	Denmark (Kingdom of)
DM	Dominica (Commonwealth of)

continues

Table 15.1, Continued
Internet Top-Level Domains

Domain	Country
DO	Dominican Republic
DZ	Algeria (People's Democratic Republic of)
EC	Ecuador (Republic of)
EDU	Education
EE	Estonia (Republic of)
EG	Egypt (Arab Republic of)
ER	Eritrea
ES	Centro de Comunicaciones CSIC RedIRIS (ESNIC)
ET	Ethiopia (Democratic Federal Republic of)
FI	EUnet Finland Oy
FJ	Fiji (Republic of)
FM	Micronesia (Federated States of)
FO	Faroe Islands
FR	France
GB	Great Britain (United Kingdom of)
GD	Grenada (Republic of)
GE	Georgia (Republic of)
GF	French Guyana
GG	Guernsey (Channel Islands, Bailiwick of)
GH	Ghana
GI	Gibraltar

Domain	Country
GL	Greenland
GN	Guinea (Republic of)
GOV	Government
GP	Guadeloupe
GR	Greece (Hellenic Republic)
GT	Guatemala (Republic of)
GU	Guam
GY	Guyana
HK	Hong Kong (Hisiangkang, Xianggang)
HN	Honduras (Republic of)
HR	Croatia/Hrvatska (Republic of)
HU	Hungary (Republic of)
ID	Indonesia
IE	Ireland
IL	Israel (State of)
IM	Isle of Man
IN	India (Republic of)
INT	International
IR	Iran (Islamic Republic of)
IS	Iceland (Republic of)
IT	Italy (Italian Republic)
JE	Jersey (Channel Islands, Bailiwick of)

continues

Table 15.1, Continued
Internet Top-Level Domains

Domain	Country
JM	Jamaica
JO	Jordan (The Hashemite Kingdom of)
JP	Japan
KE	Kenya (Republic of)
KH	Cambodia
KI	Kiribati
KN	Saint Kitts & Nevis
KR	Korea (Republic of)
KW	Kuwait (State of)
KY	Cayman Islands
KZ	Kazakhstan
LA	Lao People's Democratic Republic
LB	Lebanon (Lebanese Republic)
LC	Saint Lucia
LI	Liechtenstein (Principality of)
LK	Sri Lanka (Democratic Socialist Republic of)
LS	Lesotho (Kingdom of)
LT	Lithuania (Republic of)
LU	Luxembourg (Grand Duchy of)
LV	Latvia (Republic of)
MA	Morocco (Kingdom of)

Domain	Country
MC	Monaco (Principality of)
MD	Moldova (Republic of)
MG	Madagascar
MH	Marshall Islands (Republic of the)
MIL	Military
MK	Macedonia (The former Yugoslav Republic of)
ML	Mali (Republic of)
MN	Mongolia
MO	Macau
MP	Northern Mariana Islands
MR	Mauritania (top-level domain)
MT	Malta (Republic of)
MU	Mauritius
MV	Maldives (Republic of)
MX	Mexico (United Mexican States)
MY	Malaysia (top-level domain)
MZ	Mozambique (People's Republic of)
NA	Namibia (Republic of)
NC	New Caledonia (Nouvelle Caledonie)
NE	Niger
NET	Network
NF	Norfolk Island

continues

Table 15.1, Continued
Internet Top-Level Domains

Domain	Country
NG	Nigeria
NI	Nicaragua (Republic of)
NL	Netherlands
NO	Norway (Kingdom of)
NP	Nepal
NZ	New Zealand
OM	Oman (Sultanate of)
ORG	Organization
PA	Panama (Republic of)
PE	Peru (Republic of)
PF	French Polynesia
PG	Papua New Guinea
PH	Philippines (Republic of the)
PK	Pakistan (Islamic Republic of)
PL	Poland (Republic of)
PR	Puerto Rico
PT	Portugal (Portuguese Republic)
PY	Paraguay (Republic of)
QA	Qatar
RO	Romania
RU	Russia (Russian Federation)

Domain	Country
RW	Rwanda (Republic of)
SA	Saudi Arabia (Kingdom of)
SB	Solomon Islands
SE	Sweden (Kingdom of)
SG	Singapore (Republic of)
SK	Slovakia
SM	San Marino (Republic of)
SN	Senegal (Republic of)
SR	Telesur
SU	Soviet Union (Union of Soviet Socialist Republics)
SV	El Salvador
SY	Syria (Syrian Arab Republic)
SZ	Swaziland (Kingdom of)
TG	Togo (Republic of)
TH	Thailand (Kingdom of)
TN	Tunisia
TO	Tonga
TR	Turkey (Republic of)
TT	Trinidad & Tobago (Republic of)
TV	Tuvalu
TW	Taiwan
TZ	Tanzania (United Republic of)

continues

Table 15.1, Continued
Internet Top-Level Domains

Domain	Country
UA	Ukraine
UG	Uganda (Republic of)
UK	United Kingdom of Great Britain
US	United States of America
UY	Uruguay (Eastern Republic of)
UZ	Uzbekistan
VA	Vatican City State
VC	Saint Vincent & the Grenadines
VE	Venezuela (Republic of)
VI	Virgin Islands (US)
VN	Vietnam (Socialist Republic of)
VU	Vanuatu
WS	Samoa
YE	Yemen
YU	Yugoslavia (Federal Republic of)
ZA	South Africa (Republic of)
ZM	Zambia (Republic of)
ZR	Zaire (Republic of)
ZW	Zimbabwe (Republic of)

Subdomains in the US Domain

Within the US domain, second-level domains have been established for each state, using the standard postal abbreviations for the state domain names (NY.US for New York, for example).

RFC 1480 describes some conventions for establishing subdomains within the states (examples are taken from the RFC):

- **Locality codes.** Cities, counties, parishes, and townships (Los-Angeles.CA.US or PORTLAND.OR.US, for example).
- **CI.** City government agencies, used as a subdomain under a locality (Fire-Dept.CI.Los-Angeles.CA.US, for example).
- **CO.** County government agencies, used as a subdomain under a locality (Fire-Dept.CO.San-Diego.CA.US, for example).
- **K12.** For public school districts (John-Muir.Middle.Santa-Monica.K12.CA.US, for example).
- **CC.** All state-wide community colleges.
- **PVT.** Private schools, used as a subdomain of K12 (St-Michaels.PVT.K12.CA.US, for example).
- **TEC.** Technical and vocational schools.
- **LIB.** Libraries (<library-name>.LIB.<state>.US, for example).
- **STATE.** State government agencies (State-Police.STATE.<state>.US, for example).
- **GEN.** Things that don't fit comfortably in other categories.

Parallel to the state names, some special names have been designated under US:

- **FED.** Agencies of the federal government.
- **DNI.** Distributed national institutes, organizations with a presence in more than one state or region.

Figure 15.8 describes the structure of the US domain, including its use of state and lower-level codes.

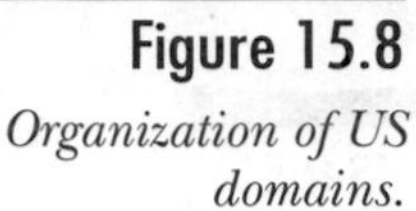

Figure 15.8
Organization of US domains.

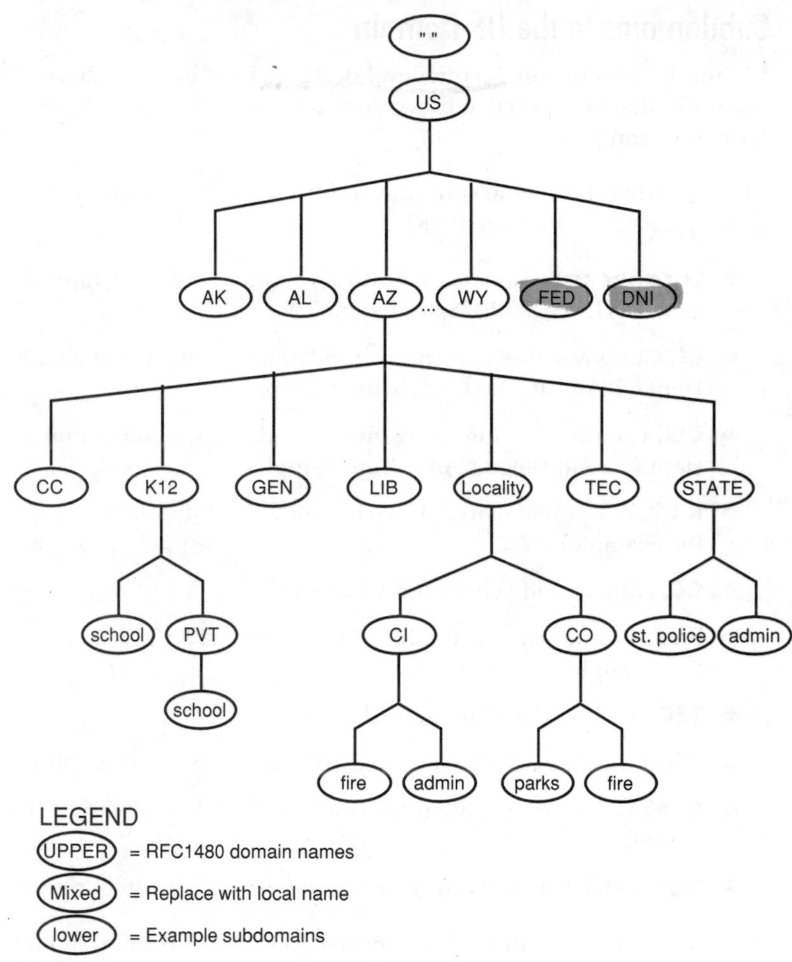

Administration of subdomains of US has been extensively delegated to local contacts. To obtain a list of contacts for the US subdomains via anonymous FTP, retrieve the file In-notes/us-domain-delegated.txt from venera.isi.edu. Other useful files are located on this host, and you should find browsing around worthwhile.

Another way to receive this list is to send an e-mail message to rfc-info@isi.edu. Put the following message in the body of the message:

```
Help: us_domain_delegated_domains
```

Note The RFC-INFO service is yet another way to obtain Internet documents, including RFCs, FYIs, STDs, and IMRs. To obtain instructions, send e-mail to rfc-info@isi.edu and type the text Help in the body of the message.

Subdomains in Non-Government Organizations

Below the second-level domain name assigned by InterNIC Registration, the organization that obtains the name is responsible for subdomain administration and has complete freedom to establish the subdomain structure. Any organization that wants to establish a subdomain must arrange for a name server to support the subdomain name space.

DNS services usually are supported on a DNS server operated by the domain's organization. Because a given DNS server can support several zones, however, establishing a new domain on an existing DNS server is possible, such as one an Internet provider operates.

Earlier examples of an organization's name space (as in figure 15.3) indicated the topmost node as the root of the tree. When an organization joins the Internet, that can no longer be the case. An organization must apply for a domain name to be a subdomain of one of the standard domains. If the organization in figure 15.3 is named Widgets, Inc., it might apply for the domain name widgets.com. In that case, their portion of the Internet name space would look like figure 15.9. It would be the responsibility of Widgets, Inc., to administer its portion of the name space, starting from the widgets domain.

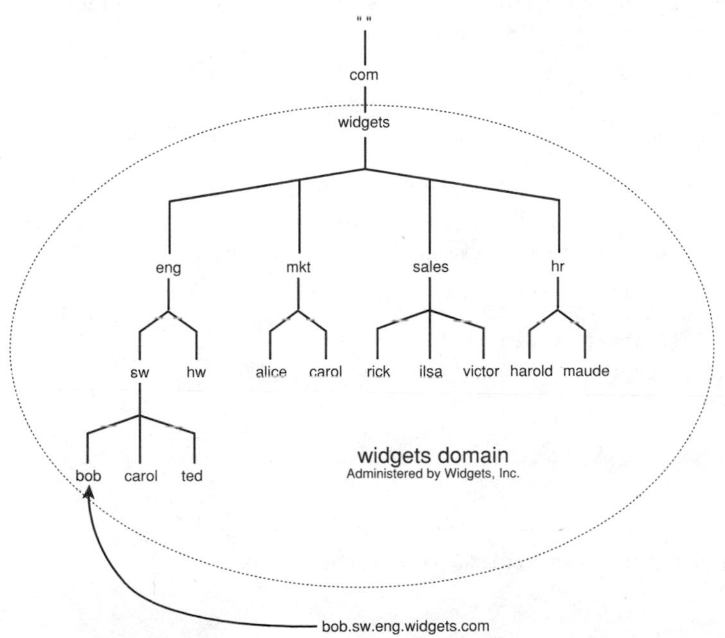

Figure 15.9

An organization in the DNS name space.

In this manner, every host on the Internet may be assigned a unique FQDN. Bob's desktop workstation would now have the FQDN bob.sw.eng.widgets.com.

Obtaining Domain Information with WHOIS

WHOIS is a "white pages" directory of people and organizations on the Internet. One way to use WHOIS is for obtaining information about top-level domains, including the contacts.

WHOIS searches are based on keywords. Each top-level domain is keyword indexed with the domain name concatenated to "-dom". To search for the com domain, for example, you would search for "com-dom".

If your host is on the Internet and has WHOIS client software, you can query WHOIS directly. To find the contact person for the edu top-level domain, enter the following WHOIS query:

```
whois -h rs.internic.net edu-dom
```

This command directs a WHOIS query using the keyword edu-dom to the host rs.internic.net. To search for top-level domains, query whois root-dom.

On the World Wide Web, use the URL http://www.internic.net to access the InterNIC web site. Enter the AT&T Directory and Databases Services and select the InterNIC Directory Services ("White Pages"). From there, you can obtain information or search the worldwide directories that are available. You can use this query page to obtain information from two WHOIS servers:

- DISA NIC for the mil domain
- InterNIC Registration Services (rs.internic.net) for point-of-contact information

An excellent way to access the InterNIC WHOIS database is to Telnet to rs.internic.net. No logon is required. Enter the command **whois** to start a WHOIS client. The following dialog shows the results of querying for EDU-DOM:

```
Whois: edu-dom
Education top-level domain (EDU-DOM)
   Network Solutions, Inc.
   505 Huntmar park Dr.
   Herndon, VA 22070

   Domain Name: EDU

   Administrative Contact, Technical Contact, Zone Contact:
```

```
      Network Solutions, Inc. (HOSTMASTER)  HOSTMASTER@INTERNIC.NET
      (703) 742-4777 (FAX) (703) 742-4811

   Record last updated on 02-Sep-94.

   Domain servers in listed order:

   A.ROOT-SERVERS.NET              198.41.0.4
   H.ROOT-SERVERS.NET              128.63.2.53
   B.ROOT-SERVERS.NET              128.9.0.107
   C.ROOT-SERVERS.NET              192.33.4.12
   D.ROOT-SERVERS.NET              128.8.10.90
   E.ROOT-SERVERS.NET              192.203.230.10
   I.ROOT-SERVERS.NET              192.36.148.17
   F.ROOT-SERVERS.NET              39.13.229.241
   G.ROOT-SERVERS.NET              192.112.36.4

Would you like to see the known domains under this top-level domain? n
```

As can be seen, it is sometimes possible to drill down to lower-level domains, although the number of subdomains frequently exceeds reporting capacity.

The preceding list contains the names and addresses of the nine name servers that service the Internet root domain. If you would like to know more about one of these hosts, you can query WHOIS as follows:

```
Whois: 128.63.2.53
Army Research Laboratory (BRL-AOS)
   Aberdeen Proving Ground, MD  21005-5066

   Hostname: H.ROOT-SERVERS.NET
   Address: 128.63.2.53
   System: SUN running Unix

   Host Administrator:
      Fielding, James L. (JLF)  jamesf@ARL.MIL
      (410)278-8929 (DSN) 298-8929 (410)278-6664 (FAX) (410)278-5077

   domain server

   Record last updated on 17-Aug-95.

Would you like to see the registered users of this host? N
Whois:
```

Mapping Addresses to Names

As described to this point, DNS is adept at resolving domain names to IP addresses. Sometimes, however, exactly the opposite is required. Given an IP address, it may be necessary to determine the domain name associated with the address. To support reverse mapping, a special domain is maintained on the Internet—the in-addr.arpa domain.

Figure 15.10 illustrates in-addr.arpa's structure. Nodes in the domain are named after IP addresses. The in-addr.arpa domain can have 256 subdomains, each corresponding to the first octet of an IP address. Each subdomain of in-addr.arpa can in turn have 256 subdomains, corresponding to the possible values of the second octets of IP addresses. Similarly, the next subdomain down the hierarchy can have 256 subdomains, corresponding to the third octets of IP addresses. Finally, the last subdomain contains records associated with the fourth octets of IP addresses.

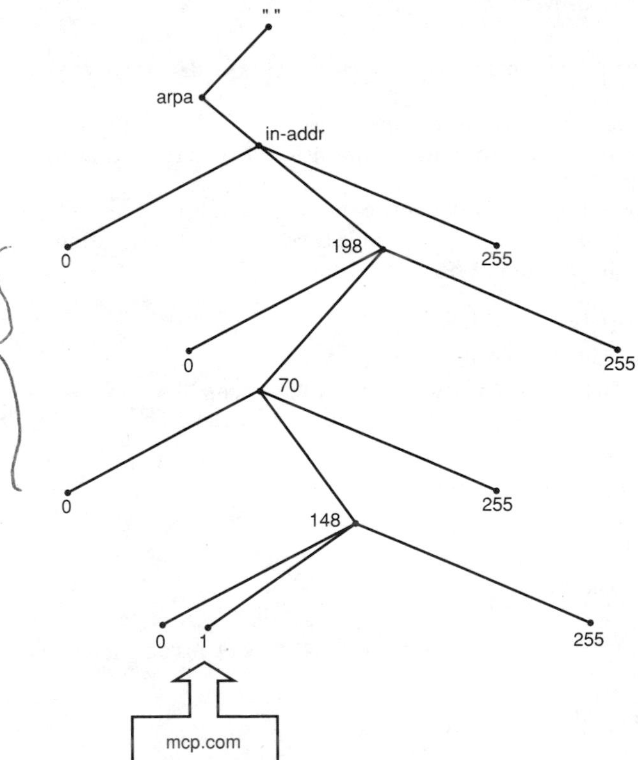

Figure 15.10
Resolving an address in in-addr.arpa.

The value of a fourth-octet resource record is the full domain names of the IP address that defines the resource record.

Figure 15.10 shows how a record could be stored in the IN-ADDR.ARPA hierarchy. The domain name mcp.com is associated with the IP address 198.70.148.1. To locate the domain name, DNS searches down the tree beginning with 198.in-addr.arpa. The search continues until reaching the resource record 1.148.70.198.in-addr.arpa. The value of that resource record is mcp.com.

DNS Under Windows NT 4

The rest of this chapter focuses on two issues: whether you need to implement DNS on your network and, if so, how to implement a DNS server on Windows NT computers.

Prior to Windows NT version 4, NT's support for DNS was rather anemic. A beta DNS server, compatible with BIND, was included with the Windows NT Resource Kit for NT Server version 3.5. This software was not particularly harmonious with the management style promoted by NT. It was configured entirely by editing BIND-compatible database files and lacked a graphic interface. It also had a reputation for instability, not surprising because it was, after all, a beta.

NA GUI-based DNS Server service is available, and it's now shipping with Windows NT Server 4. Still compatible with BIND, and in fact able to read BIND database files, the new DNS Server adds a familiar graphic interface with wizards that greatly simplify the task of maintaining the many entries that make up a DNS name space.

Additionally, the DNS server supports a feature unique to the Microsoft network environment: the use of NetBIOS names to identify computers on the network. The DNS server supports hooks into WINS that enable DNS to offer name resolution for names that it learns from WINS. As far as your Microsoft network clients are concerned, you can add DNS to the network without the necessity of manually entering your Microsoft computer names to the static DNS database. All your Microsoft hosts are maintained dynamically by the link between the DNS server and WINS.

Note Expect to see tighter links between WINS and DNS in the future, even to the extent of having WINS disappear altogether. Microsoft is committed to supporting Internet standards such as DNS and seems to be moving in the direction of eliminating WINS entirely.

Deciding Whether to Implement DNS

If your Windows TCP/IP network is not connected to non-Microsoft TCP/IP networks, you do not need DNS. WINS can provide all the naming services required on a Microsoft Windows network. Because WINS configures names to address mappings dynamically, it requires little or no maintenance to cope with network equipment changes. A user can move a portable computer from one network on the private intranet to another network and have no requirement for changes in WINS. WINS recognizes the new location of the host and adjusts its database accordingly.

You need DNS if you want to connect your TCP/IP hosts to the Internet or to a Unix-based TCP/IP network, but only if you want to enable users outside the Windows network to access your TCP/IP hosts by name. If outside users do not use services hosted on your computers, or if identifying your computers by IP address is acceptable, identifying your network hosts in DNS is not necessary.

In other words, if your network is attached to the Internet, you do not need to include your hosts in the Internet DNS tree to enable your users to connect to outside resources. You need DNS name support only if outsiders connect to resources on your network.

If you decide that hosts on your network must be identified in DNS, ask the following questions:

- Must all hosts be added to DNS or only a select few?
- How often will host name-address information change?
- Should the names of local hosts be provided by WINS?
- Will you be obtaining a domain name on the Internet?
- Will hosts under your domain name be dispersed geographically or located in a single location?

The right answers to these questions might indicate that you can hire an Internet Service Provider to manage your portion of the DNS tree. Recall from earlier discussions that a single DNS server can manage multiple zones in the DNS tree. Many commercial Internet providers will manage your zone for a fee that often is considerably less than the cost of maintaining two private DNS servers. (To provide fault tolerance, two are generally considered to be a minimum.)

Consider contracting management of your portion of the DNS tree if any or all the following circumstances apply:

- You obtain your Internet access through an Internet provider that offers DNS management as a service.

- You do not want to have local names of Windows TCP/IP hosts provided by WINS. The majority of Internet Access Providers (IAPs) run DNS on Unix computers, which do not support links to WINS.
- Your network is too small to justify training two DNS administrators, allocating a portion of their work time, and maintaining two computers with the capacity to provide DNS services.
- Your network is fairly stable and you do not need immediate posting of changes.

Consider managing your own DNS server if any, some, or all the following are true:

- You want to use WINS to provide host names of your Windows computers.
- You want local control of your organization's part of the DNS tree.
- Your network changes frequently.
- Your organization can justify the expense of administrative labor and DNS server hardware.
- Your network is local and changes infrequently so that HOSTS files may be used.

Local networks that include Unix hosts cannot use WINS for name resolution. Although DNS might seem to be the best solution for providing a local database, HOSTS files remain an option under some circumstances. Using HOSTS files generates no network traffic for name resolution, and HOSTS files can be maintained easily on a stable network. If the network changes frequently, maintaining DNS is easier than frequently distributing HOSTS files to all computers on the network.

Name Resolution with HOSTS Files

Before DNS, name resolution was accomplished by using files named HOSTS that, on Unix computers, were conventionally stored with the file name \etc\hosts. On Windows NT computers, HOSTS files are stored in the directory c:\winnt\system32\drivers\etc.

Supporting a naming service is a simple matter of editing a master HOSTS file and distributing it to all computers. To do this, you can copy the file when a user logs on to a domain, or you can use a software distribution system such as Microsoft's System Management Server.

Basically, the same tasks are involved in maintaining a master HOSTS file and maintaining DNS database files. DNS saves labor because DNS database files need not be copied to all hosts, but rather, need only be installed on the primary and backup

DNS servers. DNS begins to pay off, therefore, when your network becomes so large that keeping everyone's HOSTS file up to date becomes too labor-intensive.

Getting Ready for DNS

If your network will never be on the Internet, you can use any naming conventions for DNS. If an Internet connection is a present or future requirement, however, you must do the following things:

- Obtain one or more Internet IP network addresses.
- Obtain an Internet connection.
- Obtain a domain name in the appropriate top-level Internet domain.

If an organization already connected to the Internet agrees to let you connect to the Internet by connecting to its network, you are responsible for obtaining IP addresses and domain names. The guidelines for identifying and contacting the authority for your parent domain were discussed earlier. In these cases, IP addresses are assigned by the InterNIC Registration Service.

Increasingly, however, the principle way to connect to the Internet is to subscribe using an Internet Access Provider. IAPs are assigned blocks of IP addresses. You need to obtain an address from your IAP. Your IAP is probably also willing to help you obtain a domain name. A good IAP can greatly simplify setting up an Internet connection.

Somewhere along the line, you need to coordinate with the contact for your domain's parent domain and for in-addr.arpa to obtain authority for your domain in the DNS tree. Before you attempt to hook into Internet DNS, however, you should have your DNS system in operation.

Managing Microsoft DNS Server

Figure 15.11 illustrates an internetwork to be used as an example for configuring DNS. The University of Southern North Dakota at Hoople, a school of music (domain name: hoople.edu), operates the network. Hosts have been named after the faculty's favorite composers.

The internetwork consists of two networks connected by a multihomed host serving as an IP router. The internetwork connects to the Internet via a Cisco router. The primary DNS server will be mozart. The files configured for mozart assume a secondary name server and are set up on schubert. The details of configuring the secondary name server are discussed later in this chapter.

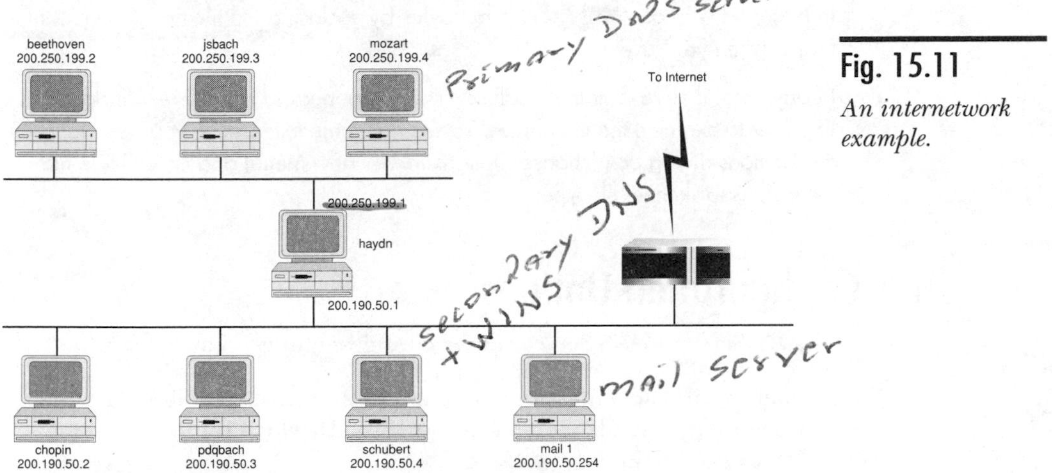

Fig. 15.11
An internetwork example.

Only the following three computers require fixed IP addresses:

- mozart is the primary DNS server.
- schubert is a secondary DNS server and also will be the WINS server.
- mail1 is the mail server.

The HOSTS file for this internetwork is as follows:

```
127.0.0.1          localhost
200.250.199.1      haydn.hoople.edu haydn papa1
200.190.50.1       haydn.hoople.edu haydn papa2
200.250.199.2      beethoven.hoople.edu beethoven
200.250.199.3      jsbach.hoople.edu jsbach jsb
200.250.199.4      mozart.hoople.edu mozart
200.190.50.2       chopin.hoople.edu chopin
200.190.50.3       pdqbach.hoople.edu pdqbach pdq
200.190.50.4       schubert.hoople.edu schubert
```

Much of the information in the HOSTS file shows up in the configuration files for DNS.

Note

You can create and modify HOSTS files with any text editor, but caution is required under Windows. Most Windows-based editors automatically append an extension to the file name when they save a file. If you save a file named HOSTS in Notepad, for example, the .txt extension is automatically added to the saved file.

In Notepad, you can override this behavior by enclosing the file name in quotation marks when you save it.

In any case, if HOSTS name resolution doesn't appear to work, use Windows NT Explorer to examine the file names. To see file name extensions, you need to open the Options dialog box (choose Options in the View menu) and check Hide file extensions for known file types.

DNS Configuration Options

Objective B.7

The Windows NT Server 4 DNS Server can be configured in two ways:

- Using database files, text files are maintained using any text editor. The DNS server accepts database files compatible with BIND, which is the most widely used DNS service on the Internet.
- Using the graphic interface, you can manage any feature of the DNS server. If desired, you do not even need to concern yourself with the formats of the BIND database files.

It is a good idea to be familiar with both techniques. If you understand how to create and maintain the BIND files, you gain several advantages. If your network is currently running a BIND DNS server, the entries in the existing server database can be imported into the Windows NT Server 4 DNS Server. Similarly, you can generate BIND database files from the DNS server if you want to export data to a BIND-based DNS server. Another significant advantage is that BIND is well documented, and you will find it easy to obtain support from other DNS managers.

On the other hand, the graphic interface has peculiar advantages that BIND lacks. Instead of creating database files in a text editor—a process prone to human error—you use familiar dialog boxes and wizards to add entries to the database. Some operations are greatly simplified by using drag-and-drop. You can also update the database dynamically, without the need to reboot the name server. BIND servers must be stopped and restarted to load new entries to the database.

This discussion begins by looking at the BIND database files. You will encounter several eccentricities when you enter data in the DNS Manager GUI, such as the use of trailing periods after fully qualified host names. It is much easier to understand these eccentricities if you have seen the data in the context of the BIND database files. Knowledge of the BIND data files also comes in handy if there is a need to copy the configuration of an existing BIND DNS server to the Microsoft DNS Server.

In the process of exploring the BIND database files, you will learn about the structure of the DNS databases, knowledge that you can apply when working with the graphic interface as well. With that background in place, this chapter shows you how to manage the DNS server graphically, creating the entire database through the GUI interface should you want to do so.

Creating BIND Database Files

When configuring DNS server using BIND database files, the files are located in the directory %systemroot%\SYSTEM32\DNS, which by default is c:\winnt\system32\dns. (Note that this directory is different from the directory used in the Windows NT 3.51 beta, which was %systemroot%\SYSTEM32\DRIVERS\ETC. If you are upgrading, you need to move the files to the new location). You need to maintain the following DNS files:

- **boot.** This file is the master configuration file. It declares all the various files used to initialize the DNS server.
- **cache.dns.** This file contains host information that establishes basic DNS connectivity. Principally, this file defines the addresses of the root name servers for the DNS.
- **127.0.0.dns.** This file includes reverse lookup data for IP numbers on the 127 (loopback) network, such as localhost.
- **reverse-netid.in-addr.arpa.dns.** For each network ID managed by the DNS server, a reverse lookup file is required to specify address-to-name mappings.
- **domain.dns.** For each domain managed by the DNS server, a forward lookup file is required to specify name-to-address mappings.

Note BIND servers use these same files without the .dns file name extension. The Microsoft DNS Manager adds the .dns extension to all data files that it creates. This chapter adheres to that convention.

The Windows NT DNS Server software includes example files for each file type. Most files require considerable editing to customize the file for local use. The following sections examine each of these files in turn.

The BOOT File

The BOOT file is responsible for the following tasks:

- Specifying the location of the directory that contains the DNS configuration files, if the location differs from the default directory.

- Declaring the domains for which the server is authoritative, and the data file that describes each domain.
- Specifying the name and location of the file that identifies the DNS root name servers.

Note The Microsoft DNS Server makes use of a BOOT file at one time only: when data are being imported from existing BIND database files for the first time. Subsequently, the data associated with the BOOT file are stored in the Registry.

Here is a possible BOOT file for the sample network:

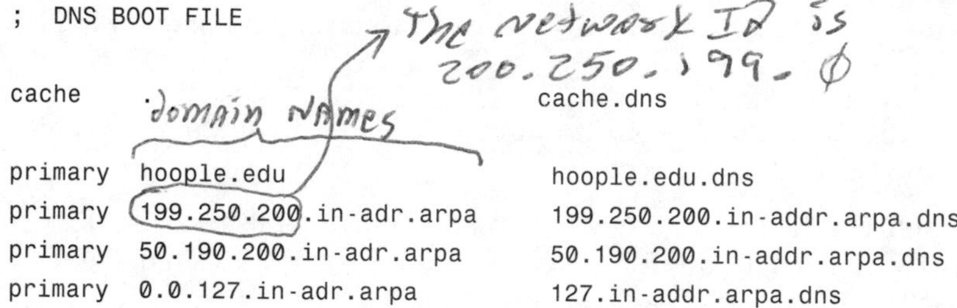

```
; DNS BOOT FILE

cache   .                            cache.dns

primary hoople.edu                   hoople.edu.dns
primary 199.250.200.in-adr.arpa      199.250.200.in-addr.arpa.dns
primary 50.190.200.in-adr.arpa       50.190.200.in-addr.arpa.dns
primary 0.0.127.in-adr.arpa          127.in-addr.arpa.dns
```

The BOOT file has two directives: primary and cache. (A secondary directive appears in BOOT files for secondary DNS servers.)

The primary directives declare the domains for which this server is authoritative, as well as the data file that contains data for each domain. This server is authoritative for four domains:

- **hoople.edu.** The file hoople.edu.dns contains the name-to-address mappings for the domain.
- **199.250.200.in-adr.arpa.** The file 199.250.200.in-addr.arpa.dns contains address-to-name mappings for this reverse-lookup domain.
- **50.190.200.in-adr.arpa.** Another reverse-lookup domain serviced by the file 50.190.200.in-addr.arpa.dns.
- **127.in-adr.arpa.** This is a reverse-lookup domain associated with the loopback address, supported by the file 127.in-addr.arpa.dns.

A primary directive is required for each of these domains. Each DNS server is authoritative for the loopback domain (127.0.0) so that attempts to resolve loopback addresses are not propagated beyond the local DNS server.

The cache directive specifies the file that is authoritative for the root domain. Unlike files specified by primary directives, which are searched during the name resolution process, entries in the cache file are held in memory to make them immediately available.

The example has stayed with the file name convention established by the Windows NT version of DNS: domain.dns files are for name domains and reverse-address.in-addr.arpa.dns files are for reverse-matching domains (in-addr.arpa).

Domain Database Files

A DNS server is responsible for portions of the overall domain name space. Each portion is called a zone. Typically, a zone consists of a specific domain, either in the forward naming domain name space or in the reverse-naming in-addr.arpa name space. The database files shown in this chapter were generated by DNS Manager but could have been created manually as well.

Each zone for which the server is authoritative must be described in a database file. By default, DNS Manager assigns the file name extension .dns to these database files. The hoople.edu.dns database file for hoople.edu is as follows:

```
;  Database file hoople.edu.dns for hoople.edu zone.
;

@                    IN  SOA  haydn.hoople.edu. peters.hoople.edu. (
                     10           ; serial number
                     3600         ; refresh
                     600          ; retry
                     86400        ; expire
                     3600       ) ; minimum TTL


;
;  Zone NS records
;
@                    IN  NS  haydn


;
;  WINS lookup record
;
@                    0  IN  WINS  200.250.199.4


;
;  Zone records
;
@                    IN  MX  10  mail1.
ftp                  IN  CNAME  jsbach.
haydn                IN  A  200.250.199.1
jsbach               IN  A  200.250.199.3
mail1                IN  A  200.190.50.254
```

```
mozart              IN  A  200.190.199.4
papa                IN  CNAME  haydn.
papa190             IN  A  200.190.50.1
papa250             IN  A  200.250.199.1
schubert            IN  A  200.190.50.4
```

The following sections examine each of the sections in the domain database. Only a few of the possible resource record types appear in this example. Table 15.2 provides a complete listing of the resource record types supported by the Microsoft DNS Server.

TABLE 15.2
Resource Record Types

Resource Record	Description
A	An address record maps a host name to an IP address.
AAAA	Also an address record, an AAAA record maps a host name to an IPv6 address.
AFSDB	An Andrew File System (AFS) database record provides the location of an AFS cell's database server or the location of a Distributed Computing Environment (DCE) cell's authenticated name server.
CNAME	A canonical name record establishes an alias, a synonym for a host name.
HINFO	A host information record provides information about the name, operating system, and CPU type of a host. RFC 1700 provides standard computer and system names for use in this record.
ISDN	An Integrated Services Digital Network (ISDN) record maps a host name to an ISDN address, a phone number for the specified ISDN resource.
MB	A mailbox record is an experimental record that identifies a DNS host with a specified mailbox. The MB record is used in association with the MG and MINFO records.
MG	A mail group record is an experimental record used to identify a mailbox that is a member of a specified mailing group, a mailing list that is identified by a DNS name.
MINFO	A mailbox information record is an experimental record type that specifies the mailbox responsible for a specific mail group or mailbox.

Resource Record	Description
MR	A mailbox rename record is an experimental record that identifies a mailbox that is the proper name of a specified mailbox.
MX	A mail exchanger record identifies the mail server for a specified DNS domain.
NS	A name server record identifies a name server for a specified DNS domain.
PTR	A pointer record associates an IP address with a host in a DNS reverse-naming database.
RP	A responsible person record identifies the person responsible for a DNS domain or host. The record includes the e-mail address and a DNS domain name that points to additional information about the responsible person.
RT	A route record identifies an intermediate host that is used to route datagrams to a specified destination host. The RT record is used in conjunction with the ISDN and X.25 resource records.
SOA	A start of authority record specifies the domain for which a DNS server is responsible. It also specifies a variety of parameters that regulate operation of the DNS server.
TXT	A text record associates text information with a record in the DNS database. TXT records could, for example, provide additional information about a host.
WINS	A Windows Internet Name Server record identifies a WINS server that can be consulted to obtain names not recorded in the DNS name space.
WINS_R	A reverse WINS record causes Microsoft DNS to use the nbstat command to resolve reverse-lookup (address-to-name) client queries.
WKS	A well-known service record describes services provided by a specific protocol on a specific adapter. Any protocol specified in the %systemroot%\system32\drivers\etc\protocols file can be specified in this record type.
X.25	An X.25 record maps a name to an X.121 address, the address format used on X.25 networks.

The Start of Authority Record

A Start of Authority (SOA) resource record is found at the beginning of each mapping database file. This block of information declares the host that is most authoritative for the domain, contact information, and some DNS server parameters.

An @ symbol at the beginning of the SOA header declares that this file defines members of the domain associated with the file in the BOOT file. Recall this entry in BOOT:

```
primary  hoople.edu                    hoople.edu.dns
```

As a result of that declaration, @ refers to the domain hoople.edu. Consequently, when the hoople.edu.dns file declares an entry for the host haydn, the directive is defining information for haydn in the hoople.edu domain. That is, the directive is defining haydn.hoople.edu. Because the domain is implied by the context established by the BOOT file, the structure of the database file is simplified, requiring less administrative effort. The IN A entry for haydn could have been entered as follows with exactly the same effect:

```
haydn.hoople.edu.         IN  A  200.250.199.4
```

Notice that haydn.hoople.edu. is terminated with a period, indicating that its origin is the root domain. Without the period indicating the origin in the root domain, DNS would understand the name as haydn.hoople.edu.hoople.edu because it would be understood in the context of the hoople.edu domain.

Caution Improper use of trailing periods is a common cause of error in DNS database files. It is well worth emphasizing the following points:

- Omit the trailing period if the host name falls within the domain defined by this database file (which is nearly always the case).
- Include the trailing period if the record fully specifies the domain name of the host being defined—that is, the record specifies the fully qualified domain name of the host.

The IN directive not surprisingly stands for Internet, one class of data that can appear in the database files. Following IN, the SOA directive declares this as a Start of Authority header.

Following the SOA directive are two Internet names:

- The first, haydn.hoople.edu., is the domain name of the name server host that is most authoritative for this domain.
- The second, peters.hoople.edu., is the e-mail address of the primary contact for this name server. The actual e-mail address is peters@hoople.edu. The @ has been replaced with a period. This e-mail name enables people to send messages when they have trouble with the name server.

Following the e-mail name are five parameters that set the operational characteristics of the DNS server, enclosed in parentheses to enable the parameters to span several lines, thereby permitting a comment to label each parameter. A comment begins with a semicolon (;) and extends to the end of the line. All comment text is for human consumption and ignored by the computer.

Note that the closing parenthesis immediately follows the final parameter, not the comment for the parameter. A parenthesis in the body of the comment would be ignored.

Without comments, the SOA record could have been entered like this:

```
@  IN  SOA  haydn.hoople.edu. peters.hoople.edu.(8 3600 600 86400 3600)
```

You probably agree that the comments make interpreting the record much easier. The five numeric parameters are as follows:

- **Serial number.** A serial number that indicates the revision level of the file. The DNS administrator increments this value each time the file is modified.
- **Refresh.** The interval in seconds at which a secondary name server checks in to download a copy of the zone data in the primary name server. The default value for DNS server is 3600, resulting in a refresh interval of one hour.
- **Retry.** The time in seconds a secondary name server waits after a failed download before it tries to download the zone database again. The default value for DNS server is 600, resulting in a retry interval of 10 minutes.
- **Expire.** The period of time in seconds that a secondary name server continues to try to download a zone database. After this time expires, the secondary name server discards data for the zone. The default value for DNS server is 86400, equivalent to 24 hours.
- **Minimum TTL.** The minimum Time to Live in seconds for a resource record. This parameter determines how long a DNS server retains an address mapping in cache. After the TTL expires for a record, the record is discarded. Short TTL values enable DNS to adjust to network changes more adroitly, but increase network traffic and loading on the DNS server. A short TTL might be appropriate in the early days, while a network evolves, but you might want to extend the TTL as the network stabilizes. The default value for DNS server is 3600, resulting in a TTL of one hour.

The WINS Record

The WINS record is specific to the version of DNS that ships with Windows NT Server 4. If an outside host queries a name from your DNS server, the server first attempts to resolve the name from DNS database files. If that is unsuccessful, the DNS server attempts to resolve the name through WINS. If a name is resolved through WINS, an address record is added to the domain database for future use.

Objective B.7

The WINS record enables DNS, WINS, and DHCP to cooperate. DNS name resolution is ordinarily static, based on manually maintained database files. With the WINS record, you can assign IP addresses dynamically with DHCP, resolve NetBIOS names to dynamic addresses with WINS, and make the name-to-address mappings available to DNS. In other words, you need not give up the advantages of DHCP dynamic address assignment to enable your network to support DNS name resolution.

The WINS record accepts one or more IP addresses that specify the WINS servers that DNS is to consult when unable to resolve an address. The following WINS record specifies two WINS servers:

```
@              IN  WINS  200.190.50.2  200.190.50.201
```

As in the SOA record, the @ refers to the domain defined by this data file. This WINS directive states, "If DNS cannot find a host in the keystone.com domain in its database, DNS should query the following WINS servers for name entries."

When DNS learns about a host from WINS, a resource record is created in the DNS database. Records created in this way are not permanent and are not archived when the database files are updated from the active DNS database. DNS will, however, no longer consult WINS regarding that name until the resource record is removed.

Note The Windows name space is a "flat" name space, unlike the hierarchical structure supported by DNS. Consequently, all names in the name space supported by a WINS server (or group of servers that replicate a common database) must be unique.

Because the WINS database does not record DNS domain names along with host names, you cannot use a given WINS name space to resolve names in multiple DNS domains. You cannot, for example, include 200.190.50.2 as a WINS server for the domains alpha.com and beta.com.

Name Server Records

A name server (NS) record must declare each primary and secondary name server that is authoritative for the zone. Name servers are declared by IN NS records. Notice that the domain servers terminate with periods, indicating that the name originates with the root.

NS records might begin with the @ specifying "the domain for this database" or the @ might be omitted, in which case the domain is implied. If the @ is omitted, the IN should not occupy the first column of the line. In other words, the following declarations are equivalent in this context:

```
hoople.edu. IN NS  mozart.hoople.edu.
@           IN NS  mozart.hoople.edu.
            IN NS  mozart.hoople.edu.
```

Address Records

Each host name that DNS resolves must be specified using an address (A) resource record—unless the name will be resolved through WINS. One example from the hoople.edu.dns database file is the following:

```
haydn       IN  A  200.250.199.1
```

Multihomed hosts require an address declaration for each network adapter, as with the host haydn in the example database file.

Note Most host names are learned from WINS. Only essential hosts, such as the DNS servers, are configured with hard-coded address records. The mappings for these hosts must be available when the DNS server is booted, and therefore cannot be learned from WINS after the server is running.

Aliases

Many networks employ aliases. In most cases, aliases are declared using CNAME ("canonical name") resource records. On the hoople.edu network, host jsbach will be configured as an FTP server. So that users can access this server with the name ftp.hoople.edu, it is necessary to establish an alias as follows:

```
ftp             IN  CNAME  jsbach
```

A more complex case is presented by multihomed computers. The aliases section of the sample database file includes three declarations related to the host haydn.edu:

```
papa            IN  CNAME  haydn
papa250         IN  A      200.250.199.1
papa190         IN  A      200.190.50.1
```

The CNAME declaration defines papa as an alias for the multihomed host haydn. DNS queries for papa or haydn are resolved to the first IP address in the configuration of haydn. A CNAME declaration maps to a canonical name, however, not to a specific network interface of the multihomed host.

Usually, applications don't care which address of a host they resolve to. When troubleshooting a network, however, you might prefer to be able to diagnose a specific interface, which is why two IN A declarations are included. papa250 and papa190 enable an administrator to ping by name a specific network attachment of haydn, for example.

The advantage of coding aliases using CNAME is that the actual IP address of the host appears in one place only. If the IP address changes, a single edit updates both the primary address map and the alias. A CNAME record does not specify a particular interface. On a multihomed host, you must use A records to establish a name for a specific interface. If the address for haydn changes, however, it is also necessary to manually edit the A records for papa250 and papa190 as well as the A record for haydn.

E-Mail Server Records

The most popular electronic mail environment in the TCP/IP world is based on a program called sendmail. If your network incorporates an electronic mail system that uses sendmail, you should add appropriate records to the zone database file.

In the sample network, sendmail is running on the host mail1.keystone.com. The following resource records support this host:

```
@                IN  MX 10  mail1.
mail1            IN  A  200.190.50.254
```

The A record specifies the IP address for mail1.keystone.com.

The MX record specifies that mail1 is an e-mail server for the keystone.com domain (specified by the @ character). If the domain is supported by more than one e-mail server, each is specified in an MX record:

```
@                  IN  MX  10  mail1
@                  IN  MX  20  mail2
```

The numbers following the MX keywords specify the priority for each mail server.

E-mail is routed to the active server with the lowest priority number—that is, 1 (10 in the example) indicates the first preferred server. In other words, if mail1 and mail2 are both active, e-mail is routed to mail1. The number parameter specifies the priority order. Priorities of 2 and 7 have exactly the same result as priorities of 10 and 20.

By including MX resource records, you make it easier for outsiders to send e-mail into your domain. E-mail can be addressed to peters@hoople.edu, for example. There's no need to address the message to peters@mail1.hoople.edu. Incoming mail is routed to the available server that has the highest priority.

Reverse-Matching Database Files

A reverse-matching (address-to-name matching) database file is required for each network ID for which the DNS server is authoritative. Recall that the file named 200.250.199 is the database for network 200.250.199, which appears in the reverse database tree as 199.250.200.in-adr.arpa.

The 199.250.200.in-addr.arpa.dns file is constructed as follows:

```
;  Database file arpa-200.250.199 for 199.250.200.in-addr.arpa.
;  Zone version:  5
@ IN SOA mozart.hoople.edu. peters.hoople.edu. (
                1      ;serial
                10800  ;refresh after 3 hours
                3600   ;retry after 1 hour
                691200 ;expire in 8 days
                86400) ;minimum TTL 1 day

;name servers
@               IN  NS  mozart.hoople.edu.

;addresses mapped to canonical names
1               IN  PTR  haydn.hoople.edu.
3               IN  PTR  jsbach.hoople.edu.
4               IN  PTR  mozart.hoople.edu.
```

Similarly, the 200.190.50.in-addr.arpa.dns file is constructed as follows:

```
;  Database file arpa-200.190.50 for 50.190.200.in-addr.arpa.
;  Zone version:  5
@ IN SOA mozart.hoople.edu. peters.hoople.edu. (
                1      ;serial
                10800  ;refresh after 3 hours
                3600   ;retry after 1 hour
                691200 ;expire in 8 days
                86400) ;minimum TTL 1 day

;name servers
@               IN  NS  mozart.hoople.edu.

;addresses mapped to canonical names
4               IN  PTR  schubert.hoople.edu.
254             IN  PTR  mail1.hoople.edu.
```

The reverse-naming files use the same Start of Authority header as the domain database file. As before, @ means "the domain specified in the BOOT file." Also, all host names are to be understood in the context of the domain name. Therefore, "4" in the IN PTR record refers to host 200.250.199.4 (which is 4.199.250.200.in-addr.arpa. in the reverse-naming database tree).

NS records declare the name servers that are authoritative for this domain.

PTR (pointer) records provide reverse mappings between IP addresses and host names. Notice that host names must be fully specified from the root domain.

The Localhost Database File

The 127.0.0.in-addr.arpa.dns file includes a reverse mapping for the localhost host name. It resembles the formats of the other reverse mapping files:

```
@ IN SOA mozart.hoople.edu. peters.hoople.edu. (
                1       ;serial
                10800   ;refresh after 3 hours
                3600    ;retry after 1 hour
                691200  ;expire in 8 days
                86400)  ;minimum TTL 1 day

;name servers
@               IN  NS  mozart.hoople.edu.

;addresses mapped to canonical names
1               IN  PTR localhost.
```

The Cache File

Objective B.7

The Cache.dns file declares name-to-address mappings to be cached in the DNS server. Essentially, cached entries define the DNS servers that are authoritative for the root domain.

If you are establishing a private TCP/IP network, the root domain will be supported by DNS servers running on your network. The records in Cache.dns will reflect this and declare entries for local DNS servers authoritative for the root domain.

In the case of hoople.edu, however, the network is connected to the Internet, and the Cache.dns file identifies the Internet root name servers. These root name servers change from time to time, and a DNS administrator should periodically check the related information files in the local cache database to make sure it is kept up to date. The official root name server list can be obtained in the following three ways:

- **FTP.** FTP the file /domain/named.root from FTP.RS.INTERNIC.NET.
- **Gopher.** Obtain the file named.root from RS.INTERNIC.NET under menu InterNIC Registration Services (NSI), submenu InterNIC Registration Archives.
- **E-mail.** Send e-mail to service@nic.ddn.mil, using the subject "netinfo root-servers.txt."

The named.root file can be used unmodified as the cache database file, although you might want to rename the file based on local database file-naming conventions. At the time of this writing, the named.root file has the following contents:

```
;       This file holds the information on root name servers needed to
;       initialize cache of Internet domain name servers
;       (e.g. reference this file in the "cache  . <file>"
;       configuration file of BIND domain name servers).
;
;       This file is made available by InterNIC registration services
;       under anonymous FTP as
;           file                /domain/named.root
;           on server           FTP.RS.INTERNIC.NET
;       -OR- under Gopher at    RS.INTERNIC.NET
;           under menu          InterNIC Registration Services (NSI)
;              submenu          InterNIC Registration Archives
;           file                named.root
;
;       last update:    Sep 1, 1995
;       related version of root zone:   1995090100
;
;
; formerly NS.INTERNIC.NET
;
.                        3600000  IN  NS    A.ROOT-SERVERS.NET.
A.ROOT-SERVERS.NET.      3600000      A     198.41.0.4
;
; formerly NS1.ISI.EDU
;
.                        3600000      NS    B.ROOT-SERVERS.NET.
B.ROOT-SERVERS.NET.      3600000      A     128.9.0.107
;
; formerly C.PSI.NET
;
.                        3600000      NS    C.ROOT-SERVERS.NET.
C.ROOT-SERVERS.NET.      3600000      A     192.33.4.12
;
; formerly TERP.UMD.EDU
;
.                        3600000      NS    D.ROOT-SERVERS.NET.
D.ROOT-SERVERS.NET.      3600000      A     128.8.10.90
;
; formerly NS.NASA.GOV
;
.                        3600000      NS    E.ROOT-SERVERS.NET.
```

```
E.ROOT-SERVERS.NET.      3600000      A      192.203.230.10
;
; formerly NS.ISC.ORG
;
.                        3600000      NS     F.ROOT-SERVERS.NET.
F.ROOT-SERVERS.NET.      3600000      A      39.13.229.241
;
; formerly NS.NIC.DDN.MIL
;
.                        3600000      NS     G.ROOT-SERVERS.NET.
G.ROOT-SERVERS.NET.      3600000      A      192.112.36.4
;
; formerly AOS.ARL.ARMY.MIL
;
.                        3600000      NS     H.ROOT-SERVERS.NET.
H.ROOT-SERVERS.NET.      3600000      A      128.63.2.53
;
; formerly NIC.NORDU.NET
;
.                        3600000      NS     I.ROOT-SERVERS.NET.
I.ROOT-SERVERS.NET.      3600000      A      192.36.148.17
; End of File
```

Notice that the names of the root name servers have been changed. You will still encounter the old names of the servers in some TCP/IP literature. The structure of the file is more clearly apparent if the comments are removed as follows:

```
.                        3600000  IN  NS     A.ROOT-SERVERS.NET.
A.ROOT-SERVERS.NET.      3600000      A      198.41.0.4
.                        3600000      NS     B.ROOT-SERVERS.NET.
B.ROOT-SERVERS.NET.      3600000      A      128.9.0.107
.                        3600000      NS     C.ROOT-SERVERS.NET.
C.ROOT-SERVERS.NET.      3600000      A      192.33.4.12
.                        3600000      NS     D.ROOT-SERVERS.NET.
D.ROOT-SERVERS.NET.      3600000      A      128.8.10.90
.                        3600000      NS     E.ROOT-SERVERS.NET.
E.ROOT-SERVERS.NET.      3600000      A      192.203.230.10
.                        3600000      NS     F.ROOT-SERVERS.NET.
F.ROOT-SERVERS.NET.      3600000      A      39.13.229.241
.                        3600000      NS     G.ROOT-SERVERS.NET.
G.ROOT-SERVERS.NET.      3600000      A      192.112.36.4
.                        3600000      NS     H.ROOT-SERVERS.NET.
H.ROOT-SERVERS.NET.      3600000      A      128.63.2.53
.                        3600000      NS     I.ROOT-SERVERS.NET.
I.ROOT-SERVERS.NET.      3600000      A      192.36.148.17
```

Each host is declared in two directives:

- **NS directive.** Declares the server by name as a name server for the root domain.
- **A directive.** Declares the server name-to-address mapping.

The NS and A directives include an additional parameter in the Cache.dns file. In early versions of DNS, a numeric parameter (here 3600000) indicated how long the data should remain in cache. In current versions of DNS, the root name server entries are retained indefinitely. The numeric parameter remains a part of the file syntax but no longer serves a function.

Creating the cache file completes configuration of the DNS database files.

Setting Up a Secondary Name Server

You should consider setting up one or more secondary name servers to prevent failure of a single name server from disrupting name resolution for your domain. The difference between primary and secondary name servers is that secondary name servers obtain their data from other name servers in a process called a *zone transfer.* Secondary name servers may obtain their data from primary or secondary name servers. This capability makes it possible to maintain the data on several name servers with only one set of master database files.

The example files in this chapter have configured the primary name server mozart. They have also anticipated establishment of a secondary name server on schubert, which this section addresses.

Install the DNS software on the secondary name server by using the same procedures used to install the primary name server. The distinction between the primary and secondary name servers is found in the structure of the BOOT file.

The DNS directory of the secondary name server needs copies of the following files:

- BOOT
- Cache.dns
- 127.in-addr.arpa.dns

The Cache.dns and 127.in-addr.arpa.dns files are identical on all DNS servers, and you do not need to create them. A Cache.dns file is created on each server when Microsoft DNS Server is installed. The required reverse-look zones, such as 127.in-addr.arpa, are established when a server is added to the DNS Manager configuration.

The BOOT file is modified for the secondary server on schubert as follows:

```
; DNS BOOT FILE

cache       .     cache

secondary  hoople.edu                  200.250.199.4  hoople.edu.dns
secondary  199.250.200.in-adr.arpa     200.250.199.4  200.250.199.in-addr.arpa.dns
secondary  50.190.200.in-adr.arpa      200.250.199.4  200.190.50.in-addr.arpa.dns
primary    0.0.127.in-adr.arpa         arpa-127.0.0.in-addr.arpa
```

schubert is a secondary name server for three zones, specified in the secondary directives. In the three secondary directives, an IP address is added to the syntax. This IP address specifies the computer that serves as the repository for the database file. schubert loads hoople.edu from mozart (IP address 200.250.199.4). During operation, schubert makes backup copies of the database files in its local DNS directory, which enables schubert to start up if mozart goes down.

A name server can be a primary for some zones and a secondary for others. The role of a name server is specified by the use of the primary and secondary directives in the BOOT file.

schubert is a primary only for the reverse-naming 127.0.0.in-addr.arpa zone. Because this information is the same on all servers, there is no sense including the records in the zone transfer.

Because the information in the cache.dns file is identical for all DNS servers, there is no sense in performing zone transfers for root name server data. Each DNS server is configured with a local Cache.dns file.

In addition to customizing the BOOT file for the secondary server, you need to add NS records for the secondary server to the database files on the primary DNS server. On the sample network, you need to add the following resource record to the hoople.edu.dns, 200.190.50.in-addr.arpa.dns, and 200.250.199.in-addr.arpa.dns files:

```
@                     IN  NS  schubert.hoople.edu.
```

Managing the DNS Server

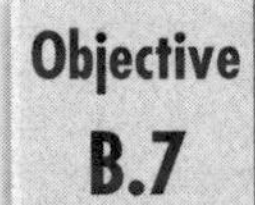

After you complete the configuration files—and check them three or four times for errors, including the correct use of trailing periods in host names—you are ready to start working with the DNS server manager. At this point, you re-enter the realm of the GUI interface.

Installing the Microsoft DNS Server

1. Install TCP/IP on the DHCP server computer. DNS servers must be configured with static IP addresses so that the addresses can be entered into host configurations.
2. Open the Network dialog box.
3. Select the Services tab.
4. Choose Add.
5. In the Network Service list, select Microsoft DNS Server and click OK.
6. Supply the path to the installation files when prompted.
7. Close the Network utility and restart the server.

Initializing the DNS Server

By default, database files for the Microsoft DNS Server are installed in %systemroot%\system32\dns. When the DNS server is installed, only a Cache.dns file is installed in this directory.

When DNS Manager is run for the first time, it attempts to initialize using database files in the %systemroot%\system32\dns directory. Depending on the contents of this directory, one of two things can happen:

- ◆ If the dns directory contains only the Cache.dns file, the DNS server is initialized with an empty database. This section assumes that only the default files are present in the dns directory.
- ◆ If you have placed a set of BIND data files in this directory, DNS Manager initializes the server database from those files. The section "Porting Data from BIND Servers" later in this chapter discusses the process of initializing the server from BIND database files.

The icon for the DNS Manager is installed in the Administrative Tools group on the Start menu. At first, no DNS servers are listed and the display is entirely uninteresting (thus no picture is provided here). The first step is to add one to the DNS Manager configuration. Figure 15.12 shows DNS Manager after a DNS server has been added.

To create a DNS server:

1. Right-click the Server List icon and select the New Server command from the displayed menus.
2. Enter the host name or IP address of the DNS server in the Add DNS Server dialog box. If you enter a host name, Microsoft DNS Server must be installed on the host. Additionally, this host must be able to resolve the host name to an IP address by using WINS or some other means.

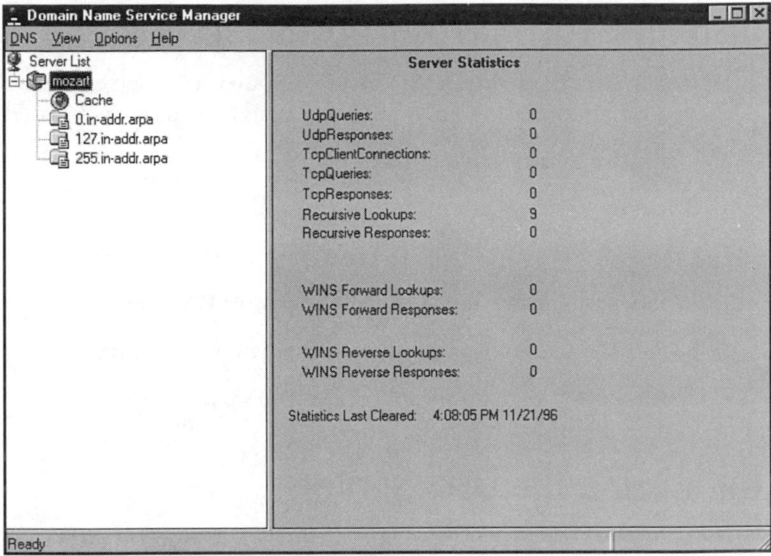

Figure 15.12
DNS Manager after a DNS server has been added.

Adding the server creates an icon for the DNS server object, which is assigned a default set of properties. In addition, the following zones are automatically created:

- **Cache.** This zone is filled with records defining the root name servers for the Internet.
- **0.in-addr.arpa.** This zone prevents reverse-lookup queries for the address 0.0.0.0 from being passed to the root name server.
- **127.in-addr.arpa.** This zone supports reverse-lookup queries for the loopback address.
- **255.in-addr.arpa.** This zone prevents broadcast name queries from being passed to the root name server.

With the exception of the Cache zone, the automatically created zones are concealed by default. To enable display of these zones, as was done to create figure 15.12, choose the Preferences command in the Options menu. Then check the Show Automatically Created Zones check box. Finally, press F5 to refresh the display and display the zone icons.

Because these zones require no maintenance on your part, you can safely leave them hidden, as was done in the other figures.

There is no need to create anything resembling the BIND boot file. The information needed to start the DNS server is continually updated as you establish the server's configuration.

Server Roles

Objective B.7

Now that you know how to install the DNS server, you need to understand the different roles that the DNS server can play. As the server is currently configured, it acts as a caching-only server. This means that the server can resolve queries sent to it by the client computers by finding and consulting with an authoritative server for the domain that you are looking for.

When you start to create your own domains, you configure at least one server as the primary server for your domain. This server loads all zone information from the local files and is the authority for the domain.

You might also configure a DNS server as a backup for your primary DNS. This is required to register with the InterNIC (they require you to have two separate name servers). The secondary server contacts its master name server—in most cases, this is the primary. You might use another secondary. If you use a secondary, however, it must be running first to ask for a zone transfer.

Adding the Reverse-Lookup Zones

Before you create a zone for the domain that is to be managed, you should create the zones that support reverse-lookups, the in-addr.arpa zones. If you create these zones first, you can populate them with PTR records automatically, as you add A records to the primary domain zone.

To create a primary reverse-lookup zone, follow these steps:

1. Right-click the icon of the primary DNS server.
2. Choose the New Zone command from the Object menu to open the Create New Zone wizard (see fig. 15.13).

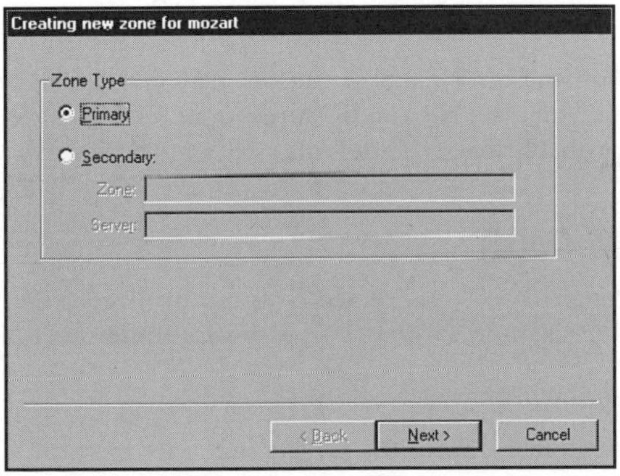

Creating new zone for mozart

Zone Type

Primary

Secondary:

Zone:

Server:

< Back Next > Cancel

Figure 15.13

Specifying whether the zone is primary or secondary.

3. Click the Primary radio button and choose Next to open the Zone Info dialog box (see fig. 15.14).

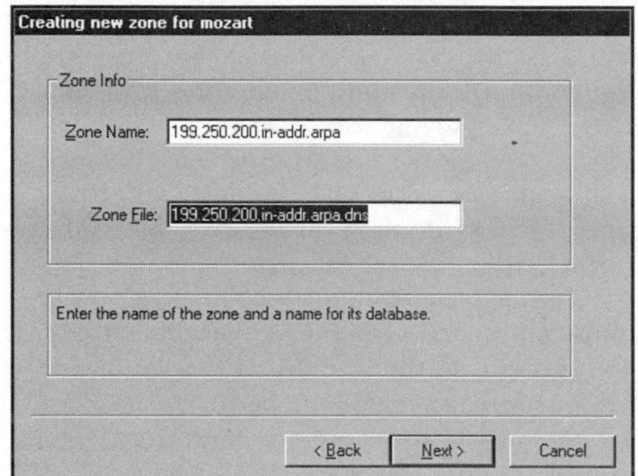

Figure 15.14

Pressing Tab automatically create the zone file name.

4. In the Zone Name field, enter the name of the reverse-lookup zone. Because this is a reverse-lookup zone, adhere to the naming convention (reverse-network_ID.in-addr.arpa). DNS server will realize this is a reverse-naming zone and configure it accordingly. To create the reverse-lookup zone for network 200.250.199.0, you enter 199.250.200.in-addr.arpa in the Zone Name field.

   Do not move to the next field except by pressing the Tab key.

5. Press Tab to automatically generate a file name in the Zone File field. The file name can be anything you want, but the default adheres to the conventions established for the Microsoft DNS Server.

6. Choose Next. You will be rewarded with the message, `All the information for the new zone has been entered.`

7. Click Finish to create the zone, or click Back to change any information you have entered.

Figure 15.15 shows DNS Manager after entry of the reverse-lookup zones required for the example network. Notice that the NS and SOA resource records have been entered for you. You can probably leave the default values for both records.

Adding a Primary Zone

Objective B.7

After the reverse-lookup zones have been created, you can begin to create the name-lookup zones. The procedure is quite similar to that shown in the preceding section:

1. Right-click the icon of the primary DNS server.

2. Select the New Zone command from the Object menu to open the Create New Zone wizard.

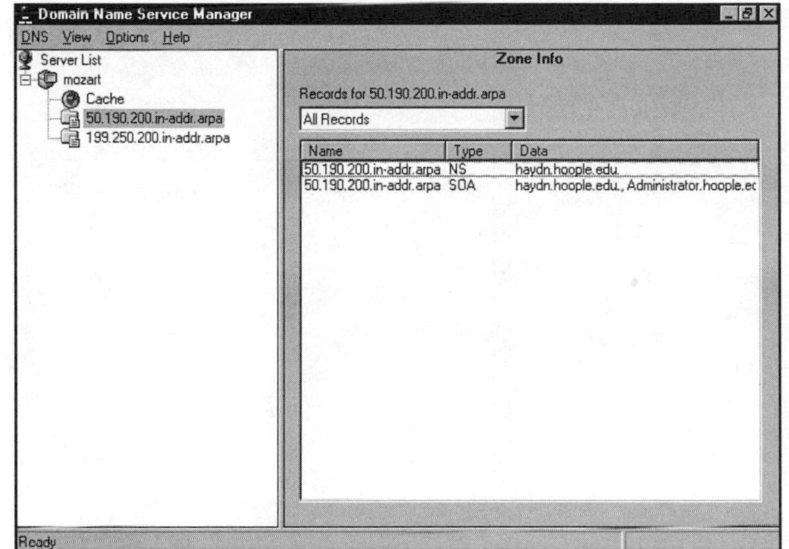

Figure 15.15

Newly created reverse naming zones.

3. Click the Primary radio button and choose Next.
4. Enter the zone name in the Zone Name field and press Tab to generate the file name. Then press Next.
5. Click Finish to create the zone, or click Back to change any information you have entered.

Figure 15.16 shows the hoople.edu zone after it has been created. Notice that the NS and SOA resource records have been created for you. You need only to create any required A records manually.

Adding Resource Records

Figure 15.17 shows DNS Manager after a variety of records have been added to the hoople.edu domain. This section and the following sections examine the creation of address, CNAME, MX, and WINS resource records.

Adding Address Records

Next you must add essential address (A) records to the name-lookup zone. You must add address records only for hosts associated with fixed IP addresses or not registered with WINS. Hosts registered with WINS can be entered into the zone database through WINS lookups.

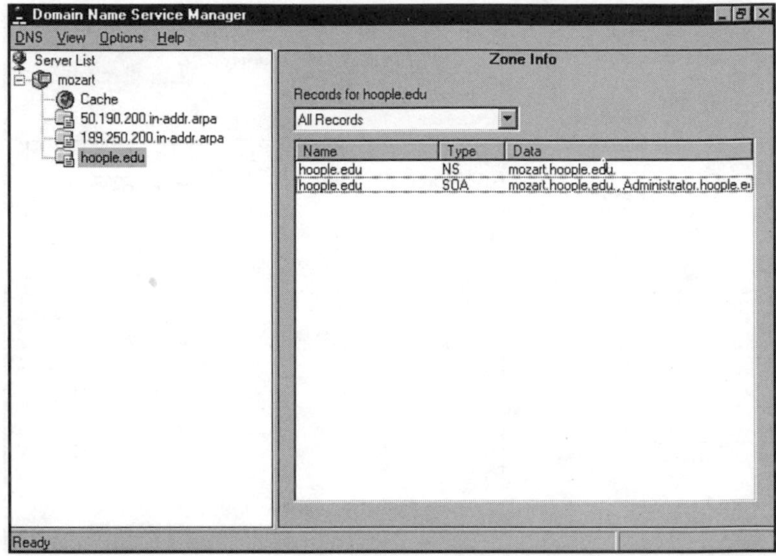

Figure 15.16 *DNS Manager with both primary and reverse-lookup zones.*

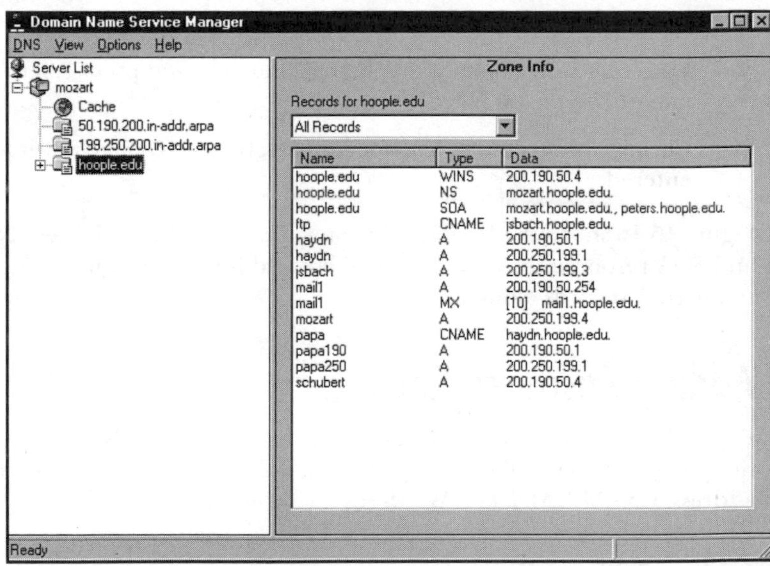

Figure 15.17 *DNS Manager with host and other records added.*

To add an address resource record, follow these steps:

1. Right-click the name-lookup zone icon (in this example, hoople.edu) and choose New Host from the object menu.

   or

   Right-click in the database area of the Zone Info pane and choose New Host from the menu.

2. In the New Host dialog box, enter the host name in the Host Name field (see fig. 15.18).

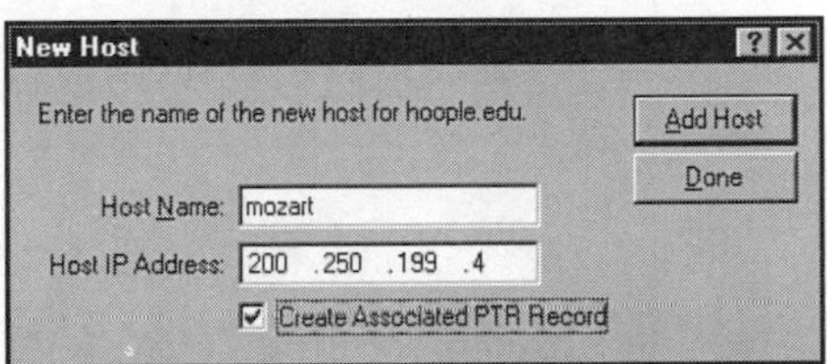

Figure 15.18
Creating a new host entry.

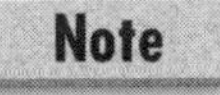

In most cases, when you are entering a host name, DNS Manager expects only the host name portion of the FQDN. When necessary, the host name is combined with the domain name to create the FQDN.

3. Enter the host's IP address in the Host IP Address field.
4. If you want to create a record in the appropriate reverse-lookup database, check Create Associated PTR Record. The reverse-lookup zone must have been previously created.
5. Choose Add Host to create the database records.
6. Repeat steps 2 through 5 to enter additional address records as required.
7. Click Done when you are finished.

When do you create a PTR record? In most cases, you want to add host addresses to the reverse-lookup zones, but there are some exceptions. In the examples created in this chapter, pointer records were created for all A records except for papa250 and papa190. Because those records were added for administrative convenience and not for public consumption, and because a PTR record for haydn already exists, entries were not added to the reverse-lookup directories. To have done so would have been to create conflicting mappings, where an IP address mapped to two host names.

Adding Other Resource Records

Besides address records, all other types of resource records are entered from the New Resource Record dialog box (see fig. 15.19). The fields you see in the Value box depend on the record type that has been selected. This section examines the procedures for creating CNAME, MX, and PTR resource records.

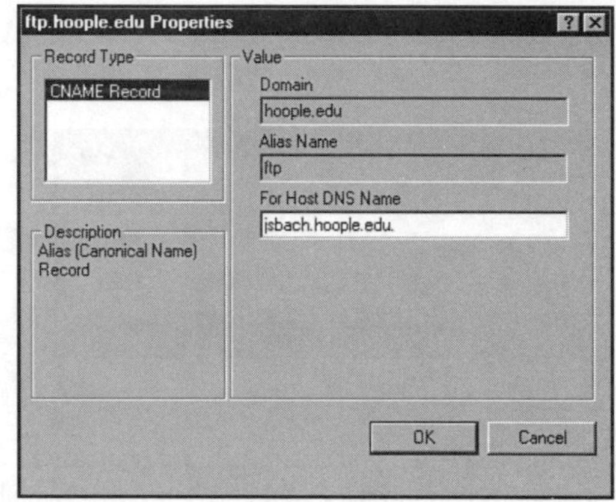

Figure 15.19
Adding a CNAME entry.

Adding CNAME Records

An alias is established by adding a CNAME record. Two aliases are required for the example network. To add a CNAME resource record, follow these steps:

1. Right-click the zone that is to contain the record.
2. Choose New Record from the Object menu to open the New Resource Record dialog box (see fig. 15.20).
3. Select CNAME Record in the Record Type list.
4. Enter an alias in the Alias Name field.
5. Enter the FQDN that is the actual name for the host in the For Host DNS Name field. Include the trailing dot when entering the name.
6. Click OK to add the record.

Adding MX Records

To add an MX resource record:

1. Right-click the zone that is to contain the record.
2. Choose New Record from the Object menu to open the New Resource Record dialog box (see fig. 15.20).
3. Enter the host name only in the Host Name field.

Note Although the description says the Host Name field is optional, I have been unable to get MX records to work without entering the host name here.

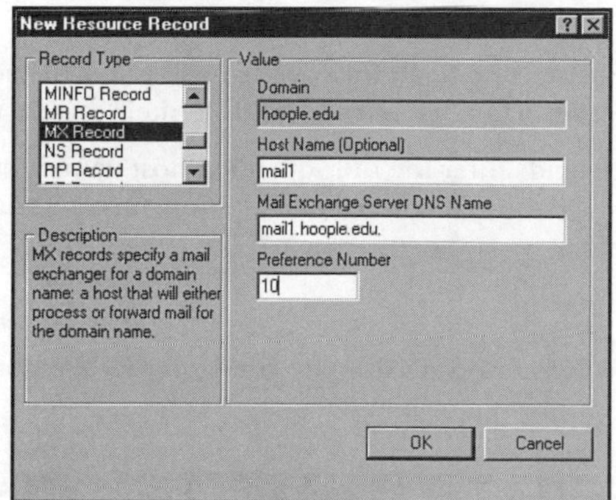

Figure 15.20

Configuring an MX (mail exchange) record.

4. Enter the FQDN of the mail exchange server in the Mail Exchange Server DNS Name field (include the trailing dot).
5. Enter a preference number in the Preference Number field.
6. Click OK to add the record.

Adding PTR Records

To add a PTR resource record to a reverse-lookup zone, perform these steps:

1. Right-click the reverse-lookup zone that is to contain the record. In the New Resource Record dialog box for a reverse-look zone, only three record types can be created (see fig. 15.21).

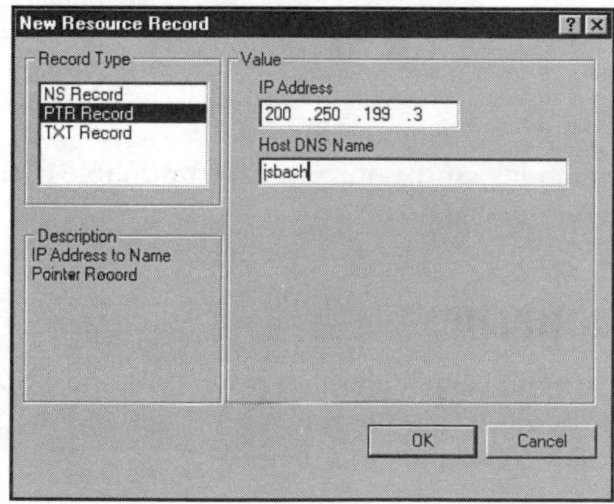

Figure 15.21

Creating a PTR record.

2. Select PTR Record in the Record Type list.
3. In the IP Address field, enter the IP address of the host. Enter the address fields in their conventional order. Do not enter the fields in their reverse order.
4. In the Host DNS Name field, enter the fully qualified host name of the host. Do not enter the host name alone. The reverse-lookup domains are not tied to a particular name domain.
5. Click OK to create the record.

Figure 15.22 shows the records for a reverse-lookup zone after PTR records have been created.

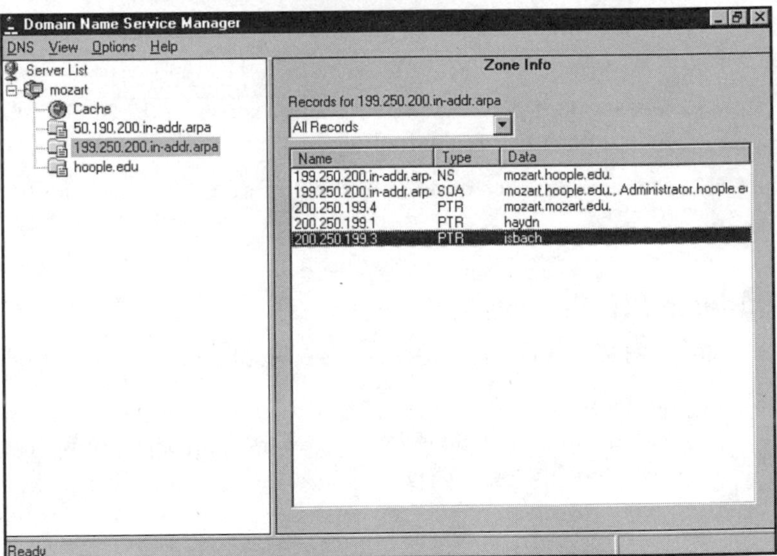

Figure 15.22
PTR records in a reverse-lookup zone.

Modifying Resource Records

You can open a dialog box to modify any resource record by double-clicking the resource record in the Zone Info dialog box.

Modifying Zone Properties

When a zone is created, it is assigned a default set of properties and a Start of Authority record is established. You should review the zone properties and the SOA record to ensure that the properties are correct for your network.

To review the zone properties, right-click the zone icon and choose Properties from the Object menu. Figure 15.23 shows the Zone Properties dialog box. Four tabs are included in the dialog box and are examined in the following sections.

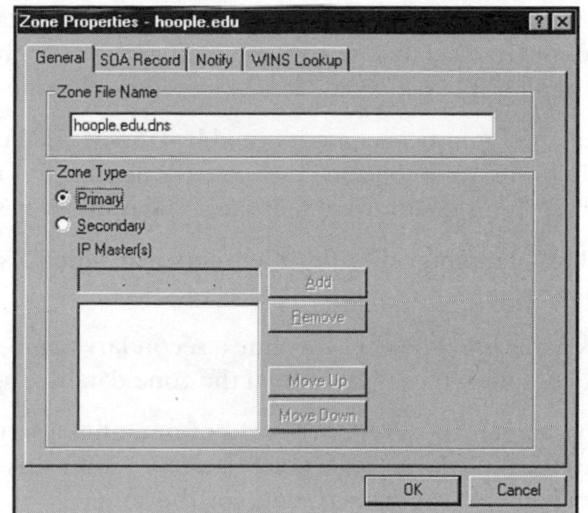

Figure 15.23

The Zone Properties dialog box.

Zone General Properties

The General Properties tab, shown in figure 15.23, has the following fields:

- **Zone File Name.** This file name specifies the file name used to create a server data file for the zone. You can change this file name at any time.
- **Primary.** When the Primary button is selected, this server is a primary DNS server for the zone. Primary DNS servers maintain a database for the zone locally on the computer on which they are running.
- **Secondary.** When the Secondary button is selected, this server is a secondary DNS server for the zone. Secondary DNS servers obtain zone data from another DNS server and do not maintain a local database for the zone.
- **IP Master(s).** If the Secondary button is selected, this list is active. You must specify the IP addresses of one or more master DNS servers, servers from which zone transfers are performed to populate the database of the secondary DNS server.

SOA Record Properties

The SOA Record tab establishes properties for the SOA record in the zone database (see fig. 15.24). The SOA record was discussed in considerable detail earlier in the chapter, but it is worth listing the fields here as well:

- **Primary Name Server DNS Name.** This field specifies the name server that appears in the SOA record and identifies the name server that is authoritative for the zone defined by this database.
- **Responsible Person Mailbox DNS Name.** This informational field identifies the contact person for this domain, typically by specifying an e-mail

address. Because the @ character has a special meaning in BIND database files, a period is substituted for the @ character in the e-mail address. In this case, peters.hoople.edu designates the e-mail address peters@hoople.edu.

- **Serial Number.** The serial number is incremented by DNS Manager each time a change is made to the contents of the zone database. Zone transfers take place when a secondary DNS server is made aware that the serial number has changed.
- **Refresh Interval.** This parameter specifies the interval at which a secondary DNS server checks to see whether a zone transfer is required.
- **Retry Interval.** This parameter specifies the time a secondary name server waits after a failed download before it tries to download the zone database again.
- **Expire Time.** This parameter specifies the period of time that a secondary name server continues to try to download a zone database. After this time expires, the secondary name server discards data for the zone.
- **Minimum Default TTL.** This parameter determines how long a DNS server retains an address mapping in cache. After the TTL expires for a record, the record is discarded. Short TTL values enable DNS to adjust to network changes more adroitly, but increase network traffic and loading on the DNS server. A short TTL might be appropriate in the early days, while a network evolves, but you might want to extend the TTL as the network stabilizes.

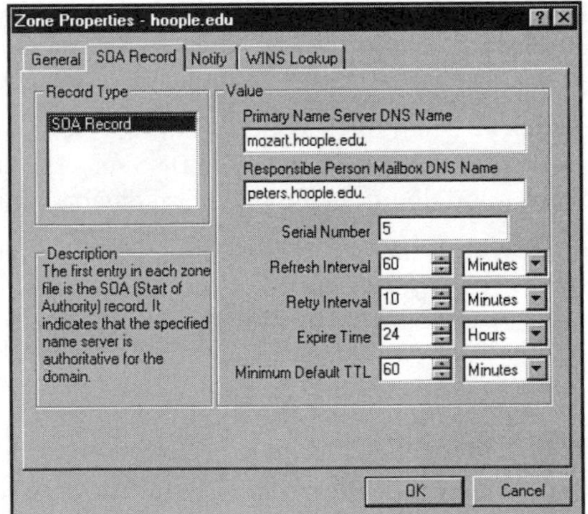

Figure 15.24
The SOA Record Properties tab.

Notify Properties

The Notify tab lists the IP addresses of secondary DNS servers that obtain zone data from this server (see fig. 15.25). A DNS server notifies servers appearing in the Notify List field when changes are made to the zone database.

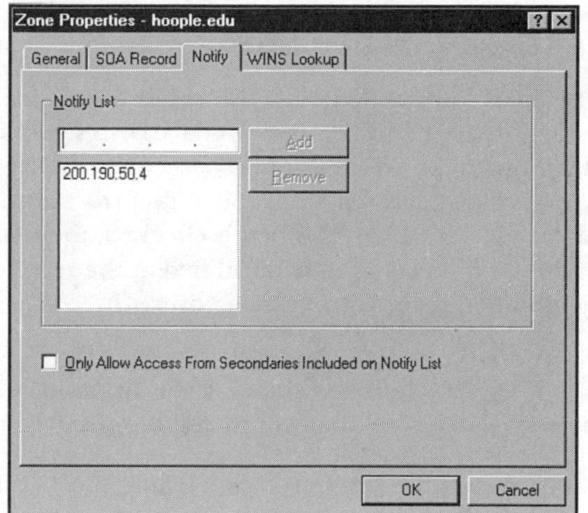

Figure 15.25

Adding a secondary DNS server to the notify list.

Zone transfers can be driven by secondary DNS servers, and it is not essential for notification to take place. If, however, you want to restrict the secondary DNS servers that can transfer records from this server, check Only Allow Access From Secondaries Included on Notify List.

WINS Lookup Properties

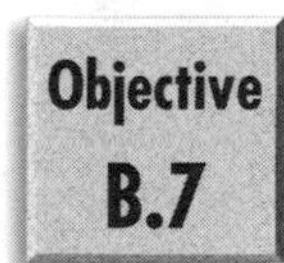

This tab is used to enable DNS Server to use WINS to resolve names that do not appear in the zone database (see fig. 15.26). This tab has three fields:

Figure 15.26

Setting the WINS lookup.

- **Use WINS Resolution.** When this box is checked, WINS lookup is enabled. A WINS resource record is added to the zone database.
- **Settings only affect local server.** When WINS resolution is enabled, this field determines how records are handled on secondary DNS servers. Ordinarily, when a record learned from WINS is sent to a secondary DNS server in a zone transfer, the record is flagged as read-only. Such records cannot be modified on the secondary server. When this box is checked, the read-only protection is removed, enabling records to be modified at the secondary DNS server and preventing modified records from being overwritten in a zone transfer.
- **WINS Servers.** When WINS resolution is enabled, this list must include the IP addresses of one or more WINS servers that will be used to resolve names.

Several advanced WINS properties can be configured by clicking the Advanced button to open the Advanced Zone Properties dialog box (see fig. 15.27). The dialog box has the following fields:

- **Submit DNS Domain as NetBIOS Scope.** NetBIOS scopes permit administrators to specify a character string (a scope ID) that is appended to NetBIOS and is used for all NetBT (NetBIOS over TCP/IP) names. The effect is that only computers having the same NetBIOS scope can communicate using NetBIOS. In the words of the Windows NT Resource Kit, "Use of NetBIOS Scope is strongly discouraged if you are not already using it, or if you use Domain Name System (DNS) on your network."

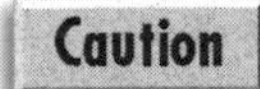

Who am I to question Microsoft? Given the many problems that can ensue if NetBIOS scopes are used, I don't recommend them. Unless they are used, there is no reason to check this box.

- **Cache Timeout Value.** The DNS Server maintains a cache of addresses that have been recently resolved via WINS. These records are retained for a limited time, determined by the settings in these fields. Long timeouts can reduce the number of calls to WINS but can increase memory demand by the DNS Server. By default, this value is 10 minutes.
- **Lookup Timeout Value.** This value determines how long DNS Server waits for a response from WINS before giving up and returning an error to the sender. By default, this value is 1 second.

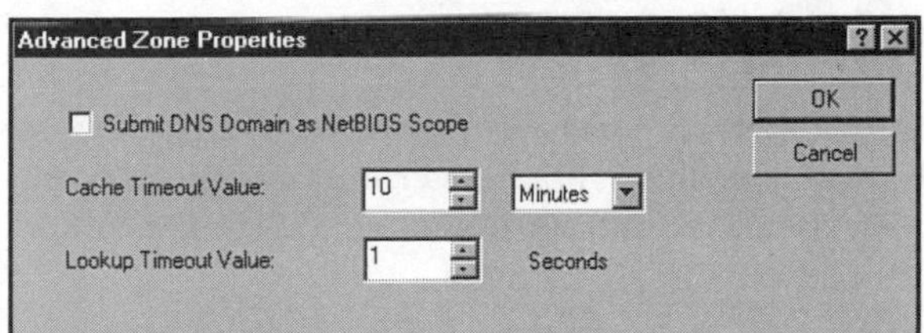

Figure 15.27
Advanced WINS lookup configuration.

Resolving Names with WINS

Very little is required to link Microsoft DNS Server with WINS:

- At least one WINS server must be operating to register hosts in the zone.
- WINS lookup must be enabled in the zone database.

The preceding section, "WINS Lookup Properties," showed how to enable WINS lookup. Figure 15.28 shows an example of a database record that has been retrieved from WINS.

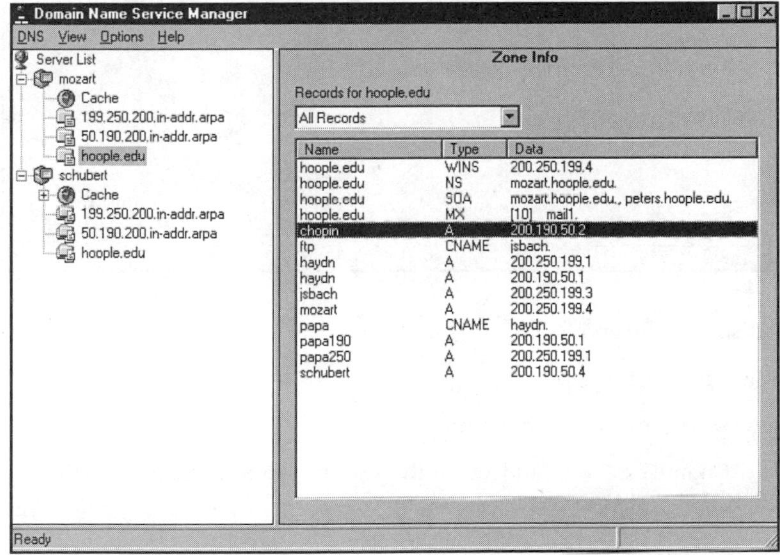

Figure 15.28
A database record that has been retrieved from WINS.

Managing Multiple DNS Servers

DNS Manager can manage many DNS servers. Besides consolidating DNS management on a single console, this capability simplifies certain operations by enabling you to use drag-and-drop to copy data. You will see how to do this in the following section, "Creating a Secondary DNS Server."

Figure 15.29 shows DNS manager with two DNS servers appearing in the Server list (no zones have been created for the second server). To add a remote DNS server to the list, perform the following steps:

Figure 15.29

DNS Manager with two zones configured.

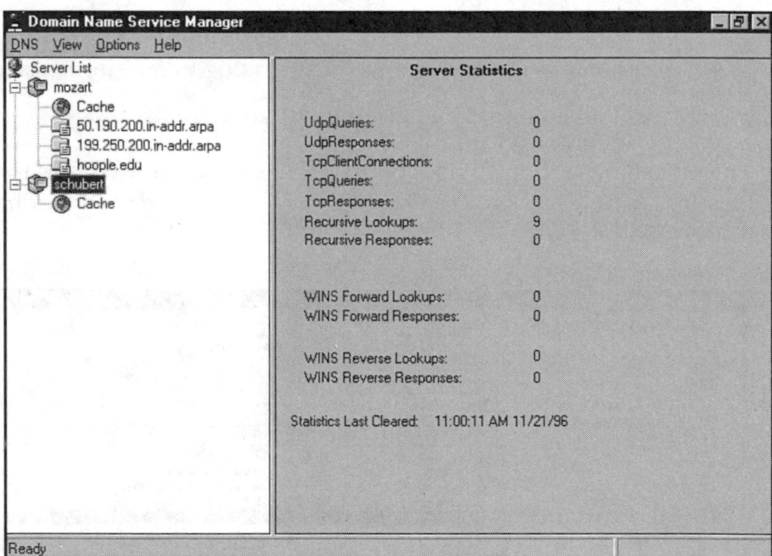

1. Install Microsoft DNS Services on the remote server.
2. Right-click the Server List icon.
3. Choose New Server in the Object menu.
4. Enter the host name or the IP address of the remote DNS server in the DNS Server field of the Add DNS Server dialog box.
5. Click OK.

Note

DNS Managers communicate with remote DNS servers by using RPCs (Remote Procedure Calls). To communicate with DNS Manager, the DNS Service must be running on the computer being managed. If DNS Manager cannot communicate with a DNS service, the icon is marked with a red X. An error message also appears in the Server Statistics box, stating that The RPC service is unavailable.

Creating a Secondary DNS Server

On the sample network, schubert will be set up as a secondary DNS sever for the hoople.edu domain. Now it is time to look at two ways to set up a secondary domain: hard and easy.

Objective B.7

The hard way is as follows:

1. Right-click the server icon and select New Zone from the Object menu.
2. Click the Secondary check box in the Creating New Zone dialog box (see fig. 15.30).

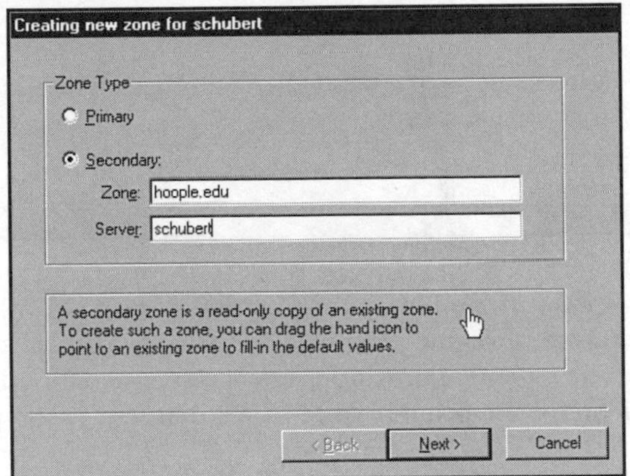

Figure 15.30
Creating a secondary zone on a DNS server.

3. Enter the zone name in the Zone field.
4. In the Server field, enter the name of the server from which zone transfers will be made.
5. Choose Next.
6. The Zone Name field will already be completed with the name of the zone that was specified in step 3. Press the Tab key in this field to generate the name for the database file in the Zone File field.
7. Press Next.
8. In the IP Masters list, specify the IP address list of at least one DNS server that will be a master server for this secondary.
9. Choose Next. Then choose Finish to create the zone.

Figure 15.31 shows the schubert server after three secondary zones have been added. Notice that the zone icon consists of two zone icons stacked one on the other, distinguishing a secondary zone from a primary zone.

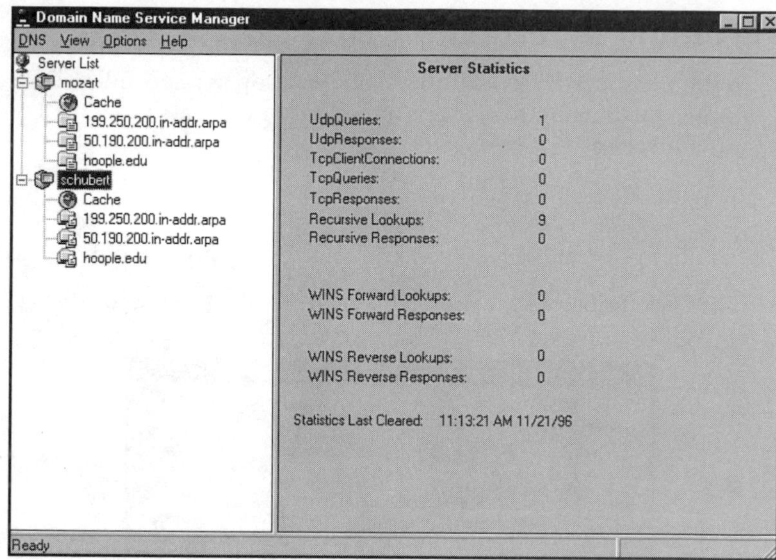

Figure 15.31
A DNS server with the secondary zone configured.

As stated earlier, there is an easy method to add the secondary zones for the two reverse-lookup zones. For this to work, the primary zone must be displayed in DNS Manager. If necessary, add the server supporting the primary zone and open the server icon to display the icon for the primary zone. After that, here's the procedure:

1. Right-click the server icon and select New Zone from the Object menu.
2. Click the Secondary check box in the Creating New Zone dialog box.
3. Look at figure 15.32. Notice a hand icon that was ignored in the previous procedure. Use the mouse to drag the hand icon and drop it on the appropriate primary zone. All the fields in the Create New Zone dialog box will be completed as required.
4. Use the Next button to review the fields in the Create New Zone dialog box.
5. Choose Finish to complete creation of the secondary zone.

If every network management task was that easy, network administrators would be out of a job.

Adding Subdomain Zones

As you have learned, the DNS name space is a hierarchy, and you can extend the name space hierarchy by adding domains below existing domains. Although the sample network has only a single domain, it is worth looking at the techniques for adding lower-level domains.

Suppose, for example, that you want to add domains, such as classic.hoople.edu and jazz.hoople.edu, to provide subdomains for various departments. This section examines the procedure.

To create a jazz.hoople.edu subdomain, perform the following steps:

1. Right-click the icon for the hoople.edu zone.
2. Choose New Domain in the Object menu.
3. In the New Domain dialog box, enter the domain name in the Domain Name field.
4. Click OK.

Subsequently, you add address records to the subdomain just as you add them to the primary domain. Figure 15.33 shows DNS Manager after two subdomains have been created. Notice that SOA and NS records are not created. The subdomain uses the same name server and SOA parameters as the primary domain.

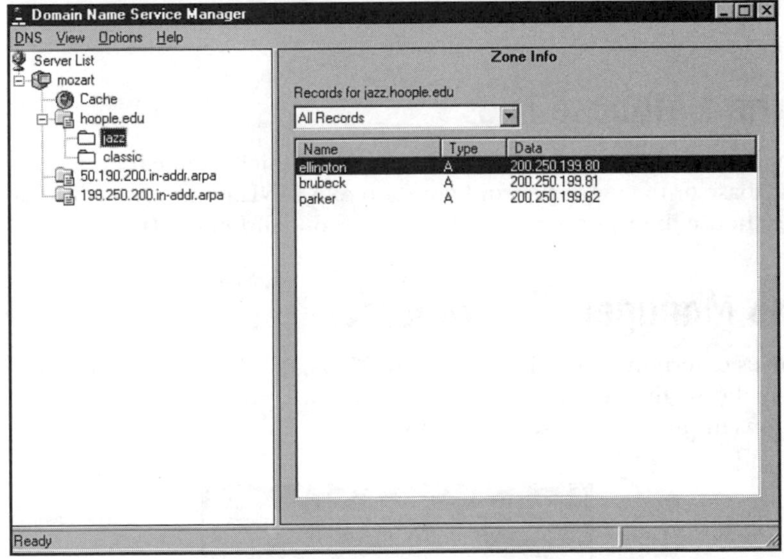

Figure 15.32

DNS Manager showing two subdomains.

Subdomains have no effect on the reverse-lookup files. The reverse-lookup database is flat and includes all hosts with the same network ID, whether or not they are in the same name domain. Figure 15.33 shows how ellington.hoople.edu is entered into the reverse-lookup database.

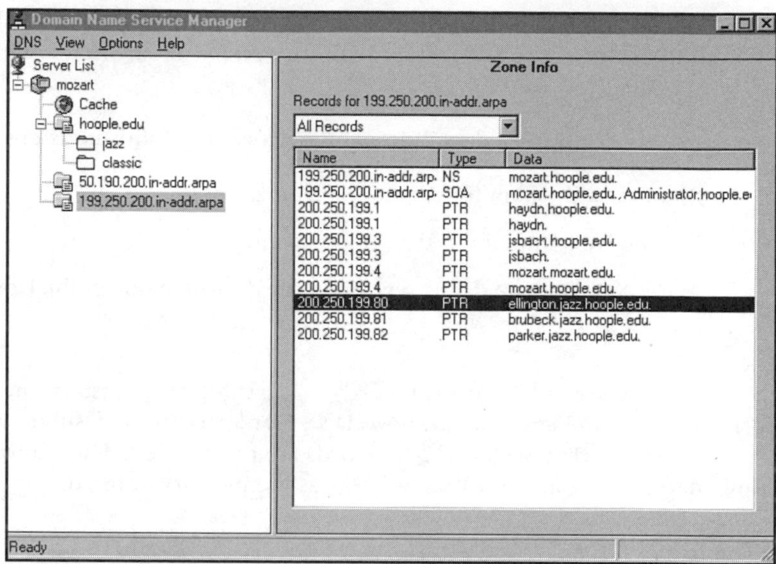

Figure 15.33
Reverse-lookup records for subdomain.

Updating the Database Files

DNS Manager maintains a standard set of BIND data files, which can be used to back up the server database or to export the configuration to a BIND name server. To back up the database, choose the Update Server Data Files command in the DNS menu.

Setting DNS Manager Preferences

Several preferences determine the behavior of DNS Manager. To open the Preferences dialog box, choose the Preferences command in the Options menu (see fig. 15.34). The options in this dialog box are as follows:

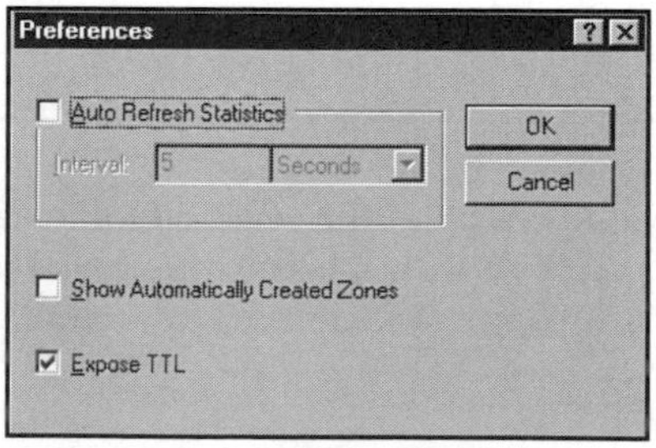

Figure 15.34
DNS Manager Preferences dialog box.

- **Auto Refresh Statistics.** Ordinarily, DNS Manager updates server statistics only when you click a server icon. If you check this check box, statistics are updated at the interval specified in the Interval field.
- **Show Automatically Created Zones.** Check this box to display the zones automatically created when a new DNS server is created.
- **Expose TTL.** Each resource record is assigned a Time to Live. Ordinarily, you don't see the value of the TTL parameter, but you can see and adjust TTL if you check this option. When Expose TTL is checked and you open the properties for a record (by double-clicking the record), a TTL field is added to the Properties dialog box (see fig. 15.35). You can change the TTL value if desired.

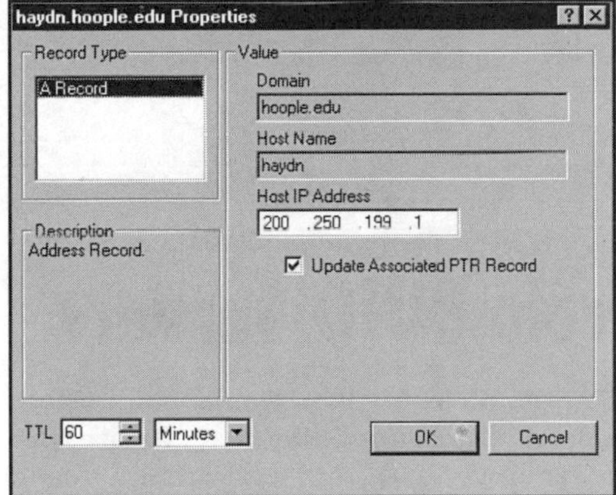

Figure 15.35

A record Properties dialog box with the TTL exposed.

DNS Server Statistics

DNS Manager maintains several statistics that describe the operation of the DNS Server. Figure 15.36 shows statistics for the mozart DNS server. These statistics give you an idea of the activity and health of the DNS server.

Ordinarily, DNS Manager does not dynamically update these statistics. You can update them manually by selecting a server icon and pressing F5. Alternatively, you can configure DNS Manager preferences so that the statistics are updated at periodic intervals. See the preceding section, "Setting DNS Manager Preferences," for the technique.

The DNS server statistics are initialized when the Microsoft DNS Server service is started. If you want to re-initialize the statistics without stopping and starting the DNS server, enter the command **DNSSTAT *servername* /CLEAR** where *servername* is the name of a computer running the DNS Server service. DNSSTAT is included with the Windows NT Server Resource Kit.

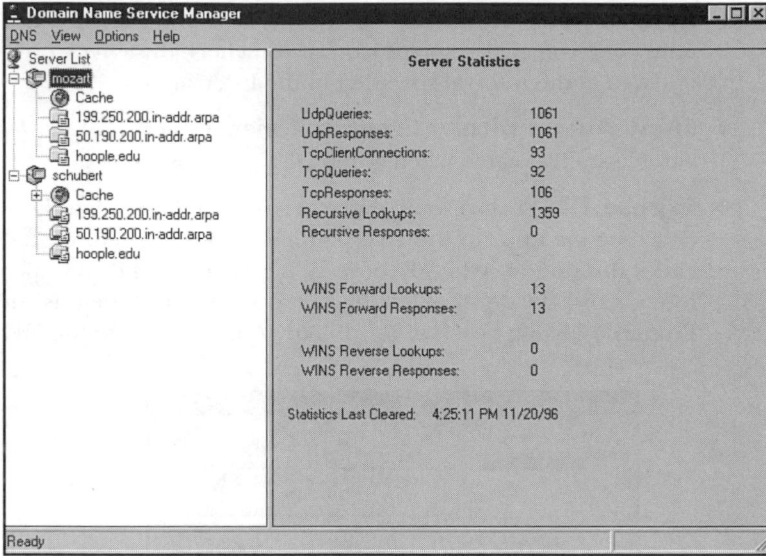

Figure 15.36
DNS Manager statistics.

Porting Data from BIND Servers

DNS Manager can import data from BIND database files, a handy feature if you want to move from a BIND name server to Microsoft DNS Server. Before attempting to port the data, assemble all the required BIND configuration files. You do not need a cache file, but you need a BOOT file as well as the database files for the various domains. Before you first start DNS Manager, place these files in the %systemroot%\system32\dns directory. Review the formats of these files carefully, making any changes that are required to make them compatible with Microsoft DNS Server.

The first time you start DNS Manager, it looks for BIND files in the dns directory. If the files are found, DNS Manager attempts to initialize the DNS server database from the BIND files. Otherwise DNS Manager initializes the DNS server with default settings from the Registry.

Subsequently, when DNS server is started, it consults the Registry for DNS server data. Any BIND files in the dns directory are ignored.

You can force DNS server to initialize from BIND files in the dns directory by changing a Registry value. Use the Registry Editor to create or modify the following value:

```
\HKEY_LOCAL_MACHINE\SYSTEM\CurrentControlSet\Services\DNS\
Parameters\EnableRegistryBoot
```

If the EnableRegistryBoot value is 1, DNS server initializes from the Registry. If the EnableRegistryBoot is 0, DNS server initializes from BIND files.

After changing the value of EnableRegistryBoot to 0, use the Service icon from the Control Panel or the Server Manager to stop and restart the Microsoft DNS Server service.

Enabling DNS Clients

Windows NT clients are configured to use DNS by editing the TCP/IP Protocol properties in the Network dialog box of the Control Panel. Also, complete the DNS tab, shown in figure 15.37, as follows:

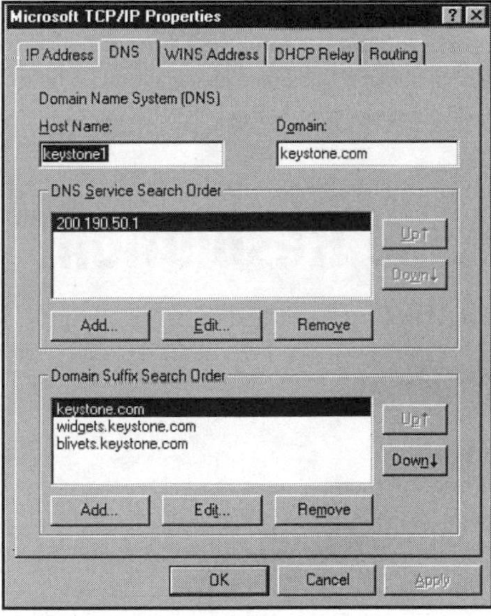

Figure 15.37
DNS Configuration tab for the TCP/IP protocol.

- **Host Name.** With Windows NT, the default DNS host name is the same as the NetBIOS computer name after removing the sixteenth hexadecimal character (which designates the service type). You can change this default name by editing the Host Name property.
- **Domain.** In this field, specify the domain name under which the host appears in the DNS name space.

Note The 15-character NetBIOS name is combined with the specified domain name to establish the FQDN for the host.

- **DNS Service Search Order.** In this list, specify the IP addresses of one or more DNS name servers. Resolution attempts query name servers in the order they appear in the search order list. Use the Up and Down buttons to adjust the search order.
- **Domain Suffix Search Order.** In this list, specify one or more domain names to be used as suffixes during attempts to resolve names not entered as fully qualified domain names. (A name that includes a period is regarded as an FQDN.) If keystone.com appears in this list and an attempt is made to resolve the name oliver, the resolver queries DNS with the name oliver.keystone.com. The suffixes are used in the order they appear in the search order list. Use the Up and Down buttons to adjust the search order.

Note If you want the DNS server to be the only method of name resolution, you can check the Enable DNS for Windows Resolution check box on the WINS Address tab.

Always include at least one domain name in the Domain Suffix Search Order list, even if it is the same as the domain specified in the Domain field. Some processes do not work properly without a domain suffix list.

Windows NT Name Resolution

As you have seen in this chapter and in Chapter 12, "NetBIOS Name Resolution," several mechanisms enable hosts to resolve names in the Microsoft TCP/IP environment:

- NetBIOS Name Cache
- NetBIOS Name Servers (WINS)
- NetBIOS broadcasts
- LMHOSTS files
- HOSTS files
- DNS servers

As you saw in Chapter 12, NetBIOS name resolution uses the methods of name resolution in a specific order. The exact order is determined by the node type set for the client. This order of resolution is used primarily for requests made by the NetBIOS API. Normally when Winsock makes a request, the order of name resolution changes to the following order:

1. **Localhost.** The first thing checked is whether the system you are looking for is your own.
2. **HOSTS file.** If your system has a HOSTS file, this file is checked to see whether the name can be resolved.

3. **DNS server.** Next your system consults the DNS server that you have just set up.
4. **WINS server.** Just like NetBIOS name resolution uses hosts name resolution for backup, host name resolution uses the NetBIOS name resolution for backup.
5. **Broadcast.** This only sees the local subnet.
6. **LMHOSTS.** If your system has an LMHOSTS file, this is the last resort before returning an error.

In Windows NT 4, however, the capability to issue NetBIOS commands to hosts names has been added. It is necessary, therefore, to look at some guidelines the system uses in determining the type of name resolution to use (host or NetBIOS).

- When using a NetBIOS command (for example, NET USE) and the host name is greater than 15 characters in length, or contains a period, NT uses host name resolution.
- When using a NetBIOS command (for example, NET USE) and the host name is less than 15 characters and does not contain periods, NT uses NetBIOS name resolution.
- When using a WinSock application (for example, FTP), NT uses host name resolution.

Nslookup

Windows NT Server 4 includes nslookup, a utility borrowed from BIND that can be used to troubleshoot DNS servers. Nslookup is a fairly elaborate tool, and this section covers only the basics. If you want greater detail, consult the Windows NT Help utility.

Nslookup is used in a command prompt window and can be used in interactive and non-interactive modes. The following section examines the non-interactive mode.

Making Non-Interactive Queries

The following dialog shows two nslookup queries. The first is a name-to-address query. The second is an address-to-name query. (If you enter an IP address, nslookup inverts the address, appends in-addr.arpa, and looks up PTR records rather than address records). Clearly, non-interactive use of nslookup is pretty elementary.

```
C:\>nslookup mozart
Server:  mozart.hoople.edu
Address:  200.250.199.4
```

```
Name:    mozart.hoople.edu
Address:  200.250.199.4
C:\>nslookup 200.190.50.4
Server:  mozart.hoople.edu
Address:  200.250.199.4

*** mozart.hoople.edu can't find 200.190.50.4: Non-existent domain
```

The first thing nslookup must do is locate a name server. It does so by consulting the addresses in the DNS Service Search Order list in the TCP/IP Properties dialog box. If nslookup cannot contact a name server in the list, it makes several attempts before moving to the next name server. For the following example, the DNS Server service was turned off. You can see the retry attempts as they time out.

```
C:\>nslookup mozart
DNS request timed out.
    timeout was 2 seconds.
DNS request timed out.
    timeout was 4 seconds.
DNS request timed out.
    timeout was 8 seconds.
*** Can't find server name for address 200.250.199.4: Timed out
DNS request timed out.
    timeout was 2 seconds.
DNS request timed out.
    timeout was 4 seconds.
DNS request timed out.
    timeout was 8 seconds.
*** Can't find server name for address 200.250.199.4: Timed out
*** Default servers are not available
Server:  UnKnown
Address:  200.250.199.4

DNS request timed out.
    timeout was 2 seconds.
DNS request timed out.
    timeout was 4 seconds.
DNS request timed out.
    timeout was 8 seconds.
*** Request to UnKnown timed-out
```

Making Interactive Queries

You can also use nslookup in interactive mode. The next dialog shows the beginning of an interactive session. The > character is the nslookup prompt.

```
C:\>nslookup
Default Server:  mozart.hoople.edu
Address:  200.250.199.4

>
```

You can enter a number of commands and queries from the nslookup prompt. The most basic are name and address queries, as in this example:

```
> mozart
Server:  mozart.hoople.edu
Address:  200.250.199.4

Name:    mozart.hoople.edu
Address:  200.250.199.4
```

By default, nslookup searches for entries in address (A) resource records. You can alter the query by specifying different resource record types, or you can search in all records. The target of a search is defined by the value of the querytype set variable (abbreviated q), which by default is set to a, resulting in address record lookups. The next listing shows how you can examine the SOA record for a domain. The first step is to use the command set q=soa, which sets the querytype to soa. Then, a query on the domain name returns the contents of the SOA resource record.

```
> set q=soa
> hoople.edu
Server:  mozart.hoople.edu
Address:  200.250.199.4

hoople.edu
        primary name server = mozart.hoople.edu
        responsible mail addr = peters.hoople.edu
        serial  = 15
        refresh = 3600 (1 hour)
        retry   = 600 (10 mins)
        expire  = 86400 (1 day)
        default TTL = 3600 (1 hour)
```

Another record type used in this chapter is MX. Here is an exchange that shows two queries for mail1. Note that when the querytype changes to mx, the contents of the MX record display.

```
> set q=mx
> mail1
Server:  mozart.hoople.edu
Address:  200.250.199.4

mail1.hoople.edu        MX preference = 10, mail exchanger = mail1.hoople.edu
mail1.hoople.edu        Internet address = 200.190.50.254
```

As a final example of using the querytype set variable, you can examine all records for a host by setting the querytype to any, as shown in this dialog.

```
> set q=any
> mail1
Server:  mozart.hoople.edu
Address:  200.250.199.4

mail1.hoople.edu        Internet address = 200.190.50.254
mail1.hoople.edu        MX preference = 10, mail exchanger = mail1.hoople.edu
mail1.hoople.edu        Internet address = 200.190.50.254
```

Want to directly examine the records in a domain? To do that, use the ls command. ls accepts a variety of arguments that focus or expand the query. In the next example, the -d parameter results in the display of all resource records in the specified domain, as determined by querying the default name server. In this case, the records fit on one screen, but long lists are presented a page at a time.

```
> ls -d hoople.edu
 hoople.edu.                      WINS
        WINS lookup info
          flags = 0 ( )
          lookup timeout = 5
          cache TTL      = 600
          server count   = 1
          WINS server = (200.190.50.4)
 hoople.edu.                      NS      mozart.hoople.edu
 ftp                               CNAME  jsbach.hoople.edu
 haydn                             A      200.190.50.1
 haydn                             A      200.250.199.1
 brubeck.jazz                      A      200.250.199.81
 ellington.jazz                    A      200.250.199.80
 parker.jazz                       A      200.250.199.82
 jsbach                            A      200.250.199.3
 mail1                             A      200.190.50.254
 mail1                             MX     10   mail1.hoople.edu
```

```
 mozart                         A      200.250.199.4
 papa                           CNAME  haydn.hoople.edu
 papa190                        A      200.190.50.1
 papa250                        A      200.250.199.1
 schubert                       A      200.190.50.4
 hoople.edu.                    SOA    mozart.hoople.edu peters.hoople.edu. (15
   _3600 600 86400 3600)
```

In the following command, the -t parameter is used with ls. The -t parameter accepts one argument, a resource record name or any name, and configures queries much like the querytype variable did in the preceding example. In this example, only address records display, but notice that the command found address records in subdomains as well.

```
> ls -t a hoople.edu.
[mozart.hoople.edu]
 hoople.edu.                    NS     server = mozart.hoople.edu
 haydn.hoople.edu.              A      200.190.50.1
 haydn.hoople.edu.              A      200.250.199.1
 brubeck.jazz.hoople.edu.       A      200.250.199.81
 ellington.jazz.hoople.edu.     A      200.250.199.80
 parker.jazz.hoople.edu.        A      200.250.199.82
 jsbach.hoople.edu.             A      200.250.199.3
 mail1.hoople.edu.              A      200.190.50.254
 mozart.hoople.edu.             A      200.250.199.4
 papa190.hoople.edu.            A      200.190.50.1
 papa250.hoople.edu.            A      200.250.199.1
 schubert.hoople.edu.           A      200.190.50.4
```

You can direct the output from ls to a file if desired. Nslookup includes a view command that permits you to list file contents without leaving nslookup. If you compare the following results to the preceding listing, you will notice that view sorts its output in alphabetic order.

```
> ls -t a hoople.edu > templist
[mozart.hoople.edu]
Received 18 records.
> view templist
 brubeck.jazz                   A      200.250.199.81
 ellington.jazz                 A      200.250.199.80
 haydn                          A      200.190.50.1
 haydn                          A      200.250.199.1
 hoople.edu.                    NS     server = mozart.hoople.edu
 jsbach                         A      200.250.199.3
```

```
 mail1                    A      200.190.50.254
 mozart                   A      200.250.199.4
 papa190                  A      200.190.50.1
 papa250                  A      200.250.199.1
 parker.jazz              A      200.250.199.82
 schubert                 A      200.190.50.4
[mozart.hoople.edu]
```

Nslookup can access only one name server at a time. If you want to query a different name server, enter the server or lserver command at the nslookup prompt, as in the following example:

```
> server schubert.hoople.edu
Server:  schubert.hoople.edu
Address:  200.190.50.4
```

Subsequent queries are directed to schubert.hoople.edu. The server and lserver commands accomplish much the same thing but differ in a significant way. lserver queries the local server, the server you started the nslookup session with, to obtain the address of the server to be switched to. server, on the other hand, queries the current default name server. If you change to a server that is not responding, nslookup is cut off from a working name server. If the current default server is not responding, you can use lserver to access the name server that was used to start nslookup, putting yourself back in business.

A lot more could be said about nslookup, but many of the options are quite advanced or specialized and are beyond the scope of this book.

Practice

In this lab, you create a DNS server and configure various hosts in it. You set up both forward and reverse name resolution. After you have the server set up, you test it using nslookup.

Exercise 1—Installing the DNS Server

In this exercise, you install the DNS server. You also configure your system to use itself as a DNS server so that you can later test the server you will set up.

If you have not installed networking, you should see the lab for Chapter 9, "Internet Information Server."

Note Important: If you have installed DNS server before and removed it, or if you have been working with BIND-compatible files, please save any files that are important and remove all files from the \%winroot%\dns directory. As you create the DNS server in this exercise, it overwrites the files in that directory; moreover, if there is a BOOT file, it could cause the installation to fail.

1. Open the Network dialog box. Choose the Protocols tab and double-click the TCP/IP protocol.
2. On the DNS tab, enter your IP address as the DNS server and click Add. Also add the domain **mcp.com** into the Domain field.
3. Click the Services tab and choose Add. From the list that appears, choose the Microsoft DNS Server and click OK.
4. Enter the directory for the NT source files.
5. Close the Network dialog box and restart your computer.

Exercise 2—Configuring DNS Domains

In this exercise, you configure a reverse lookup domain and a new primary domain called "mcp.com".

1. From the Start menu, choose Programs, Administrative Tools, DNS Manager.
2. From the menu, choose DNS, New Server. Enter your IP address and click OK.
3. To create the reverse-lookup domain, click your system's address. Choose DNS, New Zone.
4. Choose Primary and click Next
5. For the Zone, enter **53.148.in-addr.arpa** and press Tab (the file name will be filled in for you).
6. Click Next to continue and then choose Finish.
7. Ensure 53.148.in-addr.arpa is highlighted, and then choose DNS, Properties from the menu.
8. Take a moment and click each tab to familiarize yourself with the contents. On the WINS Reverse Lookup tab, check the box to Use WINS Reverse Lookup. Enter **MCP.COM** as the host domain, and click OK. There should now be a new host record.
9. Select the DNS server's address and select DNS, New Zone from the menu.
10. Select Primary and choose Next. Enter **MCP.COM** as the zone name. Press Tab to have the system fill in the file name, and then choose Next. Finally click the Finish button.

11. Ensure that the mcp.com domain is highlighted, and then right-click the domain name. From the Context menu that appears, select Properties.
12. Select the WINS Lookup tab.
13. Check the Use WINS Resolution box. Now enter your IP address in the WINS server space and choose Add.
14. Click OK to close the dialog box. There should now be a WINS record in the mcp.com domain.

Exercise 3—Adding Hosts

Now that the domains are entered, you need to add some hosts to them. To do so, follow these steps:

1. Right-click the mcp.com and choose Add Host.
2. In the New Host dialog box, add **Rob** as the Host Name and **148.53.66.7** as the Host IP Address.
3. Check the Create Associated PTR Record to create the reverse look record at the same time.
4. Choose Add Host. Now enter **Judy** as the Host Name and **148.53.66.9** as the Host IP Address.
5. Click Add Host. Then click the Done button to close the dialog box. You should now see the two new records in the DNS Manager.
6. Click the 53.148.in-addr.arpa domain and press F5 to refresh. Notice there is now a 66 subdomain.
7. Double-click the 66 subdomain. What new hosts are there?
8. There should be PTR records for the two hosts you just added.
9. Select the mcp.com domain again. Add the following hosts, ensuring that you add the associated PTR records.

Mail1	148.53.92.14
Mail2	148.53.101.80
Mail3	148.53.127.14
Web1	148.53.65.7
Web2	148.53.72.14
FTP_Pub1	148.53.99.99
FTP_Pub2	148.53.104.255
DEV	148.53.82.7

10. Close the New Host dialog box. Verify that the records were added to both the mcp.com and the reverse-lookup domain.

Exercise 4—Adding Other Records

Now that you have some hosts, you need to add a subdomain, and some other types of entries including CNAME and MX records.

1. Highlight mcp.com and choose DNS, New Domain from the menu.
2. Enter DEV as the Name for the new domain and click OK.
3. Right-click the DEV subdomain. Choose New Record. Select CNAME as the record type.
4. Enter WWW as the alias, and web2.mcp.com as the Host. (This entry is setting up WWW.DEV.MCP.COM to point to WEB2.MCP.COM.)
5. Click OK to add the record. (It should appear in the Zone Info window.)
6. Create the following CNAME entries in the mcp.com domain. Right-click mcp.com each time choosing New Record.

Alias	Host
WWW	web1.mcp.com
FTP	FTP_PUB1.mcp.com
DEV_FTP	FTP_PUB2.mcp.com

7. Create a new record in the mcp.com domain. This time choose MX as the Record Type.
8. Leave the Host blank for this record, and enter **mail1.mcp.com** as the Mail Exchange Server DNS Name. Enter **10** as the Preference.
9. Click OK to add the record. Add a second MX record for the mcp.com using **mail2.mcp.com** as the Mail Server and **20** as the Preference.
10. Now add the MX record for dev.mcp.com. To do this, right-click mcp.com and choose New Record; again this is an MX record.
11. The difference is that you include the host name. Enter **DEV** as the host, add **mail3.mcp.com** as the Mail Exchange Server DNS Name, and **10** as the preference.
12. Ensure that all the records appear to be in place and then close the DNS Manager.

Exercise 5—Testing the DNS Server

Now that the domain entries are in the DNS server, you can test the entries by using the NSLOOKUP command.

1. Start a command prompt.
2. Type the command **NSLOOKUP 148.53.101.80** and then press Enter.

   What response did you get?

   The response should show that 148.53.101.80 is mail2.mcp.com. Here you have done a reverse lookup on the IP address.
3. Using the NSLOOKUP command, find out what response the following will give you:

   148.53.66.7

   148.53.99.99

   www.mcp.com

   www.dev.mcp.com

   ftp.mcp.com

   The results should have been:

148.53.66.7	rob.mcp.com
148.53.99.99	ftp_publ.mcp.com
www.mcp.com	148.53.65.7 (webl.mcp.com)
www.dev.mcp.com	148.55.72.14 (web2.mcp.com)
ftp.mcp.com	148.53.99.99 (ftp_publ.mcp.com)

4. Start an interactive session with the name server by typing **NSLOOKUP** and pressing Enter.
5. Try the following commands:

   ls mcp.com

   ls -t mx mcp.com

   ls -d

   q=soa

   mcp.com

q=mx

mcp.com

Where is the third mail server?

dev.mcp.com

6. Press CTRL+C to exit the interactive query.
7. Close the command prompt.

Summary

Although it is new to NT, the included DNS service is a full-feature version. The DNS service provides a simple user interface and WINS integration, with the capability to configure multiple zones within a single server. The integration of the DNS server with WINS is supposed to be completed in the next release of NT where they will become a single product. This chapter has covered the DNS server in great detail and included information on the reason for DNS and how to configure the base files. With the DNS Manager, all of this becomes highly automated, and very simple.

Test Yourself

1. What organization controls the root servers?
2. What are the generic worldwide top-level domains?
3. For countries other than the U.S., what should the top-level domain normally be?
4. For the following countries, what is the top-level domain called?

   Singapore

   Greenland

   Costa Rica

   Tonga

   Zambia
5. How can you query a domain name to see who controls it?
6. What is the difference between a lookup and a reverse lookup?
7. When should you implement DNS internally?

8. In what two ways can NT Server 4's DNS be configured?
9. What is the purpose of each of the following files?

   BOOT

   Cache.dns

   127.0.0.dns

   r*everse-network_ID*.in-addr-arpa

   domain_name.dns
10. What is the SOA record?
11. Your user is at a computer called "prod172". The IP address is 152.63.85.5, and the system is used to publish to the web for a domain called "gowest.com". Give the file names and entries required for the user?
12. How do you set up Microsoft DNS Server to use the existing BIND files you have?
13. What is an MX record for?
14. Where does a secondary DNS server get zone information?
15. Can you view more than one DNS server in the DNS Manager?
16. How do you integrate WINS resolution into the DNS Server?
17. What command can you use to test the DNS server?

Test Yourself Answers

1. The root servers are maintained by InterNIC.
2. The generic worldwide domains include com, edu, net, org, and int.
3. Normally for countries other than the U.S., the top-level domain is the two-digit country code.
4. The domain suffixes are:

Singapore	SG
Greenland	GL
Costa Rica	CR
Tonga	TO
Zambia	ZM

5. You can use the WHOIS search. This can be done by using Telnet to rs.internic.net.
6. Lookup is performed to map a host name to an IP address, the reverse lookup maps the IP address to the real name.
7. If you will be connecting to the Internet, and wish to control the name resolution of many systems you should consider bringing DNS in house. Otherwise, you can have your ISP provide the service for you.
8. The DNS server in NT 4 can be configured to use the Registry, or it can use standard BIND files.
9. The purposes are as follows:

   BOOT. This contains the configuration for the DNS server. Notably it contains the names of the other files used to set up the DNS server.

   Cache.dns. This file sets basic configuration and points to the root level servers.

   127.0.0.dns. Reverse lookup file for the 127.0.0.0 network. This will contain entries for localhost.

   reverse-network_ID.in-addr-arpa. This file contains the reverse lookup information of the entire network. It is use to process queries on IP addresses.

   doamin_name.dns. Contains the name-to-IP address mapping for the domain.

10. The SOA record is the Start of Authority and configures DNS by giving information such as the name of the primary name server, the administrators e-mail, along with other parameters.
11. In “gowest.com.dns”, there would be two entries:

    ```
    prod172    IN  A     152.63.85.5
    www        IN  CNAME prod172
    ```

    And in “63.152.in-addr.arpa”, there would be only one entry:

    ```
    5.85    IN  PTR  prod172.gowest.com
    ```

12. Copy the files to the \%winroot%\system32\dns directory before starting the DNS server. The DNS server will find the files, and incorporate them automatically.
13. The MX record is the Mail Exchange record. It points to a mail server that can receive mail for a particular domain.
14. The secondary server is configured to obtain the zone information from the primary server for the zone.

15. Yes. The DNS manager provides single seat administration. Use the DNS, New Server from the menu.
16. After you have created a zone, you can edit the zone properties. On the WINS Lookup tab, you can configure DNS to use WINS for name resolution.
17. You can use the NSLOOKUP command to test the DNS server and ensure that it can resolve names.

CHAPTER 16

TCP/IP Utilities

You have already seen some of the utilities that come with Windows NT version 4. This chapter examines each of the utilities in full detail. This chapter introduces each utility and talks about where it should be used. Where necessary, this chapter also includes a demonstration. Then the discussion covers all the switches and options for each utility. The utilities are broken down into five main sections relating to their use, starting with file transfer utilities (FTP, TFTP, and RCP). Next, interactive utilities are looked at (Internet Explorer, Telnet, RSH, and REXEC), after which the printing utilities (LPR and LPQ) are revisited. The last two sections deal with trouble-shooting. First, the basic utilities are discussed (these utilities include Ping, IPCONFIG, FINGER, NSLOOKUP, HOSTNAME, NETSTAT, NBTSTAT, ROUTE, TRACERT, and ARP). The final section deals with the Network Monitor. This tool enables you to see the traffic on the network and to analyze the data being sent.

File Transfer Utilities

Objective C.1

One of the most common functions that any administrator has to do is to move files around. You can, of course, look at NT Explorer or even the Copy command at the prompt.

In this section, you add a couple more commands that you can use to transfer files. All three of the new options enable you to copy files to and from foreign hosts. This means that you can copy back and forth from a Unix system or any other system that works with these utilities rather than Microsoft's standard NetBIOS file and print-sharing utilities.

FTP

File Transfer Protocol (FTP) transfers files to and from a computer running an FTP service. FTP is an interactive system; however, you can also add switches at the command line so that the transfer can be scripted. The FTP client that comes with Windows NT is a character-based client (so that it can be scripted).

The basic command is

```
FTP hostname
```

This command opens an interactive FTP session. Figure 16.1 shows such a session where the Help commands have been brought up on-screen.

```
C:\WINNT\System32\cmd.exe - ftp ftp.microsoft.com
Microsoft(R) Windows NT(TM)
(C) Copyright 1985-1996 Microsoft Corp.

C:\>ftp ftp.microsoft.com
Connected to ftp.microsoft.com.
220 ftp Microsoft FTP Service (Version 3.0).
User (ftp.microsoft.com:(none)): anonymous
331 Anonymous access allowed, send identity (e-mail name) as password.
Password:
230-This is FTP.MICROSOFT.COM.  Please see the
 dirmap.txt file for more information.

 An alternate location for Windows NT
 Service Packs is located at:

 ftp://198.105.232.37/fixes/
230 Anonymous user logged in.
ftp> ls -l
200 PORT command successful.
150 Opening ASCII mode data connection for /bin/ls.
d---------   1 owner    group            0 May 31  1:31 bussys
d---------   1 owner    group            0 Sep 23  1996 deskapps
d---------   1 owner    group            0 Jan  4  0:53 developr
----------   1 owner    group         8012 Sep 11  1996 dirmap.htm
----------   1 owner    group         4368 Sep 11  1996 dirmap.txt
----------   1 owner    group          712 Aug 25  1994 disclaimer.txt
d---------   1 owner    group            0 Apr 21 19:11 KBHelp
----------   1 owner    group     12154016 Jun 17 10:34 ls-lR.txt
----------   1 owner    group      2947701 Jun 17 10:34 ls-lR.Z
----------   1 owner    group      1920822 Jun 17 10:34 LS-LR.ZIP
d---------   1 owner    group            0 Mar 14  2:33 MSCorp
d---------   1 owner    group            0 Oct 11  1995 peropsys
d---------   1 owner    group            0 May  1 19:09 Products
d---------   1 owner    group            0 Oct 28  1996 Services
d---------   1 owner    group            0 May  9 19:45 Softlib
d---------   1 owner    group            0 Apr  8  1996 solutions
226 Transfer complete.
1109 bytes received in 0.18 seconds (6.13 Kbytes/sec)
ftp>
```

Figure 16.1

An FTP session.

If you want to run FTP in a script, the available switches are as follows:

```
ftp [-v] [-d] [-i] [-n] [-g] [-s:filename] [-a] [-w:windowsize] [computer]
```

Table 16.1 summarizes the parameters that you can enter.

TABLE 16.1
FTP Command Line Switches

Switch	Meaning
-v	Turn off the display of remote host responses.
-n	Disable auto-logon upon initial connection.
-I	Turns off prompting during multiple file transfers.
-d	Turns on debugging mode, which displays all commands passed between the client and server.
-g	Turns off file name globbing@. This permits the use of wildcard characters in local file and path names.
-s:filename	Tells FTP to use the specified text file as a script; the commands automatically run after FTP starts.
-a	Directs FTP to use any local interface when creating the data connection.
-w:windowsize	Allows the use of a window size other than the default transfer buffer size of 4096.
Computer	Tells FTP the computer name or IP address of the remote host to which it should connect.

Most of the time, you use the FTP client in interactive mode. You should be aware of several commands when you are in this mode. Table 16.2 lists all the valid FTP commands for the Microsoft FTP client.

Table 16.2
FTP Commands

Command	Description
!	Usage: ! *command*. Specifies a command that should be run on the local computer. If *command* is left out, the local command prompt is opened.
?	Usage: ? *command*. Displays the help descriptions for FTP commands. If a command is entered, help on that command is displayed; otherwise general help comes up.
append	Usage: append *local_filename remote_filename*. Tells FTP to transfer the local file and append it to the end of the remote file. If the remote file name is not given, FTP uses the same file name as the local file name. If the local file name does not exist, FTP creates it.
ascii	Usage: ASCII. Because different systems use different bit orders internally, there can occasionally be problems transferring files. FTP has two modes: ASCII and binary. ASCII is the default. In this mode, character conversion takes place.
bell	Usage: bell. This command toggles the bell on or off. The bell is off by default. When turned on, it rings after each file transfer.
binary	Usage: binary. Changes the mode to binary from ASCII (see previous item). This should be done whenever you transfer a file so that character conversion will not take place on executable or compressed files.
bye	Usage: bye. Closes the FTP session and the window. Equivalent to Ctrl+C.
cd	Usage: cd *directory_name*. Changes the working directory on the FTP server. Same as the NT cd command.
close	Usage: close. Closes the FTP session with the remote host, but keeps you in FTP.
debug	Usage: debug. Enters the debug mode. In this mode, all commands sent between the two hosts echo to the local printer. Normally this is off.
delete	Usage: delete *filename*. Tells FTP to delete the file from the remote host.

Command	Description
dir	Usage: dir *directory filename.* Provides a listing of the directory on the remote system that you specify. The output can be directed to a file by entering a file name. Neither option is required. If the file name is omitted, only the list displays. If the directory name is omitted, the contents of the current directory display.
Disconnect	Usage: disconnect. Performs the same function as close.
get	Usage: get *remote_file local_file.* Retrieves a file from the remote host. The local_file is optional. If not given, the same name is used.
glob	Usage: glob. Toggles the glob setting on or off. Globbing permits the use of wildcards in file names. By default, this is turned on.
hash	Usage: hash. Turn the display of hash marks ("#") on or off. A hash mark displays for every block (2048 bytes) of data transferred. Default setting for hash is off.
help	Usage: help *command.* Has the same function as "?".
lcd	Usage: lcd *directory.* Local change directory changes the directory you are currently in on the local machine. If you do not include a directory name, the current directory displays.
literal	Usage: literal *parameter.* Sends a literal string to the remote FTP host. Normally a single reply code is returned.
ls	Usage: ls *directory filename.* This command has the same function as the dir command discussed earlier.
mdelete	Usage: mdelete *filename filename filename.* Multiple delete works in the same manner as the delete command, except it accepts multiple file names.
mdir	Usage: mdir *filename filename filename.* Like mdelete, this is multiple directory. It displays a listing of file names that match the pattern given.
mget	Usage: mget *filename filename filename.* Multiple get retrieves more than one file.
mkdir	Usage: mkdir *directory_name.* Creates a new directory of the given name on the remote host.

continues

Table 16.2, Continued
FTP Commands

Command	Description
mls	Usage: mls *filename filename filename*. Same as the mdir command previously mentioned.
mput	Usage: mput *filename filename filename*. Multiple put places the series of files that you specify on the remote system.
open	Usage: open *hostname port*. Opens an FTP session with the host given. The port number to open the connection can be given if the server uses something other than the default 21.
prompt	Usage: prompt. Turns on or off the prompting for each file as you use mget or mput. The option is on by default.
put	Usage: put *local_filename remote_filename*. Opposite of the get command, this takes the local file name and places it on the FTP server. If the remote file name is not given, the system uses the current file name.
pwd	Usage: pwd. Displays the name of the directory that you are currently in on the FTP server.
quit	Usage: quit. Same as the bye command, closes the connection and the FTP software.
quote	Usage: quote *parameter*. Same as the literal command previously discussed.
recv	Usage: recv *remote_filename local_filename*. Same as the get command.
Remotehelp	Usage: remotehelp command. Works in the same way as help or "?"; however, it lists the specific commands supported on the remote system.
rename	Usage: rename *old_filename new_filename*. Just like the ren command, this renames a file.
rmdir	Usage: rmdir *directory_name*. This is the same as the rd command from DOS. It removes the given directory.

Command	Description
send	Usage: send *local_filename remote_filename*. Same as the put command.
status	Usage: status. Returns the current status of your FTP connections.
trace	Usage: trace. Toggles on or off the display of each packet being sent or received. This is off by default.
type	Usage: type binary/ascii. Switches between the two data modes.
user	Usage: user *username password*. Logs you on to the remote FTP server. It should be noted that this type of logon is not secure, and that the user name and password are sent to the remote host as clear text.
verbose	Usage: verbose. Toggles the verbose mode on or off. In verbose mode, more information is displayed.

The FTP client, of course, must talk to an FTP server. FTP uses TCP to handle communications and creates a session between the two hosts. FTP is different from many other protocols in that it will use two ports. FTP uses TCP port 21 as the control port over which the interactive part of the connection flows. FTP also uses TCP port 20 to actually transfer the files.

TFTP

Trivial File Transfer Protocol (TFTP) is not used to move unimportant files. Rather, it is a connectionless file transfer protocol. TFTP is a command line system that enables you to batch a series of file transfers without creating a script such as you would have to do with FTP.

TFTP requires that there be a TFTP server on the other host. TFTP uses only one port: UDP port number 69. The TFTP command line is:

```
tftp [-i] computer [get ¦ put] remote_filename [local_filename]
```

Table 16.3 summarizes the command line switches.

Table 16.3
TFTP Command Line Switches

Switch	Description
-I	Places TFTP in binary transfer mode. Just like FTP, this moves the file byte by byte. If -i is not specified, the file is transferred in ASCII mode. This mode converts the EOL characters to a carriage return for Unix and a carriage return/line feed for personal computers.
Computer	Specifies the remote computer name.
Put	Moves the file given as the local_filename to the remote host as a file called remote_filename.
Get	Transfers the remote_filename from the remote host to the local system. If the local_filename is not given, the local file will have the same name as the remote file.
Local_filename	The name of the file on the local computer.
Remote_filename	Specifies the name of the remote file.

RCP

Remote Copy Protocol (RCP) is another method of transferring files to or from a remote host. This command copies files between an NT computer and a remote system running rshd, which is a remote shell daemon.

The parameters for the command are shown here, and table 16.4 describes them.

```
rcp [-a ¦ -b] [-h] [-r] source1 source2 ... sourceN destination
```

Table 16.4
RCP Command Line Switches

Switch	Description
-a	Sets the transfer to ASCII mode. This converts the carriage return/linefeed characters to carriage returns on outgoing files and linefeed characters to carriage return/linefeeds for incoming files.

Switch	Description
-b	Sets binary transfer mode. No carriage conversion is performed.
-h	Transfers source files marked with the hidden attribute on the Windows NT computer. Without this option, specifying a hidden file on the RCP command line has the same effect as if the file did not exist.
-r	This option copies the contents of all subdirectories starting at the source to the destination.
Source and destination	This is entered in the form [computer[.user]:]filename. Without the [computer[.user]:] portion, NT assumes the computer is the local computer. If the user portion is not entered, the current NT user name is used. When an FQDN is entered, the [.user] must be included or the top level domain name is interpreted as the user name.

If you do not include a forward slash (/) (Unix) or a backward slash (\) (DOS/Windows/NT), it is assumed to be relative to the current directory. This is the directory in which you issue the command. Therefore, if you issue the command in c:\users\default and don't use a "\" in the directory you wish to place the file in locally (or get it from), the file will be in c:\users\default or a subdirectory of it.

Remote Privileges

For the RCP command to work, you must have a valid user name for the remote system. This must either be the user name with which you logged on to Windows NT or specified on the command line.

The user name that you use must be included in the .rhosts file on the remote system. This file is used in the Unix world to determine which computers or users are allowed to use an account to use the RCP command or the RSH command (which is discussed later).

.rhosts

Like the HOSTS or LMHOSTS file, the .rhosts file is a text file. Each line is an entry that consists of a computer name, a user name, and possibly comments. The following is an example of an .rhosts file:

```
WKS917       mario
```

The .rhosts file is kept in the user's home directory on the Unix system. If you need more information about a particular vendor's version of the .rhosts file, you should check the vendor's documentation. Remember that the remote system needs to be able to resolve your computer's name; therefore, you should have your computer name added to the other computer's /ETC/HOSTS file or ensure your system is in the DNS.

Interactive Utilities

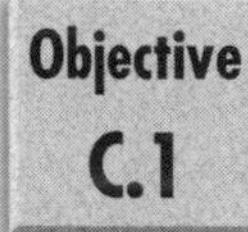

Obviously there will be times when you want to do more with the remote host than just copy a file. Currently one of the greatest examples of this is the World Wide Web. With Windows NT comes the Internet Explorer—take a quick peek at the Internet Explorer. (Although many other browsers, such as Netscape, work fine, Internet Explorer comes with NT.)

Other utilities that come with NT, however, enable you to work interactively with another system. A commonly used example is Telnet, which is a terminal emulation program that enables you to open a window that works with another system.

Two other utilities come with Windows NT: RSH and REXEC. These utilities also enable you to work with other systems. RSH enables you to open a remote shell so that you can run programs on a different computer. REXEC is a command line utility that also enables you to run programs on another computer.

When you read that Telnet, RSH, and REXEC are running on another system, that's exactly what it means. The instructions for the program are not executed by your computer, but rather are run on the processor in the other system. This is similar to the old days of dumb terminals that only opened a window that allowed you to see what the main frame was doing for you.

Internet Explorer

As you look at the Internet Explorer, you should consider what is really happening when you are surfing on the web. Essentially, all the web sites that you have visited are simple text files written in HTML. It is in fact possible to use Notepad or Edit or even Edlin (the original DOS line editor) to create a home page.

The magic of the web is neither the file format nor the stunning graphics. It is what can be done with such simple tools. Living in the age where dinosaurs come to life on the big screen, it is easy to assume that the web is more computer magic. The very simple fact is that at this point in time, there is not enough bandwidth to even begin to move the data required to handle real computer magic.

So you cheat! You take a simple file transfer utility, and you build into it a way of describing the types of files, and where they are on-screen, and where to go if a user clicks, and then you have the magic that is the web. Following is an example of a text file that came from a web site.

```
<HTML>
 <HEAD>
 <!-- $MVD$:app("MicroVision YoubExpress") -->
 <TITLE>New Riders</TITLE></HEAD>
 <BODY BACKGROUND="gm2/images/gmback.gif">
 <P>
  <TABLE CELLPADDING=1 CELLSPACING=2 BORDER=0>
    <TR>
     <TD VALIGN=CENTER><P>
            </TD>
     <TD VALIGN=CENTER><P>
      <TABLE CELLPADDING=1 CELLSPACING=2 BORDER=0>
       <TR>
        <TD VALIGN=CENTER><P ALIGN=CENTER>
         <CENTER><IMG SRC="images/nrphead2.gif" ALT="New Riders
         ➥Publishing" ALIGN=BOTTOM WIDTH=490 HEIGHT=69 BORDER=0 VSPACE=0
         ➥HSPACE=0><HR
          ALIGN=CENTER WIDTH=550 SIZE=1>
         </TD>
        </TR>
        <TR>
         <TD VALIGN=CENTER><P ALIGN=CENTER>
          <CENTER><A HREF="titles.html">New Riders titles, beginning with our
          ➥most recent releases</A>.</CENTER>
         </P><P ALIGN=CENTER>
          <CENTER>Download a trial version of Extreme 3D 2 for use with <A
          ➥HREF="http://merchant.superlibrary.com:8000/catalog/hg/PRODUCT/PAGE/
          ➥15620/bud/156205662X.html">Inside Extreme 3D 2</A> by Gary
          ➥Bouton!<BR>
          <A HREF="macdemo.sit.hqx">Macintosh</A> <A
etc …
```

Note

This is only a partial listing of the New Riders home page (otherwise it might go on for pages). If you want to see the source listing for a site in Internet Explorer, choose View, Source from the menu.

When you open the site by typing **www.newriders.com** into the File, Open dialog box, you will see the site as it is meant to be viewed (see fig. 16.2).

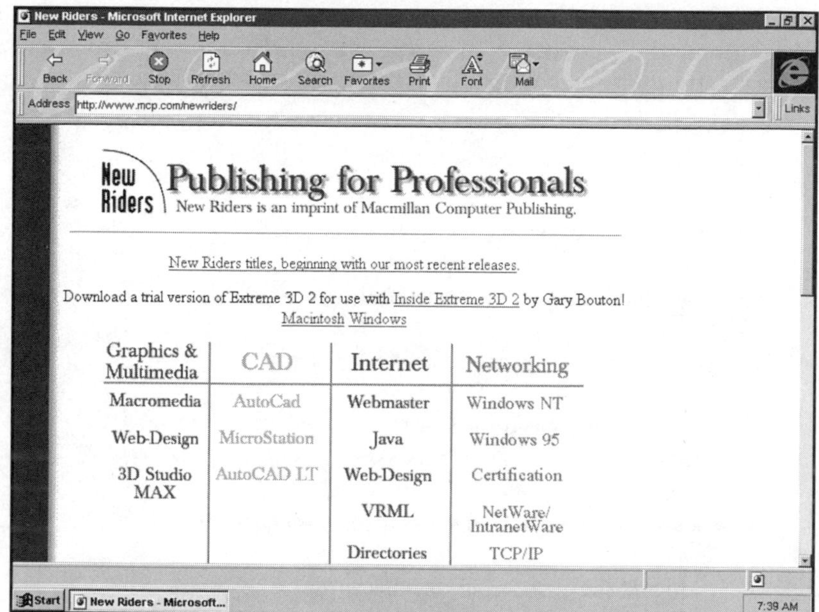

Figure 16.2

The New Riders' home page in Internet Explorer.

Configuring the Internet Explorer

You can configure a couple of items in the Internet Explorer. The following section describes the various configuration screens and tells what the pieces mean.

All the options are under View, Options. When you select this from the menu, the General tab appears (see fig. 16.3). The options for the General tab are as follows:

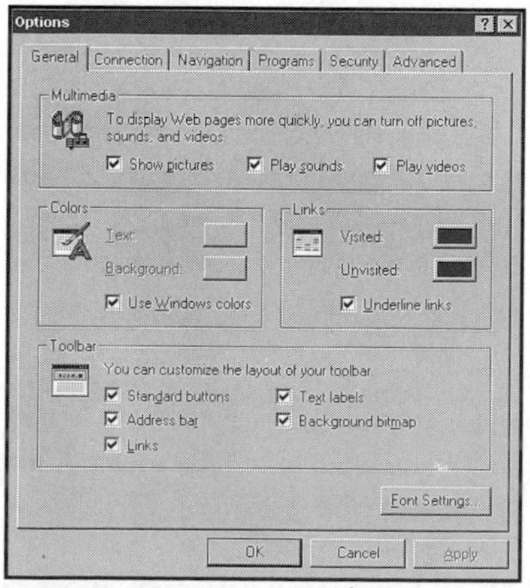

Figure 16.3

The General tab for the Internet Explorer.

- **Multimedia.** These options can increase the speed at which you move around the Internet by turning on or off the displaying or playing of pictures, sounds, and animation. Turning off the animation does not stop animated GIFs because they are considered pictures.
- **Colors.** This enables you to change the default colors for the text that will be displayed. This does not have any effect unless the designer of the page you are visiting left the text as default color.
- **Links.** Here you can set the way that you want to have the links displayed. This helps you to determine which links you have visited and which ones you have not.
- **Toolbar.** This enables you to set the toolbar preferences.
- **Font Settings.** This includes options to change the default fonts that are used while you surf the web.

In many organizations, the user must connect to the Internet by using a proxy service. This enables the organization to use any IP network address internally, but use a single valid IP address externally. Several types of proxy servers are available on the market. Microsoft itself has one available. The Connection tab in the Internet Explorer enables you to configure your browser to use a CERN-compatible proxy server (see fig. 16.4).

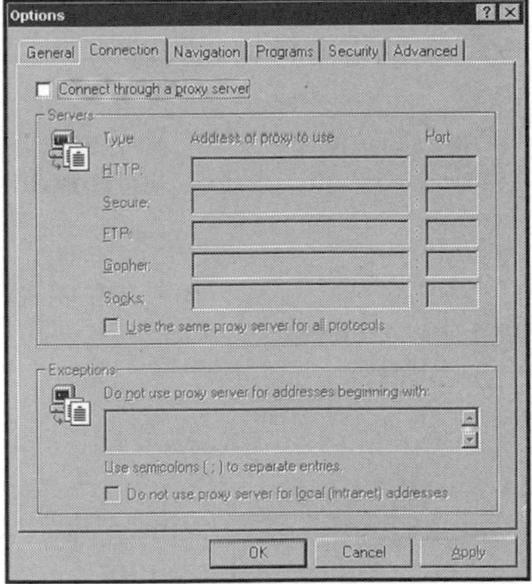

Figure 16.4

The Connection tab in the Internet Explorer.

The options available in the Connection tab are as follows:

- **Connect through a proxy server.** If this is checked, the configuration for a proxy server can be entered.

- **Servers.** In this list, you can enter the information for the major protocols that can use proxy. For each, you can enter the IP address for the system that will handle the proxy, and the port to use when contacting it.
- **Exceptions.** This enables you to enter the addresses for which you do not need to have a proxy server. These are usually internal web sites on your intranet.

The next tab in the Internet Explorer configuration is the Navigation tab (see fig. 16.5). This tab enables you to configure your Start pages and History settings.

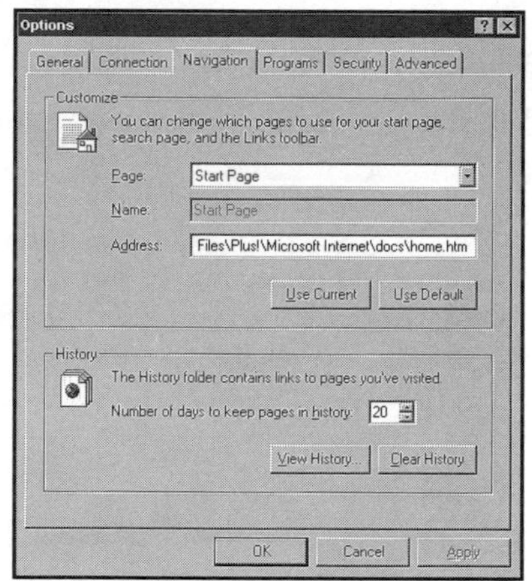

Figure 16.5
Configuring the Navigation settings for Internet Explorer.

- **Customize.** This enables you to configure your Start page (and others). To set a page, go to the page in the browser and then open this dialog box. Choose Use Current.
- **History.** When you move around on the Internet, the Internet Explorer keeps track (copies) of the last sites that you visited. The more sites you keep in history, the more disk space you use.

The Programs tab enables you to set the Mail and News Reader programs that you will use (see fig. 16.6). It also enables you to customize the programs used as helper applications. These helper applications launch if you find a site that sends you a file of that type. Following is a short description of each option:

- **Mail and news.** These settings are important because many sites refer you to a newsgroup (such as the ones in `msnews.microsoft.com`) or have a mailto item so that you can contact someone in the organization.

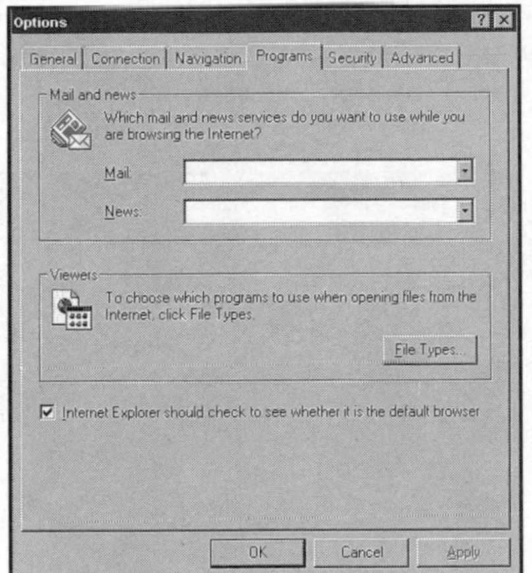

Figure 16.6

Configuring programs for Internet Explorer.

- **Viewers.** These programs are external to the Internet Explorer but are used for items such as .avi files or .wav files. When you choose the File Types button, the standard File Types dialog box appears (see fig. 16.7). From this dialog box, you can add file types or check the current settings.

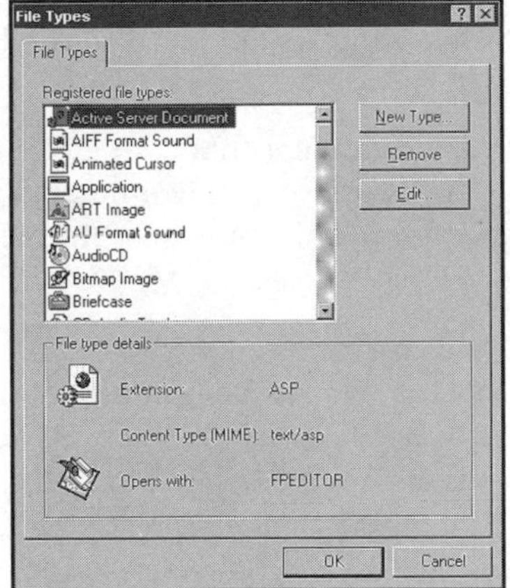

Figure 16.7

Associating file types.

- **Internet Explorer should check.** When Internet Explorer starts up, it checks to see whether it is the default browser (the executable associated with HTML and other web documents). If it is not, it asks you whether you want it to be.

The options you are looking at here are for the Internet Explorer version 3 (available for download from the Microsoft web site). This is so the Security tab can be included (see fig. 16.8). Internet Explorer now comes with a content-checking system for the Internet that blocks out certain pages based on the content rating. The ratings are currently voluntary. This is, however, an important step forward.

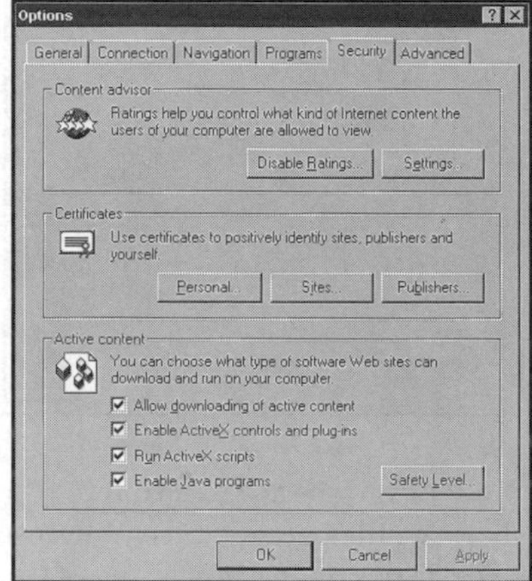

Figure 16.8

Security settings in the Internet Explorer.

The following list describes the contents of the Internet Explorer Security tab.

- **Content advisor.** This is the rating system just discussed. The two buttons that you can use are discussed shortly.
- **Certificates.** Certificates are special files that contain an encrypted signature. This enables you to verify that the site you are connecting to is the correct site, and also enables you to encrypt transmission to the site. Three main forms of encryption are used today.

Note The encryption methods that can be used today include SSL, which is the Secured Sockets Layer; PGP, or Pretty Good Privacy; and SET, or Secure Electronic Transactions. These methods are being developed to make commerce on the web work. There are many good sources of information on them. The Microsoft site has information on all of them. The RSA site, however, explains the process very well. You can find them at `www.rsa.com`.

- **Active content.** Many sites attempt to download small pieces of code to your system. The settings here enable you to determine what can be downloaded and if they will be run.

To turn on the Content Advisor, follow these steps:

1. From the Internet Explorer, choose View, Options from the menu.
2. Select the Security tab.

3. Click the Enable Rating button. You are asked to supply a password (see fig. 16.9). This prevents other users from turning off the Content Advisory.

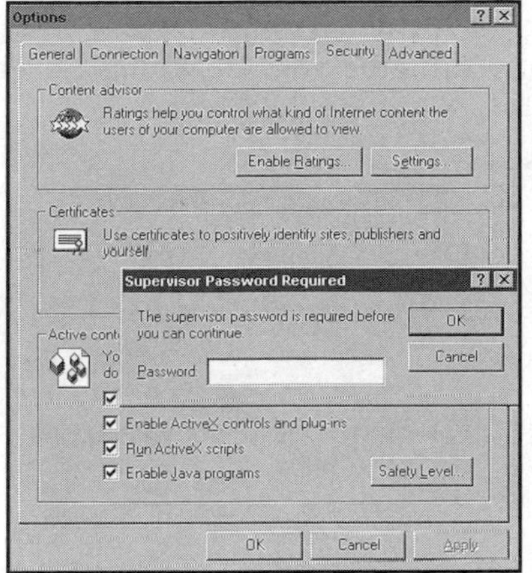

Figure 16.9

Enter a password to prevent the Content Advisor from being turned off.

4. Click the Settings button. This brings up the Configuration dialog box for the Content Advisor.

5. On the Ratings tab, choose each of the four categories: Language, Nudity, Sex, and Violence (see fig. 16.10). Choose the maximum level for each that you want to be able to be viewed.

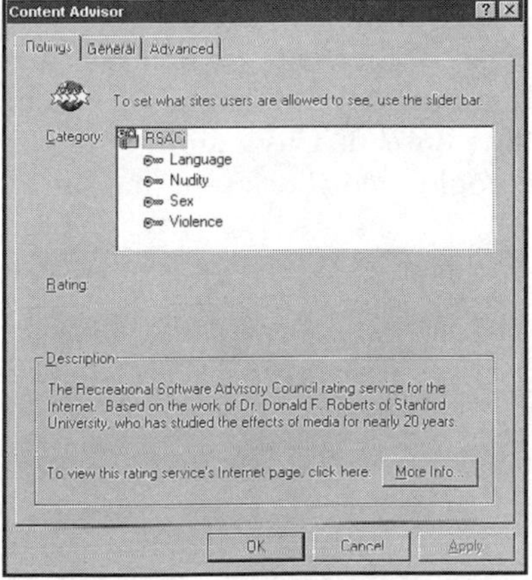

Figure 16.10

Setting the ratings levels.

6. Choose the General tab (see fig. 16.11). This enables you to configure user options. The options are as follows:

- **Users can see sites which have no rating.** As stated, this is voluntary at this point. Selecting this option prevents the display of any site that does not have a rating.
- **Supervisor can type a password to allow users to view restricted content.** This is the override setting that enables users who know the password to get into the site anyway.

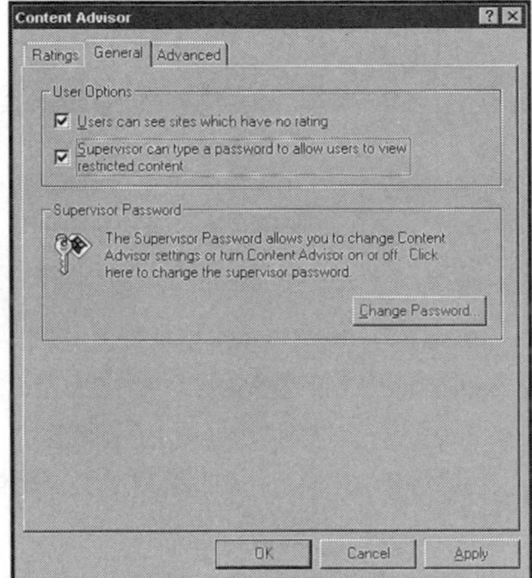

Figure 16.11
Setting the General tab options.

7. Under Supervisor Password, you can set or reset the supervisor password that can be used to override a site restriction.
8. Choose the Advanced tab (see fig. 16.12). From here, you can enter a different Rating System. This means that as other rating systems become available, you can add them to the system so that sites that use that rating system are accessible. You can also choose to use a Rating Bureau. This is another organization that keeps ratings on sites. Your system could then check with that site to find the rating.

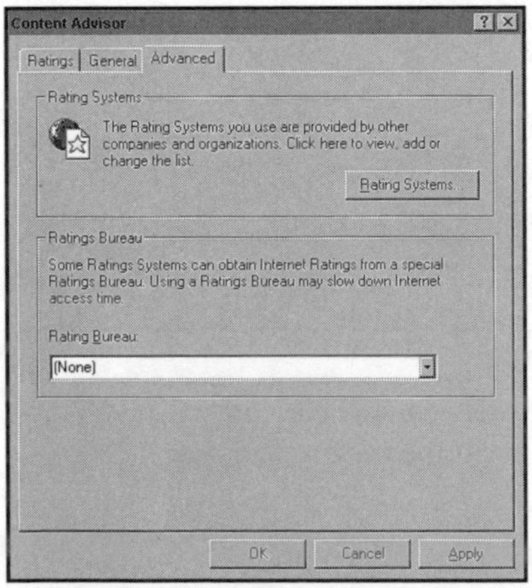

Figure 16.12
The Advanced tab of the Content Advisor.

9. Click OK to return to the Internet Explorer configuration, and then OK to return to the Internet Explorer itself.

The last tab in the Internet Explorer configuration is the Advanced tab (see fig. 16.13). This tab has the following options:

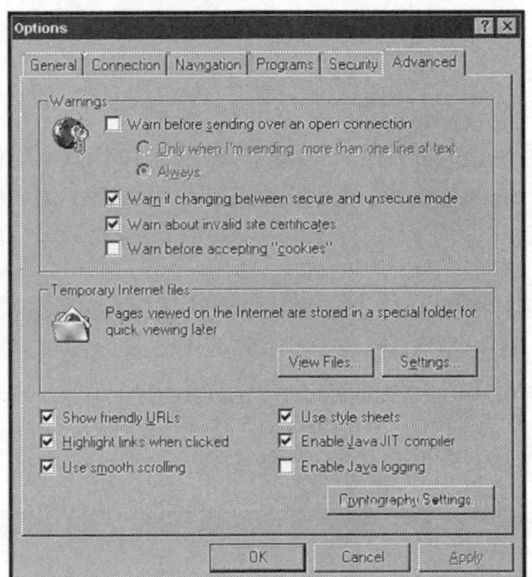

Figure 16.13
The Advanced Tab for Internet Explorer configuration.

- **Warnings.** This turns on or off the display of several warnings.
- **Temporary Internet files.** As stated before, the Internet Explorer keeps track of the pages that you visit and the copies of them. These settings enable you to view and clear the pages that you have been visiting.

The last few options describe the behavior of the browser; the options are as follows:

- **Show friendly URLs.** An URL is a Uniform Resource Locator. These are normally given as `http://www.microsoft.com/cert/exams/70-59pg.html`. This option would tell you that it was a shortcut to 70-59.html.
- **Highlight links when clicked.** This highlights a link so that you can tell the system understood. This is handy if your network connection is slow.
- **Use smooth scrolling.** Moves the screen up and down as if it is sliding rather than jumping.
- **Use style sheets.** Where applicable, the system uses built-in style sheets rather than reloading format information for every section downloaded.
- **Enable Java JIT compiler.** Tells the system to use the Just In Time compiler. This option compiles the Java script only after it is completely downloaded, which can help prevent hanging.

- **Enable Java logging.** This places a list of Java activity in a log file. This proves useful when creating pages, enabling you to test them.
- **Cryptography Settings.** Specify settings for which types of connections you will accept (SSL 2, SSL 3, and PCT) and tell the system whether to save secure pages to disk.

Telnet

Although it is sometimes surprising, many times you are still required to connect to another system using terminal emulation. This enables you to log on to the system and thereby be validated.

The Telnet screen is very simple (see fig. 16.14). For all intents and purposes, it is a dumb terminal that you run under Windows. Many versions of Telnet are available, including several that are shareware or freeware. For most purposes, however, the supplied version functions fine.

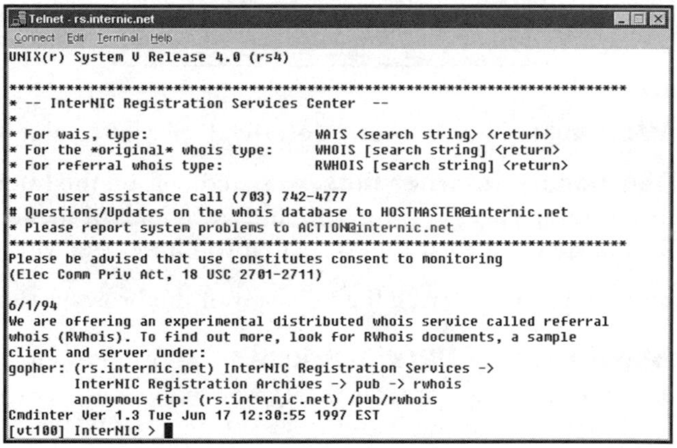

```
Telnet - rs.internic.net
Connect  Edit  Terminal  Help
UNIX(r) System V Release 4.0 (rs4)

*****************************************************************************
* -- InterNIC Registration Services Center  --
*
* For wais, type:                        WAIS <search string> <return>
* For the *original* whois type:         WHOIS [search string] <return>
* For referral whois type:               RWHOIS [search string] <return>
*
* For user assistance call (703) 742-4777
# Questions/Updates on the whois database to HOSTMASTER@internic.net
* Please report system problems to ACTION@internic.net
*****************************************************************************
Please be advised that use constitutes consent to monitoring
(Elec Comm Priv Act, 18 USC 2701-2711)

6/1/94
We are offering an experimental distributed whois service called referral
whois (RWhois). To find out more, look for RWhois documents, a sample
client and server under:
gopher: (rs.internic.net) InterNIC Registration Services ->
        InterNIC Registration Archives -> pub -> rwhois
        anonymous ftp: (rs.internic.net) /pub/rwhois
Cmdinter Ver 1.3 Tue Jun 17 12:30:55 1997 EST
[vt100] InterNIC >
```

Figure 16.14

An example of a Telnet window.

The next section discusses the steps involved for the main functions of Telnet. These are included for reference.

Connecting to a Remote Host

1. First, of course, you need to open Telnet. The easiest way to do this is to go to the Start menu and choose Run. Type **Telnet**, and press Enter. (If you want to create a shortcut, telnet.exe is in the \%winroot5\system32 directory.)
2. From the menu, choose Connect, Remote System.
3. Enter the name or IP address of the system that you want to connect to in the Host Name field.

4. If required, you can specify a port in the Port field.
5. In the TermType field, select the type of terminal that you want Telnet to emulate.

Note You must select this same emulation in the Terminal Preferences field. This tells the other functions of Telnet the emulation they should use.

When you are finished with the remote host, you can disconnect from a remote host by choosing Connect, Disconnect.

Setting the Terminal Preferences

1. Choose Terminal, Preferences from the menu (see fig. 16.15).

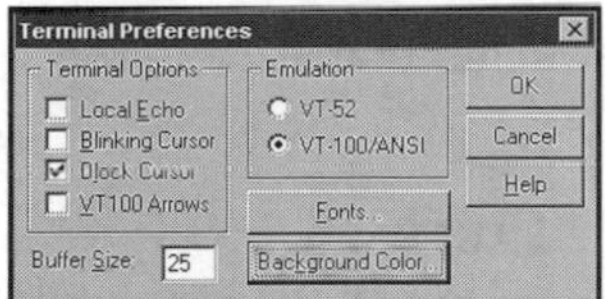

Figure 16.15
The Terminal Preferences dialog box.

2. Choose the emulation by clicking VT-52 or VT-100 (ANSI).
3. Choose other options as required (see the following list for details).

Note You should use VT-100 (ANSI) as a default. Most systems support this emulation.

The following list defines the other settings in the Terminal Preferences dialog box.

- **Local Echo.** This turns on the display of all your keyboard input.
- **Blinking Cursor.** This sets the cursor so that it blinks on-screen.
- **Block Cursor.** This tells the computer to use a block as the cursor rather than the underscore character.
- **VT100 Arrows.** This defines the character sequence sent for the arrow keys.
- **Buffer Size.** This is the number of lines that you want the terminal to keep in memory so that you can scroll through them. (The range is 25–399.)

Occasionally you will want to record the Telnet session so that you can later review it. To record a session, you need to turn on the Telnet log. To create a Telnet log, follow these steps:

1. Choose Terminal Logging.

2. Enter the file name and path where you want to keep the file.

Note If the file you enter already exists, the existing file is overwritten.

3. When you have captured the data that you wanted, select Terminal, Stop Logging.

RSH

As stated before, this enables you to open a shell on the remote system. The RSH command is run from the command line. The command and options are as follows:

```
rsh computer [-l username] [-n] command
```

Table 16.5 gives an overview of the switches that are entered.

Table 16.5
Switches for the RSH Command

Switch	Meaning
computer	Tells RSH with which system you want to connect.
-l username	This is the user name to use when connecting to the remote host. The default is the logged on user name from NT.
-n	Takes the output of the remote session and dumps it.
command	This is the command sent to the remote session.

RSH establishes a session on the remote host; it sends your command as standard (as if from the keyboard) input. It also listens for the answer and displays it on your screen. Normally the session ends when the remote command does.

REXEC

This command line utility runs commands on remote hosts that have REXEC service. REXEC requires you to authenticate your user name on the remote host before proceeding to execute the command. The syntax for the command is as follows:

```
rexec computer [-l username] [-n] command
```

Table 16.6 outlines the switches for the REXEC command.

TABLE 16.6
Switches for the REXEC Command

Switch	Description
computer	This is the name of the remote host on which you want to run the command.
-l username	The user name that you want to use as a logon on the remote system. REXEC does not automatically pass the currently logged on user name.
-n	This dumps the information returned from the command.
command	The command that you want to have executed on the remote system.

REXEC prompts you for a password and checks the user name and password with its own security system. Only if you have supplied a valid user name and password will the command execute.

Printing Utilities

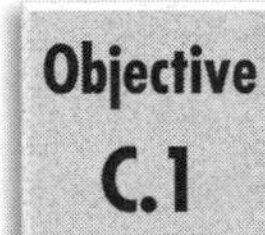

You already know that the LPR command sends a print job to a remote system that is running LPD service, and the LPQ command checks the job status. This section takes a more detailed look at these commands and all the other switches involved in printing.

LPR

As you remember, this is the Line Printer Request, the command that requests the file you give to be output to the printer that you ask for. The full command line for LPR is as follows:

```
lpr -SServer  -PPrinter [-CClass] [-JJobname] [-O option] filename
```

Table 16.7 explains all the switches.

TABLE 16.7
Command Line Switches for LPR

Switch	Description
-Sserver	The host name or IP address of the system that controls the printer.
-Pprinter	The name of the printer on the system to which you want to print.
-Cclass	The job class. This information appears on the banner page.
-Jjobname	The name of the job that you are sending. This is visible in the print queue and usually appears on the banner page.
-O option	As you saw with FTP, TFTP, and RCP, there are two ways to move files: text and binary. The default for a file going through LPR is a text file. Use -Ol (lowercase L) to tell the remote system that it is a binary file (PCL or PostScript, for example.)
filename	This is the name of the file that you want to print.

LPQ

LPQ enables you to read the status of a print queue on a remote system. The full command line for LPQ is as follows:

```
lpq -SServer  -PPrinter [-l]
```

Table 16.8 describes the switches.

TABLE 16.8
Command Line Switches for LPQ

Switch	Description
-Sserver	The host name or IP address of the system to query.
-Pprinter	The name of the printer on the remote system.
-l	This provides a lone listing of the queue, providing details about the job on the system.

Troubleshooting

One of the most important sets of utilities that you will come across is the troubleshooting utilities. You have already seen some of the utilities included. You have not, however, looked at any of them fully. This section begins to look at all these utilities.

Objective E.2

Ping

Ping is the basic troubleshooting utility. Ping (short for Packet Internet Groper) does exactly what its underwater relative does. It sends a signal and listens for the echo to come back. This is in fact a function of the ICMP (remember there were Echo Request and Echo Reply functions for ICMP) protocol (which, if you remember, resides at the IP layer). This means that you are testing the very basic parts of the TCP/IP protocol.

By default, Ping sends four transmissions of 32 bytes each. This verifies that you can connect to the host that you are pinging.

Ping has a good number of options.

```
ping [-t] [-a] [-n count] [-l length] [-f] [-i ttl] [-v tos] [-r count] [-s
➥count]
      [[-j computer-list] ¦ [-k computer-list]] [-w timeout] destination-list
```

Table 16.9 outlines these switches for you.

Table 16.9
Command Line Switches for Ping

Switch	Description
-t	This tells Ping to continue pinging until it is interrupted by the user. This is useful if you suspect cable problems because you can jiggle the wires without having to keep typing the command.
-a	This tells Ping to resolve the address to a computer name and display this as well.
-n count	This is the number of echo requests that the command should send. As you have seen, the default is four.

continues

Table 16.9, Continued
Command Line Switches for Ping

Switch	Description
-l length	By default, Ping sends 32 bytes of data (there is an error in the documentation about Ping). Using this option, you can increase the size of the echo packet that is sent. This enables you to test packets up to 8192 bytes in size, which normally causes your packets to fragment.
-f	This sets the "do not fragment" control bit in the IP header. Using this, you can determine the maximum size of the packet that can be sent to a remote host. This information can be used to optimize TCP/IP.
-i ttl	This sets the "Time to Live" in the IP header, enabling you to control how long the packet stays on the wire. You can use this to see whether your packets are occasionally being sent through alternate routes that are causing them to time out.
-v tos	This enables you to set the "Type of Service" field in the IP header. This can be used to figure out what types of service are available on remote routers and hosts.
-r count	This records the route that the packet took in the record route field. This can record from 1–9 computers as specified by the value given as count.
-s count	Tells the system to keep the timestamp information for the number of hops given.
-j computer-list	These are the systems (routers) that you want to send the packet through. They enable you to set the route that the packet takes. The maximum number you can enter is 9. The systems listed do not have to be joined directly to each other (there can be other hops between them).
-k computer-list	This is similar to the -j option. There cannot be other hops, however, between the computers listed with this switch.
-w timeout	This specifies the period Ping waits for the reply before deciding that the host is not responding.
Destination-list	This tells Ping which computer you want it to send echo requests to.

Testing Network Connectivity with Ping

The normal method of testing using Ping is to start by testing the internal loopback address (127.0.0.1). This verifies that the IP layer is functioning correctly and enables you to ping further. The next ping is normally to your own IP address to verify that the protocol has been bound to your network card correctly.

If either of these fail, there is a good chance that your IP stack has been corrupted, or that your stack did not initialize correctly. The first step in this case should always be to restart the system. Then you should go to the command prompt and check IPCONFIG to see whether you have an address. If there is no address listed, try **IPCONFIG /RENEW**.

If all else fails, this might be a good time to practice reinstalling protocols. Remember to restart your system after you have removed the protocol and before you add it back in.

The next couple of pings are to IP addresses. First you should try local addresses, making certain to use some from the low end of your subnet's range of valid host IDs and some from the high end. This is a test of the network connectivity. If you cannot ping, you might suspect your network card or cable, perhaps the adapter drivers. If you can ping some hosts but not all, you might want to look at the subnet mask to ensure that the subnet ID of the hosts is the correct subnet ID. If the mask is using too many bits, you cannot ping all local hosts.

Now you ping to a remote station. When you do this, you are checking that you can connect to and through your default gateway—in other words, you can route. This also makes certain that your subnet mask is not using too few bits. If it is, that would make remote hosts look like they were local. Again check to see that the subnet mask extracts the correct subnet ID.

Now you need to try pinging a host name. It does not really matter what the host name is, as long as the name is valid. What you are trying to do here is to ensure that the host name resolution is working correctly. If you can only ping one or two host names, check to see whether the names you can ping are in the HOSTS file. If they are, there is a problem with the DNS entry on the local machine—or maybe there is a problem with the DNS itself.

Now that you can ping all the way up to the host name, you should attempt to ping a NetBIOS name. This ensures that there is some method of NetBIOS name resolution. (Remember that the NetBIOS name resolution backs up the host's name resolution and vice versa.) Again, if it is only a couple, you can ping check the LMHOSTS file.

Note The described method of testing TCP/IP with Ping given in the preceding paragraphs is the recommended method of checking connectivity using Ping. Most people (myself included) work it the other way around, first pinging a remote host by name. This bisects all the possible problems and quickly tells you whether the TCP/IP side or the upper-layer protocols are the problem.

An example of using the PING command follows:

```
C:\>REM PING'ing by IP address

C:\>ping 198.53.147.2

Pinging 198.53.147.2 with 32 bytes of data:

Reply from 198.53.147.2: bytes=32 time=766ms TTL=105
Reply from 198.53.147.2: bytes=32 time=281ms TTL=105
Reply from 198.53.147.2: bytes=32 time=297ms TTL=105
Reply from 198.53.147.2: bytes=32 time=281ms TTL=105

C:\>REM PING'ing by host name

C:\>ping www.ibm.com

Pinging www.ibm.com [204.146.17.33] with 32 bytes of data:

Reply from 204.146.17.33: bytes=32 time=235ms TTL=237
Reply from 204.146.17.33: bytes=32 time=219ms TTL=237
Reply from 204.146.17.33: bytes=32 time=219ms TTL=237
Reply from 204.146.17.33: bytes=32 time=219ms TTL=237

C:\>ping www.microsoft.com

Pinging www.microsoft.com [207.68.137.65] with 32 bytes of data:

Reply from 207.68.137.65: bytes=32 time=234ms TTL=53
Reply from 207.68.137.65: bytes=32 time=218ms TTL=53
Reply from 207.68.137.65: bytes=32 time=219ms TTL=53
Reply from 207.68.137.65: bytes=32 time=219ms TTL=53
```

Note You will notice a great difference in the Time to Live for the packets going to www.ibm.com and www.microsoft.com. This is not uncommon. Although a router is normally only supposed to decrement the Time to Live (TTL) by 1 for every second that a packet remains in a router, some routers actually decrement by much more.

There are a couple of reasons for this. The first is the amount of traffic the router can handle. Very busy routers usually decrement by more than one to kill excess traffic. By decreasing the TTL by a large number, the router drops any packets that it cannot deal with in a reasonable period of time. The host retransmits the packet, and statistically has a fair chance of getting through the next time.

The other concern is the cost of lines. If an organization has a link for which it is paying, the organization wants its traffic to have priority. It can do this by increasing the decrement for packets that come into its network from outside.

IPCONFIG

The other main troubleshooting command that you need to be able to use is the IPCONFIG command. This is used to check that all the appropriate configuration parameters are set up in the system. You have already seen IPCONFIG a few times, just like you had seen Ping a few times (hopefully you have tried them both). The full command line is as follows:

```
ipconfig [/all ¦ /renew [adapter] ¦ /release [adapter]]
```

Table 16.10 identifies and describes the switches for the IPCONFIG command.

TABLE 16.10
Switches for the IPCONFIG Command

Switch	Description
all	Provides the full details on the configuration for the system. This often fills more than one screen. You can, however, pipe the command through the more command to display the output one screen at a time: IPCONFIG /ALL ǀ MORE.
renew [adapter]	This renews the IP lease for a specific adapter (if one is given) in the computer. With no parameter, it renews the lease for all adapters with the DHCP server.
release [adapter]	Release the IP lease that was granted by the DHCP server. This should be done before powering down a system that will move to a different subnet.

If you do not enter a parameter, IPCONFIG shows you all the basic TCP/IP configuration values. This includes the IP address and subnet mask.

Finger

This utility enables you to put the "finger" on another user on your network. The command queries the Finger service that is running on the remote system about a user that is using a remote system. The command returns basic information about who the users are, how long they have been on, and so on. This is handy if you need to shut down a system remotely.

The command line syntax is as follows:

```
finger [-l] [user]@computer [...]
```

Table 16.11 identifies and describes the switches for the Finger command.

TABLE 16.11
Switches for the Finger Command

Switch	Description
-l	Displays long information from the remote system, providing greater detail in most cases.
User	Tells the system which user you want to finger. This is the user name on which the system reports.
@computer	The computer (server) with which the users are currently working.

NSLOOKUP

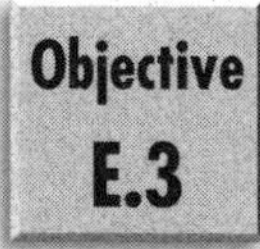

Not only have you already seen NSLOOKUP, you have used it in one of the labs. So far, you have looked at the basic functions. Here you look at all of them. The command line is as follows:

```
nslookup [-option ...] [computer-to-find ¦ - [server]]
```

Table 16.12 presents command line switches for the NSLOOKUP command.

Modes

As you may recall, NSLOOKUP uses two modes: the interactive mode, where you can work with the DNS to get a lot of information; and the non-interactive mode, used when you need to look up only a single piece of data. When you need to get at more information, you use interactive mode.

TABLE 16.12
Command Line Switches for the NSLOOKUP Command

Switch	Description
-option	Enables you to enter one or more commands from the command line. (A list of the commands follows.) For each option you want to add, enter a hyphen (-) followed immediately by the command name. Note that the command line length needs to be less than 256 characters.
Computer-to-find	This is the host about which you want to find information. It is processed using the default server, or if given, using the specified server.

Interactive Commands

You have already seen the interactive mode for the NSLOOKUP command. To enter the interactive mode, you need only to type **NSLOOKUP**. There are a couple of points worth noting about interactive mode:

- You can interrupt commands at any time by pressing Ctrl+C.
- Just like the prompt, the command line length needs to be less than 256 characters.
- If a computer on your network is named after an NSLOOKUP command, preceding it with the backslash character (\) causes it to be treated as a computer name.
- Any unrecognized command is treated as a computer name.

Several different errors can be returned. The next list covers the errors that you might encounter:

- **Timed out.** The DNS server did not respond to the request within an acceptable period of time. (This is set by the timeout parameter.)
- **No response from server.** Your system was not able to open the DNS port on the computer name given or the default DNS. This could mean there is a name problem, or the server is down.
- **No records.** The name that you requested was either entered incorrectly, or there is no record for it in the database.
- **Non-existent domain.** The name you are attempting to look up is in a domain that is not registered. There was no reference to the domain for the system you entered, even starting with the root server.

- **Connection refused.** The server does not have an account for you. You are not authorized to perform that function or see those records.
- **Network is unreachable.** Either the system refused your connection (as previously described), or the server you are attempting to work with is on a network currently unavailable.
- **Server failure.** The DNS server cannot fulfill your request because of internal database problems. This means your server needs a little (serious) attention.
- **Refused.** Generally this is also an authorization problem. You have rights to query part of a database, but not all.
- **Format error.** The DNS server did not understand the request, and it suspects that the request was not formatted correctly. This might be an NSLOOKUP problem.

NSLOOKUP Commands

When you are working in interactive mode, you can use many commands. You can also set some values. The following list explains them:

- **help.** This provides a list of basic commands.
- **exit.** This closes the connection and returns you to the prompt (or desktop if this was run through Start, Run).
- **finger.** This enables you to finger the users or a user on a system with the NSLOOKUP command. Just typing **finger** brings up information on the last system that you found. Usage: Afinger [username] [> filename] | [>> filename]@
- **ls.** This returns a list of information from a DNS domain. By default this output includes both computer names and IP addresses. Usage: Als [option] dnsdomain [> filename] | [>> filename]@
    - **-t querytype.** This lists all the records of a given type. The record types are listed under querytype.
    - **-a.** This lists all the CNAME entries from the DNS server.
    - **-d.** This dumps all the records that are in the DNS server.
    - **-h.** This returns information on the DNS server's CPU and operating system.
    - **-s.** This returns the well-known services for hosts in the DNS domain.
    - **domain.** This lists the information for the domain that you enter.
    - **filename.** This specifies a file name to which the output of the command should be redirected.

- **lserver.** Based on the resolution in the local server, this changes to a default server. The only difference between this and the server command occurs if you enter a host name for the DNS server. In this case, the system uses the local DNS server to resolve the name. Usage: Alserver dnsname@
- **root.** This changes the default server to the root server for the Internet domain name space. Currently this is ns.nic.ddn.mil. Usage: Aroot@
- **server.** This changes to a new DNS server, as discussed in the lserver section. Resolution of the new DNS server's IP address is handled by the current default server.
- **set.** This command enables you to set any of a number of variables that change the function of the NSLOOKUP command. The form of the command is Aset keyword[=value]@. Following is a list of keywords that you can enter:
    - **all.** Outputs all the current values for the configuration settings. This information includes the default server and host.
    - **cl[ass].** This parameter changes the class of the query. The default is to include all the IN. Entries from the server. The choices for the class variable are as follows:
        - **IN.** Internet class
        - **CHAOS.** Chaos class
        - **HESIOD.** MIT Athena Hesiod class
        - **ANY.** Any of the preceding classes in this list
    - **[no]deb[ug].** This is similar to a verbose mode switch. With the debugging turned on, the display includes more information about the packets that are sent and about the information received. Usage: Aset [no]deb[ug]@
    - **[no]d2.** Like Adeb@ and Anodeb@, this turns on the exhaustive debugging mode. This causes every piece of information being sent back and forth to be printed. Usage: Aset [no]d2"
    - **[no]def[name].** Turns the default domain option on or off. The default domain option automatically appends the default domain if you enter a query for a name without giving the FQDN. Usage: Aset [no]def[name]@
    - **do[main].** This enables you to set the default domain name to the name given. If, for example, you will be searching for several names in the ScrimTech.com domain, you can set the domain value, and set Aset def@ to turn on the use of the default domain names. Usage: Aset do[main]=name@

- **[no]ig[nore].** If this parameter is set, packet truncation errors are ignored. Usage: Aset [no]ig[nore]@
- **po[rt].** This changes the default Winsock port used to send queries to the DNS server. Usage: Aset po[rt]=value@
- **q[uerytype].** This changes the default type of query that is made. Several values can be entered for this command. The following list identifies and explains these values. Usage: Aset q[uerytype]=value@
    - **A.** This searches for AA@ type records in the DNS server. This is the default setting.
    - **ANY.** This includes a listing of any and all systems listed in the DNS server.
    - **CNAME.** This searches for alias names in the DNS server.
    - **GID.** This searches for the entries that are group identifiers in the server.
    - **HINFO.** This looks for the DNS server's SPU and operating system information.
    - **MB.** This searches the DNS server for the mail domain.
    - **MG.** This looks for Mail Group records in the DNS server.
    - **MINFO.** This searches for information on mailboxes or mail lists.
    - **MR.** This finds mail rename domain information.
    - **MX.** This looks for mail exchange records in the DNS server.
    - **NS.** This looks for any name server records that exist in the DNS server.
    - **PTR.** This seeks out the reverse name resolution records in the DNS server.
    - **SOA.** This displays the Start of Authority record information from the DNS server.
    - **TXT.** This returns any text information that resides in the DNS server.
    - **UID.** This searches for user ID information in the DNS server.
    - **UINFO.** This looks for user information in the DNS server.
    - **WKS.** This queries the DNS server for well-known service descriptions.
- **[no]rec[urse].** If recurse is turned on, it tells the DNS server that it should search for the information in other DNSs. This treats your query as a recursive query and forces the DNS server, if required, to do an iterative query to the other DNS servers. Usage: Aset [no]rec[urse]@

- **ret[ry].** This sets the number of retries. Each time a query times out, your system attempts to query the DNS server again until this number is reached. (Note: The timeout is doubled each time.) Usage: Aset ret[ry]=number@
- **ro[ot].** Sets the name of the root-level server. This changes the computer that is contacted with the root command. Usage: Aset ro[ot]=host name@
- **[no]sea[rch].** If this is turned on, the system appends each of the names in the DNS Domain Search order to the end of the host given if the value that you are searching for does not end with a period. Usage: Aset [no]sea[rch]@
- **set srchl[ist].** This enables you to enter a domain suffix search order different from the one entered in the DNS tab of the TCP/IP Configuration dialog box. Usage: ASet srchl[ist] name1/name2/...@
- **ti[meout].** Configures the starting timeout for queries made to the DNS server. As previously noted, every time the query is not answered, the DNS timeout is doubled. Usage: Aset ti[meout]=number@
- **ty[pe].** This is the same as the querytype discussed earlier. Usage: set ty[pe]=value
- **[no]v[c].** Specifies whether to use a virtual circuit to send to the server. If a virtual circuit is requested, TCP is used. Otherwise, UDP is used. Usage: Aset [no]v[c]@

- **view.** This sorts and lists the output of the previous ls commands.

HOSTNAME

This is a very simple command. It displays the current host name. The syntax is as follows:

```
Hostname
```

On a computer, HOSTNAME looks like this:

```
C:\>HOSTNAME
tawni

C:\>
```

Note In the case of this computer, there was no domain information entered in the DNS tab of the TCP/IP Configuration dialog box.

NETSTAT

As you have seen, the NETSTAT command is useful for determining the types of connections that you have made on the TCP/IP stack. This shows all connections, including the connections made using NetBIOS over TCP/IP. The full syntax of this command is as follows:

```
netstat [-a] [-e] [-n] [-s] [-p protocol] [-r] [interval]
```

Table 16.13 summarizes the command line switches available with NETSTAT.

TABLE 16.13
Command Line Switches for the NETSTAT Command

Switch	Description
-a	This shows every connection and the listening ports which are normally not displayed.
-e	This displays network card statistics. It can be combined with the -s option.
-n	This shows the information using the IP addresses rather than host names.
-s	This shows statistics per protocol. Normally statistics are given for TCP, UDP, ICMP, and IP. The -p switch can be used to select a subset of these.
-p protocol	This displays connections for only the protocol given in the switch. Normally this can be TCP or UDP. In conjunction with the -s switch, however, you can specify TCP, UDP, ICMP, or IP.
-r	This shows the content of the routing table.
Interval	This continues to display statistics. Interval is the update frequency, after which new statistics are gathered and displayed on-screen.

Figure 16.16 shows what is output when the NETSTAT command is used.

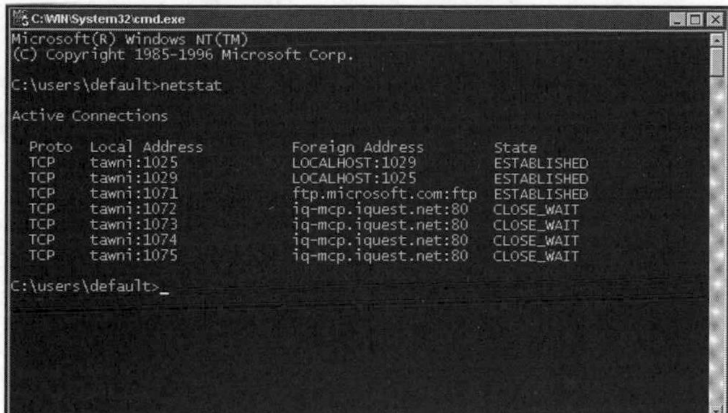

Figure 16.16

Output from the NETSTAT command.

The information displayed by NETSTAT includes the following:

- **Foreign Address.** This is the IP address or host name and WinSock port of the remote host with which you are communicating. If the port is initializing, an asterisk (*) displays.
- **Local Address.** This is your computer's IP address or host name and the port that you are using to connect to the remote host.
- **Proto.** This is the name of the protocol being used for the connection.
- **State.** This displays the state of TCP connections that you are viewing. The state can be any one of the following:
  - **CLOSED.** The TCP session has been closed.
  - **FIN_WAIT_1.** The connection is being closed.
  - **SYN_RECEIVED.** A session request has been received.
  - **CLOSE_WAIT.** The connection is being closed.
  - **FIN_WAIT_2.** The connection is being closed.
  - **SYN_SEND.** A session is being requested.
  - **ESTABLISHED.** A session currently exists between the systems.
  - **LISTEN.** A service has done a passive open on a port.
  - **TIMED_WAIT.** The session is currently waiting for activity from the other computer.
  - **LAST_ACK.** Your system has made a last acknowledgment.

NBTSTAT

This diagnostic command displays protocol statistics and current TCP/IP connections using NBT (NetBIOS over TCP/IP). This command is available only if the TCP/IP protocol has been installed.

```
nbtstat [-a remotename] [-A IP address] [-c] [-n] [-R] [-r] [-S] [-s] [interval]
```

You have already read about some of the command line parameters for this command. Table 16.14, however, identifies and explains all the switches.

TABLE 16.14
Switches for the NBTSTAT Command

Switch	Description
-a remotename	This lists the names that another host has registered on the network. Remotename is the computer name of the other host.
-A IP address	Basically the same as the preceding command, but you can specify the IP address rather than the name.
-c	This displays all the names that are in the NetBIOS Name Cache and the IP address that they map to.
-n	This lists all the names that your computer has. If they have been registered, they are marked as such.
-R	This command purges and reloads the NetBIOS Name Cache. The cache is reloaded from the LMHOSTS file if one exists, using the entries marked with #PRE.
-r	This lists all the names that your computer has resolved and the IP address from them. The difference from the -c switch is that preloaded names are not listed when using the -r switch.
-S	Lists all the current sessions that have been established with your computer. This includes both the client and server sessions.
-s	This is basically the same as the -S switch, but the system attempts to resolve the IP addresses to a host name.
interval	This is the interval in seconds at which the computer should redisplay the information on-screen.

Output from the NBSTAT command is shown in figure 16.17.

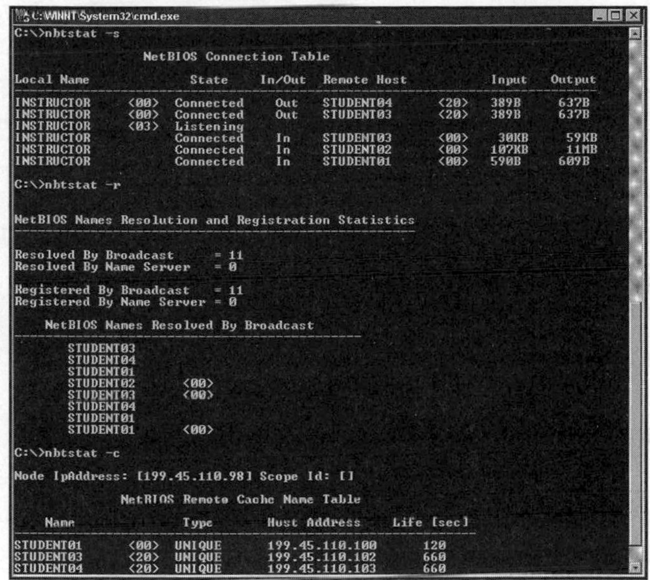

Figure 16.17

Output from the NBTSTAT command.

The column headings generated by the NBTSTAT utility have the following meanings:

- **Input.** The number of bytes of information received.
- **Output.** The number of bytes of information sent.
- **In/Out.** The direction in which the connection was made—with Out to the other computer, or In from it.
- **Life.** The time remaining before the cache entry is purged.
- **Local Name.** The local name used for the session.
- **Remote Host.** The name on the remote host being used in this session.
- **Type.** The type of name resolved.
- **State.** The state of the connection. Possible states include the following:
    - **Connected.** A NetBIOS session has been established between the two hosts.
    - **Associated.** Your system has requested a connection, and has resolved the remote name to an IP address. This is an active open.
    - **Listening.** This is a service on your computer that is currently not being used. This is a passive open.

- **Idle.** The service that opened the port has since paused or hung. No activity is possible until the service resumes.
- **Connecting.** At this point, your system is attempting to create a NetBIOS session. The system is currently attempting to resolve the name of the remote host to an IP address.
- **Accepting.** A service on your system has been asked to open a session, and is in the process of negotiating the session with the remote host.
- **Reconnecting.** After a session has dropped (often due to time out), your system is trying to reconnect.
- **Outbound.** The TCP three-way handshake is in process. This establishes the Transport layer session used to establish the NetBIOS session.
- **Inbound.** Same as outbound. This, however, is a connection being made to a service on your system.
- **Disconnecting.** The remote system has requested a session be terminated, so the session is being shut down.
- **Disconnected.** Your system is requesting a session be terminated.

ROUTE

As you saw, the ROUTE command can be used to manipulate the routing table on a Windows NT-based computer. The format for the command is as follows:

```
route [-f] [-p] [command [destination] [mask subnetmask] [gateway] [metric
costmetric]]
```

Table 16.15 reviews the switches available for the ROUTE command.

TABLE 16.15
Switches for the ROUTE Command

Switch	Description
-f	This flushes all the entries in the routing table.
-p	If used with the ADD command, it makes the route persistent (by storing it in the Registry). If it is used with the PRINT command, it displays only registered persistent routes.

Switch	Description
Command	This is the activity to perform. The valid commands are PRINT (displays the routing table on-screen), ADD (adds a route to the routing table), DELETE (removes a command from the routing table), and CHANGE (to change the gateway address for a route that already exists).
destination	This is the network ID to which packets might be sent. IP calculates the network ID for all packets that it will send and checks the routing table to see where they should be sent.
Mask subnet mask	This is the subnet mask that tells the IP layer how to calculate the network ID to which the system will send the information.
gateway	This is the IP address to which packets for the network being described will be sent. If this is a network to which the system is attached, the address is one of the network cards. Otherwise, the address is the next router that must be on a network to which the system is attached.
metric cost	This enables you to assign the metric value used in determining the route that a packet takes. Routes with a lower metric are usually preferred. The cost can be any number from 1–9,999, although anything over 15 is meaningless.

Note Although you can use host names for the destination or gateway, your system must be capable of resolving them. This can be done by using the standard host name resolution, or with a NETWORKS file that is in the\%winroot%\system32\drivers\etc directory.

It you are performing PRINT or DELETE operations, you can use wildcards for the destination or gateway addresses. You can also omit the gateway address.

NETWORKS File

The following is an example of a NETWORKS file. Like the HOSTS and LMHOSTS file, the NETWORKS file is a plain-text file.

```
loopback     127
carleton     185.42
ottawa       207.122.108
youstern      162.25
```

The complete format for entries in the file is as follows:

```
network name network number  aliases #  comment
```

- **Network name.** This is the name that you use to represent the network.
- **Network number.** The Network ID for this network; the trailing 0s are not required.
- **Aliases.** Other names that might be used to refer to the same network.
- **# comments.** Everything entered after a # sign is considered a comment.

TRACERT

The TRACERT command can be used to view the path that any packet would take as it travels through the network. The TRACERT command tells your system to use ICMP to trace where the packet travels as it travels the network. The command is as follows:

```
tracert [-d] [-h maximum_hops] [-j computer-list] [-w timeout] target_name
```

Table 16.16 identifies and describes the switches for the TRACERT command.

Table 16.16
Switches for the TRACERT Command

Switch	Description
-d	Tells TRACERT not to resolve the host names for the routers.
-h maximum_hops	Tells TRACERT the maximum number of hops to be traced to the destination.
-j computer-list	Tells TRACERT to use this list of computers as the route to the destination host.
-w timeout	The timeout value for each reply that TRACERT waits for. Entered in milliseconds.
Target_name	The name or IP address of the system you want to reach.

TRACERT determines the route taken to a destination by sending many ICMP Echo Request packets, each with a different Time to Live value. Because all routers along the path are required to decrement the TTL by at least 1 before forwarding it, the TTL effectively becomes a hop count. When the TTL on a packet reaches 0, the router sends back an ICMP Time Exceeded message to the source system.

Therefore, TRACERT can determine the route by sending the first Echo Request with a TTL of 1 and then incrementing the TTL by 1 on each subsequent transmission until the target responds or the maximum TTL is reached. The route is determined by examining the ICMP Time Exceeded messages sent back by intermediate routers. Note that some routers silently drop packets with expired TTLs and will be invisible to TRACERT.

The following is an example of a TRACERT session:

```
C:\>REM Trace by IP Address

C:\>tracert 199.45.110.97

Tracing route to 199.45.110.97 over a maximum of 30 hops

  1   141 ms   141 ms   140 ms  annex4.intranet.ca [206.51.251.55]
  2   156 ms   141 ms   141 ms  cisco2.intranet.ca [206.51.251.10]
  3   219 ms   171 ms   141 ms  spc-tor-6-Serial3-3.Sprint-Canada.Net
      ➥[206.186.248.85]
  4   156 ms   156 ms   157 ms  core-spc-tor-1-fddi0/0.Sprint-Canada.Net
      ➥[204.50.251.33]
  5   219 ms   219 ms   219 ms  sl-pen-15-H11/0-T3.sprintlink.net
      ➥[144.228.165.25]
  6   421 ms   579 ms   609 ms  sl-pen-11-F8/0/0.sprintlink.net [144.228.60.11]
  7     *        *        *     Request timed out.
  8   297 ms   453 ms     *     331.atm11-0.cr2.ewr1.alter.net [137.39.13.230]
  9   250 ms   500 ms   469 ms  105.Hssi4-0.CR2.CLE1.Alter.Net [137.39.58.173]
 10   250 ms   266 ms   266 ms  119.Hssi4-0.GW1.BUF1.Alter.Net [137.39.31.61]
 11   281 ms   266 ms   297 ms  uunetcabuf-gw1.ALTER.NET [137.39.142.6]
 12   250 ms   281 ms   282 ms  vl151.f000.bb1.tor1.uunet.ca [205.150.242.94]
 13   266 ms   250 ms   281 ms  vl20.f000.backbone3.toronto.uunet.ca
      ➥[142.77.180.1]
 14   250 ms   265 ms   266 ms  max1.toronto.uunet.ca [142.77.1.210]
 15   281 ms   329 ms   390 ms  199.45.110.34
 16     *      312 ms     *     199.45.110.97
 17   422 ms   547 ms     *     199.45.110.97
 18   312 ms   360 ms   312 ms  199.45.110.97

Trace complete.

C:\>REM Trace by Host Name

C:\>tracert www.Microsoft.com
```

```
Tracing route to www.Microsoft.com [207.68.156.61]
over a maximum of 30 hops:

  1   140 ms   156 ms   141 ms  annex4.intranet.ca [206.51.251.55]
  2   140 ms   141 ms   140 ms  cisco2.intranet.ca [206.51.251.10]
  3   140 ms   157 ms   156 ms  spc-tor-6-Serial3-3.Sprint-Canada.Net
      ➥[206.186.248.85]
  4   156 ms   172 ms   156 ms  core-spc-tor-1-fddi0/0.Sprint-Canada.Net
      ➥[204.50.251.33]
  5     *      219 ms   250 ms  sl-pen-15-H11/0-T3.sprintlink.net
      ➥[144.228.165.25]
  6   219 ms   219 ms   250 ms  sl-pen-17-F6/0/0.sprintlink.net [144.228.60.17]
  7     *        *        *     Request timed out.
  8   875 ms   250 ms     *     sl-chi-20-P0/0/0-155M.sprintlink.net
      ➥[144.232.0.134]
  9   218 ms   235 ms   234 ms  sl-chi-20-H1/0-T3.sprintlink.net
      ➥[144.228.10.61]
 10   219 ms   234 ms   235 ms  sl-sea-6-F0/0.sprintlink.net [144.228.90.6]
 11   500 ms   281 ms   344 ms  sl-mic-3-h0-T3.sprintlink.net [144.228.96.22]
 12   500 ms   375 ms   297 ms  207.68.145.53
 13   250 ms   250 ms   235 ms  207.68.156.61

Trace complete.

C:\>
```

The preceding listing shows two different TRACERT sessions—one going to an IP address and the other to a host name. In the case of the host name, notice that it has resolved the name to an IP address and has then proceeded to trace the route to the IP address. Another point should be made about the traces shown. In the first example, the information being sent goes first through a local ISP (intranet). They connect to Sprint Canada, which passes the information to Sprintlink in the United States. The information then comes back to Canada via Alter.Net and then into uunet. You can cross from one provider to another only at certain places, and your information needs to travel to that site to move around the Internet. This more than anything else causes the slowness that often frustrates users on the Internet.

ARP

You know that ARP is responsible for mapping the IP address to a MAC address. Obviously then, the ARP command is used to view and modify the cache of addresses that the ARP command has resolved. The possible command lines are as follows:

```
arp -a [IP_address] [-N [local_MAC_address]]
arp -d IP_address [local_MAC_address]
arp -s IP_address remote_MAC_address [local_MAC_address]
```

Table 16.17 identifies and describes the switches used with the ARP command.

TABLE 16.17
Switches Used with the ARP Command

Switch	Description
-a	Displays the IP addresses and MAC addresses that have been resolved. If a single IP address is entered, only the resolution of that address is shown.
-g	Performs the same function as -a.
IP address	The IP address of the system being added, deleted, or that you want to view.
-N	Shows the ARP cache entries for only the given MAC address.
Local_MAC_address	Where the network card for the ARP cache you want to work with is kept.
-d	Deletes the ARP cache entry from the local_MAC_address. (This can be omitted if there is only one card.)
-s	Adds a static mapping to the ARP cache. Static mappings in the ARP cache do not remain in memory after a system restart. However, the entry remains in memory until the system is restarted, or it is specifically removed.
Remote_MAC_address	The MAC address of the remote machine.

Network Monitor

Network Monitor extends your capability to manage the network by enabling you to capture network data for detailed examination. You can look inside the frames to perform a detailed analysis of the network's operation.

Objective D.1

Network Monitor is equipped with a wide variety of protocol parsers, which are modules that examine network frames to decode their contents. Among the 62 or so included protocol parsers are many you will recognize from discussions in this book, including Ethernet, Token Ring, IPX, IP, TCP, and PPP. A complete discussion of the protocol parsers is, however, far beyond the scope of this book.

As shipped with Windows NT 4, Network Monitor has one significant limitation: Network Monitor can capture only those frames that originate from or are delivered to the computer on which Network Monitor is running, including broadcast and multicast frames that the computer receives or originates. You cannot use Network Monitor to monitor frames associated with other computers on the network.

Note

To monitor the entire network from a single computer, you need Microsoft's Systems Management Server (SMS), which includes a more powerful version of Network Monitor. SMS can monitor network traffic associated with any computer that is running a Network Monitor Agent. (Agents are proxy programs that collect data and forward them to another computer for analysis.) The Network Monitor Agent is included with Windows NT 4.

Ordinarily, computers on a network are selective and only receive frames addressed to them. As shipped with Windows NT 4, Network Monitor is designed to work with standard network adapter cards, which in part accounts for the restriction that Network Monitor can capture only those frames that originate from or are delivered to the computer on which Network Monitor is running. Network Monitor works with NDIS 4.0, new with Windows NT 4, to capture network data with little or no degradation in computer performance.

The SMS Network Monitor (more correctly the full version, as you can obtain it separately) captures network traffic in promiscuous mode, meaning that it can capture all network data regardless of the destination of the frames. This enables SMS to monitor any computer running a Network Monitor Agent. Capturing data in promiscuous mode is intense work, however, and performance suffers on the computer running SMS. Therefore, monitoring the network with SMS Network Monitor is an activity best reserved for a dedicated network management computer. (On some network types, such as Token Ring, special network adapters are required to support promiscuous mode. Because the Network Monitor included with Windows NT 4 does not operate in promiscuous mode, special network adapters are not required.)

SMS has other capabilities as well, including hardware inventory management and software management, as well as the capability to take over a station across the network.

Installing Network Monitor

The following steps detail how to install the Network Monitor:

1. Open the Network dialog box.
2. Choose the Services tab and click the Add button.
3. Choose either the Network Monitor Agent or the Network Monitor Tools and Agent. The following list briefly describes each of the choices:
   - **Network Monitor Agent.** Choose this option if this computer will be monitored by another computer running the SMS.
   - **Network Monitor Tools and Agent.** Choose this option if this computer will be used to collect and analyze network data. This option also installs the Network Monitor Agent, which enables SMS to monitor this computer remotely.
4. Click OK to add the Service. When prompted, enter the source files directory.
5. Click OK to close the Network dialog box, and then restart the system.

Network Monitor is added to the Administrative Tools group of the Start menu. Network Monitoring Agent is added to the Control Panel as the Monitoring Agent utility. You must restart the computer to activate Network Monitor.

Setting Up Network Monitor Security

The data captured by Network Monitor can include very sensitive information. Suppose, for example, that you are logging on to a terminal session with a remote computer that does not use encrypted logons. Data frames sent to the remote computer would include your password in clear text, and the password could be discovered by any user with access to the Network Monitor. You should, therefore, prevent unauthorized users from using Network Monitor by assigning the following two types of passwords:

- **Capture password.** Used to restrict the users who can use Network Monitor to capture and display statistics and data associated with this computer.
- **Display password.** Used to determine which users can open previously saved capture files.

A capture password also restricts SMS access to the Network Monitor Agent. SMS can be used to capture data from a given agent only when the capture password is known.

To assign or change the Network Monitor passwords, perform the following procedure:

1. Open the Monitoring Agent utility in the Control Panel to open the Configure Network Monitoring Agent dialog box (see fig. 16.18).

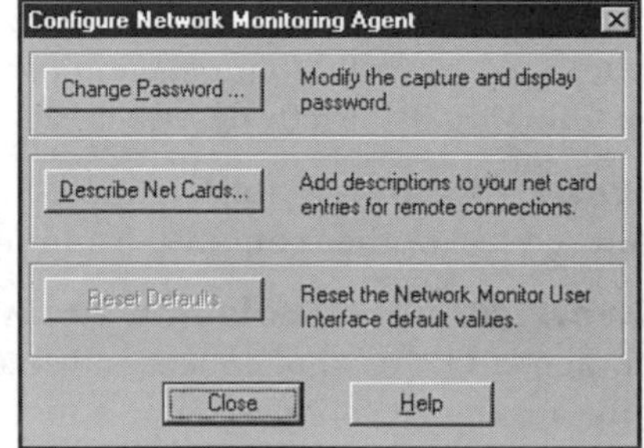

Figure 16.18
Options used to configure the Monitoring Agent utility.

2. Choose Change Password to open the Network Monitoring Password Change dialog box (see fig. 16.19).

Network Monitoring Password Change

You can control access to Network Monitor with two types of passwords. The Display password will restrict a user to viewing only previously saved capture files. The Capture password allows the user to capture data, as well as to view capture files.

Old Capture Password
Password: ********
Enter the old capture password for validation.

Display Password
Password: *******
Confirm: *******
This password will only grant permission to view previously saved capture files.

Capture Password
Password: *********
Confirm: *********
This password will grant permission to capture frames and to view capture files.

OK | Cancel | No Password | Help

Figure 16.19
Configuring Network Monitor passwords.

3. To remove all passwords, choose No Password. Click OK.

4. To change the capture password, first enter the current password in the Old Capture Password field.

5. To specify a display or capture password, complete the appropriate Password field. Then enter the password again in the associated Confirm field to verify the entry.

6. Click OK when passwords have been specified as desired. Then exit the Monitoring Agent utility.

Describing Your Network Cards

When one computer will be monitored by another, you should enter descriptions for each of the network adapters in the Network Monitor Agent. These descriptions enable the administrator monitoring the network to more easily identify the computer's network interfaces.

To describe network cards, follow these steps:

1. Open the Monitoring Agent dialog box in the Control Panel to open the Configure Network Monitoring Agent dialog box (refer to fig. 16.18).
2. Choose Describe Net Cards to open the Describe Net Cards dialog box (see fig. 16.20). In the figure, a description has been entered for the E100B1 adapter. The E100B2 adapter has not yet been described.

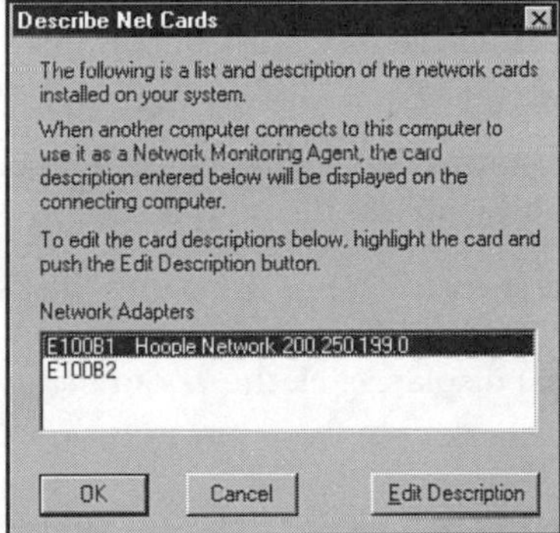

Figure 16.20
Describing network cards.

3. To change the description of a network adapter, select the entry and choose Edit Description to open a Change Net Card Description dialog box. Enter a new description and then click OK.
4. Repeat step 3 for each network card to be described.

Capturing Network Frames

Figure 16.21 shows the Network Monitor Capture window. The window contains the following four panes:

◆ **Graph Pane.** This pane includes bar charts that dynamically display current activity. The five bars in this pane are % Network Utilization, Frames Per Second, Bytes Per Second, Broadcasts Per Second, and Multicasts Per Second. You can display or hide this pane by clicking the Toggle Graph Pane button. (A line in the % Network Utilization bar designates the highest utilization encountered during the current capture. The numbers at the right ends of the other bars describe the highest measurement encountered.)

- **Total Statistics.** This pane displays cumulative network statistics. These statistics summarize network traffic in five areas: Network Statistics, Capture Statistics, Per Second Statistics, Network Card (MAC) Statistics, and Network Card (MAC) Error Statistics. You can display or hide this pane by clicking the Toggle Total Statistics Pane button.
- **Session Statistics.** This pane displays statistics about sessions currently operating on the network. You can display or hide this pane by clicking the Toggle Total Session Statistics Pane button.
- **Station Statistics.** This pane displays statistics about sessions in which the computer is participating. You can display or hide this pane by clicking the Toggle Total Station Statistics Pane button.

When capturing is active, network frames are captured into a buffer that is limited in size. When the buffer fills, older data is discarded to make room for new entries. Control capture status using the following options in the Capture menu: Start, Stop, Stop and View, Pause, and Continue. These functions can also be controlled by using buttons in the toolbar (see fig. 16.21).

Figure 16.21 was prepared while a capture was taking place. The information in the various panes is updated dynamically while capturing is active.

If you want, you can focus on the activity in one of the panes. Just select the pane and click the Zoom Pane button in the toolbar. The pane you selected expands to fill the available space. To return to normal display, click the Zoom Pane button again.

Saving Captured Data

After you are finished, choose Stop in the Capture menu to stop the capture. The data in the capture buffer can now be analyzed as required, or it can be saved for future study.

Creating an Address Database

When you first capture data in Network Monitor, most devices are identified by their physical network addresses (such as their MAC addresses). Data captured in figure 16.21 identifies most computers by their physical network addresses.

Because it is easier to associate a name with a computer rather than having to memorize MAC addresses, Network Monitor includes a feature that identifies the NetBIOS names of computers from which data is captured.

To build the address database, start capturing data on the network and let Network Monitor continue to collect data for an extended period of time. As traffic is generated, computers are added to the Session Statistics and Station Statistics panes, identified by their network addresses.

After capturing a large number of frames, stop capturing. Then choose the Find All Names command in the Capture menu. The frames in the capture buffer are scanned and the names are added to the address database. During future capture operations, computers are identified by name (see fig. 16.21).

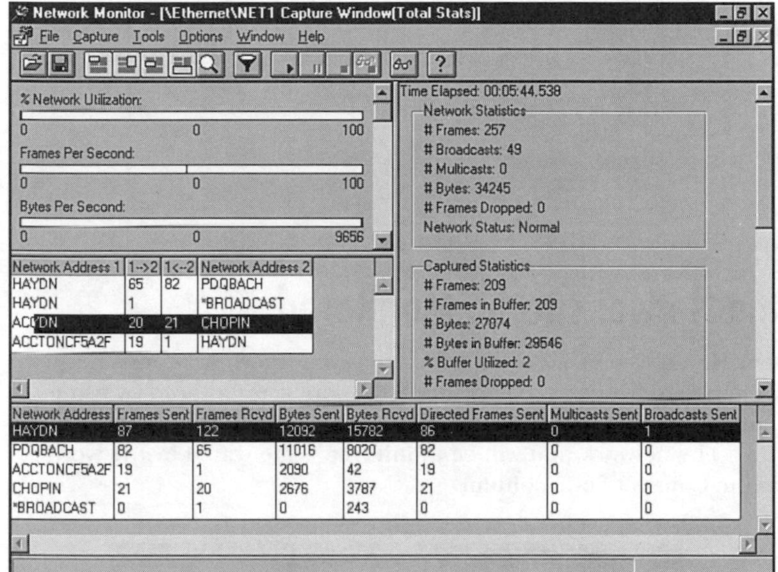

Figure 16.21

Computers identified by name in the Network Monitor.

Note

A bit of luck is required to capture frames that include computer names. Each time you capture data, collect names and add them to the database until the list is complete. You can save the names so that they remain after Network Monitor is closed.

You can view the address database, shown in figure 16.22, by choosing the Addresses command in the Capture menu. Notice in the figure that a given computer can be represented by multiple entries, associated with different protocols and network types.

In the Address Database dialog box, you can add, edit, and delete specific entries. You can save the database to a file with an .adr extension and load existing address files. The default address database, which is used unless you load another, is saved as Default.adr.

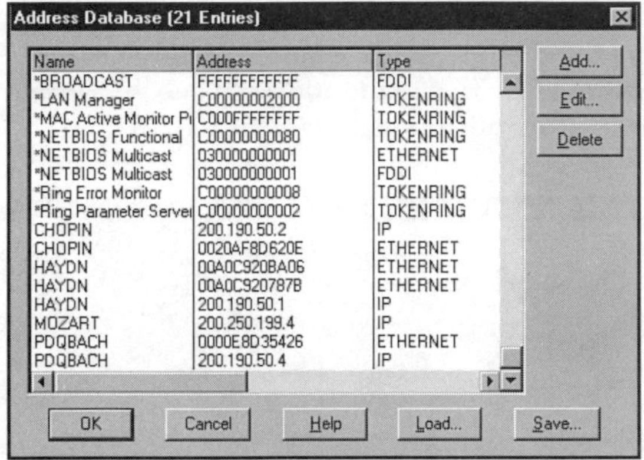

Figure 16.22

Viewing the address table.

Selecting the Network to be Monitored

When the Network Monitor computer is attached to two or more networks, it can monitor only one at a time. You can specify which network is monitored by using the Networks command in the Capture menu to open the Select Capture Network dialog box (see fig. 16.23). The network that will be monitored is identified by the word CONNECTED in the Connect State column.

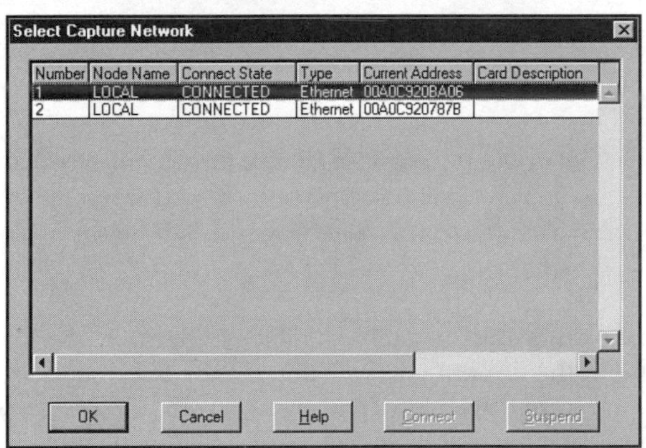

Figure 16.23

Selecting the connected network.

To change the connected network, select the network and choose Connect.

Managing the Capture Buffer

The data captured by Network Monitor is stored using system memory in a capture buffer. Due to lower performance of hard disks, disk storage cannot be used without the risk of losing frames during the capture process.

Ideally, the capture buffer should reside entirely in RAM. Virtual memory can be used, but frames might be lost. Therefore, setting the size of the capture buffer involves compromise. If the buffer is too small, it will not be large enough to capture a reasonable sample of network traffic. If the capture buffer is too large, part of it might be swapped into virtual memory and the efficiency of network data capture might be impaired.

To adjust the size of the capture buffer, choose the Buffer Settings command in the Capture menu to open the Capture Buffer Settings dialog box (see fig. 16.24). In the Buffer Size (in MB) field, adjust the size of the capture buffer as desired. By default, the maximum size of the capture buffer is 8 MB less than the amount of RAM installed in the computer. To maximize the amount of RAM available for the capture buffer, stop as many applications as possible. Ideally, only Network Monitor should be running.

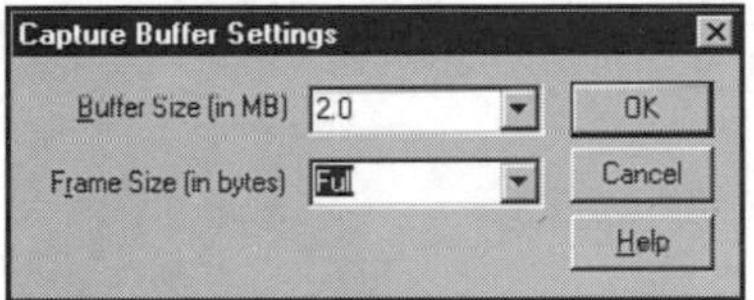

Figure 16.24
Configuring the capture buffer.

On a busy network, captured frames can quickly fill a capture buffer. In many cases, to ensure that the frames you need are captured, you need to capture more frames than will fit in the capture buffer at one time. Fortunately, the most critical bytes are often found at the beginning of the frame. In many cases, you can use the capture buffer more efficiently by capturing only the frame header to obtain the information you need. In other cases, you need only capture the header and a limited portion of the data field.

The Frame Size (in bytes) field in the Capture Buffer Settings dialog box specifies the number of bytes to be captured from the start of each frame that is captured. By default, the value of this field is Full, indicating that complete frames are to be captured. Suppose, however, that you are capturing data from an Ethernet network, and that you require only the bytes in the Ethernet frame headers, which make up the first 22 bytes of the frame. In that case, you can set the value of the Frame Size (in bytes) field to 64 (the smallest setting). Other size increments are available.

Avoiding Dropped Frames

When data is being captured, a significant part of the computer's processing capacity is required to dynamically update the Network Monitor display. When the CPU is busy, frames might be lost. You can reduce CPU loading by placing Network Monitor in dedicated capture mode.

Choose the Dedicated Capture Mode command in the Capture menu. When capturing is active, the Dedicated Mode dialog box displays (see fig. 16.25). If capturing is currently stopped, the Dedicated Mode box displays when capturing is started.

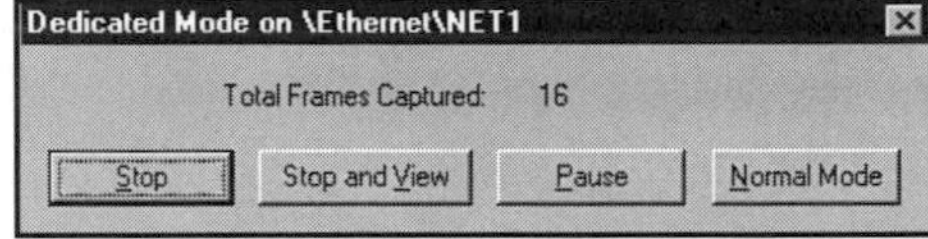

Figure 16.25
Capturing in dedicated mode.

When capturing in dedicated mode, only the number of captured frames is updated in the display. You can stop and pause capturing in the Dedicated Mode dialog box. If you choose Normal Mode, capturing continues while the full Network Monitor window displays. If you choose Stop and View, capturing stops and the Capture window displays. See the section "Examining Captured Data" later in this chapter for a discussion of the Capture window.

Using Capture Filters

On a large network, the volume of data can overwhelm you unless you have a way of focusing on specific types of data. Capture filters enable you to specify which types of frames will be captured, enabling you to capture data from a specific subset of computers or protocols.

Capture filters determine which frames will be stored in the capture buffer. All frames are reported in the performance statistics, however, regardless of any capture filter that might be in effect.

Structures of Capture Filters

Figure 16.26 shows the default capture filter, which is organized as a decision tree. Filters consist of three sets of criteria, connected by AND keywords. Frames are captured only if they meet all three of the following criteria: SAP/ETYPE, address, and pattern match.

The following sections describe the capture filter criteria.

SAP/ETYPE Filters

The frames associated with specific protocols are identified by hexadecimal numbers referred to as SAPs or ETYPEs. By default, Network Monitor captures frames matching all supported protocols. You can, however, restrict capturing to specific protocols by selecting the SAPs and ETYPEs that will pass through the filter.

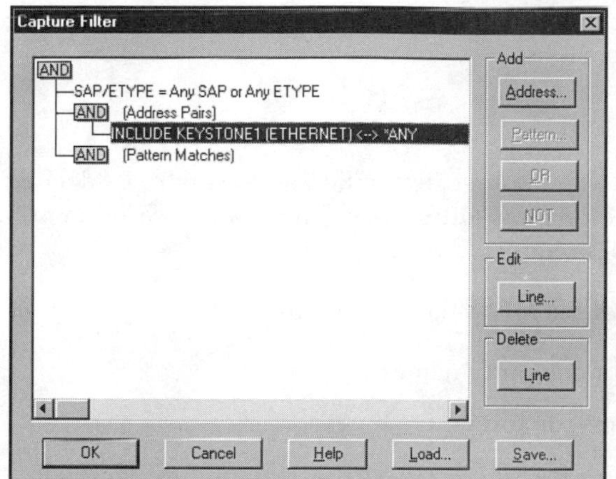

Figure 16.26

The default capture filter.

ETYPEs (EtherTypes) and SAPs (service acccss points) are used to specify the upper-laycr protocols associated with a frame. An EtherType of 800 hex is associated with the IP protocol, for example. An EtherType of 8137 hex is associated with NetWare running on an Ethernet II LAN.

To establish capture filters for specific SAPs or ETYPES, select the SAP/ETYPE= line in the Capture Filter dialog box. Then choose Line in the Edit box to open the Capture Filter SAPs and ETYPEs dialog box (see fig. 16.27). Network Monitor captures frames matching protocols specified in the Enabled Protocols list. By default, all supported ETYPEs and SAPs are shown in this list.

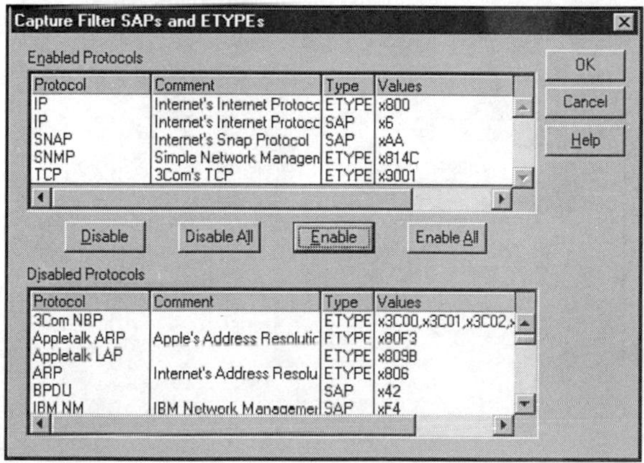

Figure 16.27

Filtering SAPs and ETYPEs.

To disable protocols, use the Disable and Disable All buttons to move protocols to the Disabled Protocols list. Figure 16.27 shows several protocols that have been disabled in this way.

To enable disabled protocols, use the Enable and Enable All buttons to move protocols to the Enabled Protocols list.

Address Filters

Every frame is associated with a source-destination address pair. By default, frames are captured for all source-destination address pairs. You can, however, limit capturing to specific address pairs if desired.

An address pair consists of the following components:

- A source address (or computer name)
- A destination address (or computer name)
- A direction arrow (-->, <--, or <->) specifying direction(s) in which traffic should be monitored
- The keyword INCLUDE or EXCLUDE, specifying whether frames should or should not be captured for this address pair

Address pairs are established in the Address Expression dialog box (see fig. 16.28). Open this dialog box as follows:

- To edit an existing address pair, select the entry in the entry under (Address Pairs) and choose Line in the Edit box, or double-click the entry.
- To create a new address pair, select any line in the (Address Pairs) section and choose Address in the Add box, or double-click the (Address Pairs) line.

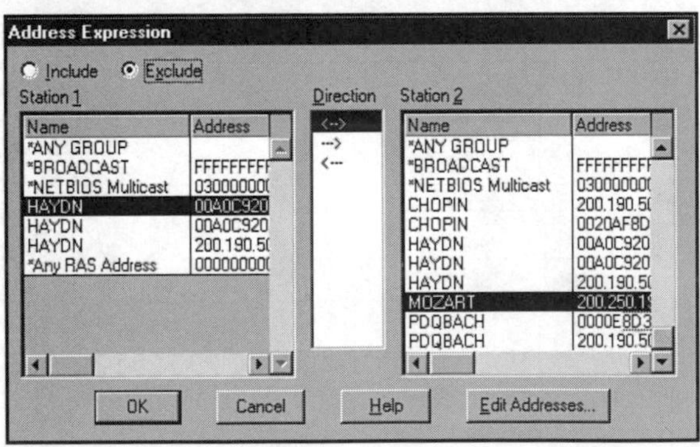

Figure 16.28
Filtering on Address Pairs.

You can specify up to four address pairs. Suppose you want to display all traffic between the HAYDN server and clients, but you want to ignore traffic with the MOZART server. The following address pairs establish a filter to accomplish that goal:

```
INCLUDE HAYDN <-> ANY
EXCLUDE HAYDN <-> MOZART
```

Figure 16.28 shows the establishment of the EXCLUDE HAYDN <-> MOZART filter.

When multiple address pairs are specified, EXCLUDE statements have priority. If a frame matches an EXCLUDE statement, it will not be captured even though it might also match one or more INCLUDE statements.

Data Pattern Filtering

In some cases, you may want to filter frames, depending on whether they include a specific pattern of bytes. In that case, you must specify one or more entries in the Pattern Matching section.

A pattern consists of the following two components:

- **The pattern of bytes to be matched.** These can be specified as a series of hexadecimal numbers or as a string of ASCII characters.
- **An offset that specifies the position of the bytes in the frame.** The offset can specify the position relative to the beginning of the frame or relative to the end of the topology header. (An offset of 0 specifies the first byte, which is 0 bytes from the beginning of the frame. Therefore, an offset of 19 specifies the twentieth byte of the frame.) Specify the offset from the beginning of the topology header if the topology protocol permits variable length headers, such as Ethernet or Token Ring MAC frames.

You don't get much help when constructing capture filters based on data patterns. When you need to analyze frames based on data patterns, you might find it easier to construct data filters instead. As the following section shows, considerable expertise is built into the expression editor, which knows the structures of the headers for all the supported protocols.

Clearly, to set up filters you must have a thorough understanding of the structures of the frames on your LAN. It is, unfortunately, beyond the scope of this book to consider the details of the message structures associated with the various protocols supported by Windows NT.

To add a filter, select the (Pattern Matches) line and choose Pattern in the Add box, or double-click the (Pattern Matches) line. This opens the Pattern Match dialog box (see fig. 16.29).

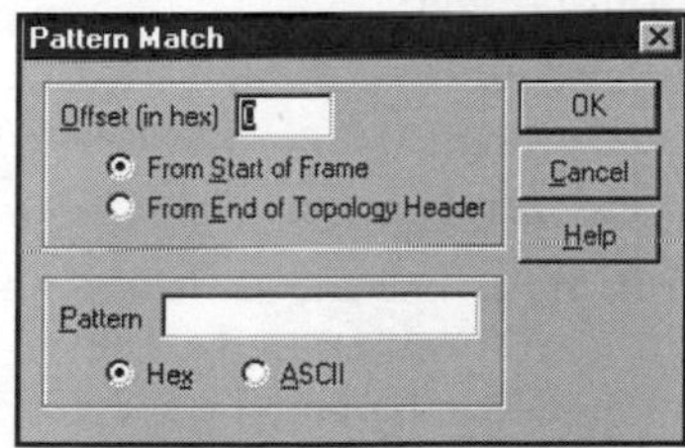

Figure 16.29

Entry form for a Pattern Match filter.

Using Logical Operators

When two or more patterns have been entered, you can set up complex filtering criteria using AND, OR, and NOT logical operations. Select the line to receive the logic operator and choose AND, OR, or NOT in the Add box. After you add a logical operator, you can drag around the operators and expressions to construct the logic tree that you require.

The logical operators function as follows:

- An AND branch of the tree will be true if all the expressions under the AND are true. Otherwise, the AND branch will be false.
- An OR branch of the tree will be true if any of the expressions under the OR are true. The OR branch will be false if all the expressions under the OR are false.
- A NOT will be true if the expression under the NOT is false. A NOT will be false if the expression under the NOT is true.

Note Pattern matching is the one place in this book that enters the esoteric realm of Boolean algebra. The programmers among you will be comfortable enough, but readers new to Boolean logic should be wary when setting up complex filters. It is quite easy to get the logic wrong and to establish filters that misbehave in mysterious ways. If you aren't capturing the frames you want, check the logic in your capture filter.

Using Capture Triggers

On occasion, you may want to have an action occur when a particular network situation occurs. A trigger describes a set of network conditions and an action that takes place when the conditions are met.

To define a capture trigger, choose the Trigger command in the Capture menu to open the Capture Trigger dialog box (see fig. 16.30). The following trigger types can be selected:

- **Nothing.** No triggers are specified. This is the default setting.
- **Pattern match.** The trigger is initiated when a specified pattern is identified in a captured frame. Specify the pattern in the Pattern box.
- **Buffer space.** The trigger is initiated when the free buffer space falls below the threshold specified in the Buffer Space box.
- **Pattern match then buffer space.** The trigger is initiated when the pattern specified in the Pattern box is identified, followed by a free buffer space that falls below the threshold specified in the Buffer Space box.
- **Buffer space then pattern match.** The trigger is initiated when the free buffer space falls below the threshold specified in the Buffer Space box, followed by the detection of a frame that includes the pattern specified in the Pattern box.

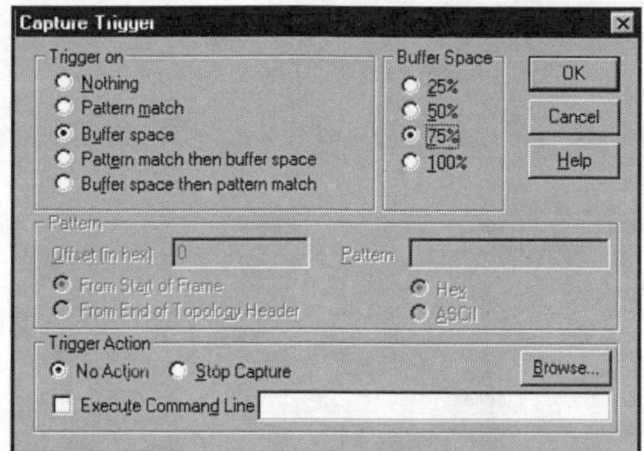

Figure 16.30
Establishing a capture trigger.

When the trigger occurs, one of three events can take place, as specified in the Trigger Action box:

- **No Action.** No action is taken when the trigger occurs.
- **Stop Capture.** Capturing will halt when the trigger occurs. This option ensures that the frame that initiated the trigger remains in the capture buffer.
- **Execute Command Line.** The command specified is executed when the trigger occurs. Include the path and command to be executed.

Saving Capture Data

After you have stopped capturing data, you can save the contents of the capture buffer for later analysis. Use the Save command in the File menu to save the capture buffer in a file with a .cap extension. Load previously saved data with the Open command in the File menu.

Examining Captured Data

After frames have been captured, you can examine them in considerable detail. To examine captured frames, do one of the following:

- When capturing is active, click the Stop and View Capture toolbar button, choose the Stop and View option in the Capture menu, or press Shift+F11.
- When capturing is stopped, click the Display Captured Data toolbar button, choose the Display Captured Data option in the Capture menu, or press F12.

Any of these actions opens the Capture dialog box (see fig. 16.31). At first, this dialog box includes one pane, which lists all frames currently in the capture buffer.

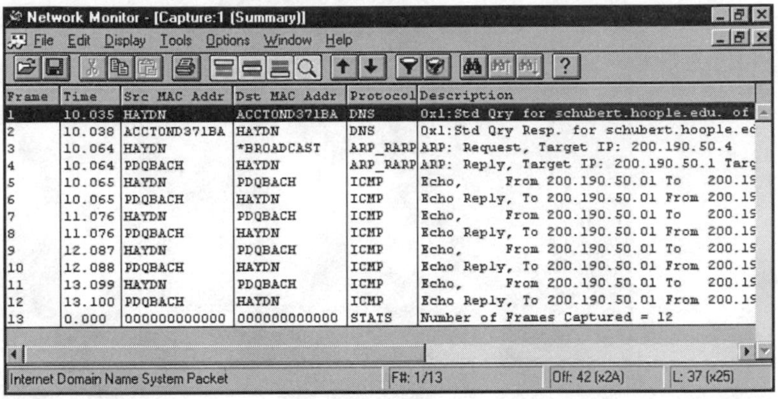

Network Monitor - [Capture:1 (Summary)]

File Edit Display Tools Options Window Help

Frame	Time	Src MAC Addr	Dst MAC Addr	Protocol	Description
1	10.035	HAYDN	ACCTOND371BA	DNS	0x1:Std Qry for schubert.hoople.edu. of
2	10.038	ACCTOND371BA	HAYDN	DNS	0x1:Std Qry Resp. for schubert.hoople.ed
3	10.064	HAYDN	*BROADCAST	ARP_RARP	ARP: Request, Target IP: 200.190.50.4
4	10.064	PDQBACH	HAYDN	ARP_RARP	ARP: Reply, Target IP: 200.190.50.1 Targ
5	10.065	HAYDN	PDQBACH	ICMP	Echo, From 200.190.50.01 To 200.19
6	10.065	PDQBACH	HAYDN	ICMP	Echo Reply, To 200.190.50.01 From 200.19
7	11.076	HAYDN	PDQBACH	ICMP	Echo, From 200.190.50.01 To 200.19
8	11.076	PDQBACH	HAYDN	ICMP	Echo Reply, To 200.190.50.01 From 200.19
9	12.087	HAYDN	PDQBACH	ICMP	Echo, From 200.190.50.01 To 200.19
10	12.088	PDQBACH	HAYDN	ICMP	Echo Reply, To 200.190.50.01 From 200.19
11	13.099	HAYDN	PDQBACH	ICMP	Echo, From 200.190.50.01 To 200.19
12	13.100	PDQBACH	HAYDN	ICMP	Echo Reply, To 200.190.50.01 From 200.19
13	0.000	000000000000	000000000000	STATS	Number of Frames Captured = 12

Internet Domain Name System Packet | F#: 1/13 | Off: 42 (x2A) | L: 37 (x25)

Figure 16.31

The Capture dialog box showing captured frames.

The capture consists of a single ping event in which HAYDN (the host running Network Monitor) pinged pdqbach.hoople.edu by name. As you determine from the Description column, the sequence begins with a DNS query to determine the IP address of pdqbach, together with a response from the DNS server. Next, an ARP request and ARP reply establish the physical address of a DNS server. Finally, a series of ICMP Echo and Echo Reply datagrams comprise four repeated pings.

To examine details for a frame, double-click the entry for the frame. In figure 16.32, an ICMP Echo datagram has been opened. The panes are as follows:

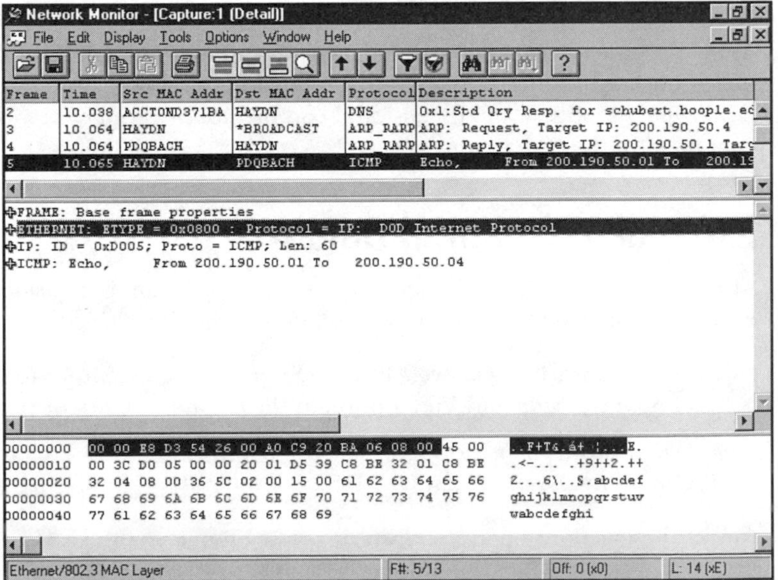

Figure 16.32

The Capture dialog box showing all panes.

- **Summary Pane.** This pane includes a one-line summary of each frame in the capture buffer.
- **Detail Pane.** This pane displays the contents of the frame, organized by Protocol layer.
- **Hex Pane.** This pane displays the data in the pane in hexadecimal and in ASCII characters. The bytes that are highlighted are associated with the protocol section that is highlighted in the Detail Pane.

The following sections discuss the Summary and Detail Panes.

The Summary Pane

The Summary Pane briefly describes each frame held in the capture buffer. To open a frame for detailed analysis, select the entry for that frame in the Summary Pane.

The source and destination computers are identified by the Src MAC Address and Dst MAC Address fields. If a name database has been created, NetBIOS names appear in place of hexadecimal physical addresses.

The Protocol field describes the protocol associated with the frame.

As you can see, the entries in the Description column can be reasonably clear (for example, "Echo Reply, To 200.190.50.01"), but they can also be downright obscure. To decode the descriptions, you need to learn the operational details of the protocols being analyzed.

The Detail Pane

Unless you are knowledgeable enough to undertake a byte-by-byte analysis of the data, the Detail Pane will probably be the pane that occupies most of your analytical effort. This pane translates the data in the various header layers into human-readable form.

In figure 16.33, the Detail Pane was expanded by selecting the pane and clicking the Zoom Pane button.

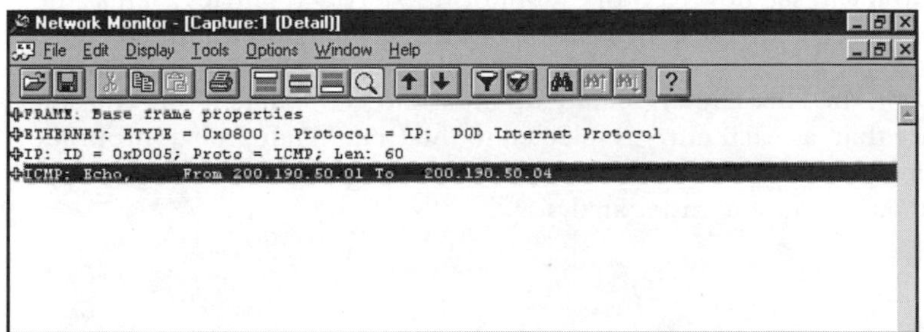

Figure 16.33

The Detail Pane.

The frame that is represented is an ICMP Echo frame. In figure 16.34, notice that some entries are tagged with a + to the left, indicating that the entry can be expanded by clicking the + to show greater detail. To illustrate the significance of the discussion in Part I, it is worthwhile to open each entry and examine the details.

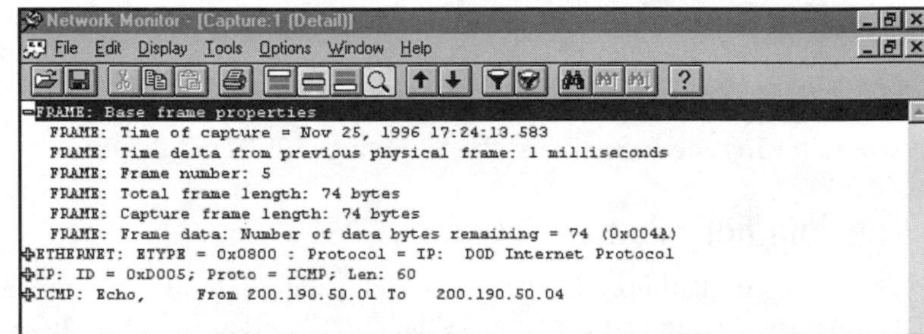

Figure 16.34

An example of the FRAME layer.

First, notice the layers of encapsulation:

- **FRAME.** This layer describes the raw characteristics of the frame at the physical layer.
- **ETHERNET.** This layer describes the MAC sublayer characteristics.
- **IP.** This layer describes the IP protocol encapsulation of the ICMP message.
- **ICMP.** Here at last is the ICMP message itself.

It is time to open each of these layers for a more detailed examination. (After opening the entry, the + changes to a –, indicating that the entry is fully expanded.) First, the FRAME layer, containing raw frame data, is shown in figure 16.35. Notice in the decoding that there is no notion of the frame's purpose or type of data at this layer. There is only the notion that the frame consists of a certain number of bytes to be transmitted.

In figure 16.35, the ETHERNET entry has been expanded. Each entry under the ETHERNET heading corresponds to a field in the Ethernet frame format. Within the example entry, you can see how Network Monitor has decoded entries such as the destination and source addresses, the frame length, and the length of the data field.

In this screen shot, the Hex Pane is included, which shows the data in raw, hexadecimal form. Notice that, as each entry is selected in the Detail Pane, the appropriate bytes are illuminated in the Hex Pane. This gives you an appreciation for the way the Detail Pane translates data for easier analysis.

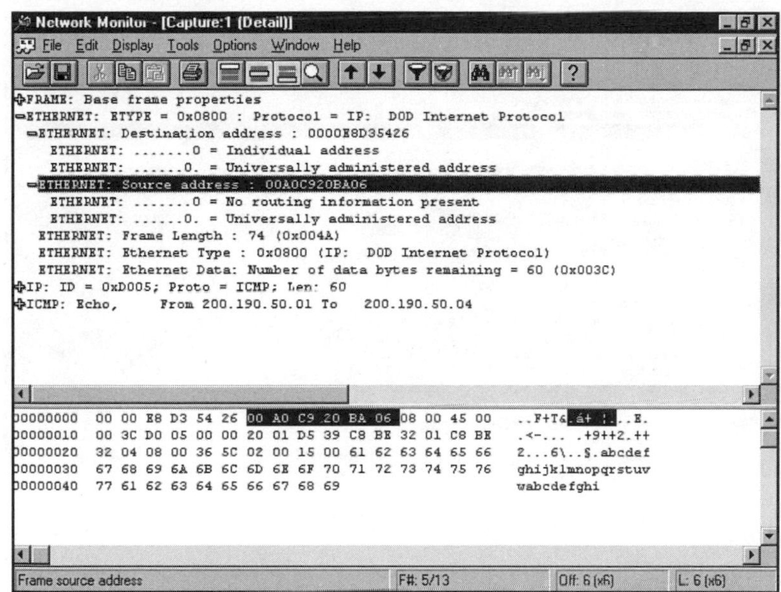

Figure 16.35

Details of the Ethernet frame.

When you select a field in the Detail Pane, the legend at the bottom of the window provides the following useful information about the field:

- A brief description of the field is shown.
- **F#.** This box designation specifies the frame's position in the capture buffer. F# 4/10, for example, designates that this is the fourth of 10 frames captured.
- **Off:.** This box specifies the offset of the selected byte from the start of the frame. Off: 74(x4A), for example, specifies that the selected byte is offset 74 (decimal) bytes (4A hex) from the first byte of the frame. The first byte of the frame has an offset of 0. (This field is a valuable guide when setting up capture and display filters.)
- **L:.** This box specifies the length of the field in bytes.

Figure 16.36 expands the data at the IP datagram level. Both the IP: Service Type and the IP: Flags Summary have been expanded to show their contents. Given your experience in earlier chapters, you should be able to interpret the contents of this datagram.

Finally, in figure 16.37, you come to the ICMP payload.

Clearly, given the complexity of the data, there is nothing easy about protocol analysis. Your understanding of this information can go a long way when it is necessary to troubleshoot your network.

Figure 16.36

Details of the IP datagram header.

```
Network Monitor - [Capture:1 (Detail)]
File Edit Display Tools Options Window Help
+FRAME: Base frame properties
+ETHERNET: ETYPE = 0x0800 : Protocol = IP:  DOD Internet Protocol
-IP: ID = 0xD005; Proto = ICMP; Len: 60
  IP: Version = 4 (0x4)
  IP: Header Length = 20 (0x14)
 -IP: Service Type = 0 (0x0)
    IP: Precedence = Routine
    IP: ...0.... = Normal Delay
    IP: ....0... = Normal Throughput
    IP: .....0.. = Normal Reliability
  IP: Total Length = 60 (0x3C)
  IP: Identification = 53253 (0xD005)
 -IP: Flags Summary = 0 (0x0)
    IP: .......0 = Last fragment in datagram
    IP: ......0. = May fragment datagram if necessary
  IP: Fragment Offset = 0 (0x0) bytes
  IP: Time to Live = 32 (0x20)
  IP: Protocol = ICMP - Internet Control Message
  IP: Checksum = 0xD539
  IP: Source Address = 200.190.50.1
  IP: Destination Address = 200.190.50.4
  IP: Data: Number of data bytes remaining = 40 (0x0028)
+ICMP: Echo,     From 200.190.50.01 To   200.190.50.04
Summary of the IP packet    F#: 5/13    Off: 14 (xE)    L: 20 (x14)
```

Figure 16.37

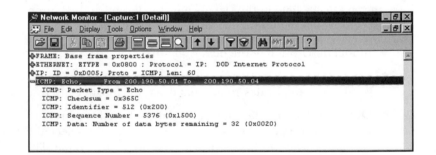

Details of the ICMP echo message.

```
Network Monitor - [Capture:1 (Detail)]
File Edit Display Tools Options Window Help
+FRAME: Base frame properties
+ETHERNET: ETYPE = 0x0800 : Protocol = IP:  DOD Internet Protocol
+IP: ID = 0xD005; Proto = ICMP; Len: 60
-ICMP: Echo,     From 200.190.50.01 To   200.190.50.04
  ICMP: Packet Type = Echo
  ICMP: Checksum = 0x365C
  ICMP: Identifier = 512 (0x200)
  ICMP: Sequence Number = 5376 (0x1500)
  ICMP: Data: Number of data bytes remaining = 32 (0x0020)
```

Display Filters

Okay, you have collected a buffer full of frames and you want to focus your attention on just a few without scrolling through the thousands that are available? No problem, just design a display filter. Choose Filter in the Display menu to open a dialog box with which you can design a display filter. Display filters are a bit different from capture filters, so it's necessary here to take a brief look at the procedure.

Figure 16.38 shows the Display Filter dialog box, showing the default filter that displays frames for all protocols and computer addresses.

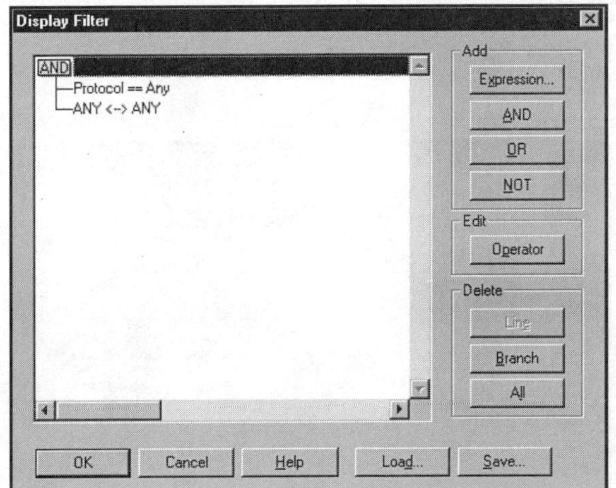

Figure 16.38

The default Display Filter dialog box.

Adding Expressions

To add an expression to the display filter, select the line that will precede the new expression and choose Expression in the Add box to open the Expression dialog box (see fig. 16.39). This dialog box has three tabs, enabling you to enter expressions based on three types of properties: address, protocol, and property. Figure 16.39 shows the Address tab.

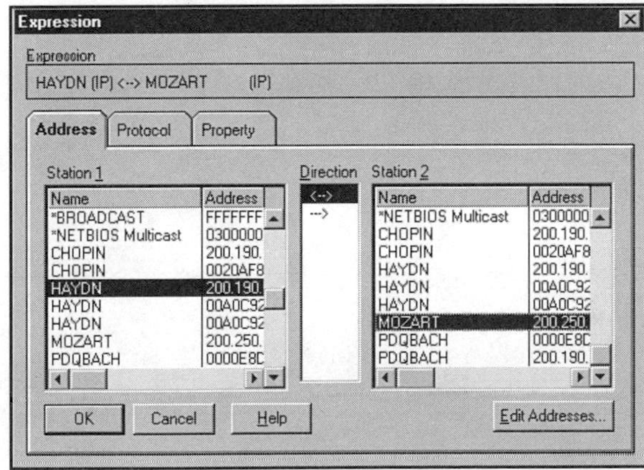

Figure 16.39

Constructing an address expression for a display filter.

Address expressions specify the addresses of two computers whose frames are to be captured together with a direction specification. As you select entries for Station 1, Direction, and Station 2, the expression you are constructing displays in the Expression box.

The Protocol tab enables you to enable and disable filters for specific protocols (see fig. 16.40). If a protocol is listed in the Disabled Properties list, frames for that protocol do not display.

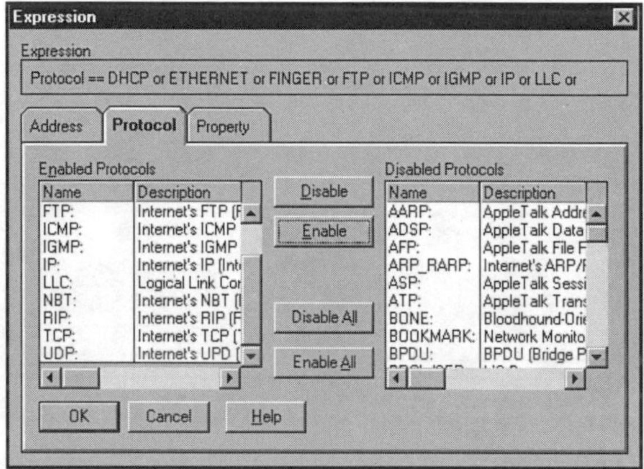

Figure 16.40

Constructing a protocol expression for a display filter.

The Property tab is used to construct filters based on data patterns (see fig. 16.41). As you saw, you receive no help when establishing data patterns for capture filters. Considerable help is available, however, when constructing display filters.

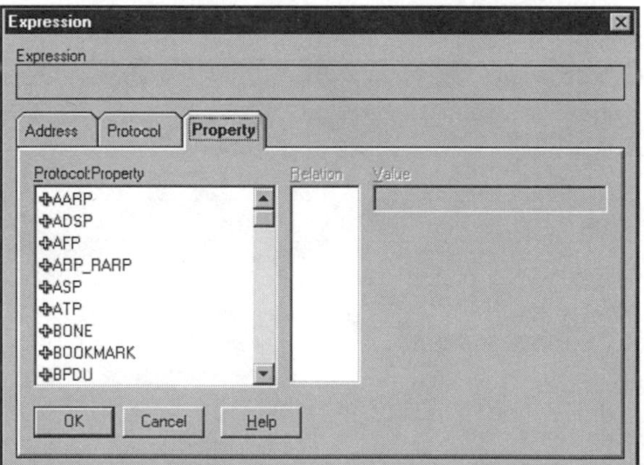

Figure 16.41

The display filter Property tab.

You can open each of the protocols in the Protocol Property list to list the data fields in the protocol header. In figure 16.42, the IP protocol has been expanded to reveal the fields of an IP datagram header. After selecting Destination Address, a list of valid options is revealed in the Relation list. And, although you could have manually entered a hex number in the Value field, usually you can select one of the predefined options based on the IP addresses that Network Monitor has learned. After selecting CHOPIN, the IP address was entered automatically.

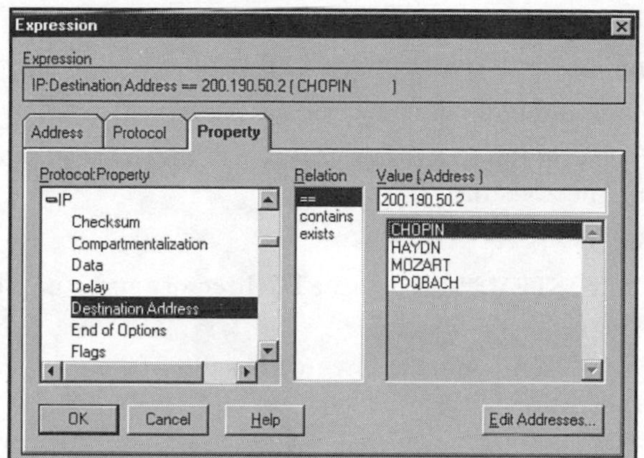

Figure 16.42

Constructing a protocol property expression for a display filter.

It is clearly easier to construct display filters rather than capture filters. You may want to filter in two stages. To avoid having unwanted frames cluttering the capture buffer, construct capture filters to limit the general categories of frames that are captured, perhaps sorting by protocol (using SAP or ETYPE filters). Then use display filters to zoom in on the details and isolate specific frames.

Using Logical Operators

You can use AND, OR, and NOT operators to modify the expressions in display filters. To add a logical operator to an expression, select the expression and choose AND, OR, or NOT. The easiest way to organize the structure of the logic tree is to drag around expressions and operators.

To change a logical operator in a display filter, click the operator icon. The icon changes from AND to OR to NOT with each click.

Practice

The following exercise gives you a chance to try several of the commands that you have looked at here. This lab requires that you have networking installed and that you have IIS installed.

Exercise 1—Using the FTP Command to Move Files

In this exercise, you work with the FTP command to try to move some files around. This exercise refers to the standard locations. If you have installed components in other locations, please substitute these locations.

1. Copy a group of files into the C:\INETPUB\FTPROOT directory.
2. Start an FTP session to your system by using FTP 127.0.0.1.
3. Log on as anonymous and enter anything for the password.
4. Attempt to list the files on the FTP server (use ls -l.) Can you see the files you copied? (You should be able to.)
5. Exit the FTP session (press Ctrl+C).
6. Go to the C:\WINNT\SYSTEM32\DRIVERS\ETC directory and copy SERVICES to SERVICES.GOOD.
7. Edit the SERVICES file and delete the line that has the FTP entry (leave the FTP_DATA entry).
8. Save the file and then shut down and restart your computer.
9. Go to the Internet Service Manager, and double-click the FTP service. Change the port from 21 to 9999. Ensure that Allow only anonymous is not selected.
10. On the Directories tab, double-click the Home directory. Ensure both the Read and Write check boxes are selected.
11. Click OK. You should receive a warning that the changes will not take effect until you restart the service.
12. Stop and restart the FTP service.
13. Attempt again to connect using FTP 127.0.0.1. Were you able to? (No. The FTP client attempts to connect to port 21 by default.)
14. Start an FTP session, type **FTP,** and press Enter.
15. Try to open your site using OPEN 127.0.0.1 4021. Does this work? (This should enable you to connect.)
16. Start another DOS prompt. Enter **NETSTAT**.
17. Enter your administrator account and password to log on.
18. Switch to binary by typing **BINARY**.
19. Enter the command ls -l. You should receive a listing of the files that you put in the directory.
20. Choose a file and type **GET *filename.ext*.** The file should transfer to the current directory. Type **! DIR** to check.
21. Rename the local file name using **! ren *filename.ext filename.RJS*.**
22. Put a copy back on the FTP server using **PUT *filename.RJS*.**
23. Verify by using **ls -l**.
24. Close the FTP session by using **BYE**.

You will want to change the port and security back to their original state. Also copy SERVICES.GOOD over the top of the SERVICES file.

Exercise 2—Entering and Removing Entries from the ARP Cache

This exercise requires that you actually be connected to a network. You look at the ARP cache and try entering and removing static entries from it.

1. View the current ARP cache by using **arp -a**.
2. Ping a host on your network by using *ping host_ip_address* and view the ARP cache again by using **arp -a**.
3. Is there a new entry? (There should be an entry for the system you pinged.)
4. Ping `www.microsoft.com`.

   Is this a new entry? (There should now be another entry in the ARP cache.)
5. Ping `www.intel.com`.

   Is there a new entry? (No. Both of the preceding addresses will have to find the router, and will have resolved the same IP to MAC address for it.)
6. Ping your default gateway.
7. Enter the following command, substituting your ARP -s *your_gateway_address* B4-D5-F7-D3-B4-B7
8. Check the ARP cache by using **arp -a**.
9. Ping your default gateway. Were you successful? (No. The system attempts to reach the default gateway at the supplied MAC address.)
10. Try pinging different sites that you know of on the Internet. Could you? (No. You will not be able to pass your default gateway.)

Remove the static address, arp -d your_gateway_address.

Exercise 3(A)—Using the Network Monitor and Agent

In this exercise, you use the Network Monitor and Agent to view ARP requests. At the very least, you need to have a functioning network card in your system for this.

1. Open the Network dialog box. From the Services tab, choose Add.
2. Select the Network Monitor and Agent from the list and then click OK.
3. Enter the directory for your NT source files.
4. Click OK to close the Network dialog box.
5. When prompted, restart your system.

This exercise requires that you know three IP addresses (other than your own). You will need an address local to your subnet, an address that is currently remote (but wouldn't be if your subnet mask covered one less octet), and the address of your router.

To figure this out, try calculating all the valid hosts on the network you are on (see Chapter 6, "Subnetting"). The following is an example employing the addresses used in most of the exercises.

IP address 148.53.66.7 with a subnet mask of 255.255.192.0

The valid hosts on this subnet are 148.53.64.1 to 148.53.127.254. Currently all addresses from 148.53.128.1 to 148.53.191.254 are remote. They won't be, however, if 255.255.0.0 is used as a subnet mask. Therefore, the local host is any number in the first range, and the remote is any number in the second range.

Viewing an ARP Broadcast

In this part of the exercise, you look at a simple ARP broadcast.

1. Start a command prompt and also start the Network Monitor.
2. In the Network Monitor, choose Capture, Start.
3. Switch to the command prompt and ping the local host. (It doesn't matter whether you see it.)
4. Switch back to the Network Monitor. Choose Capture, Stop and View.
5. A list of the packets sent or received by your system appears.
6. One of the first should be a ARP:Request. Double-click it.
7. Expand the packet completely. (Click the plus signs so that all the packet is in view.)
8. In the packet, find the target MAC and IP addresses.
9. Was the IP address the one you entered? Yes.
10. What is the MAC address? All 0s. At this point the address is unknown.
11. If the ping worked on your system, look in the Summary Pane at the top of the screen. What is the next packet that you received? It should be an ARP:Reply.

Viewing ARP Broadcasts for Remote Hosts

Now you perform the same exercise. This time, however, you use a remote host address.

1. In the Network Monitor, choose File, Close. This closes the window with the captured data.
2. Choose Capture, Start. A message appears asking whether you want to save the data. Choose No.
3. Switch to the command prompt and ping the remote host. (It doesn't matter whether you see it.)
4. Switch back to the Network Monitor. Choose Capture, Stop and View.

5. Find the ARP:Request packet, and double-click it.
6. Expand the packet completely.
7. In the packet, find the target MAC and IP addresses.
8. Was the IP address the one you entered? No, it should be the address of the router.
9. What is the MAC address? All 0s. At this point, the address is unknown.
10. If the ping worked on your system, look in the Summary Pane at the top of the screen. What is the next packet that you received? (It should be an ARP:Reply from the router.)

Changing the Subnet Mask

Now you change your subnet mask and check the packet again.

Open the Network dialog box. From the Protocol tab, double-click the TCP/IP protocol.

Change the last non-0 number to a zero (make a note of it so that you can put it back later). In the case previously discussed, the subnet mask was 255.255.192.0, so it changes to 255.255.0.0.

Note If you use DHCP, run IPCONFIG from the command prompt and note the values. For the duration of the exercise, enter this information as a static IP address. Remember to set it back after the exercise.)

Click OK on the TCP/IP Configuration dialog box and on the Network dialog box. Then restart your system.

1. Start the Network Monitor and a command prompt.
2. Choose Capture, Start.
3. Switch to the command prompt and ping the local host.
4. Now ping the remote host.
5. Switch back to the Network Monitor. Choose Capture, Stop and View. (There should be two ARP Request packets.)
6. Find the first ARP:Request packet, and then double-click it.
7. Expand the packet completely.
8. In the packet, find the target MAC and IP addresses.
9. Was the IP address the one you entered? (Yes. The local host IP address.)
10. In the Summary Pane, highlight the second ARP:Request.

11. What IP address was this packet to? (This was sent directly to the remote host IP address.)
12. What IP address should this packet have been sent to? (The router as it was in the last exercise.)
13. What effect does this have on communications? (The use of it enables you to communicate with some but not all hosts. Any host on the local subnet is fine, as well as some remote hosts. The other subnet in this organization will be invisible.)

Summary

You need to use many different utilities when working with TCP/IP. This chapter has covered the basic utilities that come with Windows NT 4. By now you should understand the different utilities and which ones you should use in different circumstances.

Test Yourself

1. How should you use Ping to test a TCP/IP connection?
2. Which utility enables you to see all the IP type connections to your system?
3. What command can you use to purge and reload the NetBIOS Name Cache?
4. What utility enables you to see the packets coming into and out of your computer?
5. What utilities can be used to copy files?
6. What is the main difference between FTP and TFTP?
7. What is the purpose of TRACERT?
8. What are the three switches for the IPCONFIG utility? What do they do?
9. How long will a static ARP cache entry remain in the cache?
10. When using the RSH and RCP commands, where must your name be listed?
11. If an FTP server is set to use port 6374, how do you start a session with it?
12. What two emulation modes does Telnet support? Which is more common?
13. What can the Network Monitor that comes with NT capture?
14. How does TRACERT trace a route?
15. What command can you use to get information on the users currently on a system?

16. If you have a text file name Myfile.txt, what LPR command can be used to print it to a printer called PRT23 which is on a system with the IP address of 148.53.64.7?
17. How do you start an interactive NSLOOKUP session?
18. How do you list all the mail servers in a given domain?
19. What command can you use to check the status of your print job on a printer called PRT77 that is run by a Unix print server called BOX7?
20. How can you view the routing table of your computer?
21. In the case of a REXEC command, which CPU actually runs the instructions?

Test Yourself Answers

1. Using Ping you should:

   ping 127.0.0.7

   ping *your_IP_address*

   ping *local_hosts_ip_address*

   ping *remote_hosts_ip_address*

   ping *host_name*

   ping *NetBIOS_name*
2. You can use NETSTAT -a. This displays all connections for both clients and services using WinSock.
3. The NBTSTAT -R command performs this function.
4. The Network Monitor captures the packets moving into and out of your system.
5. Three utilities can be used to copy files: FTP, TFTP, and RCP.
6. FTP is a connection-oriented file transfer utility that uses TCP as the Transport layer protocol. TFTP is connectionless and uses UDP as a transport protocol.
7. The TRACERT utility enables you to trace the path your packet takes as it moves across the network.
8. The switches are as follows: /ALL (this displays detailed information about the adapters and the system in general), /RELEASE (this releases an IP address that has been supplied by a DHCP server), and /RENEW (this forces a DHCP client to renew its IP address and thereby the configuration information).
9. Static entries in the ARP cache remain until the system is restarted or the entry is cleared by being deleted.
10. In using these commands, your name must be listed in the .rhosts file on the system with which you are communicating.

11. First you start the FTP client, and then issue the OPEN command, giving the host name followed by the port number: OPEN FTP.HOST.NET 6374, for example.
12. Telnet works with both VT100 and VT52 emulation. The VT100 is more common.
13. The Network Monitor that comes with NT can only capture packets sent to or from your system. The version that comes with SMS (Systems Management Server) can capture packets from any system that has the monitor agent installed.
14. Because a router that discards a packet is supposed to return an ICMP message saying the packet is discarded, TRACERT can trace the route by sending multiple packets to the target system with different Time to Live values. The first would have a TTL of 1, the second would have a TTL of 2, and so forth. This causes every router in the path to drop the packet and therefore identify itself in the ICMP message.
15. The Finger command reports information on the current users of a system.
16. The command would be LPR -S148.53.64.7 -PPRT23 MYFILE.TXT.
17. To start an interactive NSLOOKUP session, type **NSLOOKUP** and press Enter.
18. You can use an NSLOOKUP session and enter the command **ls-t mx domain**.
19. The command is LPQ -SBOX7 -PPRT77.
20. The command is ROUTE PRINT.
21. The CPU on the remote host runs the instructions.

CHAPTER 17

Management Utilities: SNMP and the Performance Monitor

A big part of the job of any network administrator is the actual administration of the network. This means taking care of the day to day operations—in other words, management. If you have a small network with 500 or 600 stations and 10 to 20 servers, the management is fairly simple.

What happens though if you have 5,000 or 6,000 stations on your network and 500 or 600 servers? As well, assume that the servers are a mix of NT, Unix, and Netware. The management of this type of network is obviously more complex than that of a smaller network. Now take the example one step further; you must somehow manage a large group of computers on the Internet—spread out physically across the entire world.

As you may have guessed, the problems can become enormous. Therefore in the early days of the Internet, the problem needed to be addressed. Another protocol was developed, and more standards were created that enabled managers to reach out across the network to manage not only servers but also the physical devices such as the routers and bridges, Ethernet hubs, Token Ring maus (multistation access units), and so on.

SNMP Roles

The protocol that was developed was the Simple Network Management Protocol (SNMP). The SNMP protocol essentially has two main pieces. These are the following:

- **SNMP Managers.** These are stations that have SNMP management software installed. The Management software handles querying the devices that it manages and also looks for alert conditions on the network.
- **SNMP Agents.** This is the part of the protocol that sits in the devices and responds to the requests of the Management software. The Agent is also responsible for sending alerts to the managers on the network.

SNMP is a very simple protocol. The SNMP protocol uses UDP (on port 161) packets to send and receive the information sent back and forth between the Management software and the SNMP Agent.

In total, you can use the following four commands in the SNMP protocol:

- **GET.** This command comes from a Manager, and tells the Agent to return the current value for a particular setting (the number of user accounts in the system, for example).
- **GET-NEXT.** This tells the Agent to return the value for the next setting that it has. (This could be used to get the name of each service in sequence.)
- **SET.** When a Manager sends this packet, it includes a value. The Agent sets the value of a given setting to whatever is sent. (Set a value—very few values can be set in this way.)
- **TRAP.** Occasionally the Agent sends a TRAP. This indicates an alert condition and is intended to alert the Manager to the condition. (An unauthorized unit has sent an SNMP packet to the system, for example.)

MIBs (Management Information Base)

If an SNMP Agent is going to return values to a Manager or set values that it receives from the Manager, there must be some known data structure that can be addressed easily over the network. The structure used by the SNMP protocol is the Management Information Base (MIB). Different MIBs can be supported. NT supports four main MIBs.

MIBs were started by the International Standards Organization, and are broken down in much the same way that the DNS structure is. That is, there is a root to the MIBs, and then you go down a level and there are a few branches, and so on until you get to the MIBs that deal with the Internet (see fig. 17.1).

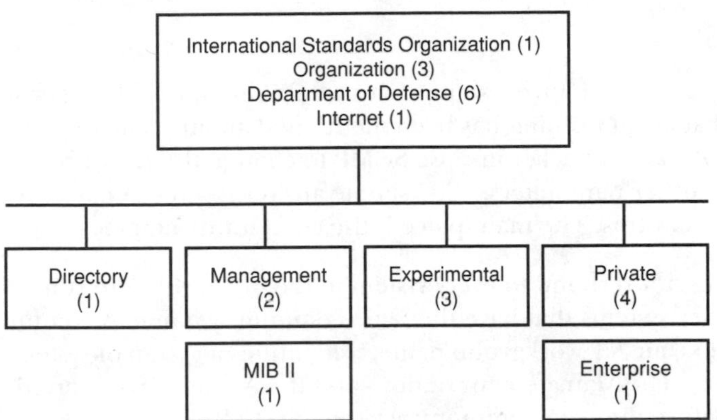

Figure 17.1
Breakdown of MIBs that affect TCP/IP and NT.

In figure 17.1, you can see that there is an Internet MIB II. The full name of the MIB is "International Standards Organization \ Organization \ Department of Defense \ Internet \ Management \ MIB II." If you had to send all of this, the packet size for the SNMP packets would increase dramatically.

You might have noticed that all the listed parts of the MIB are also numbered. If you look at the name this way, it is ".1.3.6.1.2.1." This is obviously a lot easier to deal with from the network point of view. For the humans that are involved, however, it makes little to no sense. Can *you* tell what ".1.3.6.1.4.1.311.1.2.1.18" is? No. This is not something the average computer user would know. This means that Management software needs to have a copy of the MIB that provides a translation between the value and the name of the object.

Windows NT 4 supports the following four MIBs:

- **Internet MIB II.** Used for the standard TCP/IP objects. This makes possible the management of stations and routers through an entire intranet or on the Internet. Currently, 171 objects can be managed using this MIB.
- **LAN Manager MIB II.** A group of 90 objects that deal with NT itself. This makes possible the management of Windows NT workstations and servers that have the SNMP agent installed.
- **DHCP MIB.** Because this is a simple protocol (DHCP that is), only 14 objects need to be managed in the MIB.
- **WINS MIB.** This is a Microsoft-specific protocol. Therefore a Microsoft MIB with 70 objects can be managed.

Windows NT comes with an SNMP Agent, currently Microsoft has not released a Management Tool. Instead, Microsoft has included a Manager API, and intends to allow others to produce the software.

Communities

If this was all there was to the entire system, chaos would reign over the network. You may have noticed that as yet nothing has been mentioned about security. If there is no security on SNMP, can't a hacker just use SNMP to change the IP address of any system? What about other parameters? The simple answer is—yes. A couple of things, however, prevent this. The main piece is the community name.

An SNMP Agent does not respond to every system in the world that can run SNMP. It responds only to other systems that have the same community name. A community name is very much like an NT workgroup name; it identifies a group of systems managed as one unit. The Management stations and the Agents must share the same community name before they can communicate (see fig. 17.2).

Figure 17.2

A sample network with community names.

Figure 17.2 shows two management stations—one is in community CA, the other is in community CB. There are six other stations in community CA that the CA Management station can work with, and only three stations that the CB Management station can work with.

You can take a couple of other security measures. The most important one if you connect to the Internet is to filter UDP port 161 at the router. This means that you cannot manage the network across the Internet (unless you use PPTP; see the next chapter). Others, however, cannot do so either.

You can also tell the Agent software to which management systems it can respond. In this way, you can also prevent internal hackers from taking over workstation management.

Installing and Configuring SNMP

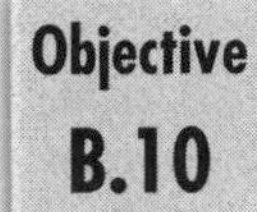

Now that you have an understanding of the concepts of SNMP, look at the actual installation of the SNMP Agent on Windows NT. This is a simple process, you just follow these steps:

1. Open the Network dialog box.
2. From the Services tab, choose Add.
3. From the dialog box, choose the SNMP Agent (see fig. 17.3).

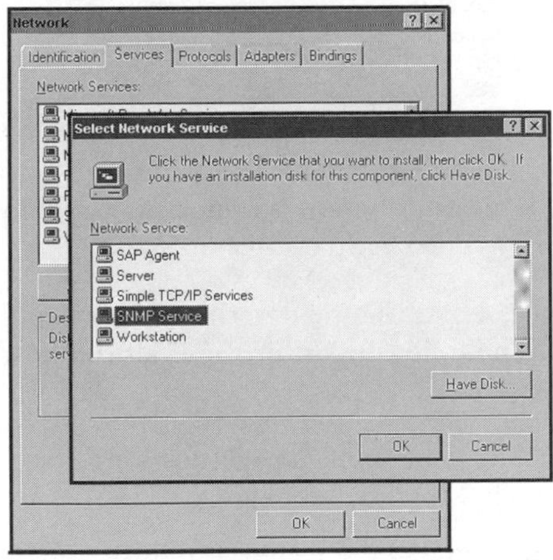

Figure 17.3
Adding the SNMP Agent.

4. Click OK, and then enter the directory for your NT source files.
5. Click OK to close the Network dialog box.
6. The SNMP Agent asks for its configuration. Enter the information for your network (see the following sections), and then choose OK.
7. When prompted, restart your system.

In the configuration for the SNMP service, there are three tabs. The next sections discuss the options that are on each of the tabs.

The Agent Tab

The Agent tab provides the basic information about the SNMP agent, and what the SNMP agent handles. Figure 17.4 shows the Microsoft SNMP Properties Agent tab.

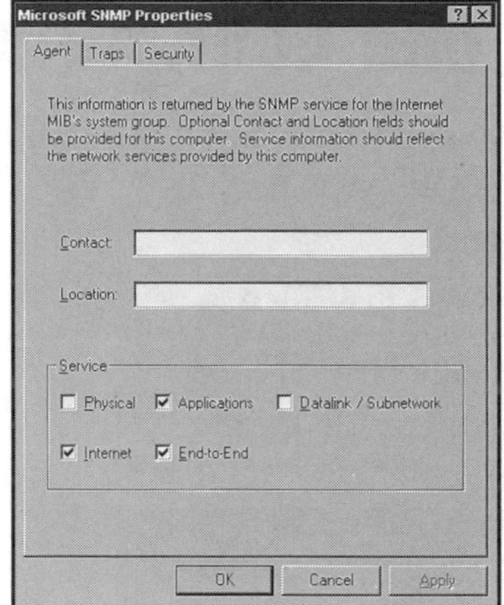

Figure 17.4
The Agent tab.

This tab has two main sections. The first section is the Name and Location of the contact person for this system. This information is optional, although it makes finding the system easier in the case of a Trap event.

There is also a series of five check boxes. These describe the service that the computer provides to the network. The following list provides a brief description of each of the services:

- **Physical.** This option needs to be set if the Windows NT system will be managing any physical devices such as network repeaters.
- **Applications.** This should always be selected. It tells the Agent that the NT system will run software that will use TCP/IP.
- **Datalink / Subnetwork.** Use this if the NT system will be managing a bridge.
- **Internet.** This option needs to be selected if the NT system will be acting as an IP router.
- **End-to-End.** This option tells the agent software that the system will participate in IP hosts-to-host communications. This options should always be selected.

The Traps Tab

This sets the destination for Traps to be sent to. Because a single host might be a member of more than one community, you can set Trap destinations for each of the community names. Figure 17.5 shows the Traps tab.

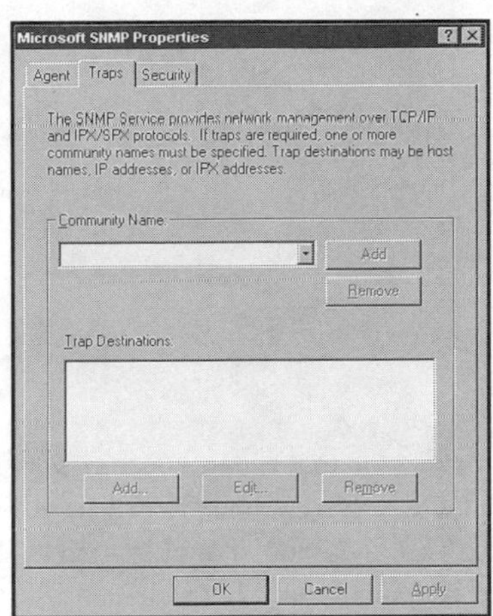

Figure 17.5

The Traps tab.

To add a Trap destination, follow these steps:

1. Choose the community name from the list, or click Add to add it.
2. Click the Add button for the hosts and enter either the IP address or the host name for the management station that should receive the Traps.

The Security Tab

This tab is important because it establishes the community name or names that this system will be part of. It also enables you to set authentication Traps and the Managers that you should respond to. Figure 17.6 shows what this tab looks like.

The options that can be set from this tab include the following:

- **Send Authentication Trap.** This sends an event Trap to the Manager of the system (set on the Traps tab) if a host that is not within your community or that is not listed in the lower section attempts to send you an SNMP packet.
- **Accepted Community Names.** This is a list of the community names to which the system responds. The default community name is public. You should remove this and enter the community name that you wish to use.

Figure 17.6

The Security tab.

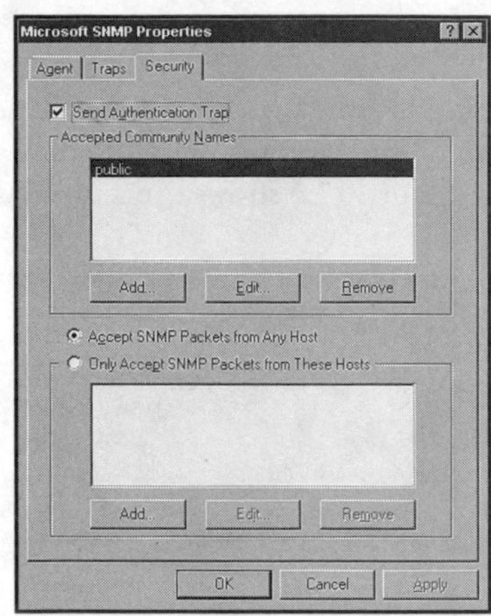

Note Although it is advisable to change to a different community name rather than use "public" for the Agent software, that community should remain on the Management software. Because "public" is the default, it enables you to still control the system even if the SNMP service is removed and reinstalled.

- **Accept SNMP Packets from Any Host.** This enables any system with Management software that uses the community name entered to access information about the system.

  or

- **Only Accept SNMP Packets from These Hosts.** This limits the number of hosts that can manage this system remotely. For better security, this should be set.

Testing SNMP

A handy utility enables you to test the SNMP installation—the SNMPUTIL, which can be found in the Windows NT 4 Resource Kit. The command is very simple:

```
snmputil command IP_address community_name object_ID
```

You can use the following three commands with the SNMPUTIL command:

- **get.** Gets the value of the object requested.
- **getnext.** Gets the value of the next objext.
- **walk.** Steps through the MIB branch that was given.

Figure 17.7 shows the SNMPUTIL being used to extract some information from a system. The information is fairly cryptic. Remember that you will want to use an SNMP manager such as HP's Openview.

```
D:\CFS>snmputil walk 152.42.65.2 public .1.3.6.1.4.1.77
Variable = .iso.org.dod.internet.private.enterprises.lanmanager.lanmgr-2.common.comVersionMaj.0
Value    = OCTET STRING - 4

Variable = .iso.org.dod.internet.private.enterprises.lanmanager.lanmgr-2.common.comVersionMin.0
Value    = OCTET STRING - 0

Variable = .iso.org.dod.internet.private.enterprises.lanmanager.lanmgr-2.common.comType.0
Value    = OCTET STRING - <0x03><0x00><0x00><0x00>

Variable = .iso.org.dod.internet.private.enterprises.lanmanager.lanmgr-2.common.comStatStart.0
Value    = INTEGER - 866931176

Variable = .iso.org.dod.internet.private.enterprises.lanmanager.lanmgr-2.common.comStatNumNetIOs.
Value    = Counter - 6

Variable = .iso.org.dod.internet.private.enterprises.lanmanager.lanmgr-2.common.comStatFiNetIOs.0
Value    = Counter - 0

Variable = .iso.org.dod.internet.private.enterprises.lanmanager.lanmgr-2.common.comStatFcNetIOs.0
Value    = Counter - 0

Variable = .iso.org.dod.internet.private.enterprises.lanmanager.lanmgr-2.server.svDescription.0
Value    = OCTET STRING -

Variable = .iso.org.dod.internet.private.enterprises.lanmanager.lanmgr-2.server.svSvcNumber.0
Value    = INTEGER - 13

Variable = .iso.org.dod.internet.private.enterprises.lanmanager.lanmgr-2.server.svSvcTable.svSvcE
77.80
Value    = OCTET STRING - SNMP

Variable = .iso.org.dod.internet.private.enterprises.lanmanager.lanmgr-2.server.svSvcTable.svSvcE
.114.118.101.114
Value    = OCTET STRING - Server

Variable = .iso.org.dod.internet.private.enterprises.lanmanager.lanmgr-2.server.svSvcTable.svSvcE
.111.111.108.101.114
Value    = OCTET STRING - Spooler
```

Figure 17.7

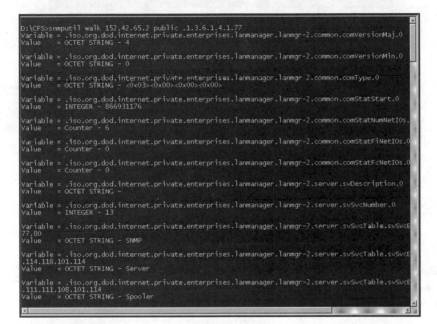

Output from the SNMPUTIL.

Performance Monitor

Objective D.1

Although this might seem to be a strange place to include information on the Performance Monitor, it does make sense if you know that the TCP/IP counters for the Performance Monitor are not installed unless the SNMP Agent is installed.

The next few sections discuss the various counters added to the Performance Monitor when you install the SNMP Agent. For each of the counters, a brief description is included. Before that, however, the following section quickly reviews the Performance Monitor.

Using Performance Monitor

The Performance Monitor is a very powerful tool for checking the performance of your system. Because a detailed discussion of the Performance Monitor is inappropriate here, this section provides only an overview. (Performance Monitor is unto itself subject enough for a book.)

When you open Performance Monitor, a screen similar to the one shown in figure 17.8 appears. This is one of the four views that can be used in Performance Monitor.

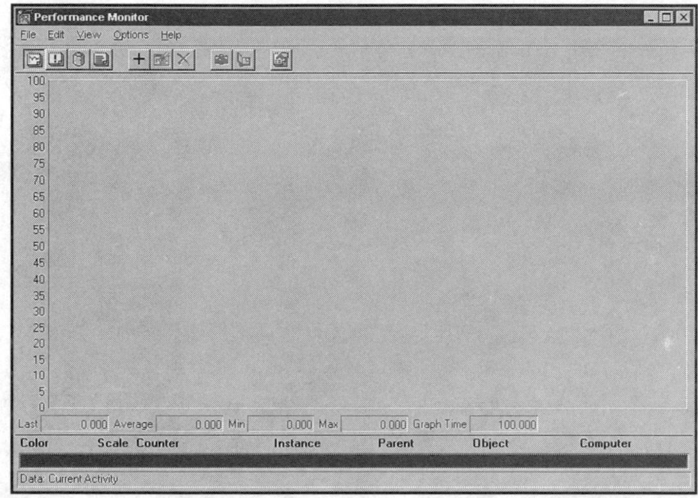

Figure 17.8

The Performance Monitor.

The Chart view shown here enables you to monitor real-time activity on the computer. Although empty at the moment, it is easy to add items to the chart. To do this, choose Edit, Add to Chart from the menu. The dialog box shown in figure 17.9 appears.

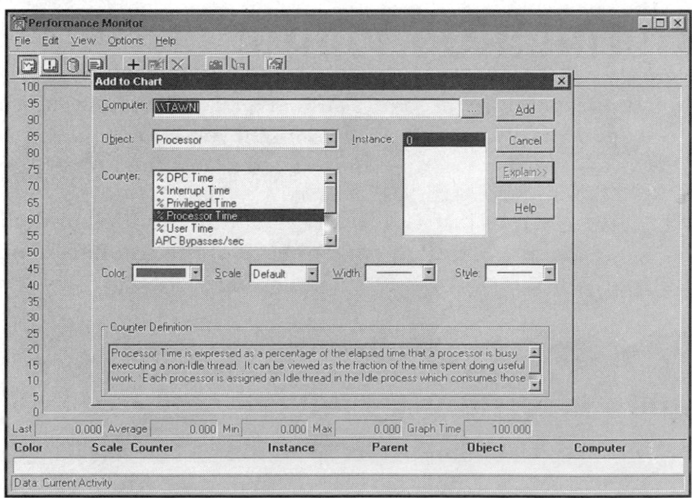

Figure 17.9

Adding entries to the chart.

Many options are available. To summarize, these include the following:

- **Computer.** Using this option, you can select the computer that you wish to monitor. In this way, you can get a better view of what is really happening because the monitoring process does not have to run the system that you will be monitoring. To select a different computer, click on the ellipsis (...) at the end of the computer field. A list of the computers in your workgroup appears.
- **Object.** After you have chosen the computer that you wish to monitor, you should choose the object. Objects represent the categories or areas that you can monitor.
- **Counter.** Within each of the different objects is a series of counters that enable you to see how this object is performing.
- **Instance.** With some objects, you can choose which instance of the object you want to look at. If your system has more than one processor, for example, you may want to look at each of the processors. To do this, choose the Instance. The same applies to the hard disks in your system.

Note

This book is not on Performance Monitor. A couple of quick points, however, should be passed on. First, the disk objects (Logical Disk and Physical Disk) cannot report any information unless you turn on disk performance monitoring. To do this, you type **"diskperf -y"** at the command prompt and restart your system.

Note also that there are two separate objects for the processors in the system. There is the Processor object that enables you to see each individual processor and report on it, and there is the System object that combines all the processors together and treats them like a single object.

A final note: There is no need to memorize the Performance Monitor counters. You need only be aware of what types of counters are available because there is a description available in the Performance Monitor. The counters are included here to give you the opportunity to review the counters and know what type of information is available.

Figure 17.10 shows an example of a chart with a few options enabled.

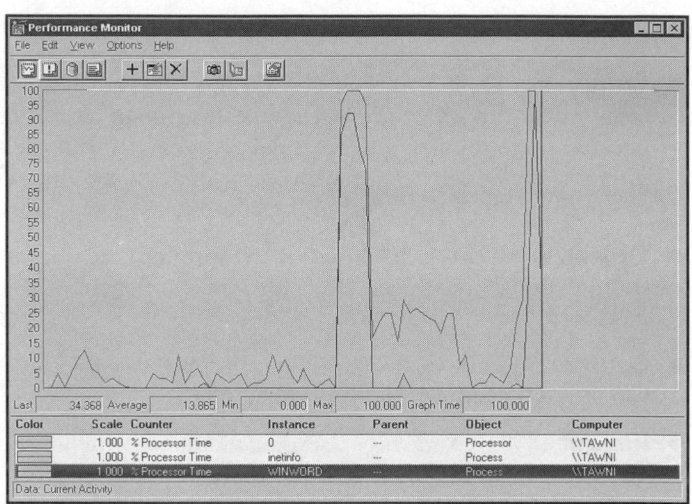

Figure 17.10

An active Performance Monitor.

Counters for Internet Control Messaging Protocol (ICMP)

The following is a list of the counters available for the ICMP object:

- **Messages Outbound Errors.** This is the number of ICMP messages that your computer did not send due to internal problems with ICMP.
- **Messages Received Errors.** This counter gives the number of ICMP messages received but determined to have errors.
- **Messages Received/sec.** This is the number of ICMP messages received in total per second. (This includes any packets received in error.)
- **Messages Sent/sec.** This is the number of ICMP messages being sent by the system.
- **Messages/sec.** This is the total of the Messages Received/sec and Messages Sent/sec.
- **Received Address Mask.** The number of ICMP Address Mask Requests received.
- **Received Address Mask Reply.** This is the number of ICMP Address Mask Reply messages received.
- **Received Destination Unreachable.** The number of Destination Unreachable messages received.
- **Received Echo Reply/sec.** The number of ICMP Echo Reply messages received.

- **Received Echo/sec.** This is the number of ICMP Echo messages received.
- **Received Parameter Problem.** The number of ICMP Parameter Problem messages received.
- **Received Redirect/sec.** The number of ICMP Redirect messages received per second.
- **Received Source Quench.** This is the number of ICMP Source Quench messages received.
- **Received Time Exceeded.** The number of ICMP Time Exceeded messages received.
- **Received Timestamp Reply/sec.** The number of Timestamp Reply messages received per second.
- **Received Timestamp/sec.** The number of Timestamp Requests messages received per second.
- **Sent Address Mask.** The number of Address Mask Requests that were sent.
- **Sent Address Mask Reply.** The number of Address Mask Reply messages that were sent.
- **Sent Destination Unreachable.** The number of Destination Unreachable messages that were sent.
- **Sent Echo Reply/sec.** This is the number of Echo Reply messages sent per second.
- **Sent Echo/sec.** The number of Echo messages sent per second.
- **Sent Parameter Problem.** The number of Parameter Problem messages your system has sent.
- **Sent Redirect/sec.** Total number of Redirect messages your system has sent.
- **Sent Source Quench.** This is the number of Source Quench messages sent by your system.
- **Sent Time Exceeded.** The number of ICMP Time Exceeded messages sent by you.
- **Sent Timestamp Reply/sec.** The number of Timestamp Reply messages sent per second.
- **Sent Timestamp/sec.** The rate of Timestamp Requests sent.

Counters for Internet Protocol

The following list describes the counters available for the Internet Protocol:

- **Datagrams Forwarded/sec.** On a multihomed system acting as a router, this is the number of IP datagrams received by your system where the final IP destination was another system. Therefore, these packets were routed. This counter includes any packets bound for a network for which you have added a route in your routing table.
- **Datagrams Outbound Discarded.** This is the number of IP datagrams that your system could not forward. This counter includes only the packets discarded because of internal problems, lack of memory, and so on. Packets discarded due to errors are handled in other counters.
- **Datagrams Outbound No Route.** This is the number of IP datagrams that your system has received (or created) for which no route was found to the destination network. An ICMP message is sent to the host that originated the datagram, and the datagram is discarded.
- **Datagrams Received Address Errors.** If the IP datagram includes an incorrect address, it is discarded. An ICMP message is sent, and the datagram is discarded.
- **Datagrams Received Delivered/sec.** This is a count of the IP datagrams received and delivered to the appropriate protocol per second.
- **Datagrams Received Discarded.** This is the number of IP datagrams intended for your system that were discarded due to internal IP problems such as a lack of memory.
- **Datagrams Received Header Errors.** This is the number of IP datagrams that your system received where there was an error of some sort in the IP header. These datagrams will be discarded.
- **Datagrams Received Unknown Protocol.** Part of the IP header describes the protocol that the datagram should be delivered to. This is the number of IP datagrams for which your system does not include the protocol that is in the header. The datagram will be discarded.
- **Datagrams Received/sec.** This is the number of IP datagrams received per second by your computer, including those that will be forwarded.
- **Datagrams Sent/sec.** This is the number of packets sent to your IP layer from your local system that are bound for transmission by the IP layer. This does not include any datagrams to be routed by your system.
- **Datagrams/sec.** This is the total number of datagrams sent to your system (not including those to be routed) and sent by your system.

- **Fragment Re-assembly Failures.** The number of IP datagrams that are fragments your system must re-assemble but cannot.
- **Fragmentation Failures.** This is the number of IP datagrams that your system has attempted to fragment yet could not for some reason. This is usually due to the DF (Don't Fragment) flag in the IP header being turned on.
- **Fragmented Datagrams/sec.** This is the number of IP datagrams that your system is having to fragment per second.
- **Fragments Created/sec.** The number of fragments that your system generated per second.
- **Fragments Re-assembled/sec.** This is the number of fragments that your system has re-assembled per second.
- **Fragments Received/sec.** This is the number of IP datagram fragments that your system has received per second.

Counters for NetBIOS Over TCP/IP

This area has only the following few counters:

- **Bytes Received/sec.** This is the number of bytes that your system has received of the NetBIOS over TCP/IP connections that it has with other systems.
- **Bytes Sent/sec.** The number of bytes that your system has sent over all the NetBIOS over TCP/IP connections.
- **Total Bytes/sec.** The total number of bytes that your system has sent or received over the NetBIOS over TCP/IP ports (TCP ports 137, 138 and 139).

Counters for Transmission Control Protocol

The following list identifies the counters that are available for TCP connections:

- **Connection Failures.** This gives the number of times TCP connections have gone directly to the CLOSED state from a state of SYN-SENT or SYN-RCVD. It also includes the number of times a TCP connection has gone to the LISTEN state from a SYN-RCVD state.
- **Connections Active.** This is the number of transitions to the SYN-SENT state from the CLOSED state.
- **Connections Established.** The number of connections in which the current state is ESTABLISHED or CLOSE-WAIT.

- **Connections Passive.** The number of transitions to the SYN-RCVD state from the LISTEN state.
- **Connections Reset.** The number of times connections have gone to the CLOSED state from either the ESTABLISHED state or the CLOSE-WAIT state.
- **Segments Received/sec.** The total number of TCP segments (packets) being received per second.
- **Segments Retransmitted/sec.** The number times per second that your system must retransmit a TCP segment due to there being no acknowledgment causing the retransmit timer to expire.
- **Segments Sent/sec.** This is the number of TCP segments that your system transmits per second.
- **Segments/sec.** The total number of segments sent or received using the TCP protocol per second.

Counters for User Datagram Protocol

And finally, the following list identifies the counters for the User Datagram Protocol:

- **Datagrams No Port/sec.** The number of UDP datagrams received for which there is no service listening on the Winsock port.
- **Datagrams Received Errors.** UDP datagrams that could not be delivered for any reason other than there being no service listening on the port.
- **Datagrams Received/sec.** The number of UDP datagrams delivered to UDP users per second.
- **Datagrams Sent/sec.** The number of UDP datagrams sent from your system per second.
- **Datagrams/sec.** Total of all UDP datagrams either sent or received.

Chart Settings for Performance Monitor

Several settings affect the way the chart works. To set preferences for the chart, choose Option, Chart from the menu. A dialog box like that shown in figure 17.11 appears.

Figure 17.11
Chart options in Performance Monitor.

The following options are available:

- **Legend.** Turns the display of the legend at the bottom of the chart on.
- **Value Bar.** Controls the display of the information at the bottom of the graph, this includes the following:
    - **Last.** The last recorded value
    - **Average.** The average of the values for the period given in Graph Time.
    - **Min/Max.** The minimum and maximum values that have been recorded in this session.
    - **Graph Time.** The period of time shown on the graph.
- **Vertical Grid.** Displays vertical gridlines.
- **Horizontal Grid.** Displays horizontal gridlines
- **Value Labels.** Controls whether the list of values is shown down the side or not.
- **Gallery.** This enables you to switch between a regular graph and a histogram.
- **Vertical Maximum.** This option sets the top value of the graph scale.
- **Update Interval.** Tells Performance Monitor how often to update the graph.

The Log Setting

The Chart view of the Performance Monitor is very good for watching the current data (see fig. 17.12). You will, however, frequently want to view the activity over a longer period of time. To do this, you can create a log file that contains the counters for all instances of the objects that you select. Once collected, you can view this information in either the Chart view or the Report view. As previously mentioned, this is an overview of Performance Monitor, so it does not cover the Report view.

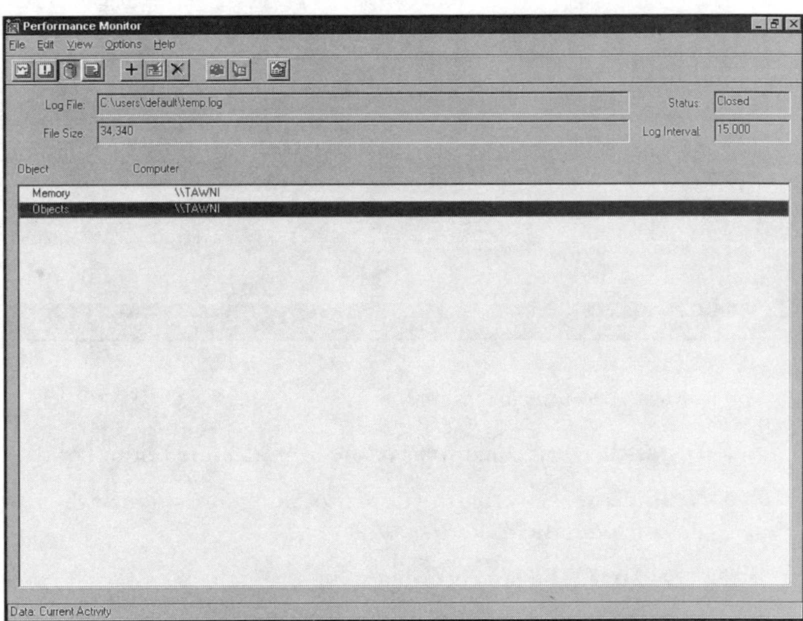

Figure 17.12
The Log view of the Performance Monitor.

Creating a log is fairly simple. To do so, follow these steps:

1. Choose View, Log from the Performance Monitor menu.
2. Then choose Edit, Add to Log. A dialog box appears asking which objects you want to log (see fig. 17.13).

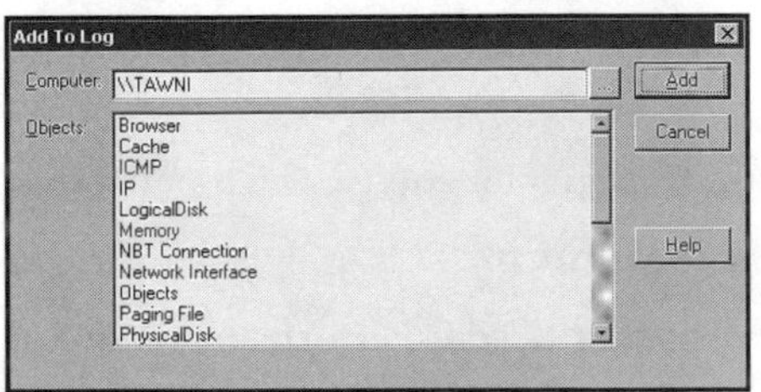

Figure 17.13
Add To Log options.

3. Select the items that you want to log from your system or any system or the network that you have administrator privileges for.
4. Click Cancel when everything that you want to log is listed.
5. Choose Options, Log from the menu. This brings up a dialog box in which you enter information about where to store the log (see fig. 17.14).

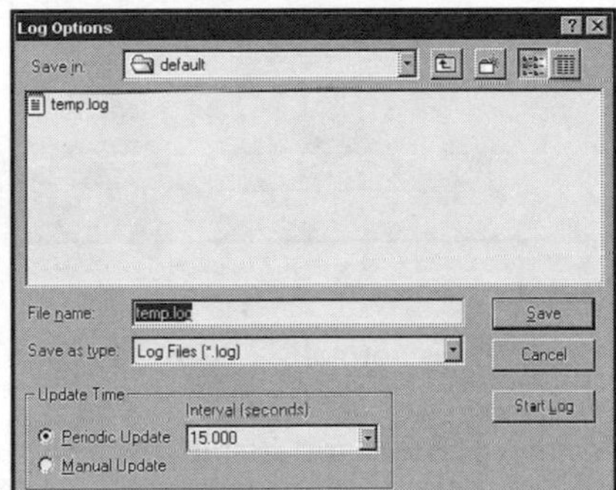

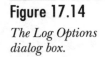

Figure 17.14

The Log Options dialog box.

6. Enter the log file name, and then check the Periodic Update value. Then click Start Log.
7. When you have finished logging, go back to Options, Log on the menu and choose Stop Log.

Log files can grow very rapidly if you are not careful. Ensure that the Periodic Update value is sufficiently high that your log does not fill your disk. You can see the size of the log on the log screen.

Using a Log File

After you have created a log file, you will want to view the contents. The Chart view usually handles this. To use the information in a log, perform these steps:

1. Go to the Chart view of the Performance Monitor.
2. Choose Options, Data From the dialog box that appears (see fig. 17.15).
3. Choose Log File and enter the name of the file. Then click OK.

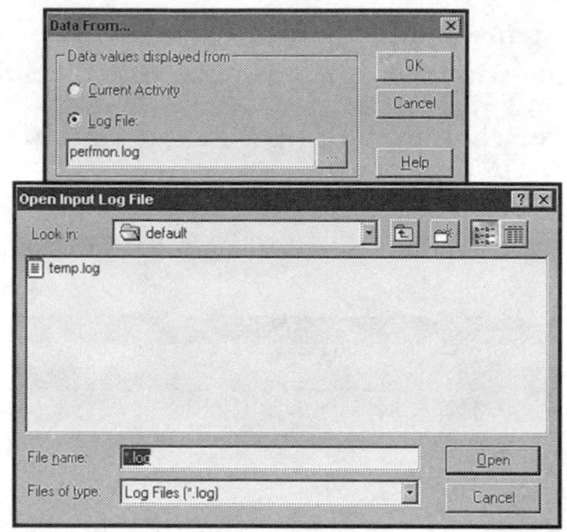

Figure 17.15
The Data From dialog box.

Note Nothing displays at this point. This is normal.

As done before, you can now add the counters and instances to the chart (Edit, Add to Chart). You can only add to the chart for objects that you logged.

One of the advantages of logging is that you can zoom in on a particular time period. To do so, follow these steps:

1. Add the items you wish to view to the chart.
2. Choose Edit, Time Window. A dialog box appears (see fig. 17.16). From this dialog box, choose the period of time that you want to view.

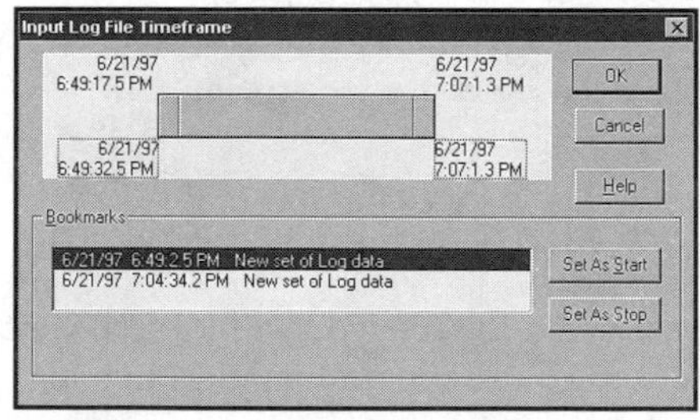

Figure 17.16
The Input Log File Timeframe dialog box.

3. Slide the handles along the time window until you have the period you want to view. Black bars on the chart in the background tell you where you are.
4. Click OK. The display updates (see fig. 17.17).

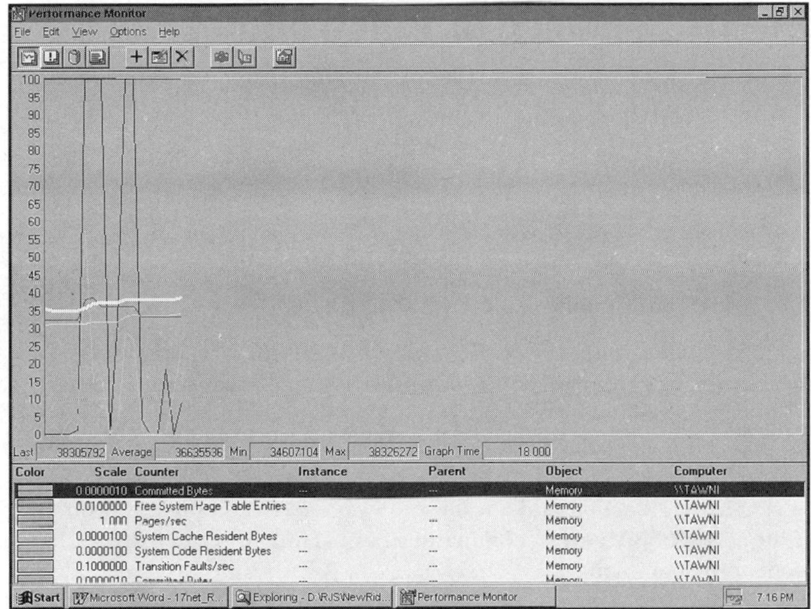

Figure 17.17

The Chart window after a timeframe is applied.

Practice

This lab covers using the SNMP Agent, and also examines the Performance Monitor. You need to have network connectivity of some nature for some parts of this lab. You also need a few megabytes of disk space.

Exercise 1—Installing the Protocol

The first step in working with SNMP is to install the protocol. In this exercise, you install the SNMP Agent.

1. Open the Network dialog box. Click the Services tab.
2. Choose Add, and select the SNMP Agent. Click OK and enter the source directory.
3. Choose Close on the Network dialog box and restart your system when prompted.

Exercise 2—Using SNMPUTIL to Test SNMP

In this lab, you need a copy of the SNMPUTIL. You can find this in the Windows NT Resource Kit. If you do not have the Resource Kit, you can also find it on the Internet.

1. Start a command prompt.
2. Enter the following commands:

   SNMPUTIL get 127.0.0.1 public .1.3.6.1.4.1.77.1.2.2.0

   SNMPUTIL get 127.0.0.1 public .1.3.6.1.4.1.77.1.2.24.0
3. Verify the numbers that you received. To verify the first number, open the Services icon in the Control Panel and count the number of services started.

   To Verify the second number, open the User Manager for Domains, and count the number of users.
4. In User Manager for Domains, add a test user. Switch to the command prompt, and enter the second SNMPUTIL command again. (Hint: You can use the Up arrow to repeat the command.)
5. Verify that the user you added increased the number. Enter the following command:

   SNMPUTIL walk 127.0.0.1 public .1.3.6.1.4.1.77.1.2.25

Note You will want to increase the number of lines in the command prompt in some cases. To do this, click the Control Menu box in the upper-left corner of the window. Select Properties and on the Layout tab change the height value to a higher number (I tend to use 300).

   Are all the users listed? (They should be.)

6. Open the Services icon from the Control Panel again. Stop the Server service. It warns you that this also stops the Computer Browser service. This is fine.
7. Re-enter the command:

   SNMPUTIL get 127.0.0.1 public .1.3.6.1.4.1.77.1.2.2

   Did the number change? (It should be two less than before.)
8. Verify the services are not running. Enter the following command:

   SNMPUTIL walk 127.0.0.1 public .1.3.6.1.4.1.77.1.2.3.1.1

   Are the services that you stopped listed? (They shouldn't be.)

   Because the Server service is stopped, how can you retrieve the information?

The system is using the Winsock interface, not the NetBIOS interface. The Server service is a NetBIOS server. Because you are communicating over Winsock directly, you can use the SNMP Agent service, which is bound directly to UDP port 161.

9. Restart the Server Service and the Computer Browser Service.

10. Optionally, you can enter the following command. It gives you a list of all the information in the LAN Manager MIB.

    SNMPUTIL wa

    lk 127.0.0.1 public .1.3.6.1.4.1.77

    You probably want to redirect the information to a file. The other starting points for MIBs are:

    .1.3.6.1.2.1 - Internet MIB II

    .1.3.6.1.4.1.311 - DHCP and WINS MIBs

Exercise 3—Monitoring Real-Time Performance

In this exercise, you use the Performance Monitor to monitor real-time performance. You work with FTP to generate statistics and see how heavy the load is.

1. First you need to create a large file. You can use the Performance Monitor to do this. Open the Performance Monitor and choose View, Log.

2. Choose Edit, Add to Log. Select the first object in the list and then Shift-click the last object. Click Add, Done.

3. From Options, Log, enter the name **C:\INETPUB\FTPROOT\TEST.LOG** (if you installed the FTPROOT directory elsewhere, use that directory). Set the Periodic Update to 1 second. Then choose Start Log.

4. When the log reaches 2 MB in size, choose Options, Log from the menu and click Stop Log. (This should only take one or two minutes.)

Note As you can see from the preceding step, the log file can fill up quickly. This is something to keep in mind if you create log files that span long periods of time.

5. Switch back to the Chart view (View, Chart) and add the following objects/counters to the chart (Edit, Add to Chart):

    IP - Datagrams/sec

    ICMP - Received Echo Reply/sec

ICMP - Sent Echo/sec

ICMP - Received Time Exceeded

TCP - Connections Established

TCP - Segments/sec

UDP - Datagrams/sec

6. Set the vertical maximum for the chart to 30. You can do this by using Options, Chart and entering the value in the Vertical Maximum field.

   Your screen should now look like that shown in figure 17.18.

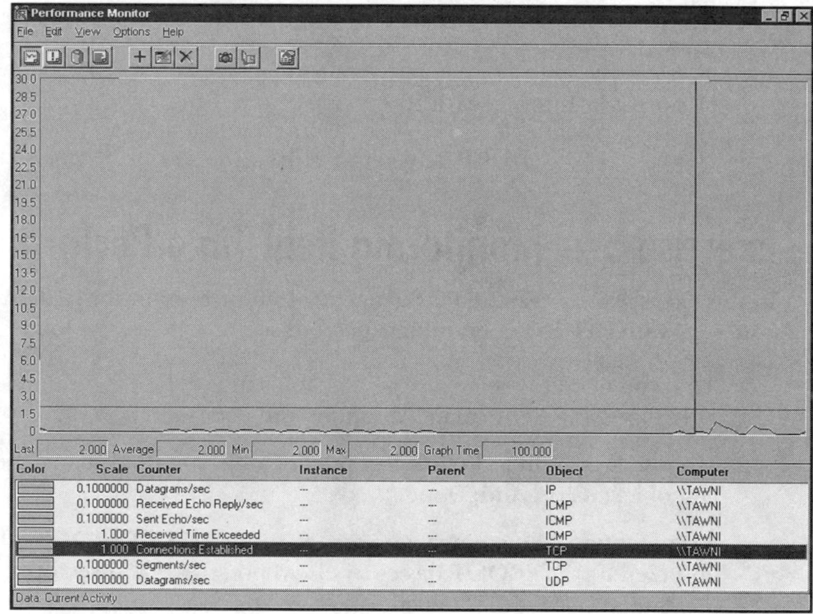

Figure 17.18

An example of how the Performance Monitor window should look.

7. Start a DOS Prompt, and log on to your FTP server. (FTP 127.0.0.1.)

Note If you have problems logging on, check that the port is back to 21. This was changed in the lab for Chapter 9.

   What changes in Performance Monitor? Two more sessions are showing in Performance Monitor.

8. List the files on the FTP server.

9. Switch to binary mode, and retrieve the file you created (Test.log).

Is there activity in the Performance Monitor? Yes. There should be two more connections, and the number of IP:Datagrams/sec and TCP:Segments/sec should both rise dramatically.

10. Close the FTP session.

Exercise 4—Logging TCP/IP Activity

In this exercise, you observe the information created during a TRACERT, and then log the same information. The Performance Monitor should still be running with the same settings as before.

1. Start a command prompt.
2. Ensure that you are connected to the network and then issue the following command:

   TRACERT WWW.COMAT.COM.SG

   What do you see? There is an small increase in the traffic, and the ICMP:Received Time Exceeded increases steadily (in my case, right off the scale).

   Does this make sense? Yes. Because the TRACERT command sent a series of ICMP Echo Requests, with incrementing Time to Live values, there should be an increase in traffic. Because the packets being sent are intended to time out, there should also be the steady increase in the ICMP:Received Time Exceeded.
3. Change the scale so that 2 is the top. Select the ICMP:Received Time Exceeded and press Delete to remove it. Also remove the TCP:Connections Established.
4. Perform the trace again. After the trace, click each of the values, and note the values shown.

   Where are Echo Replies received?

   Only one set (the value will probably read less than this), the last Echo Request sent, eventually reached the host. All the other requests timed out.
5. Switch to the Log view (View, Log). Add the ICMP object to the log by using Edit, Add to Log. (You can clear any existing items by using File, New Log Settings.)
6. Set the Options, Log so that the file is captured to ICMP.log and the Periodic Update is “0.1”.
7. Start the log, and repeat the trace once more. Stop the log when you are finished. (This file could be over 1 MB in size.)
8. Switch to the Chart view, and select Options, Data From. Enter the file name for the log you just created.

9. Add the following to the chart:

   ICMP - Received Echo Reply/sec

   ICMP - Sent Echo/sec

10. Select the ICMP:Received Echo Reply/sec. What is the average value? Multiply the value by the time in the Graph Time. How many Echo Replies were received?

    The received value will vary. The calculated value, however, is around 3 (probably a little less). If you think about the TRACERT command, it always shows three values; this is because it always sends three Echo Requests.

11. Verify the number of hops. Take the average of ICMP:Echo Sent/sec and multiply this by the Graph Time. Take the result and divide by three. What do you get?

    You should get approximately the same number as the number of hops.

Summary

This chapter covered SNMP and the Performance Monitor. As you have seen, SNMP is a very simple protocol that can be used to look at the information stored in a Management Information Base. This enables Management software (such as HP's Open View) to read information from an NT system. If you intend to use SNMP, you must purchase SNMP Management software. (You could use SNMPUTIL, but you would need to memorize all the numbers. This is not realistic.) SNMP is installed, however, whether you are using it directly or not. This occurs so that the Performance Monitor counters function correctly.

This chapter also provided an overview of Performance Monitor. Because you will monitor many different aspects of NT with this tool, you need to spend a good deal of time learning how to use it fully.

Test Yourself

1. What three things do you gain if you install the SNMP Agent?
2. What areas can you watch in Performance Monitor?
3. What utility can be used to test the SNMP Agent after it is installed?
4. For an SNMP Manager to be able to request information from an Agent, what conditions must be true?

5. What is the default community name?
6. If you are having problems communicating with an SNMP Agent within your community, what else can you check?
7. Can you use SNMP across the Internet?
8. What is the UDP port used by SNMP?
9. There are four commands in the SNMP protocol. What are they? Which system initiates the command?
10. What is a MIB?
11. What MIBs does NT use?
12. What two types of data can you view in the Performance Monitor?
13. What are the steps to create a log file using Performance Monitor?
14. For each of the following, choose the object and counter that you would use in the Performance Monitor:
    a. You want to know how much data is sent using NetBIOS networking.
    b. You are having problems transferring a file by using NetBIOS networking. You suspect transmission problems.
    c. FTP is running slowly. The file does, however, eventually get to the destination.
    d. An application that you are developing uses UDP as the transfer protocol. You have tested the application on several machines, but one of them will not respond. You suspect that the application has not bound to the port correctly.
    e. You implement an NT system as an IP router. Your clients are complaining that their network access is slower now. What counter might you look at on the router to determine the problem.
    f. You want to watch the counters used for TRACERT. What are the main object/counters that you should look at?

Test Yourself Answers

1. With the SNMP Agent you will get the following: an SNMP Agent, the SNMP Management API, and the TCP/IP Performance Monitor counters are added.
2. The following new objects are added to Performance Monitor: ICMP, IP, NBT, TCP, and UDP.

3. The SNMPUTIL from the NT Resource Kit can be used to test the SNMP Agent.
4. The Agent and Manager must at least share a common community name.
5. Public is the default community name.
6. The Agent might be configured to accept SNMP packets from only a limited number of SNMP Mangers. In this case, your management station needs to be added.
7. Theoretically, yes. Most routers, however, are set to filter the UDP port for SNMP so that the threat of outside intrusion is reduced.
8. SNMP runs on UDP port 161.
9. The Manager sends the get, get-next, and set commands. The Agent responds to those commands, and also sends Traps when significant events occur.
10. A MIB or Management Information Base is a group of manageable objects that can be accessed using the SNMP protocol.
11. Four MIBs come with Windows NT. They are Internet MIB II, LAN Manager MIB II, DHCP MIB, and WINS MIB.
12. The Performance Monitor enables you to view either current activity or information stored in log files.
13. If you want to create a log file in Performance Monitor, you perform the following steps:

    Open Performance Monitor and choose View, Log.

    Choose Edit, Add to Log and choose the objects you want to log.

    Choose Options, Log and give the log a name and update frequency. Then choose Start Log.

    Choose Options, Log. Then choose Stop Log when you have finished the log.
14. a. Log the Bytes Sent/sec from the NBT connection. When the log is complete, multiply the average for this counter by the total time of the log.

    b. You can use several counters from the ICMP object to handle this. The key one is Messages Received/sec. This tells you whether you are receiving ICMP (which handles error reporting) messages. This helps determine whether the problem is the network or not.

    c. Again, you can use the ICMP object, but you would also want to look at TCP - Segments Retransmitted/sec. Because FTP uses the TCP protocol, a slowness is usually a result of lost packets or packets where the retransmit timer has expired.

d. In this case, the object is obvious—UDP. The counter that enables you to test the theory is the Datagrams No Ports/sec. This enables you to see the number of times a UDP datagram was sent and there was nothing there to listen.

e. You would want to look at the IP object for this (as routing takes place at the IP layer). Some of the counters that you might look at are Datagrams Received/sec (total incoming traffic), Datagrams Forwarded/sec (the number that need to be forwarded), Datagrams Outbound Discarded (the number of datagrams that timed out and so on), Datagrams Outbound No Route (this tells you that your router needs more routing information), and Datagrams Received Address Errors (the number that will be discarded because the address was wrong). One other one you could look at is Fragmentation Failures. This is caused, however, by the Do Not Fragment flag, which would be set by the client.

f. When you look at the TRACERT, you need to look at ICMP counters. Specifically, you need to look at Sent Echo/sec, Received Echo Reply/sec, and Received Time Exceeded.

CHAPTER 18

Remote Access Service and TCP/IP

In today's day and age of mobile executives on the go, system administrators are faced with providing dial-in access to the corporate network. As well, it is increasingly important for the system administrators to be able to dial into their network and handle administrative tasks from home. The process called Remote Access Service, provided by Windows NT, enables them to do this. This chapter investigates the process of remote access and the Remote Access Service server (RAS), both what is and is not possible.

This chapter is broken into two main sections. The first section covers the basics of RAS and NT. Although this section is not specific to NT, you must understand RAS before you can understand how to relate it to NT. The second part of the chapter, starting around the section entitled "Configuring RAS to Dial Out," deals more directly with TCP/IP and configuring RAS to use it.

Before you look at using the NT Remote Access Service server, you should take some time to understand exactly what the RAS server is all about, and the limitations that it has. The Remote Access Service provides a dial-in capability for Windows NT Workstation and Windows

NT Server. This capability was extended to include Windows 95 with the release of Service Pack 1 for that product.

The major difference in the version is just the capabilities. The version that comes with Windows NT Workstation and with the recent update to Windows 95 are both intended to enable a user to dial into a single machine. Both these versions have an inbound connection limit of one. Although this does enable a user to reach his or her office machine, it does not facilitate the number of connections required for a dial-in server.

Microsoft has tested the version of RAS that comes with NT Server with up to 256 inbound connections. This means that NT Server can become a very powerful dial-in server. This discussion first looks at the RAS server that comes with NT Server. Remember, though, that the discussion also applies to the other version of RAS.

Understanding RAS

The Remote Access Service server enables multiple users to dial in to your network. The users can then use the services of the RAS server or the services of the entire network. This extends to the capability to send packets out of your router and to "surf" the Internet. Before a user is allowed to dial in to your RAS server, the user needs to have dial-in permissions. In NT 4, you can grant this permission through the User Manager for Domains.

Note You will notice that there seems to be a difference between Remote Access Service and Remote Access Service (RAS) server. This is intentional; RAS is the overall product that enables you to both dial out and allows others to dial in. The component that allows others to dial in is the RAS server.

One of the properties that you can set as you create accounts is the dial-in permission. Figure 18.1 shows a User Properties dialog box from the User Manager for Domains. Notice the last icon is the Dialin icon.

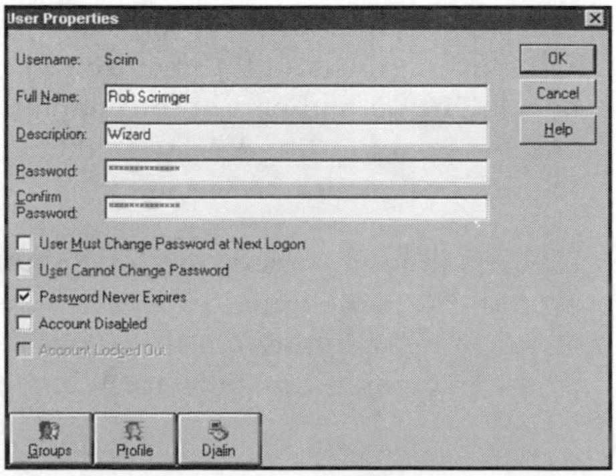

Figure 18.1

A User Properties dialog box showing the Dialin icon.

When you click the Dialin icon, a dialog box like the one shown in figure 18.2 appears. You can either grant the user dial-in permission or not. Further, you can request callback security. There are three types of callback security, as follows:

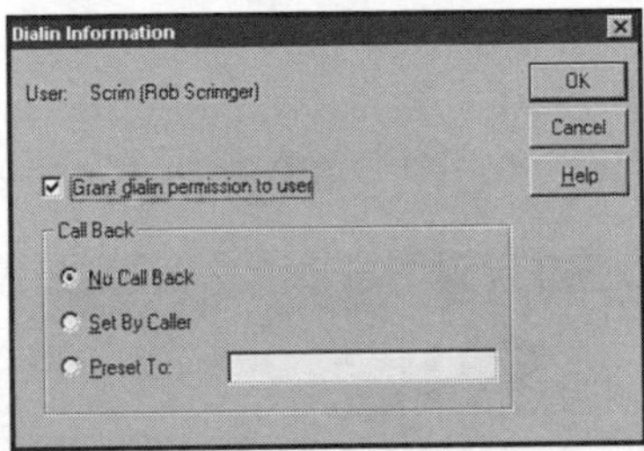

Figure 18.2
The options for dial-in permissions.

- **Preset To.** This enables you to enter a number. The user must be calling from this number, otherwise the system hangs up and calls the number back to verify the user.
- **Set By Caller.** This allows the user to enter the phone number from which he or she is calling. The system hangs up and then calls back to the number entered. This is not for security. If you have a group of users that travel often, however, this enables them to dial in without accumulating excessive phone charges. The charges are centralized at the corporate office.
- **No Call Back.** Select this if you do not wish to configure callback security.

Of course for anyone to succeed in dialing in to the network, the RAS server must be installed. Not only does RAS need to be installed on the server, the client must also have RAS installed. Installing RAS on NT is straightforward, and the steps are as follows:

1. Open the Network dialog box (right-click the Network Neighborhood).
2. From the Services tab, choose the Remote Access Server.
3. Click OK and enter the location of your NT source files.
4. Click OK to close the Network dialog box.

Note At this point, you may get a warning message that there are no RAS devices in your system (see fig. 18.3). If you do, click Yes to install the drivers for your modem. If you have no RAS devices, click No and this aborts the installation. See the section entitled "Installing Modems," later in this chapter.

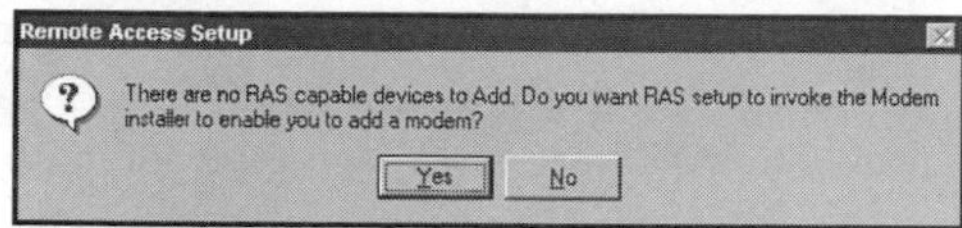

Figure 18.3

You may get a warning that no RAS devices exist.

5. A dialog box appears asking you which device you want to use (see fig. 18.4). From this list, choose the modem or modems that you want to use for RAS.

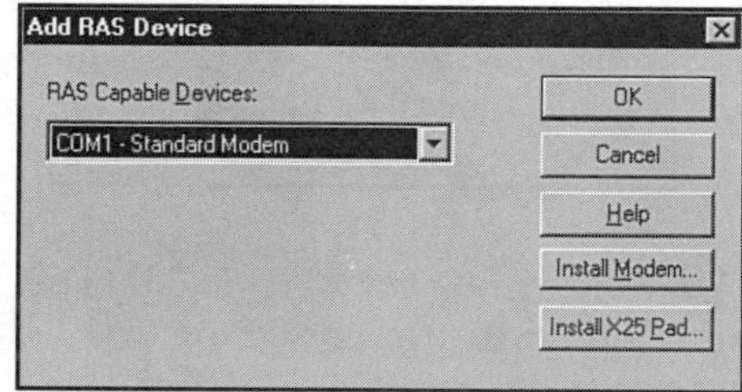

Figure 18.4

The RAS Installation dialog box.

6. Next you will see the RAS Setup dialog box (see fig. 18.5). From this dialog box, you can configure how you want RAS to work on your computer.

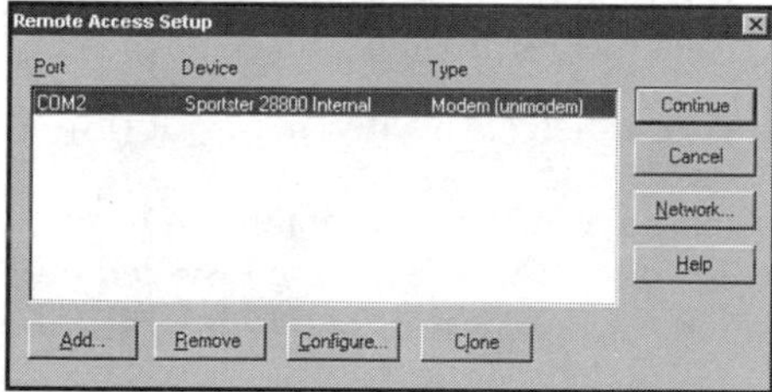

Figure 18.5

The RAS Setup dialog box.

7. From the RAS Setup dialog box, choose the Port Usage button to tell the system how you want to have the port used. As you can see in figure 18.6, the port usage can be dial-in, dial-out, or both. After selecting the appropriate setting, click OK.

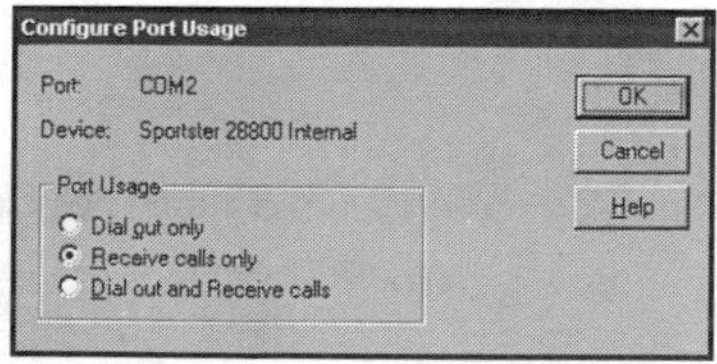

Figure 18.6

Configure RAS port usage.

8. After you configure the RAS port usage, you want to configure the network settings. Click the Network button from the RAS Setup dialog box. Another dialog box appears, asking you about the network settings (see fig. 18.7). Click OK after you have configured these (discussed later in the chapter).

9. Click the Continue button to close the RAS Setup dialog box. Then click OK to close the Network dialog box.
10. When prompted, select Yes to restart your system.

Installing the Hardware

Before you can install modems or X.25 (an older standard for network modems), you must install serial ports to support the hardware. To add serial ports, use the Ports dialog box in the Control Panel.

Note RAS also supports ISDN. Consult the manufacturer's literature if you are installing an ISDN device. They are usually installed as if they are a network card.

Adding Serial Ports

Figure 18.7 shows the Ports dialog box. In this example, COM1 is available.

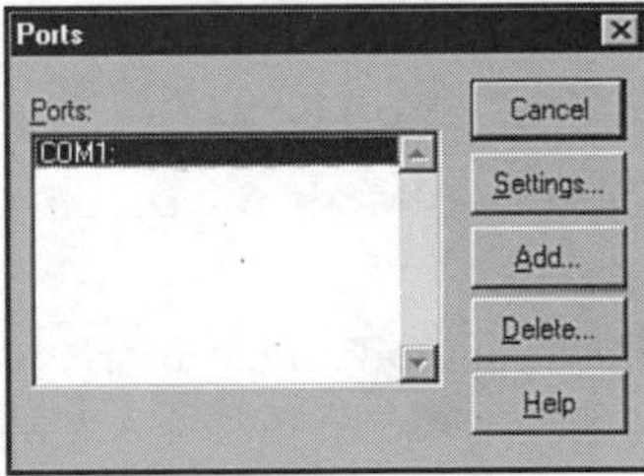

Figure 18.7

The Ports dialog box.

Under the PC architecture, for interrupts 1 through 8, lower-number interrupts have the highest priority. COM2, typically serviced by interrupt 3, has a higher priority than COM1, which is ordinarily serviced by interrupt 4. Consequently, for the best performance, you should connect a modem to COM2 whenever possible.

To add a serial port, click Add to open a dialog box in which you enter the following information:

- COM port number
- Base I/O port address
- Interrupt request line (IRQ)
- FIFO enabled

To change the settings for a port, select the port and click Settings. From the Settings dialog box, you can configure the following settings:

- Baud rate
- Data bits
- Parity
- Stop bits
- Flow control

You can click the Advanced button in the Settings dialog box to reconfigure the port number, port address, interrupt request line, and FIFO enabled settings for the port.

After one or more serial ports are available, you can install modems on the ports.

Installing Modems

Before installing Dial-Up Networking, you should configure at least one communications device (such as a modem or ISDN card—these can also be configured during the installation of Dial-Up Networking). Modems are installed using the Modem utility on the Control Panel as follows:

1. Open the Modem dialog box in the Control Panel.
2. If no modem is installed, the Install New Modem Wizard is invoked automatically.
3. Windows NT is very adept at detecting modem hardware. In the majority of cases, you should not check `Don't detect my modem; I will select it from a list.`
4. Choose Next. The wizard scans your COM ports and attempts to identify a modem. The modem may not be identified by brand. A standard Hayes-compatible modem is identified as a Standard Modem.

Note Even though your modem may qualify as a generic Standard Modem, you should attempt whenever possible to purchase modems that are on the approved equipment list for Windows NT. Subtle differences between modems may make non-approved modems interact poorly with RAS. In any case, if you have a problem with RAS and call Microsoft for support, Microsoft won't be very willing to assist if your modem isn't approved.

5. If you don't like the modem choice, choose Change. You can then select a specific make and model.

6. Choose Next when you are satisfied with the modem choice.
7. When the computer informs you `Your modem has been set up successfully,` choose Finish.

If at least one modem has been installed, the Modems Properties dialog box looks like figure 18.8. You can use this dialog box to add, remove, and change the properties of modems. Choosing Add starts the Install New Modem wizard.

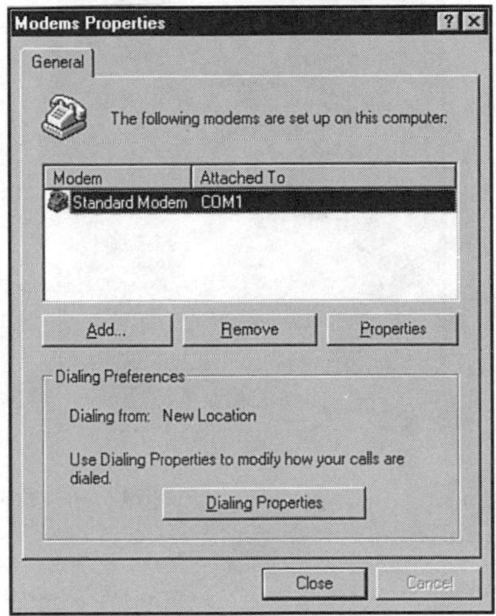

Figure 18.8

The Modems Properties dialog box after a modem is installed.

To change the properties of a modem, select the modem in the Modem dialog box and choose Properties. Doing so brings up two tabs that enable you to configure the modem (see figs 18.9 and 18.10).

The General tab has three settings:

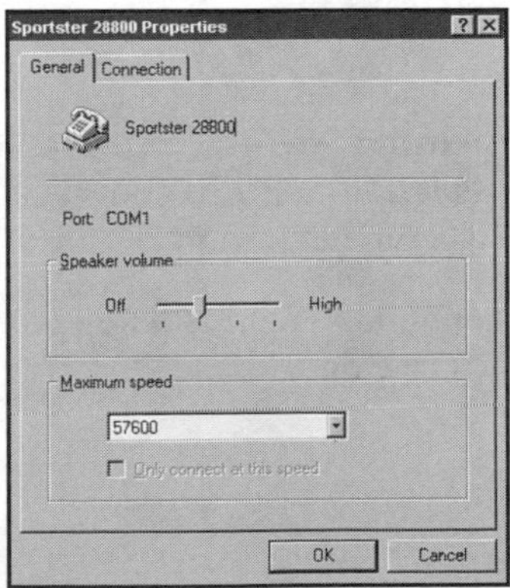

Figure 18.9

The General tab of the Modems Properties dialog box.

- **Port.** Describes the COM port to which the modem is connected.
- **Speaker volume.** Determines the loudness of the modem speaker.
- **Maximum speed.** Specifies the maximum speed at which software should attempt to operate the modem.

The Connection tab enables you to configure the following modem properties:

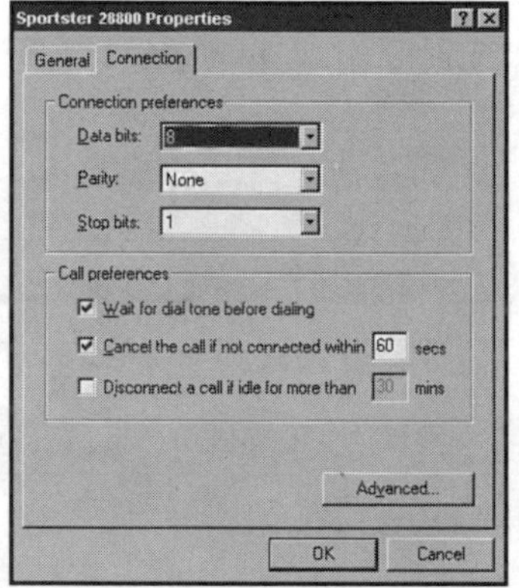

Figure 18.10
The Connection tab of the Modems Properties dialog box.

- **Data bits.** Specifies the size of the data character to be used, with 8 bits being both the most common and the default setting.
- **Parity.** Specifies the type of parity to be used. The most common setting, and the default, is None.
- **Stop bits.** Specifies the stop bits to be sent after a data character is sent. 1 is the most common setting and is also the default.
- **Wait for dial tone before dialing.** When checked (the default), the modem does not commence dialing until after detecting a dial tone.
- **Cancel the call if not connected within ... secs.** Check this option if calls should time out if a specified number of seconds elapses before a call connects, and then specify a time in seconds.
- **Disconnect a call if idle for more than ... mins.** Check this option if connections should be terminated if no traffic is generated within a specified period of time, and then specify a time in minutes.

The Advanced button on the Connection tab opens a dialog box in which you can configure several advanced properties (see fig. 18.11):

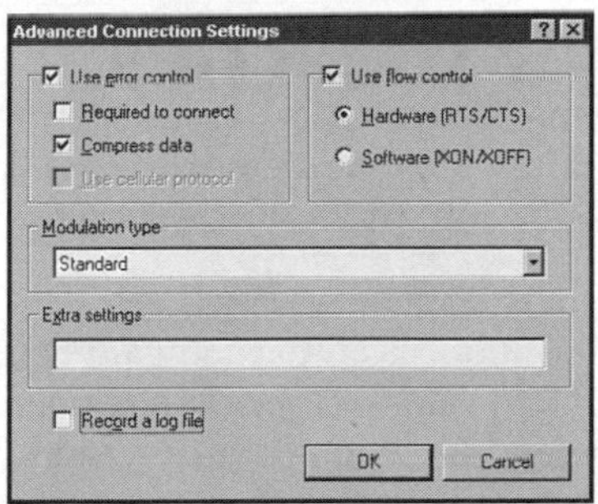

Figure 18.11
The Advanced Connection Settings dialog box.

- **Use error control.** Check this box if error control protocols will be in use. If error control is enabled, select one or more of the following error control protocols:
  - **Required to connect.** If this option is checked, error control should be used. Modems at either end of the connection must agree on an error control protocol. If this option is not checked, connections can be established without error control in effect.
  - **Compress data.** Checking this option enables modems to compress data. The modems must be capable of communicating using a common data-compression protocol.
  - **Use cellular protocol.** Check this option if the modem will communicate through a cellular telephone link.
- **Use flow control.** Check this option if flow control will be used to regulate data transfer between the modems. Select one of the following flow control methods:
  - **Hardware (RTS/CTS).** Hardware flow control uses wires in the serial interface cable to signal when the modem is ready to receive data. Hardware flow control is more efficient than software flow control because extra traffic is not generated.
  - **Software (XON/XOFF).** Software flow control consists of sending special XON and XOFF characters to start and stop data transmission. Software flow control is generally used only when hardware flow control is not supported.
- **Modulation type.** Under some circumstances, this field is used to configure nonstandard modulating techniques.
- **Extra settings.** This field accepts setup codes in addition to the codes specified by the modem's standard settings.
- **Record a log file.** Check this field to log events related to this modem. The log file can be useful for troubleshooting communication problems.

Setting Telephony Properties

With the advent of the laptop computer, an increased need has arisen for the user to configure and reconfigure the dialing properties settings for the system that they are using to dial in to their networks.

This can be complicated by the amount of travel that some users do. The capability to reconfigure a laptop to dial in from different locations often meant the technical staff spent a good deal of time either writing very detailed instructions on how to configure the dialing properties for the software used, or on the phone walking users through the complicated screens.

Microsoft has addressed this need by including a Telephony API that handles the configuration of the location that you are dialing from, enabling the technical staff to pre-set locations from which the user typically dials. As well, the addition of locations is easy enough that even users can configure new dialing locations. This section quickly covers the addition of locations, and the options available for configuring locations.

To access the telephony settings, use the Control Panel and open the Telephony icon. A dialog box appears (see fig. 18.12).

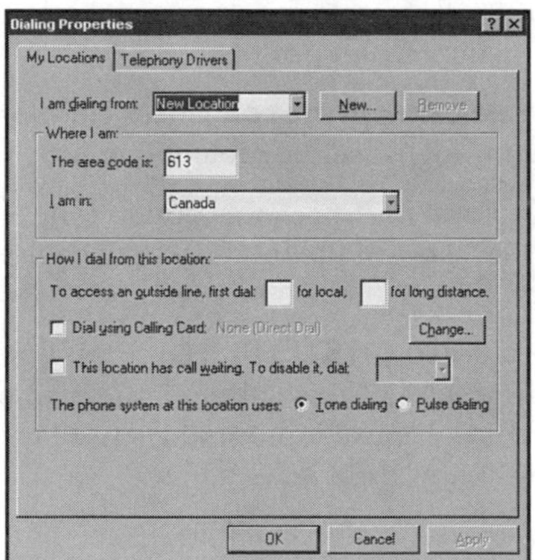

Figure 18.12

The Dialing Properties dialog box.

The properties that you can set from this dialog box include the following:

- **I am dialing from.** This is the location that you want to edit. To add a new location, type the name in here and click the New button. To remove a location, select it from the drop-down list and then click Remove.
- **The area code is.** This is the area code for this location. This tells the Telephony API that the call is either local or long distance.
- **I am in.** Tells the system what country you are in. The system then knows the country code for your location.

- **To access an outside line, first dial.** This enables you to put in two different dialing prefixes. The first is to get a phone line for local, the second gets you long distance. If you dial 9 for an outside line and then 1 for long distance, the entries are 9 and 91 respectively.
- **Dial using Calling Card.** This enables your system to automatically enter the calling card information for the phone system you are using. Click the Change button to enter calling card numbers. A dialog box appears (see fig. 18.13).

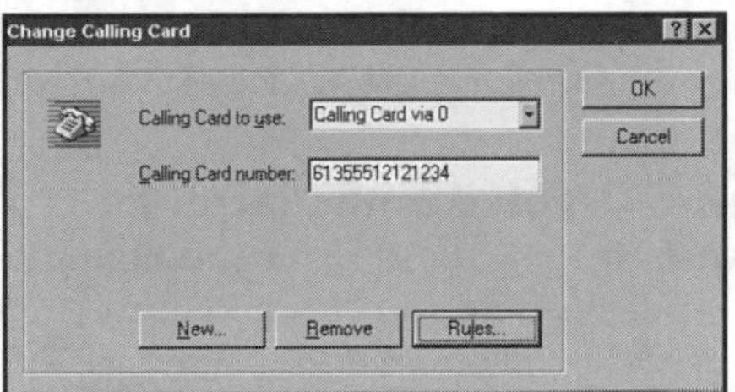

Figure 18.13
Adding calling card information.

- **This location has call waiting. To disable it, dial.** Because a call waiting tone will at least cause errors on a modem connection, and possibly disconnect you, you should always disable it before you dial. This enables you to do so automatically. Note that it does not turn call waiting back on automatically.
- **The phone system at this location uses.** Some locations still use pulse dialing. Here you can tell the system to use pulse so that you can connect from such a location.

Configuring RAS to Dial Out

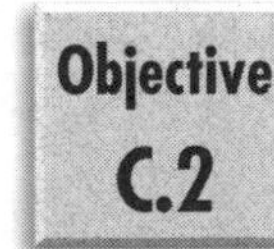

Before you can use RAS to dial in to a server, you must configure a couple of areas. First, you need to configure RAS to enable you to dial out and tell the service which protocols you want to dial out using. You can do this by configuring the Remote Access Service in the Network dialog box.

To configure Remote Access Service to dial out, follow these steps:

1. Open the Network dialog box.
2. On the Services tab, double-click Remote Access Service.
3. Select the modem you want to use, and click the Port Usage button. Choose the appropriate setting.
   - **Dial out only.** This enables you to place outgoing calls.
   - **Receive calls only.** Other users can dial in.
   - **Dial out and Receive calls.** Gives you both.

4. Click the OK button to close the Port Usage dialog box.
5. Open the Network Configuration dialog box by clicking the Network button.
6. Select the network protocols that you dial out using.
7. Select the security setting that you want to use. The settings are as follows:
   - **Allow any authentication including clear text.** This choice facilitates the broadest range of encryption options, including clear text. This setting is useful with clients that do not support logon data encryption.
   - **Require encrypted authentication.** This option enables a wide variety of clients to connect using MS-CHAP, MD5-CHAP, and SPAP encryption.
   - **Require Microsoft-encrypted authentication.** This option requires clients to support MS-CHAP, the most secure authentication supported by RAS. If this option is selected and you check Require data encryption, all data transferred between the client and the server are encrypted using the RSA Data Security Incorporated RC4 algorithm.
8. Choose Enable Multilink if required. If this option is checked, RAS can use multiple physical links (modems) as a single logical bundle to give you the combined speed of all the links. Bundling is a common technique used with ISDN links. This requires that both ends of the connection allow Multilink, and that sufficient phone lines are available.
9. Click OK to close the Network Configuration dialog box.
10. Click Continue to close the Remote Access Setup dialog box, and then click OK to close the Network dialog box.

Note Some encryption algorithms were just mentioned. Just so you know, here is a quick overview of each.

CHAP, Challenge Handshake Authentication Protocol, adds considerable security to the RAS session. When a connection is being established, the CHAP server sends a random challenge to the client. The challenge is used to encrypt the user's password, which is returned to the server. This has two advantages: the password is encrypted in transit, and an eavesdropper cannot forge the authentication and play it back to the server at a later time because the challenge is different for each call.

MS-CHAP is the most secure protocol supported by RAS. MS-CHAP, also known as RSA Message Digest 4 (MD4), uses the RC4 algorithm to encrypt all user data during the RAS session.

PAP, the Password Authentication Protocol, is a clear-text authentication protocol associated with PPP. PAP authentication should be used only when dialing in to servers that do not support authentication, such as SLIP and PPP servers.

SPAP, the Shiva Password Authentication Protocol, is supported only on the RAS server and is an implementation of PAP on Shiva remote client software.

Dial-Up Networking

Objective C.2

Now that the configuration for the Remote Access Service has been completed, you need to add the entries to Dial-up Networking. This is actually where you will keep the information about each of the locations that you will dial in to. Dial-up Networking can be found either in My Computer or the control panel.

Dial-up Networking enables you to dial out to an Internet access provider using either the Point-to-Point (PPP) or the Serial Line Interface Protocol (SLIP). SLIP is an older, very simple protocol that performs well but provides few amenities. PPP is a more recent protocol that provides more reliable communication and a number of options that automate session configuration and logon. As a result of the advantages of PPP, it is the preferred protocol for the majority of Internet access providers.

Adding Phonebook Entries

The Dial-up Networking application is used to manage your dial-up configurations and to connect to remote locations. After you learn how to manage phonebook entries, you are ready to dial out to RAS and other servers.

The first time you start Dial-up Networking, you see this message: `The phonebook is empty`. Click OK to add an entry. When you click OK, you are shown the New Phonebook Entry wizard. You need to configure at least one phonebook entry to use Dial-up Networking. The wizard requires the following information:

- A name for the new phonebook entry
- Whether you are calling the Internet
- Whether it is okay to send your password in plain text if requested by the server
- If you are calling a non-Windows NT server, whether the server expects you to enter logon information after connecting
- The phone number (and alternate phone numbers if available)
- Whether the phonebook entry will use telephony dialing properties

Using the New Phonebook Entry wizard, the steps to add an entry are as follows:

1. Enter a name in the first dialog box and then click Next (see fig. 18.14).
2. You are asked what type of system you are calling (see fig. 18.15).
3. Next you are asked for the phone number. Here you also enter alternate phone numbers if you want, which enable your system to try all the numbers and use whichever one works. If you want the system to automatically know where you are dialing from, check the Use Telephony check box.

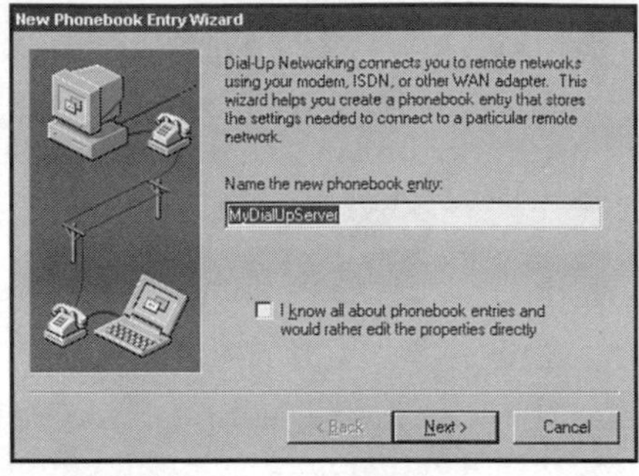

Figure 18.14

The New Phonebook Entry wizard, first dialog box.

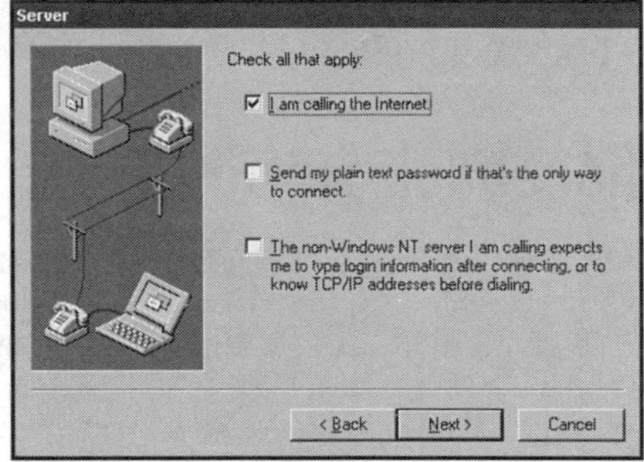

Figure 18.15

Configuring the type of server.

4. After you click the Next button, the system comes up and tells you that you are finished. Click the Finish button.

When the phonebook entry is completed, it resembles what you see in figure 18.16.

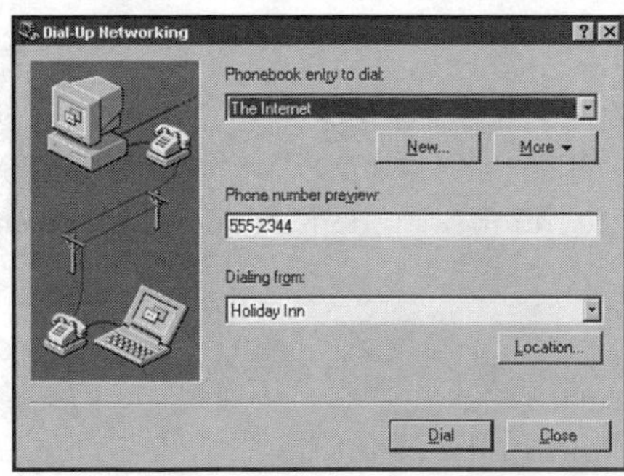

Figure 18.16

An entry in the phonebook.

From this screen, you can perform several options, including the following:

- **New.** Creates a new phone entry, using the same wizard that you just saw.
- **More.** This brings up several different options. Figure 18.17 shows these options, which include the following:

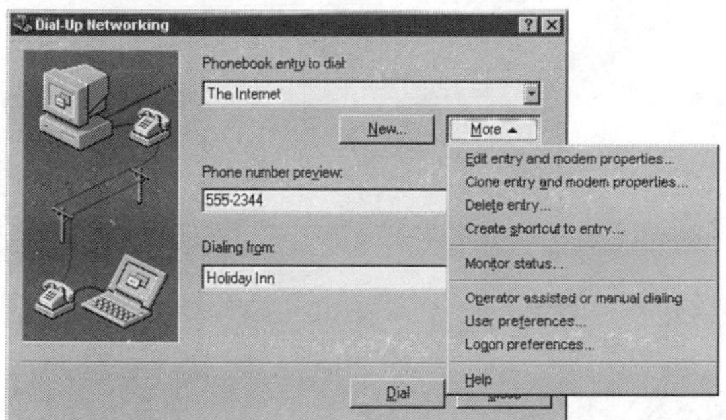

Figure 18.17

The options on the More menu.

- **Edit entry and modem properties.** Using this option, you can change the properties for this dial-up entry (this is discussed in more detail later).
- **Clone entry and modem properties.** If you will add another dial-up service similar to an existing one, you can use this to copy one that you already have working.
- **Delete entry.** Removes the entry.
- **Create shortcut to entry.** This adds an icon to your desktop that you can use to connect to the entry (see fig. 18.18).

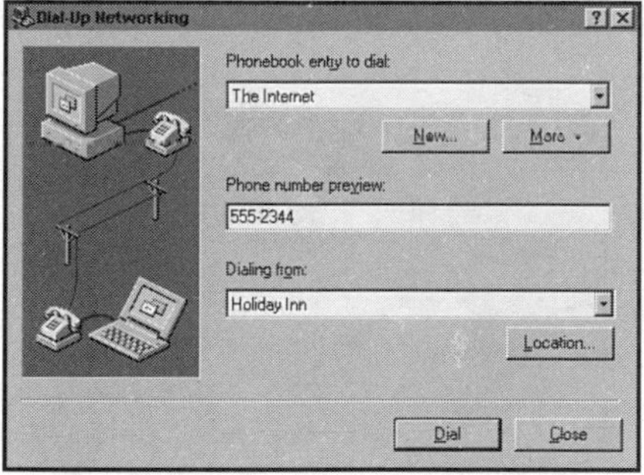

Figure 18.18

A Dial-up Networking shortcut.

- **Monitor Status.** This opens the Dial-up Networking Monitor (discussed later).
- **Operator assisted or manual dialing.** In some cases, you need to dial the number yourself. This enables you to do so. If you choose this option, dialing is still done normally. You can, however, see a dialog box that tells you when to dial (see fig. 18.19). If this is set, a check mark appears in front of the entry.
- **User preferences.** Used to view or set your preferences for dialing (discussed shortly).

Figure 18.19

The Manual Dialing dialog box.

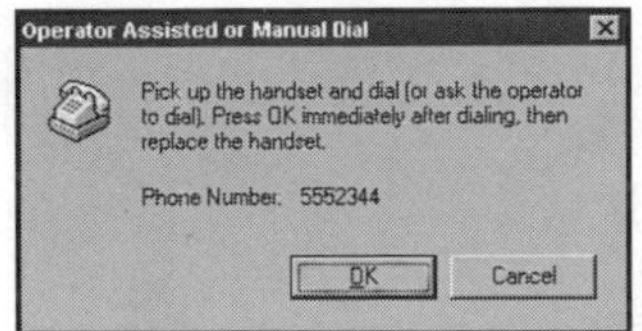

- **Logon preferences.** This sets your logon preferences (also discussed shortly).
- **Help.** Opens the RAS help.

- **Phone Number preview.** You can change the phone number here if you want. If you change the number, it is saved (see fig. 18.16).
- **Dialing From.** This enables you to choose the telephone location that you are dialing from (see fig. 18.16).
- **Location.** Enables you to temporarily change the dialing prefix and/or suffix used to dial the number (see fig. 18.16).

Editing Entries

You can edit a phonebook entry in two ways. You can either return to Dial-up Networking, or you can right-click a shortcut on the desktop and choose Edit Entry, Modem Properties. In either case, the dialog box like that shown in figure 18.20 appears.

Figure 18.20

The Edit Phonebook Entry Properties dialog box.

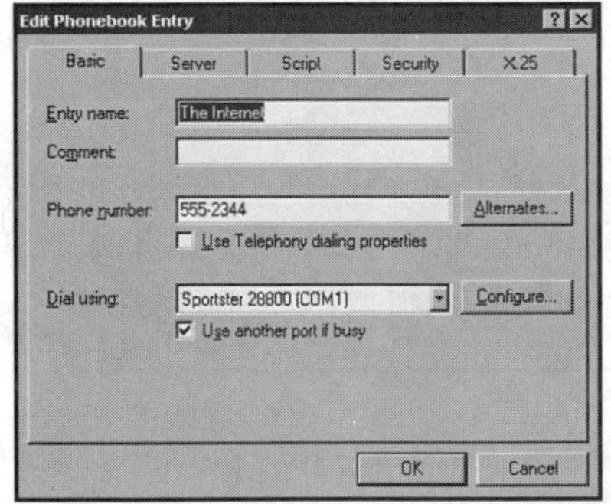

Most of the entries on-screen you have already seen. There are, however, two items that you should notice. First, if you use Multilink, this is where you configure it. To configure Multilink, perform these steps:

1. From the Dial using drop-down list, select Multiple Lines.
2. Choose Configure, and a dialog box appears (see fig. 18.21). Configure a separate phone number for each line.

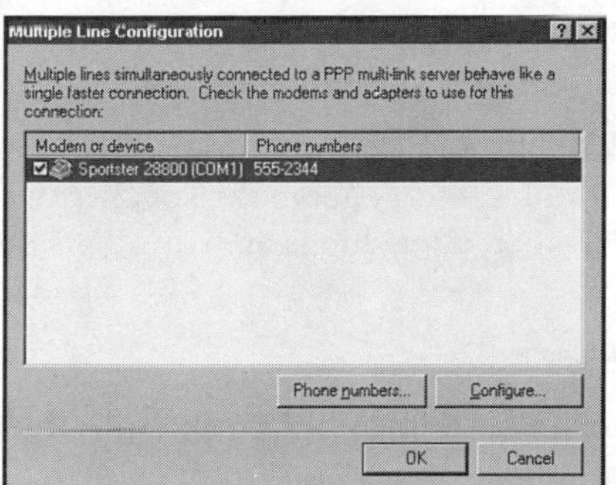

Figure 18.21
The Multiple Line Configuration dialog box.

Note Figure 18.21 shows only one modem. If there were multiple modems, you could configure each with a separate phone number.

3. For each modem listed, choose Phone numbers and enter the number or numbers for that line.
4. If required, choose Configure to set the properties for the modem for that connection.

The other item to notice on the General tab of the Edit Phonebook Entry tab is the Configure button. It also brings up a dialog box (see fig. 18.22).

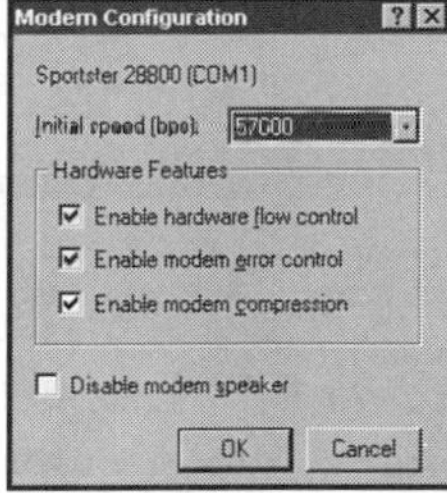

Figure 18.22
The Modem Configuration dialog box for a phonebook entry.

The options in the Modem Configuration dialog box are as follows:

- **Initial speed (bps).** Enter the highest speed supported by your modem. Modems negotiate down from that speed when a connection is established. (Setting this speed above what is supported can cause the modem to function incorrectly.)
- **Enable hardware flow control.** Typically hardware flow control should be enabled.
- **Enable modem error control.** Modem error control can be used if modems at both ends support the same error control protocol.

- **Enable modem compression.** In most cases, software compression performs better and modem compression should be disabled.
- **Disable modem speaker.** If you don't want to hear the beeps, disable the speaker. In most cases, you will want to enable the speaker during early testing phases, but may want to disable it after things are running smoothly.

Server Protocol Properties

The Server tab defines the protocols used to communicate with the server (see fig. 18.23). Options in this tab are as follows:

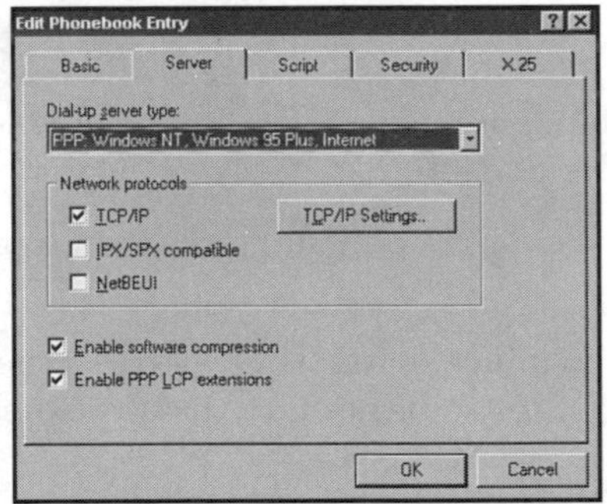

Figure 18.23
The Server tab for a phonebook entry.

- **Dial-up server type.** In this field, you have three choices that determine the type of line protocol that you use. A line protocol essentially replaces the frames that you find on a local area network in that they are used to move the data between hosts. You have the following three choices for line protocol:
  - **PPP: Windows NT, Windows 95 Plus, Internet.** The Point-to-Point Protocol (PPP) is the most commonly used protocol for TCP/IP dial-up services. This is the default and the best all-around choice. You can use PPP with all supported protocols.
  - **SLIP: Internet.** The Serial Line Internet Protocol (SLIP) is an older Internet protocol that is losing popularity. SLIP is less reliable and has fewer features than PPP, but is more efficient and provides somewhat better performance. When SLIP is selected, only TCP/IP is available as a protocol option.
  - **Windows NT 3.1, Windows for Workgroups 3.11.** This option selects an older RAS protocol not usable on the Internet.

- **Network protocols.** You must check TCP/IP in this box to enable TCP/IP support.
- **Enable software compression.** This option is checked by default and configures the communication software to compress and decompress communications data. It is unproductive and unnecessary to enable both hardware (modem) and software (protocol) compression. Typically, software compression is more efficient, particularly on higher-end computers. Software compression is not supported by the SLIP protocol.
- **Enable PPP LCP extensions.** LCP is a component of newer PPP implementations, but is not supported by older PPP servers. Try deselecting this box if problems occur when using PPP.

After TCP/IP has been checked, you can click the TCP/IP Settings button to access the TCP/IP Settings dialog box. The contents of the dialog box depend on whether you have selected PPP or SLIP. Figure 18.24 shows the PPP TCP/IP Settings dialog box, which has the following options:

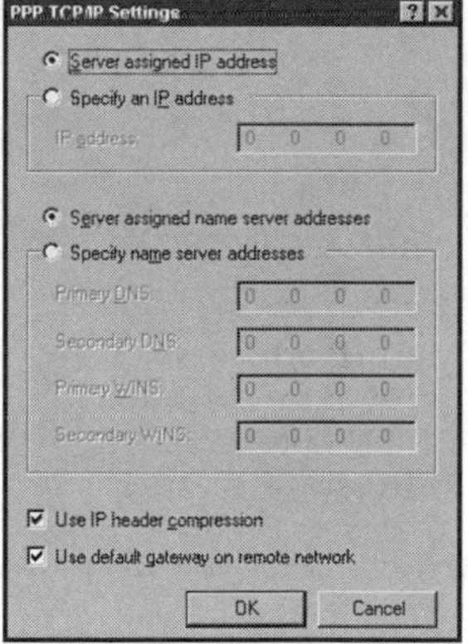

Figure 18.24
TCP/IP settings for PPP connections.

- **Server assigned IP address.** Check this option if the PPP dial-in server will assign an IP address to you. This is the most common situation.
- **Specify an IP address.** Select this option and specify an IP address in the IP address field if the PPP server does not assign an IP address.
- **Server assigned name server addresses.** Select this option if the PPP dial-in server adds the address of a DNS server to your configuration when you dial in. This is less commonly done than automatic IP address assignment.
- **Specify name server addresses.** Select this option to manually specify the IP addresses of DNS and WINS name servers.

- **Use IP header compression.** Header compression—also known as Van Jacobson IP header compression, or VJ header compression—is almost always used to reduce the amount of traffic. Check with the manager of the dial-in server to determine whether header compression is used.
- **Use default gateway on remote network.** This option applies to computers connected to local networks at the same time they are dialing remotely. When this option is checked, packets that cannot be routed to the local network are routed to the default gateway on the remote network.

Figure 18.25 shows the SLIP TCP/IP Settings dialog box. This might be used when connecting to an Internet access provider. You must complete the following fields:

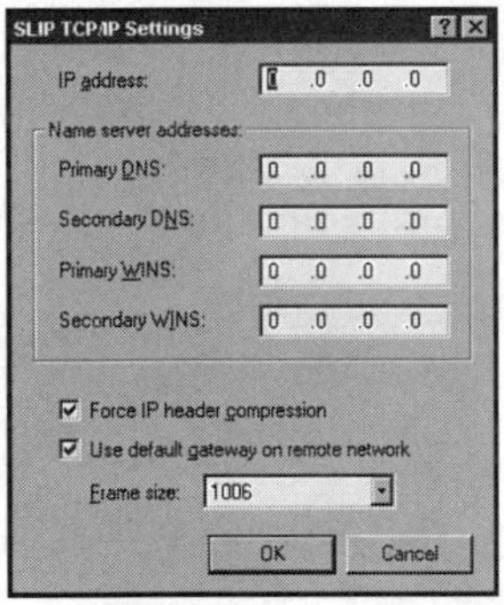

Figure 18.25
TCP/IP configuration for SLIP connections.

- **IP address.** SLIP cannot supply an IP address.
- **Primary DNS.** SLIP cannot supply a DNS server address. Optionally, you can supply a secondary DNS server address.
- **Force IP header compression.** Check this option if the SLIP server uses header compression.
- **Use default gateway on remote network.** This option applies to computers connected to a local network at the same time they are dialing remotely. When this option is checked, packets that cannot be routed to the local network are routed to the default gateway on the remote network.
- **Frame size.** This value determines the size of frames that will be used. Adjust this value if required for the SLIP server. Frame sizes of 1006 and 1500 can be selected.

Script Properties

Figure 18.26 shows the Script tab. Scripts are text files that contain commands that automate dial-in events such as logon. You can add different scripts to each entry to automate that entry. The details of scripts are beyond the scope of this book, but are discussed in the Windows NT Server documentation.

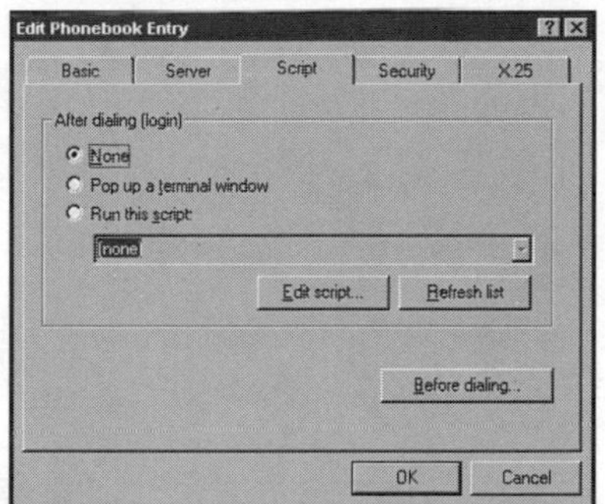

Figure 18.26

The Script tab.

Scripts are typically unnecessary when dialing in to PPP servers. PPP includes the Password Authentication Protocol (PAP), which automates the acceptance of user IDs and passwords. Because no automation is available for SLIP, however, scripts may be of benefit.

The Script tab provides options for scripts to be executed after dialing. The options are as follows:

- **None.** No script will be executed. This is the default and works with most PPP servers.
- **Pop up a terminal window.** If this option is selected, a terminal window opens when a connection is established. The terminal is used to accept the user's password and other required logon information.
- **Run this script.** If this option is selected, enter the path name for a script file. You can choose Edit Scripts to create and modify script files.

You can also specify scripting to take place before dialing. Choose Before Dialing to open the Before Dialing Script dialog box.

Security Properties

The Security tab, shown in figure 18.27, determines the types of encryption used when you dial this entry. Each server that you connect with could use a different form of security. This entry must match that of the server, otherwise you cannot connect. The option chosen must match the requirements of the server. These settings are the same as discussed earlier.

If you select Accept only Microsoft encrypted authentication, you can check Use current username and password. Checking this box instructs Dial-up Networking to automatically use your Windows NT user name and password when dialing out.

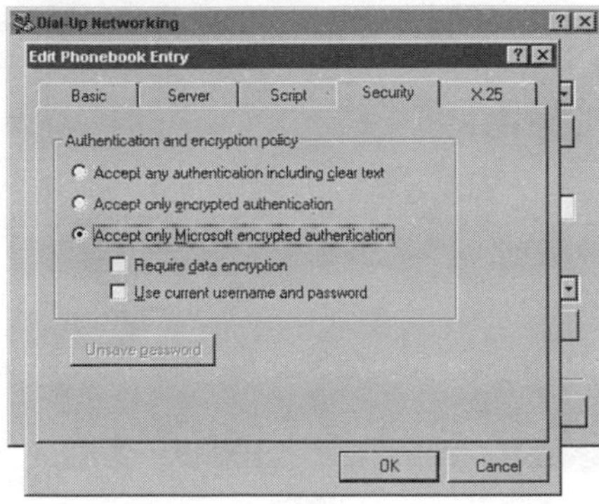

Figure 18.27
The Security tab.

X.25

You can use the last tab to configure this link if you are using X.25. As shown in figure 18.28, little configuration is required. The fields include the following:

- **Network.** Here you should choose the name of the X.25 network that you will be calling.
- **Address.** The X.25 address of the dial-in server that you wish to call.
- **User Data.** This field enables you to enter extra information required by the dial-in server that you will connect to across the X.25 network.
- **Facilities.** Enables you to enter parameters for any additional facilities that you want to request from your x.25 provider.

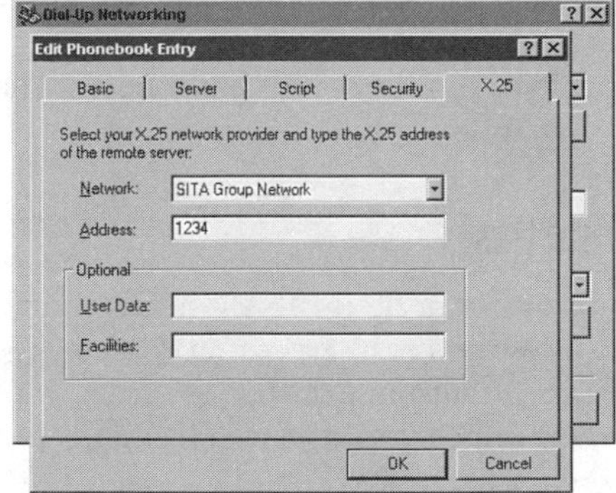

Figure 18.28
X.25 configuration.

Dialing with a Phonebook Entry

After you have created the entries that you want to dial, the next step is to use the entry. You can do this either by double-clicking the shortcut (if you created one) or by opening the Dial-up Networking dialog box, selecting the entry, and choosing Dial. What happens next depends on two factors:

- Whether the host is a RAS server or a TCP/IP network
- Whether the host is configured for dial-back operation

Here is the sequence of events that take place when you use Dial-up Networking to call a RAS server:

1. Select a phonebook entry from the Phonebook entry to dial field. (Or double-click the shortcut.)
2. Verify the entry in the Dialing from field. You can select another location by choosing Location. New locations must be entered using the Telephony utility in the Control Panel.
3. Verify the number in the Phone number preview field. If the number is not complete and correct, check the configuration for the location.
4. Choose Dial to open the Connect to The Internet dialog box (see fig. 18.29).

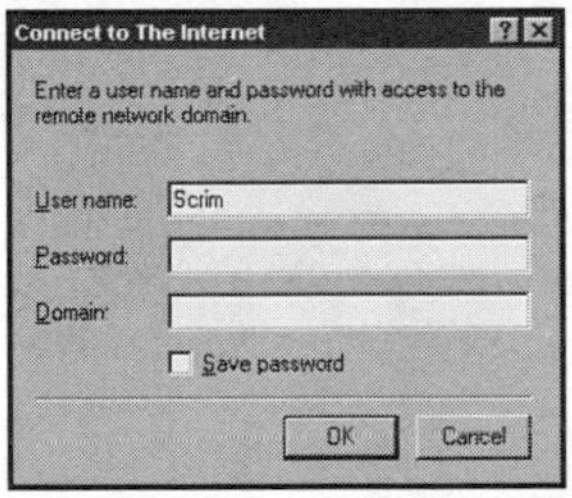

Figure 18.29

Entering connection information.

5. Complete the fields in the Connect dialog box as follows:
    - **User name.** Enter your user name on the destination network. This field and the Password field are completed with your Windows network user name if you checked Use current username and password in the Security tab when configuring this phonebook entry.
    - **Password.** Enter your password on the destination network.
    - **Domain.** If you are dialing to a RAS server, enter the domain you want to log on to. If you are dialing a non-RAS server, clear this field.
    - **Save password.** Check this field if you want to have your password saved with the phonebook entry. This can be hazardous. Saving your password enables any user who has access to your computer to dial your remote account without entering a password.

    Choose OK after you have configured the Connect dialog box.

6. The client dials and enters a conversation with the RAS server.
7. The RAS server sends a challenge to the client.
8. The client sends an encrypted response.
9. The server checks the response against its database.
10. If the response is valid, the server checks for remote access permissions.
11. If callback is enabled, the server disconnects, calls the client, and completes steps 6 through 10 again.
12. Next, a message box informs you that the connection is complete. At this point, you can specify two actions that will take place when you make future connections:
    - **Close on dial.** If this box is checked, the Dial-up Network application closes when a connection is established.
    - **Do not display this message again.** If this box is checked, you will not see this message in the future when a connection is completed.
13. When the session is complete, choose the Hang Up button in the Dial-up Networking application. You must reopen the application if you checked Close on dial in step 12. You can also right-click the Dial-up Networking icon on the taskbar and choose Disconnect.

You are now connected. The connection mimics a direct network connection, and you can use any applications appropriate to the environment. You can use Windows NT applications, for example, to access files on a remote RAS server. Or you can use WinSock-compatible applications to access remote TCP/IP services such as those on the Internet.

User Preferences

You can set a number of preferences for yourself using Dial-up Networking. This section reviews the settings and describes them for you. To edit the User Preferences, you need to get into the Dial-up Networking dialog box and choose More, User Preferences. This brings up the User Preferences dialog box (see fig. 18.30).

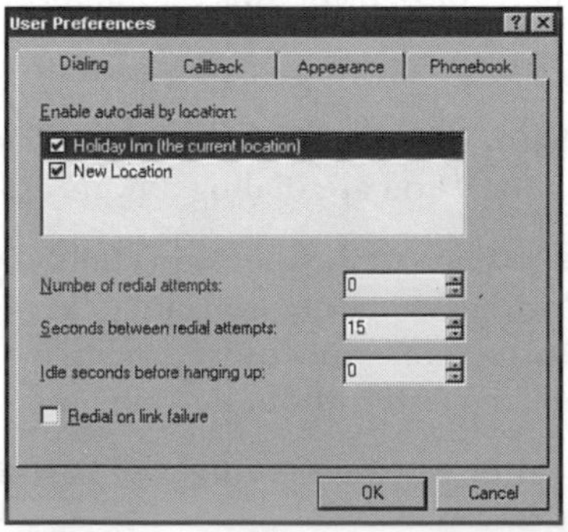

Figure 18.30

User Preferences Dialing tab.

The options that you can set here include the following:

- **Enable auto-dial by location.** Auto-dial automatically reconnects you to the dial-in server if you choose a network option after you have disconnected. If the system goes to redial, you usually get a dialog box similar to the one shown in figure 18.31.

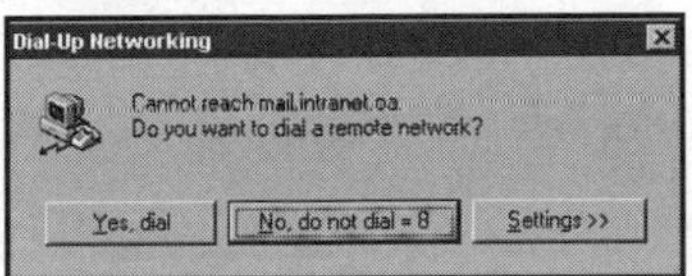

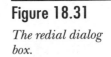

Figure 18.31

The redial dialog box.

- **Number of redial attempts.** This is the number of times that the system should attempt to redial a connection if the first attempt does not succeed.
- **Seconds between redial attempts.** This is the number of seconds the system should wait before trying an unsuccessful number again.
- **Idle seconds before hanging up.** If you have enabled the Auto-dial for the location that you are dialing from, this automatically disconnects the session after the number of seconds you specify.
- **Redial on link failure.** This option automatically reconnects to the dial-in server if the line fails. This functions only if the Auto-dial is configured for the location from which you are dialing.

Callback

As you will see when the discussion turns to talk about configuring the server, there is a setting for callback security. Three settings are available for callback (as discussed earlier). From this tab, you set the callback security for a phonebook entry.

The Callback settings are used if the Callback to a User Defined Number option is chosen (you will see this in the "Configuring a RAS Server" section). The options for Callback are as follows:

- **No, skip the callback.** Choosing this option forces the server to accept the connection now.
- **Maybe, ask me during dial when server offers.** Brings up a dialog box during dialing where you can choose to accept the callback or not.
- **Yes, call me back at the numbers below.** Always accept the callback. If you choose this option, you should enter the phone number in the Call me back at section of this option. When you select the option, you can choose Edit and enter the phone number in the dialog box that appears (see fig. 18.32).

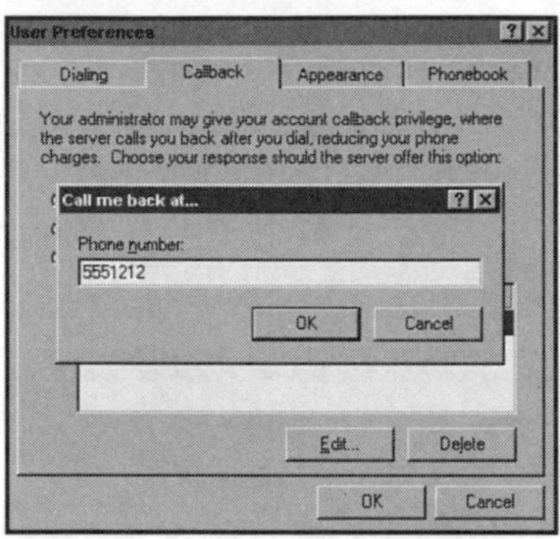

Figure 18.32
Entering a callback number.

Appearance

The Appearance tab could also be called the Behavior tab (see fig. 18.33). It deals with the way that Dial-up Networking interacts with you. The options available are as follows:

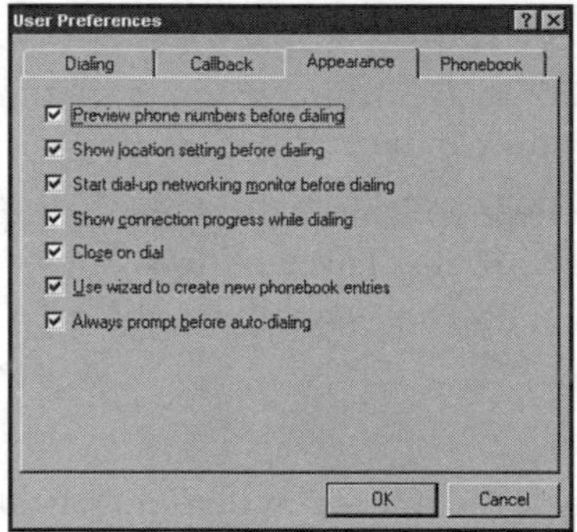

Figure 18.33
The Appearance tab.

- **Preview phone numbers before dialing.** Forces the Dial-up Networking to show the phone number before you dial. This gives you the opportunity to change the number ad hoc.
- **Show location settings before dialing.** This enables you to override the setting for dialing a prefix and suffix before you dial. This temporarily overrides the location settings.
- **Start dial-up networking monitor before dialing.** Starts the Dial-up Networking Monitor (see the following section of the same name) before dialing.
- **Show connection progress while dialing.** When you dial, you see the status in the connecting dialog box. Deselecting this option turns that off.

- **Close on dial.** Closes Dial-up Networking after you have dialed the number and connected to the system. This leaves the Dial-up Networking Monitor running.
- **Use wizard to create new phonebook entries.** You can choose to add the properties for new phonebook entries yourself.
- **Always prompt before auto-dialing.** This forces the display of the dialog box shown in figure 18.31.

Phonebook

The Phonebook tab enables you to switch between different phonebooks stored on the system (see fig. 18.34). You enter three options: the system phonebook, your personal phonebook, or another phonebook.

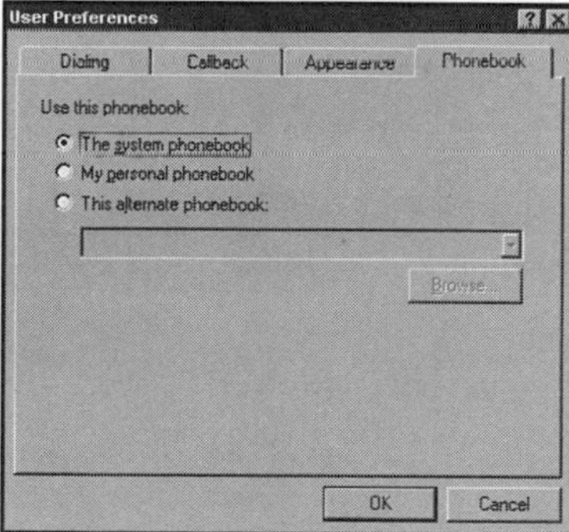

Figure 18.34
The phonebook settings.

Logon Preferences

The logon preferences are basically the same as the user preferences. They do, however, affect the one entry in the phonebook.

Dial-Up Networking Monitor

After you have started a session, an icon is added to the status bar or a new window is available on the taskbar (see fig. 18.35). This is the Dial-up Networking Monitor. This utility enables you to perform many different functions, and also provides you with information about the current connection.

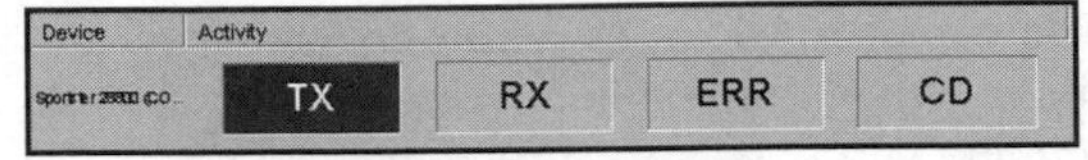

Figure 18.35
The Dial-up Networking Monitor icon and dialog box.

When the monitor is running as an icon or as a dialog box, you can right-click to bring up a quick menu. The main items on the quick menu are as follows:

- **Open Dial-Up Monitor.** This brings up the Dial-up Networking Monitor. From the networking monitor, you can view connection statistics and set preferences.
- **Dial.** This lists all the phonebook entries and enables you to dial any of them (see fig. 18.36).

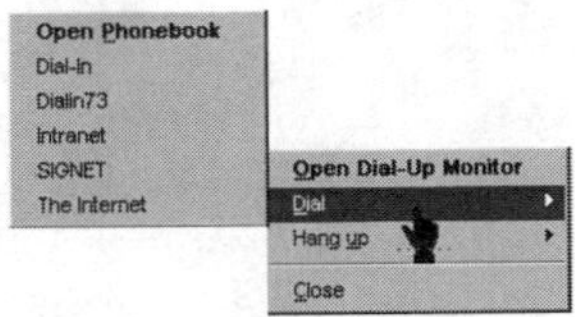

Figure 18.36
The quick menu from the icon.

- **Hang up.** Disconnect for the current session; however, the monitor stays active so that you can redial quickly.

Monitor Settings

When you open the Dial-up Networking Monitor, by default you see the connection information on the Status tab for the current connection (see fig. 18.37). There are different items on the screen that are not covered here. The functions available are as follows:

- **Reset.** This resets all the counter variables shown on-screen.
- **Details.** Shows information about the names with which you have connected.
- **Hang up.** Disconnects from the dial-in server.

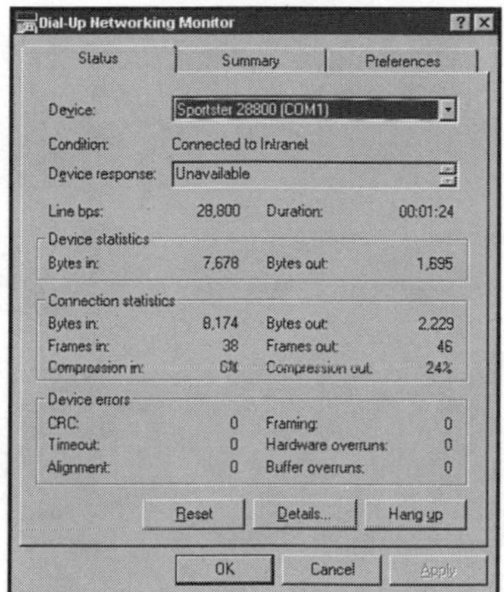

Figure 18.37

The Dial-Up Networking Monitor Status tab.

The Summary Tab

Most of the time, the Summary tab will not be of much use (see fig. 18.38). You can use this tab to determine which modem you must connect to which service. This also enables you to see whether the multilink session with a server has been correctly established.

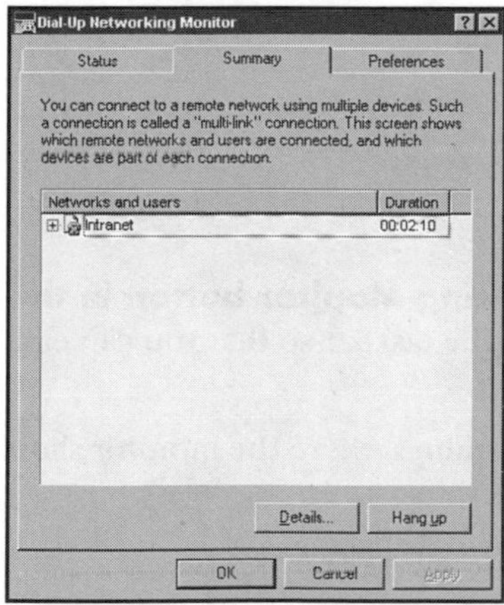

Figure 18.38

The Summary tab.

The options available are the basically the same as those on the Status tab.

- **Details.** This gives you information about the names you were registered with (see fig. 18.39).
- **Hang up.** Disconnects from the server.

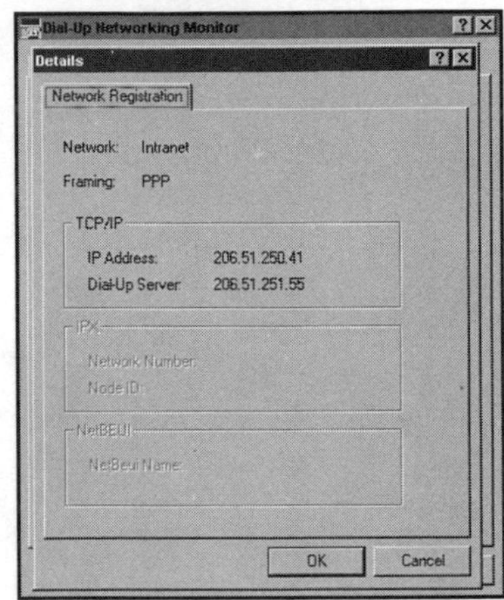

Figure 18.39
The Details tab.

Preferences

The Preferences tab enables you to customize the way the monitor works (see fig. 18.40). Many options are available on this tab, including the following:

- **Play a Sound.** Enables you to set up when sounds (beeps) will play. The events that you can set include the following:
  - When a connection is made
  - When a connection is dropped
  - When data is sent or received
  - When a line error occurs
- **Include Dial-Up Networking Monitor button in the task list.** This adds the Dial-up Monitor to the taskbar so that you can easily switch to it during a connection.
- **Show status lights.** Determines where the monitor should show status lights. The options are as follows:
  - As an icon next to the taskbar clock
  - As a window on the desktop. If you choose to have the monitor as a window, you can also choose the following:
    - Display the window's title bar
    - Always on top

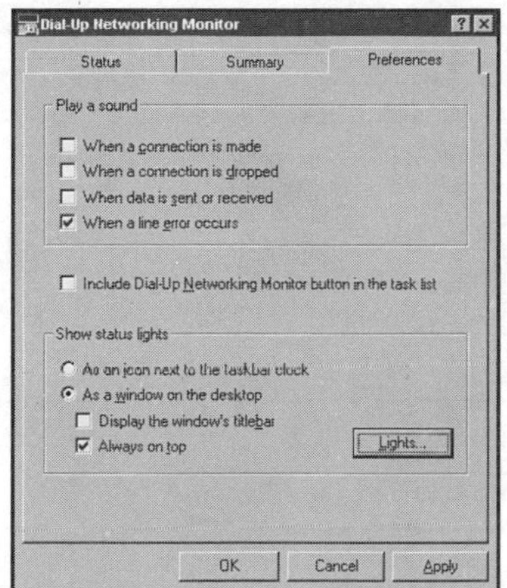

Figure 18.40

The Preferences tab.

Using RAS as an Internet Router

Objective C.2

After RAS has been configured and tested, you can configure RAS as a router that enables other users on your network to access the Internet. Performance is limited by the slow bit rates supported by analog modems, but routing through RAS is one possible way to connect multiple users to the Internet.

To configure RAS as an Internet router, you need the following:

- A PPP connection to the Internet
- An Internet Class C network address or a valid IP subnet and subnet mask, assigned by your Internet access provider
- A domain name and name server if you want to have your local computers identified through DNS
- A Windows NT computer configured with a high-speed modem and serial card

Figure 18.41 illustrates a Windows network that uses RAS to route traffic to the Internet. To configure a network with a RAS Internet router, perform the following steps:

1. Configure your local TCP/IP hosts with IP addresses that have been assigned to your site. The RAS gateway connects your local network to the Internet through a router, and it is essential that your network be configured with legitimate Internet addresses.
2. Configure the default gateway for all TCP/IP computers to the IP address that matches the LAN adapter card in the RAS server.
3. On the RAS server, use regedt32 to add a value to the Registry in the following key:

```
\HKEY_LOCAL_MACHINE\System\CurrentControlSet
      \Services\RasArp\Parameters
```

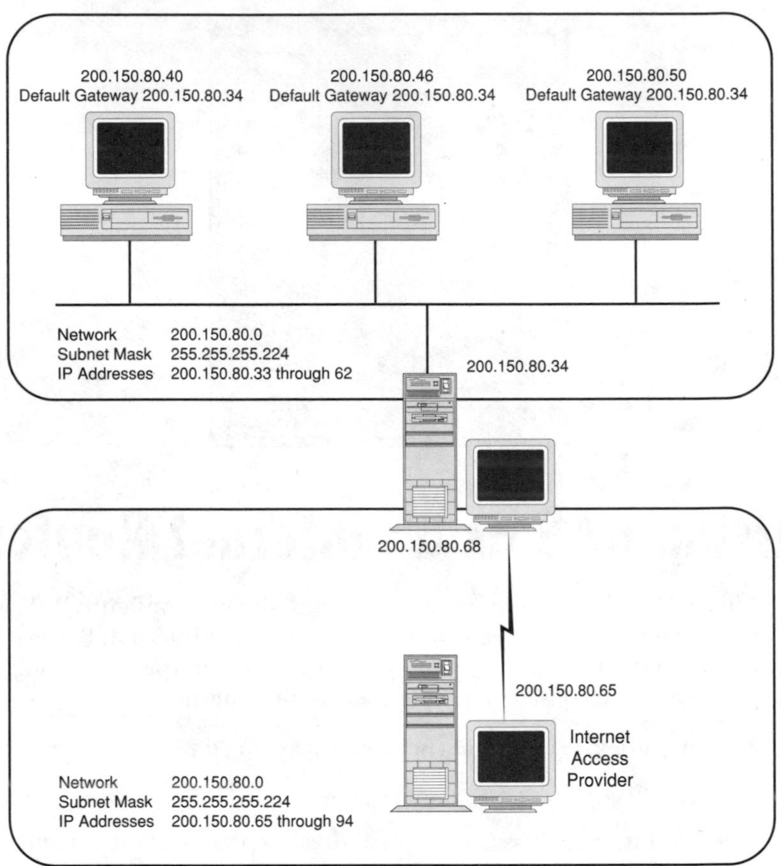

Figure 18.41

Using RAS as a router.

The value to add is:

- Name: DisableOtherSrcPackets
- Data Type: REG_DWORD
- Value: 0

This value ensures that packets routed through the RAS server retain the IP addresses of the clients that originated the packets.

4. In the Network dialog box, examine the TCP/IP properties to ensure that routing is enabled.

5. Obtain the IP address of your Internet default router from your ISP. Add a static route to the RAS gateway's routing table that defines the router as a default gateway for the RAS server. The command will resemble the following:

   route -p add 0.0.0.0 mask 0.0.0.0 ipaddress

6. Establish a phonebook entry on the gateway RAS server for your ISP. When you connect with this phonebook entry, the RAS server is established as an Internet gateway.

Configuring a RAS Server

As RAS is already installed, configuring the system to act as a RAS server is just a matter of configuration. You need to change the configuration in only the following three places:

Objective C.2

- **RAS Setup.** You need to set the port up to receive calls and set up the Network settings for inbound connections.
- **User Manager for Domains.** This is optional. You can, however, grant the dial-in permission using the User Manager for Domains.
- **RAS Administrator.** You use the Remote Access Administrator to both configure (to a limited degree) and monitor the RAS service.

RAS Setup

The first thing that you need to do in the RAS Setup dialog box is to set the port usage to at least Receive calls. To do this, perform the following steps:

1. Open the Network dialog box and choose the Services tab.
2. Click the Remote Access Service and choose Properties.
3. Choose the port (or ports) that you will use as dial-in ports and click Configure.
4. Select either Receive calls or Dial out and Receive calls.
5. Click OK to close the Port Usage dialog box.

Now you need to configure the way that the network will work with systems that dial in. You do this in the Network Configuration dialog box (see fig. 18.42).

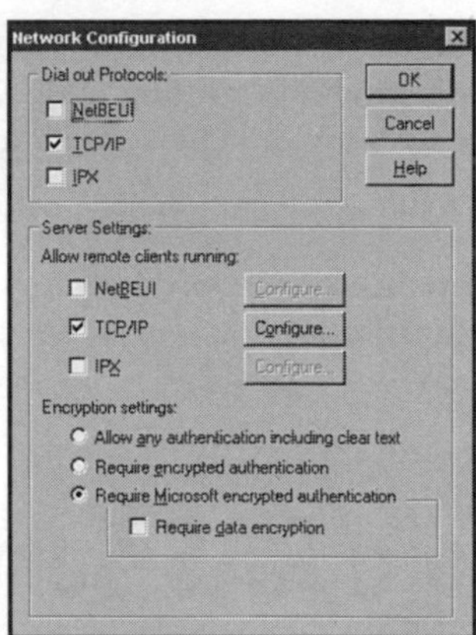

Figure 18.42
The Network Configuration dialog box.

There are two main items that you need to set:

- **Network Protocols.** These are the protocols that users can dial in with. Any protocol that you want to use must be installed as a protocol on your system. The RAS service must be able to bind with the protocol.
- **Encryption Settings.** Any encryption setting that you choose here must also be supported by the client on the other end.

Network Protocols

Because the encryption settings have already been covered in previous sections of this chapter, this section concentrates on the Network Protocols. Three protocols can be used to dial in: NetBEUI, NWLINK, and TCP/IP. It might seem useless to talk about the settings for NetBEUI or for NWLINK, but either of these protocols can be used to dial in to a TCP/IP network. Later, this chapter discusses the NetBIOS Gateway, which enables NetBEUI and NWLINK clients to dial in and use the services (NetBIOS only) of a network that runs only TCP/IP.

The configuration of NetBEUI and NWLINK is very simple and are not discussed in this chapter. Suffice to say that if you can configure TCP/IP on the dial-in server, you can handle the configuration of the other two protocols.

The configuration for TCP/IP is fairly easy. After you have selected TCP/IP as a protocol, click the Configure button to its right. The RAS Server TCP/IP Configuration dialog box appears (see fig. 18.43). The options available in this dialog box are as follows:

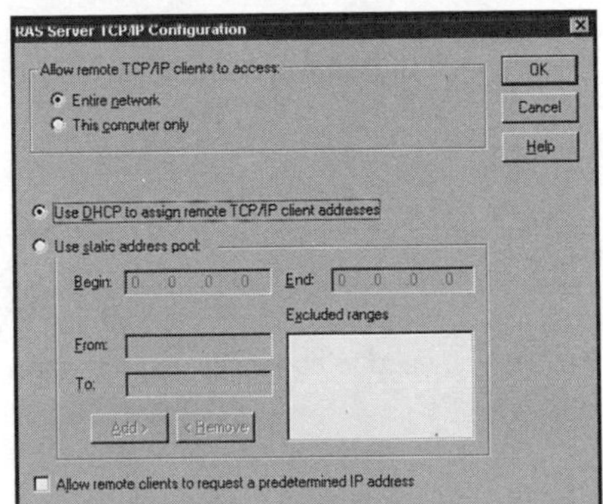

Figure 18.43
The RAS Server TCP/IP Configuration dialog box.

- **Allow remote TCP/IP clients to access.** There are two options here. These options are available for all the possible dial-in protocols.
  - Entire network
  - This computer only
- **Use DHCP to assign remote TCP/IP client addresses.** Tells the dial-in server to use the DHCP server to allocate TCP/IP addressing and configuration to the remote client. In the DHCP server, these leases have small telephones on the icons.
- **Use static address pool.** This enables you to choose a range of addresses that are only used to service the dial-in clients. The options are similar to configuring a DHCP scope.
- **Allow remote clients to request a predetermined IP address.** This is required in some environments where the IP address is used as another layer of security. This requires that the dial-in server be on the user's subnet.

NetBIOS Gateway

As you have now seen many times, Microsoft networking is based on NetBIOS. This means that originally the dial-in clients were also based on NetBIOS—both the Windows for Workgroups and the NT 3.1 clients were NetBIOS only. The RAS 1.1a for DOS is also NetBIOS.

This will obviously cause some problem if you want to use the dial-in service to connect to all the network resources (unless there is only on subnet). NetBIOS cannot be routed. To overcome this shortfall, Microsoft developed the NetBIOS Gateway.

Basically, what the gateway does is to accept an SMB (you might remember that is a Server Message Block) over the non-TCP/IP dial-in connection and forward the SMB on behalf of the client to the correct server using TCP/IP.

Note Remember that TCP/IP utilities require the use of Winsock. If there is no Winsock layer, these utilities do not function. Therefore you cannot route to other networks using a non-TCP/IP connection, nor can you connect to Unix or IPX/SPX hosts in your own network. To do this, you need to connect using the appropriate protocol.

Remote Access Admin

After everything is in and running, you can use the Remote Access Admin program to monitor and configure the RAS server (see fig. 18.44). This program is in the Administrative Tools group on the Start menu.

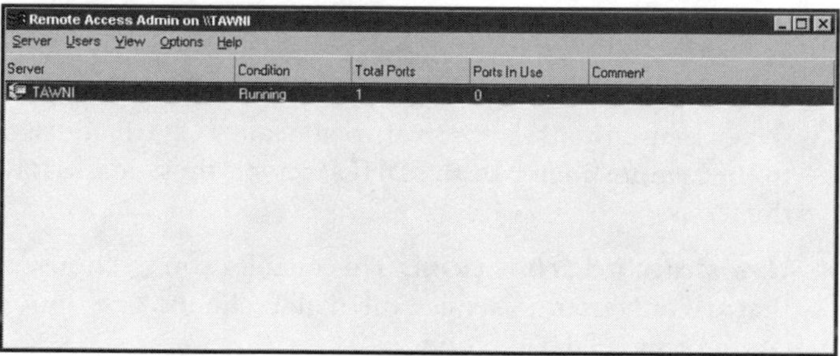

Figure 18.44
The Remote Access Admin.

You can find several basic functions on the Server menu. The following are two important items:

- **Communications Ports.** This brings up the Communications Ports dialog box, which enables you to check the Port Status for any of the ports connected to the server (see figs. 18.45 and 18.46).

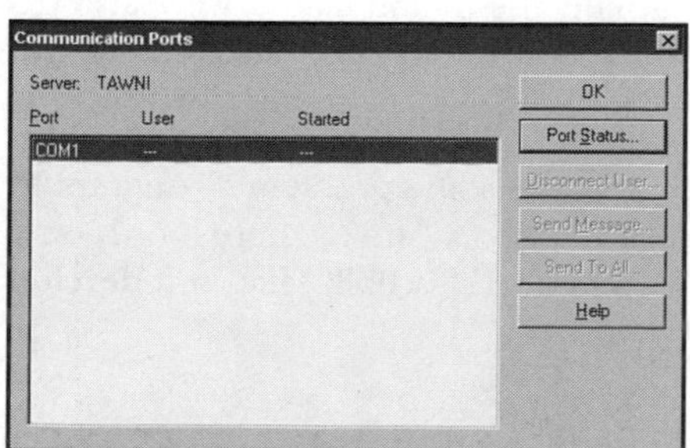

Figure 18.45
The Communications Ports dialog box.

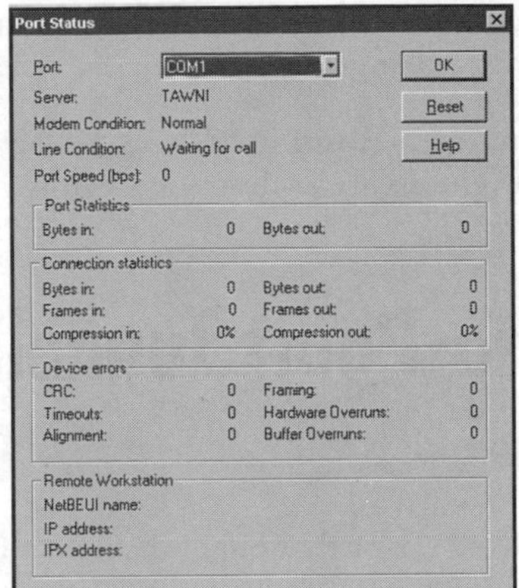

Figure 18.46

The Port Status dialog box.

- **Select Domain or Server.** This option enables you to handlc thc administration of other servers from one system. A Select Domain enables you to enter a computer or domain name (see fig. 18.47).

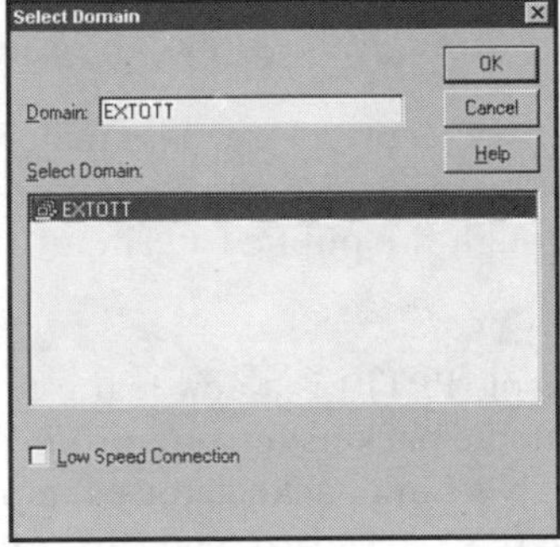

Figure 18.47

The Select Domain dialog box.

You also need to provide users with the dial-in permission. You can do this from the Users item on the menu by choosing Permissions (see fig. 18.48).

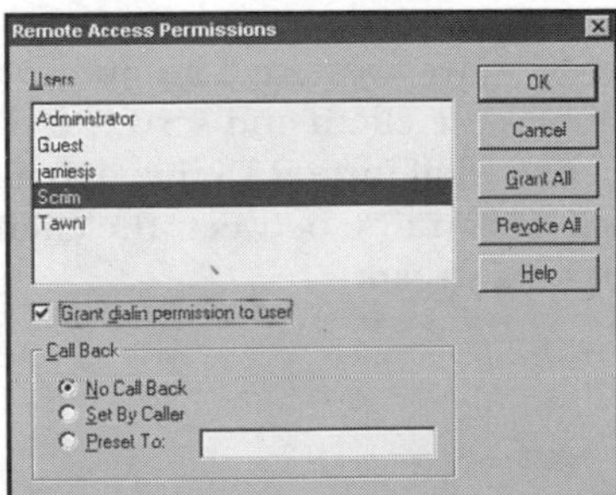

Figure 18.48

Assigning user permissions.

From this dialog box, you can select a user and check the Grant dialin permission to user check box to enable the user to dial in to the server.

If a user is given dial-in permission, you may wish to set the callback security. This is done in the CallBack section. The options are as described before.

Using the Point-to-Point Tunneling Protocol

Using RAS, you can construct a dial-in server that enables clients to access your network from anyplace in the world. RAS works well and provides a high level of security. What more could you want?

Lower cost, for one thing. If you have dozens of users calling in via RAS, you can run up a lot of long-distance charges. If your network is connected to the Internet, you might begin to wonder whether your users could connect to your network by dialing in to the Internet. They would be making a local call to an ISP, and their traffic would be routed to your RAS server for free through the global Internet. Nice and cheap!

Unfortunately, the Internet is not a very secure place. The majority of traffic is not encrypted and is vulnerable to eavesdropping. Sensitive communications should always be secured when it passes through the public Internet. Until recently, however, RAS has not had that capability.

The Point-to-Point Tunneling Protocol (PPTP) is a new feature in Windows NT version 4. PPTP uses tunneling to enable packets for one protocol to be carried over networks running another protocol. NWLink packets, for example, can be encapsulated inside IP packets, enabling the IPX packets to be transported through the TCP/IP world of the Internet. PPTP has the added benefit of enhancing security because it works hand-in-hand with the encryption capability of RAS.

Consider the following two scenarios for using PPTP. In figure 18.49, both the RAS client and the RAS server are directly connected to the Internet. A PPTP tunnel between the client and the server establishes a secure communication channel between them. The use of PPTP enables the client and server to connect via the Internet, without a need for the client to dial in to RAS through a switched connection. While communicating, RAS encrypts traffic between the client and server, providing a secure communications data stream.

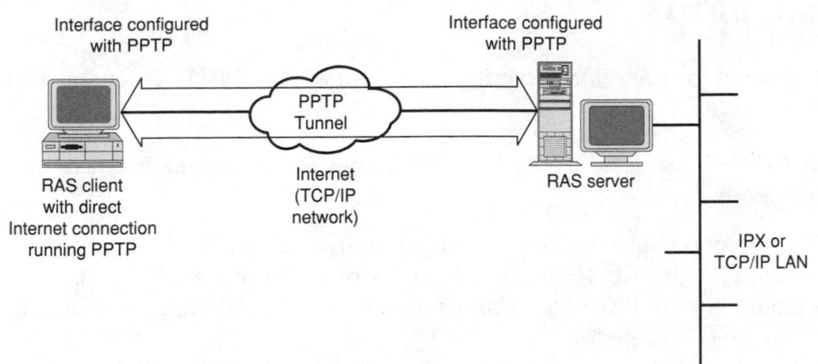

Figure 18.49

A client and server communicating using PPTP over the Internet.

A slightly more elaborate example is shown in figure 18.50. The RAS server is connected to a LAN running NWLink. By establishing a PPTP tunnel through the Internet, the client can connect with the NWLink network even though it is communicating through the TCP/IP Internet. This is accomplished by loading the NWLink protocols on the client together with PPTP. The client dials in to the Internet and opens a PPTP tunnel with the RAS server. From that point, the NWLink packets are encapsulated in PPP packets for transfer through the Internet. The RAS server unencapsulates the PPP packets to recover the NWLink messages, which are forwarded to the LAN.

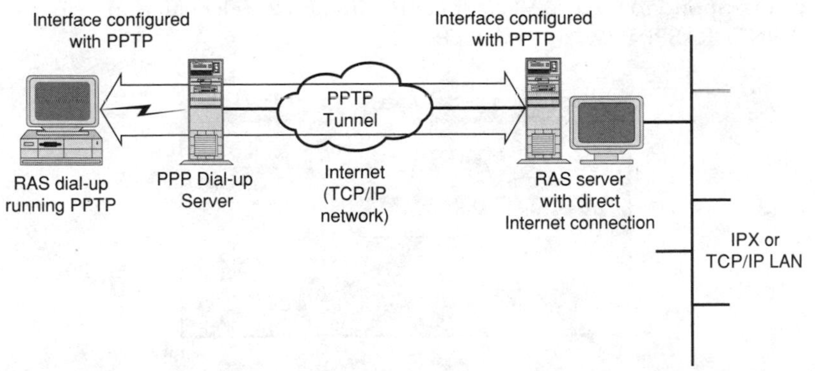

Figure 18.50

Using PPTP to communicate with a NWLink network.

Microsoft refers to PPTP tunnels as virtual private networks (VPNs) because they establish a logical private network that runs over the public network infrastructure.

PPTP configuration is not difficult. The following sections show how to configure PPTP support on the RAS server and client.

Configuring PPTP

PPTP must be enabled for each RAS server or client that will use PPTP. To enable PPTP, follow these steps:

1. Using the Network dialog box, install the Point-To-Point Tunneling Protocol in the Protocols tab.
2. After the protocol is copied from the installation disks, the PPTP Configuration dialog box appears (see fig. 18.51). The Number of Virtual Private Networks specifies the number of PPTP connections that will be supported. In the example, two VPNs will be established.

Figure 18.51
PPTP Configuration dialog box.

3. Next, the RAS setup utility is started. Here, you add the virtual ports that support the VPNs that you want to establish.
4. Choose Add to open the Add RAS Device dialog box (see fig. 18.52). The example shows an open RAS Capable Devices list, showing you the two virtual ports that correspond to the two VPNs specified in Step 2. Select an entry (for example VPN1 - RASPPTPM) and click OK.

Figure 18.52
Adding VPN devices.

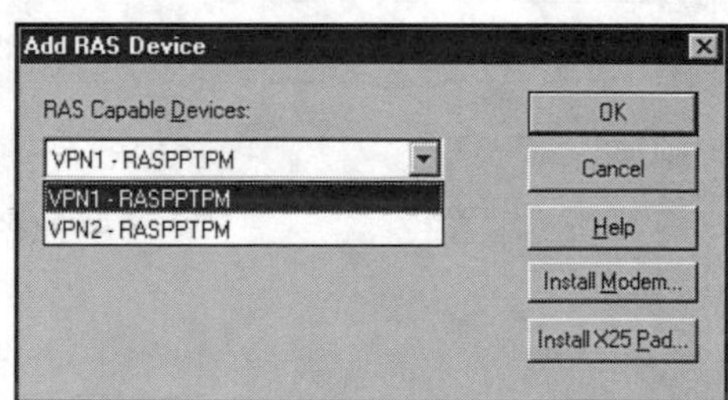

5. In the Remote Access Setup dialog box, select each new entry and choose Configure to open the Configure Port Usage. Select one of the following options to define how the port will be used: Dial out only, Receive calls only, or Dial out and Receive Calls.

   For a PPTP client, at least one VPN port must be configured to permit dial-out.

   For a PPTP server, at least one VPN port must be configured to permit receiving calls.
6. Repeat Steps 4 and 5 for each VPN device you want to add. Figure 18.53 shows Remote Access Setup after both VPNs have been added.

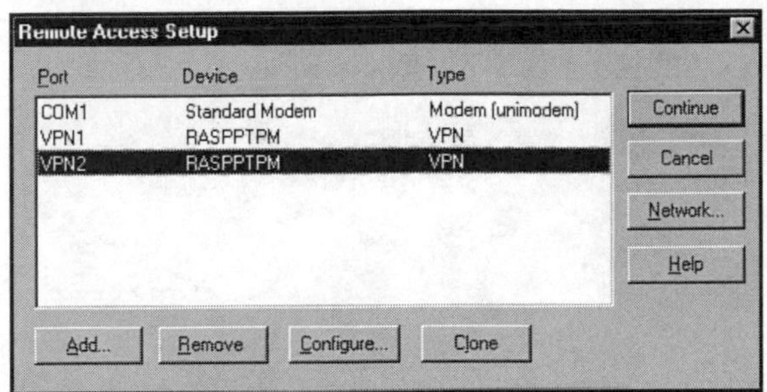

Figure 18.53

RAS Setup after VPNs are configured.

7. After all virtual devices have been added, choose Continue.
8. When you are returned to the Protocols tab, choose Close.
9. Restart the computer.

Enabling PPTP Filtering

After PPTP is installed, the RAS server supports both PPTP and non-PPTP connections, a potential security hole. If you want, you can enable PPTP filtering, disabling support for any traffic except PPTP.

To enable PPTP filtering, perform the following steps:

1. Select the Protocols tab in the Network dialog box.
2. Select TCP/IP Protocol and choose Properties.
3. Select the IP Address tab.
4. Select a network adapter for which PPTP filtering is to be enabled.
5. Click Advanced.
6. Check Enable PPTP Filtering.
7. Repeat steps 4 through 6 for each interface that will support PPTP filtering.
8. Restart the computer to activate the changes.

Monitoring Server PPTP Support

You can monitor the PPTP ports in the RAS Server Admin utility by choosing the Communication Ports command in the Server menu. As shown in figure 18.54, VPN ports are listed with modem ports and can be managed in the same way. Ports appear only if they are configured to receive calls. Dial-out only ports are not listed.

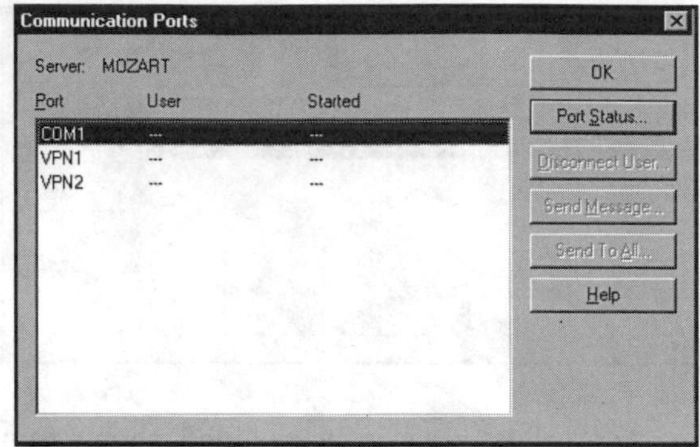

Figure 18.54
The Communication Ports dialog box showing VPN ports.

Enabling Client PPTP Support

When a client is dialing in to the Internet, establishing a PPTP tunnel to the RAS server has the following two steps:

- The client establishes a dial-up connection to the Internet through an Internet access provider.
- The client establishes a PPTP connection to the RAS server.

When a client is directly connected to the Internet, it is unnecessary to establish a dial-up connection. The procedure for starting a PPTP connection to the RAS server, however, remains the same.

To establish a PPTP connection, you need to create a special entry in the Dial-up Networking phonebook. This entry, an example of which appears in figure 18.55, has two distinguishing characteristics:

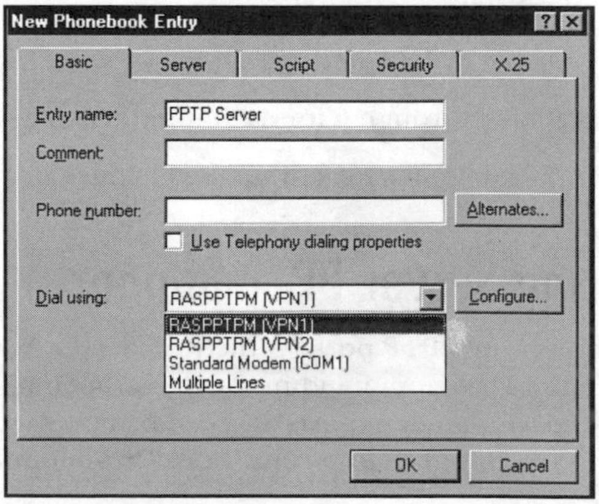

Figure 18.55
The client PPTP connection.

- The Dial using field is configured with one of the VPN virtual devices added to the RAS configuration when PPTP was installed. In figure 18.55, the field has been pulled down to show the available ports. VPNs appear in this list only if they have been configured to support dial-out.
- The Phone number preview field is completed with the DNS name or the IP address of the PPTP server.

Creating a dial-up connection to PPTP has the following two steps:

1. In Dial-up Networking, run the phonebook entry that connects to your IAP using a telephone number and a modem.
2. After the connection is established, run the phonebook entry that connects to the PPTP tunnel using a DNS host name or IP address.

If the client is directly connected to the Internet, it is only necessary to run the phonebook entry that creates the PPTP tunnel.

Practice

In this lab, you install the Remote Access Service. If you have already done this, you can skip to Exercise 2. If you do not have a modem, you can follow the instructions in Exercise 0, which installs a false modem.

Exercise 0—Adding a Null Modem

In this exercise, you install a null modem that enables those of you without a modem to proceed through some of the remaining exercises.

1. Open the Control Panel and double-click the Modems icon.
2. Click the Add button. This brings up the Modem Installer.
3. Choose `Don't detect my modem, I will select it from a list`, and then click Next.
4. The list of manufacturers and models appears. From the Standard Modem Types choose Dial-Up Networking Serial Cable between 2 PCs and then click Next.
5. Choose any available port and click Next. NT installs your modem. When the next screen appears, choose Finish.
6. Click OK to close the Modem Installer.

Exercise 1—Installing Remote Access Service

In this exercise, you install the Remote Access Service. If you already have this installed, skip to exercise 2.

1. Open the Network dialog box, and then from the Services tab choose Add.
2. From the list, choose the Remote Access Service. Click OK, and when prompted enter the source files directory.
3. Choose Close on the Network dialog box. When prompted, select the Null Modem or the modem you already had.
4. From the RAS Setup dialog box, choose Configure, and select Dial Out. Click OK to return to the RAS Setup dialog box.
5. Click the Continue button.
6. When prompted, restart your system.

Exercise 2—Creating Phonebook Entries

You now create a new phonebook entry. This exercise walks you through all the information required to create a real phonebook entry.

1. Open the My Computer icon and double-click Dial-up Networking.
2. As this is the first time you have run Dial-up Networking, you are informed that the phonebook is empty and are asked to add a new entry.

Note If you have already used Dial-up Networking, you can click the New button and you will be in the same position.

3. For the Name, enter **Test Entry Number 1** and then click Next.
4. Select the first (I am calling the Internet) and third (The non-Windows NT server) check boxes. Then select Next.
5. Enter **555-3840** as the phone number and click Next.
6. Select PPP as the protocol and click Next.
7. Choose Use a terminal window from the next screen and then click Next.
8. Assuming the server provides you an address, click Next.
9. Enter **148.53.66.7** as the DNS server and click Next.
10. Now you have entered all the information. Click Finish.

Exercise 3—Editing Phonebook Entries

In this exercise, you work with editing a phonebook entry and the preferences.

1. To create a shortcut to the entry, choose More, Create a shortcut to the entry.
2. Accept the default name (Test Entry Number 1.rnk).
3. Close the Dial-Up Networking dialog box.
4. On the Desktop, right-click the icon and choose Edit entry and modem properties.
5. Add the alternate numbers **555-9930** and **555-6110**. To do this, click the Alternates button, type the first number in the New phone number field, and click Add. Do the same for the second number.
6. Click OK to save the changes.
7. You have created a script for this entry and wish to use it. Right-click the icon on the desktop and choose Edit entry and modem properties.
8. Select the Script tab and click Run this Script.
9. From the drop-down list, choose PPPMENU.SCP.
10. Click the Server tab and Enable software compression.
11. Click OK to save the changes.

Exercise 4—Configuring RAS as a Server

In this exercise, you set up the Remote Access Service to act as a RAS server. This enables others to dial in to your machine.

1. Open the Network dialog box and choose the Services tab.
2. Click the Remote Access Service and click the Properties button.
3. In the dialog box that appears, select the Null Modem cable (or the modem you are using) and select Configure.
4. Click the Dial Out and Receive Calls option and then click OK to close the dialog box.
5. Click the Network button. From here, ensure that TCP/IP is configured in the Server Settings.
6. Click the Configure button beside TCP/IP and choose Use static address pool.
7. Enter **148.53.90.0** as the Begin address and **148.53.90.255** as the end address. Click OK to close the dialog box and then click OK again to close the Server Settings.

8. Click Continue to return to the Network dialog box and then choose Close.
9. You need to restart your computer.

Exercise 5—Assigning Permissions

You now provide your users with dial-in permissions and review the Remote Access Admin program.

1. Start the User Manager for Domains (User Manager works fine in this case).
2. Choose User, New User and enter the following information:

Username	Bilbo
Full name	Bilbo Baggins
Description	Hobbit (small with furry feet)
Password	Blank

3. Click the Dialin icon and check the Grant dial-in permission.
4. Click OK to close the Dial-in dialog box and then click OK to add the user.
5. Close User Manager for Domains.
6. Open the Remote Access Admin program from the Administrative Tools group.
7. Choose Users, Permissions from the menu. Click on Bilbo's name in the list. Does he have dial-in permission? (He should.)
8. Choose the account you logged on as. If you do not have dial-in permission, grant it to yourself.

Summary

The era where a user could sit at a stand-alone computer is long past and the privilege of users to communicate with each other long ago moved from a few technical users into the mainstream. Any serious networking product that hopes to compete in today's market must provide a facility for users who travel or work from home. Remote Access Services is the Microsoft solution that enables this to happen. As stated in the introduction, this chapter covered both the basics of RAS: installing and configuring, as well as the relationship of RAS with the TCP/IP protocol.

Test Yourself

1. What service does RAS provide?
2. How many inbound RAS connections can Workstation handle? Server?
3. What dial-in protocols does Windows NT support?
4. When users dial in, can they talk to only the system that they dial in to?
5. What is Multilink?
6. What is callback security? What configurations can you have?
7. What are the three options that you can set for Port Usage?
8. What network protocols will the RAS server support?
9. Can a user who dials in using NetBEUI use the services of a remote server that communicates using TCP/IP?
10. What is the purpose of the Telephony API?
11. Where can you enable a log that records all the communications between the modem and the system?
12. Can the Telephony API be set to turn off the call waiting?
13. What types of security does the RAS server accept?
14. Can you enter more than one phone number per phonebook entry?
15. How do you create a shortcut to a phonebook entry?
16. What do you have to change to use a different DNS for a phonebook entry?
17. What condition must be met before you can select a frame size of 1006 or 1500 bytes?
18. If your dial in server requires you to log on, and this cannot be scripted, what can you do?
19. How many forms can the Dial-up Networking Monitor take?
20. What does Auto dial do for you?
21. What events can cause the Dial-up Networking Monitor to make a sound?
22. Where can you grant a user dial-in permissions?
23. From where does the IP address for a client come?
24. What is the purpose of PPTP?
25. How does PPTP show up in the Remote Access Admin?

Test Yourself Answers

1. RAS provides dial-in networking for Windows NT Workstation and Server.
2. There is a one-connection limit on inbound RAS when you are working with NT Workstation. Server has been tested with up to 256 inbound connections.
3. Windows NT enables you to dial out using either PPP (Point-to-Point Protocol) or using SLIP (Serial Line Internet Protocol). The dial-in for Windows NT only supports PPP.
4. Depending on the configuration of the protocol that they use to dial in, they are allowed to see either the one computer that they dial in to, or they can see the entire network.
5. Multilink is a special protocol that enables a user to use more than one modem to connect to a RAS server. It should be noted that the Multilink protocol does not work with the callback security.
6. Callback security causes the RAS server to call back the client. There are three forms of callback security: None (no callback is done); Set by Caller (This enables the caller to enter the number he is at. Although this does not necessarily increase security, it reduces the long distant charges for the user.); Preset. (This requires that the users be at a specific phone number. Therefore they can only call from a known location.)
7. A port can be used for Dial Out, Receive Calls, or both.
8. The RAS server enables you to call in using NetBEUI, NWLink, and TCP/IP. These are configured in the RAS Setup under the Network button.
9. If the server is using NetBIOS, the user can call in using NetBIOS (or anything else). The RAS Server uses a system called a NetBIOS Gateway to forward the SMB request to the other server over the TCP/IP protocol.
10. The Telephony API enables you to set up Windows NT with different locations. You can choose the location that you are calling from and the system will know whether the call is local or long distance, what the dialing codes are, and even what calling card to use.
11. This feature is turned on in the Advanced Properties of the modem that you want to record communications with.
12. Yes. This is configured in the General settings for the location. Note of course that it will not turn the call-waiting back on.
13. The RAS server can be configured to accept most types of authentication. This includes clear text, MS-CHAP, MD5-CHAP, and SPAP.
14. Yes. Using the Alternates button on the General tab of an entries property dialog box you can enter as many phone numbers as you like.

15. From the Dial-up Networking dialog box, choose the entry and then select More, Create shortcut to entry.
16. This configuration is done under the TCP/IP settings for the entry that is on the Servers page.
17. You need to be dialing in to the server using the SLIP protocol. This is the only case where you have the choice of frame size.
18. You can configure the entry to bring up a terminal window that enables you to enter a user name and password as you are logging on.
19. The Dial-up Networking Monitor can be either an icon on the taskbar (beside the clock) or a window on your screen.
20. The Auto dial feature automatically reconnects to a server that you were using if you have disconnected. It also enables you to configure your system to automatically disconnect after a given idle period to save communications costs.
21. The monitor can be configured to make a sound when a connection is made, data is sent, data is received, or line errors occur.
22. This can be done either from the User Manager for Domains or from the Remote Access Admin program.
23. The client's IP address will come from a DHCP server, a static pool of addresses you configure, or they could select their own. Normally the address comes from a DHCP server.
24. This enables you to configure users that already have a service provider to connect to the corporate network in a secure fashion across the Internet.
25. PPTP connections appear as VPNs or Virtual Private Networks. PPTP enables you to then tunnel (or encapsulate) other protocols within it for transmission over the network.

PART V

Microsoft TCP/IP Implementation

19 Troubleshooting TCP/IP 561

20 Designing a TCP/IP Intranetwork.................... 589

CHAPTER 19

Troubleshooting TCP/IP

One of the major activities that a systems professional must perform is troubleshooting the network problems. You can take several basic steps in the troubleshooting process. This chapter covers the basic troubleshooting of the TCP/IP stack and a theory of troubleshooting found by many professionals to have worked over the past few years.

This chapter also introduces you to some of the specific things that go wrong in the different services and protocols discussed earlier in this book. This chapter, even this whole book, cannot cover all the possible problems that might occur on your network. Instead, this chapter intends to point out some of the common mistakes.

The Basics

You should, of course, check some very basic things. If you have worked in the industry, these should all be very familiar to you. The simple things are often overlooked for the more complicated answers, notably if you are working in a new operating system. The tendency when you move to a new operating system is to blame that operating system for the problems that are occurring.

Where Is the Problem?

When you deal with the problem that can creep into a large network installation, it is important to figure out where the problem is. Spending countless hours at a user's workstation, attempting to correct a problem is frustrating for you and for your user. Thus before you plunge into the bits of the computer, you should consider that there are two ends to every connection. Some things to consider include the following:

- **Is this the only user affected?** If it is, the problem is likely the user's workstation.
- **Can more than just this user not use the service, yet others can?** If this is the case, look for some common thread in these users. Is it possible they are all on one subnet, or all using the same network protocol (that the users still working are not)?
- **Can any user use the service?** If not, you should look at the server.

As you look at these points, you can check a couple of quick things with the aid of the user. If he or she is the only user having a problem, the first choice is to have the user restart the computer.

If that does not solve the problem (often it does), try pinging the user to see whether you can get to him. If you can, a permissions problem is likely or possibly he has a corrupted application. The possibility of a computer/user interface problem also exists.

If the problem is with more than one user, the problem is more critical. If you find that all the affected users are on one subnet, it could be one of several things:

- **Configuration in the router is gone.** This could mean that another router is down between them and the server with which they are attempting to work. (Use TRACERT to see where the problem is.)
- **Dead router.** You can tell this by attempting to ping their subnet. If you can't, you should look at the router.

- **One of a group of servers for the application is down.** You use Performance Monitor to check that there is activity for the service in question. You might also try pinging the system to see whether the system is the problem or perhaps its subnet is down.
- **All these users have a NetBIOS scope ID.** If this is the case, check that the server has the same scope ID.

What Changed?

One of Newton's laws of physics states that a body in motion remains in motion unless acted upon by an outside force. Normally the same can be said of computers. A computer that is working remains working unless acted upon by some outside force. Thus one of the first things to determine is what has changed.

Keeping in mind that most of the problems discussed here deal with the client/server environment, you should have a clue as to which end to look at. Some items to consider if you think the problem is at the server end include the following:

- **Has there been an upgrade to the server?** When server software is upgraded, there is always a risk—despite what the vendor says—that some of the clients that you are currently using will have a problem with the new version. If the software has been upgraded lately, you should consider checking this and possibly upgrading the client or clients as required (or removing the upgrade).
- **Has a file restore been done recently?** If the user or users involved only recently had rights to the software added, the permissions on restored files might cause a problem.
- **Has the user recently been granted other rights?** In this case or if the user was migrated recently, check to see whether the permissions are correct. As well, if the user has been granted rights recently, he was probably added to another group. Has the user logged off and back on to update his access token?
- **Is the server running?** If many users are complaining about the same thing, perhaps the server has crashed. If the server has had recent hardware upgrades, check the Event Log and/or NT Diagnostics to verify that the server's hardware is running as it should.

The other end of the connection is the client station. All too frequently, the client station is the problem. You can encounter many causes for the problems on the client stations. A few basic things you should look for are the following:

- **Check for INI files in the Windows NT installation directory.** INI files are still created by many of the 16-bit programs, including games. Users occasionally attempt to install these sorts of applications (or others). Sort the output by date. You can see the last application install. If the system is an NT system, check the Event Log; many of the events tell you what happened.

- **Check for new hardware.** Check for hardware that has been added (or removed) that could cause the problem. Examples here could include a sound board, which almost always competes with the network card for memory addresses. Perhaps there is no longer enough memory to enable the application to run. Also check to see whether the system has been serviced recently. Perhaps hardware was changed at that point.
- **Determine whether the application has ever worked on this station.** If the user is new to the company, or to this position, he may be used to other software and hardware. What worked in the user's old job will not necessarily work in the new job.
- **Check the IP configuration.** The possibility always exists that the system is configured wrongly. Notably, check the IP address and subnet mask to verify that the system is going to generate the correct subnet ID. Check that the router is on that subnet. Also verify that name resolution functions correctly.
- **Check the name resolution.** If the user can connect to the IP, the problem might be name resolution. Verify the DNS and/or WINS servers are running, also check that the HOSTS, LMHOSTS, and NETWORKS files are correct.
- **If the problem is connectivity, don't forget to check the obvious.** Is it plugged in? Is the jack a live jack?
- **If you get a bad command or file name error, you should still check the path.**

If all else fails, you can now consider this a problem. Problems are annoying, but resolving them is one of life's greater thrills. The next thing you need to do is start to delve into the nuts and bolts of how the application works. This requires that you become familiar with the ports that are used and what sort of transmissions are required.

Note On many occasions, I have been able to ping a server, yet unable to use the DNS server that was on the server. In a case like this, the service itself had stopped responding.

Computers are very simple by their nature—they move bits of data from point A to point B. They manipulate the information in the processor and move it back. If you can figure out the path that the data has to take from point A to point B, you can effectively troubleshoot the problem.

Consider an example of a user who is attempting to download a file from an FTP server. Many things can go wrong. Depending on what is wrong, the effect on other applications could be none or total. The following list outlines all the parts that come into play during this transfer:

1. The user selects Start, Run.
2. The user enters the FTP command.
3. The system creates a memory space for the process and initializes it.
4. The FTP executable is searched for in this order: current directory, and then each directory in the path in the order they are entered.
5. The application is loaded into the memory space.
6. Control of the thread for the process is passed to the application.
7. The user gets a prompt (which uses the video subsystem from NT).
8. The user enters the destination host (www.microsoft.com).
9. FTP actively opens the name service port and sends a query to the DNS server.
10. The transport protocol (UDP in this case) takes the data and bundles it. The UDP datagram and pseudo header is passed to IP.
11. IP looks at the address of the DNS server and performs the ANDing process to see whether it is local or remote (local in this case).
12. ARP checks the ARP cache for an entry to the DNS server IP address (there is none).
13. ARP now creates an ARP broadcast and asks IP to send it.
14. IP takes the ARP broadcast and passes it to the NDIS drivers.
15. NDIS packages the datagram in a frame, and sends it on the wire.
16. Every system on the wire now receives the frame and examines it. If the frame is for the system, it grabs it.
17. On the DNS server (if it is local; otherwise the router), the Network layer passes the frame up to IP as a datagram.
18. IP gives the frame to ARP. ARP adds the information to its cache, and creates a reply that it gives to IP.
19. IP passes this to the Network layer, which then sends the information to the other system's MAC address.
20. The MAC layer on the other system receives the frame and passes it to IP.

21. IP passes it to ARP, which adds the information to cache, and hands the MAC address back to IP (ARP is always local).
22. IP now takes the UDP datagram and creates an IP datagram. This is passed to NDIS with the MAC address.
23. NDIS in the client's host sends directly to NDIS on the DNS server.
24. NDIS on the DNS server (which in this case is NT) receives the datagram and passes it to the IP layer.
25. IP decodes the header information and passes the UDP datagram to UPD.
26. UDP decodes the UDP datagram and passes the request for name resolution to the name service port.
27. The DNS service receives the request and checks its database.
28. If there is a match (if there wasn't, this book would be fifty pages longer), the information is packaged as a Name Query Reply and passed back to the UDP name service port.
29. UDP receives the information, bundles it, and passes the UDP datagram and pseudo header to the IP layer.
30. IP checks whether the address is local or remote (local in this case).
31. IP checks with ARP for a MAC address.
32. ARP checks the cache, finds it, and returns the address to IP.
33. IP passes the datagram to NDIS with the MAC address. NDIS sends the data as a frame (or frames) to the MAC on the client computer.
34. NDIS on the client passes the frame to IP as a datagram.
35. IP decodes the header and passes it to UDP.
36. UDP decodes the datagram and passes the information to the FTP software over the name service port.

Note Ports for name service resolution and name service server are different.

37. The client now has the target IP address. FTP actively opens a port above 1023.
38. FTP passes a session request to TCP over the port.
39. TCP creates a TCP segment that contains the SYN flag and pseudo header, which are passed to IP.

40. IP checks whether the host is local or remote. In this case, it is remote.
41. IP checks the routing table, and finds the default gateway as the route.
42. IP consults ARP for the MAC address of the router.
43. ARP checks the ARP cache. (This is long enough. If the address isn't there, several of the previous steps could be repeated.)
44. IP creates the IP datagram and forwards it to NDIS.
45. NDIS forwards the datagram as a frame to the local destination, which is the router.
46. The Network layer (which may not be NDIS) on the router receives the frame and passes it to IP.
47. IP checks the address to see whether it is local (it's not).
48. IP checks the routing table for a route. It finds one on a local subnet.
49. IP checks with ARP for the MAC address.
50. Luckily the MAC address is in cache (or there would be steps 12 to 21 again).
51. IP packages the datagram and passes it to the Network layer.
52. The Network layer passes the frame to the next hop.
53. Steps 46 to 52 are repeated for each hop until the destination host receives the packet.
54. The NDIS layer of the other host passes the request to the IP layer.
55. IP decodes the header and passes it to TCP.
56. TCP creates the acknowledgment and informs the port of activity.

Note This is not the complete series of steps. It is intended, however, to give you the idea of how detailed you can and sometimes have to get. After 56 steps, the client application and host service are not even communicating yet. As an extra exercise, try to figure out all the other steps required to complete the file transfer.

The point of the preceding note is twofold: First, it should help you remember that there is lot more going on than double clicking; second, it should give you an appreciation of the number of pieces that all have to work to make TCP/IP actually function.

Tools and Utilities

Objective E.2

Before going into each of the services and what can go wrong with them, take a look at some of the tools that help you find the problems. Some of the tools have already been discussed. Others are introduced here because they are not specific to TCP/IP—but neither are the errors that will seem to be TCP/IP-related.

- Ping
- IPCONFIG
- NETSTAT
- NBTSTAT
- ROUTE
- TRACERT
- ARP
- Network Monitor
- Performance Monitor
- Event Viewer
- NT Diagnostics

Ping

The uses of Ping are by now well documented. This is the utility that enables you to verify the basic network connectivity and the function of the TCP/IP protocol stack.

IPCONFIG

This utility has also been discussed quite a bit. The IPCONFIG utility enables you to verify that your system is correctly configured and that all the information is in fact entered. You can also use this utility with DHCP system to RENEW their addresses. This can cause confusion if the host has just moved to another subnet and is still trying to use the old address.

NETSTAT

NETSTAT is used to check the status of the TCP/IP connections. This helps you to determine which port or ports are not working. It can also verify that any services that you are running are using the correct ports.

NBTSTAT

If you can use TCP/IP Winsock communications, NBTSTAT can be used to check the status of connections that you are attempting with other systems over NetBIOS. This can also help to see whether the problem that you are facing is one of name resolution.

ROUTE

Using the ROUTE command, you can check that the system has the routes that you expected. This is very important in the case of an environment that does not use dynamic routing, or if preferred routes are entered on some workstation that are later moved.

TRACERT

If you can talk to the local network but not the intranet, your problem might be a bad route to the other system. The TRACERT utility enables you to check that router and specify different routes that you think might work better.

ARP

ARP enables you to verify that no static ARP entries exist. You can also see what entries are in the ARP cache, which enables you to verify that ARP is functioning correctly.

Network Monitor

When all else fails, you might be required to check the actual packets flowing on the network. Network Monitor enables you, at the very least, to check the information moving in and out of your system. If you work with the full Network Monitor that comes with Systems Management Server, you can check the data going in and out of a remote system.

Performance Monitor

From the brief look at Performance Monitor in Chapter 17, "Management Utilities: SNMP and the Performance Monitor," hopefully you gained the impression that it is a powerful tool that enables you to check on not only the network components, but all parts of the NT system. If networking is slow, there is always the possibility that there are other pieces causing the problem. This tool enables you to look at processor usage for each and every process that runs on the system and track it over a period of time.

You can also check the general condition of the network if you look at the ICMP counters because they enable you to see the number of errors coming back to your station.

Event Viewer

The Event Viewer is a critical troubleshooting tool. This is where all the different parts of the system report errors. The Event Viewer actually is a fancy log file that keeps track of the following three different logs for you:

- **System.** In this log, you find all the major system errors. This includes the DNS server not being able to start, the network card not being found, and duplicate IP addresses.
- **Security.** If you enable auditing, the system records all the audited events in this log. This includes any unsuccessful attempts to log, or attempted use of resources for which the users did not have rights.
- **Application.** Any of the Back Office applications that you install report their system errors in the Applications Log. This will usually be Microsoft products. Other vendors are, however, beginning to embrace the sense of a single error log.

Figure 19.1 shows the Event Viewer screen. Notice the highlighted Event Log entry in the Event Log. When you are looking for a problem in the Event Log, you should always start at this entry and move up the event.

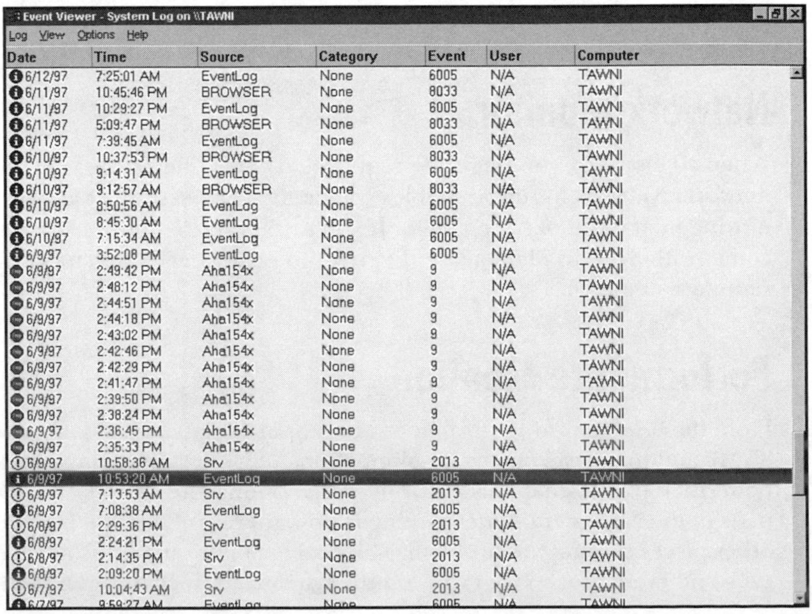

Figure 19.1

The Event Viewer.

Event Viewer - System Log on \\TAWNI

Log View Options Help

Date	Time	Source	Category	Event	User	Computer
6/12/97	7:25:01 AM	EventLog	None	6005	N/A	TAWNI
6/11/97	10:45:46 PM	BROWSER	None	8033	N/A	TAWNI
6/11/97	10:29:27 PM	EventLog	None	6005	N/A	TAWNI
6/11/97	5:09:47 PM	BROWSER	None	8033	N/A	TAWNI
6/11/97	7:39:45 AM	EventLog	None	6005	N/A	TAWNI
6/10/97	10:37:53 PM	BROWSER	None	8033	N/A	TAWNI
6/10/97	9:14:31 AM	EventLog	None	6005	N/A	TAWNI
6/10/97	9:12:57 AM	BROWSER	None	8033	N/A	TAWNI
6/10/97	8:50:56 AM	EventLog	None	6005	N/A	TAWNI
6/10/97	8:45:30 AM	EventLog	None	6005	N/A	TAWNI
6/10/97	7:15:34 AM	EventLog	None	6005	N/A	TAWNI
6/9/97	3:52:08 PM	EventLog	None	6005	N/A	TAWNI
6/9/97	2:49:42 PM	Aha154x	None	9	N/A	TAWNI
6/9/97	2:48:12 PM	Aha154x	None	9	N/A	TAWNI
6/9/97	2:44:51 PM	Aha154x	None	9	N/A	TAWNI
6/9/97	2:44:18 PM	Aha154x	None	9	N/A	TAWNI
6/9/97	2:43:02 PM	Aha154x	None	9	N/A	TAWNI
6/9/97	2:42:46 PM	Aha154x	None	9	N/A	TAWNI
6/9/97	2:42:29 PM	Aha154x	None	9	N/A	TAWNI
6/9/97	2:41:47 PM	Aha154x	None	9	N/A	TAWNI
6/9/97	2:39:50 PM	Aha154x	None	9	N/A	TAWNI
6/9/97	2:38:24 PM	Aha154x	None	9	N/A	TAWNI
6/9/97	2:36:45 PM	Aha154x	None	9	N/A	TAWNI
6/9/97	2:35:33 PM	Aha154x	None	9	N/A	TAWNI
6/9/97	10:58:36 AM	Srv	None	2013	N/A	TAWNI
6/9/97	10:53:20 AM	EventLog	None	6005	N/A	TAWNI
6/9/97	7:13:53 AM	Srv	None	2013	N/A	TAWNI
6/9/97	7:08:38 AM	EventLog	None	6005	N/A	TAWNI
6/8/97	2:29:36 PM	Srv	None	2013	N/A	TAWNI
6/8/97	2:24:21 PM	EventLog	None	6005	N/A	TAWNI
6/8/97	2:14:35 PM	Srv	None	2013	N/A	TAWNI
6/8/97	2:09:20 PM	EventLog	None	6005	N/A	TAWNI
6/7/97	10:04:43 AM	Srv	None	2013	N/A	TAWNI
6/7/97	9:59:27 AM	EventLog	None	6005	N/A	TAWNI

The first thing that is done when Event Log starts is to write that entry (just about always, occasionally there is one entry before, normally a network card). Double-click the entry and then you will see the details (see fig. 19.2). You can continue up the list of events by using the Previous button (although it seems backward).

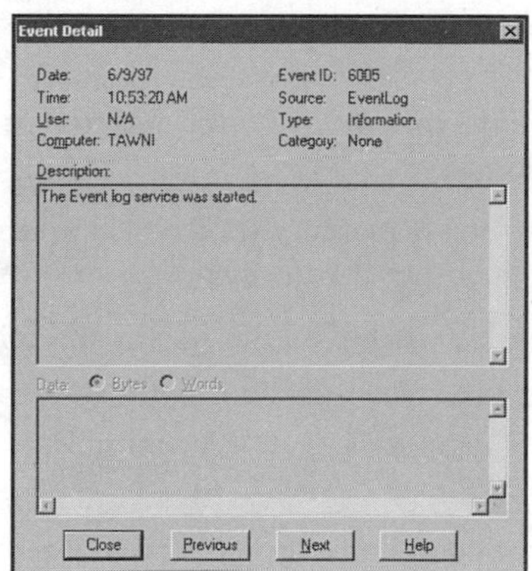

Figure 19.2

The Event Detail dialog box.

NT Diagnostics

Another useful tools is the NT Diagnostic application (see fig. 19.3). In NT 4, this tool not only enables you to look at the current system, but also enables you to see other systems on the network. Several tabs on the NT Diagnostics tool enable you to see the information about a system. These are as follows:

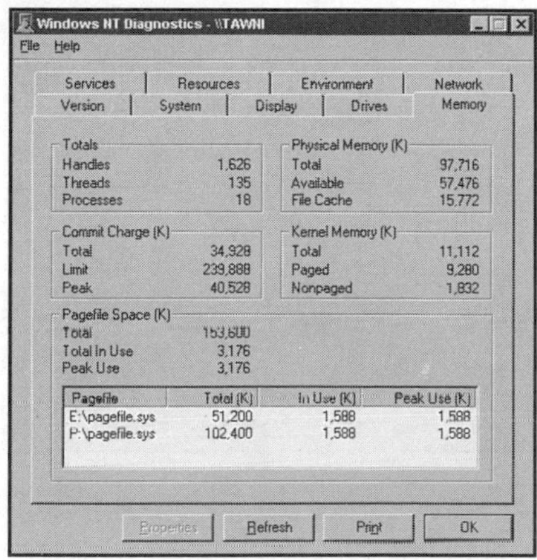

Figure 19.3

The Windows NT Diagnostics screen.

- **Version.** The version and registration information for the version of NT currently installed on the system.
- **System.** Information about the HAL (Hardware Abstraction Layer), BIOS, and CPUs in the system.
- **Display.** Tells you what the current resolution of the system and the chip set and drivers used are.
- **Drives.** Enables you to see the disk drives connected to a system. This enables you to see sector/cluster and so on.
- **Memory.** Describes the available memory (both real and virtual) and what memory is committed to the different types of processes on the system.
- **Services.** List all the services available on the system and tells you whether they are running.
- **Resources.** The IRQ, base memory I/O, DMA channels, and so on, and what pieces of hardware are using them.
- **Environment.** The environment variables set for the users and the system.
- **Network.** General information about your connection to the network, as well as information on the transports, settings, and some statistics.

To connect across the network, you can choose File, Select Computer. This gives you a different screen that shows all the tabs across the top (see fig. 19.4).

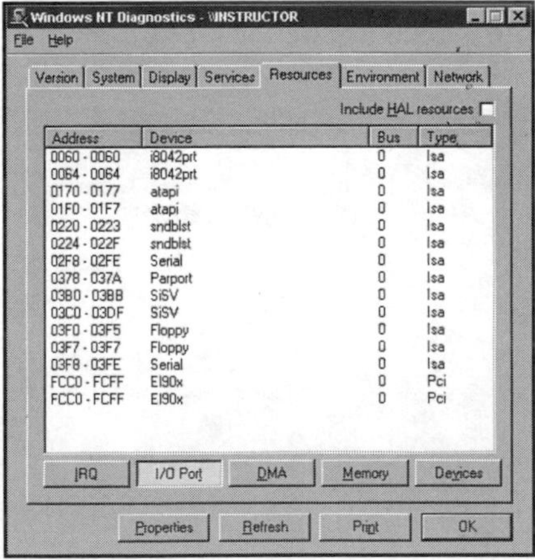

Windows NT Diagnostics - \\INSTRUCTOR
File Help
Version System Display Services Resources Environment Network
Include HAL resources
Address Device Bus Type
0060 - 0060 i8042prt 0 Isa
0064 - 0064 i8042prt 0 Isa
0170 - 0177 atapi 0 Isa
01F0 - 01F7 atapi 0 Isa
0220 - 0223 sndblst 0 Isa
0224 - 022F sndblst 0 Isa
02F8 - 02FE Serial 0 Isa
0378 - 037A Parport 0 Isa
03B0 - 03BB SiSV 0 Isa
03C0 - 03DF SiSV 0 Isa
03F0 - 03F5 Floppy 0 Isa
03F7 - 03F7 Floppy 0 Isa
03F8 - 03FE Serial 0 Isa
FCC0 - FCFF El90x 0 Pci
FCC0 - FCFF El90x 0 Pci
IRQ I/O Port DMA Memory Devices
Properties Refresh Print OK

Figure 19.4
Diagnostics on a remote system.

Note You can print the information for both a local system or a remote system. Click the Print button in the dialog box.

Checking Connectivity

The first step is to confirm that the TCP/IP stack is configured. This is best done by running the IPCONFIG /ALL command that you can find on most clients (in Windows 95, this would be WINIPCFG). This enables you to see that the configuration is in fact correct and that the system is running as it should.

Because the series of steps that you should go through in checking the TCP/IP connection has already been covered, the following list should be little more than review.

1. Ping 127.0.0.1.
2. Ping your_IP_address.
3. Ping local_IP_address.
4. Ping remote_IP_address.
5. Ping host_name (this could be on your network or an FQDN—Fully Qualified Domain Name—such as www.learnix.com).
6. Ping NetBIOS_name.

These important steps ensure that the network itself can pass data from one point to another. Ping, however, only ever tests part of the process. Remember that Ping is handled at the IP layer. (This is required so that you can ping a router.)

To fully test the communications between two hosts, you need to try to establish sessions between the two hosts. You can do this in many ways. It is easiest if services are running on both hosts.

If the system in question is running the Personal Web Server, Peer Web Server, or IIS, you can try a WWW or FTP connection to verify that you can communicate. If the system is running DNS, try NSLOOKUP to see whether the system is running. If SNMP is installed (as might be for monitoring the system with Performance Monitor), you can use the SNMPUTIL.

If the system is using NBT to allow for NetBIOS communications, you can try NET VIEW \\system_name. Better still, if the system is an NT system, use Server Manager.

If the IPCONFIG and Ping commands work, you want to verify that the services that you need to communicate with the system can talk to the other host—in other words, the services are listening on the correct ports.

Note Again I have found that restarting a system usually clears up the problem. If not, you can often uninstall the service and reinstall it.

Troubleshooting TCP/IP Services

The different applications all have problems associated with them in particular. This text has covered a lot of different protocols and applications, and now covers some of the things that can go wrong with them.

The Internet Information Server

IIS is generally fairly stable. You can, however, occasionally have problems with it. You can do the following few common things to ensure that users can work with the services:

- Ensure TCP/IP is functioning correctly.
- Ensure the port is the standard port number that is used.
- If you made a change to the service, make sure that you stop and start the service.
- Ensure that if you have any scripts, the directories they are in have Execute permissions.
- If your site uses reverse lookup for verification, make sure name resolution is functioning.
- If you are creating virtual servers, make sure they are removed if the IP addresses are used.
- Ensure DHCP addressing is not used for the IIS site.
- Make sure the correct entries are in the DNS server if you work with the Internet.
- If users cannot connect, ensure the IUSR_computername account exists and the password is correct in the Service Properties and the User Manager.

TCP/IP Printing

Printing is a problem in all networks. Using TCP/IP can add a few differences that you should be aware of:

- Job does not print or comes out all garbled. This is likely a print driver problem. With this type of printer, you have to install the driver locally.
- Text jobs are fine; however, other jobs come out strange. This is normally a problem with using the LPD command. Ensure that you are setting the -0l option to tell the remote host the job is binary.

- If you use host names, ensure name resolution works.
- If you are hosting, ensure the TCP/IP Print Server service is started (this is not automatic).

DHCP

DHCP is a great relief to the system administrator. In some situations, however, DHCP can cause problems. Things to be aware of include the following:

- Ensure at all times that DHCP addresses are never used as static addresses.
- Make sure that if you are using a DHCP backup scheme, the server ranges do not overlap.
- If a client cannot get an address, ensure there is a scope for the client's subnet and that it is active. Make sure there is a DHCP boot relay agent if the routers do not forward BOOTP broadcasts.
- Consider using IPCONFIG /RENEW in the logon script. Although this increases the load on the DHCP server, you can be assured that the users will have the current options.
- Make sure you do not use the Unlimited lease period. This will mean that client stations never update their configuration.

WINS

Objective E.3

WINS also enables you to resolve many problems, notably with NetBIOS over TCP/IP networking. Although the system is fairly simple, things can still go wrong:

- If a client cannot resolve addresses, make sure the client is set up to use WINS and that the address is right.
- Remember that not all clients can register with WINS. Thus if you must resolve their names, you need to add static mappings.
- The WINS server should be able to handle 10,000 computers, but that is excessive. Where needed, place WINS servers near clients. WINS should never be slower than local broadcast.
- Remember that pull replication can be set up for timed intervals. Therefore you should use this over slow links.
- For non-WINS clients, you should set up a proxy agent on their subnet. Otherwise, they can't resolve names across the intranet.

Note

The TCP/IP advanced configuration has a setting for NetBIOS Scope ID. This was included in NT 3.5 and remains in NT 4 for compatibility. The scope ID works like the SNMP community name discussed in Chapter 17—only systems with the same scope ID can talk to each other using NetBIOS. It does not, however, affect Winsock communications. Scope ID is not recommended for most networks. If you are having a NetBIOS communications problem, however, you might wish to check that a Scope ID has not been added by mistake.

The Browser Service

Objective E.3

The Browser service is not really TCP/IP-specific. Some concerns are important, however, when browsing on a TCP/IP network if you do not use WINS:

- Even if the clients can see the remote computer, they need to be able to resolve the IP address before they can connect.
- LMHOSTS files are required for the domain controllers to facilitate browsing and domain activity.
- Computers can remain in the browse list for 51 minutes after they crash. This is something you need to make users understand.
- Logon is handled by broadcast unless a #DOM tag exists in the LMHOSTS files.

DNS

The DNS service is new to NT 4, and it is a very welcome addition. Microsoft DNS has many strong features. There are, however, issues as well:

- To register with the InterNIC (rather than having your ISP handle your domain), you need a primary and secondary DNS server.
- If the DNS server does not have a resolution, it must go to the root servers and back down. This often takes longer than the client timeout value.
- If you want to be able to provide reverse lookup, you must create the in-addr.arpa domain.
- WINS integration is configured differently for the DNS Domains and the reverse lookup. Ensure you turn them both on.
- You can always use NSLOOKUP to test the DNS resolution.
- If DNS was installed before, and you are re-installing, you might need to remove the boot file from the \%winroot%\system32\dns directory.

Summary

One of the most rewarding feelings is fixing a problem that you have struggled with for a long period of time. This chapter has presented a basic strategy for finding and eliminating problems with TCP/IP being used with Windows NT. The best approach to troubleshooting is to look at all the places the data has to get through, and determine from that where the problem resides.

Test Yourself

This exercise presents several difference scenarios. For each of these, you are presented with a network not working in an optimum way. The questions after the network drawings give you a chance to determine what is wrong with the network.

Scenario 1—Troubleshooting an FTP Server

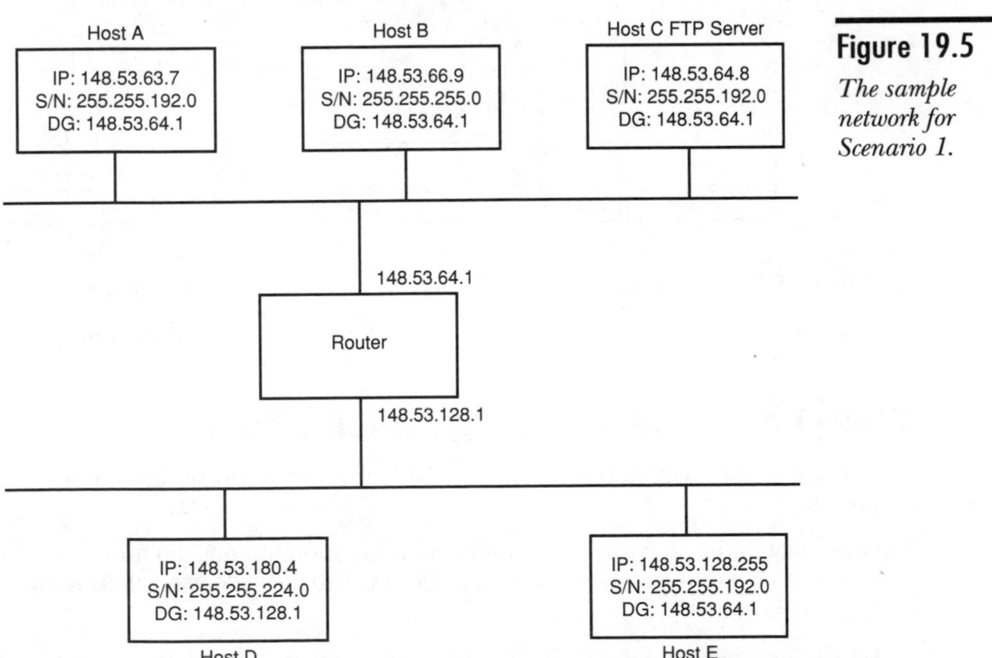

Figure 19.5 *The sample network for Scenario 1.*

1. Which systems can talk to the FTP server?
2. Why can't the other systems talk to the FTP Server?
3. What should the correct values be?
4. After you correct the problem, your clients still cannot connect to the FTP server. What other settings could you check?

Scenario 2—A Subnetting Problem

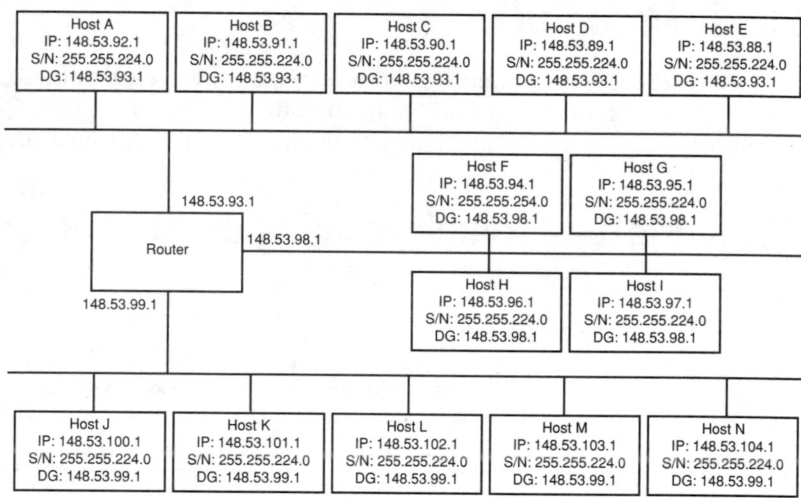

Figure 19.6
The sample network for Scenario 2.

1. Which of the hosts in this system will not be able to communicate? Why?
2. Is there any way in which you can fix this problem by changing the subnet mask?

Scenario 3—Finding Configuration Errors

1. In the network diagram shown in figure 19.7, what errors in configuration are present?
2. Given that in the scenario shown there are never more than 2,000 hosts per subnet, which of the two subnet masks (255.255.240.0 or 255.255.248.0) is the better subnet mask?
3. Which hosts need to have their IP configuration changed to use the subnet mask 255.255.248.0 as the subnet mask for the entire network?

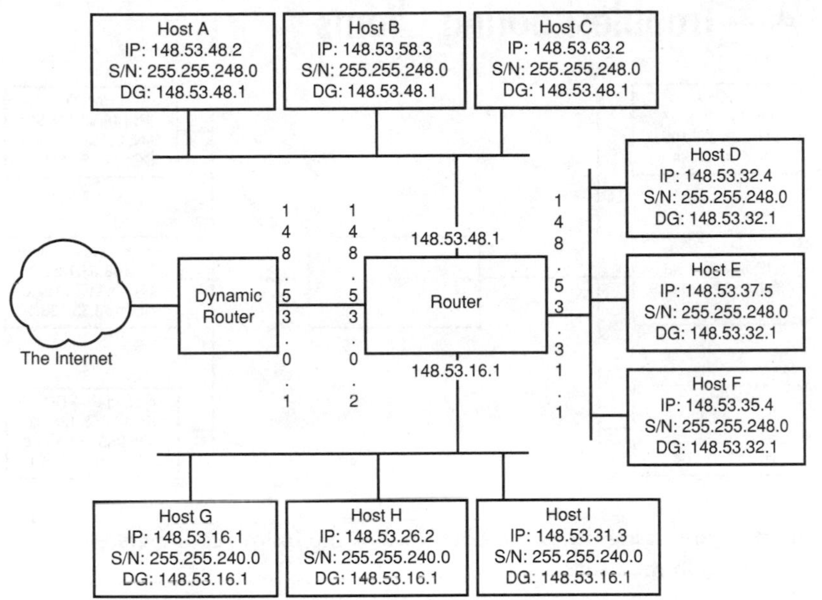

Figure 19.7

The sample network for Scenario 3.

4. Given the subnet mask of 255.255.248.0, and the contents of the routing table for router J (see table 19.1), is this routing table correct? If required, what can you do to correct the problem?

TABLE 19.1
Router Table for Router at J

Network	Subnet Mask	Gateway
148.53.56.0	255.255.248.0	148.53.56.1
148.53.32.0	255.255.248.0	148.53.32.1
148.53.24.0	255.255.248.0	148.53.24.1
148.53.0.0	255.255.0.0	148.53.0.1
0.0.0.0	0.0.0.0	148.53.0.1

Scenario 4—Troubleshooting Clients

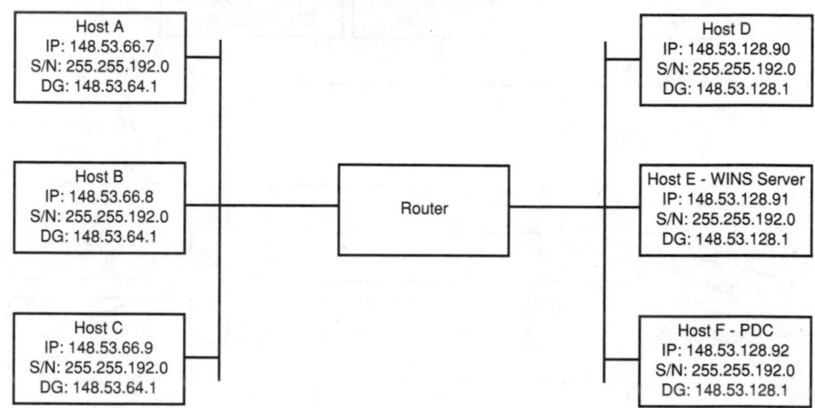

Figure 19.8
The sample network for Scenario 4.

The user at station A cannot log on to the domain. For the following file systems, what could you do to help the user?

1. LAN Manager for OS/2 client
2. Windows Version 3.1

Consider that the following changes are made to the scenario: the system marked as B became a BDC, and the WINS server does not exist. What would be required to facilitate domain activity (that is, domain logon and security accounts manager database replication)?

Scenario 5—Client Configuration Problems

In this exercise, the following network is assumed.

1. For each of the following exhibits, determine what the problem is, the effect of the problem, and a solution.

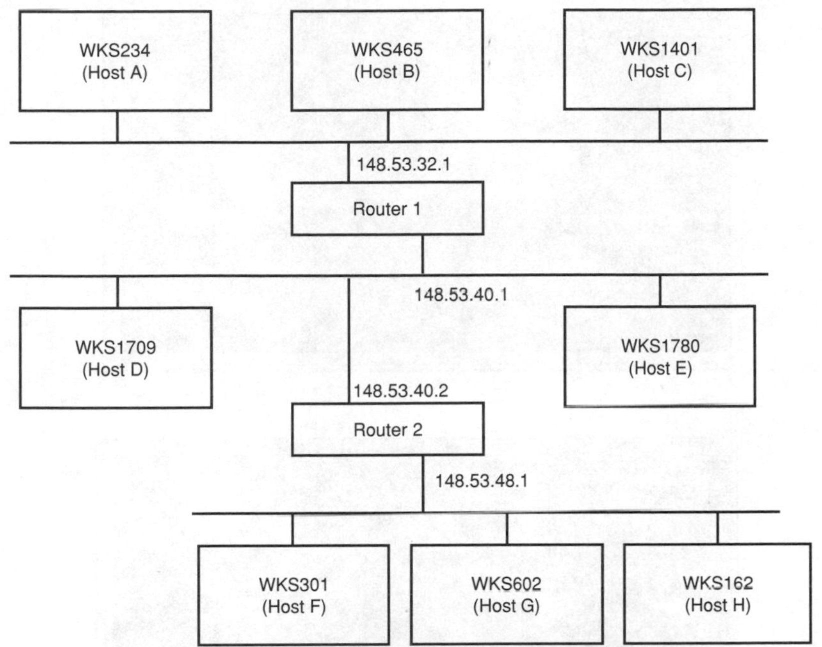

Figure 19.9

The sample network for Scenario 5.

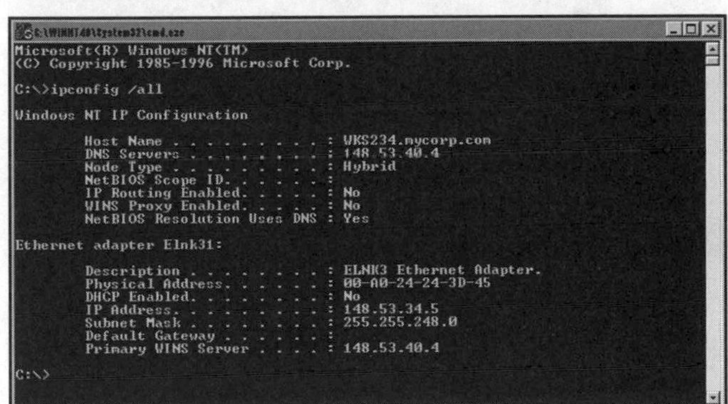

Figure 19.10

IP configuration for Host A.

Figure 19.11

IP configuration for Host C.

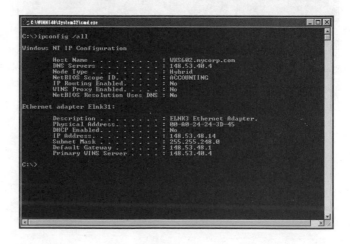

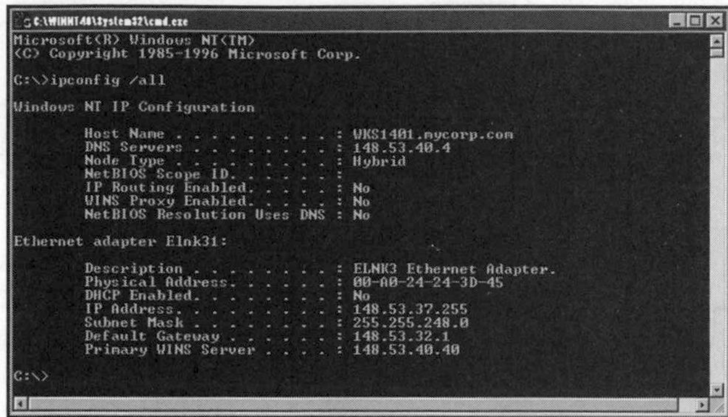

Figure 19.12

IP configuration for Host D.

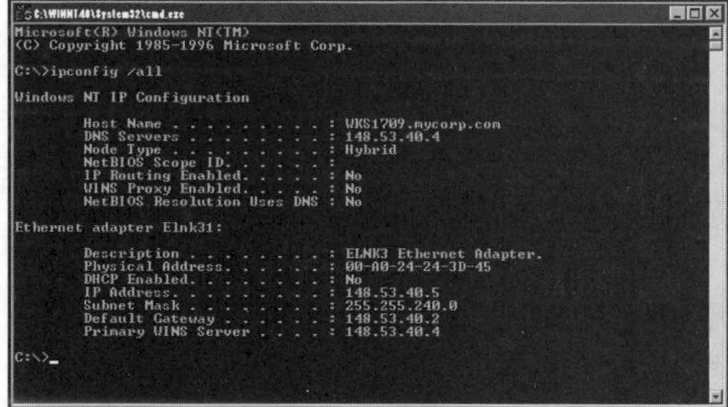

Figure 19.13

IP configuration for Host G.

```
C:\WINNT40\System32\cmd.exe

C:\>ipconfig /all

Windows NT IP Configuration

        Host Name . . . . . . . . . : WKS602.mycorp.com
        DNS Servers . . . . . . . . : 148.53.40.4
        Node Type . . . . . . . . . : Hybrid
        NetBIOS Scope ID. . . . . . : ACCOUNTING
        IP Routing Enabled. . . . . : No
        WINS Proxy Enabled. . . . . : No
        NetBIOS Resolution Uses DNS : No

Ethernet adapter Elnk31:

        Description . . . . . . . . : ELNK3 Ethernet Adapter.
        Physical Address. . . . . . : 00-A0-24-24-3D-45
        DHCP Enabled. . . . . . . . : No
        IP Address. . . . . . . . . : 148.53.48.14
        Subnet Mask . . . . . . . . : 255.255.248.0
        Default Gateway . . . . . . : 148.53.48.1
        Primary WINS Server . . . . : 148.53.40.4

C:\>
```

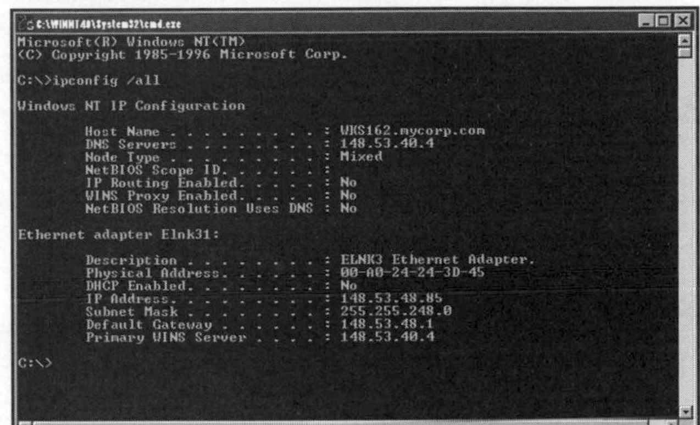

Figure 19.14

IP configuration for Host H.

Test Yourself Answers

Scenario 1

1. The only system that can talk to the FTP server is the FTP server itself.
2. The problems are as listed here:

   System A has an invalid IP address for the subnet. The subnet that the system is on is 148.53.64.0. The IP address is not valid because it falls outside the range of valid addresses.

   System B cannot communicate because it will see the FTP server as a remote system due to the incorrect subnet mask. According to system B, it is on subnet 148.53.66.0. The FTP server is on 148.53.64.0.

   System D also has a problem with its subnet mask. In this case, the system sees the other hosts as being remote. The default gateway, however, is also on a remote subnet. The system sees this and does not even try to reach the default gateway.

   System E can talk to any systems on the local subnet, but the gateway address that has been entered is incorrect. The gateway is again on a different subnet. The system will not even attempt to connect to it.

3. Table 19.2 lists the correct values.

TABLE 19.2
Possible Values for Network 1

System	IP address	Subnet Mask	Default Gateway
A	148.53.64.7	255.255.192.0	148.53.64.1
B	148.53.64.8	255.255.192.0	148.53.64.1
D	148.53.180.4	255.255.192.0	148.53.128.1
E	148.53.128.255	255.255.192.0	148.53.128.1

4. Some of the items that you might check include the following:
   - Is the FTP Server service running?
   - Because many hosts cannot connect, check the service port number.
   - Check that the FTP Server service has been restarted if there were any changes made. (You would probably just stop and start the service.)
   - Verify that you can ping the client stations. Re-initialize the TCP/IP stack (reboot).

Scenario 2

1. Both hosts F and G are unable to communicate. In the scenario given here, their IP address actually belong on the first subnet. There is also a problem in that the second and third subnets will have the same subnet ID and therefore routing will not be possible.
2. No. Because the three subnets all have hosts that have similar IP addresses, there is no way.

Scenario 3

1. The errors are as follows:
   - There are two subnet masks on this network. This is not an actual error; there will be times when it is required to have two subnet masks, and even times when this is desirable. Using multiple subnet masks, however, does require a good deal more attention be paid to the network as a whole.
   - Host G requires a different IP address, or a different subnet mask. (Here you see an example of where the multiple subnet architecture can lead to errors.)
   - The gateway on the second network is incorrect (the subnet with Hosts D, E, and F). This causes some large problems for the network. The router

(I) will have two possible routes to the network called 148.53.16.0. It can route either through 148.53.16.1 or 148.53.31.1, depending on the subnet mask the router is using. Even without the issue of two routes, the users at D, E, and F will not be able to communicate because they are in subnet 32.0, and both of the gateways will be in a different subnet.

- The last paragraph outlines a problem that will only be compounded by the problem with Host I. Host I has a duplicate IP address with the router. This means that the other hosts on this subnet (H and G) will possibly not be able to send to the world (or any other subnet). This depends on which system started up first, the router or Host I.

2. A subnet mask of 255.255.248.0 provides the required number of hosts per subnet while still providing the maximum number of subnets available for the network to expand.

3. The changes required are as follows:

   - Host A needs a new IP address that brings it into the 148.53.56.0 subnet.
   - The router for the first subnet (top) also has to be brought into the 148.53.56.0 subnet.
   - The router for the second subnet (right) also needs to have a new address that brings it into the subnet with the hosts.
   - Host I requires a new IP address. This address should be in the 148.53.24.0 subnet.
   - The router for the third subnet needs to be added to the 148.53.24.0 subnet as well, probably at 148.53.24.1.

4. No. The routing table is not correct and will not work. There will a problem in that network 148.53.56.0, 148.53.32.0, and 148.53.24.0 are all parts of the network called 148.53.0.0. This will cause the router to be unsure as to whether to send packet for those three networks to the actual subnet or on to the Internet. In others words, there is no guarantee that the information will ever reach the destination.

   To fix the problem, change the network used for the connection to the Internet. Currently the network that sits between the dynamic router and the router at J is 148.53.0.0. Thus the dynamic router believes that all the information is for a local network and looks for the host on the network between the dynamic router and the NT router that is at J. To fix this problem, you have to give the subnet that exists between the dynamic and static routers a subnet ID such as 148.53.16.0. This also enables you to have hosts sitting on the outside of the network. This would enable the entire network to function correctly.

Scenario 4

1. The LAN Manager for OS/2 client cannot use the WINS server for either the name registration/release feature or for the name resolution feature. In this case, you can do two things. You would want to add a static mapping for the client into the WINS database, and you would want to enable one of the other systems on the subnet with this host to act as a proxy server.
2. The thing to remember about Windows 3.1 is that it will normally use the MS-Client 3.0 for MS-DOS. This client can use a WINS server for the name resolution functions. Other than checking that the name does not already exist, however, there is no name registration/release interaction. In this case, you want to create a static mapping in the WINS data to the host. You also want to run the SETUP.EXE that is in the C:\NET directory to add the WINS server address to the system. (This will be stored in the SYSTEM.INI in the same directory.)
3. There would need to be some way for the domain controllers to be able to see each other and recognize each other as domain controllers. This can be handled by the LMHOSTS file. There would need to be two entries in the LMHOSTS file, one for each of the two domain controllers shown on the network. They would both be marked with the #DOM tag and probably the #PRE in the file. The client stations will not require any modification; the domain logon is handled by broadcast. In that case, however, the hosts on either network cannot log on if the domain controller on the local subnet goes down. Therefore every host requires the LMHOSTS file with the name of the two domain controllers and the #DOM tag.

Scenario 5

1. The solutions are:

Host A

In this particular host, there are two potential problems: the system is set to use the DNS server for NetBIOS Name Resolution, and the system has an incorrect default gateway.

The fact that it is using the DNS server for NetBIOS Name Resolution is not necessarily a problem. The DNS, however, must be using the same names as the NetBIOS names used on the network, otherwise the system cannot communicate with the other system on the network.

The larger of the two problems is the default gateway, with the default gateway being either not entered or wrong. (If the default gateway is not on the same subnet, the system will refuse to display it.) The system cannot communicate off the network. This means that name resolution is limited to the local network using broadcasts.

The first part of the solution is very simple: Use the correct default gateway address of 148.53.32.1. This enables the system to communicate with the whole intranet. The second part, should the system use DNS for NetBIOS Name Resolution, is a larger question. This depends on whether the system is supposed to or not. If not, clear the check box that tells the system to use DNS for NetBIOS Name Resolution (on the WINS tab in the TCP/IP configuration).

Host C

The error on this system is straightforward. The effects of the configuration error, however, are far reaching. The error is the WINS server address that is configured incorrectly. This system cannot resolve the name on the local subnet. This is slow because the attempts to reach the WINS server need to time out first. The system can then resolve the local names. The system can reach the DNS server in this case. If the user is patient enough, and if the DNS is using the same names as the NetBIOS names, the resolution will take place (remember the two methods back each other up). The system would, however, take a long time to resolve the address in this manner.

Interestingly enough, the system would have absolutely no problems with the resolution of host names because the DNS server is in place. This can cause confusion because the system might seem to work with some systems and not others. The solution to the problem is very simple: just enter the correct WINS server address.

Host D

If you look closely at the configuration for the Host D, you will notice that it has the default gateway set to 148.53.40.2. This indicates that the system is intending to communicate primarily over that router to the hosts on the third subnet.

There is not a problem. It will never be able to reach the users on the third subnet. The subnet mask in this case is wrong. It is the users on the first subnet that the system will not be able to reach. The subnet mask for this host indicates that all the systems from 148.53.32.1 to 148.53.47.255 are local to itself. This means that the hosts on the third subnet (Host D will see this as 148.53.48.1 to 148.53.63.254) appear as remote. All the systems on the first subnet, however, will return the same subnet ID.

The solution of course is to just fix the subnet mask. This will enable the system to correctly determine the remote hosts from the local hosts.

Host G

The problem with Host G is not exactly an error. The system has been given a NetBIOS Scope ID of ACCOUNTING. This means that it can communicate only with hosts that have the same scope ID. This is not necessarily an error. If the system is meant to be secure, this provides that security.

The system can still communicate with all other stations using the TPC/IP stack. It should be noted that other stations can still communicate with this host over the TCP/IP stack as well. This means that if the IIS server (for example) had been installed on the system, other hosts on the network could get at it through this opening.

On the NetBIOS side, the system can communicate only with systems of the same NetBIOS scope. This does not include the WINS server. Thus all address resolution must be done by broadcast. The error (if it is one) can be corrected by removing the NetBIOS scope ID from this host.

Host H

The problem with this host is subtle. There is no connectivity problem. This host will continue to be able to communicate over the network. The only real symptom is how slow the connection process will be.

The problem is the type of NetBIOS name resolution. The host appears completely normal if the TCP/IP (Winsock) stack is used. If the system attempts to connect to a NetBIOS host, however, it uses M-Node resolution. This means that it always attempts to broadcast first and then use the WINS server.

In this case, you need to remove the entry NodeType (or set it to 0x8) in the Registry under, `HKEY_LOCAL_MACHINE\System\CurrentControlSet\NetBT\Parameters`. Removing this key enables the system to determine the node type automatically and restore it (after restarting) to an H-Node setting.

CHAPTER 20

Designing a TCP/IP Intranetwork

In the chapters leading up to this one, you have seen all the pieces of TCP/IP that are available in Windows NT specifically, and from Microsoft in general. This chapter attempts to bring the pieces together to look at the overall implementation of a TCP/IP intranetwork. This chapter doesn't go into any procedural specifics; refer to the specific chapters for that information.

Just as in project management, most of the work is done during the planning or design phase. Therefore, this part is covered in detail. For the purposes of the discussion, this chapter walks through the planning of a network for an organization referred to as Corporation X.

Corporation X is a multinational corporation with major centers in Ottawa, Canada; Sydney, Australia; Cape Town, Republic of South Africa; and London, United Kingdom. Corporation X has series of smaller branch offices throughout the world. Figure 20.1 is a map showing these four major centers, as well as the branch offices.

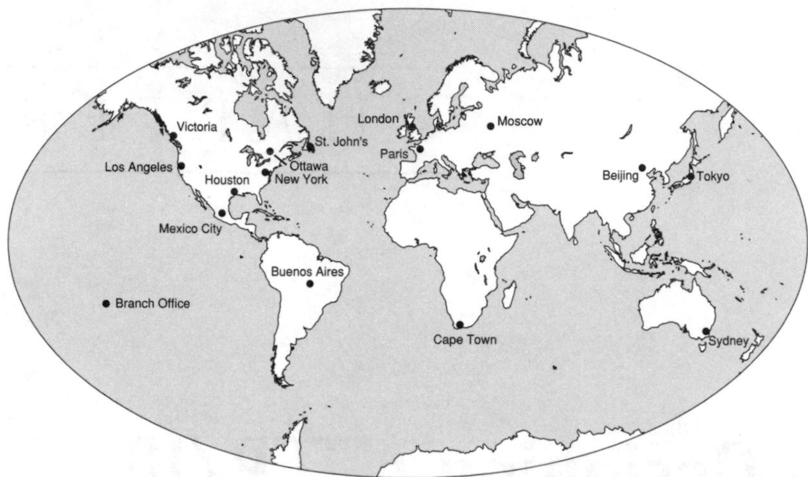

Figure 20.1
Corporation X's office locations.

As you can see, there are 11 different branch offices. Before proceeding, you need to find out a little more about the organization. You need to know several things about all the various sites for Corporation X. You also need to know what the corporation wants from the network. Some of the questions that you need to ask might include:

- How many users at each site?
- How many more locations will you add?
- Do users travel from location to location?
- How will you handle electronic mail?
- Do you want Internet access? For everyone?
- Do users need access to local resources only, or do they need access to the entire network?

If you have worked with NT for awhile, you will notice that the questions are the same that could be asked for planning a domain model.

This company plans on providing both Internet and intranet access to all employees. As well, information needs to flow easily from location to location because teams are often drawn up from human resources across the entire organization.

Obviously, the organization requires a strong communications backbone. As well, some provision must be made for the sales and technical staff who travel frequently but still need to be in contact via e-mail.

Before deciding on a communications structure, you need to determine the number of users in each location, and, more importantly, the budget. Corporation X provides the following list of staff distribution at its main locations:

- Ottawa: Corporate Headquarters
- 6,732 users distributed as follows:
    - 87 Executives
    - 3,156 Production staff
    - 672 Head Office support staff
    - 960 Accounting staff
    - 873 Research & Development staff
    - 352 Sales staff
    - 632 General Administration staff
- London: European Headquarters
- 2,462 users, as follows:
    - 14 Executives
    - 78 local Head Office support staff
    - 400 Accounting staff
    - 798 Research & Development staff
    - 651 Sales Staff
    - 521 General Administration staff
- Cape Town: African Regional Headquarters
- 1,462 users, as follows:
    - 62 Executives
    - 132 local Head Office support staff
    - 341 Accounting staff
    - 198 Research & Development staff
    - 632 Sales staff
    - 87 General Administration staff
- Sydney: Asia-Pacific Zone Headquarters
- 3,263 users, as follows:
    - 153 Executives
    - 632 local Head Office support staff

- 345 Accounting staff
- 406 Research & Development staff
- 965 Sales staff
- 762 General Administration staff

Corporation X also provides table 20.1, which gives the information for each of the branch locations:

TABLE 20.1
Users at Branch Locations

Branch	Admin	Sales	Technical
Victoria	127	253	187
Los Angeles	169	375	318
Mexico City	217	485	230
Houston	125	632	240
New York	146	496	300
Buenos Aires	289	682	120
St. John's	205	110	132
Paris	150	469	327
Moscow	259	182	51
Beijing	98	770	244
Tokyo	140	563	198

The Technical staff (including Research & Development) and the Sales staff travel often and require dial-in access from around the world. They all use laptops that have both PCMCIA modems and network cards. The Executives also travel, but normally not as often. They generally do not require dial-in, but visit the other offices where they need to be able to connect to the network and log on to their accounts.

Corporate information is kept on each of the main sites. Region-specific information, however, is kept in the appropriate branch office. This information needs to be available to all users.

Looking at IP

The starting point is deciding what sort of requirement exists for IP addresses. Corporation X currently holds the Class B address 148.53.0.0. The main connection to the Internet is through a router located in Ottawa, which is directly connected to the backbone. The Class B address can be broken down, as you know (see Chapter 6, "Subnetting"), into different numbers of networks and number of hosts per. Table 20.2 shows the breakdown.

Table 20.2
Possible Combinations of Networks and Hosts

Bits in Subnet	Networks	Hosts
2	2	16,382
3	6	8,190
4	14	4,094
5	30	2,046
6	62	1,022
7	126	510
8	254	254

The deciding factor in the subnetting scheme is the number of hosts desired per subnet. The table 20.3 gives you a look at the possibilities, and the number of subnets needed in each case.

Table 20.3
Subnets Required

Location	254 Subnets 254 hosts per	126 Subnets 510 hosts per	62 Subnets 1,022 hosts per
Ottawa	27	14	7
London	10	5	3

continues

TABLE 20.3, CONTINUED
Subnets Required

Location	254 Subnets 254 hosts per	126 Subnets 510 hosts per	62 Subnets 1,022 hosts per
Cape Town	6	3	2
Sydney	13	7	4
Victoria	3	2	1
Los Angeles	5	3	2
Mexico City	4	2	1
Houston	4	2	1
New York	4	2	1
Buenos Aires	5	3	2
St. John's	2	1	1
Paris	4	2	1
Moscow	2	1	1
Beijing	5	3	2
Tokyo	4	2	1
Total	54	29	17
Available	254	126	62

Any of these network choices works. A personal preference is to use a 7-bit mask, because that means that 126 networks are available, but require only 29. This facilitates a great deal of expansion for the future because each of the remaining 97 subnets can hold 510 hosts.

Linking the Sites

The next step is to look at the links between the different locations. Because there will be a lot of information going across the links, the connection speeds will be high.

This means that the designer for the network needs to sell the cost of the high bandwidth to the customer. Figure 20.2 shows the proposed network links.

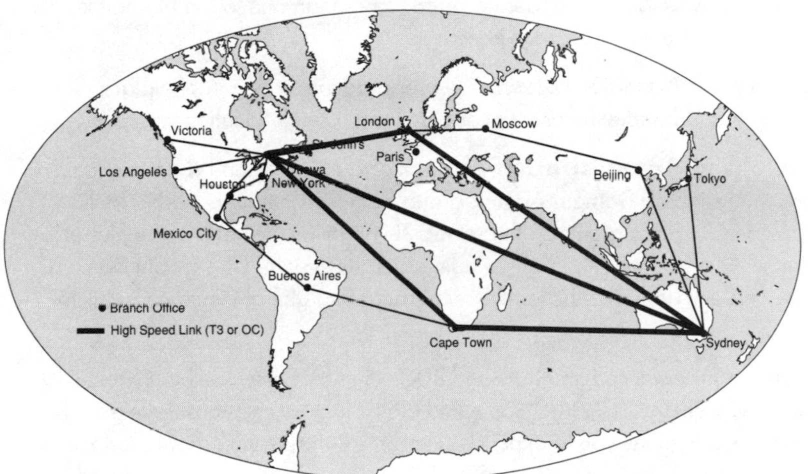

Figure 20.2

Desired WAN links for Corporation X.

The links shown here provide complete redundancy of routes (see Chapter 7, "Routing") for the network system. They do, however, also represent a significant investment.

The next step is to determine the domain model that will be implemented in this network. In this case, all the main offices handle the account administration for their areas. All the branch offices run as resource domains, enabling them to handle some of their own administration.

Therefore the model in this case will be a multiple master domain. There will be four account/resource domains and the rest (11) acting as resource domains only. Each of the resource domains (where the users are physically located) needs to trust the account domains (where the user accounts are), and the account domains will trust each other in this model.

Trust Relationship Review

As you should already have some understanding of a trust relationship, I have simply included their use here. As a quick refresher, I have included an overview here.

To understand trust relationships, you need to understand a domain. A Windows NT *domain* can be defined as a group of users and computers tied together into a logical unit for the purposes of administration. This enables a single administrator to handle

continues

many different systems over a vast area. A single Windows NT domain can span a WAN or other connections and still provide three main things:

- **Single User Logon.** The user never has more than one logon no matter how many servers the user needs to access.
- **Centralized Administration.** The user accounts are all in one place. This enables you to handle the account activity from a single location.
- **Centralized Administration of Resources.** When an NT system joins a domain, the global Domain Admins group from the domain is added to the local Administrators group on the server. This provides anyone in the global Domain Admins group the right to administer the system. (The global Domain Users group is added to the local Users group, and global Domain Guests to the local Guests.)

To handle the points just listed, the PDC and BDC computers discussed in Chapter 14, "The Browser Service and TCP/IP,"" come into play. The trust relationship takes this single domain and enables you to expand it into an enterprise scenario. Perhaps this method is not as simple as some others; STDS (Street Talk Directory Services) and NDS (Netware Directory Services), for example, can be easier in some ways. But it works.

Essentially, the trust relationship enables a user who has an account to log on at a computer that is part of a different domain. This user has only the rights normally granted to the user and cannot read any information from the host domain unless his account from the authenticating domain allows access. All the user can do is use the computer to get at his own information on the network.

Trust relationships are normally drawn as an arrow. This arrow points to the user accounts. Hence the term account domain (or trusted domain, as the domain will need to be trusted to verify the user is who he says he is). If a domain trusts another domain, it does not even need to have user accounts, the user accounts can reside in the other domain. In this way, it is possible to separate the management of the computer systems from the management of the user accounts. The primary purpose of a trust relationship is to make this separation possible, and to enable users from any domain to access resources across the entire enterprise.

According to Microsoft, you can have up to 40,000 users in a single domain, but no groups and no computers. 26,000 is suggested with only one computer per user and a limited number of groups. Somewhere between those numbers is what can be put into an accounts domain if trusts are used. This is possible as the machine accounts are removed, leaving more space for the user accounts.

Another point that needs to be considered is the dial-in capability (see Chapter 18, "Remote Access Service and TCP/IP"). With Corporation X, the Sales and Technical staff are not always near an office and therefore dial-in in the usual sense will not work. In this case, Corporation X needs to work with ISPs in the countries it intends to do business in, to use the services of these ISPs to facilitate dial-in. This makes the use of the PPTP protocol possible. Therefore, Corporation X requires a series of RAS servers set up in Ottawa that use only PPTP (in Ottawa because this is where the corporation connects to the Internet).

In doing this, Corporation X saves money on expensive dial-in equipment and the maintenance of it. To aid the implementation of this, the local dial-in numbers for the ISPs from around the world can be gathered and then locations added to the Telephony API for major cities in the world. This can be pre-installed in the laptops as they are sent to the users.

With all this in mind, you should now be able to put together the domain model and the subnets. Figure 20.3 outlines the domains involved and the trust relationships. Figure 20.4 breaks down the Class B network to different subnets. (In the diagram, the 148.53 prefix was dropped for clarity.)

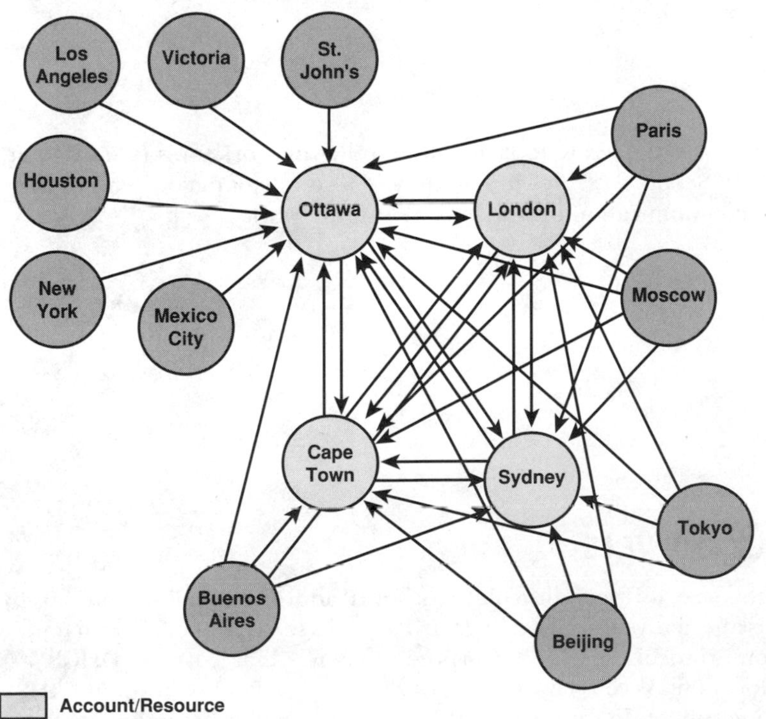

Figure 20.3

The domains and trust relationships.

Note

In figure 20.3 I have not drawn all the trust relationships. Please take it as reading that the North American resource domains do in fact trust the other account domains. The figure would be too messy otherwise.

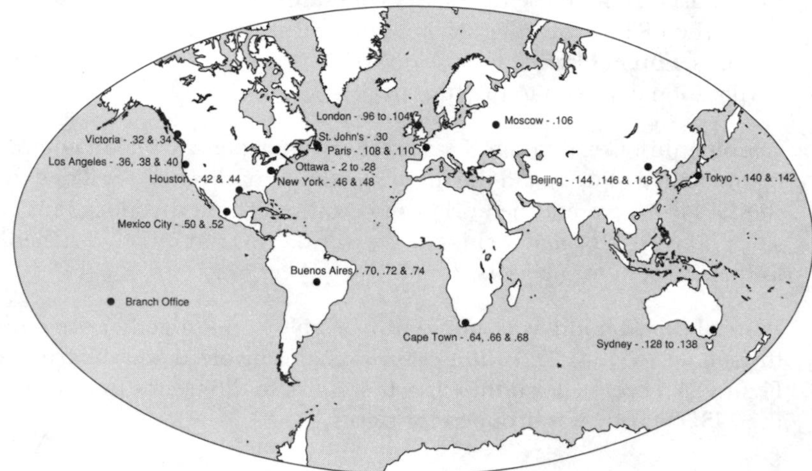

Figure 20.4
Breaking down the 148.53 network.

Services

Objective B.1

In designing a network, you need to look at adding other network tools (see Chapter 8, "Microsoft TCP/IP Services"). You will want to add a couple of major items to this network to enable communication over the entire intranetwork.

DHCP servers

WINS servers

DNS servers

IIS

RAS server

Adding DHCP Servers

In an intranet of this size, it is very difficult to assign IP addresses to all the stations by hand. The obvious alternative is to install a DHCP server (see chapter 11, "Dynamic Host Configuration Protocol (DHCP)"). Corporation X needs at least one DHCP server per major location. As you have seen, however, a few locations (most in fact) need more than one subnet. In cases where this is so, you call on the services of the DHCP Relay agent. Neither of these services are overly resource intensive. They are added on to other servers. Probably this will be added to the BDC role.

Adding WINS Servers

If you assign the IP addresses using DHCP, there needs to be something that enables you to keep track of the location of each and every computer name on this network—some way to resolve the NetBIOS names of the computer to the actual IP addresses. This is a case for WINS (see Chapter 13, "The Windows Internet Name Service"). In this case, however, there needs to be more than one WINS server. This means configuring WINS replication so that the systems all around the world can see each other.

The replication of the WINS databases requires making some decisions about the traffic that the corporation is willing to put up with. In this case,about fifteen different locations need to be serviced. If possible, it is best to avoid the resolution of names across the WAN links that bring all the offices together.

The answer is simple, but brings up some other questions. A WINS server is placed on each of the networks that require the service. This means that there are fifteen WINS servers. To enable a user sitting in Cape Town to use the resource of the systems in Victoria, the user's computer must be capable of resolving the NetBIOS names of systems in Victoria. Therefore the WINS server on the network in Cape Town needs to be able to resolve the names for systems in Victoria.

Because of the need to be able to resolve names for systems around the world, replication is required. Currently four main sites are connected by very high bandwidth links. This enables the information to flow between them easily. For these sites, there is enough bandwidth to enable the WINS server to use push & pull replication. The information in the WINS servers at these locations can then be exchanged with the information in the WINS servers at the remote locations for each of the sites.

There could, therefore, be a problem if a WINS server in any of the primary locations ever went down. To relieve this consideration, two WINS servers are configured in each of the main locations, with an extra in Ottawa. This provides the required backup.

In any of the locations, the systems are configured to use the local WINS server as the primary WINS server, and the main WINS server in the closest headquarters office as the backup WINS server. In this way, there is a constant source of duplication.

The replication should be configured so that the main WINS server pulls the information from the servers in the branch offices, as well as pushes the changes to the other servers. The pull frequency in this case needs to reflect the network traffic. About once every hour, however, should work fine. The system could then push only on every 100 to 1,000 changes to the other servers.

Adding DNS Servers

There is also the matter of being able to use the Internet. In this scenario, all the Internet traffic is forwarded to the Ottawa Headquarters, and from there it is fed directly to the Internet. This means that given the high-speed (and expensive) links that this organization has put in place, it will take only a few hops to get to the Internet, and then out to the final destination. Finding the final destination on the Internet requires some method of resolving FQDN-type names to actual IP addresses. This can be handled by the DNS (see Chapter 15, "Microsoft DNS Server") service that comes with Windows NT 4.

In this case, there will be more than one type of DNS server. Because the WINS service makes the address of any system in the organization available for NetBIOS, the WINS service in the Ottawa Headquarters is used to enable the main DNS to revolve the IP addresses requested from the outside world. To do this, the domain name registration that is sent to the InterNIC contains the IP addresses and names of at least two servers in Ottawa that are set up to handle the CorpX domain. These servers are configured to enable them to use the WINS server to handle both forward and reverse name lookup features.

These servers are the servers that resolve the requests of the outside world for the location of WWW or FTP servers. Remember that you need at least two servers to register a domain name, because the InterNIC requires that you have backup.

Corporation X also needs a series of servers that enable the users in Corporation X to resolve the IP addresses of systems outside their network. The servers should, of course, be close to the user so that as the user visits a site more and more, the user does not have to search halfway around the world to find the location of the system that he is looking for.

Each location, therefore, can be configured (possibly each subnet) with the location of a DNS server. The server can be any local NT server that has the DNS service installed. These DNS servers, however, would be configured to act as caching-only servers, forwarding the request for the name resolution to the main DNS servers in Ottawa.

Adding the Internet Information Server

Another item to look at is the servers that will provide Corporation X with a presence on the Internet. There is a need for both a WWW server and an FTP server. Because of the type of dial-in that will be configured, there is no need for the corporation to provide secured WWW or FTP services. It has already been decided that because all the other components of the network use Microsoft products, the WWW and FTP services will also be provided by Microsoft.

The Corporation will use the Internet Information Server 3.0 (see Chapter 9, "Internet Information Server") to handle the provision of these services to the rest of the world. These will be configured on as close to the actual Internet as possible. This means that all the web sites will be hosted in the Ottawa location. There is a problem, however, with the regional content. This is an important issue for the corporation, and the corporation wants to handle it with a minimum of frustration.

Because IIS 3.0 makes the use of virtual servers possible, there are two different ways that the local content can be handled. In some cases, the connection to the site in Ottawa will be slow, because of the number of networks that a client from another company will be required to go through. In these cases, Corporation X has decided that it will use the services of a local Internet provider, and will just create a sub-domain in the main web servers that will enable them to point at the address of the system that will host the Internet site.

For situations where there will not be a major hit on the performance of the system, the local office is given a directory on a server at its location. This directory will be called from the main web server, and either a virtual server or a virtual directory will be created on the main server to point at the directory on the local server.

The same sort of decision also carries over to the use of the FTP server. Either the corporate DNS resolves the IP address as an address in the local country that handles the FTP services, or the virtual directories capabilities of IIS 3.0 are used to enable users to point an alias at the local directories.

The RAS Server

The RAS servers all need to be in the Ottawa location (see Chapter 18, "Remote Access Service and TCP/IP"). Because Corporation X will use PPTP (Point-to-Point Tunneling Protocol), there is no need for the systems to actually use modems. Instead there will be multiple virtual private networks that will be defined. The systems will be in Ottawa so that they can connect as quickly as possible to the Internet.

In this case, there is a need for many RAS servers, given the number of users that will need to connect other RAS servers from remote locations. A decision needs to be made as to the number of users that should be connected to any RAS server. As a general guideline, there normally should never be more than 64 in-bound connections per RAS server unless the server is using multiple processors. Even then, as the users attempt to connect over the network, the system will slow significantly.

Using a Proxy Server

A proxy is something that acts on your behalf if you cannot handle something yourself. In this case, that means that you make a request to a proxy server and it actually forwards the request to another server to retrieve the information that you are requesting.

The upshot is that you talk to the proxy server with any address that you want to use, and it forwards the request to the correct proxy server. Corporation X, for example, has 15 offices. If it were to use the proxy server, Corporation X could have used a mere 15 IP addresses rather than the 65,534 that did in fact get used. In the worst case scenario, 15 Class C addresses might have been used; that's still a lot less that the single Class B.

Internally, you will run what is known as a PNA (Private Network Address). This means that no one ever knows your address, and you send your requests to the proxy server. The proxy server goes out and gets the page and returns it. In the case of Microsoft Proxy server, this page is retained. This means that if you return to the page, all the system needs to do is determine whether the original has been updated. If not, it can give the page from cache.

Summary

You now have come full circle, from the notes in the introduction to actually sitting down and planning the general characteristics of a network. What has been presented here is not the end point—there is a great deal more to planning a network. You have seen here the initial planning for the TCP/IP portion of the network implementation. In many cases, there will already be a network in place and more effort will be required to plan the transition than the actual network. This chapter was intended to help you start thinking about all the different services that you have been introduced to in this text and where they will fit into the network. The following Test Yourself section gives you a chance to try this out.

Test Yourself

This lab presents several scenarios that enable you to walk through the planning phase of the network. Read each of the scenarios carefully and then take some time to draft out the possible solutions that you could implement using Windows NT Server and Workstation. In most cases, the scenarios attempt to give you more information than actually required, something you will find is a common characteristic of Microsoft test questions as well.

You should bear in mind as you look at the scenarios that there is no one right answer. There will often be several different ways to perform the functions described. The secret in this case is to understand what the client organization is about, and what the organization can afford. In the scenario presented in the main body of this chapter, the organization was a large international organization. It had the required resources to acquire the lines that would enable it to communicate. Not all the organizations given here have these types of resources.

Scenario 1—Designing a High-Security Network

This scenario is based on an organization called LockTite.Data. It is a computer security consulting outfit. Its primary business is security audits of other companies' computer networks. There are currently four different locations that it works out of. It needs to service all the North American continent from these locations.

LockTite.Data currently has four locations. These are Vancouver, San Francisco, Toronto, and New Orleans. There are few actual administration staff, but they are all in the head office (in New Orleans). The sizes of the offices are as follows:

- **Vancouver.** 45 technical staff, 8 administration. Most of the time there will be between 15 and 20 technical staff in the office working on projects; the remainder will be at the client site. The administrative staff is always in the office.
- **San Francisco.** Here there is a technical staff of 64, and administrative staff of 10. Normally, there will be about 30 technical staff in the office, working on projects in addition to the administrative staff.
- **Toronto.** This is the newest office for the company. There are 28 employees in this location, 6 of whom are administrative.
- **New Orleans.** The office serves as both a branch office and the headquarters for the company on a continental level. There are 23 staff who handle accounting and payroll for all the locations. The technical staff is broken into two parts in this branch. There is a small group of about 12 that provides backup to the technical staff in the rest of the country, and a field staff of 89. Usually there are 20–30 of the field staff in-house at any time.

The field staff is normally on the road doing the audits and configurations for the clients. The rest of the time, they are in the branch working on projects for other customers, or upgrading their skills. When they are in the branch, they use one of a group of shared workstations that provide a location for them to connect their laptops.

Each location provides a web site for the clients in their area to browse. This also includes discussion groups that enable the users to talk online with some of the technical staff. Each site is also connected to the Internet and communications between the offices need to pass over these connections. They do, however, need to be secured.

Obviously, the maximum security available is required for the organization. This goes both for the internal networks as well as for the communication to the other branches.

Scenario 2—Planning to Use the Internet as Your WAN

In this scenario you have been asked to set up the networking requirements for an organization called Twosl. It is a small organization located in Kingston, Jamaica. Twosl provides certified instructors for Microsoft courses to Authorized Technical Education Centers. Unfortunately, Twosl is so busy that it does not have time to set up its own network and has contracted you to handle the job.

In this case, Twosl has an ISDN link to a local ISP, and three permanent IP addresses from that service provider. Twosl wants to handle all its own servers, and wants to register the name Twosl.com with the InterNIC. It has a small office that it rents in an executive suite of offices. This provides Twosl with an office to work from. Twosl currently handles bookings for 50 MCTs (Microsoft Certified Trainers).

Scenario 3—Creating a Private Network

In this scenario, the company is a large international system integrator. For the most part, the company does not require general access to the Internet; it needs only exchange e-mail with clients and provide a simple web site managed from an office in North America.

It has offices in several different cities across the world; the head office is in Dundee, Scotland. The organization wants to connect all the offices via high-speed links, and thinks that the TCP/IP protocol suite is best suited to the challenge.

Test Yourself Answers

Keeping in mind that there is technically more than one way to solve each situation; following are the best solutions for each scenario.

Solution to Scenario 1

You should look at several things that make sense in this case. These points are listed here:

- The technical staff must be able to dial in to the network. This is handled by RAS (because this is an NT book).
- There is a requirement for talk to the other networks. This can be done using a leased line that could link each of the offices. (This will cost a fair amount of money.) The organization already has a link to each office from the Internet, so you might have considered using the PPTP function built into NT to enable the networks to connect over a secure connection.
- The internal network is, in this case, separate from the external network. This enables the organization to secure its internal network using a protocol other than the TCP/IP protocol. This makes it far more difficult for external hackers to break through the TCP/IP portion of the network (the outside portion) and get into the inside. In this case, any protocol is usable on the internal side of the network.
- IIS provides the services required for the organization to make the web presence. IIS 3.0 facilitates many different types of functions, including the capability to include code in the web pages to handle functions such as a chat room. Internal users could be given a choice of connecting to the external or internal networks (because the internal will not run TCP/IP). In this case, the internal network could run IPX/SPX. Proxy could be used to enable the users from the internal site to surf the external side while still protecting the internal network.
- Because there is a possibility that the technical staff will be moving outside the four cities in which the branches are located, an internal RAS server (using IPX/SPX) could be configured for their dial-in requirements. This could also be configured to use callback security that enables the users to set a phone number if they wish to.

Solution to Scenario 2

In this case, the solution is very simple: You install three Windows NT servers. On two of the servers, you run the DNS server. One is used for the primary DNS for the domain TWOSL.COM and the other is used as a secondary server. This enables the organization to register its name with the InterNIC, because there are two servers that respond to the TWOSL.COM domain name. The other server are used to provide mail services using the Commercial Internet Mail server available from Microsoft. IIS is installed on any one of the systems; whichever one is used requires a second hard disk, enabling you to secure the site to some degree by using NTFS permissions. The MCTs associated with Twosl will be given one account and be expected to connect to the server using NetBIOS. (Remember the LMHOSTS file. This enables the system to locate the Twosl server from anywhere on the Internet so that the instructors can connect to the server in order to download files.)

Solution to Scenario 3

In this case, the organization uses its own network to provide data services around the network. This means that there is no need to worry about addressing what the organization will use internally. (I would use a Class B address to allow for a large number of networks and hosts/network. Any class of address, however, will do.)

For interactions with the Internet, the organization uses a single Class C that can be provided by an ISP in North America. At this site, the organization sets up several proxy servers that enable the organization to connect with the outside world and provide an extra level of security by logging access to the Internet and allowing only some ports to come in.

There will also be a connection here for the internal mail service to use SMTP (Simple Mail Transfer Protocol) to transfer mail to hosts around the world. The IIS server is set up here, and the various locations can connect to various shares on its drive to add content. The content is copied to an internal server to enable the internal users to connect to the web site and to provide a backup server.

PART VI

Appendices

A *Overview of the Certification Process* *609*

B *All About TestPrep* *619*

APPENDIX A

Overview of the Certification Process

To become a Microsoft Certified Professional, candidates must pass rigorous certification exams that provide a valid and reliable measure of their technical proficiency and expertise. These closed-book exams have on-the-job relevance because they are developed with the input of professionals in the computer industry and reflect how Microsoft products are actually used in the workplace. The exams are conducted by an independent organization—Sylvan Prometric—at more than 700 Sylvan Authorized Testing Centers around the world.

Currently Microsoft offers four types of certification, based on specific areas of expertise:

- **Microsoft Certified Product Specialist (MCPS).** Qualified to provide installation, configuration, and support for users of at least one Microsoft desktop operating system, such as Windows 95. In addition, candidates may take additional elective exams to add areas of specialization. MCPS is the first level of expertise.
- **Microsoft Certified Systems Engineer (MCSE).** Qualified to effectively plan, implement, maintain, and support information systems with Microsoft Windows NT and other Microsoft

advanced systems and workgroup products, such as Microsoft Office and Microsoft BackOffice. The Windows NT Server 4.0 exam can be used as one of the four core operating systems exams. MCSE is the second level of expertise.

- **Microsoft Certified Solution Developer (MCSD).** Qualified to design and develop custom business solutions using Microsoft development tools, technologies, and platforms, including Microsoft Office and Microsoft BackOffice. MCSD also is a second level of expertise, but in the area of software development.
- **Microsoft Certified Trainer (MCT).** Instructionally and technically qualified by Microsoft to deliver Microsoft Education Courses at Microsoft authorized sites. An MCT must be employed by a Microsoft Solution Provider Authorized Technical Education Center or a Microsoft Authorized Academic Training site.

The following sections describe the requirements for each type of certification.

Note For up-to-date information about each type of certification, visit the Microsoft Training and Certification World Wide Web site at http://www.microsoft.com/train_cert. You must have an Internet account and a WWW browser to access this information. You also can call the following sources:

- Microsoft Certified Professional Program: 800-636-7544
- Sylvan Prometric Testing Centers: 800-755-EXAM
- Microsoft Online Institute (MOLI): 800-449-9333

How to Become a Microsoft Certified Product Specialist (MCPS)

Becoming an MCPS requires you pass one operating system exam.

Windows NT Server 4.0 is not the only operating system you can be tested on to get your MCSP certification. The following list shows the names and exam numbers of all the operating systems from which you can choose to get your MCPS certification:

- Implementing and Supporting Microsoft Windows 95 #70-63
- Implementing and Supporting Microsoft Windows NT Workstation 4.02 #70-73

- Implementing and Supporting Microsoft Windows NT Workstation 3.51 #70-42
- Implementing and Supporting Microsoft Windows NT Server 4.0 #70-67
- Implementing and Supporting Microsoft Windows NT Server 3.51 #70-43
- Microsoft Windows for Workgroups 3.11–Desktop #70-48
- Microsoft Windows 3.1 #70-30
- Microsoft Windows Operating Systems and Services Architecture I #70-150
- Microsoft Windows Operating Systems and Services Architecture II #70-151

How to Become a Microsoft Certified Systems Engineer (MCSE)

MCSE candidates need to pass four operating system exams and two elective exams. The MCSE certification path is divided into two tracks: the Windows NT 3.51 track and the Windows NT 4.0 track.

Table A.1 shows the core requirements (four operating system exams) and the elective courses (two exams) for the Windows NT 3.51 track.

TABLE A.1
Windows NT 3.51 MCSE Track

Take These Two Required Exams (Core Requirements)	Plus, Pick One of the Following Operating System Exams (Core Requirement)	Plus, Pick One of the Following Networking Exams (Core Requirement)	Plus, Pick Two of the Following Elective Exams (Elective Requirements)
Implementing and Supporting Microsoft Windows NT Server 3.51 #70-43	Implementing and Supporting Microsoft Windows 95 #70-63	Networking Microsoft Windows for Workgroups 3.11 #70-46	Microsoft SNA Server #70-12

continues

Table A.1, Continued
Windows NT 3.51 MCSE Track

Take These Two Required Exams (Core Requirements)	Plus, Pick One of the Following Operating System Exams (Core Requirement)	Plus, Pick One of the Following Networking Exams (Core Requirement)	Plus, Pick Two of the Following Elective Exams (Elective Requirements)
AND Implementing and Supporting Microsoft Windows NT Workstation 3.51 #70-42	*OR* Microsoft Windows for Workgroups 3.11–Desktop #70-48	*OR* Networking with Microsoft Windows 3.1 #70-47	*OR* Implementing and Supporting Microsoft Systems Management Server 1.0 #70-14
	OR Microsoft Windows 3.1 #70-30	*OR* Networking Essentials #70-58	*OR* Microsoft SQL Server 4.2 Database Implementation #70-21
			OR Microsoft SQL Server 4.2 Database Administration for Microsoft Windows NT #70-22
			OR System Administration for Microsoft SQL Server 6 #70-26
			OR Implementing a Database Design on Microsoft SQL Server 6 #70-27
			OR Microsoft Mail for PC Networks 3.2–Enterprise #70-37

Take These Two Required Exams (Core Requirements)	Plus, Pick One of the Following Operating System Exams (Core Requirement)	Plus, Pick One of the Following Networking Exams (Core Requirement)	Plus, Pick Two of the Following Elective Exams (Elective Requirements)
			OR Internetworking Microsoft TCP/IP on Microsoft Windows NT (3.5–3.51) #70-53
			OR Internetworking Microsoft TCP/IP on Microsoft Windows NT 4.0 #70-59
			OR Implementing and Supporting Microsoft Exchange Server 4.0 #70-75
			OR Implementing and Supporting Microsoft Internet Information Server #70-77
			OR Implementing and Supporting Microsoft Proxy Server 1.0 #70-78

Table A.2 shows the core requirements (four operating system exams) and elective courses (two exams) for the Windows NT 4.0 track. Tables A.1 and A.2 have many of the same exams listed, but there are distinct differences between the two. Make sure you read each track's requirements carefully.

TABLE A.2
Windows NT 4.0 MCSE Track

Take These Two Required Exams (Core Requirements)	Plus, Pick One of the Following Operating System Exams (Core Requirement)	Plus, Pick One of the Following Networking Exams (Core Requirement)	Plus, Pick Two of the Following Elective Exams (Elective Requirements)
Implementing and Supporting Microsoft Windows NT Server 4.0 #70-67	Implementing and Supporting Microsoft Windows 95 #70-63	Networking Microsoft Windows for Workgroups 3.11 #70-46	Microsoft SNA Server #70-12
AND Implementing and Support- Microsoft Windows NT Server in the Enterprise #70-68	*OR* Microsoft Windows for Workgroups 3.11–Desktop	*OR* Networking with Microsoft Windows 3.1 #70-47	*OR* Implementing and Supporting Microsoft Systems Management Server 1.0 #70-14
	OR Microsoft Windows 3.1 #70-30	*OR* Networking Essentials #70-58	*OR* Microsoft SQL Server 4.2 Database Implementation #70-21
	OR Implementing and Supporting Microsoft Windows NT Workstation 4.02 #70-73		*OR* Microsoft SQL Server 4.2 Database Administration Microsoft Windows NT #70-22
			OR System Administration for Microsoft SQL Server 6 #70-26
			OR Implementing a Database Design on Microsoft SQL Server 6 #70-27

Take These Two Required Exams (Core Requirements)	Plus, Pick One of the Following Operating System Exams (Core Requirement)	Plus, Pick One of the Following Networking Exams (Core Requirement)	Plus, Pick Two of the Following Elective Exams (Elective Requirements)
			OR Microsoft Mail for PC Networks 3.2–Enterprise #70-37
			OR Internetworking Microsoft TCP/IP on Microsoft Windows NT (3.5–3.51) #70-53
			OR Internetworking Microsoft TCP/IP on Microsoft Windows NT 4.0 #70-59
			OR Implementing and Supporting Microsoft Exchange Server 4.0 #70-75
			OR Implementing and Supporting Microsoft Internet Information Server #70-77
			OR Implementing and Supporting Microsoft Proxy Server 1.0 #70-78

How to Become a Microsoft Certified Solution Developer (MCSD)

MCSD candidates need to pass two core technology exams and two elective exams. Table A.3 shows the required technology exams, plus the elective exams that apply toward obtaining the MCSD.

Caution The "Implementing and Supporting Microsoft Windows NT Server 4.0" (#70-67) exam does *not* apply toward any of the MCSD requirements.

TABLE A.3
MCSD Exams and Requirements

Take These Two Core Technology Exams	Plus, Choose from Two of the Following Elective Exams
Microsoft Windows Operating Systems and Services Architecture I #70-150	Microsoft SQL Server 4.2 Database Implementation #70-21
AND Microsoft Windows Operating Systems and Services Architecture II #70-151	*OR* Developing Applications with C++ Using the Microsoft Foundation Class Library #70-24
	OR Implementing a Database Design on Microsoft SQL Server 6 #70-27
	OR Microsoft Visual Basic 3.0 for Windows–Application Development #70-50
	OR Microsoft Access 2.0 for Windows–Application Development #70-51
	OR Developing Applications with Microsoft Excel 5.0 Using Visual Basic for Applications #70-52
	OR Programming in Microsoft Visual FoxPro 3.0 for Windows #70-54

Take These Two Core Technology Exams	Plus, Choose from Two of the Following Elective Exams
	OR Programming with Microsoft Visual Basic 4.0 #70-65
	OR Microsoft Access for Windows 95 and the Microsoft Access Development Toolkit #70-69
	OR Implementing OLE in Microsoft Foundation Class Applications #70-25

Becoming a Microsoft Certified Trainer (MCT)

To understand the requirements and process for becoming a Microsoft Certified Trainer (MCT), you need to obtain the Microsoft Certified Trainer Guide document (MCTGUIDE.DOC) from the following WWW site:

http://www.microsoft.com/train_cert/download.htm

On this page, click on the hyperlink MCT GUIDE (mctguide.doc) (117 KB). If your WWW browser can display DOC files (Word for Windows native file format), the MCT Guide displays in the browser window. Otherwise, you need to download it and open it in Word for Windows or Windows 95 WordPad. The MCT Guide explains the four-step process to becoming an MCT. The general steps for the MCT certification are as follows:

1. Complete and mail a Microsoft Certified Trainer application to Microsoft. You must include proof of your skills for presenting instructional material. The options for doing so are described in the MCT Guide.
2. Obtain and study the Microsoft Trainer Kit for the Microsoft Official Curricula (MOC) course(s) for which you want to be certified. You can order Microsoft Trainer Kits by calling 800-688-0496 in North America. Other regions should review the MCT Guide for information on how to order a Microsoft Trainer Kit.
3. Pass the Microsoft certification exam for the product for which you want to be certified to teach.
4. Attend the MOC course for which you want to be certified. This is done so you can understand how the course is structured, how labs are completed, and how the course flows.

Caution You should use the preceding steps as a general overview of the MCT certification process. The actual steps you need to take are described in detail in the MCTGUIDE.DOC file on the WWW site mentioned earlier. Do not misconstrue the preceding steps as the actual process you need to take.

If you are interested in becoming an MCT, you can receive more information by visiting the Microsoft Certified Training (MCT) WWW site at `http://www.microsoft.com/train_cert/mctint.htm` or by calling 800-688-0496.

APPENDIX B

All About TestPrep

The electronic TestPrep utility included on the CD-ROM accompanying this book enables you to test your Windows NT Server 4 knowledge in a manner similar to that employed by the actual Microsoft exam. When you first start the TestPrep exam, select the number of questions you want to be asked and the objective categories in which you want to be tested.

Although it is possible to maximize the TestPrep application, the default is for it to run in smaller mode so you can refer to your Windows NT Desktop while answering questions. TestPrep uses a unique randomization sequence to ensure that each time you run the program you are presented with a different sequence of questions—this enhances your learning and prevents you from merely learning the expected answers over time without reading the question each and every time.

Question Presentation

TestPrep emulates the actual Microsoft Internetworking Microsoft TCP/IP on Microsoft Windows NT 4.0 (#70-59), in that radial (circle) buttons are used to signify only one correct choice, while check boxes (squares) are used to signify multiple correct answers. Whenever more than one answer is correct, the number you should select is given in the wording of the question.

You can exit the program at any time by choosing the Exit key, or you can continue to the next question by choosing the Next key.

Scoring

The TestPrep Score Report uses actual numbers from the Internetworking Microsoft TCP/IP on Microsoft Windows NT 4.0 (#70-59) exam. For TCP/IP, a score of 750 or higher is considered passing; the same parameters apply to TestPrep. Each objective category is broken into categories with a percentage correct given for each of the categories.

Choose "Show Me What I Missed" to go back through the questions you answered incorrectly and see what the correct answers are. Choose Exit to return to the beginning of the testing routine and start over.

Non-Random Mode

You can run TestPrep in Non-Random mode, which enables you to see the same set of questions each time, or on each machine. To run TestPrep in this manner, you need to create a shortcut to the executable file and place the CLASS parameter on the command line calling the application, after the application's name. For example:

```
C:\TESTENG\70_67.EXE CLASS
```

Now, when you run TestPrep, the same sequence of questions will appear each time. To change the sequence but stay in Non-Random mode (for example, if you're in a classroom setting, where it is important that everyone see the same questions), choose Help, Class Mode on the main screen. This lets you enter a number from 1 to 8 to select a predefined sequence of questions.

Instructor Mode

To run TestPrep in Instructor mode (seeing the same set of questions each time, or on each machine), create a shortcut to the executable file, and place the INSTR parameter following CLASS on the command line calling the application, after the application's name. For example:

```
C:\TESTENG\70_67.EXE CLASS INSTR
```

Now, when you run TestPrep, the same sequence of questions will appear each time. Additionally, the correct answer will be marked already, and the objective category from which the question is coming will be given in the question. To change the sequence of questions that appear, choose Help, Class Mode on the main screen. This prompts you to enter a number from 1 to 8 to select a predefined sequence of questions; increment that by 100 and the sequence will be presented in Instructor mode.

Flash Cards

As a further learning aid, you can use the FLASH! Electronic Flash Cards program to convert some of the questions in the database into a fill-in-the-blank format. Run the FLASH! program and select the categories on which you want to be tested. The engine then goes through the database in sequential order and tests your knowledge without multiple choice possibilities.

INDEX

Symbols

0x0, 283
0x1, 283
0x1B, 284
0x1F, 284
0x20, 284
0x21, 284
0x3, 284
0x6, 284
0xBE, 284
0xBF, 284
44 WINS/NBNS Servers (DHCP configuration), 269
  adding to a scope, 269-270
46 WINS/NBT Node Type (option 46), 269
  adding, 271

A

A (resource record type), 354
A field (WINS database), 275
AAAA (resource record type), 354
abbreviations
  country domains, 329-338
  US domain, subdomains, 339-341
  world-wide domains, 328
accessing
  directories, WWW servers, 164
  web sites, 177
account domains, 596
accounts, configuring IUSR_*computername* account, 160-161
acknowledgment numbers, 69
activating
  Content Advisor (Internet Explorer), 420-422
  DHCP scopes, 212
active connections, 60
active leases
  deleting, 209
  managing, 206-208, 212
  properties, modifying, 208-209
  viewing, 206-208
Active Leases dialog box, 207, 272
active open, 56
Adapter Bus Location dialog box, 139
adapter card drivers, 36, 38-43
Add Reserved Clients dialog box, 210
Add Services dialog box, 189
Add WINS Server dialog box, 273
adding
  address records, 371-373
  DHCP servers to a network, 598
  DNS
    names, 172
    servers, 600
  expressions to display filters, 469-471
  IIS to a network, 177, 600-601
  MX records, 374-375
  network adapters, 139-140
  option 44 (DHCP) to a scope, 269-270
  phonebook entries, 521-524
  preloaded entries to Name Cache, 237
  primary zones, 370
  proxy servers to a network, 602
  PTR records, 375-376
  RAS (Remote Access Server) to a network, 601
  replication partners, 289-290
  resource records, 371-376
  reverse-lookup zones, 369-370
  serial ports to RAS, 513-514
  static mappings, 281-282
  subdomain zones, 384-385
  WINS servers to a network, 599
Address Display (Preferences dialog box option), 276
Address Expression dialog box, 460

address filters, 460-461
address records, 359
adding, 371-373
Address Resolution Protocol, *see* ARP
addresses (IP)
ANDing, 48-49
binary, 24-26
Class A, 26
Class B, 26
Corporation X, 593
Class C, 26
configuring, 171-172
host IDs, 24
locating, 80-83
MAC, 80
Name Cache, 237-238
network IDs, 24
octets, 24
Private Network Address, 94
subnetting, 94, 96-105
administration, DNS domains, 324-325
Advanced Microsoft TCP/IP Configuration dialog box, 269
Advanced Network Services, *see* ANS
Advanced tab, WWW Server Properties, 166
AFP (Apple File Protocol), 37
AFSDB (resource record type), 354
Agent tab (SNMP Properties), 484
agents, 450
aliases, 323, 359-360
CNAME declaration, 359
ANDing, 47-49
announcements, 300, 314
ANS (Advanced Network Services), 18
API (Application Programming Interface), 34
APIProtocolSupport (DHCP parameter), 224-225
Appearance option (phonebook entries), 534-535
Application layer (TCP/IP model), 32, 42
components, 43-45
NetBIOS, 45-46
Winsock, 43-45, 56-61
host communications, 43
Application log (Event Viewer), 570
Application Programming Interface, *see* API
Application/File System Drivers layer (Microsoft Networking), 34, 36
applications
IIS (Internet Information Server), installing, 154-158
printing from, 187
Applications checkbox (SNMP Properties Agent tab), 484
architecture
Microsoft networks, 34-36
adapter card drivers, 38-43
Application layer, 36
layers, 35-38
NDIS layer, 38
TDI layer (Transport Driver Interface), 36-37
ARP (Address Resolution Protocol), 49, 81, 138, 448-449, 569
broadcasts, viewing, 474-475
ARP cache, 83
ARP command, 83
ARP packets, 82
ARPA (Advanced Research Project Agency), 18
ARPAnet, 18
attributes, files, 47

B

B-Node (Broadcast), 247
backing up WINS database, 284-285
Backup Browsers, 300-301, 305
Backup On Termination (WINS Server Configuration dialog box option), 279
BackupDatabasePath (DHCP parameter), 225
BackupInterval (DHCP parameter), 225
BcastNameQueryCount (Broadcast parameter), 238
BcastQueryTimeout (Broadcast parameter), 239
BDCs (Backup Domain Controllers), Backup Browsers, 306
#BEGIN_ALTERNATE tag, 241
Berkeley Internet Name Domain, *see* BIND
Berkeley Standard Distribution, *see* BSD
binary, 24-26
overview, 94-96
subnet IDs, calculating, 99-100
binary addresses, 24
BIND (Berkeley Internet Name Domain)
database files, creating, 351
servers, 325
porting data, 388-389
stub resolvers, 325
bindings, 38, 140-141
LANA (Local Area Network Adapter), 38
Bindings tab (Network Settings dialog box), 140-141

bits
file attributes, ANDing, 47-49
masking, 48
subnet mask requirements, 97-98
BOOT file, 351-353
BOOTP (Boot Protocol), 130
DHCP, 198
bridges, 114
Broadcast, B-Node, 247
broadcasting, 63, 238-239
ARP, viewing, 474
BOOTP (Boot Protocol), 130
broadcast packets, 81
broadcast traffic, 236
browser elections, 305-307
configuring parameters, 238-239
Name Release, 237
browser elections
causes, 306
tie breaking, 306
browser list, updating, 301, 303-304
Browser service, troubleshooting, 576
browsers
configuring, 304-305
domains, 307-308
elections, 305-307
Master Browser, 300
web, Internet Explorer, 414-424
browsing, 300-307, 314
subnets, 308-314
BSD (Berkeley Standard Distribution), 18
building address database, 454-455
byte stream communication, segments, 73
Bytes Received/sec (NBT counter), 493
Bytes Sent/sec (NBT counter), 493

C

cache
directives, 352
files, 362-365
CacheTimeout (Name Cache parameter), 238
calculating
first host IDs, 102
last host IDs, 103
subnet masks, 101
hosts, 98-99
subnets, 101
subnetwork IDs, 99-102
Callback option (phonebook entries), 533
callback security, 511
capture buffer, managing, 456-457
Capture Buffer Settings dialog box, 457
capture data
saving, 463
viewing, 463-471
Detail Pane (Network Monitor), 465-467
Summary Pane (Network Monitor), 465
capture filters, 458-461
capture triggers, 462-463
capturing
frames 453-454, 457
CD-ROM TestPrep Utility, 619-620
certification exams
MCPS, 610-618
MCSD, 616-618
MCSE, 611-618
MCT, 617-618
Challenge Handshake Authentication Protocol, *see* CHAP
challenge/response protocol, 163
challenges, 260
CHAP (Challenge Handshake Authentication Protocol), 520
characterization data files, 186
chart settings, Performance Monitor, 494-495
Chart view (Performance Monitor), 488
checksum, 69
choosing home directories for IIS installation, 156
Class A addresses, 26
Class B addresses, 26
Corporation X, 593
Class C addresses, 24-26, 103
for Class A supernets, 105
supernetting, 104
clearing Name Cache, 237
client stations
hardware, troubleshooting, 564
troubleshooting, 563-564
client/server environment, troubleshooting, 563-568
clients
DHCP, enabling, 205-206
DNS, enabling, 389-390
RAS server, enabling PPTP support, 550-551
WINS
DHCP, 269-272
installing, 268-272
static IP address configuration, 268
WINS proxy configuration, 268-269
CNAME records, 354
CNAME declaration, 359
adding, 374
column headings, NBSTAT command, 443-444

command line switches
FTP, 407
IPCONFIG, 433
LPQ, 428
LPR, 428
NETSTAT, 440
NSLOOKUP
command, 435
Ping, 429-430
RCP, 412-413
TFTP, 412
commands
ARP, 83
FTP, 408-412
NBSTAT, column
headings, 443-444
NSLOOKUP (interactive
mode), 436-445
REXEC, 426-427
ROUTE, 78, 114, 569
ROUTE PRINT, 119
RSH, 426
communication, between redirectors and servers, 33
communities, 482-483
compacting databases, 286-287
DHCP databases, 214
comparing
addresses, binary versus
decimal system, 24-26
bridges to routers, 114
UDP to TCP, 75
components
Application layer (TCP/
IP model), 43-45
NetBIOS, 45-46
WinSock, 43-45, 56-61
Microsoft networking
Application/File System drivers, 34, 36
Microsoft networks,
adapter card
drivers, 36
Computer (Performance Monitor Chart view option), 489
Computer Name field (WINS database), 275
Computer Names: LAN Manager-Compatible (Preferences dialog box option), 277
computers, multihomed, 260
concepts, DHCP servers, 198-201
Configure Network Monitoring Agent dialog box, 452-453
configuring
broadcast parameters,
238-239
browsers, 304-305
DHCP
options, 217-221
parameters, 221-226
DNS options, 350-351
DNS servers, 350-351
IIS Gopher service,
175-176
IIS for TCP/IP installation, 154
Internet Explorer,
416-424
IP addresses, 171-172
IPCONFIG utility, 568
IUSR_*computername*
account, 160-161
Name Cache, 238
NBNS parameters, 244
Network Monitor,
security, 451-452
PPTP for RAS servers,
548-549
proxy servers
EnableProxy parameter, 269
RAS, 541-546
dialing out, 519-521
RAS as a router, 539-541
Remote Access Admin, 544-546
serial ports, 514
services, FTP, 174
SNMP (Simple Network
Management Protocol),
483-486
static mappings,
281-282
TCP/IP, 138
virtual
directories, 168-169
servers, 170-176
WINS clients
DHCP, 269-272
proxy servers, 268-269
static IP addresses, 268
WINS
parameters, 291-295
replication, 599
server properties, 277-279
WWW server (IIS),
161-173
Confirm Deletion of Static Mappings & Cached WINS servers (Preferences dialog box), 277
connecting
LPD servers, 189-191
physical printers, port
monitors, 187-188
to remote hosts, 424-425
Connection Failures (TCP counter), 493
Connection tab (Modem Properties dialog box), 516
connection-oriented data transfer, NetBIOS, 33
connection-oriented traffic, 61
connectionless data transfer, NetBIOS, 33
connections
monitoring, 535-538
NETSTAT utility, 568
Connections Active (TCP counter), 493
Connections Established (TCP counter), 493
Connections Passive (TCP counter), 494
Connections Reset (TCP counter), 494
connectivity
networks, testing with
Ping, 431-434
troubleshooting, 573

Content Advisor (Internet Explorer), activating, 420-422
control bits, 69
convergence, 120
converting print files, 187
Corporation X (sample TCP/IP intranet implementation), 589-592
 branch locations, 592
 Class B addresses, 593
corrupted DHCP databases, 215-216
Counter (Performance Monitor Chart View option), 489
counters
 ICMP object, 490-491
 Internet Protocol, 492-493
 NBT object, 493
 TCP (Transmission Control Protocol), 493-494
 UDP (User Datagram Protocol), 494
country domains, 329-338
creating
 address databases, 454-455
 DHCP databases, 216-217
 DHCP reservations, 210-211
 DNS servers, 367-368
 IP datagrams, 84-86
 Performance Monitor log files, 496-497
 scopes, 203-204
 secondary DNS servers, 383-384
 sessions, 72
 subnet masks, 98
 virtual directories, 168-169
 virtual servers, home directories, 172-173
Creating New Zone dialog box, 383
custom subnet masks, creating, 98

D

daemons, 129
DARPA, *see* ARPA
data link control layer, 32
data offset, 69
data segments
 headers, 68-71
  fields, 68
  pseudo headers, 71
  TCP headers, 68-70
  UDP header, 70-72
data transfer mode, 61
data types (Registry), 223
Database Backup Path (WINS Server Configuration dialog box option), 279
database files
 configuring DNS server, 350-351
 DHCP, 213
 domain database files, 353-360
 localhost, 362
 reverse-matching, 360-362
 updating, 386
Database Initialized (WINS server statistic), 274
DatabaseCleanupInterval (DHCP parameter), 225
DatabaseLoggingFlag (DHCP parameter), 225-226
DatabaseName (DHCP parameter), 226
DatabasePath (DHCP parameter), 226
databases
 address, creating, 454-455
 compacting, 286-287
 DHCP
  compacting, 214
  corrupted, 215-216
  creating, 216-217
  managing, 213-217
  reconciling, 216
  repairing, 215-216
 files, creating BIND database files, 351
 WINS
  backing up, 284-285
  configuring static mappings, 281-282
  replicating, 287-291
  restoring, 285-286
  scavenging, 286-287
  viewing, 274-276
datagrams, 78
 fields, 84-86
 fragmentation, 86-87
 IP, creating, 84-86
 retransmitting, 87
 transmission, error detection, 87-88
 see also packets
Datagrams Forwarded/sec (Internet Protocol counter), 492
Datagrams No Port/sec (UDP counter), 494
Datagrams Outbound Discarded (Internet Protocol counter), 492
Datagrams Outbound No Route (Internet Protocol counter), 492
Datagrams Received Address Errors (Internet Protocol counter), 492
Datagrams Received Delivered/sec (Internet Protocol counter), 492
Datagrams Received Discarded (Internet Protocol counter), 492
Datagrams Received Errors (UDP counter), 494
Datagrams Received Header Errors (Internet Protocol counter), 492
Datagrams Received Unknown Protocol (Internet Protocol counter), 492

Datagrams Received/sec
Internet Protocol counter, 492
UDP counter, 494
Datagrams Sent/sec
Internet Protocol counter, 492
UDP counter, 494
Datagrams/sec
Internet Protocol counter, 492
UDP counter, 494
Datalink / Subnetwork checkbox (SNMP Properties Agent tab), 484
DbFileNm parameter, 291
deactivating DHCP scopes, 212
decimal system, IP addresses, 25-26
DECPSMON.DLL, 187
default DHCP options, managing, 218-219
defining capture triggers, 462
deleting
active leases, 209
DHCP scopes, 212
describing network cards, 453
designations of protocol standards, 21
destination address, 86
Destination ports, 69
Detail Pane (Network Monitor), viewing capture data, 465-467
detailed information, viewing with WINS manager, 279-280
Detailed Information dialog box, 279
development, TCP/IP, 17-18
RFC (Request for Comments), 19-22
devices, installing modems 514-521
DHCP (Dynamic Host Configuration Protocol), 130
44 WINS/NBNS Servers (option 44), 269
adding to a scope, 269-270
46 WINS/NBT Node type (option 46), 269
adding, 271
BOOTP, 198
clients, enabling, 205-206
configuration options, 217-221
databases
compacting, 214
corrupted, 215-216
creating, 216-217
managing, 213-217
repairing, 215-216
IP addresses, 198
parameters
APIProtocolSupport, 224-225
BackupDatabasePath, 225
BackupInterval, 225
DatabaseCleanupInterval, 225
DatabaseLoggingFlag, 225-226
DatabaseName, 226
DatabasePath, 226
RestoreFlag, 226-232
Registry values, editing, 223-224
reservations
creating, 210-211
establishing, 209-211
managing client-specific options, 219-220
RFC1533 DHCP, options, 220-223
scopes
activating, 212
deactivating, 212
deleting, 212
setting up, 202-205
servers
adding to networks, 598
concepts, 198-201
installing, 202-212
managing multiple, 213
operation, 198-201
starting, 214-215
stopping, 214-215
troubleshooting, 575
WINS clients, 269-272
DHCP Boot Relay Agent, 130
DHCP database files, 213
DHCP MIB, 481
DHCP Options: Global dialog box, 271
DHCP Options: Scope dialog box, 270
DHCP Relay Agent, 148-149
installing, 226-227
DHCP Scopes dialog box, 216
DHCPDICOVER (DHCP process), 200
DHCPOFFER (DHCP process), 200
DHCPREQUEST (DHCP process), 200
dial-in capability, domains, 597
dial-up networking, 521-530
phonebook entries
Appearance option, 534-535
Callback option, 533
dialing, 530-535
editing, 524-532
Phonebook option, 535
Dial-Up Networking Monitor, 535-538
Preferences tab, 538
Summary tab, 537
dialing out (RAS), 519-520
dialog boxes
Active Leases, 207, 272

Adapter Bus Location, 139
Add Reserved Clients, 210
Add Services, 189
Add WINS Server, 273
Address Expression, 460
Advanced Microsoft TCP/IP Configuration, 269
Capture Buffer Settings, 457
Configure Network Monitoring Agent, 452-453
Creating New Zone, 383
Detailed Information, 279
DHCP Options: Global, 271
DHCP Options: Scope, 270
DHCP Scopes, 216
Directory Properties, 167-168, 172-173
Microsoft TCP/IP Properties, 137
Modem, 514
Monitoring Agent, 453
Network, 483
Network Card Setup, 139
Network Settings, 120, 134-141, 171, 189, 242, 266
Bindings tab, 140-141
Identification tab, 134-135
Protocols tab, 136-138
Services tab, 136
Port Usage, 541
Preferences, 276
Printer Ports, 190
Properties, 159
Property, 167-168
Pull Partner Properties, 290
Push Partner Properties, 289
RAS Setup, 541-544
Replication Partners, 289, 291
Set Filter, 276
Show Database, 274
Static Mappings, 282
TCP/IP Configuration, 115, 475
TCP/IP Properties, 171
TCP/IP Settings, 242
Terminal Preferences, 425
TPC/IP Settings, 243
WINS Server Configuration, 277

directories
home, 167-168
IIS, testing, 179
properties, editing, 167
virtual, 168
configuring, 168-169
WHOIS, 342-343
WWW servers, accessing, 164

Directories tab (WWW Server Properties), 163

Directory Properties dialog box, 167-168, 172-173

display filters, 468-471
adding expressions, 469-471
logical operators, 471

displaying
node types, 249-250
WINS databases, 274-276

DLC (Data Link Control), 37

DNS (Domain Name Service), 64, 128
address records, 359
aliases, 323, 359-360
BOOT files, 351-353
cache files, 362-365
clients, enabling, 389-390
configuring options, 350-351
country domains, 329-338
domain name space, 321-324
domain administration, 324-325
e-mail server records, 360
fully qualified names, 321
hierarchies, 320-321
implementing, 346-347
name resolution, 245
names, adding, 172
nodes, 321
NS records (Name Server), 358-359
overview, 320-345
preparing for, 348
primary zones, adding, 370-371
properties, 146-147
queries, resolving, 325-327
resolvers, 325
resource record types, 354-355
reverse mapping, 344-345
reverse-lookup zones, adding, 369-370
servers, 131
adding, 600
creating, 367-368
initializing, 367-368
installing, 367
managing, 348-387
managing multiple, 382
statistics, 387
troubleshooting with Nslookup, 391-396
zones, 368
SOA resource record (Start of Authority), 356-357
subdomains, 323
non-government organizations, 341-342
US domain, 339-341
zones, adding, 384-385
troubleshooting, 576
WHOIS, 342-343
Windows NT, 345
WINS record, 357-358

world-wide
domains, 328
zone properties, modify-
ing, 376-380
zones, 324
properties, 377

DNS Manager
BIND servers, porting
data, 388-389
DNS server statistics, 387
preferences, 386-387

documentation
IIS (Internet Informa-
tion Service), 157
IIS 2.0 (Internet
Information Service),
157

DOD (Department of Defense)
ARPA (Advanced
Research Project
Agency), 18
development of TCP/IP,
17-18
GOSIP (Government OSI
Protocols), 23

DOD Advanced Research Project Agency, *see* ARPA

DOD protocol suite, *see* TCP/IP

#DOM:domain_name tag, 240, 576

Domain Announcements, 314

domain browser list, 310

domain controllers, synchronization, 310

domain database files, 353-360

Domain group names, 283

Domain Master Browsers, 304

Domain Name Group, 313

Domain Name Service, *see* DNS

Domain Name Space, 321-324
organization, 327-342

domains
administration, 324-325
BDCs, Backup
Browsers, 306
browsers, 307-308
browsing, 306-307
country domains,
329-338
dial-in capability, 597
multiple master domain
model, linking sites in
TCP/IP implementa-
tion, 594-598
traffic
handling with LMHOSTS, 309-313
handling with WINS, 313
trust relationships,
595-606
trusted domains, 596
world wide, 328
zones, 353

DoStaticDataInit parameter, 292

downloading from FTP servers, troubleshooting, 565-567

draft standards, 21

drivers
graphics drivers, 185-186
Microsoft networking
Adapter Card Drivers, 36-37
Application/File System drivers, 34, 36
PLOTTER.DLL, 186
print drivers, 185-186
characterization data files, 186
PSCRIPT.DLL, 186
RASDD.DLL, 185

duplicate IP addresses, 137

Dynamic Host Configuration Protol, *see* DHCP

dynamic routing, 115, 118-120
RIP routing, 119-124

E

e-mail server records, 360

EDIT command, 239

editing
DHCP Registry values,
223-224
directory properties, 167
LMHOSTS file, 239
phonebook entries,
524-532
static mappings, 282

editors
IP Address Array Editor,
270
Registry, configuring
WINS parameters,
291-295

elections, 305-307
tie breaking, 306

EMF (Enhanced Metafile), 184

EnableProxy parameter, 269

EnableRegistryBoot parameter, 389

enabling
DHCP clients, 205-206
DNS clients, 389-390
NBT, 313-315
PPTP filtering for RAS
servers, 549
PPTP support, RAS server
clients, 550-551

#END_ALTERNATE tag, 241

End to End checkbox (SNMP Properties Agent tab), 484

Enhanced Metafile, *see* EMF

error detection, datagram transmission, 87-88

Ethernet frames, 86

ETYPE filters, 458-460

Event Viewer, 570-571

evolution, TCP/IP, 17-18

exams
- certification
  - *MCPS, 610-618*
  - *MCSD, 616-618*
  - *MCSE, 611-618*
  - *MCT, 617-618*
- TestPrep Utility (CD-ROM), 619-620
  - *instructor mode, 621*
  - *non-random mode, 620-621*
  - *question presentation, 620-621*
  - *score report, 620-621*

exercises
- Adding an Alias to the FTP Server, 179
- Adding Client Reservations, 230
- Adding Hosts, 398
- Adding Other Records, 399
- Adding Scope and Global Options in the DHCP server, 228
- Adding Static Mappings to the Database, 296
- Changing the IUSR_*computername* Password, 177
- Checking the Information, 230
- Configuring a DHCP Scope, 228
- Configuring a Second DHCP Scope, 230
- Configuring DNS Domains, 397
- Creating a Demonstration Printer, 194
- Creating a Simple LMHOSTS File, 251
- Entering and Removing Entries from the ARP Cache, 473
- Hooking Up to the LPD Service, 195-196
- Installing IIS, 176
- Installing the DHCP Server, 228
- Installing the DNS Server, 396
- Installing the Protocol, 499
- Installing the TCP/IP Printing Service, 193
- Installing the WINS Server, 295
- Learning About WINS Server, 296
- Logging TCP/IP Activity, 503
- Monitoring Real-Time Performance, 501
- Sample LMHOSTS, 251
- Testing the DNS Server, 400
- Turning On the TCP/IP Print Server, 194
- Using Network Monitor and Agent, 473
- Using SNMPUTIL to Test SNMP, 500
- Using the FTP Command to Move Files, 471

experimental standards, 21

expressions, adding to display filters, 469-471

extensions
- country domains, 329-338
- US domain, subdomains, 339-341
- world-wide domains, 328

Extinction Interval (WINS Server Configuration dialog box option), 278

extinction intervals, setting, 278

Extinction Timeout (WINS Server Configuration dialog box option), 278

extracting network IDs from IP addresses, 95

F

FAQs (Frequently Asked Questions), 22

fault tolerance, WINS servers, 267

Federal Networking Council, 19

fields, 68
- packets, 84-86
- WINS database, 275
- WWW Server Properties, Service tab, 162

File and Print Sharing, 312

file restores, troubleshooting, 563

file transfer utilities, 406-414
- RCP (Remote Copy Protocol), 412-414
  - *.rhosts file, 413-414*
  - *remote privileges, 413*
- TFTP (Trivial File Transfer Protocol), 411-412

files
- .rhosts, 413-414
- attributes, 47
- BOOT, 351-353
- cache files, 362-365
- characterization data files, 186
- database
  - *configuring DNS server, 350-351*
  - *creating BIND database files, 351*
  - *reverse-matching, 360-362*
- DHCP database, 213
- domain database, 353-360
- downloading from FTP server, 565-567
- EMF, 184
- HOSTS, 244-245
  - *name resolution, 347-348*
- hosts.txt, 239
- J50.log, 286
- LMHOSTS, 239-242, 309-313
  - *editing, 239*
  - *modifying, 311-313*
- LMHOSTS.SAM, 239
- localhost database files, 362

log files (Performance Monitor), creating, 496-497
printer interface files, 186
PSCRIPT1, 187
Wins.mdb, 286
Winstmp.mdb, 286

filters
address, 460-461
capture, 458-461
display filters, 468-471
ETYPE, 458-460
logical operators, 462
PPTP, enabling, 549
SAP, 458-460

finding IP address mappings, 263

Finger utility, 434

first host IDs, calculating, 102

flags, *see* fields

FLASH! Electronic Flash cards, TestPrep Utility, 621

FQDN (Fully Qualified Domain Name), 244

fragment offset, 85

Fragment Reassembly Failures (Internet Protocol counter), 493

fragmentation
datagrams, 86-87
headers, 86-87

Fragmentation Failures (Internet Protocol counter), 493

Fragmented Datagrams/sec (Internet Protocol counter), 493

Fragments Created/sec (Internet Protocol counter), 493

Fragments Re-assembled/sec (Internet Protocol counter), 493

Fragments Received/sec (Internet Protocol counter), 493

frames
capture filters, 458-461
captured, saving, 454
capturing, 453-454
preventing lost frames, 457
filters
address, 460-461
ETYPE, 458-460
logical operators, 462
SAP, 458-460
monitoring, Network Monitor, 449-471
see also datagrams

framing packets, Network Access layer, 50

Frequently Asked Questions, *see* FAQs

FrontPage, 161

FTP (File Transfer Protocol), 406-411
command line switches, 407
commands, 408-412

FTP Directories tab (FTP service), 175

FTP servers, downloading files, troubleshooting, 565-567

FTP service
configuring, 174
FTP Directories tab, 175
Messages tab, 174

Fully Qualified Domain Name, *see* FQDN

fully qualified domain name (FQDN), 321-322

FYI (For Your Information), 22

G

Gallery (Performance Monitor chart setting), 495

gateways, *see* routers

GDI (Graphics Device Interface), 184

General tab (Modem Properties dialog box), 515

GET (SNMP command), 480

get (SNMPUTIL command), 486

Get command, 57

GET-NEXT (SNMP command), 480

getnext (SNMPUTIL command), 486

global DHCP options, managing, 218-219

goals of TCP/IP development, 17

Gopher services (IIS), configuring, 175-176

GOSIP (Government OSI Protocols), 23

Government OSI Protocols, *see* GOSIP

graphic interface, configuring DNS server, 350-351

Graphics Device Interface, *see* GDI

graphics drivers, 185-186

H

H-node, name resolution, 264-265

H-Node (Hybrid Node), 247-249

handshake, 72

hardware
RAS, installing, 513-517
troubleshooting, 564

header checksum, 85

headers, 68-71, 86
fields, 68
IP, 84
pseudo headers, 71
TCP headers, 68-70
UDP header, 70-72
format, 70

hierarchies, DNS, 320-321

HINFO (resource record type), 354

historical standards, 21

history of TCP/IP, 17-18
RFC (Request for Comments), 19-22

HKEY_LOCAL_MACHINE
browser parameters, 305
WINS Registry parameters, 291-295
home directories, 167-168
choosing for installation, 156
creating, 172-173
Horizontal Grid (Performance Monitor chart setting), 495
host communications, Winsock, 43
host IDs
first, calculating, 102
last, calculating, 103
TCP/IP, 24
host names, 244
HOSTNAME, 64, 439
hosts
IIS, identifying, 154
remote, connecting, 424-425
HOSTS file, 64, 244-245
HOSTS files, name resolution, 347-348
hosts.txt, 239
HPMON.DLL, 187
HTML (Hypertext Markup Language), 157
HTTP (HyperText Transfer Protocol), 22
HTTP services, configuring, 161-173
Hybrid (H-Node) name resolution, 248-249
Hypertext Markup Language, *see* HTML
HyperText Transfer Protocol, *see* HTTP

I

IAB (Internet Activities Board), 18-19
see also IETF, IRFT
ICMP (Internet Control Messaging Protocol), 49-50, 490
ICMP object counters, 490-491
ICMP packets (Internet Control Messaging Protocol), 87-88
Icon field (WINS database), 275
Identification tab (Network Settings dialog box), 134-135
identifying, IIS host, 154
IDs, subnetwork, 99-102
IETF (Internet Engineering Task Force), 19-20
IIS (Internet Information Server) 128-129
adding, 177
adding to networks, 600-601
directory, testing, 179
FTP services, configuring, 174
FTP Directories tab, 175
Messages tab, 174
Gopher services, configuring, 175-176
home directories, choosing for installation, 156
installing, configuring TCP/IP, 154-158
IUSR_*computername* account, configuring, 160-161
managing, 158-176
passwords
changing, 177-178
troubleshooting, 178-179
services, pausing, 159
troubleshooting, 574
views, selecting, 160
WWW server (IIS), configuring, 161-173
implementing
DNS, 346-347
TCP/IP intranets
linking networks, 594-598
sample IP address requirements, 593-594
subnet requirements, 593-606
#INCLUDE tag, 240
informational standards, 21
initializing DNS servers, 367-368
initiating replication, 287-288, 290-291
InitTimePause parameter, 292
installing
DHCP Relay Agent, 226-227
DHCP servers, 202-212
DNS servers, 367
initializing, 367-368
IIS (Internet Information Server), 154-158
identifying a host, 154
modems, 514-521
Network Monitor, 451
printers, 188
RIP, 120
services, TCP/IP printing, 189
SNMP (Simple Network Management Protocol), 483-486
TCP/IP, 134-149
WINS clients, 268-272
DHCP configuration, 269-272
static IP address configuration, 268
WINS proxy configuration, 268-269
WINS server, 265-267
see also uninstalling
Instance (Performance Monitor Chart View option), 489
interactive queries, 393-396
interactive utilities, 414-426
Internet Explorer, 414-424
configuring, 416-424
REXEC, 426-427
RSH, 426
Telnet, 424-426

Intermediate nodes, 321
International Standards Organization, *see* ISO
Internet
defined, 18
directories, WHOIS, 342-343
DNS (Domain Name Server), 128
Federal Networking Council, 19
IIS (Internet Information Server)
installing, 154-158
Internet Service Manager (ISM), 159
managing, 158-176
troubleshooting, 574
supernetting, 104-108
TCP/IP, advantages, 22-24
web sites, accessing, 177
Internet layer, subnet masks, 47
Internet Activities Board, *see* IAB
Internet checkbox (SNMP Properties Agent tab), 484
Internet Control Messaging Protocol, *see* ICMP
Internet Engineering Steering Group, 20
Internet Engineering Task Force, *see* IETF
Internet Explorer, 414-424
configuring, 416-424
Content Advisor, activating, 420-422
Internet Group Management Protocol, 50
Internet Information Server, *see* IIS
Internet layer (TCP/IP model), 42, 46-50
Address Resolution Protocol, 49
ANDing, 47-49
Internet Control Messaging Protocol, 49-50
Internet Group Management Protocol, 50
Internet Protocol (IP layer), 46-49
Internet MIB II, 481
Internet Official Protocol Standards, 21
Internet Protocol (IP layer), 46-49
counters, 492-493
subnet masks, 47
Internet Research Task Force, *see* IRFT
Internet Server Application Programming Interface, *see* ISAPI
Internet Service Manager (IIS), 159
Internet Society, 19
Internic web site, 22
intervals
extinction, setting, 278
renewal, setting, 278
IP (Internet Protocol)
configuration, troubleshooting, 564
counters, 492-493
IP Address Array Editor, 270
IP address field, (WINS database), 275
IP address mappings, locating, 263
IP address spoofing, 167
IP addresses, 24-26
ANDing, 48-49
Class A, 26
Class B, 26
Class C, 26
configuring, 171-172
DHCP, 198
intranet implementation, sample requirements, 593-594
Name Cache, 237-238
name resolution
WINS, 258-265
see also name resolution
network IDs, extracting, 95
resolution, modifying LMHOSTS file, 311
special names, recognizing, 282-284
subnetting, 94, 96-105
host IDs, 102-103
planning, 97
supernetting, 104-108
IP datagrams, 86
creating, 84-86
fragmentation, 86-87
IP headers, 84
IP layer, subnet masks, 78
IPCONFIG, 433-434, 568
switches, 144
IPCONFIG utility, 144-145
IR (Internet Registry), 327
IRFT (Internet Research Task Force), 19
ISAPI (Internet Server Application Programming Int, 129, 153
ISDN (resource record type), 354
IsDomainMaster parameter, 305
ISO (International Standards Organization)
MIB (Management Information Base), 480
OSI (Open Systems Interconnection), 23
IUSR_*computername* account, 157
configuring, 160-161

J-L

J50.log, 286
keys, 222
LAN Manager MIB II, 481
LANA (Local Area Network Adapter) Number, 38
last host IDs, calculating, 103
Last Replication Time: Admin Trigger (WINS server statistic), 274

Last Replication Time: Net Update (WINS server statistic), 274
Last Replication Time: Periodic (WINS server statistic), 274
layers
  Internet Layer, 46-50
  IP (Internet Protocol) layer
    creating IP datagram, 84-86
    IP headers, 84
    subnet masks, 78
  Microsoft networks, 34-36
    adapter card drivers, 38-43
    Application layer, 36
    NDIS (Network Driver Interface Specification), 35, 38
    TDI (Transport Driver Interface), 36-37
  OSI reference model, 32
leaf nodes, 321
leases
  active
    managing, 206-208
    modifying properties, 208-209
    viewing, 206-208
  managing, 212
Legend (Performance Monitor chart setting), 495
LEXMON.DLL, 187
Line Printer Daemon, *see* LPD
Line Printer Request, *see* LPR
linking networks with TCP/IP, 594-598
LMHOSTS, 64, 309-313
  browsing, 310-313
    domain browser list, 310
  domain traffic, handling, 309-313
LMHOSTS file, 239-242
  modifying, 312-313
  troubleshooting, 241-242
LMHOSTS.SAM, 239
Local Area Network Adapter, *see* LANA
localhost database files, 362
LOCALMON.DLL, 187
locating
  addresses, 80-83
  sources of problems, 562-568
Log Detailed Events (WINS Server Configuration dialog box option), 279
log files (Performance Monitor), creating, 496-497
LogDetailedEvents parameter, 292
LogFilePath parameter, 292
Logging Enabled (WINS Server Configuration dialog box option), 279
Logging tab, WWW Server Properties, 164
LoggingOn parameter, 293
logical connections, 38
logical operators, 462, 471
  ANDing, 47-49
logical printers
  port monitors, 187-188
  printer pools, 188
  see also printers
logon validation, 308
logons, 308-309
  challenge/response, 163
loop back tests, 25
LPD (Line Printer Daemon), 129
  sharing printers, 191-192
  servers, connecting, 189-191
LPQ, 428
LPR (Line Printer Request), 129, 427-428
LPR Port monitor (Line Printer Request), 190-191
LPRMON.DLL, 187

M

M-Node (Mixed Node), 247-248
MAC address, 80
MaintainServerList parameter, 305
Management Information Base, *see* MIBs
management stations, 482
managing
  active leases, 206-208
  capture buffer, 456-457
  DHCP, client-specific options for reservations, 219-220
  DHCP databases, 213-217
  DNS servers, 348-387
  IIS (Internet Information Server), 158-176
  leases, 212
  multiple DNS servers, 382
  multiple servers, DHCP, 213
  WINS servers, 272-287
manual database restoration, 286
mappings
  IP addresses, locating, 263
  reverse mapping, 344-345
  static
    configuring, 281-282
    editing, 282
masking, 48
masks, subnet, 78
  modifying, 175-476
Master Browsers, 300, 306
  browse list, 301
  browser list, updating, 303-304
maximum transfer unit, *see* MTU
MB (resource record type), 354
McastIntvl parameter, 293
McastTtl parameter, 293

MCPS (Microsoft Certified Product Specialist) certification
- exams, 610-618
- operating systems, 610-618
- qualified functions, 609

MCSD (Microsoft Certified Solution Developer) certification
- exams, 616-618
- operating systems, 616-618
- qualified functions, 610

MCSE (Microsoft Certified Systems Engineer) certification
- exams, 611-618
- operating system exams, 611-618
- qualified functions, 609
- Windows NT 4.0, exam requirements, 614-618

MCT (Microsoft Certified Trainer) certification
- exams, 617-618
- operating systems, 617-618
- qualified functions, 610
- Web site, 618

MD4 (RSA Message Digest 4), 520

Messages Outbound Errors (ICMP object counter), 490

Messages Received Errors (ICMP object counter), 490

Messages Received/sec (ICMP object counter), 490

Messages Sent/sec (ICMP object counter), 490

Messages tab (FTP service), 174

Messages/sec (ICMP object counter), 490

MG (resource record type), 354

#MH tag, 241

MIBs (Management Information Base), 480-481

Microsoft
- certification types, 609-618
- DNS servers, managing, 348-365
- Internet Information Server, *see* IIS
- networks, 32-40
  - *adapter card drivers, 38-43*
  - *layering, 34-36*
  - *NDIS layer, 38*
  - *protocols, 35*
  - *TDI layer (Transport Driver Interface), 36-37*

Microsoft Browser Service, 300-304
- configuring browsers, 304-305
- *see also* browsers

Microsoft Certified Product Specialist, *see* MCPS

Microsoft Certified Professional Program, 610

Microsoft Certified Solution Developer, *see* MCSD

Microsoft Certified Systems Engineer, *see* MCSE

Microsoft Certified Trainer, *see* MCT

Microsoft Certified Training Web site, 618

Microsoft Official Curricula (MOC), 617

Microsoft Online Institute (MOLI), 610

Microsoft SNMP Properties Agent tab, 484

Microsoft SNMP Properties Security tab, 485-486

Microsoft SNMP Properties Traps tab, 485-486

Microsoft TCP/IP Properties dialog box, 137

Microsoft Training and Certification Web site, 610

Migrate On/Off (WINS Server Configuration dialog box option), 279

MINFO (resource record type), 354

Mixed (M-Node) name resolution, 248

models (networking) TCP/IP, 42-50

Modem Configuration dialog box
- options, 525-526
- Script tab, 528-529
- Security tab, 529
- Server tab, 526-528

Modem dialog box, 514

modems
- installing, 514-521
- Modem Configuration dialog box
  - *Script tab, 528-529*
  - *Security tab, 529*
  - *Server tab, 526-528*

Modes (NSLOOKUP function), 434

modifying
- active lease properties, 208-209
- LMHOSTS file, 311, 312-313
- network adapters, properties, 140
- scopes, 205
- subnet masks, 475-476
- zone properties, 376-380

monitoring
- frames, Network Monitor, 450-471
- frames with Network Monitor, 449-471
- ports, PPTP, 549
- WINS servers, 273-274

Monitoring Agent dialog box, 453

MR (resource record), 355

MTU (Maximum Transfer Unit), 86

multihomed
- computers, 260
- names, 283
- systems, installing a WINS server, 266

multiple master domain model
TCP/IP implementation, linking sites, 594-598
trust relationships, 595-606
Multiprotocol Router, 129
MX records, 355
adding, 374-375

N

Name Cache (NetBIOS), 264-265
name management, 61
NetBIOS, 33
Name Query, 236
name refresh requests, 261
name registration, 258-260
name registration queries, 258-260
Name Release, 237, 244
name release requests, 262
name resolution, 63-64, 237-245
B-Node (Broadcast), 247
broadcasting, 238-239
DNS, 245
H-Node (Hybrid), 248-249, 264-265
HOSTS files, 244-245, 347-348
LMHOSTS, 239-242
browsing, 310-313
domain browser list, 310
M-Node (Mixed node), 248
NetBIOS, 308-314
LMHOSTS, 309-313
viewing node types, 249-250
NetBIOS name cache, 237-238
NetBIOS Name Server, 242-244
order of resolution, 246-250
P-Node (Peer-to-Peer), 248
troubleshooting, 564
Windows NT, 390-391
WINS, 258-265, 381
challenges, 260
multihomed computers, 260
name registration, 258-260
NetBIOS name release, 262-263
NetBIOS name renewal, 261-262
troubleshooting, 575-576
name servers, 324
NAMEQUERY REQUEST, 260
NAMEQUERY RESPONSE, 260
NAMEREGISTRATION REQUEST, 258
NAMEREGISTRATION RESPONSE, 259
names
community names, 482-483
host, 244
mapping, 344-345
resolving
B-Node (Broadcast), 247
H-Node (Hybrid), 248-249
M-Node (Mixed), 248
P-Node (Peer-to-Peer), 248
WINS, 381
WINS process, 263-268
special, recognizing, 282-284
Domain group names, 283
multihomed names, 283
normal group names, 283
NameServerPort (NBNS parameter), 244
NameSrvQueryCount (NBNS parameter), 244
NameSrvQueryTimeout (NBNS parameter), 244
National Science Foundation, *see* NSF
nbdatagram, 62
nbname, 62
NBNS (NetBIOS Name Server), 242-244
parameters, configuring, 244
nbsession, 62
NBSTAT, column headings, 443-444
NBSTAT command, switches, 62-63
NBT (NetBIOS over TCP/IP), 61-63
enabling, 313-315
NBTSTAT, 62-63, 442-444, 569
NBTSTAT -n, 264
NBTSTAT -R, 237, 241
NBTSTAT -r, 237
NCP (Netware Core Protocol), 36
NDIS (Network Driver Interface Specification), 35
bindings, 38
NDS (Netware Directory Services), 596
NET USE, 63
NetBEUI (NetBIOS Extended User Interface), 37
NetBIOS (Network Basic Input/Output System), 45-46
broadcast, 63
commands, NBTSTAT, 62-63
HOSTNAME, 64
LMHOSTS, 64
names, refreshing, 261
name resolution, 63-64, 237-245
broadcasting, 238-239
DNS, 245
HOSTS file, 244-245
LMHOSTS file, 239-242

NetBIOS name cache, 237-238
NetBIOS Name Server, 242-244
see also NetBIOS name resolution
node types
B-Node (Broadcast), 247
H-Node (Hybrid), 247, 248-249
M-Node (Mixed), 248
P-Node (Peer-to-Peer), 248
server service, 33
services, 32-33, 62
SMB (Server Message Block), 33
NetBIOS Datagram Service, 62
NetBIOS Datagram Service port, 300
NetBIOS gateway, RAS server configuration, 543-544
NetBIOS name cache, 63, 264-265
see also Name Cache
NetBIOS name query, 243
NetBIOS name release, 262-263
NetBIOS name renewal, 261-262
NetBIOS name resolution, 308-314
LMHOSTS, 309-313
browsing, 310-313
domain browser list, 310
LMHOSTS file, modifying, 312-313
node types, displaying, 249-250
order of resolution, 246-250
NetBIOS Name Server, 242-244
NetBIOS Name Service, 62
NetBIOS Name Service port, 236
NetBIOS over TCP/IP, *see* NBT
NetBIOS Session Service, 62
NETLOGON service, 308
NETSTAT, 440-441, 568
NETSTAT command, 60
switches, 60-61
Netware Core Protocol, *see* NCP
Netware Directory Services, *see* NDS
Network Access (TCP/IP model), 42
Network Access layer, 50
network adapter cards, binding protocols, 38
network adapters
adding, 139-140
properties, modifying, 140
removing, 140
Network Basic Input/Output System, *see* NetBIOS
Network Card Setup dialog box, 139
network cards, descriptions, 453
Network Settings dialog box, 120, 134-141, 171, 189, 242, 266, 483
Bindings tab, 140-141
Identification tab, 134-135
Protocols tab, 136-138
Services tab, 136
Network Driver Interface Specification, *see* NDIS
network frames, capturing, 454
Network IDs
extracting from IP addresses, 95
TCP/IP, 24
Network Information Center (Stanford Research Institute), 239
Network Interface Card, *see* NIC
network layers, 32
Network Monitor, 449-471, 569
address databases, creating, 454-455
capture buffer, managing, 456-457
capture data
saving, 463
viewing, 463-471
capture triggers, 462-463
display filters, 468-471
adding expressions, 469-471
logical operators, 471
frames, capture filters, 458-461
installing, 451
managing capture buffer, 456-457
network cards, describing, 453
network frames, capturing, 453-454
networks, selecting for monitoring, 456
security, 451-452
WINS special name, 284
network traffic
promiscuous mode, 450
WINS servers, 267
networks
adapters, adding, 139-140
adding proxy servers, 602
bindings, 140-141
bridges, 114
browsers
domains, 307-308
elections, 305-307
connections, monitoring, 535-538
connectivity
testing with Ping, 431-434
troubleshooting, 573
DNS servers, adding, 600

domains
browsing, 306-307
dial-in capability, 597
handling traffic, 313
trust relationships, 595-606
zones, 353
frames
capture filters, 458-461
capturing, 453-454
monitoring, 449-471
IIS (Internet Information Server), adding, 600-601
Internet Layer, 46-50
IP addresses
configuring, 171-172
subnetting, 94, 96-105
IP layer
creating IP datagram, 84-86
IP headers, 84
subnet masks, 78
Microsoft, 32-40
adapter card drivers, 36, 38-43
Application layer, 36
layering, 34-36
NDIS layer, 38
protocols, 35
TDI layer (Transport Driver Interface), 36-37
monitoring, 456
OSI reference model (Open Systems Interconnection), 32
packets
fields, 84-86
ICMP (Internet Control Messaging Protocol), 87-88
sending, 80-83
print devices
installing, 188
port monitors, 187-188
printer pools, 188
printers, sharing, 191-192
protocols, SNMP (Simple Network Management Protocol), 480
RAS (Remote Access Server), 510-513
adding, 601
adding phonebook entries, 521-524
adding serial ports, 513-514
callback security, 511
configuring servers, 541-546
dial-up networking, 521-530
dialing out, 519-520
dialing with phonebook entries, 530-535
installing, 511-517
X.25, 530
resources, browsing, 300-307
routers, 114, 539-541
convergence, 120
dynamic routing, 118-120
static routing, 115-118
Windows NT, 115-120
routing, 78-80
servers, 598-601
Backup Browser, 300-301
connecting to LPD servers, 189-191
DHCP (Dynamic Host Configuration Protocol), 598
Master Browser, 300
WINS, 599
subnet masks, bit requirements, 97 98
subnets
browsing, 308-314
troubleshooting, 562-563
supernets, Class A addresses, 105
TCP/IP, linking, 594-598
TCP/IP model, 42-50
components, 43-45
Transport layer protocols, 45-46
TCP/IP printing services, installing, 189
Transport layer, *see* Transport layer
troubleshooting, 562-567
locating problems, 562-568
WINS servers, multiple, 267
workgroups, browsing, 306-307
see also subnets
NETWORKS file, ROUTE command, 445-446
New Pull Partner Default Configuration: Start Time (Preferences dialog box option), 277
New Push Partner Default Configuration:Update Count (Preferences dialog box option), 277
NIC (Network Interface Card), 114
nodes
B-Node (Broadcast), 247
DNS, 321
fully qualified names, 321
H-Node (Hybrid), 247-249
name resolution, 264-265
M-Node (Mixed), 248
P-Node (Peer-to-Peer), 248
viewing, 249-250
#NOFNR tag, 240
Non Browsers, 305
non-government organizations, subdomains, 341-342
non-interactive queries, 391-392
NoOfWrkThds parameter, 293
normal group names, 283
NS record (Name Server), 355, 358-359

NSF (National Science Foundation), 18
NSFnet, 18
NSLOOKUP, 434-439, 576
interactive commands, 435-436
interactive mode, commands, 436-445
Nslookup, 391-396
NT Diagnostics, 571-572
numbers
see also binary
subnet, 99
numeric parameters, SOA (Start of Authority resource record), 357
NWLink (Netware Link), 37

O

Object (Performance Monitor Chart View option), 489
objectives of TCP/IP development, 17
objects
NBT (NetBIOS over TCP/IP), counters, 493
TCP (Transmission Control Protocol), counters, 493-494
UDP (User Datagram Protocol), counters, 494
objects (Performance Monitor)
ICMP, counters, 490-491
Internet Protocol, counters, 492-493
octets, 24
online documentation
IIS (Internet Information Service), 157
IIS 2.0 (Internet Information Service), 157
Open Shortest Path First, *see* OSPF
Open Systems Interconnection, *see* OSI
opening
interactive FTP session, 406
IP Address Array Editor, 270
operating systems, MCSE exams
Windows NT 3.51, 611-618
Windows NT 4.0, 614-618
operation of DHCP servers, 198-201
operators (logical), ANDing, 47-49
option 44 (DHCP), 269
adding to a scope, 269-270
option 46 (DHCP), 269
adding, 271
options
DHCP configuration, 217-221
DNS configuration, 350-351
Messages tab (FTP service), 174-181
RFC1533 DHCP, 220-223
WWW Server Properties
Advanced tab, 166-167
Directories tab, 163
Logging tab, 164-166
order of name resolution, 246-250
organization, Domain Name Space, 327-342
OSI reference model (Open Systems Interconnection), 23, 32
layers, 32
OSPF (Open Shortest Path First), 119

P

P-Node (Peer-to-Peer Node), 247-248
Packet Internet Groper, *see* Ping
packet switching, 17-18
packets
ARP (Address Resolution Packets), 82
broadcast, 81
fields, 84-86
framing, Network Access layer, 50
ICMP (Internet Control Messaging Protocol), 87-88
sending, 80-83
see also datagrams
PAP (Password Authentication Protocol), 520
parameters
broadcast, configuring, 238-239
DHCP
APIProtocolSupport, 224-225
BackupDatabase Path, 225
BackupInterval, 225
configuring, 221-226
DatabaseCleanup Interval, 225
DatabaseLoggingFlag, 225-226
DatabaseName, 226
DatabasePath, 226
RestoreFlag, 226-232
DNS server, EnableRegistry Boot, 389
Name Cache, configuring, 238
NBNS, configuring, 244
numeric, SOA (Start of Authority resource record), 357
proxy servers, EnableProxy, 269

WINS, configuring, 291-295
pass through authentication, 308
passive open, 56
Password Authentication Protocol, *see* PAP
passwords
changing, 177-178
testing, 178
troubleshooting, 178-179
pausing IIS services, 159
Peer-to-Peer (P-Node) name resolution, 248
Performance Monitor, 487-498, 569-570
chart settings, 494-495
chart view, 488
viewing log files, 497-498
log files, creating, 496-497
NBT object, counters, 493
NetBIOS over TCP/IP object, counters, 493
TCP (Transmission Control Protocol), counters, 493-494
UDP (User Datagram Protocol), counters, 494
phonebook entries
adding, 521-524
dialing, 530-535
editing, 524-532
user preferences, 532-535
Phonebook option (phonebook entries), 535
Physical checkbox (SNMP Properties Agent tab), 484
physical layer, 32
physical printers
port monitors, 187-188
printer pools, 188
see also printers
Ping, 429-433, 568
command line switches, 429-430
Ping (Packet Internet Groper), 141-144
PJL (Printer Job Language), 187
PJLMON.DLL, 187
planning
subnets, 97
virtual servers, 169-170
WINS server installation, 265-267
PLOTTER.DLL, 186
plotters, 186
PLOTUI.DLL, 186
PNA (Private Network Address), 602
port monitors, 187-188
LPR Port monitor (Line Printer Request), 190-191
Port Usage dialog box, 541
porting data from BIND servers, 388-389
ports, 56
PPTP monitoring, 549
source ports, 69
Positive Name Query Response, 236
PostScript printers, 186
PotentialBrowsers, 305
PPTP monitoring ports, 549
PPTP (Point-to-Point Tunneling Protocol), 546-551
PPTP filtering, RAS servers, enabling, 549
#PRE tag, 240
preferences
DNS Manager, 386-387
WINS Manager, 276-277
Preferences dialog box, 276
preparing for
DNS, 348
IIS installation, 154-155
presentation layer, 32
primary directives, 352
primary zones, adding, 370
print drivers, 185-186
characterization data files, 186
print interface, 186
print process
port monitor, 187-188
print processors, 187
print spooler, 186
Windows NT, print drivers, 185-186
print processors, 187
print spoolers, 186
printer interface, 186
Printer Job Language, *see* PJL
printer pools, 188
Printer Ports dialog box, 190
printers
installing, 188
jammed, troubleshooting, 186
sharing, 191-192
see also plotters
printing
LPD (Line Printer Daemon)
port monitors, LPR Port monitor (Line Printer Request), 190-191
troubleshooting, 574-575
Windows NT, 184-188
printing utilities, 427-428
LPQ, 428
LPR (Line Printer Request), 427-428
PriorityClassHigh parameter, 293
Private Network Address, *see* PNA
problems, *see* troubleshooting
promiscuous mode, 450
properties
DNS, 146-147
network adapters, modifying, 140
scopes, 202
SOA records, 377-378
telephony, 518-519
WINS address, 147-148
WINS server, configuring, 277-279

WWW servers, managing, 161-173
zone, 377

Properties dialog box, 159

Property dialog box, 167-168

proposed standards, 21

protocols
Address Resolution Protocol, 49
AFP (Apple File Protocol), 37
binding, 38
BOOTP (Boot Protocol), 130
configuring for RAS servers, 542-543
DHCP, DHCP Relay Agent, 148-149
DLC (Data Link Control), 37
FTP (File Transfer Protocol), 406-411
commands, 408-412
Internet Control Messaging Protocol, 49-50
Internet Group Management Protocol, 50-54
Microsoft networking, 35
NCP (Netware Core Protocol), 36
NetBEUI (NetBIOS Extended User Interface), 37
NetBIOS (Network Basic Input/Output System), 32
name resolution, 63-64
services, 32-33, 62
NWLink (Netware Link), 37
PAP (Password Authentication Protocol), 520
PPTP (Point-to-Point Tunneling Protocol), RAS servers, 546-551
RFCs, requirement levels, 22
RIP (Routing Internet Protocol), 119
installing, 120
SLIP (Serial Line Interface Protocol), 521
SNMP
communities, 482-483
installing, 483-486
MIBs (Management Information Base)
testing, 486-487
SNMP (Simple Network Management Protocol), 480
standards
designations, 21
RFCs (Requests for Comments), 19-22
TCP (Transmission Control Protocol), 71-75
overview, 46
TCP/IP (Transmission Control Protocol/ Internet Protocol), 37
advantages, 22-24
development, 17-18
host IDs, 24
installing, 134-149
network IDs, 24
OSI reference model (Open Systems Interconnection), 32
testing configuration, 141-145
Transport Layer, 45-46
Transport protocols, 37
UDP (User Datagram Protocol), 75
overview, 46

Protocols tab (Network Settings dialog box), 136-138

proxy servers
adding to a network, 602
PNA (Private Network Address), 602
WINS clients, 268-269

PSCRIPT.DLL, 186

PSCRIPT1 files, 187

PSCRPTUI.DLL, 186

pseudo headers, 68, 71, 78

PTR records, 355
adding, 375-376

Pull Parameters: Initial Replication (WINS Server Configuration dialog box option), 278

Pull Partner Properties dialog box, 290

pull partners
adding, 289-290
replication, initiating, 287-288

push & pull replication, 599

Push Parameters: Initial Replication
(WINS Server Configuration dialog box option), 279

Push Partner Properties dialog box, 289

push partners
adding, 289-290
replication, initiating, 287-288

Q

queries
DNS queries, resolving, 325-327
interactive, 393-396
name registration, 258-260
non-interactive, 391-392
WHOIS, 342-343
see also challenges

R

RAS (Remote Access Server), 510-513
adding to a network, 601
callback security, 511
CHAP (Challenge Handshake Authentication Protocol), 520

dial-up networking, 521-530
adding phonebook entries, 521-524
dialing out, 519-520
dialing with phonebook entries
Appearance option, 534-535
Callback option, 533
Phonebook option, 535
hardware, installing, 513-517
installing, 511-513
modems, installing, 514-521
phonebook entries
dialing, 530-535
editing, 524-532
user preferences, 532-535
PPTP, configuring, 548-549
routing, 539-541
serial ports
adding, 513-514
configuring, 514
servers
configuring protocols, 542-543
NetBIOS gateway, 543-544
PPTP (Point-to-Point Tunneling Protocol), 546-551
Remote Access Admin, 544-546
telephony properties, configuring, 518-519
X.25, 530
RAS Server service, WINS special name, 284
RAS Setup dialog box, 541-544
RASDD.DLL, 185
RASDDUI.DLL, 186
Raster printers, 185
RCP (Remote Copy Protocol), 412-414
.rhosts file, 413-414
command line switches, 412-413
remote privileges, 413
reassembling datagrams, 86-87
Received Address Mask (ICMP object counter), 490
Received Address Mask Reply (ICMP object counter), 490
Received Destination Unreachable (ICMP object counter), 490
Received Echo Reply/sec (ICMP object counter), 490
Received Echo/sec (ICMP object counter), 491
Received Parameter Problem (ICMP object counter), 491
Received Redirect/sec (ICMP object counter), 491
Received Source Quench (ICMP object counter), 491
Received Time Exceeded Number of ICMP (ICMP object counter), 491
Received Timestamp Reply/sec (ICMP object counter), 491
records
address, 359
adding, 371-373
CNAME, adding, 374
e-mail server, 360
MX records, adding, 374-375
NS (Name Server), 358-359
PTR, adding, 375-376
resource, adding, 371-376
SOA, properties, 377-378
WINS, 357-358
WINS database
displaying, 274-276
fields, 275
see also aliases
redirectors, 33
RefreshInterval parameter, 294
registration
name, 258-260
renewing, 261-262
see also name registration
Registry Editor
browsers, configuring, 305
configuring Name Cache, 238
data types, 223
DHCP values, editing, 223-224
DHCP parameters
APIProtocolSupport, 224-225
BackupDatabase Path, 225
BackupInterval, 225
configuring, 221-226
DatabaseCleanup Interval, 225
DatabaseLoggingFlag, 225-226
DatabaseName, 226
DatabasePath, 226
RestoreFlag, 226
keys, 222
WINS parameters, configuring, 291-295
Relay Agent
DHCP, 148-149
installing, 226-227
DHCP Boot, 130
Remote Access Admin, 544-546
Remote Access Server, *see* RAS
Remote Copy Protocol, *see* RCP
remote hosts
ARP broadcasts, viewing, 474-475
connecting, 424-425
remote privileges, RCP, 413
remote procedure call, *see* RPC

removing
active leases, 209
network adapters, 140
TCP/IP protocols, 138-139
Renewal Interval (WINS Server Configuration dialog box option), 278
renewal intervals, setting, 278
renewing name registration, 261-263
repairing DHCP databases, 215-216
Replicate Only With Partners (WINS Server Configuration dialog box option), 279
replication
initiating, 287-288, 290-291
manual initiation, 290-291
WINS database, 287-291, 599
replication partners, adding, 289-290
Replication Partners dialog box, 289, 291
Request for Comments, *see* RFC
requests
name refresh, 261
name release, 262
requirement levels, RFCs, 22
requirements of TCP/IP intranet implementation, IP addresses, 593-594
reservations
client-specific options, managing, 219-220
DHCP
creating, 210-211
establishing, 209-211
resolvers, 325
resolving
DNS queries, 325-327
names, 237-245
B-Node (Broadcast), 247
broadcasting, 238-239
DNS, 245
H-Node (Hybrid), 248-249
HOSTS file, 244-245
HOSTS files, 347-348
LMHOSTS file, 239-242
M-Node (Mixed), 248
NetBIOS, 308-314
NetBIOS Name Cache, 237-238
NetBIOS Name Server, 242-244
order of resolution, 246-250
P-Node (Peer-to-Peer), 248
troubleshooting, 575-576
Windows NT, 390-391
WINS, 258-265, 381
WINS process, 263-268
resource records, 354-355
adding, 371-376
address records, adding, 371-373
CNAME records, adding, 374
MX records, adding, 374-375
PTR records, adding, 375-376
SOA (Start of Authority), 356-357
resources, browsing, 300-307
see also browsers
responses
name refresh responses, 262
NAMEQUERY RESPONSE, 260
NAMEREGISTRATION RESPONSE, 259
Positive Name Query Response, 236
RestoreFlag (DHCP parameter), 226-232
restoring WINS database, 285-286
restrictions, TCP/IP addresses, 25-26
retransmitting datagrams, 87
reverse mapping, 344-345
reverse-lookup zones, adding, 369-370
reverse-matching database files, 360-362
REXEC, 426-427
switches, 427
RFC (Request for Comments), 19-22
FAQs (Frequently Asked Questions), 22
FYI (For Your Information), 22
requirement levels, 22
RFC 1591, 327
RFC 2000, 21
RFC1533 DHCP options, 220-223
RFCs supported by Microsoft NT TCP/IP, 132-134
.rhosts file, 413-414
RIP (Routing Internet Protocol), installing, 119-120
RIP routing, 119-124
disadvantages, 120
root name servers, 327
root nodes, 321
ROUTE, 444-446
NETWORKS file, 445-446
ROUTE command, 78, 114, 569
ROUTE PRINT command, 119
routers, 114
convergence, 120
dynamic routing, 118-120
RIP routing, 119-124

Multiprotocol Router, 129
RAS, 539-541
RIP routing, disadvantages, 120
see also gateways
static routing, 115-118
Windows NT, 115-120
routing, 78-80
Routing Internet Protocol, *see* RIP
routing protocols, RIP (Routing Internet Protocol), 119
installing, 120
routing tables, 80
three-subnet network, 118
two-subnet network, 116
RP (resource record), 355
RPC (remote procedure call), 184
RSA Message Digest 4, 520
RSH, 426
RT (resource record), 355

S

S field (WINS database), 275
sample HOSTS file, 245
sample TCP/IP implementation
IP address requirements, 593-594
subnets, 593-594
networks, linking, 594-598
SAP Filters, 458-460
saving
capture data, 463
captured frames, 454
scavenging, 286-287
scope DHCP options, managing, 218-219
scopes
creating, 203-204
DHCP
activating, 212
deactivating, 212
deleting, 212
setting up, 202-205
modifying, 205
secondary DNS servers, creating, 383-384
secondary name servers, establishing, 365-366
security
Network Monitor, 451-452
configuring, 451-452
spoofing, 167
Security log (Event Viewer), 570
Security tab (SNMP Properties), 485-486
segments, 73
fragmentation, 86-87
Segments Received/sec, (TCP counter), 494
Segments Retransmitted/sec, (TCP counter), 494
Segments Sent/sec, (TCP counter), 494
Segments/sec, (TCP counter), 494
selecting
home directories for IIS installation, 156
IIS views, 160
networks for monitoring, 456
sending
datagrams, error detection, 87-88
packets, 80-83
sendmail, 360
Sent Address Mask (ICMP object counter), 491
Sent Address Mask Reply (ICMP object counter), 491
Sent Destination Unreachable (ICMP object counter), 491
Sent Echo Reply/sec (ICMP object counter), 491
Sent Echo/sec (ICMP object counter), 491
Sent Parameter Problem (ICMP object counter), 491
Sent Redirect/sec (ICMP object counter), 491
Sent Source Quench (ICMP object counter), 491
Sent Time Exceeded (ICMP object counter), 491
Sent Timestamp Reply/sec (ICMP object counter), 491
Sent Timestamp/sec (ICMP object counter), 491
Sequence numbers, 69
serial ports, adding to RAS, 513-514
server services, 300-307
browsers
configuring, 304-305
domains, 307-308
Server Start Time (WINS server statistic), 273
Server Statistics: Auto Refresh (Preferences dialog box option), 277
servers, 598-601
announcements, 300
Backup Browser, 300-301
BIND, 351
porting data, 388-389
browsers, elections, 305-307
communication with redirectors, 33
DHCP (Dynamic Host Configuration Protocol)
adding, 598
concepts, 198-201
installing, 202-212
managing multiple, 213
starting, 214-215
stopping, 214-215
DNS (Domain Name Server), 128
adding, 600
configuring, 350-351

creating, 367-368
enabling clients, 389-390
implementing, 346-347
initializing, 367-368
installing, 367
managing, 348-387
managing multiple, 382
preparing, 348
resource record types, 354-355
statistics, 387
zones, 368
IIS (Internet Information Server), adding to networks, 600-601
LPD, connecting, 189-191
Master Browser, 300
name servers, 324
names, secondary, 367-387
print servers, print processing, 187
proxy servers, adding to a network, 602
RAS (Remote Access Server)
adding to a network, 601
configuring, 541-546
configuring PPTP, 548-549
configuring protocols, 542-543
NetBIOS gateway, 543-544
PPTP (Point-to-Point Tunneling Protocol), 546-551
Remote Access Admin, 544-546
see also RAS
root name servers, 327
secondary DNS servers, creating, 383-384
virtual
configuring, 170-176
planning, 169-170
WINS
adding, 599
adding to WINS Server Manager, 273
adding replication partners, 289-290
browsing, 314
configuring properties, 277-279
fault tolerance, 267
initiating replication, 290-291
installing, 265-267
managing, 272-287
monitoring with WINS Server Manager, 273-274
network traffic, 267
viewing detailed information, 279-280
WWW, configuring, 161-173

Servers View (IIS), selecting, 160

Service tab, WWW Server Properties fields, 162

services, 59-60
Browser services, troubleshooting, 576
browsers, domains, 307-308
DNS, troubleshooting, 576
FTP
configuring, 174
FTP Directories tab, 175
Messages tab, 174
Gopher service (IIS), configuring, 175-176
IIS (Internet Information Service)
configuring IUSR_computername account, 160-161
installing, 154-158
Internet Service Manager (IIS), 159
managing, 158-176
Microsoft Browser Service, 300-304
configuring browsers, 304-305
see also browsers
NetBIOS (Network Basic Input/Output System), 32-33
NETLOGON, 308
RAS, 510-513
adding phonebook entries, 521-524
adding serial ports, 513-514
callback security, 511
dial-up networking, 521-530
dialing out, 519-520
dialing with phonebook entries, 530-535
installing, 511-513
installing hardware, 513-517
X.25, 530
TCP/IP, 23
TCP/IP printing, installing, 189
troubleshooting, 574-576
Windows NT, 129-131
DHCP (Dynamic Host Configuration Protocol), 130
DNS Server, 131
IIS (Internet Information Server), 129
Line Printer Daemon, 129
WINS (Windows Internet Name Service), 130-131
WINS, name registration, 259
WWW server (IIS), configuring, 161-173

Services tab (Network Settings dialog box), 136
session layer, 32
session management, 61
NetBIOS, 33
sessions
byte stream communication, 73
creating, 72
interactive FTP, opening, 406
TRACERT, 447-448
SET (SNMP command), 480
Set Filter dialog box, 276
settings
Dial Up Networking Monitor, 536-541
renewal intervals, 278
Telnet, Terminal preferences, 425-426
WINS Manager preferences, 276-277
setting up DHCP scopes, 202-205
SFMMON.DLL, 187
sharing printers, 191-192
Shiva Password Authentication Protocol, *see* SPAP
Show Database dialog box, 274
Simple Network Management Protocol, *see* SNMP
sites
Microsoft Certified Training, 618
Microsoft Training and Certification, 610
sample TCP/IP implementation, linking, 594-598
web, Internic, 22
Size (Name Cache parameter), 238
Sliding Windows adjusting size, 73-75
SLIP (Serial Line Interface Protocol), 521
SMB (Server Message Block), 32-33
SMS (Systems Management Server), 450
SMS Network Monitor, 450
SNMP (Simple Network Management Protocol), 480
communities, 482-483
configuring, 483-486
installing, 483-486
MIBs (Management Information Base), 480-481
testing, 486-487
SNMP Agents, 480
SNMP Managers, 480
SNMP Properties Agent tab, 484
SNMP Properties Security tab, 485-486
SNMP Properties Traps tab, 485-486
SNMPUTIL, 486-487
SOA (Start of Authority) resource record, 355
numeric parameters, 357
record properties, 377-378
source address, 86
source ports, 69
special names, 282-284
spoofing, 167
spoolers, *see* print spoolers
standards, 21
Internet Official Protocol Standards, 21
RFCs (Requests for Comments), 19-22
Stanford Research Institute, Network Information Center, 239
starting DHCP servers, 214-215
Starting Version Count (WINS Server Configuration dialog box option), 279
static IP address configuration, WINS clients, 268
static mappings configuring, 281-282
editing, 282
Static Mappings dialog box, 282
static routing, 115-118
statistics, DNS server, 387
Statistics Cleared (WINS server statistic), 274
STDS (Street Talk Directory Services), 596
stopping DHCP servers, 214-215
Street Talk Directory Services, *see* STDS
stub resolvers, 325
subdomain zones, adding, 384-385
subdomains, 323
non-government organizations, 341-342
US domain, 339-341
subnet IDS, 102-103
subnet masks, 47, 78
bit requirements, 97-98
calculating, 101
creating, 98
hosts, calculating, 98-99
modifying, 475-476
three bit, 100-101
subnets
browsing, 308-314
calculating, 101
requirements, sample TCP/IP implementation, 593-606
troubleshooting, 562-563
subnetting, 94, 96-105
class C addresses, 103
host IDs, 102-103
planning, 97
subnet masks, bit requirements, 97-98
see also supernetting

subnetwork IDs, 99-102
Summary Pane (Network Monitor), viewing capture data, 465
supernetting, 104-108
Class A addresses, 105
class C addresses, 104
support, TCP/IP, installing, 136-138
switches
ARP command, 449-478
Finger command, 434
FTP, 407
IPCONFIG, 144, 433
LPQ, 428
LPR, 428
NBSTAT command, 62-63, 442
NETSTAT, 440
NETSTAT command, 60-61
NSLOOKUP command, 435
Ping, 429-430
RCP, 412-413
REXEC command, 427
ROUTE command, 444-445
RSH command, 426
TFTP, 412
TRACERT command, 446
Sylvan Prometric Testing Centers, 610
synchronization, 308, 310
System log (Event Viewer), 570

T

tables, routing, 80
three-subnet network, 118
two-subnet routers, 116
tags, 240-241
TCP (Transmission Control Protocol), 23, 71-75
byte stream communications, 73
comparing to UDP, 75
overview, 46
sessions, creating, 72
Sliding Windows, 73-76
adjusting size, 74-75
TCP headers, 68-70
TCP/IP (Transmission Control Protocol/Internet Protocol), 37
addresses
classes, 24
octets, 24
restrictions, 25-26
see also IP addresses
advantages, 22-24
configuring, 138
configuring for IIS installation, 154
history, 17-18
RFC (Request for Comments), 19-22
host IDs, 24
implementation, subnet requirements, 593-606
installing, 134-149
NETSTAT utility, 568
network IDs, 24
OSI reference model (Open Systems Interconnection), 32
Ping, 568
printing, troubleshooting, 574-575
printing services, installing, 189
properties, overview, 145-149
protocols, 23
removing, 138-139
services, troubleshooting, 574-576
testing configuration, 141-145
Windows NT, 128-134
TCP/IP Configuration dialog box, 115, 475
TCP/IP model, 42-50
Transport layer protocols, 45-46
TCP/IP Properties dialog box, 171
TCP/IP Settings dialog box, 242
TDI (Transport Driver Interface) layer, 35-37
telephony properties, 518-519
Telnet, 424-426
Terminal Preferences dialog box, 425
testing
IIS directory, 179
network connectivity, 431-434
passwords, 178
SNMP, 486-487
TCP/IP configuration, 141-145
TestPrep Utility (CD-ROM), 619-620
instructor mode, 621
non-random mode, 620-621
question presentation, 620-621
score report, 620-621
TestPrep Utility
FLASH! Electronic Flash cards, 621
instructor mode, 621
non-random mode, 620-621
question presentation, 620-621
score report, 620-621
TFTP (Trivial File Transfer Protocol), 411-412
command line switches, 412
three-bit subnet masks, 100-101
three-way handshakes, 72
tie breaking, 306

Time to Live, ***see*** **TTL**
Timestamp field (WINS database), 275
token rings, 86
TombstoneInterval parameter, 294
TombstoneTimeout parameter, 294
tools, 568-572
Total Bytes/sec (NBT counter), 493
Total Queries Received (WINS server statistic), 274
Total Registrations (WINS server statistic), 274
Total Releases (WINS server statistics), 274
TPC/IP Settings dialog box, 243
TRACERT, 446-448, 569
traffic
- domains
  - *handling with LMHOSTS, 309-313*
  - *handling with WINS, 313*
- networks, monitoring, 450-471

transfers, zone, 378
Transmission Control Protocol, ***see*** **TCP**
transmitting datagrams
- error detection, 87-88

Transport layer (TCP/IP model), 42, 32
- pseudo headers, 71
- TCP headers, 68-70
- UDP (User Datagram Protocol), 75
- UDP header, 70-72

Transport Layer protocols, 45-46
Transport protocols, 37
TRAP (SNMP command), 480
Traps tab (SNMP Properties), 485-486
trees, DNS, 320-321
troubleshooting, 562-567
- Browser service, 576
- client stations, 563-564
- connectivity, 573
- DHCP, 575
- DNS, 576
- DNS servers with Nslookup, 391-396
- duplicate IP addresses, 137
- file restores, 563
- hardware, 564
- IIS (Internet Information Server), 574
- IP configuration, 564
- jammed printers, 186
- LMHOSTS file, 241-242
- locating sources of problems, 562-568
  - name resolution, 564
    - *WINS, 575-576*
- passwords, 178-179
- printing, 574-575
- servers, upgrades, 563
- services, 574-576
- tools and utilities, 568-572
- user rights, 563
- Windows for Workgroups, browser elections, 306
- WINS, 575-576

troubleshooting utilities, 429-449
- ARP, 448-450
- Finger, 434
- HOSTNAME, 439
- IPCONFIG, 433-434
- NBTSTAT, 442-444
- NETSTAT, 440-441
- NSLOOKUP, 434-439
  - *interactive commands, 435-436*
- Ping, 429-433
- ROUTE, 444-446
  - *NETWORKS file, 445-446*
- TRACERT, 446-448

trust relationships, 595-606
trusted domains, 596
TTL (Time to Live), 85, 326
TXT (resource record), 355

U

UDP (User Datagram Protocol), 75
- comparing to TCP, 75
- overview, 46

UDP header, 70-72
- format, 70

UDP port 137
- *see also* NetBIOS Name Service port

UNC (Universal Naming Convention), 169
uninstalling
- *see also* installing
- TCP/IP protocols, 138-139

Unix
- BSD (Berkeley Standard Distribution), 18
- daemons, 129

Update Interval (Performance Monitor chart setting), 495
updating
- browser list, 303-304
- configurations, DHCP clients, 272
- database files, 386

upgrading servers, troubleshooting, 563
US domain, subdomains, 339-341
user accounts, 1USR_*computername* account, 157
- configuring, 160-161

User Datagram Protocol, ***see*** **UDP**
user logons, 308-309
user rights, troubleshooting, 563
UseSelfFndPntrs parameter, 294

utilities, 568-572
ARP, 569
Dial-Up Networking Monitor, 535-538
Event Viewer, 570-571
file transfer, 406-414
RCP (Remote Copy Protocol), 12-414
FTP (File Transfer Protocol), 406-411
commands, 408-412
interactive, 414-426
Internet Explorer, 414-424
REXEC, 426-427
RSH, 426
Telnet, 424-426
IPCONFIG, 144-145, 568
NBTSTAT, 569
NETSTAT, 568
Network Monitor, 449-471, 569
capture triggers, 462-463
installing, 451
managing capture buffer, 456-457
saving capture data, 463
security, 451-452
Nslookup, 391-396
NT Diagnostics, 571-572
Performance Monitor, 569-570
Ping, 141-144, 568
printing, 427-428
LPQ, 428
LPR (Line Printer Request), 427-428
see also Performance Monitor
SNMPUTIL, 486-487
TFTP (Trivial File Transfer Protocol), 411-412
TRACERT, 569
troubleshooting, 429-449
ARP, 448-450
Finger, 434
HOSTNAME, 439
IPCONFIG, 433-434
NBTSTAT, 442-444
NETSTAT, 440-441
NSLOOKUP, 434-439
Ping, 429-433
ROUTE, 444-446
TRACERT, 446-448

V

Validate Cache of "Known" WINS Servers at Startup Time (Preferences dialog box option), 277
Value Bar (Performance Monitor chart setting), 495
Value Labels (Performance Monitor chart setting), 495
Verify Interval (WINS Server Configuration dialog box option), 278
VerifyInterval parameter, 295
Version ID field (WINS database), 275
Vertical Grid (Performance Monitor chart setting), 495
Vertical Maximum (Performance Monitor chart setting), 495
viewing
active leases, 206-208
ARP broadcasts, 474
capture data
Detail Pane (Network Monitor), 465-467
Summary Pane (Network Monitor), 465
captured data, 463-471
node types, 249-250
Performance Monitor log files, 496-497
remote hosts, ARP broadcasts, 474-475
WINS database, 274-276
WINS Manager, detailed information, 279-280
views, IIS, selecting, 160
virtual directories, 163, 168
configuring, 168-169
virtual servers, 163
configuring, 170-176
directory properties, 173
planning, 169-170

W

walk (SNMPUTIL command), 486
web browsers
Internet Explorer, 414-424
configuring, 416-424
Web sites
Microsoft Certified Training, 618
Microsoft Training and Certification, 610
web sites
accessing, 177
Internic, 22
WHOIS, 342-343
Windows for Workgroups, browser elections, 306
Windows Internet Name Service, *see* WINS
Windows NT
configuring for DNS server use, 245
DHCP (Dynamic Host Configuration Protocol), 130
DHCP clients, updating configurations, 272
DNS (Domain Name Server), 128, 131, 345
domain model, browsers, 307-308
IIS (Internet Information Server), 129
configuring IUSR_computername account, 160-161
configuring WWW server, 161-173

installing, 155
Internet Service Manager, 159
managing, 158-176
see also IIS
Line Printer Daemon, 129
MCSE exams, 614-618
Multiprotocol Router, 129
name resolution, 390-391
Nslookup, 391-396
NT Diagnostics, 571-572
Performance Monitor, 487-498
print drivers, 185-186
print process, 184-188
print processors, 187
print spooler, 186
Remote Access Server, *see* RAS
routers, 115-120
dynamic routing, 118-120
RIP routing, 119-124
static routing, 115-118
services, 129-131
tags, 240-241
TCP/IP support, 128-134
Windows NT 3.51, MCSE exams, 611-618
Windows NT Challenge/Response, 162
Windows NT Server 4 DNS Server
configuring, 350-351
see also DNS
WINPRINT.DLL, 187
WINS (Windows Internet Name Service), 130-131, 243, 258-265
adding servers to a network, 599
browsing, 314
challenges, 260
clients
DHCP, 269-272
installing, 268-272
static IP address configuration, 268
WINS proxy servers, 268-269
Domain Name Group, 313
monitoring with WINS Server Manager, 273-274
multihomed computers, 260
name registration, 258-260
services, 259
name resolution, 263-268, 381
NBT, enabling, 313-315
NetBIOS name release, 262-263
NetBIOS name renewal, 261-262
parameters, configuring, 291-295
special names, 282-284
Domain group names, 283
multihomed names, 283
normal group names, 283
troubleshooting, 575-576
WINS (resource record), 355
WINS Address tab (Network dialog box), 147-148
WINS database
backing up, 284-285
compacting, 286-287
replicating, 287-291
restoring, 285-286
scavenging, 286-287
static mappings, configuring, 281
WINS databases, viewing, 274-276
WINS Manager
detailed information, viewing, 279-280
preferences, 276-277
static mappings, adding, 281-282
WINS MIB, 481
WINS record, 357-358
WINS Server Configuration dialog box, 277
WINS Server Manager, 272-287
adding WINS servers, 273
WINS database, viewing, 274-276
WINS servers, monitoring, 273-274
WINS servers
adding to WINS Server Manager, 273
clients
DHCP, 269-272
installing, 268-272
static IP address configuration, 268
WINS proxy servers, 268-269
fault tolerance, 267
installing, 265-267
network traffic, 267
properties, configuring, 277-279
push & pull replication, 599
replication, initiating, 290-291
replication partners, adding, 289-290
Wins.mdb, 286
WINS_R (resource record), 355
WinSock, 43-45, 56-61
active open, 56
host communications, 43
name resolution, 390-391
NETSTAT command, switches, 60-61
passive open, 56

Winstmp.mdb, 286
WKS (resource record), 355
workgroups,
browsing, 306-307
world-wide domains, 328
WWW server (IIS)
configuring, 161-173
directories, accessing, 164
WWW Server Properties
Advanced tab, 166-167
Directories tab, 163-164
Logging tab, 164-166
Service tab, fields, 162-163

X-Z

X.25, 355, 530

zone database, zone transfers, 378
Zone Properties dialog box
Notify Properties tab, 378
SOA Record Properties tab, 377-378
WINS Lookup Properties tab, 379-404
zone transfers, 378
zones, 324, 353
DNS server, 368
primary, adding, 370
properties, 377
modifying, 376-380
reverse-lookup, adding, 369-370
subdomain zones, adding, 384-385

Technical Support:

If you cannot get the CD/Disk to install properly, or you need assistance with a particular situation in the book, please feel free to check out the Knowledge Base on our Web site at **http://www.superlibrary.com/general/support**. We have answers to our most Frequently Asked Questions listed there. If you do not find your specific question answered, please contact Macmillan Technical Support at **(317) 581-3833**. We can also be reached by email at **support@mcp.com**.